MW00528418

THE NEW AMERICAN COMMENTARY

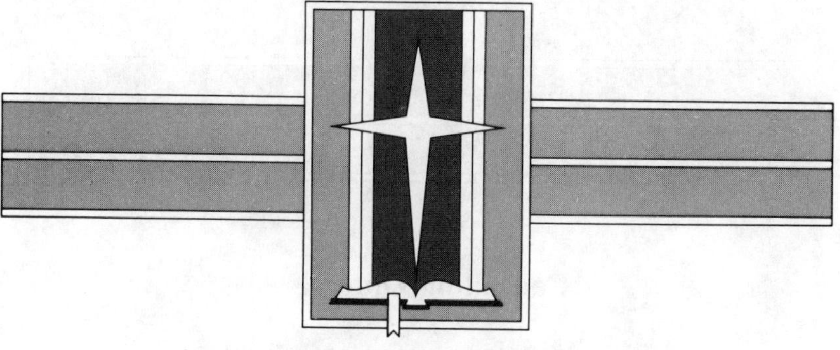

An Exegetical and Theological Exposition of Holy Scripture

THE NEW AMERICAN COMMENTARY

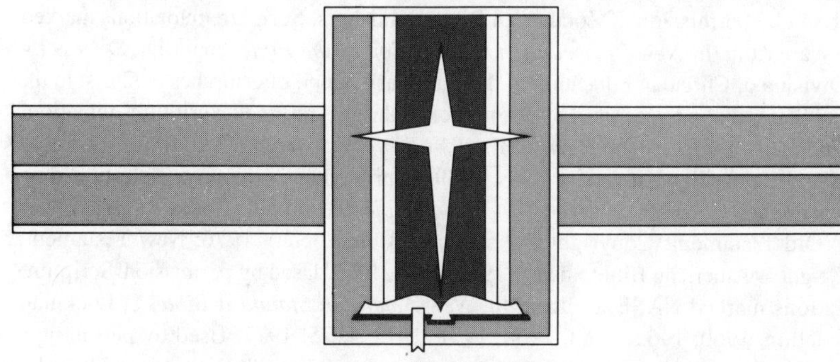

Volume 20

MICAH
NAHUM, HABAKKUK, ZEPHANIAH

Kenneth L. Barker
Waylon Bailey

Nashville, Tennessee

ISBN 0–8054–0120–2
Dewey Decimal Classification: 224.90
Subject Heading: BIBLE. O.T. MICAH
Library of Congress Catalog Number: 98–40576
Printed in the United States of America
01 00 99 98 4 3 2 1

Library of Congress Cataloging-in-Publication Data

Barker, Kenneth L.
Micah, Nahum, Habakkuk, Zephaniah / Kenneth L. Barker, Waylon Bailey.
p. cm. — (The new American commentary ; v. 20)
Includes bibliographical references and indexes.
ISBN 0–8054–0120–2 (hardcover)
1. Bible. O.T. Micah—Commentaries. 2. Bible. O.T. Nahum–Commentaries. 3. Bible. O.T. Habakkuk—Commentaries. 4. Bible. O.T. Zephaniah—Commentaries. I. Bailey, D. Waylon. II. Title. III. Series.
BS1615.3.B37 1998
224'.9077—dc21

To my wife Isabelle

And my children Ken, Pat, Ruth, and David and their families

From a husband, father, and grandfather

Who loves them and thanks God for them

Kenneth L. Barker

To Martha,
"The delight of my eyes" (Ezek 24:16)
and
to our children, Anna, Emily,
and Chris

Waylon Bailey

Authors' Prefaces

MICAH

Based on my experience as a Bible translator (NIV, NIrV, NASB), I have often said, "If you want to discover how little you really know, become involved in translating all the books of the Bible from Hebrew, Aramaic, and Greek into English or any other language." The same applies to writing a commentary. I have never been more cognizant of my own inadequacies than when attempting to do justice to the exquisite Book of Micah. Certainly my appreciation for the book has been vastly enhanced. Now my earnest prayer to God is that the pastors, students, and Bible teachers who refer to this commentary on Micah will be as blessed and edified in using it as I was in writing it.

I wish to thank Ray Clendenen for honoring me by inviting me to make this contribution to the distinguished NAC series. Special thanks go to my wife, Isabelle, for putting the complete text into the computer. My greatest debt of gratitude is owed to my "Sovereign Lord" (Mic 1:2) and incomparable God (Mic 7:18) for granting me such a high privilege and enabling me to finish the work. In the words of the hymn title, "To God Be the Glory."

—Kenneth L. Barker

NAHUM, HABAKKUK, ZEPHANIAH

The Word of God continues to speak. Primarily, it does so because it has come from the living God. The Bible speaks to us because it is rooted in history and because we live in a historical context. While culture and cultural mores have changed, human nature has not changed. God spoke to the needs of human nature in the past; He continues to speak to us as well. We will face the same needs related to human nature in the third millennium that people faced six hundred years before the time of Jesus.

In the new millennium, we will want to know that God is still in control of history. We will face the recurring problems presented by human sin, and we will need to know that the righteous shall live by faith.

My hope is that the reader will be helped with interpreting the text for the contemporary situation and that the relevance for the present time will be clear. The work of the interpreter is not only what the text meant in the past but also how it applies in the contemporary time.

My love for the Word of God and for the Old Testament in particular started with the encouragement of loving Christian parents and a nurturing church. After being called to preach, I was immeasurably motivated by two professors who specialized in the Old Testament. Each one communicated the Word of God with power and compassion. Each one possessed a Christ-like spirit and demonstrated that spirit in daily living.

At Samford University in Birmingham, Alabama Dr. Sigurd Bryan taught students the Old Testament from a perspective which took the text seriously and showed the importance of understanding the history, background, and theological outlook of the text. He also showed the Bible's relevance for contemporary living. Dr. Bryan prepared the way for my later specializing in Old Testament at New Orleans Baptist Theological Seminary.

Dr. John Olen Strange at New Orleans Seminary introduced me to the Hebrew language. Dr. Strange became my teacher, mentor, colleague, and, most importantly, friend. In 1985, I had the privilege of authoring a Hebrew grammar with him. I have missed him greatly since his passing in January, 1995.

I wish to thank the faculty and administration of New Orleans Baptist Theological Seminary for their support and encouragement. I was privileged to serve for seventeen years under the leadership of President Landrum Leavell. During that time I experienced an uncommon fellowship with Godly men and women who loved, lived, and taught the message of a loving God.

I wish to thank Mike Smith, David Dockery, and Ray Clendenen and the editorial staff of the *New American Commentary* for the confidence that they have expressed in me and for the help that they have given in the presentation of this volume. I am particularly indebted to Trent Butler for his invaluable assistance in revising the original manuscript for publication.

I also wish to thank the congregation of the First Baptist Church in Covington, Louisiana, the congregation which I am privileged to serve as pastor. They have encouraged me to teach the Word and to show its importance for our age. This congregation has a vision to make God known in our world. I am indebted for their love and support.

My wife, Martha, and our daughters, Anna and Emily, serve as constant sources of strength. They have encouraged me in my life's work and have helped me make life meaningful.

My hope is that the prophecies of Nahum, Habakkuk, and Zephaniah may come alive to the reader. May the Word of God through these prophets help us in the worst of times to "rejoice in the Lord … [and] be joyful in God [our] savior" (Hab 3:18).

—Waylon Bailey

Editors' Preface

God's Word does not change. God's world, however, changes in every generation. These changes, in addition to new findings by scholars and a new variety of challenges to the gospel message, call for the church in each generation to interpret and apply God's Word for God's people. Thus, THE NEW AMERICAN COMMENTARY is introduced to bridge the twentieth and twenty-first centuries. This new series has been designed primarily to enable pastors, teachers, and students to read the Bible with clarity and proclaim it with power.

In one sense THE NEW AMERICAN COMMENTARY is not new, for it represents the continuation of a heritage rich in biblical and theological exposition. The title of this forty-volume set points to the continuity of this series with an important commentary project published at the end of the nineteenth century called AN AMERICAN COMMENTARY, edited by Alvah Hovey. The older series included, among other significant contributions, the outstanding volume on Matthew by John A. Broadus, from whom the publisher of the new series, Broadman Press, partly derives its name. The former series was authored and edited by scholars committed to the infallibility of Scripture, making it a solid foundation for the present project. In line with this heritage, all NAC authors affirm the divine inspiration, inerrancy, complete truthfulness, and full authority of the Bible. The perspective of the NAC is unapologetically confessional and rooted in the evangelical tradition.

Since a commentary is a fundamental tool for the expositor or teacher who seeks to interpret and apply Scripture in the church or classroom, the NAC focuses on communicating the theological structure and content of each biblical book. The writers seek to illuminate both the historical meaning and contemporary significance of Holy Scripture.

In its attempt to make a unique contribution to the Christian community, the NAC focuses on two concerns. First, the commentary emphasizes how each section of a book fits together so that the reader becomes aware of the theological unity of each book and of Scripture as a whole. The writers, however, remain aware of the Bible's inherently rich variety. Second, the NAC is produced with the conviction that the Bible primarily belongs to the church. We believe that scholarship and the academy provide an indispensable foundation for biblical understanding and the service of Christ, but the editors and authors of this series have attempted to communicate the findings of their research in a manner that will build up the whole body of Christ. Thus, the commentary concentrates on theological exegesis while providing practical, applicable exposition.

THE NEW AMERICAN COMMENTARY's theological focus enables the reader to see the parts as well as the whole of Scripture. The biblical books vary in content, context, literary type, and style. In addition to this rich variety, the editors and authors recognize that the doctrinal emphasis and use of the biblical books differs in various places, contexts, and cultures among God's people. These factors, as well as other concerns, have led the editors to give freedom to the writers to wrestle with the issues raised by the scholarly community surrounding each book and to determine the appropriate shape and length of the introductory materials. Moreover, each writer has developed the structure of the commentary in a way best suited for expounding the basic structure and the meaning of the biblical books for our day. Generally, discussions relating to contemporary scholarship and technical points of grammar and syntax appear in the footnotes and not in the text of the commentary. This format allows pastors and interested laypersons, scholars and teachers, and serious college and seminary students to profit from the commentary at various levels. This approach has been employed because we believe that all Christians have the privilege and responsibility to read and seek to understand the Bible for themselves.

Consistent with the desire to produce a readable, up-to-date commentary, the editors selected the *New International Version* as the standard translation for the commentary series. The selection was made primarily because of the NIV's faithfulness to the original languages and its beautiful and readable style. The authors, however, have been given the liberty to differ at places from the NIV as they develop their own translations from the Greek and Hebrew texts.

The NAC reflects the vision and leadership of those who provide oversight for Broadman Press, who in 1987 called for a new commentary series that would evidence a commitment to the inerrancy of Scripture and a faithfulness to the classic Christian tradition. While the commentary adopts an "American" name, it should be noted some writers represent countries outside the United States, giving the commentary an international perspective. The diverse group of writers includes scholars, teachers, and administrators from almost twenty different colleges and seminaries, as well as pastors, missionaries, and a layperson.

The editors and writers hope that THE NEW AMERICAN COMMEN-

TARY will be helpful and instructive for pastors and teachers, scholars and students, for men and women in the churches who study and teach God's Word in various settings. We trust that for editors, authors, and readers alike, the commentary will be used to build up the church, encourage obedience, and bring renewal to God's people. Above all, we pray that the NAC will bring glory and honor to our Lord who has graciously redeemed us and faithfully revealed himself to us in his Holy Word.

SOLI DEO GLORIA
The Editors

Abbreviations

Bible Books

Gen
Exod
Lev
Num
Deut
Josh
Judg
Ruth
1, 2 Sam
1, 2 Kgs
1, 2 Chr
Ezra
Neh
Esth
Job
Ps (pl. Pss)
Prov
Eccl
Song
Isa
Jer
Lam
Ezek
Dan
Hos
Joel
Amos
Obad
Jonah
Mic
Nah
Hab
Zeph
Hag
Zech
Mal
Matt
Mark
Luke
John
Acts
Rom
1, 2 Cor
Gal
Eph
Phil
Col
1, 2 Thess
1, 2 Tim
Titus
Phlm
Heb
Jas
1, 2 Pet
1, 2, 3 John
Jude
Rev

Apocrypha

Add Esth	*The Additions to the Book of Esther*
Bar	*Baruch*
Bel	*Bel and the Dragon*
1,2 Esdr	*1, 2 Esdras*
4 Ezra	*4 Ezra*
Jdt	*Judith*
Ep Jer	*Epistle of Jeremiah*
1,2,3,4 Mac	*1, 2, 3, 4 Maccabees*
Pr Azar	*Prayer of Azariah and the Song of the Three Jews*
Pr Man	*Prayer of Manasseh*
Sir	*Sirach, Ecclesiasticus*
Sus	*Susanna*
Tob	*Tobit*
Wis	*The Wisdom of Solomon*

Commonly Used Sources

AASOR	Annual of the American Schools of Oriental Research
AB	Anchor Bible
ABR	*Australian Biblical Review*
ABD	*Anchor Bible Dictionary,* ed. D. N Freedman
ABW	*Archaeology and the Biblical World*
AC	An American Commentary, ed. A. Hovey
AcOr	*Acta orientalia*
AEL	M. Lichtheim, *Ancient Egyptian Literature*
AJBI	*Annual of the Japanese Biblical Institute*
AJSL	*American Journal of Semitic Languages and Literature*
Akk.	Akkadian
AnBib	Analecta Biblica
ANET	*Ancient Near Eastern Texts,* ed. J. B. Pritchard
Ant.	*Antiquities*
AOAT	Alter Orient und Altes Testament
AOS	American Oriental Society
AOTS	*Archaeology and Old Testament Study,* ed. D. W. Thomas
ArOr	Archiv orientální
AS	Assyriological Studies
ATD	Das Alte Testament Deutsch
ATR	*Anglican Theological Review*
AusBR	*Australian Biblical Review*
AUSS	*Andrews University Seminary Studies*
AV	Authorized Version
BA	*Biblical Archaeologist*
BAGD	W. Bauer, W. F. Arndt, F. W. Gingrich, and F. W. Danker, *Greek-English Lexicon of the New Testament*
BALS	Bible and Literature Series
BARev	*Biblical Archaeology Review*
BASOR	*Bulletin of the American Schools of Oriental Research*
BDB	F. Brown, S. R. Driver, and C. A. Briggs, *Hebrew and English Lexicon of the Old Testament*
BETL	Bibliotheca ephemeridum theologicarum lovaniensium
BFT	Biblical Foundations in Theology
BHS	*Biblia hebraica stuttgartensia*
Bib	*Biblica*
BibOr	Biblica et orientalia
BibRev	*Bible Review*
BJRL	*Bulletin of the Johns Rylands University Library*
BKAT	Biblischer Kommentar: Altes Testament
BN	*Biblische Notizen*
BO	*Bibliotheca orientalis*
BSac	*Bibliotheca Sacra*
BSC	Bible Student Commentary
BST	Bible Speaks Today
BT	*The Bible Translator*
BurH	*Buried History*
BZ	*Biblische Zeitschrift*
BZAW	Beihefte zur ZAW
CAD	*The Assyrian Dictionary of the Oriental Institute of the University of Chicago*

CAH	*Cambridge Ancient History*
CB	Century Bible
CBSC	Cambridge Bible for Schools and Colleges
CBC	Cambridge Bible Commentary
CBQ	*Catholic Biblical Quarterly*
CBQMS	Catholic Biblical Quarterly Monograph Series
CC	The Communicator's Commentary
CCK	*Chronicles of Chaldean Kings,* D. J. Wiseman
CD	Cairo *Damascus Document*
CGTC	Cambridge Greek Testament Commentaries
CHAL	*Concise Hebrew and Aramic Lexicon,* ed. W. L. Holladay
Comm.	J. Calvin, *Commentary on the First Book of Moses Called Genesis,* trans., rev. J. King
COT	*Commentary on the Old Testament, C. F. Keil and F. Delitzsch*
CSR	*Christian Scholar's Review*
CT	*Christianity Today*
CTR	*Criswell Theological Review*
CurTM	*Currents in Theology and Mission*
DAH	*Dictionary of Classical Hebrew,* ed. D. J. A. Clines
DOTT	*Documents from Old Testament Times,* ed. D. W. Thomas
DSS	Dead Sea Scrolls
EAEHL	*Encyclopedia of Archaeological Excavations in the Holy Land,* ed. M. Avi-Yonah
EBC	Expositor's Bible Commentary
Ebib	Etudes bibliques
EDBT	*Evangelical Dictionary of Biblical Theology,* W. A. Elwell, ed.
EE	*Enuma Elish*
EDNT	*Exegetical Dictionary of the New Testament*
EGT	*The Expositor's Greek Testament*
EncJud	*Encyclopaedia Judaica* (1971)
ErIsr	*Eretz Israel*
ETL	*Ephermerides theologicae lovanienses*
EvBC	Everyman's Bible Commentary
EV(s)	English Version(s)
EvQ	*Evangelical Quarterly*
ExpTim	*Expository Times*
FB	Forschung zur Bibel
FOTL	Forms of Old Testament Literature
Gk.	Greek
GKC	Gesenius's Hebrew Grammar, ed. E. Kautzsch, trans. A. E. Cowley
GTJ	*Grace Theological Journal*
HAR	*Hebrew Annual Review*
HAT	Handbuch zum Alten Testament
HBD	*Harper's Bible Dictionary,* ed. P. Achtemeier
HBT	*Horizons in Biblical Theology*
HDR	Harvard Dissertations in Religion
Her	Hermeneia
HKAT	Handkommentar zum Alten Testament
HS	*Hebrew Studies*
HSM	Harvard Semitic Monographs

HT Helps for Translators
HTR *Harvard Theological Review*
HUCA *Hebrew Union College Annual*
IB *Interpreter's Bible*
IBC Interpretation: A Bible Commentary for Teaching and Preaching
IBD *Illustrated Bible Dictionary,* ed. J. D. Douglas and N. Hillyer
IBS *Irish Biblical Studies*
ICC International Critical Commentary
IDB *Interpreter's Dictionary of the Bible,* ed. G. A. Buttrick, et al.
IDBSup Supplementary volume to *IDB*
IBHS B. K. Waltke and M. O'Connor, *Introduction to Biblical Hebrew Syntax*
IBS *Irish Biblical Studies*
ICC International Critical Commentary
IDB *Interpreter's Dictionary of the Bible,* ed. G. A. Buttrick
IDBSup Supplementary Volume to *IDB*
IEJ *Israel Exploration Journal*
IES Israel Exploration Society
IJT *Indian Journal of Theology*
Int *Interpretation*
INT Interpretation: A Bible Commentary for Teaching and Preaching
IOS *Israel Oriental Society*
ISBE *International Standard Bible Encyclopedia,* rev. ed., G. W. Bromiley
ITC International Theological Commentary
ITQ *Irish Theological Quarterly*
JAAR *Journal of the American Academy of Religion*
JAARSup *Journal of the American Academy of Religion,* Supplement
JANES *Journal of Ancient Near Eastern Society*
JAOS *Journal of the American Oriental Society*
JBL *Journal of Biblical Literature*
JBR *Journal of Bible and Religion*
JCS *Journal of Cuneiform Studies*
JEA *Journal of Egyptian Archaeology*
JETS *Journal of the Evangelical Theological Society*
JJS *Journal of Jewish Studies*
JNES *Journal of Near Eastern Studies*
JNSL *Journal of Northwest Semitic Languages*
JPOS *Journal of Palestine Oriental Society*
JPST Jewish Publication Society Torah
JRT *Journal of Religious Thought*
JSJ *Journal for the Study of Judaism in the Persian, Hellenistic, and Roman Period*
JSOR *Journal of the Society for Oriental Research*
JSOT *Journal for the Study of the Old Testament*
JSOTSup JSOT—Supplement Series
JSS *Journal of Semitic Studies*
JTS *Journal of Theological Studies*
JTSNS *Journal of Theological Studies, New Series*
JTT *Journal of Translation and Textlinguistics*

KAT	Kommentar zum Alten Testament
KB	L. Koehler and W. Baumgartner, *Lexicon in Veteris Testamenti libros*
KB^3	L. Koehler and W. Baumgartner, *The Hebrew and Aramaic Lexicon of the Old Testament,* trans. M. E. J. Richardson
KD	*Kerygma und Dogma*
LBBC	Layman's Bible Book Commentary
LBI	Library of Biblical Interpretation
LCC	Library of Christian Classics
LLAVT	E. Vogt, *Lexicon Linguae Aramaicae Veteris Testamenti*
LSJ	Liddell-Scott-Jones, *Greek-English Lexicon*
LTQ	*Lexington Theological Quarterly*
LW	*Luther's Works. Lecture's on Genesis,* ed. J. Pelikan and D. Poellot, trans. G. Schick
LXX	Septuagint
MT	Masoretic Text
NAB	New American Bible
NASB	New American Standard Bible
NAC	New American Commentary, ed. R. Clendenen
NB	*Nebuchadrezzar and Babylon,* D. J. Wiseman
NBD	*New Bible Dictionary,* ed. J. D. Douglas
NCBC	New Century Bible Commentary
NEB	New English Bible
NIB	The New Interpreter's Bible
NICNT	New International Commentary on the New Testament
NICOT	New International Commentary on the Old Testament
NIDOTTE	*The New International Dictionary of Old Testament Theology and Exegesis , ed. W. A. VanGemeren*
NJB	New Jerusalem Bible
NJPS	New Jewish Publication Society Version
NKZ	*Neue kirchliche Zeitschrift*
NovT	*Novum Testamentum*
NRSV	New Revised Standard Version
NRT	*La nouvelle revue the' ologique*
NTS	*New Testament Studies*
NTT	Norsk Teologisk Tidsskrift
OBO	Orbis biblicus et orientalis
Or	*Orientalia*
OTL	Old Testament Library
OTP	*The Old Testament Pseudepigrapha,* ed. J. H. Charlesworth
OTS	*Oudtestamentische Studiën*
OTWSA	*Ou-Testamentiese Werkgemeenskap in Suid-Afrika*
PCB	*Peake's Commentary on the Bible,* ed. M. Black and H. H. Rowley
PEQ	*Palestine Exploration Quarterly*
POTT	*Peoples of Old Testament Times,* ed. D. J. Wiseman
PTMS	Pittsburgh Theological Monograph Series
PTR	*Princeton Theological Review*
RA	*Revue d'assyriologie et d'archéologie orientale*
RB	*Revue biblique*
REB	Revised English Bible
ResQ	*Restoration Quarterly*

RevExp	*Review and Expositor*
RSR	Recherches de science religieuse
RTR	*Reformed Theological Review*
SANE	Sources from the Ancient Near East
SBLDS	Society of Biblical Literature Dissertation Series
SBLMS	Society of Biblical Literature Monograph Series
SBLSP	Society of Biblical Literature Seminary Papers
SBT	Studies in Biblical Theology
SJT	*Scottish Journal of Theology*
SJLA	Studies in Judaism in Late Antiquity
SLJA	*Saint Luke's Journal of Theology*
SOTI	*A Survey of Old Testament Introduction,* G. L. Archer
SP	Samaritan Pentateuch
SR	Studies in Religion/Sciences religieuses
ST	*Studia theologica*
STJD	Studies on the Texts of the Desert of Judah
Syr.	Syriac
TD	*Theology Digest*
TDNT	*Theological Dictionary of the New Testament, ed. G. Kittel and G. Friedrich*
TDOT	*Theological Dictionary of the Old Testament,* ed. G. J. Botterweck anxd H. Ringgren
Tg(s).	Targum(s)
TJNS	Trinity Journal—New Series
TLZ	*Theologische Literaturzeitung*
TNTC	Tyndale New Testament Commentaries
TOTC	Tyndale Old Testament Commentaries
TrinJ	*Trinity Journal*
TS	*Theological Studies*
TWAT	*Theologisches Wörterbuch zum Alten Testament,* ed. G. J. Botterweck and H. Ringgren
TWOT	*Theological Wordbook of the Old Testament*
TynBul	*Tyndale Bulletin*
UF	*Ugarit-Forschungen*
Ug.	Ugaritic
UT	C. H. Gordon, *Ugaritic Textbook*
Vg	Vulgate
VT	*Vetus Testamentum*
VTSup	Vetus Testamentum, Supplements
WBC	Word Biblical Commentaries
WEC	Wycliffe Exegetical Commentary
WTJ	*Westminster Theological Journal*
WMANT	Wissenschaftliche Monographien zum Alten und Neuen Testament
ZAW	*Zeitschrift für die alttestamentliche Wissenschaft*
ZDMG	*Zeitschrift der deutschen morgenländischen Gesellschaft*
ZDPV	*Zeitschrift des deutschen Palätina-Vereing*
ZPEB	*Zondervan Pictorial Encyclopedia of the Bible*
ZTK	*Zeitschrift für katholische Theologie*

Contents

Divided Monarchies
Scale of Miles
0
25
50
Scale of Kilometers
0
25
50
75
Mediterranean Sea
(Great Sea)
Phoenicia
Aram
Ammon
Israel
Moab
Judah
Philistia
Edom
Arabian Desert
Desert of Paran
Beirut
Sidon
Damascus
Ijon
Mt. Hermon
Tyre
Dan
Kedesh
Hazor
Acco
Kinnereth
Sea of Kinnereth
Ashtaroth
Hannathon
Golan
Mt. Carmel
Yarmuk River
Mt. Tabor
Edrei
Dor
Lo Debar
Megiddo
Jezreel
Taanach
Beth Shan
Mt. Gilboa
Ramoth Gilead
Ibleam
Jordan River
Jabesh Gilead
Samaria
Tirzah
Mahanaim
Socoh
Penuel
Mt. Ebal
Mt. Gerizim
Shechem
Zarethan
Jabbok River
Succoth
Aphek
Shiloh
Joppa
Rabbah of the Ammonites
Bethel
Gezer
Gibeon
Heshbon
Aijalon
Jericho
Bezer
Mt. Nebo
Beth Shemesh
Jerusalem
Medeba
Ashdod
Azekah
Bethlehem
Gath
Jahaz
Moresheth Gath
Kedemoth
Ashkelon
Mareshah
En Gedi
Dead Sea (Salt Sea)
Wilderness of Judah
Dibon
Gaza
Lachish
Aroer
Hebron
Arnon River
Arad
Beersheba
Kir Hareseth
Wadi el-Arish
Zoar
Tamar
Kadesh Barnea
Bozrah

Micah

INTRODUCTION OUTLINE

INTRODUCTION

1. Historical Setting

According to the first verse of the book, Micah's prophetic ministry fell within the reigns of Jotham, Ahaz, and Hezekiah, kings of Judah. The relevant background Scriptures covering that period are 2 Kgs 15:32–20:21; 2 Chr 27–32; Isaiah 7; 20; 36–39. The following charts will be helpful in negotiating some of the chronology of Micah's time. All dates, of course, are B.C.[1]

Kings of Judah

Jotham	Ruled for Uzziah 750–740
	Official reign 750–735
	Lived three more years 735–732
Ahaz	Co-regent with Jotham 744/3–735
	Then he ruled 735–715
	Sixteen-year reign counted from Jotham's death 732–715
Hezekiah	Co-regent with Ahaz 729–715
	Then he ruled 715–686

Kings of Israel

Menahem	752–742
Pekahiah	742–740
Pekah	Rival rule in Gilead 752–740
	Sole reign in Samaria 740–732
Hoshea	732–722

Kings of Assyria

Tiglath-pileser III[2]	745–727
Shalmaneser V	727–722
Sargon II	721–705
Sennacherib	705–681

Selected Dates and Events

734	Tiglath-pileser III's campaign against Philistia; Aramean and Israelite war against Judah after retreat of Assyrians from Philistia; Ahaz makes an alliance with Tiglath-pileser
733	Assyrian invasion of Aram (Syria)

[1] For historical treatments of the period from the mid-eighth century B.C. to the death of King Hezekiah in 686, see J. Bright, *A History of Israel*, 3d ed. (Philadelphia: Westminster, 1981), 269–309, E. H. Merrill, *Kingdom of Priests: A History of Old Testament Israel* (Grand Rapids: Baker, 1987), 391–430, and W. C. Kaiser, Jr., *A History of Israel* (Nashville: Broadman & Holman, 1997), 357–81. For a good archaeological survey of the period from 734 to 586 B.C., see E. Stern, "Israel at the Close of the Period of the Monarchy: An Archaeological Survey," *BA* 38 (1975): 26–54. For the most part, I follow the chronology of E. R. Thiele for the reigns of the kings of Israel and Judah (*The Mysterious Numbers of the Hebrew Kings* [Grand Rapids: Zondervan, 1983]).

[2] Tiglath-pileser was also called Pul in 1 Chr 5:26, where the following "and" in the KJV should be rendered "even," "namely," or "that is." Appropriately the Hebrew verb that follows in that verse is singular: "He took [the Israelites] into exile." We now know that the Babylonians called Tiglath-pileser "Pulu," which must have been his throne name in Babylon. (Pulu has been shortened to Pul in Hebrew.)

732	Damascus, north Transjordan, and Galilee conquered by Assyrians
722–721	Shalmaneser V and Sargon II conquer Samaria (Sargon involved only in mopping-up operations)
715	Hezekiah begins religious reforms, including cleansing of temple
712	Sargon captures Ashdod[3]
702–701	Hezekiah's illness; Sennacherib's threat to Judah and Jerusalem, but Jerusalem escapes; Babylonian representatives from Merodach-Baladan (in exile at the time) visit Hezekiah; Hezekiah granted fifteen more years to live

Both Israel under the reign of Jeroboam II (793–753 B.C.) and Judah under Uzziah (792–740) had enjoyed a long period of material and economic prosperity. Unfortunately it was also a time of political, social, moral, and religious corruption. Bright notes that, with the death of Jeroboam II in 753 B.C., the history of the Northern Kingdom of Israel became "a tale of unmitigated disaster." Israel's "internal sickness" erupted into anarchy at the very time that Assyria revived to pose its greatest threat. "Within twenty-five short years [Israel] had been erased from the map."[4]

The picture in Judah was almost as dark. The situation certainly grew worse with Ahaz's pagan practices. Only the reforms under Hezekiah and Josiah postponed the agony of God's discipline.

Uzziah (also known as Azariah) was succeeded on the throne of Judah in Jerusalem by his son Jotham in 740 B.C. (2 Kgs 15:32). Jotham had ruled for his father 750–740 (2 Kgs 15:5–7). Although Jotham "did what was right in the eyes of the LORD" (2 Kgs 15:3), he did not remove the "high places" (v. 4), which apparently were "assimilated from pagan Baal worship and used for the worship of the LORD in a syncretistic fashion" (2 Kgs 15:34–35).[5] There is also a parenthetical note that in his days "the LORD began to send Rezin king of Aram and Pekah son of Remaliah against Judah" (2 Kgs 15:37). This refers to the anti-Assyrian coalition that led to war in 734 B.C. between Judah and an alliance of Pekah (Israel) and Rezin (Aram).

Meanwhile, Jeroboam II was succeeded on the throne of Israel in Samaria by Zechariah (ruled six months), Shallum (one month), Menahem (ten years), Pekahiah (two years), and Pekah (twenty years). All except Menahem were assassinated. In his annals Tiglath-pileser III indicated that in 743 B.C. he

[3] In 1963 three fragments of an Assyrian stele commemorating Sargon's victory were discovered at Ashdod; see K. N. Schoville, *Biblical Archaeology in Focus* (Grand Rapids: Baker, 1978), 204, 300.

[4] Bright, *History of Israel*, 269–70.

[5] NIVSB, 2 Kgs 16:4 n.; cf. 1 Kgs 15:14 n.

marched west with his army and exacted tribute from Carchemish, Hamath, Tyre, Byblos, Damascus, and Samaria (Menahem). After Hoshea assassinated Pekah in 732, Tiglath-pileser also claimed that he put Hoshea on the throne of Israel and received ten talents of gold and one thousand talents of silver from him as tribute.[6]

In Judah, Ahaz succeeded his father, Jotham, as king in 735 B.C., though Jotham continued to live until at least 732. Ahaz became so paganized that he "even sacrificed his son in the fire" (2 Kgs 16:3), in spite of God's warning through Moses not to practice this rite (Lev 18:21; Deut 18:10). Sacrificing children to the Ammonite god Molech was common in Phoenicia and other surrounding countries. Although the exact form and origin of this sacrifice have been debated, Hartley convincingly defends an actual burning (see Jer 7:30), and Jones persuasively argues for its practice in Phoenicia and other places.[7]

Rezin of Aram and Pekah of Israel invaded Judah but could not overpower Ahaz (2 Kgs 16:5). They wanted to depose Ahaz and replace him with "the son of Tabeel" (Isa 7:6) in order to gain another ally in their anti-Assyrian coalition. It was during this period that Isaiah confronted Ahaz with the issue of faith and the prophecy of Immanuel ("God is with us," Isa 7:1–17). But Ahaz appealed to Tiglath-pileser for help and gave him the temple treasure (2 Kgs 16:7–8). The name "Jehoahaz [=Ahaz] of Judah" appears on a list of rulers who brought tribute to the powerful Assyrian king in 734 B.C.

Tiglath-pileser complied with Ahaz's request for help by attacking Damascus, destroying it, and deporting its inhabitants to the eastern part of the Assyrian Empire in 732 B.C. (2 Kgs 16:9). This fulfilled Amos's prophecy about the Arameans (Amos 1:5; 9:7). Ahaz went to Damascus to meet Tiglath-pileser. While there he saw an altar and sent a sketch of it (along with detailed plans) to the priest Uriah, who had it built before Ahaz arrived back in Jerusalem. Ahaz offered sacrifices on it instead of on the bronze altar for burnt offerings the Lord had established (2 Kgs 16:9–18). Tiglath-pileser not only defeated the Arameans of Damascus but also conquered the northern parts of the kingdom of Israel and reduced Judah to a vassal state.

In 732 B.C. Hoshea succeeded Pekah as king of Israel (after assassinating him; see above and 2 Kgs 15:30), and in 727 Shalmaneser V succeeded Tiglath-pileser in Assyria. When Hoshea stopped paying tribute to Shalmaneser, the latter began a three-year siege of Samaria (725–722) that resulted in its fall. Apparently Shalmaneser died in December of 722 and was immediately replaced by Sargon II (some scholars suspect foul play). In his

[6] Documentation for this and other references to Assyrian royal annals may be found in *ANET,* 282–88 (esp., 283 for Menahem and 284 for Hoshea).

[7] J. E. Hartley, *Leviticus,* WBC (Dallas: Word, 1992), 333–37; G. H. Jones, *1 and 2 Kings,* 2 vols., NCB (Grand Rapids: Eerdmans, 1984), 2:533–34.

annals Sargon takes credit for Samaria's capture, but his role was hardly more than a mopping-up operation. Sargon also boasts that he deported 27,290 Israelites to other parts of the Assyrian Empire (see 2 Kgs 17:6; cf. 2 Kgs 16:9 for Tiglath-pileser's similar action to the citizens of Damascus ten years earlier). Such deportations became official Assyrian policy, but in Israel's case they also were fulfillments of the curses for disobedience to the Sinaitic covenant (Lev 26:14–15,33,38; Deut 28:15,36–37,64–65). Assyria was indeed "the rod of [God's] anger" (Isa 10:5). Yet Israel's covenant Lord provided hope (Lev 26:40–45).

The next section of Kings (2 Kgs 17:7–23) provides theological reasons for the downfall of Samaria (i.e., the Northern Kingdom of Israel). The reasons include sin, ingratitude and spurning God's grace, idolatry and polytheism, pagan practices, worshiping at high places and sacred stones and Asherah poles, ritual prostitution, stubbornness, covenant breaking, the golden calves at Bethel and Dan, astral cults, worshiping the Canaanite god Baal, sacrificing sons and daughters to the Ammonite god Molech, divination, and sorcery.

The next part of Kings (2 Kgs 17:24–41) deals with repopulating Samaria and the results of that action. Sargon II and later kings of Assyria transplanted other captured peoples from various areas of the Assyrian Empire to the newly vacated towns in the Northern Kingdom of Israel. These peoples intermarried with the northern Israelites who had been left in the land. Eventually they came to be known as the Samaritans. At first, theirs was a syncretistic religion: "They worshiped the LORD, but they also served their own gods" (2 Kgs 17:33). Later, however, the Samaritans rejected polytheism and followed Moses' teachings, including monotheism. They became responsible for the Samaritan Pentateuch (for Samaritans in the NT, see Luke 10:25–37; John 4:4–26,39–43; Acts 8:4–25).

In the meantime, Ahaz was succeeded on Judah's throne by Hezekiah, who was recognized as a righteous king (2 Kgs 18:3). When Hezekiah began his sole reign in 715 B.C., he embarked on a course of sweeping reforms, including reopening and purifying the temple, whose doors had been shut by his father Ahaz (2 Chr 28:24; 29:3–5). He was particularly praised for his trust in the Lord (2 Kgs 18:5).

Probably sometime shortly after Sennacherib became the new king of Assyria in 705 B.C., Hezekiah ceased paying the annual tribute to the Assyrians (2 Kgs 18:7). So in 701 Sennacherib captured all of Judah's fortified cities and laid siege to Jerusalem (2 Kgs 18:13–17; see introduction to Mic 1:8–16). In his own annals he boasts, "As for Hezekiah, the Judean, who did not submit to my yoke, forty-six of his strongly fortified cities as well as the villages of their environs … I surrounded and conquered; 200,150 people … I brought here and counted as booty. As for him, like a bird in a cage I shut him up in

Jerusalem, his royal city."[8] He does not claim that he captured Jerusalem. The reason for such silence is clear from 2 Kgs 19:35–36 (see comments on Mic 1:9).

During Sennacherib's siege of Jerusalem, Hezekiah sent his officials to Isaiah to apprise him of the situation and to request his prayers "for the remnant that still survives" (2 Kgs 19:4). But who constitutes this "remnant"? Broshi cites archaeological evidence that Jerusalem's population increased by three to four times about 700 B.C. He explains this as due to immigration from Samaria following its fall in 721 and from the towns Sennacherib took in 701 in Judah.[9] So the Southern Kingdom of Judah now became the "remnant" of all Israel (see comments and note on Mic 3:10).

Isaiah responded to Hezekiah's request by telling him not to be afraid. Sennacherib would eventually return to Nineveh and would there be assassinated (corroborated by ancient records).[10]

At this point things became somewhat more complicated for Sennacherib, for he heard that Tirhakah, the Cushite king of Egypt, "was marching out to fight against him" (2 Kgs 19:9).[11] When Sennacherib heard about Tirhakah's military action against him, he sent a letter to Hezekiah warning him not to be deceived into thinking that God would deliver Jerusalem. Doubtless he hoped that Hezekiah would surrender the capital. But Hezekiah spread the letter out before the Lord in the temple and prayed (2 Kgs 19:14–15). He asked the Lord to rescue him and his people, "so that all kingdoms on earth may know that you alone, O LORD, are God" (v. 19). Isaiah declared the Lord's answer: Sennacherib would return by the way he came (v. 28). "He will not enter this city" (v. 32). The Lord concluded, "I will defend this city and save it, for my sake and for the sake of David my servant" (v. 34).

---

[8] Translation mine (cf. *ANET*, 288).

[9] M. Broshi, "The Expansion of Jerusalem in the Reigns of Hezekiah and Manasseh," *IEJ* 24 (1994): 21, 26.

[10] See *ANET*, 288; cf. H. W. F. Saggs, *The Might That Was Assyria* (London: Sidgwick & Jackson, 1984), 103.

[11] Much debate has swirled around Tirhakah, since he did not become king of Cush (Nubia) and Egypt until 690 B.C. But there is a solution to the problem. In 701 Tirhakah was a prince because he was the brother of the new pharaoh Shebitku, who sent Tirhakah with an army to help Hezekiah withstand the Assyrian siege. But the biblical narrative does not end in 701; it continues the story down to the death of Sennacherib in 681 (2 Kgs 19:37), which is nine years after Tirhakah had become king of Nubia and Egypt. Thus the biblical record, from the perspective of 681, refers to Tirhakah by the title he had at that time instead of the one he bore in 701— much as we refer to President Clinton even when describing events in his life before he became president. K. A. Kitchen concludes, "Unaware of the importance of these facts, and badly misled by a wrong interpretation of some of Tirhakah's inscriptions [e.g., regarding his age in 701 (actually he was at least twenty)], Old Testament scholars have often tumbled over each other in their eagerness to diagnose hopeless historical errors in Kings and Isaiah, with multiple campaigns of Sennacherib and what not—all needlessly" (*The Bible in Its World* [Exeter, U.K.: Paternoster, 1977], 114).

That night the angel of the Lord killed 185,000 Assyrian soldiers. (The Greek historian Herodotus refers to a bubonic plague as the cause of these deaths.) So Sennacherib withdrew and returned to Nineveh. There two of his sons assassinated him in 681 B.C. (vv. 35–37). Unfortunately this supernatural deliverance of Jerusalem probably helped to give rise "to the dogma of the inviolability of Zion that in no small way contributed to its ultimate destruction."[12]

The narrative continues (2 Kgs 20:1–11) with an account of Hezekiah's illness and extension of life (702–686 B.C.). The last historical event recorded in Kings involving Hezekiah was his reception of envoys from Babylon who represented Merodach-Baladan (vv. 12–19). This visit probably occurred in 703 or 702 B.C. It precipitated Isaiah's prophecy of the Babylonian exile some 115 years in advance (v. 17). The prediction is amazing since it was uttered during the period of Assyria's ascendancy. It fits nicely with Micah's similarly amazing prophecy in Mic 3:12 (see also 4:10).

The closing verses of the account of Hezekiah's reign (2 Kgs 20:20–21) mention the tunnel he built. It can still be seen (and walked through!) and is where the Siloam Inscription was located. It is dated probably around 702 B.C., when preparations were being made for Sennacherib's siege. It describes the digging that took place by the two crews who started at the two ends, and then the breaking through to each other. I translate it as follows:

> This was its boring through (or tunneling), and this was the manner of the boring through: While the miners were still swinging their picks toward each other and while there were still three cubits to be bored through, the voice of each calling to the other was heard, because there was a split in the rock on the right and on the left [=running from south to north]. Then on the day of the boring through, the miners each struck to meet the other, pick against pick. And the water flowed from the source to the pool for 1,200 cubits, and 100 cubits was the height of the rock above (or over) [=up to ground level] the heads of the miners.[13]

Incidentally, since the tunnel is almost eighteen hundred feet long, it indicates that the cubit was about eighteen inches at that time. Recently an attempt was made to redate the Siloam Inscription hundreds of years later to the Hasmonean era (long after Hezekiah). However, as Hendel has demonstrated, the forms of the Hebrew letters fit those of Hezekiah's time, not the Hebrew script of the period of the Hasmoneans.[14]

---

[12] D. J. Clark, "Micah," IBC, ed. F. F. Bruce et al. (Grand Rapids: Zondervan, 1986), 929; see also comments on Mic 3:11.

[13] Cf. *ANET*, 321; J. C. L. Gibson, *Textbook of Syrian Semitic Inscriptions, Volume 1: Hebrew and Moabite Inscriptions* (Oxford: Clarendon, 1971), 21–23.

[14] R. S. Hendel, "The Date of the Siloam Inscription …," *BA* 59 (1996): 233–37.

2. Author and Unity

Among biblical scholars there is a near consensus that most of the material in the first three chapters of this book comes from the prophet Micah. However, opinion is greatly divided regarding the authorship, date, unity, and authenticity of Micah 4–7, and thus regarding the unity of the book as a whole. R. K. Harrison points out that the first major objection to the unity and authenticity of the book came from Bernhard Stade in 1881, "who roundly denied that Micah wrote chaps. 4 and 5 and extended his views to include chaps. 6 and 7."[15] Stade was followed by many other critical scholars, who refined his views somewhat but generally agreed on exilic and/or postexilic dates for Micah 4–7.

J. D. Davis lists and rebuts six reasons the book's integrity has been impugned:[16]

First, the Assyrian and Babylonian exiles are presupposed (1:8–16; 2:12–13; 4:10; 7:7–20). But this is a problem only to those who reject supernatural predictive prophecy. Actually such exiles could be expected as punishment for breaking the terms of the Sinaitic covenant (Deut 28:31–37,47–53).

Second, the book presents glowing pictures of a future Messianic era (2:13; 4:1–8; 5:2–8). Again this is a problem only to those who cannot accept the possibility of long-range prophecies.

Third, universalism—the inclusion of Gentiles in divine blessing—is announced (4:1–3; 7:12,16–17). But this could have been anticipated at least as early as Gen 12:3; 49:10.

Fourth, prophecies such as the overthrow of Zion by its enemies seem to contradict others such as a world attack on Zion and its failure (3:12; but cf. 4:11–13). The two ideas, however, are not inconsistent because two different occasions are in view.

Fifth, sacred stones and Asherah poles are condemned, according to some critics, prior to late preexilic reforms pertaining to such objects at the pagan high places (5:13–14). But this objection assumes that Deuteronomy's condemnation of such things (Deut 7:5; 12:2–4) was not Mosaic in origin but originated centuries later. The prophets are best seen not as innovators but as reformers, calling God's people back to the covenant obedience and faithfulness that were first announced through Moses in the Pentateuch.[17] Besides, Hosea, who began his ministry even earlier than Micah, condemned the same kinds of things (Hos 2:13; 4:12; 8:4–6; 10:1–2).

---

[15] R. K. Harrison, *Introduction to the Old Testament* (Grand Rapids: Eerdmans, 1969), 922–23.

[16] J. D. Davis, *A Dictionary of the Bible* (Grand Rapids: Baker, 1954), 498–99.

[17] W. F. Albright, *The Biblical Period from Abraham to Ezra* (New York: Harper & Row, 1963), 71.

Sixth, the book proclaims both threat and promise. This "mixed" message, however, is common enough in other prophetic books. J. I. Alfaro says, "Micah, like other contemporary prophets, alternates oracles of doom and denunciation with oracles of hope and salvation."[18] If certain scholars solve such "problems" by excising the promises, are they not guilty of trimming the prophecies to suit their own theories? In fact, if Micah left us no oracles of salvation, he would be unlike most other prophets, who hold out promise and hope as well as announcing threat and doom.[19]

Although H. Gunkel's own methods were often arbitrary, he nevertheless justly protested against the whole procedure of many modern critics: "The reigning school of literary criticism is all too zealous to explain as not genuine the passages which do not exactly fit in with its construction of the history, or which are hard to be understood by the modern investigator."[20] In other words, most critical views are based on "certain presuppositions that predetermine their conclusions."[21]

If one's presuppositions or preunderstandings recognize the reality and validity of supernatural revelation, divine inspiration, miracles, and predictive prophecy (including long-range predictions), most of the "problems" evaporate. Furthermore, the "lack of agreement among critical scholars [about Mic 4–7] leaves their conclusions open to question."[22] M. F. Unger maintained: "The unsound theory of the evolutionary development of Israel's religious concepts, which erroneously insists that certain theological ideas found in Micah were not developed until a later date, has no objective evidence to support it."[23] Harrison concludes, "There is in fact no convincing proof that can be adduced against the authenticity of the oracular material in chapters 4 to 7."[24] And so we conclude that the entire prophecy of Micah—modern negative critics to the contrary notwithstanding—is the work of the

---

[18] J. I. Alfaro, *Justice and Loyalty: A Commentary on the Book of Micah*, ITC (Grand Rapids: Eerdmans, 1989), 8.

[19] See L. M. Luker, "Beyond Form Criticism: The Relation of Doom and Hope Oracles in Micah 2–6," *HAR* 11 (1987): 285–301.

[20] H. Gunkel, *Genesis*, 113; quoted by J. Orr, *The Problem of the Old Testament* (New York: Scribner, 1906), 96.

[21] C. H. Bullock, *An Introduction to the Old Testament Prophetic Books* (Chicago: Moody, 1986), 112.

[22] A. K. Helmbold, "Micah the Prophet," *ZPEB*, ed. M. C. Tenney et al., 5 vols. (Grand Rapids: Zondervan, 1975), 4:214.

[23] M. F. Unger, *Introductory Guide to the Old Testament* (Grand Rapids: Zondervan, 1951), 348.

[24] Harrison, *Introduction to the Old Testament*, 924.

prophet Micah.[25]

As for the man himself, little is known about Micah. He was from Moresheth (1:1), probably the same as Moresheth Gath (1:14). Obviously Moresheth was near Gath, one of five cities that made up the Philistine pentapolis. Moresheth has been identified with Tell el-Judeideh,[26] a small village situated almost twenty-five miles southwest of Jerusalem and about six miles north-northeast of the military fortress at Lachish.

A little over a century after Micah predicted the fall of Jerusalem (3:12), Jeremiah prophesied the same fate for the temple, the city, and its people (Jer 26:6,9,11). The priests and false prophets wanted to have Jeremiah executed. After listening to Jeremiah's defense (Jer 26:12–15), the officials and the people disagreed with that opinion (Jer 26:16). To help rescue Jeremiah, some elders appealed to the parallel case of Micah (Jer 26:17–19). They pointed out that, like Jeremiah, Micah had prophesied that Jerusalem would become a ruin and "the temple hill a mound overgrown with thickets" (quoting Mic 3:12). They further indicated that instead of executing Micah, King Hezekiah feared the Lord and sought his favor, so that the Lord relented and did not allow King Sennacherib to destroy Jerusalem at that time. This argument, together with Ahikam's support, was sufficient to save Jeremiah's life (Jer 26:24).

Since Micah was a younger contemporary of Isaiah, G. L. Robinson noted the following comparisons between the two:[27]

ISAIAH	MICAH
courtier in Jerusalem	rustic from obscure village
statesman	evangelist, sociologist
dealt with political issues	dealt with personal religion and social morality

The content of the book reveals that Micah had a "deep sensitivity to the social ills of his day, especially as they affected the small towns and villages of his homeland."[28]

Micah's name is an abbreviated form of *Mîkāyāhû* (cf. "Micaiah" in 2 Chr 17:7), meaning "Who is like Yahweh/the LORD?" (cf. 7:18; Exod 15:11; Ps 89:6). The incomparability of God is one of Micah's themes.

---

[25] For typical approaches and conclusions different from mine, see the discussions in D. R. Hillers, *Micah,* Her (Philadelphia: Fortress, 1984), 1–4; J. L. Mays, *Micah: A Commentary*, OTL (Philadelphia: Westminster, 1976), 21–33; H. W. Wolff, *Micah: A Commentary* (Minneapolis: Augsburg, 1990), 17–27; cf. G. Stansell, *Micah and Isaiah: A Form and Tradition Historical Comparison* (Atlanta: Scholars Press, 1988). For additional evidence of the unity of the book see the following structural analysis, p. 31ff.

[26] Y. Aharoni, *The Land of the Bible*, trans. A .F. Rainey (London: Burns & Oates, 1967), 292.

[27] G. L. Robinson, *The Twelve Minor Prophets* (1926; reprint, Grand Rapids: Baker, 1967), 96.

[28] NIVSB, Introduction to Micah: Author.

3. Date

The Book of Micah dates itself to the reigns of Jotham, Ahaz, and Hezekiah, kings of Judah (1:1). The maximum period for Micah's prophetic ministry would be 750–686 B.C. (see the chart on Kings of Judah on p. 22). The minimum time would be 735–715. Most scholars place his activity somewhere between these two extremes, though few would begin his ministry much earlier than 735 or end it later than 700. This means that Micah's ministry overlapped those of Isaiah (ca. 740–681) and Hosea (ca. 750–715). But his ministry was closest to that of Isaiah in both time and place (Judah; see introduction to 4:1–5 on the similarity of Mic 4:1–3 and Isa 2:2–4).

Here are two representative views of the date. "The bulk of his recorded prophetic oracles were uttered in the period 725–710."[29] "It is in [the period of Ahaz] that much of Micah's invective against social ills is best placed."[30] If Micah himself reduced his messages to writing, the date for the earliest written form of his work would be ca. 700 or shortly after. If one of his disciples arranged his messages in their present form, the date would be the early seventh century B.C. If a later editor collected and organized his messages, the date would still need to be fairly early in the seventh century in order to allow time for his prophecy of the fall of Jerusalem (3:12) to become familiar enough to be quoted in Jer 26:18 ca. 608 B.C.

4. Literary Analysis

(1) Structure

For the most part, the Book of Micah is a collection of short prophetic messages delivered by the prophet Micah. It contains twenty such literary subunits or pericopes, which were compiled and organized into a symmetrical structure. But what is that structure?

D. G. Hagstrom has identified four major, possible structures that have been proposed by various scholars.[31] The first has three major divisions: 1–3; 4–5; 6–7. He has two objections to this option: First, this partitioning of the book is "based primarily on a critical evaluation of its compositional history, rather than its present shape."[32] Second, it "also involves the elimination (or relocation) of 2:12–13 as a misplaced later interpolation."[33] He concludes,

---

[29] Helmbold, "Micah the Prophet," 215.

[30] Clark, "Micah," 928.

[31] D. G. Hagstrom, *The Coherence of the Book of Micah: A Literary Analysis, SBLDS* 89 (Atlanta: Scholars Press, 1988), 13–22; see also J. T. Willis, "The Structure, Setting, and Interrelationships of the Pericopes in the Book of Micah" (Ph.D. diss., Vanderbilt University, 1966).

[32] Hagstrom, *The Coherence of the Book of Micah*, 14.

[33] Ibid.

"This partitioning thus tends to obscure the logical literary arrangement of the book."[34] Those who prefer this structure understand chaps. 1–3 as stressing judgment, 4–5 hope, and 6–7 judgment and hope. Yet all three sections contain both judgment and hope.

The second structure has four major divisions: 1–3; 4–5; 6:1–7:6; 7:7–20. Hagstrom also objects to this proposal: "Once again the chief rationale put forth in support of this outline has to do with content. … Again, this partitioning is also argued on the basis of the history of the formation of the book of Micah."[35]

The third structure has two major divisions: 1–5; 6–7. In this division chaps. 1–5 are usually taken as addressed mainly to the nations and 6–7 primarily to Israel. The first part ends with a threat of judgment on the nations (5:15) and the second with a hymn to God's compassion (7:18–20). This approach, however, oversimplifies the diverse materials in the two major sections. Hagstrom raises no serious objections to this third possibility. The reason will become clear shortly.

The fourth structure has three major divisions: 1–2; 3–5; 6–7. With this structure each major section opens with a summons to "hear" (from the same Hebrew verb in each instance) and a specification of addressee. And each of the three sections displays the pattern, "judgment and salvation." Willis further refined this approach, stressing the role of symmetry in the final arrangement of the book:

> The general arrangement of the book seems to conform to a [sic] A(1–2)–B(3–5)–A(6–7) pattern. In the first and third divisions, the doom sections are much longer than the hope sections, whereas in the central division, the hope section is much longer than the doom section. It is striking that the first and third sections are composed of four pericopes each: (a) a covenant lawsuit (1:2–7 in I and 6:1–8 in III), (b) a lament (1:8–16 in I and 7:1–6 in III), (c) an explanation … for the impending catastrophe in the form of a reproach (2:1–11 in I and 6:9–16 in III), and (d) a hope oracle (2:12–13 in I and 7:7–20 in III). To include chap. 3 as part of the first section or portions of chap. 5 as part of the last would destroy this symmetry.[36]

Willis's analysis is compelling, though Hagstrom concludes, "Of the four structural proposals treated above, the latter two are clearly the better options. … Both present certain advantages; both entail certain difficulties."[37] But he ends up favoring the twofold division: 1–5; 6–7.[38] One difficulty Hagstrom

---

[34] Ibid.

[35] Ibid., 15.

[36] Willis, "The Structure of Mic. 3–5 and the Function of Mic. 5:9–14 in the Book," *ZAW* 81 (1969): 197; quoted by Hagstrom, *The Coherence of the Book of Micah*, 19.

[37] Hagstrom, *The Coherence of the Book of Micah*, 21.

[38] Ibid., 27.

sees with the threefold division (the last option above) is that *šim ʿû* ("Hear, Listen") occurs not only at 1:2; 3:1; 6:1 but also at 3:9; 6:2,9. But there is no literary law that states that a given Hebrew verb (in this case an imperative) cannot be used as a major division marker and still perform its usual syntactical function within a division.

Another difficulty Hagstrom finds is that 3:1 begins with a *waw* consecutive "imperfect" form in Hebrew ("*And* I said"), which seems to suggest that chap. 3 should be connected with and continue chap. 2 instead of beginning a new division. But this is probably placing too much weight on a waw consecutive—more weight than it can bear. For example, the NIV translates *wāʾōmar* "*Then* I said." Besides, the Book of Leviticus starts with a waw consecutive form (*wayyiqrāʾ,* "He [The LORD] called"). Even if one argues that the waw consecutive links Leviticus sequentially to Exodus, it nonetheless occurs at the beginning of a new major division in Leviticus. Moreover, Amos 1:2 also starts a major division with a *waw* consecutive form. Finally, it may even be possible that in certain contexts (such as Mic 3:1) the *waw* consecutive simply became a conventional way of distinguishing the old preterite form from the imperfect. Regrettably, there is still no scholarly consensus on the precise syntactical function of the *waw* consecutive in some contexts.[39] However, it is now generally agreed that the "imperfect consecutive" can at times even be used as a pluperfect (past perfect) in "dischronologized" narrative. Strictly speaking, this function would denote, not sequential action, but antecedent action.[40] Thus not all *waw* consecutive "preterites" are sequential.

Therefore Willis's analysis probably is to be preferred. Childs agrees: "The Book of Micah gives every evidence of being arranged in a clear pattern of alternating sections of judgment and salvation."[41] He then lays out the three cycles:

First cycle:	judgment (1:2–2:11)
	salvation (2:12–13)
Second cycle:	judgment (3)
	salvation (4–5)
Third cycle:	judgment (6:1–7:7)
	salvation (7:8–20)

Numerous scholars accept this understanding of the structure. Some critics question the authenticity of the salvation (or redemption or deliverance) ora-

[39] E. L. Greenstein, "On the Prefixed Preterite in Biblical Hebrew," *HS* 29 (1988): 7–17, as well as other articles in this same issue; *IBHS*, 466–78, 543–62.

[40] Barker, *The Accuracy of the NIV* (Grand Rapids: Baker, 1996), 19–20 (see also footnotes there).

[41] B. S. Childs, *Introduction to the Old Testament as Scripture* (Philadelphia: Fortress, 1979), 431.

cles, but the themes of judgment and salvation (or restoration or blessing) from the same prophet are common enough elsewhere in the prophetic literature. The outline at the end of this introduction reflects this three-cycle structure.

(2) Literary Forms

All of the following literary forms are represented in the Book of Micah:

Cycle One

1:1	Title
1:2–7	Divine covenant lawsuit (or legal procedure)
(1:3–4	Theophany)
1:8–16	Lament
2:1–5	Woe oracle (message of judgment)
2:6–11	Disputation
2:12–13	Salvation oracle

Cycle Two

3:1–4	Divine covenant lawsuit
3:5–8	Disputation
3:9–12	Judgment oracle
4:1–5	Eschatological salvation oracle
4:6–8	Eschatological salvation oracle
4:9–10	Mixed judgment and salvation oracle
4:11–13	Mixed judgment and salvation oracle
5:1–4	Mixed judgment and salvation oracle
5:5–6	Salvation oracle
5:7–9	Salvation oracle
5:10–15	Salvation oracle

Cycle Three

6:1–8	Divine covenant lawsuit	
6:9–16	Divine covenant lawsuit	
7:1–7	Lament	
7:8–20	Prophetic liturgy, with four subunits:	
	7:8–10	A psalm of trust
	7:11–13	A promise of restoration
	7:14–17	A prayer, the Lord's answer, and the response
	7:18–20	A hymn of praise to God

The commentary on each pericope includes its genre category, though occasionally such classifications were arrived at tentatively. For the most part, the literary forms identified agree with R. L. Smith's work.[42]

[42] R. L. Smith, *Micah-Malachi,* WBC (Waco: Word, 1984), 1–60.

(3) Stylistic Features

Robinson describes Micah's general style: "Vividness and emphasis, lightning flashes of indignation at social wrongs, rapid transitions from threatening to mercy, vehement emotion and sympathetic tenderness, rhetorical force, cadence and rhythm at times elevated and sublime,—these are among the prophet's outstanding literary characteristics."[43] Like Isaiah, Micah makes abundant use of figures of speech (e.g., 1:4–5,7; 3:2–3; 4:3–4,12–13) and vigorous language. He employs alliteration and assonance (e.g., 2:4,6,11; 5:1). Micah is also known for his wordplays *(paronomasia)*. The classic example is 1:10–16 (see comments there and the NIV translators' textual footnotes on vv. 10–15).

5. Hebrew Text

The Dead Sea Scrolls have generally confirmed the value and validity of the Masoretic Text (MT, the traditional Hebrew text of the OT), so it should be given primacy. Harrison writes, "A midrash on the text of Micah, recovered in a fragmentary condition from Qumran, lends support to the traditional Hebrew text."[44] Cross adds, "Actually, the most important of the Murabbaʿât finds, a magnificent scroll of the Minor Prophets from the second century A.D., came to light early in 1955."[45] He concludes that "the text of the Murabbaʿât manuscript of the Twelve Prophets … is virtually identical with the Masoretic consonantal tradition."[46] Only rarely have I felt constrained to depart from the MT in Micah. For example, in 6:16 preference was given to the LXX "the peoples" (i.e., "the nations") over the MT "my people," and in 7:19 "our iniquities" (some Hb. MSS, the LXX, Syr. and Vg.) was preferred over "their iniquities" (most Hb. MSS).

6. Purpose, Themes, and Message

(1) Purpose

It has been said that one of the purposes of the prophets was to comfort the afflicted and to afflict the comforted. Craigie puts it like this: "Micah has been called the 'conscience of Israel,' and certainly the substance of his message was designed to prick the conscience of those who had long since abandoned

[43] Robinson, *The Twelve Minor Prophets*, 104.

[44] Harrison, *Introduction to the Old Testament*, 925.

[45] F. M. Cross, Jr., *The Ancient Library of Qumran and Modern Biblical Studies* (1961; reprint Grand Rapids: Baker, 1980), 18–19.

[46] Ibid., 19, n. 23.

the integrity of Israel's faith."[47] Micah appears to have had a threefold purpose: first, to present the nature of God's complaint against his covenant people (1:2–7; 2:6–11; 3:1–4,9–12; 6:1–16); second, to proclaim the Lord's certain punishment of their many sins (3:8); and third, to predict God's sure salvation to come, centering in the appearance of the Davidic Messianic Deliverer (5:2).

E. R. Clendenen has noted the absence in Micah of an instruction message or exhortation as is typical of a prophetic book. He has suggested that the covenant context of the prophets might have supplied such an exhortation as "Return to the LORD your God and obey him with all your heart and with all your soul (Deut 30:2; also v. 10; 4:29–30; Lev 26:40–45; 2 Chr 7:14). Furthermore, "Micah's expression of confidence in 7:7 may be intended as a form of exhortation": "But as for me, I watch in hope for the LORD, I wait for God my Savior; my God will hear me." The significance of this, Clendenen suggests, is that "after God's judgment had removed from Israel every reason for arrogance, the believing remnant should watch prayerfully for the Lord's deliverance, trusting in His promises. Even in the midst of judgment Israel should not simply cry out in pain but should trust His wisdom and power and, like a woman in labor, should look for His purposes to be accomplished (4:9–10)."[48]

(2) Themes

One emphasis is clearly stated in 3:8 and is closely related to one of Micah's chief purposes: Israel's and Judah's sin and transgression. But the same God who must punish such sin also promises to deliver, restore, and bless his people again. He hates idolatry, injustice, rebellion, breach of covenant, empty ritualism, and sin of any kind; yet he delights to pardon the penitent. The section on Theological Teaching also reflects dominant themes (see p. 37ff.). Key passages include 1:2; 3:8–12; 5:1–4; 6:2,6–8; 7:18–20.

(3) Message

Although Micah lived in a small town almost twenty-five miles southwest of Jerusalem, he displayed a surprising knowledge of the social abuses and civic corruption in the capital city. As champion of the poor, he denounced the unscrupulous officials who oppressed poor farmers. It has been said that pinched peasant faces peer from between his words. Robinson states, "His

---

[47] P. C. Craigie, *The Old Testament: Its Background, Growth, and Content* (Nashville: Abingdon, 1986), 192.

[48] E. R. Clendenen, "Micah," in *The Holman Concise Bible Commentary* (Nashville: Broadman & Holman, 1998), 364–65.

whole message might almost be summed up in this one sentence: Those who live selfish and luxurious lives, even though they offer costly sacrifices, are vampires in the sight of God, sucking the life-blood of the poor. His words fairly quiver with feeling."[49] Because of Micah's condemnation of social injustice and religious apostasy, he has been dubbed the "Amos of the Southern Kingdom."

The book has a vital, much-needed message for today, and it applies to people in any age and of every generation. For God always requires justice, faithful covenant love, and humble obedience to him. Indeed, his most famous rhetorical question and reply probably is 6:8: "What does the Lord require of you? To act justly and to love mercy and to walk humbly with your God."

The writers of the New Testament found Micah to be important enough to cite. Matthew 2:6 quotes Mic 5:2 as fulfilled in Jesus, the Messianic Ruler and royal Shepherd from Bethlehem. Since the verse is applied to the Messiah by the chief priests and teachers of the law, it demonstrates that the Jewish religious leaders of Jesus' day understood Mic 5:2 as a Messianic prophecy, though they did not agree that it was fulfilled in Jesus. The same Jewish expectation concerning the origin of the Messiah is expressed in John 7:42. Matthew 10:35–36 applies the principle of Mic 7:6 to the disturbance of society caused by Jesus' own ministry. The universalism of the vision of peace seen in Mic 4:1–3 reflects a spirit not unlike that of Jesus in Mark 11:17: "My house will be called a house of prayer for all nations."

Other predictions in the book include the destruction of Samaria which occurred at the hand of Shalmaneser V and his successor Sargon II (1:6–7); the invasion of Judah by Sennacherib (1:9–16); the fall of Jerusalem and the temple (3:12); the deportation to Babylon (4:10); the return from exile and the restoration to the land of Judah (2:12–13; 4:9–10); peace and joy under a theocratic government and the spiritual supremacy of Israel (4:1–8,13; 7:11,14–17).

The preceding summary indicates that Micah's message basically alternates between oracles of doom and oracles of deliverance. To express it in terms of Rom 11:22, it alternates between God's sternness and his kindness.

7. Theological Teaching

(1) The Lord

If we accept "God's Rule or Kingdom (or Kingdom and Covenant)" as the central focus (or at least the dominant theme) of biblical theology,[50] Micah's

---

[49] Robinson, *The Twelve Minor Prophets*, 96–97.

[50] Barker, "The Scope and Center of Old and New Testament Theology and Hope," in *Dispensationalism, Israel and the Church*, ed. C. A. Blaising and D. L. Bock (Grand Rapids: Zondervan, 1992), 305–18.

contribution to such a theological center would be this: The Lord "registers his complaint against his covenant people. His punishment of their sin is certain, but so are his sure salvation and the restoration to come, centering in the appearance of the Davidic Messianic Deliverer (e.g., 2:12–13; 4:1–8; 5:2–5)."[51] This "center" will now be expanded further through a synthesis of how the Lord is described, what he does, and what he desires.

HOW HE IS DESCRIBED. The Lord is characterized as LORD (his personal, faithful, redemptive covenant name Yahweh, 1:1, etc.), universal Sovereign (1:2; 4:13b), Divine Warrior (1:3–4), Judge (1:3–5; 6:2), "Breaker" (2:13), King (2:13; 4:7–8), Redeemer (4:10; 6:4a), omniscient (4:12), omnipotent (4:4; 5:4), Lord (or Master, 1:2; 4:13b), Shepherd (5:4; 7:14), majestic (5:4), God (4:2,5; 5:4; 6:8; 7:7), great (5:4), righteous (6:5b; 7:9), exalted (6:6), Savior (7:7), light (7:8), angry (7:9), incomparable (7:18), gracious and merciful (7:18b), compassionate (7:19), true and faithful and loving (7:20).

WHAT HE DOES. The Lord reveals his word (1:1; 4:4), judges his people (1:3–5; 7:4), punishes them for their sin (1:12; 2:3; 3:4,12; 6:13–14,16), restores and leads them (2:12–13; 4:6–8), teaches his ways to the nations (4:2), settles disputes between them as royal Judge (4:3), redeems his people (4:10; 6:4a), enables them to overcome their enemies (4:13a), shepherds his flock (5:4; 7:14), gives his people security (4:4; 5:4), becomes the source of their peace (5:5b), delivers them (5:6; 6:4a), brings charges against them (6:2), provides leaders for them (6:4b), performs righteous acts for them (6:5b), appoints discipline for them (6:9), saves them (7:7), responds to their prayer (7:7), shows his wrath to them when necessary (7:9), brings them into the light (7:9), protects them (7:14a), provides what they need (7:14b), performs wonders or miracles for them (7:15), pardons and forgives them (7:18–19), delights to show them his faithful covenant love (7:18b), has compassion on them (7:19), and keeps covenant with them (7:20).

WHAT HE DESIRES. What the Lord desires from his covenant people, as well as from others, is uprightness (2:7; 7:2), justice (3:1,8), obedience (4:2; 5:15; 6:8), good stewardship (4:13b), listening to him (6:1,9), remembering his mighty acts (6:5), knowing his righteous acts (6:5b), what is good (6:8), acting justly (6:8), showing faithful covenant love (6:8; 7:2), humility (6:8), the fear of God (6:9; 7:17), wisdom (6:9), hoping for the Lord (7:7), and waiting for him (7:7).

(2) Israel and the Nations

According to the prophet Micah, the people of Israel would be disciplined for sin by their covenant Lord, but they would be restored. Their Suzerain

---

[51] Ibid., 311.

would allow them to be exiled, but he would bring them home again (2:12–13). They would be forced to go to Babylon, but the Lord would redeem them (4:10). Many nations would gather against them, but their King would enable them to be victorious (4:12–13). Nations such as Assyria would invade their land, but their Messianic Ruler would deliver them and give them peace and safety (5:2–9). The Lord would use their enemies to bring Israel down, but they would rise again thanks to their covenant God's forgiveness and restoration—all because of his faithfulness to the covenant blessings promised to Abraham and Jacob (6:13,16; 7:8,18–20).

The Gentile nations, too, Micah says, would be recipients of the Lord's covenant blessings. They would make pilgrimages to his temple at Mount Zion to worship him, to be instructed by him, and to have him settle international disputes as royal Judge (4:2–3; 7:12,16–17).

The hermeneutical approach to prophecy (regarding the place of the church, Israel, and the Gentile nations in God's program and kingdom) followed in this commentary is very similar to that of C. H. Spurgeon, which he expressed splendidly in a little work worth summarizing here.

The nations of the earth will be joined to the Lord, Spurgeon explains, so that "while Jerusalem remains the city of the Great King, the faithful among the people of all nations shall be, as it were, a suburban population to the chosen city, and the kingdom of the Messiah shall extend far and wide." Furthermore, Jerusalem will be rebuilt "in more than her former splendor," the Jews will be restored to their land, and the Messiah will be enthroned "as a prince of the house of David." It is difficult to understand many portions of Scripture apart from such an interpretation.

Although "the fixing of dates and periods has been exceedingly injurious to the whole system of premillennial teaching," Spurgeon admits, the personal return and earthly reign of Christ is still clear in Scripture. At his coming he will gather the Jews, and Jerusalem will become "the metropolis of the new empire which shall then extend from pole to pole, from the river even to the ends of the earth." If this is a correct interpretation of prophecy, Spurgeon points out, we may read the whole of Scripture and understand it; we have "the key to every sentence."

Furthermore, it seems to be "in perfect harmony with all the doctrines of the gospel." God certainly did elect the Jews, making a covenant with Abraham. If God were to cast away his people whom he foreknew, "it might augur to us the ill foreboding that mayhap He might cast away His spiritual seed also, and that those who were chosen as the spiritual seed of Abraham might yet be cut off from the olive into which they had been grafted. If the natural branches are cast away forever, why not the grafted branches too?" But the God who made a covenant with Abraham has not gone back on his word. "They shall possess the land, their feet shall joyously tread its fruitful acres yet again," and "of their rightful portion no robber will despoil them."[52]

(3) Judgment on Sin

Because Israel's covenant Lord is holy, righteous, and just, he not only gives his people the blessings of the covenant for obedience but also sends its curses on them for disobedience. In the Book of Micah itself, the sins condemned include idolatry (1:7; 5:13–14), prostitution (including religious prostitution, 1:7), plotting evil and carrying it out (2:1), coveting the property of others and taking it through fraud (2:2), rejection of true prophets and following false prophets (2:6,11), robbery (2:8), taking advantage of women and children (2:9), oppression (3:1–3), distortion of justice (3:9), bloodshed (3:10), bribery (3:11), ill-gotten gains (4:13), depending on military power instead of the Lord (5:10–11), witchcraft (5:12), cheating (6:10–11), violence (6:12), lies and deception (6:12), following the practices of Omri and Ahab (6:16), and hostility within families (7:6).

Alfaro summarizes the sins condemned especially in Micah 2–3: "The real god of the existing society was money, Mammon, and everything else was intended for his service; the poor were the main sacrificial victims. All those who had power, whether political, judicial, economic, or religious, used it for evil and for their own advantage."[53] Oesterly and Robinson conclude, "The conditions depicted for us by the eighth-century prophets, Amos, Hosea, Isaiah, and Micah, made the ruin of the country not merely intelligible but inevitable."[54]

(4) Salvation and Restoration

The oracles of judgment are counterbalanced by oracles of salvation (i.e., deliverance, restoration, and blessing). Here the covenant Lord promises to regather his people and restore them (2:12–13), to make the temple greater than ever before in order to become the worship and learning center for all nations (4:1–5), to reign over his restored flock in Zion (4:6–8), to send a Davidic Ruler (to be born in Bethlehem) whose greatness would extend to the ends of the earth (5:1–4), to enable his people to triumph over their enemies (5:7–9), to rid them of the things that once caused them to stumble (5:10–15),

---

[52] C. H. Spurgeon, "God's Sense Stands First: On the Literality of Prophecy (Zechariah 2:1–5)" (Pasadena, Tex.: Pilgrim Publications, n.d.), a one-page reprint. For similar sentiments expressed by C. L. Feinberg, see Barker, "Zechariah," EBC 7 617; see also Barker, "The Scope and Center of Old and New Testament Theology and Hope," 318–28.

[53] Alfaro, *Justice and Loyalty*, 21.

[54] W. O. E. Oesterly and T. H. Robinson, *An Introduction to the Books of the Old Testament* (New York: World, 1958), 235.

and to show faithfulness and unfailing covenant love to Abraham and Jacob (and thus to their descendants, 7:18–20).

8. Interpreting Micah

An additional clarification needs to be delineated here concerning the hermeneutical approach to prophecy referred to previously. The approach followed in this commentary includes the principle of progressive fulfillment. What that means is that certain prophecies are of such a nature that they are progressively fulfilled (i.e., in stages). Prophecies sometimes require two or more stages in order to fulfill the whole picture seen by the prophet. Conceptually, each stage is necessary to "fill to the full" the total content of what the prophet envisioned. And the fulfillment of one part is part of the fulfillment of the whole—a guarantee that the remaining events will definitely follow. Each stage becomes typological of the later stage[s], (i.e., of the fulfillment[s] yet to come).

To illustrate, many Messianic prophecies involve two stages in the progressive fulfillment of the whole, and these stages correspond to the two advents of the Messiah and to both the present and future aspects of the Messianic kingdom. The classic example of this prophetic principle is the very promise of the coming Messiah. If we had been living in the old-covenant era, we probably would have anticipated only one Messianic appearance. But in the new-covenant era we discover through the progress of revelation and fulfillment that there are actually two advents of the Messiah. It further becomes clear that to fulfill everything predicted of the Messiah and his work, both stages of the Messiah's coming are essential. Thus the promise of the advent of the Messiah is progressively fulfilled in the two stages.

Examples of this principle at work in Micah may be seen in the exposition of 2:12–13; 4:1–5,11–13; 5:1–4; 7:11–13. Additional illustrations may be found elsewhere.[55]

---

[55] For the full discussion with further examples, see Barker, "The Scope and Center of Old and New Testament Theology and Hope," 323–28.

OUTLINE OF MICAH

I. The Title (1:1)

II. First Cycle: The Judgment and Restoration of Israel and Judah (1:2–2:13)

1. The Judgment of Israel and Judah (1:2–2:11)
2. The Restoration of a Remnant (2:12–13)

III. Second Cycle: Indictment of Judah's Leaders but Judah's (and Israel's) Future Hope (3:1–5:15)

1. Indictment of Judah's Leaders (3:1–12)
2. Future Hope (4:1–5:15)

IV. Third Cycle: God's Charges against Judah Primarily and the Ultimate Triumph of God's Kingdom (6:1–7:20)

1. God's Charges against Judah Primarily (6:1–7:7)
2. The Ultimate Triumph of God's Kingdom (7:8–20)

SECTION

I. THE TITLE (1:1)

[1]The word of the LORD that came to Micah of Moresheth during the reigns of Jotham, Ahaz and Hezekiah, kings of Judah—the vision he saw concerning Samaria and Jerusalem.

The title identifies the prophetic messenger, the source of his message, where he was from, the period of his ministry, how he received his message, and the recipients of his message. The messenger-prophet was Micah. To what has been said concerning him in the introduction,[1] J. M. P. Smith would add these words: "He was not misled by false standards of value to place too high an estimate upon those things which perish with the using. He had Amos's passion for justice and Hosea's heart of love."[2]

1:1 The source of Micah's message was "the word of the LORD." This is a "technical term for the prophetic word of revelation."[3] So even though Micah is not called a prophet and the book contains no record of his call (but cf. 3:8), he is nonetheless a true prophet because the Lord revealed his prophetic word to him. That is why he can declare with full divine authority, "This is what the LORD says" (3:5; cf. 2:3). That the word of the Lord "came" to Micah is indicative of the vitality of the divine word in the Old Testament. This so-called word-event formula occurs about thirty times in Jeremiah and some fifty times in Ezekiel. When reference is made to the coming of the Lord's word, the historical character of that word is in view—its character as an event.[4] Elsewhere God's word not only "comes" but also "comes true," or is fulfilled (cf. Isa 55:8–11).

In the ancient Near East, the word of a god was thought to possess inherent power, guaranteeing its effect. In the Akkadian epic *Enuma Elish* (4:19–28), for example, the destructive and restorative power of the Babylonian god Marduk's word is considered to imply his right to rule above all others.[5] Sim-

---

[1] For Micah as a person and the meaning of his name, see Introduction ("Author and Unity," p. 28).

[2] J. M. P. Smith, *A Critical and Exegetical Commentary on the Books of Micah, Zephaniah and Nahum*, ICC (Edinburgh: T & T Clark, 1911), 18.

[3] O. Grether, quoted by W. H. Schmidt, "דָּבַר *dābhar*; דָּבָר *dābhār*," *TDOT*, 3:111.

[4] W. Zimmerli, ibid., 113.

[5] *ANET*, 66.

ilarly, the Lord's efficacious word, which can both destroy and restore, suggests his right to absolute sovereignty. He alone is the Great King, and he reigns supreme. And one of the ways he demonstrates his sovereignty and superiority is by speaking and fulfilling his dynamic word. Of course, the power of God's word resides not in magic but in his will.[6]

For the place of Micah's origin (Moresheth), see Introduction (p. 28). For the period of his ministry, see Introduction (p. 31).

According to the NIV, the Lord communicated his message to Micah through a "vision," which Micah "saw." Actually the noun "vision" does not occur in the Hebrew text, but the verb "saw" by itself can occasionally mean "saw in a vision" (the noun is from the same Hebrew root as the verb). Here, however, the notion of seeing (a vision?) may be used in the more general sense of receiving a divine revelation or a prophecy from the inspiring Spirit of the Lord (3:8; cf. 1 Sam 3:1; Prov 29:18; Isa 1:1; 2:1; Obad 1). Such an understanding is strengthened by the fact that the Hebrew text in reality says that Micah "saw the word of the LORD"; that is, the Lord's word (message) was revealed to him and he received it.[7]

The word (message) that the Lord gave Micah concerned "Samaria and Jerusalem." Samaria is mentioned first probably because the opening pericope contains a prophecy against Samaria (1:6–7) and because Micah wanted to use what would happen to Samaria as a warning to Judah and Jerusalem (1:8–9,12). After this, Samaria is no longer in view in the book except where the term "Israel" includes Israelite refugees who fled to Judah and Jerusalem.

Samaria, of course, was the capital of the Northern Kingdom of Israel, so it represented the entire Northern Kingdom. The city had been founded by King Omri (885–874 B.C.; 1 Kgs 16:23–24). It lay seven miles northwest of Shechem and rose approximately three hundred feet above the surrounding fertile valleys (cf. Isa 28:1). Although the site was an ideal location for a nearly impregnable capital city, it fell to the Assyrians in 722–721 B.C. Yet no destruction of Samaria was as complete as that by John Hyrcanus, who razed it to the ground in 108 or 107 B.C. Herod the Great rebuilt it and named it Sebaste in honor of the Roman emperor Augustus (in Gk. *Sebastos*=Augustus).

Archaeologists have uncovered the ruins of Omri's palace at Samaria and a fortress dating to the time of the dynasties of Omri and Jehu. A burned layer has been attributed to the conquest of the city in 722–721 B.C. Also discovered at the site were the Samaria ostraca (broken pieces of pottery containing writing). They probably date to the time of Jeroboam II (793–753 B.C.). They

---

[6] K. L. Barker, "Zechariah," EBC 7:605. For a discussion of the signification of "the LORD" as the personal name of God, see my chapter, "The Lord Almighty," in *The Making of the NIV*, ed. K. L. Barker (Grand Rapids: Baker, 1991), 104–8, 161.

[7] A. Jepsen supports this interpretation for such contexts. Cf. "חָזָה *chāzāh*, etc.," *TDOT* 4:280–90.

are basically receipts telling about oil, barley, wine, and other commodities being received in Samaria. They also have written on them the names of the individuals involved. Many of the names have the name of the Canaanite god Baal in them. This fits the pictures of apostasy painted by the eighth-century prophets, such as Micah.[8] Finally, beautiful ivory work was uncovered there. "The group of ivory objects found in Samaria is the most important collection of miniature art from the Iron Age discovered in Israel."[9] All the ivory work clarifies references such as 1 Kgs 22:39; Amos 3:15; 6:4. The ivories date to the ninth and eighth centuries B.C.

Just as Samaria was the capital of Israel, so Jerusalem was the capital of Judah. As such, Jerusalem stood for the entire Southern Kingdom. King David captured it from its Canaanite inhabitants about 1003 B.C. (2 Sam 5:6–10) and made it his capital city (for all Israel at that time). One of its pre-Davidic Canaanite kings was Melchizedek (Gen 14:18, where it is called Salem in the time of Abraham; cf. Ps 76:2; Heb 7:1–3). Another was Adoni-Zedek (Josh 10:1).

The city is referred to by name in Egyptian Execration Texts of the nineteenth to eighteenth centuries B.C. It is also mentioned in the Amarna letters of the fourteenth century (as "Urusalim") and in Sennacherib's inscriptions of the seventh century (as "Ursalimmu"). Excavators have identified the millo or retaining walls that David and his successors had to repair from time to time, though the nature of the millo is debated.[10] Fragments of two Proto-Aeolian capitals are the only evidence of a public building from the period of the monarchy. Remains of an Israelite settlement on the western hill from the eighth century B.C. on have been found.[11] As far as the time of Micah is concerned, Y. Shiloh "found considerable evidence of building activity in the eighth century which he thinks probably points to the work of Hezekiah (Isa 22:9–11; 2 Chr 32:3–5,30)."[12]

---

[8] J. A. Thompson, *The Bible and Archaeology* (Grand Rapids: Eerdmans, 1982), 138–39.

[9] N. Avigad, "Samaria," *EAEHL* 4:1044; see pp. 1041–43 for the palace, burned layer, and ostraca.

[10] See, e.g., P. L. Garber, "Millo," *ISBE* 3:361–62.

[11] B. Mazar, K. Kenyon, and M. Avi-Yonah, "Jerusalem," *EAEHL* 2:580–97.

[12] W. H. Mare, *The Archaeology of the Jerusalem Area* (Grand Rapids: Baker, 1987), 9.

SECTION OUTLINE

II. FIRST CYCLE (1:2–2:13)
 1. The Judgment of Israel and Judah (1:2–2:11)
  (1) The Divine Warrior Comes to Judge Samaria and Israel (1:2–7)
  (2) Micah Laments the Coming Invasion of Judah (1:8–16)
  (3) Woe to Wealthy and Oppressive Land-grabbers (2:1–5)
  (4) The Wealthy Wicked and Their False Prophets versus Micah and His God (2:6–11)
 2. The Restoration of a Remnant (2:12–13)

II. FIRST CYCLE (1:2–2:13)

Here begins the first cycle of judgment and salvation (see Literary Analysis: "Structure," p. 31). The judgment theme is presented in 1:2–2:11 and the salvation or restoration theme in 2:12–13.

1. The Judgment of Israel and Judah (1:2–2:11)

(1) The Divine Warrior Comes to Judge Samaria and Israel (1:2–7)

2Hear, O peoples, all of you,
listen, O earth and all who are in it,
that the Sovereign LORD may witness against you,
the Lord from his holy temple.

3Look! The LORD is coming from his dwelling place;
he comes down and treads the high places of the earth.
4The mountains melt beneath him
and the valleys split apart,
like wax before the fire,
like water rushing down a slope.
5All this is because of Jacob's transgression,
because of the sins of the house of Israel.
What is Jacob's transgression?
Is it not Samaria?
What is Judah's high place?
Is it not Jerusalem?

6"Therefore I will make Samaria a heap of rubble,
a place for planting vineyards.
I will pour her stones into the valley

and lay bare her foundations.
7 All her idols will be broken to pieces;
all her temple gifts will be burned with fire;
I will destroy all her images.
Since she gathered her gifts from the wages of prostitutes,
as the wages of prostitutes they will again be used."

The literary form is a divine covenant "lawsuit" (or at least "legal procedure") and a theophany (vv. 3–4). "Lawsuit" is in quotation marks because the suitability of the term has been questioned. G. W. Ramsey prefers "complaint speech."[1] M. De Roche argues that "lawsuit" is a "modern technical term that has no real Hebrew equivalent" and that "the loose application of modern technical terminology to the OT can cause grave misunderstandings."[2] He believes that the difference between a *rîb* and a lawsuit is that a *rîb* is a contention or grievance, "while a lawsuit is a particular way of solving a contention."[3] He concludes that "the terms 'prophetic lawsuit' and 'covenant lawsuit' should be abandoned."[4] Although De Roche probably has overreacted, it might be preferable here to use C. Westermann's term "legal procedure,"[5] particularly since the Hebrew word *rîb* does not occur in this pericope. Certainly some sort of legal process is involved because testimony is given, charges are brought, and sentence is pronounced.

In this first literary subunit, the peoples of the world are summoned to hear what the Lord—as Plaintiff, Witness, and royal Judge—will testify against them. He also is described as Divine Warrior leaving his heavenly temple to descend to the earth and tread on the mountains, which melt under him (1:2–4). God's coming (theophany) is due to the sins of the people. This sets the stage for what follows in vv. 5–7, where the focus is narrowed. In particular, Samaria—the capital of the Northern Kingdom of Israel—is to be destroyed, primarily because of idolatry. The Lord will use the Assyrians to bring about the destruction.

1:2 The pericope opens with the imperative *šimᶜû*, a call to "Hear." The same Hebrew verb form marks the beginning of the second and third cycles of judgment and salvation (3:1; 6:1). In most contexts (including this one) to "hear" in Hebrew means more than to receive information by ear. It means to

[1] G. W. Ramsey, "Speech-Forms in Hebrew Law and Prophetic Oracles," *JBL* 96 (1977): 46.

[2] M. De Roche, "Yahweh's *Rîb* against Israel: A Reassessment of the So-Called 'Prophetic Lawsuit' in the Preexilic Prophets," *JBL* 102 (1983): 564.

[3] Ibid., 569.

[4] Ibid., 574; for a more positive view of "prophetic lawsuit," see T. C. Butler, "Announcements of Judgment," in *Cracking Old Testament Codes*, ed. D. B. Sandy and R. L. Giese, Jr. (Nashville: Broadman & Holman, 1995), 163–64.

[5] C. Westermann, *Basic Forms of Prophetic Speech*, trans. H. C. White (London: Lutterworth, 1967), 199.

listen, understand what is being said, and respond to it appropriately.[6] The addressees are "all peoples," a reference to all nations, as shown by the parallel (more literally "those who fill the earth"). God is about to call the nations to account. As Allen puts it, "Micah's God is no provincial deity but the universal Overlord to whom all nations must render account."[7] Isaiah 3:13–14 (in the MT) has a similar movement from the peoples of the world to the Lord's own chosen people. Motyer notes: "Divine judgment often has a universal setting. … The reason for this is that judgment is one aspect of the day of the Lord when his just account is settled against all without exception."[8] In view of that day Micah prophesies the impending judgments on Samaria (Israel) and Jerusalem (Judah).

The purpose of the previous summons is next stated: "that the Sovereign LORD may witness against you."[9] When Adonai *(ʾădōnāy)* and Yahweh *(YHWH)* occur together (as here), "Sovereign" is an accurate rendering of Adonai (usually Lord, in contradistinction to *YHWH,* usually LORD).[10] As Master of everything, He rules over all (see 1:3; 4:13). "Witness" reflects the legal or court setting. The Lord of the universe will testify against "you." Keil construes "you" as a reference to Samaria and Jerusalem (v. 1).[11] But it is preferable and more natural to take the nearest antecedent: all peoples (nations). The Lord's indictment of Israel and Judah is tantamount to an indictment of all. If he indicts his own chosen but sinful people, then certainly the other nations stand indicted; for their behavior is at least as bad, if not worse (5:15; 7:16–17). The pattern of the divine judgment motif narrowing from the broader realm to the more focused area occurs elsewhere (Isa 34:1–2,5ff.; Amos 1–2).

God is further described as the Lord who testifies "from his holy temple." The primary reference here is to God's heavenly temple (v. 3; Ps 11:4; Jonah 2:7; Hab 2:20; Zech 2:13).[12] The temple, as the place of God's throne, was by definition "holy" (Ps 65:4; Jonah 2:4). The root idea of the Hebrew word for

[6] BDB, 1033–34; H. J. Austel, "שָׁמַע," *TWOT* 2:938.

[7] L. C. Allen, *The Books of Joel, Obadiah, Jonah and Micah,* NICOT (Grand Rapids: Eerdmans, 1976), 269.

[8] J. A. Motyer, *The Prophecy of Isaiah: An Introduction and Commentary* (Downers Grove: InterVarsity, 1993), 62.

[9] When two volitional forms occur together, as here (imperative followed by jussive), the second signifies purpose or result (*IBHS,* 577).

[10] K. L. Barker, "Zechariah," EBC 7:632 n. on 4:14; note bibliographical references there.

[11] C. F. Keil, "The Twelve Minor Prophets," in *Biblical Commentary on the Old Testament,* C. F. Keil and F. Delitzsch, trans. J. Martin (Grand Rapids: Eerdmans, 1949), 1:426.

[12] The Hebrew word used here for "temple" (הֵיכָל) is ultimately derived from Sumerian *é.gal,* literally "great house" (cf. Akk. *ekallu,* "royal palace," in *CAD* 4:52–61). In Hebrew it came to be used for either "palace" or "temple" (BDB, 228). Either is appropriate for King Yahweh, since the ark of the covenant represented his throne in his earthly temple.

"holy" is "separate" or "set apart."[13] In Isa 6:1–5 the ascription of holiness to the Lord begins with the Lord seated as King on a throne, high and exalted. Thus the Lord is "separated" spatially from his creation. Then, too, there is a close connection between the Lord's holiness and his kingship. Isaiah saw the Lord on his majestic throne in the year that Judah lost one of its better kings (Uzziah) after a long and prosperous reign. So the Lord is "separated" from the frailties of human rulers. Isaiah 6:3 closely associates the Lord's regal glory (his manifested character) with his holiness. After seeing the vision, Isaiah's first utterance declared the Lord to be King (6:5). The temple was holy in the sense that it was set apart to King Yahweh for his holy purposes and functions in his service and for his glory.[14]

1:3–4 King Yahweh now appears in a theophany as Divine Warrior in preparation for punishing his covenant-breaking people. "The Lord is coming" and "he comes down" describe his intervention in history (Pss 18:9; 96:13; 144:5; Isa 26:21; 31:4; 40:10; 64:1–3; Zech 2:10; 14:3; Mal 3:1). The participle *yōṣēʾ* ("is coming") probably is best taken as indicating imminent action (*futurum instans*), which can be translated "is about to come."[15] The Lord's "dwelling place" is his holy temple in heaven (v. 2). Treading the high places of the earth speaks of conquest. "High places" could refer to pagan shrines (v. 5), but in view of "mountains" (v. 4) the term probably here means "heights," as in Amos 4:13. Since God comes down to earth, he is not just transcendent (v. 2) but immanent (v. 3). He is the sovereign Lord of history, nations, earth, and its peoples. He intervenes. He acts. He conquers and judges.

Verse 4 describes the effects of the theophany. When the Lord appears, there are disturbances in nature. Similar theophanic phenomena are found in Exod 19:16–19; 20:18,21; Judg 5:4–5,20–21; Ps 18:7–15; Nah 1:2–6; Hab 3:3–15. J. E. Smith fittingly asks, "How could mere man stand in the presence of such a God when the most substantial of earth's topography cannot endure his coming?"[16] These verses provide the divine perspective on the events that were to occur in the latter eighth century B.C. when Shalmaneser and Sennacherib invaded Israel and Judah. "The Lord was coming not to save Israel from her enemies, but to deal with her as an enemy."[17]

---

[13] N. H. Snaith, *The Distinctive Ideas of the Old Testament* (New York: Schocken, 1964), 24–32, 42–50.

[14] Barker, "Zechariah," in EBC 7:620–21.

[15] C. von Orelli, *The Twelve Minor Prophets*, trans. J. S. Banks (1897; reprint, Minneapolis: Klock & Klock, 1977), 191; *IBHS*, 627. B. K. Waltke states, "The participle with הִנֵּה normally denotes an imminent future situation" ("Micah," in *The Minor Prophets*, 3 vols., ed. T. E. McComiskey [Grand Rapids: Baker, 1993], 2:618). Similarly, the following verbs (perfects with *waw* consecutive) are oriented toward the future ("will come down," "will tread," etc.). The כִּי before הִנֵּה introduces the theophany as further explanation of v. 2.

[16] J. E. Smith, *The Minor Prophets* (Joplin, Mo.: College Press, 1994), 286.

[17] J. R. Riggs, *Micah*, BSC (Grand Rapids: Zondervan, 1987), 22.

The first simile ("like wax ...") probably is intended to go with mountains melting; the second ("like water ..."), with the valleys splitting apart. The NIrV nicely captures that thought: "The mountains will melt under him/ like wax near a fire./ The valleys will be broken apart/ by water rushing down a slope."

1:5 Limburg notes the shocking effect of v. 5. The Lord's coming is usually to deliver his people in response to their prayers (e.g., Ps 144:5; Isa 13:5–9; 19:1; 26:21; 30:27; 40:10; 59:19–20; 64; 66:15). But in this case he comes in judgment on Israel (cf. 3:8; Amos 5:18–20).

> "But why should this be?" those hearing these words would ask. What wrongdoing could bring about such a terrifying intervention of the Lord? Verse 5 gives a partial hint: The wrongdoing is centered in the capital cities of both the north and the south.[18]

"All this" refers to the Lord's coming in judgment (vv. 3–4). The reason for it is here said to be Jacob's transgression and the sins of the house of Israel. The primary nuance of *pešaʿ* ("transgression") is "rebellion."[19] Jacob (another name for Israel because he fathered the twelve tribes) had rebelled against the Mosaic or Sinaitic covenant and against the Lord (King) of the covenant and his rule. The key concrete idea of *ḥāṭāʾ* (the Heb. root behind "sins") is "missing the mark/target, failure, falling short of the divine standard, et cetera" (Judg 20:16; Job 5:24; Prov 8:36; 19:2; cf. Rom 3:23); but it has semantically developed into the more common idea of "offense" or "sin" in general.[20] The rebellious acts, sins, offenses, and failures are listed in passages such as 1 Kgs 14:15–16; 16:30–33; 2 Chr 28:1–4,24–25. Israel and the first occurrence of *Jacob* theoretically could refer to either the entire nation or the Northern Kingdom alone. The second occurrence of Jacob, however, is a clear reference to the Northern Kingdom because it is coupled with Samaria and distinguished from Judah. Micah uses *Israel* for the whole covenant people (1:14–15; 2:12; 5:2; 6:2), for the Northern Kingdom (1:13), and for the Southern Kingdom (3:1,8–9; 5:1,3).

Micah raises and answers two rhetorical questions. There probably is metonymy of effect for cause here, so that the sense is: "What is the cause of Jacob's rebellion? What is the cause of Judah's high place?"[21] The answer is supplied: Samaria and Jerusalem are! Once again the NIrV brings out that idea: "Who is to blame/ for the wrong things Jacob has done?/ Samaria!/ Who is to blame for the high places/ where Judah's people worship other gods?/ Jerusalem!" But these capitals, in turn, represent the seats of power—corrupt

---

[18] J. Limburg, *Hosea-Micah*, INT (Atlanta: John Knox, 1988), 166.

[19] Snaith, *The Distinctive Ideas of the Old Testament*, 61–64.

[20] G. H. Livingston, "חָטָא (*ḥāṭāʾ*)," *TWOT*, 277–79.

[21] E. W. Bullinger, *Figures of Speech Used in the Bible* (1898; reprint, Grand Rapids: Baker, 1968), 565.

leadership had infected the whole land. So Micah will later condemn, in particular, all the civil and religious leaders. The use of Hebrew *mî* ("Who?") instead of *mâ* ("What?") probably is a deliberate personification of the two cities and their inhabitants (especially their leaders). The "high place" was a pagan center of idolatry (2 Kgs 18:4; 2 Chr 28:25; Amos 7:9). Actually the Hebrew word is plural ("high places"), though it could be repointed as singular construct. Obviously Hezekiah's reforms had not yet taken place. And since Samaria had not been captured at this point either, these words were uttered prior to 722 B.C.

1:6 Micah quotes God in vv. 6–7, pronouncing the sentence and judgment on Samaria for the transgression referred to in v. 5. The prophecy recorded here began to be fulfilled even during Micah's lifetime when Assyria captured Samaria in 722–721 B.C. (2 Kgs 17:3–6), though complete destruction was not effected until John Hyrcanus inflicted it in 108 or 107 B.C. Destruction of any kind in 722 has been denied by some (e.g., R. L. Smith[22]). However, if Avigad is correct, a burned layer may be attributed to this earlier period (see comments and notes on Samaria in 1:1).[23] So some destruction may have taken place, followed by rapid rebuilding, renovation, and restoration. The Divine Warrior's use of Assyria to carry out his judgment or conquest in this pericope and the next one is similar to his use of Babylonia in 3:12; 4:9–10; 5:1 and of Alexander and Greece in Zech 9:1–8.

Some of the language here is the same as or similar to that pertaining to the destruction of Jerusalem in 3:12 ("heap of rubble" in both; "a place for planting vineyards" and "plowed like a field"; "temple gifts" and "temple hill"). Samaria's stones could be thrown or pushed down into the valley below because the city was built on a hill (see comments on v. 1). A modern tourist can stand on that hill today and see nothing but ruins.

1:7 The idolatrous nature of "Jacob's transgression" (v. 5) is elaborated in this verse and God's intention "to abolish all forms of idolatrous worship, worship that flagrantly violated the first and second commandments (Exod 20:3–5)."[24] Therefore Samaria's idols, religious prostitution, and wealth would also be annihilated. Ahab and Jezebel had increased such idolatry and pagan worship in the Northern Kingdom of Israel (1 Kgs 16:29–33), and Baalism and all its trappings continued down to the fall of Samaria. The immoral and idolatrous practices referred to here constituted a blatant violation of Deut 23:17–18.

The "temple gifts" (*ʾetnan,* used three times in this verse, also translated

---

[22] R. L. Smith, *Micah–Malachi,* WBC (Waco: Word, 1984), 18.

[23] N. Avigad, "Samaria," *EAEHL* 4:1041; cf. L. F. DeVries, *Cities of the Biblical World* (Peabody, Mass.: Hendrickson, 1997), 230.

[24] W. P. Brown, *Obadiah through Malachi,* Westminster Bible Companion (Louisville: Westminster John Knox, 1996), 35.

“wages”) were the gifts the people of Samaria gave to the shrine prostitutes as part of pagan fertility rites. Because of such practices, prostitution in the Old Testament is frequently a symbol for idolatry or spiritual adultery and unfaithfulness (Exod 34:15–16; Judg 2:17; Ezek 23:29–30). The NIrV makes the meaning of the last sentence of the verse clearer: “Samaria collected gifts that were paid to temple prostitutes. / So the Assyrians will use the gifts / to pay their own temple prostitutes.” That is to say, the invading Assyrians (722–721 B.C.) would transfer the wealth Samaria had acquired from its idolatry to their own temples, where it would be used again for immoral and idolatrous worship (2 Kgs 17:6–18). The divine punishment fits the crime. No wonder Israel’s covenant Lord and King decided that it was time for the Northern Kingdom to cease as a separate national entity! (For further application of the principle involved here, see Prov 1:19; Isa 33:15–16; Jas 4:13–14.)

(2) Micah Laments the Coming Invasion of Judah (1:8–16)

8Because of this I will weep and wail;
I will go about barefoot and naked.
I will howl like a jackal
and moan like an owl.
9For her wound is incurable;
it has come to Judah.
It has reached the very gate of my people,
even to Jerusalem itself.
10Tell it not in Gath;
weep not at all.
In Beth Ophrah
roll in the dust.
11Pass on in nakedness and shame,
you who live in Shaphir.
Those who live in Zaanan
will not come out.
Beth Ezel is in mourning;
its protection is taken from you.
12Those who live in Maroth writhe in pain,
waiting for relief,
because disaster has come from the LORD,
even to the gate of Jerusalem.
13You who live in Lachish,
harness the team to the chariot.
You were the beginning of sin
to the Daughter of Zion,
for the transgressions of Israel
were found in you.
14Therefore you will give parting gifts

to Moresheth Gath.
The town of Aczib will prove deceptive
to the kings of Israel.
15I will bring a conqueror against you
who live in Mareshah.
He who is the glory of Israel
will come to Adullam.
16Shave your heads in mourning
for the children in whom you delight;
make yourselves as bald as the vulture,
for they will go from you into exile.

The literary genre or form of this unit is that of a lament. The section is framed by an inclusio, the concept of mourning in vv. 8,16.[25] It seems clear from vv. 8–9 that the fall of Samaria portends a similar fate for Jerusalem and Judah, so the prophet Micah laments. He sees an invading army, doubtless that of King Sennacherib of Assyria in 701 B.C.[26] Twelve cities, including even Jerusalem, are in its path. Desolation, refugees, and hostages are the result. Wordplays on the names of the cities and towns are designed to express at least part of the nature of their judgment. Some of the cities are well known, such as Jerusalem, Lachish, and Adullam, while the location of others is uncertain. Although the first oracle was addressed to the nations and specifically announced the fall of Samaria, this pericope indicates that Judah and Jerusalem were Micah's principal concern.

1:8 "Because of this" refers to the coming Assyrian capture of Samaria (vv. 6–7). Now Micah perceives that Judah and Jerusalem will also suffer at the hands of Assyria (vv. 9–16). As history has shown, it would happen approximately twenty years later. So between 1:2–7 and 1:8–16 a period of two decades has been telescoped. Micah's heart (undoubtedly reflecting the heart of God) is broken as he contemplates the fate of Samaria (v. 8). He is filled with compassion as he considers what will also happen to Judah and Jerusalem (v. 9).[27] He is much like Jeremiah in Jer 8:21–9:1, like the Lord himself in Hos 11:8–9, like Amos in Amos 7:1–6, and like Paul in Rom 9:2–3; 10:1.

Going "barefoot"[28] is a sign of mourning in 2 Sam 15:30. "Naked" here

[25] For a description of this genre, see T. Longman III, "Lament," in Sandy and Giese, *Cracking Old Testament Codes*, 197–215.

[26] See Introduction: "Historical Setting" (pp. 25–27).

[27] In Hebrew the verbs "weep ... wail ... go about" are cohortatives of resolve.

[28] The *kethiv*, שׁילל, occurs only here. The *qere*, שׁוֹלָל, which is also in the Qumran Scroll and many Hb. manuscripts, occurs in Job 12:17,19 where it is translated "stripped." It probably derives from שׁלל, "pull out" (BDB) but may also derive from שׁלל, "plunder" (Ibn Ezra, R. Gordis, *The Book of Job* [N.Y.: Jewish Theological Seminary of America, 1978], 139, and elsewhere). Its occurrence only with the verb הלך ("walk") suggests the meaning "barefoot" as probably correct. Cf. D. R. Hillers, *Micah,* Her (Philadephia: Fortress, 1984), 22.

means stripped of one's outer and inner robes and so clothed only in a loincloth (1 Sam 19:24; Isa 20:2–4; cf. John 21:7).[29] Micah, like Isaiah, may actually have walked barefoot through Jerusalem while wearing only a loincloth. His sadness was so great that he howled like a jackal and moaned (or screeched) like an owl. The mournful, sobbing cry of the jackal[30] is used symbolically of a man lamenting his bitter fate in Job 30:29, where both jackal and owl occur together again. The Hebrew word for "owl" *(yaᶜănâ)* is usually assigned the meaning "ostrich." However, some scholars connect it to an Arabic etymological cognate with the root idea of "desert." So the entire Hebrew phrase *(bĕnôt yaᶜănâ)* would mean literally "daughters of the desert," hence "desert owls" or "eagle owls" or simply "owls" (REB "desert-owl").[31]

1:9 "For" introduces the reason for Micah's grief, namely, the implications of Samaria's fall for Judah and Jerusalem (cf. Isa 10:11). Samaria's "wound"[32] refers to the judgment about to overtake it. That wound is described as "incurable."[33] It will spread like a cancer to the Southern Kingdom.[34] The covenant nation is similarly portrayed in Isa 1:5–6; 17:11 (here, too, the incurable pain is brought by the Assyrians); Jer 8:22; 14:17; 30:12–17.

---

[29] Cf. S. R. Driver, *Notes on the Hebrew Text and the Topography of the Books of Samuel* (Oxford: Clarendon, 1913), 160; B. V. Seevers, "עָרוֹם," *NIDOTTE* 3:532–33.

[30] "I will howl" is lit. "I will make mourning" (אֶעֱשֶׂה מִסְפֵּד), which uses the same root (ספד) as "I will weep" (אֶסְפְּדָה). מִסְפֵּד also occurs in v. 11, translated "mourning." "The primary sense [of ספד] appears to be that of wailing" (R. W. L. Moberly, "Lament," *NIDOTTE* 4:869). See also Gen 50:10; 2 Sam 1:11–12; 3:31; 1 Kgs 13:30; Jer 6:26; 22:18; 34:5; Amos 5:16.

[31] *Fauna and Flora of the Bible*, 2d ed. (New York: UBS, 1980), 60–61.

[32] When a verb occurs before its subject in a clause, it is quite common in Hebrew for it to be singular even when the subject is plural as here (lit., "For incurable [singular] are her wounds"). Some scholars prefer revocalizing "wounds" as singular ("wound") or repointing "her wounds" to read "Yah's (=Yahweh's) wound" (Hillers, *Micah,* 22), but such alterations are unnecessary. In view of analogous phenomena elsewhere, the MT can be considered original.

[33] See Jer 30:12, where אָנוּשׁ is parallel to נַחְלָה, "beyond healing" (from חלה, "be weak, ill"; cf. Jer 10:19). See also *DCH* 1:344–45.

[34] The verb נָגַע, "reached," means basically to touch and is often used of affliction by God (cf. Gen 12:17; 2 Kgs 15:5; Job 19:21; Ps 73:5; Isa 53:4). See M. A. Grisanti, "נגע," *NIDOTTE* 3:22–24. After בָּאָה, "it has come"—a feminine verb form referring back to feminine "wound(s)"—one would have expected the feminine in the continuation, "It has reached." Instead, the verb form is masculine. But when one examines all the data in the Hebrew Bible dealing with grammatical agreement (and disagreement!), one discovers considerable inconsistency in such matters. For example, in the Book of Ruth there are several instances of masculine pronouns and verb forms where the feminine would have been anticipated. As M. Held once remarked, "Language is not mathematics." Now it would be possible here to read the subject of "has reached" as "He," referring either to the enemy or to the Lord himself. However, there is no compelling need to do so. "It" is more natural in the context and is acceptable in view of the known phenomena of Hebrew grammar and syntax.

The wound or injury to Jerusalem was inflicted by King Sennacherib of Assyria in 701 B.C. (Isa 36:1), though Jerusalem did not fall until the summer of 586 (Isa 37:33–37; 39:5–7). The gate of a city was the location of judicial, commercial, and administrative activity (cf. Gen 19:1; Ruth 4:1–4). Hillers interprets "Jerusalem" as in apposition to "the gate of my people," explaining that Jerusalem was "the center of political and religious life for the people." He says "gate" is "a kind of synonym for 'city' in Isa 14:31." He also notes the phrase in Obad 13 and Ruth 3:11.[35] After Sennacherib conquered most of Judah, he did reach the gate of Jerusalem, but he did not take the city at that time (see Historical Setting, pp. 25–27).

1:10 Here begins Micah's description of Sennacherib's destruction and/or capture of several cities or towns in Judah.[36] All of them except Jerusalem were only a few miles from Micah's native town (Moresheth Gath) and were situated in the Shephelah district—the foothills between the Mediterranean coastal plain and the central mountain range of Judah. Verses 10–16 feature many striking wordplays that Moffatt attempts to reflect in his English translation of 1:10–16. The cities' names are connected to their judgment:

> Weep tears at Teartown (Bochim),
> grovel in the dust at Dustown (Beth–ophrah),
> fare forth stripped, O Fairtown (Saphir)!
> Stirtown (Zaanan) dare not stir,
> Beth–êsel …
> and Maroth hopes in vain;
> for doom descends from the Eternal
> to the very gates of Jerusalem.
> To horse and drive away, O Horsetown (Lakhish),
> O source of Sion's sin,
> where the crimes of Israel centre!
> O maiden Sion, you must part with
> Morêsheth of Gath;
> and Israel's kings are ever balked
> at Balkton (Achzib).
> I will march the conqueror on you yet,
> O men of Mareshah;
> and Israel's pomp shall perish utterly.

---

[35] Hillers, *Micah,* 23.

[36] C. S. Shaw, however, believes that the general period of the anti-Assyrian coalition of Aram, Israel, and other states against King Ahaz and Judah (and ultimately against Assyria) is in view (ca. 734–732 B.C.), but he resorts to rather radical surgery on the MT to obtain the desired sense ("Micah 1:10–16 Reconsidered," *JBL* 106 [1987]: 223–29). It is more natural to take these verses as a prophecy (in the form of a lament) of what Assyria would do not only to Samaria and Israel but also to Judah and Jerusalem (cf. Isa 10:28–32). So understood, vv. 10–16 would be a logical development from vv. 1–9.

Israel, shave your head and hair,
in mourning for your children dear,
shave it like a vulture's, bare;
for they are lost to you.

The towns listed in these verses comprise a part of the destructive march of the Assyrian army under Sennacherib to the gates of Jerusalem in 701 B.C. Sennacherib himself proudly portrayed the defeat of Lachish (1:13) on a wall of his palace and boasted of having King Hezekiah of Jerusalem shut up like "a bird in a cage."[37] But Sennacherib does not claim that Jerusalem fell at this time. That would not happen until the destructive march and siege by the Neo-Babylonian army under Nebuchadnezzar in 588–586 B.C.

The section begins with a quotation from David's lament over Saul and Jonathan in 2 Sam 1:20: "Tell it not in Gath." The reason for the quotation probably is to relate the anticipated fall of the house of David (v. 16 and later in the book) to the fall of the house of Saul (2 Sam 1:20). The wordplay here involves assonance in the Hebrew for "Gath" and "Tell" *(bĕgat ʾal taggîdû).*[38] "Tell it not in Gath" introduces a funeral lament over Judah. Micah did not want the pagan people of Gath to have the pleasure of gloating over the downfall of God's people (cf. Pss 30:1; 89:49–51). Gath has been identified as Tell es-Safi. It was the closest of the Philistine cities to Judah's borders.[39]

Micah also did not want the nearby Philistines of Gath to see his people weeping over the devastation to be brought by Sennacherib. There is assonance in the Hebrew for "weep" *(tibkû)* and "at all" *(bākô).* Hebrew *bākô* is sometimes construed as a contraction of *bĕʿakkô* ("in Acco") to maintain the parallel with "in Gath," hence "weep not in Acco." But Waltke has persuasively demonstrated the unlikelihood of such a possibility.[40] For one thing, the textual evidence for it is weak. For another, Acco lies north of Mount Carmel, whereas the other known towns in the pericope (besides Jerusalem) are within a ten-mile radius of Micah's native town, Moresheth Gath. Pusey notes that Gath probably had now ceased to be of any account. This shows how David's elegy lived in the hearts of Judah—that his words are used as a proverb when its original application probably was lost. True, since Gath itself was reduced, its inhabitants might rejoice the more maliciously over the sufferings of Judah. But David mentions it as a chief seat of Philistine strength; now its strength was gone.[41]

As a sign of mourning over the coming catastrophe, those who live in Beth

[37] W. P. Brown, *Obadiah through Malachi,* 37.

[38] R. F. Youngblood, "1, 2 Samuel," EBC 3:812.

[39] E. Stern, "Tell es-Safi," *EAEHL* 4:1024–27.

[40] Waltke, "Micah," 2:627.

[41] E. B. Pusey, *The Minor Prophets*, 2 vols. (Grand Rapids: Baker, 1950 repr.), 2:22.

Ophrah are told to "roll in the dust" (cf. Isa 47:1).[42] The location of this town has not yet been determined, though some locate it in the eastern Shephelah. The name means "house (or temple) of dust." The wordplay on the sense is obvious: Those who live in House of Dust are to roll in the dust.

1:11 The location of Shaphir, Zaanan, and Beth Ezel is uncertain, though some identify the first with Khirbet el-Qom, west of Hebron, and the last with Deir el-Asal, about ten miles southwest of Hebron. "Shaphir" means "pleasant." Its inhabitants are commanded to leave in nakedness and shame, the condition of prisoners (Isa 20:4). So the "pleasant" ones would endure a very unpleasant experience as they joined the more than 200,000 captives Sennacherib took away on this expedition (according to his own annals). "Zaanan" sounds like the Hebrew for "come out," but those who live there will not "come out."[43] "Beth Ezel" suggests the meaning "house (or temple) of protection," but its citizens are in great mourning because its "protection" is removed from Shaphir. Although the verse is difficult, the NIrV probably captures the sense as well as any other version: "You who live in the town of Shaphir, / leave in shame and without your clothes. / Those who live in Zaanan / won't come out to help you. / The people in Beth Ezel will sob. / They won't be able to help keep you safe."

1:12 "Maroth" is also of uncertain location. The wordplay hinges on a dual meaning for *ṭôb,* "relief." The word *ṭôb* can mean "sweetness," contrasting with *mārâ,* "bitter" (Ruth 1:20), which sounds like "Maroth"; or it can mean "good," contrasting with "disaster" (*rāᶜ,* which can mean "evil").[44] The suffering inhabitants of Maroth wait for "good"; instead, the Lord will send "disaster." Pusey comments: "Losing the true Good, man lost all other good, and dwelling in the bitterness of sin and provocation, he dwelt indeed in bitterness of trouble."[45] The Hebrew for "has come" (lit. "has come down") is actually a prophetic perfect and should have been rendered as future ("will come"). In fact, in several places in this pericope it would have been preferable to use the English future instead of the NIV's present or past. The "disaster" would reach "even to the gate of Jerusalem" (cf. v. 9). This is precisely what happened in 701 B.C. So how could there be any hope for the people of Maroth? Many other towns of Judah had already fallen, and King Sennacherib and his Assyrian army were laying siege at the city gates and walls of Jerusalem, with King Hezekiah shut up inside "like a bird in a cage." But it was not

---

[42] "Roll" (imperative) follows the MT *qere* instead of the *kethiv* ("I have rolled").

[43] יָצְאָה is here construed as a prophetic perfect or perfect of confidence; for this syntactical function of the perfect, see *IBHS,* § 30.5.1e, (examples 38–39).

[44] רָע *(rāᶜ),* "evil, disaster," "is the 'evil' someone does and the 'disaster' he encounters in consequence" (G. Fohrer, "Twofold Aspects of Hebrew Words," in *Words and Meanings*, ed. P. P. Ackroyd and B. Lindars [Cambridge: University Press, 1968], 102).

[45] Pusey, *The Minor Prophets*, 2:24.

God's will for Jerusalem to fall at that time. Jerusalem's actual demise was delayed until 586 B.C.

1:13 Lachish has been identified with Tell ed-Duweir. It was one of the largest cities in Judah and was located almost thirty miles southwest of Jerusalem and only six miles southwest of Moresheth Gath. Rehoboam had fortified Lachish (2 Chr 11:9) so that it guarded the main approach to the capital city from that district. It had a massive city wall twenty feet thick and a defensive gateway comparable to the ones at Gezer, Hazor, and Megiddo. It was one of the last of the forty-six cities to fall to Sennacherib in 701 B.C. (2 Kgs 18:13; 2 Chr 32:9). The siege and the following procession of plunder are depicted on bas-reliefs found in Sennacherib's palace at Nineveh. Later the city was rebuilt, and Jer 34:7 indicates that in 588 B.C., when King Nebuchadnezzar was leading his Neo-Babylonian army against Judah, the only fortified cities left were Jerusalem, Lachish, and Azekah. A cache of ostraca (letters written on fragments of pottery) was found at Lachish dating from this time. Letter 4 from the commander of an outlying garrison indicates that the nearby city of Azekah had already fallen: "We are watching for the fire-signals of Lachish … for we cannot see Azekah."[46] This Hebrew military communique seems to have been written in feverish haste as the Babylonian army was closing in.

The people of Lachish are told to harness the team of horses to the chariot (lit., "harness the chariot to the team") in order to escape the onslaught of King Sennacherib's Assyrian army. The wordplay here involves alliteration and assonance between Lachish (Hb. *lākîš*) and "team" (lit. "to the team," Hb. *lārekeš*). The singulars are collectives, of course. The last half of the verse is difficult. But again the NIrV seems to capture the sense intended: "You trust in military power. / That was the beginning of sin / for the people of Zion. / The wrong things Israel did / were also done by you." It is instructive that "military power" (horses and war chariots) would be demolished by the Lord (5:10). "Transgressions" (NIV) could have been more precisely rendered "rebellious acts" (see comments on v. 5). The last "you" of the verse may refer to the people of Lachish in particular or, more generally, of Judah. If the latter, "Israel" would definitely be restricted to the Northern Kingdom (in fact, it could be so restricted in either case).

1:14 "Therefore" connects this verse with what has preceded and thus would most likely mean "Because Judah has adopted the evil practices of the Northern Kingdom of Israel." Judah and Jerusalem probably are addressed ("you") from here to the end of the chapter, which would be natural enough since Jerusalem and Zion were just mentioned in vv. 12–13 and since the feminine singular verb ("give") quite frequently refers to Jerusalem.

---

[46] DeVries, *Cities of the Biblical World,* 208–14.

There appears to be a wordplay on the meaning suggested by the name "Moresheth" ("inheritance, possession"). Judah will have to part with its inheritance or possession, symbolized by the parting gifts (lit. "wedding gifts, dowry"). Moresheth also sounds like *mĕʾōreśet* ("betrothed"). Somewhat as a daughter goes to a new and strange place in marriage, so the people of Moresheth will go into exile to strange surroundings. Or perhaps the sense is that as a father gives a "wedding gift" to his daughter when she marries and leaves, so Judah must give up Moresheth to Assyria. The "dowry" paid may refer to Hezekiah's payment of silver and gold to Sennacherib at Lachish (2 Kgs 18:13–16).

Aczib probably is Tell el-Beida, situated about halfway between Adullam and Moresheth Gath. The wordplay is clear in the Hebrew text between *ʾakzîb* (Aczib) and *ʾakzāb* ("deceptive")—"Deception Town" will prove "deceptive." In Jer 15:18 "deceptive" is used of a brook that has dried up. Aczib will be as undependable and disappointing as a dried-up brook because its people won't be able to give any help to the kings of Israel in stopping the Assyrian juggernaut. Israel could refer to the whole covenant nation or to Judah alone; many northerners had fled to Judah by 701 B.C. anyway.

"Town" is literally "houses." Waltke prefers to follow Demsky in construing "houses" as "workshops" or "factories" and taking it as indicating economic loss.[47] In support of "town," R. L. Smith explains that the kings (the plural is perhaps a way of speaking of the whole royal house or of a coregency involving Hezekiah and Ahaz) of Israel expected help in resisting the Assyrians but found none in Aczib.[48] One problem with Waltke's (and Demsky's) interpretation is that elsewhere when *bayit,* "house," is used in the sense of "workshop," the nature of the work is specified. In 1 Chr 4:21 it is linen work; in Jer 18:2 it is the work of a potter. Here in Mic 1:14 no such work is specified. Furthermore, as Hillers points out, this passage speaks not of "loss" but of "something that deceives or disappoints."[49] So while "workshops" is semantically possible, "town" seems more likely.

1:15 God ("I") now speaks directly through his prophet, as in vv. 6–7. He declares that he will bring a conqueror against those who live in Mareshah.[50] The conqueror, of course, was King Sennacherib of Assyria in 701 B.C. Mareshah has been identified as Tell Sandahanna, located about halfway between Lachish and Moresheth Gath. Archaeological excavations at the tell turned up an inscription mentioning the Sidonian community "residing in

[47] Waltke, "Micah," 2:631; A. Demsky, "The Houses of Achzib. A Critical Note on Micah 1:14b," *IEJ* 16 (1966): 211–15. Allen inclines toward this view as well (*Joel, Obadiah, Jonah and Micah*, 282).

[48] R. L. Smith, *Micah–Malachi*, 22.

[49] Hillers, *Micah*, 27.

[50] As in 1 Kgs 21:29, אָבִי ("I will bring") is defective for אָבִיא.

Marisa," thus confirming the identification.[51] Mareshah sounds like the Hebrew for "conqueror" (*hayyōrēš* from *yāraš*, "dispossess, take possession") and that is the wordplay here. Its people would be conquered and dispossessed.

The second half of v. 15 is literally "To Adullam the glory of Israel will come." If "glory" functions as a surrogate for God (as in 1 Sam 15:29), the NIV is correct in adding "He who is" for clarity. And the thought would be that Israel's glorious King would come to Adullam in judgment (cf. 1:3; Adullam probably is Tell esh-Sheikh Madkur, just northeast of Aczib). However, it seems best in this context to take "glory" as a reference to Israel's leaders (see Isa 5:13). Then the idea would be: "Israel's glorious leaders will have to run away / and hide in the cave of Adullam" (NIrV). In either case, David's experience in 1 Sam 22:1 and 2 Sam 23:13 is evoked, hinting that his dynasty is threatened and its royal and other government officials are going to be exiled (v. 16). Thus vv. 10–15 (where various cities in Judah are about to fall) begin and end with allusions to David (see comments on v. 10). And the stage is nicely set for the last verse of the pericope.

1:16 As in v. 14 the "you" is feminine singular, so Jerusalem/Zion (ultimately Judah) is being addressed. "Shave your heads in mourning" renders a verb phrase consisting of two Hebrew verbs *(qorḥî wāgōzzî)* that would be more literally, "Shave and shear," or "Make yourselves bald [taking the singular as collective] and cut your hair." In the second half of v. 16 "make yourselves as bald as the vulture" is more literally, "enlarge your baldness like a vulture." This makes it easier to see the final wordplay of the pericope, involving the same Hebrew root: "Make yourselves bald *(qorḥî)* ... enlarge your baldness *(harḥibî qorḥātēk)*." A mourning rite is in view. Only certain kinds of cutting the hair and beard were prohibited in the Pentateuch (Lev 19:27; 21:5 [priests]; Deut 14:1). Partial or extensive baldness continued to symbolize mourning (cf. Isa 3:17,24; 15:2; Jer 48:37; Amos 8:10). In the simile the griffon vulture is referred to because it has no feathers on its head and neck.

Jerusalem's (or Judah's) "children" were the inhabitants (particularly the leaders, royal and otherwise) of all the towns previously mentioned. The reason for such extreme lamentation is that these "children" will "go from you into exile." In fact, it is so certain that the Hebrew prophetic perfect is used, "will go into exile." It is as good as done. In 722–721 B.C. and following, the Assyrians took into exile many from the Northern Kingdom of Israel. Now the same thing is to happen to Judah in 701. Sennacherib boasts that he deported over two hundred thousand captives from these and other cities. Probably also present here is a hint of the ultimate fall of Jerusalem and the ensuing Babylonian exile in 586 (see 3:12; 4:10).

---

[51] M. Avi–Yonah, "Mareshah (Marisa)," *EAEHL* 3:782, 789.

What could have precipitated such a coming of the Divine Warrior in severe judgment on his covenant people? In 2:1–11 Micah states the reasons for the previous devastation, charging that those in positions of leadership, wealth, power, and control were guilty of the sins of greed, covetousness, oppression, corruption, fraud, and theft. And their highly paid false prophets predicted nothing but prosperity for them, thus encouraging them in their evil acts. These and other sins brought stern discipline from their covenant Lord. There is a warning here for his new covenant people as well. Such sins do bring judgment. People reap what they sow (Gal 6:7–8). So do nations, whether Israel or America or any other modern power.

(3) Woe to Wealthy and Oppressive Land-grabbers (2:1–5)

1Woe to those who plan iniquity,
to those who plot evil on their beds!
At morning's light they carry it out
because it is in their power to do it.
2They covet fields and seize them,
and houses, and take them.
They defraud a man of his home,
a fellowman of his inheritance.
3Therefore, the LORD says:
"I am planning disaster against this people,
from which you cannot save yourselves.
You will no longer walk proudly,
for it will be a time of calamity.
4In that day men will ridicule you;
they will taunt you with this mournful song:
'We are utterly ruined;
my people's possession is divided up.
He takes it from me!
He assigns our fields to traitors.'"

5Therefore you will have no one in the assembly of the LORD to divide the land by lot.

The literary genre is a woe oracle (message of judgment). Klein, Blomberg, and Hubbard use 2:1–5 as an example of a "Woe Speech," having (1) a declaration of woe, (2) an explanation of offenses (basic statement and amplification), (3) a messenger formula, and (4) a prediction of doom.[52] All these elements or components are present in this pericope. Westermann's analysis is similar. He makes reference to 2:1–4 as a prophetic judgment

[52] W. W. Klein, C. L. Blomberg, and R. L. Hubbard, Jr., *Introduction to Biblical Interpretation* (Dallas: Word, 1993), 295.

speech to the nation, having (1) an introduction (woe), (2) an accusation, (3) a development of the reason for the judgment, (4) a messenger formula, (5) an intervention by God, and (6) the results of that intervention.[53]

Some keep 2:1–11 together as a single unit (see Introduction: "Structure"), but it seems preferable to treat the two parts separately: 2:1–5 as a woe oracle and 2:6–11 as a disputation. The judgment in vv. 1–5 is against a certain group of wealthy men who devise wicked schemes at night to seize houses and lands from unsuspecting farmers. Their slogan is "Might makes right." But their plots will boomerang: Their own lands will be snatched from them by the Assyrians.

2:1 The Hebrew for "woe" is *hôy,* which is used of threats in prophetic literature. Here it castigates the greed of the wealthy and powerful. Since *hôy* also is used in funeral laments, it suggests that such schemers are as good as dead. Three verbs characterize the land-grabbers: "plan," "plot," and "carry out." Evil acts begin with evil thoughts. Two words for sin are used: "iniquity" and "evil." "Iniquity" here refers to abuse of power in illegal and unethical machinations, resulting in social injustice. "Evil" refers to things that are wicked in God's eyes (cf. Gen 39:9; 2 Sam 11:27).

The wealthy oppressors were so filled with greed that they were plotting their next move even before they got out of bed in the morning (something the Lord hates, according to Prov 6:18). But a better use of waking hours would have been to think about the Lord (Ps 63:6). As soon as daylight came, they carried out their evil plans to increase their riches at the expense of the poor. They could do it because they controlled the power structures of their society, believing that "might makes right."[54] The very ease with which they did what was wrong shows how evil their manipulations were. Amos likewise condemns such people (Amos 8:5–6). Mammon (money) was their god (cf. Matt 6:24; Luke 16:11–13). The more they had, the more they wanted. No wonder Isaiah pronounces a similar woe of judgment on them (Isa 5:8)! Proverbs 3:27 provides a better use of power: "Do not withhold good from those who deserve it, / when it is in your power to act."

2:2 The wicked schemes of v. 1 spring from greed or covetousness, "which is idolatry" (Col 3:5) and a violation of the Tenth Commandment

[53] Westermann, *Basic Forms of Prophetic Speech,* 175; see also Butler, "Announcements of Judgment," 163.

[54] יֶשׁ־לְאֵל יָדָם ("It is in their power to do it") could be more literally rendered "there is to the power of their hand." The idiom also occurs in Gen 31:29: יֶשׁ־לְאֵל יָדִי (NIV, "I have the power"), lit., "there is to the power of my hand." On the latter text R. Wakely comments: "This text describes a classic case of the kind of imbalance of power between two parties that, humanly speaking, is almost guaranteed to lead to might prevailing over right. However, as a result of God's intervention in favor of the weaker party, whose labor has been unjustly exploited by the one in power, justice prevails" (*NIDOTTE* "אֵל," 1:399). See also Deut 28:32; Neh 5:5.

(Exod 20:17; Deut 5:21). Sin begins in the heart (Matt 15:19). The following verbs are intended to cast the schemers' actions in a negative light: "seize ... take ... defraud." Perhaps because of indebtedness they foreclose on fields and houses of other human beings—probably with help from crooked courts (cf. Amos 5:12). So they take a poor victim's inheritance (family land handed down from ancestors). According to covenant law, land was supposed to remain in the family.[55] Ultimately it belonged to the covenant Lord (Lev 25:23). Yet the land barons were cheating others out of their homes and landed property.

2:3 "Therefore"—because of the aforementioned sins of the influential and wealthy classes of Israelite society—divine judgment was about to fall.[56] In v. 1 the rich, oppressive landowners were "planning ... evil"; now the Lord is "planning" (the same Hb. verb as in v. 1) "disaster" (the same Hb. root as "evil" in v. 1) against "this people."[57] "Many are the plans in a man's heart, but it is the LORD's purpose that prevails" (Prov 19:21). Those "who do harm will experience harm."[58] The disaster probably was the Assyrian captivity of 722–721 B.C. and perhaps the Assyrian invasion of 701 (see comment on "disaster" in 1:12). From this they would not be able to extricate themselves (lit. "from which you cannot remove your necks"). The Assyrian yoke of exile would be like a heavy ox yoke on them. As Fausset put it, "They who will not bend to God's 'easy yoke' (Matt. xi. 29,30) shall feel His iron yoke."[59] Then they will no longer walk in proud defiance of God and his laws. The Hebrew word for "calamity" is the same as that for "disaster" at the beginning of the verse and is repeated at the end for emphasis.

2:4 When the disaster comes, the rich landowners will be mocked. "Men will ridicule you" is literally "he will lift up against you a *māšāl*." The Hebrew word *māšāl* is most likely used here with the negative sense of a "taunt song." The Hebrew for "they will taunt you with this mournful song" features alliteration: *nāhâ nĕhî nihyâ*. Micah loves to employ such literary devices for greater poetic effect. He next uses assonance: *šādôd nĕšaddunû* ("We are utterly ruined"). Others will play the role of the landowners and will mock them with these words. In v. 1 the oppressing classes ruined others; now the tables are turned. Their enemies will divide up their land. The Lord will

---

[55] See Lev 19:13; 25:10,13 (Year of Jubilee); Num 27:1–11; 36:1–12 (Zelophehad's daughters); 1 Kgs 21:1–19 (Naboth's vineyard).

[56] For the messenger formula ("the LORD says") see Barker, "Zechariah," EBC 7:607.

[57] "People" is Hb. מִשְׁפָּחָה, usually "family" or "clan" but here used of the entire people or nation (as in Jer 8:3). It may be used here because of the reference in v. 2 to family inheritance.

[58] H. W. Wolff, *Micah: A Commentary*, trans. G. Stansell (Minneapolis: Augsburg, 1990), 79.

[59] A. R. Fausset, "Jeremiah-Malachi," in *A Commentary Critical, Experimental and Practical on the Old and New Testaments*, 6 vols., by P. Jamieson, A. R. Fausset, and D. Brown (Grand Rapids: Eerdmans, 1967), 4:590.

take it away from the scheming land-grabbers in Israel. He will give their fields to the treacherous Assyrians (see Isa 33:1 and note there in NIVSB). In v. 2 the greedy land barons seized the fields of their helpless victims; now the Lord takes those fields and turns them over to enemies. So the rich are dispossessed of their ill-gotten property. All this will happen in fulfillment of the curses for covenant disobedience (Lev 26:33; Deut 28:49–68). "Blessings abused are at last removed."[60]

2:5 "Therefore"—because the guilty parties have dealt with their neighbors' fields unjustly—they will not have anyone left in the Lord's covenant community (due to being in exile) who can use a measuring line to divide up the land by lot (cf. Josh 14:2; 18:8,10). So they will be cut off from the promises of the Lord's people. It is punishment in kind. Craigie observes: "Those who had a desperate greed for land and power had made their personal goals a kind of god. And those who would worship land in its acquisition would also learn the emptiness of land in its loss."[61]

(4) The Wealthy Wicked and Their False Prophets versus Micah and His God (2:6–11)

6"Do not prophesy," their prophets say.
"Do not prophesy about these things;
disgrace will not overtake us."
7Should it be said, O house of Jacob:
"Is the Spirit of the LORD angry?
Does he do such things?"

"Do not my words do good
to him whose ways are upright?
8Lately my people have risen up
like an enemy.
You strip off the rich robe
from those who pass by without a care,
like men returning from battle.
9You drive the women of my people
from their pleasant homes.
You take away my blessing
from their children forever.
10Get up, go away!
For this is not your resting place,
because it is defiled,
it is ruined, beyond all remedy.
11If a liar and deceiver comes and says,

---

60 Ibid., 593.

61 P. C. Craigie, *Twelve Prophets*, 2 vols. (Philadelphia: Westminster, 1985), 2:19.

'I will prophesy for you plenty of wine and beer,'
he would be just the prophet for this people!"

Literarily the form is a disputation, in which Micah and his God complain bitterly against those who snatched houses and fields from unsuspecting victims (see preceding section).[62] Micah quotes the false prophets of these greedy oppressors in 2:6–7a. His wicked listeners could not accept his message of doom. They found it offensive and commanded him to stop preaching such things. They could not believe that disaster and disgrace would overtake them because they thought God would not do such things. But God himself enumerates the crimes of these wicked men, such as taking the very robes off travelers' backs and driving women and children from their homes (vv. 7b–9). Such wicked men follow false prophets (v. 11). The pericope is framed by occurrences of the verb "prophesy" (vv. 6,11).

2:6 Micah speaks, quoting the reaction of false prophets. Once again he employs assonance: *ʾal-taṭṭipû yaṭṭîpûn lōʾ-yaṭṭipû lāʾēlleh* (lit. " 'Do not prophesy,' they [= their false prophets] prophesy. 'They [= Micah and other true prophets] must not prophesy about these things' "). The verb *nāṭap* (lit. "drop, drip") is sometimes used in contexts like this of letting words drop from one's mouth.[63] The plural verb form *taṭṭipû* must be addressed to Micah and the other true eighth-century prophets. All judgment prophecy is rejected by these charlatans. "Their" refers to the wealthy, oppressive land-grabbers of vv. 1–5, who support such prophets. Many of the same greedy oppressors had attempted to silence Amos and Isaiah (Amos 7:16; Isa 30:10). As Brown puts it: "Like Amaziah's attempt to silence Amos (Amos 7:12–13), Micah's detractors order him to cease such negative preaching."[64] "These things" refers to the condemnations of vv. 1–2 and the judgments of vv. 3–5. "Disgrace" sums up the disaster, calamity, and ruin predicted in vv. 3–4. It was all inconceivable to those in power.[65] Yet Jeremiah asks a relevant question in Jer 5:31: "The [false] prophets prophesy lies, the priests rule by their own authority, and my people love it this way. But what will you do in the end?"

2:7 Micah continues to quote the wealthy and corrupt oppressors and/or

---

[62] See R. D. Patterson, "Old Testament Prophecy," in *A Complete Literary Guide to the Bible*, ed. L. Ryken and T. Longman III (Grand Rapids: Zondervan, 1993), 303. He maintains that the "desired effect in ... disputation speeches is to leave the opponent devoid of further argumentation and resigned to the divine decision."

[63] As R. Hess explains, all the *hiphil* uses except Amos 9:13 describe prophetic preaching ("נטף," *NIDOTTE* 3:97).

[64] Brown, *Obadiah through Malachi*, 41.

[65] "Overtake" is contingent on reading יַסִּג as יַשִּׂג, *hiphil* from נשׂג, "overtake, reach" rather than *niphal* from סוג, "turn back, withdraw" (BDB, 691; *HALOT*, 727, 744). It is not uncommon for a verb to be masculine singular even with a feminine plural subject when the verb appears before its subject, as here (GKC § 145o).

their false prophets in the first part of the verse. Micah's point is that they should not doubt the fact of God's righteous indignation. The Lord does indeed act in judgment (vv. 1–6: "Woe. ... disaster. ... calamity. ... ruined. ... disgrace"). Unlike the use of "Jacob" in 1:5, "house of Jacob" here refers to the entire nation. "Is angry?" translates a verb *(qāṣar)* meaning "be short." It can be understood as an idiom meaning "Does the LORD become impatient?" (as in Prov 14:29, where *qĕṣar rûaḥ,* "quick-tempered" [lit. "short of spirit"], is used as the opposite of *ʾerek ʾappayim,* "patient" [lit. "slow to anger"]; Job 21:4). The false prophets were teaching erroneously that the Lord's patience had no limits (cf. not only Exod 34:6–7a but also 34:7b!).

Beginning in the middle of the verse Micah quotes God, who continues to speak through the end of v. 12; then Micah speaks again. The main point the Lord makes in v. 7b is that if the greedy land barons would live uprightly (like those they were cheating), they would be the recipients of his blessing instead of his judgment. At this time their ways were not upright (or straight) but crooked.[66]

2:8–9 The Lord next lists some of the specific sins of his people. First, he charges them with attacking innocent passers-by as if they were enemies—"the powerless are the prey of the powerful."[67] Their goal was to take the rich robes of their unsuspecting and helpless victims. The latter thought they were as safe as soldiers returning from a battle they had won. It is possible that the regulations of Exod 22:26–27 and Deut 24:10–13 were also being broken. Those laws specified that if someone had to give his cloak as a pledge for a loan, it had to be returned by sunset so he would have something to cover his body while sleeping. If *ʾeder* ("rich [robe]") is a case of haplography (accidental scribal deletion) and the correct reading is *ʾadderet,* it probably should be rendered as simply "cloak" (as in 1 Kgs 19:13).[68] So the "real enemies are not the Assyrian armies or any other outside force but those within the community who profit at its expense."[69]

Second, in v. 9 the Lord charges the oppressors with dispossessing women of their pleasant homes (cf. v. 2). The women may have been widows; if so, the homes would be the ones they inherited from their husbands. Widows were especially vulnerable to exploitation (cf. Mark 12:40). Third, the Lord charges the rich and powerful with depriving the apparently fatherless chil-

---

[66] In its literal use the root ישׁר refers to something "straight, level, or flat," and when applied figuratively to human behavior it describes it as "right, honest, upright, conduct that does not go astray or out of bounds" (L. Alonso-Schökel, "יָשַׁר *yāšar,*" *TDOT 6:465–66).*

[67] Allen, *Joel, Obadiah, Jonah and Micah,* 296.

[68] The root speaks of something "magnificent, majestic, splendid," or "excellent" (C. J. Collins, "אדר," *NIDOTTE* 1:275–77). Collins favors regarding *ʾeder* as an alternative form of *ʾadderet,* "which always refers to a mantle or robe" (pp. 276–77).

[69] Brown, *Obadiah through Malachi,* 41.

dren of the women (widows?) of his blessing permanently. They not only dispossessed women but also disinherited their children. Due to the previous action, the children were left without property, money, and security. Clark reminds us that "Micah's declarations retain a pressing relevance in a world in which such conditions continue."[70] Covetousness and greed are still having the same devastating results for defenseless women and children and the unprotected poor.[71] The oppressors "robbed men of their clothes, women of their homes, and children of their inheritance. Was God not right to send judgment against such wicked individuals?"[72]

2:10 In v. 8 the oppressors among God's people "rose up" like an enemy to increase their wealth and power at the expense of others among their own people; now the Lord tells them to "get up" and prepare to leave their ill-gotten land and other possessions behind (the Hb. verb is *qûm* in both verses). They are to go away into exile. Their wrongfully acquired land will no longer be their secure resting place and possession. The reason given is that they defiled it with their sins and ruined it beyond all remedy. Nothing but exile awaits. Others will take over their property acquired by fraud and oppression. In v. 9 they evicted women from their homes; now the Lord evicts them from his land, fulfilling Lev 18:24–28.[73]

2:11 Just as this literary unit began with false prophets, so it ends with them. Here such a prophet is called a liar and deceiver, obviously because he does not tell the truth and so leads others astray.[74] His message is one of peace and prosperity ("plenty of wine and beer").[75] The sinful, covenant-breaking people deserve that kind of prophet. Anyone who promises greater affluence will gain a hearing. According to 3:5,11 false prophets are happy to oblige with "feel-good messages" so long as their hearers feed them and pay them enough money. The tests of true prophets are given in Deut 13:1–3; 18:14–22: A prophet's message must not contradict or disagree with the previous revelation of truth through true prophets (cf. Isa 8:19–20), and his predictions must come true. These prophets failed on both counts.

We are still plagued by false prophets and false teachers both inside and

[70] D. J. Clark, "Micah," in *The International Bible Commentary*, ed. F. F. Bruce et al. (Grand Rapids: Zondervan, 1986), 931.

[71] For a fuller treatment of these weak and helpless members of society, see R. D. Patterson, "The Widow, the Orphan, and the Poor in the Old Testament and the Extra-Biblical Literature," *BSac* 130 (1973): 223–34.

[72] J. M. Boice, *The Minor Prophets*, 2 vols. complete in one edition (Grand Rapids: Kregel, 1996), 2:24.

[73] The *piel* תְּחַבֵּל should perhaps be repointed as a *pual*, תְּחֻבַּל.

[74] רוּחַ characterizes the lies of the liar and deceiver as "windy" or "empty" (BDB, 924); cf. Job 6:26; 16:3; Jer 5:13.

[75] Micah uses another wordplay with alliteration and assonance: *šeqer* ("liar") and *šēkār* ("beer"). The latter is related to Akk. *šikaru* ("beer").

outside the church. We still have charlatans and hucksters who "peddle the word of God for profit" (2 Cor 2:17). Jesus issued a warning about them (Matt 24:4–5,10–11,23–24). So did Paul and John (1 Tim 4:1–2; 1 John 2:18–19; 4:1–3). Such so-called ministers may masquerade as "apostles of Christ," but in reality they are "false apostles" and servants of Satan (2 Cor 11:13–15). They will exist as long as there are people who "will gather around them a great number of teachers to say what their itching ears want to hear" (2 Tim 4:3–4). A. T. Robertson comments, "This is the temptation of the merely 'popular' preacher, to furnish the latest tickle."[76] It is better to serve Christ and his church in such a way that one will be commended rather than condemned. W. Cowper put it like this:

> I venerate the man whose heart is true,
> Whose hands are pure, whose doctrine and whose life,
> Coincident, exhibit lucid proof
> That he is honest in the sacred cause.
> To such I render more than mere respect,
> Whose actions say that they respect themselves.[77]

2. The Restoration of a Remnant (2:12–13)

12"I will surely gather all of you, O Jacob;
I will surely bring together the remnant of Israel.
I will bring them together like sheep in a pen,
like a flock in its pasture;
the place will throng with people.
13One who breaks open the way will go up before them;
they will break through the gate and go out.
Their king will pass through before them,
the LORD at their head."

The literary genre is a salvation or deliverance oracle[78] in which the Lord as royal Shepherd promises to gather a remnant of his people like sheep in a

[76] WP 4:629–30.

[77] Quoted in W. J. Deane et al., "Micah," in *The Pulpit Commentary,* 23 vols., ed. H. D. M. Spence and J. S. Exell (Grand Rapids: Eerdmans, 1983), 14:34.

[78] J. L. Mays construes these verses as an oracle of judgment, with Yahweh leading his people *into* exile (*Micah*, OTL [Philadelphia: Westminster, 1976], 4–5,28,73–76). But this seems to be an unnatural reading of the actual language (B. S. Childs, *Introduction to the Old Testament as Scripture* [Philadelphia: Fortress, 1979], 431–32). J. M. P. Smith goes so far as to say, "It is impossible to find anything but words of encouragement and comfort here" (*A Critical and Exegetical Commentary on the Books of Micah, Zephaniah and Nahum*, ICC [Edinburgh: T & T Clark, 1911], 68). For a good analysis of salvation oracles, see W. A. VanGemeren, "Oracles of Salvation," in Sandy and Giese, *Cracking Old Testament Codes*, 139–55.

pen (2:12). Then, as their King, he leads them out through the city gate (2:13). The scope of the passage probably extends beyond restoration from exile to the Messianic Kingdom. Perhaps the hope envisaged here is fulfilled progressively (cf. 5:2–4).

2:12 As Deane observed, "the prophet, without any preface, introduces abruptly a promise of restoration after exile, a type of the triumph of Messiah."[79] Sudden transitions are common in the prophetic books (cf. a similar transition from threat to promise of restoration in Hos 1:9–10). The ultimate and complete fulfillment of this verse will coincide with the fulfillment of Rom 11:26. The promise is that even though Jacob/Israel (probably referring to the entire nation, north and south) will be taken into exile (1:8,16; 2:4,10; 4:10), a remnant will return. Isaiah often refers to the remnant that will survive God's judgment on the nation and will take possession of the land (Isa 4:3; 6:13; 10:20–22; 11:11,16; 46:3).

Here God, as royal Shepherd, will gather his scattered people like sheep in a pen (cf. 4:6, where the same Hb. verbs [*ʾāsap,* "gather," and *qābaṣ,* "assemble/bring together"[80]] are used). Although his people may be reduced to a remnant in exile, in the future they will be restored and will become a great throng. Some understand these words (and those of v. 13) as fulfilled in Jerusalem's deliverance from King Sennacherib's siege (701 B.C.; cf. 1:12); others, in the restoration from Babylonian exile; and still others, in the final regathering and salvation yet to come in the eschaton. Perhaps it is best to see it as another case of progressive fulfillment of prophecy.[81] "The place will throng with people" is literally "They [i.e., fold and pasture] will murmur/roar with people,"[82] that is, there will be a great commotion due to the throng of people.

2:13 Apparently Micah's quotation of the Lord ends in v. 12, and now Micah himself takes up the strain. He identifies the one who will accomplish Israel's restoration as "One who breaks open," "King," and "the LORD" (using the redemptive covenant name of Israel's Suzerain, Yahweh). The verse begins with a prophetic perfect in the Hebrew text ("will go up"), stressing the certainty of the action. Rabbinic interpretation refers this verse to the Messiah and Redeemer.[83]

---

[79] Deane, "Micah," 20.

[80] In the third line of 2:12, "bring … together" translates a third verb שׂים ("put/place") plus adverb יַחַד ("together").

[81] For a development of what is meant by progressive fulfillment, see Introduction: "Interpreting Micah" and Barker, "The Scope and Center of Old and New Testament Theology and Hope," in *Dispensationalism, Israel and the Church*, ed. C. A. Blaising and D. L. Bock (Grand Rapids: Zondervan, 1992), 323–28.

[82] BDB, 223.

[83] K. Cathcart and R. P. Gordon, *The Targum of the Minor Prophets* (Wilmington: Michael Glazier, 1989), 117.

The Lord is first described as "the Breaker,"[84] who opens up the way and leads his people out of the lands where they have been scattered. The significance of the epithet is then explained: The Lord's action enables his people to break through the city gate and exit the place of their confinement. Second, the Lord is described as their "King," who "will pass through before them," as he did when they came up out of Egypt (Exod 13:21; Deut 1:30–33; Isa 63:9). Third, he is described as "the LORD," who will pave the way ahead of them, further emphasizing his leadership. The ultimate, complete fulfillment of vv. 12–13 extends to the future coming of the Messiah and even to his second advent and millennial reign for the final stage in the progressive fulfillment of the whole (cf. 4:1–8; 5:2–9; Ezek 20:33–44; Zech 9:9–10; Matt 24:30–31; Rev 11:15; 19:6–9,11–16; 20:1–6).

[84] Participle from פָּרַץ, "break out, break through, make a breach." The perfect tense of the verb also occurs in the second line of v. 13, translated "break through." Cf. Gen 38:29; 2 Sam 6:8; 2 Kgs 14:13; Neh 1:3; 4:3; Job 16:14; Ps 80:12; Prov 25:28; Eccl 10:8; Isa 5:5; Amos 4:3. The word can also have the idea of "spreading out" or "overflowing" (Gen 28:14; 30:30,43; Exod 1:12; Job 1:10; Isa 54:3). See also G. Brin, "Micah 2,2–13: A Textual and Ideological Study," *ZAW* 101 (1989): 118–24.

SECTION OUTLINE

III. SECOND CYCLE (3:1–5:15)
   1. Indictment of Judah's Leaders (3:1–12)
      (1) Guilty Civil Leaders (3:1–4)
      (2) Peace Prophets and Micah (3:5–8)
      (3) Corrupt Leaders and Zion's Fall (3:9–12)
   2. Future Hope (4:1–5:15)
      (1) Zion's Future Exaltation (4:1–5)
      (2) Restoration of a Remnant and Zion (4:6–8)
      (3) From Distress to Deliverance (4:9–10)
      (4) From Siege to Victory (4:11–13)
      (5) From Helpless Ruler to Ideal King (5:1–4)
      (6) The Ideal King Will Deliver His People (5:5–6)
      (7) The Remnant among the Nations (5:7–9)
      (8) Obliteration of Military Power and Pagan Worship (5:10–15)

III. SECOND CYCLE (3:1–5:15)

Here begins the second cycle of judgment and salvation (see Introduction, p. 34). The judgment theme is presented in 3:1–12 and the salvation or restoration theme in 4:1–5:15.

1. Indictment of Judah's Leaders (3:1–12)

(1) Guilty Civil Leaders (3:1–4)

1Then I said,
"Listen, you leaders of Jacob,
you rulers of the house of Israel.
Should you not know justice,
2you who hate good and love evil;
who tear the skin from my people
and the flesh from their bones;
3who eat my people's flesh,
strip off their skin
and break their bones in pieces;
who chop them up like meat for the pan,
like flesh for the pot?"

[4]Then they will cry out to the LORD,
but he will not answer them.
At that time he will hide his face from them
because of the evil they have done.

Although some construe this unit as a judgment oracle, the literary form probably is a divine covenant "lawsuit" (see introduction to 1:2–7), in which God charges that the civil leaders or rulers of his people act like cannibals. They should know and practice justice; instead, they hate what is good and love evil. They betray the trust placed in their leadership. They will cry out to the Lord, but he will not answer them. What a contrast these leaders are to the good and great Shepherd of 2:12!

3:1 The function of the phrase (one word in Hebrew) "then I said" could be to separate chaps. 3–5 from chaps. 1–2.[1] The pericope opens with the imperative *šimᶜû,* a call to "Listen" or "Hear" (see comments on 1:2). The same Hebrew verb form marks the beginning of the first and third cycles of judgment and salvation (1:2; 6:1). The addressees are the "leaders" or "rulers" (including judges in the courts) of Jacob/Israel, here referring to Judah (vv. 9–12) but including the northerners who had fled there. The government itself was the problem. The "establishment" was controlled by corrupt public officials who winked at (and even participated in) all the unjust and oppressive practices Micah has been condemning up to this point. The rhetorical question that follows ("Should you not know justice …?") implies, of course, that as leaders they should know justice.[2] This "use of the interrogative is altogether different from our idiom, since it serves merely to express the conviction that the contents of the statement are well known to the hearer and are unconditionally admitted by him."[3]

In this context "know" is most likely "used as a technical term for recognition of the treaty stipulations as binding."[4] The treaty stipulations would refer to those of the Sinaitic covenant that pertain to the execution of justice. The leaders should recognize them as binding. "Justice" *(mišpāṭ)* links all three literary units in Micah 3 (see vv. 8–9). Eichrodt correctly asserts concerning "justice":

> [It] is no abstract thing, but denotes the rights and duties of each party arising out of the particular relation of fellowship in which they find themselves. In this way everyone has his own special *mĭspāṭ:* the king, the Deity, the priest, the firstborn son, the Israelites as a group, and so on. The task of righteousness

---

[1] See also Introduction: "Literary Analysis: Structure," pp. 33–34.

[2] For other uses of ידע ("know") with object מִשְׁפָּט ("justice") see Ps 147:20; Jer 5:4,5; 8:7; Ezek 20:11.

[3] GKC § 150e.

[4] H. B. Huffmon, "The Treaty Background of Hebrew *Yādaᶜ*," *BASOR* 181 (1966): 33.

is to render this justice, and the claims which it implies, effective in the proper way, so that the good of all those united in the one community of law may be safeguarded.[5]

At the broadest level, there is a sense in which justice ultimately has in view the proper ordering of all society. This more comprehensive meaning also seems called for in Isa 42:1,4, where justice is presented as the mission of the Messianic Servant of the Lord. He will establish a proper order on earth. Lindsey maintains that "any translation less comprehensive than 'a right order' or a similar phrase fails to take account of the far-reaching accomplishments purposed for Yahweh's Servant. The Servant's task is to rectify within history all aspects and phases of human existence—moral, religious, spiritual, political, social, economic, and so forth."[6] Again he notes that *mišpāṭ* "describes the totality of the just order that the Servant will cause to prevail on the earth."[7] That is precisely what the rulers and leaders of Micah's time had failed to do. In a more practical vein, "Perhaps it is not amiss to suggest that as the Lord's servants today, we too are to strive to help bring about such a proper and just ordering of all society (cf. Mic 6:6–8)."[8] Craigie observes: "'Justice,' Disraeli said in a speech to the House of Commons (1851), 'is truth in action.' Injustice, as Micah saw so clearly, was falsity in action throughout every key realm of society."[9]

3:2–3 Judah's and Jerusalem's corrupt leaders and judges failed to recognize the covenant stipulations as authoritative. They did nothing to establish a proper and spiritual order in the covenant community. They should have loved what is good and hated evil (Amos 5:15; Rom 12:9) by protecting the rights of all members of society. Instead, they were guilty of doing exactly the opposite. Occurrences of "evil" at the beginning of v. 2 and the end of v. 4 mark off these verses (i.e., an inclusio) as a unit comprising the charge and God's corresponding judgment (on "evil" see comments on 1:12; 2:1).

"Tear" begins a series of figures of speech describing the cruel, brutal, and inhumane way the leaders were treating the people (note the verbs "tear … eat … strip off … break … chop").[10] Instead of shepherding them, the civil leaders are pictured as exploiting and oppressing them like animals that are being

---

[5] W. Eichrodt, *Theology of the Old Testament*, 2 vols., trans. J. A. Baker (Philadelphia: Westminster, 1961), 1:241.

[6] F. D. Lindsey, *The Servant Songs: A Study in Isaiah* (Chicago: Moody, 1985), 44.

[7] Ibid., 49.

[8] K. L. Barker, "Zechariah," EBC, 7:646.

[9] P. C. Craigie, *Twelve Prophets*, 2 vols. (Philadelphia: Westminster, 1985), 2:26.

[10] "Tear" translates גזל, often rendered "rob" or "seize" in other contexts, as in 2:2; Isa 10:2. It refers to taking something from someone by force (cf. 2 Sam 23:21; Job 24:9). It can also refer to stealing (Lev 5:21[6:2]) or extortion (Lev 5:23[6:4]). See W. R. Domeris, "גזל," *NIDOTTE* 1:844–45.

butchered, cooked, and prepared for eating (on "like meat for the pan, like flesh for the pot," cf. 1 Sam 2:13–14). They are like the so-called shepherd-leaders of Ezek 34:2–11 and like the foolish, worthless shepherd of Zech 11:15–17.[11] G. A. Smith observed, "While Micah spoke he had wasted lives and bent backs before him. … Pinched peasant-faces peer between all his words."[12]

3:4 "Then" and "At that time" refer to the time of divine judgment. When that day comes, the guilty leaders will cry out to the Lord for help in their time of need, but he will not respond—"a just retribution on those who refused to hearken to the cry of the poor and needy."[13] It is the principle of Prov 21:13 at work: "If a man shuts his ears to the cry of the poor, / he too will cry out and not be answered." The Lord will hide his face (of favor and blessing) from such heartless people. It is punishment in kind, measure for measure. The practice of injustice (or sin in any form) leads to alienation from God (Isa 59:1–4). Unfortunately corrupt civil leaders are still very much with us. The verse closes with the reason for the awful silence of God: their "evil" and cruel behavior (see v. 2). They have refused to honor their covenant obligations.

(2) Peace Prophets and Micah (3:5–8)

5This is what the LORD says:
"As for the prophets
who lead my people astray,
if one feeds them,
they proclaim 'peace';
if he does not,
they prepare to wage war against him.
6Therefore night will come over you, without visions,
and darkness, without divination.
The sun will set for the prophets,
and the day will go dark for them.
7The seers will be ashamed
and the diviners disgraced.
They will all cover their faces
because there is no answer from God."

8But as for me, I am filled with power,

---

[11] See Barker, "Zechariah," 679–80.

[12] G. A. Smith, *The Book of the Twelve Prophets*, vol. 1: "Amos, Hosea and Micah" (New York: A. C. Armstrong, 1899), 394.

[13] Deane et al., "Micah," 36. The appropriateness of the retribution is highlighted by the last word in v. 4, מַעַלְלֵיהֶם, translated "they have done." It echoes the word מֵעֲלֵיהֶם, lit. "from upon them," which occurs in vv. 2 and 3.

with the Spirit of the LORD,
and with justice and might,
to declare to Jacob his transgression,
to Israel his sin.

In the previous literary unit the civil leaders (including corrupt judges) were the target of divine and prophetic condemnation; here the focus is on false prophets. The form is another disputation (see introduction to 2:6–11), in which God through Micah accuses the false prophets of preaching for money and asserts that they have no vision or message from God. They "had developed what J. L. Sicre calls 'a theology of oppression' which seeks to rationalize injustice with religious arguments, false oracles, and visions, which serve to calm the conscience of the oppressors who thus can enjoy their wealth without scruples."[14] The "clergy had become as corrupt as the judiciary."[15] Micah, however, speaks by the power and Spirit of God (v. 8).

3:5 The messenger formula ("This is what the LORD says") introduces this pericope (see 2:3).[16] "Prophets" *(nĕbîʾîm)* normally refers to "those who are called by God to be his spokesmen,"[17] but here they are counterfeits who lead God's people astray. Such so-called prophets are also denounced in Lam 2:14: "The visions of your prophets / were false and worthless; / they did not expose your sin / to ward off your captivity. / The oracles they gave you / were false and misleading." To the people who fed them, they proclaimed a message of "peace" *(šālôm)* and prosperity (cf. Jer 6:14);[18] against those who did not, they declared a holy war[19] and announced nothing but doom (see comments on 2:11; cf. 2 Tim 4:3–4). They made themselves God's enemies, "whose end is destruction, whose god is their belly, and whose glory is in their shame—who set their mind on earthly things" (Phil 3:19, NKJV). "Love of filthy lucre is especially unseemly in him who exercises the sacred ministry."[20] Mays adds, "Money talked louder than God" to these false prophets.[21]

---

[14] J. I. Alfaro, *Justice and Loyalty: A Commentary on the Book of Micah*, ITC (Grand Rapids: Eerdmans, 1989), 35.

[15] P. C. Craigie, *Twelve Prophets*, 2:28.

[16] See Barker, "Zechariah," 7:607.

[17] Ibid., 605–07.

[18] הַנֹּשְׁכִים בְּשִׁנֵּיהֶם וְקָרְאוּ שָׁלוֹם is lit., "Those who bite with their teeth and proclaim peace." The opposite situation is וַאֲשֶׁר לֹא־יִתֵּן עַל־פִּיהֶם וְקִדְּשׁוּ עָלָיו מִלְחָמָה, which could be rendered "but against the one who does not put [something] in their mouth they declare holy war."

[19] The end of v. 5, וְקִדְּשׁוּ עָלָיו מִלְחָמָה, is lit. "they consecrate against him a war." The expression "consecrate war" also occurs in Jer 6:4; Joel 3:9[Hb. 4:9].

[20] A. R. Fausset, "Jeremiah-Malachi," in *A Commentary Critical, Experimental and Practical on the Old and New Testaments*, 6 vols., by P. Jamieson, A. R. Fausset, and D. Brown (Grand Rapids: Eerdmans, 1967 repr.), 4:595.

[21] J. L. Mays, *Micah: A Commentary*, OTL (Philadelphia: Westminster, 1976), 83.

Brown also observes that "the perversion of the ministerial office still runs rampant today."[22] The true prophet Micah, on the other hand, rebuked Judah's sin (v. 8) and predicted destruction and exile (v. 12; 4:10).

3:6–7 "Therefore," because the false prophets were misleading the people by promising them the light of God's favor and peace for monetary gain, the darkness of God's judgment will descend on them (cf. Amos 5:18–20). The Lord will give them no revelation of his word—once again the awful silence of God (see comments on v. 4). "Therefore their knowledge of God will be darkened."[23] There will be "a famine of hearing the words of the LORD" (Amos 8:11). These money-driven, peace-and-prosperity prophets used their prophetic gifts improperly, so God will take those gifts away from them (cf. Jer 14:14–15). The punishment will fit the crime. It is better not to speak at all than to declare a message that leads others astray.

In v. 7 the prophets are called "seers" (see comments on 1:1; cf. 1 Sam 9:9). They will become ashamed and disgraced because their oracles will be shown to be "delusions of their own minds" (Jer 14:14; cf. Zech 13:4). They are also called "diviners," a reference to those who secure information or guidance from a deity by checking omens. These prophets "conjure up visions on demand just as pagan diviners create omens" (see 3:11).[24] All of them will cover the lower half of their faces (lit. "their upper lip" or "their mustache"), a gesture of ceremonial uncleanness in Lev 13:45 and of grief in Ezek 24:17 but here primarily a sign of shame and humiliation (note the same thought in 7:16). The reason ("because") for their disappointment and disillusionment is the same as that in v. 4 ("he will not answer them")—"there is no answer from God." "Micah's diagnosis warns that it is still possible for a theologian to become more concerned about fees than faith, about honoraria than honor."[25]

3:8 "But as for me"—a sharp contrast is drawn between the true prophet Micah and the false prophets of the preceding verses. First, Micah asserts that he is filled with power. The Hebrew preposition *ʾet-* ("with") should perhaps here be read with the preceding clause in the sense, "I am filled with power by the help of the Spirit" (cf. Gen 4:1).[26] The false prophets were motivated by greed, but Micah was empowered by the Spirit of the Lord for his prophetic ministry. All true prophets were the Lord's Spirit-filled messengers (see 2 Pet 1:20–21). Such empowerment is related to the Spirit's enablement for the New Testament gospel mission as well (Acts 1:8).

---

[22] W. P. Brown, *Obadiah through Malachi*, Westminster Bible Companion (Louisville: Westminster John Knox, 1996), 45.

[23] H. W. Wolff, *Micah: A Commentary*, trans. G. Stansell (Minneapolis: Augsburg, 1990), 104.

[24] Mays, *Micah*, 84.

[25] J. Limburg, *Hosea-Micah*, INT (Atlanta: John Knox, 1988), 177.

[26] R. J. Williams, *Hebrew Syntax: An Outline*, 2d ed. (Toronto: University of Toronto, 1976), 58–59 (345).

Second, Micah claims that he is filled with justice (see comments on v. 1). Third, he declares that he is filled with might. This has been defined as "a holy courage that enables him to face any danger in delivering his testimony."[27] The purpose of such an endowment is next stated: to declare to Judah (see v. 10) its sin (see Introduction, p. 36; cf. Isa 58:1; for "transgression" and "sin" see comments on 1:5). The church and the world desperately need prophetic messengers like Micah today.

(3) Corrupt Leaders and Zion's Fall (3:9–12)

9Hear this, you leaders of the house of Jacob,
you rulers of the house of Israel,
who despise justice
and distort all that is right;
10who build Zion with bloodshed,
and Jerusalem with wickedness.
11Her leaders judge for a bribe,
her priests teach for a price,
and her prophets tell fortunes for money.
Yet they lean upon the LORD and say,
"Is not the LORD among us?
No disaster will come upon us."
12Therefore because of you,
Zion will be plowed like a field,
Jerusalem will become a heap of rubble,
the temple hill a mound overgrown with thickets.

This oracle of indictment and judgment seems to be a summary of all that Micah has been saying to the various groups of leaders in Jerusalem—both civil and religious, now including the priests. Because of their covenant-breaking sins and crimes, Jerusalem and the temple will be destroyed.

3:9–10 Because v. 8 is true of Micah, he proceeds with his forceful, Spirit-inspired message. Verse 9 is an illustration of his courage in denounc-

---

[27] Deane et al., "Micah," 37. "The strength conveyed by the word *gĕbûrâ* is a gift from God" (R. Wakely, "גבר," *NIDOTTE* 1:812). Cf. Job 39:19–20; Isa 11:2; 28:6; 30:15. Wakely also explains: "Ultimate power belongs to Yahweh (1 Chr 29:11–12), and it is from his sovereign rule that humans derive any potential they may have. … Yahweh's power is inextricably linked to righteousness, goodness, justice, steadfast love, and faithfulness (Pss 89:13–14[14–15]; 145:6–17; Mic 3:8)" (p. 813). Our share in "the divine *gĕbûrâ* … manifests itself not only in terms of physical strength, but in spiritual qualities as well—particularly wisdom, understanding, counsel, knowledge, and the fear of Yahweh" (p. 814). In the OT, Yahweh is so essentially connected to this concept that "it is scarcely surprising that in the rabbinic age, when the name of Yahweh was no longer uttered, the word *gĕbûrâ* became one of the substitutes for God's proper name" (p. 814). Cf. Matt 26:64.

ing sin (see comments on v. 8). The "leaders" and "rulers" (see comments on v. 1) were examples of injustice and wickedness rather than of righteousness. "Hear" *(šimᶜû)* introduces a smaller literary unit, not a major division (see Introduction: "Literary Analysis: Structure," p. 33). "Jacob" and "Israel" refer to Judah here (see also v. 12). The leaders are charged with despising "justice" (see comments on v. 1). They show their attitude toward it by not practicing it.[28] Micah also accuses them of distorting or twisting "all that is right" (lit. "everything that is straight"; see the use of the word *yāšār* ["upright"] in 2:7; 7:2,4). They make crooked all that should be straight and upright. They pervert what is right and fair.

The leaders (probably here including prophets, priests, judges, and other governmental leaders) are further condemned as those who build Zion/Jerusalem with bloodshed and wickedness or violence (v. 10). "It was urban renewal with a vengeance, a new Jerusalem that cost the lives of men."[29] Vawter says that the meaning is "that they have squeezed the slender resources of their victims by nothing short of bloodshed to provide the brick and mortar for their flamboyant municipal works."[30] A woe of divine judgment is pronounced on such people in Hab 2:12. Jerusalem's wealth and power had come at a very heavy price. "Abuse of the sacred is … the worst of transgressions."[31]

3:11 All classes of leaders are now included in Micah's scathing denunciation. Prophets, priests, judges, and other governmental rulers alike betrayed their trust. Jerusalem's (and Judah's) leaders judged favorably for a bribe (see 7:3). Like Samuel's sons (1 Sam 8:3), they were the opposite of Samuel (1 Sam 12:3). Such perversion of justice through bribery was explicitly prohibited in Pentateuchal law (Exod 23:8; Deut 16:19; cf. Isa 1:23; 5:23). The priests made their teaching ministry a source of gain. It was their duty to teach the law and decide controversies (Lev 10:11; Deut 17:9,11), not to enrich themselves beyond their tithes by charging extra for their services. And the false prophets sold their oracles or divinations, divorcing what should have been a spiritual ministry from ethics, morality, and integrity (see v. 5). "The love of money is a root of all kinds of evil" (1 Tim 6:10). Boice comments:

> What troubled Micah (and God far more) was the sin in the courts, palaces, and temple. All three branches of government were corrupt. Worse yet they

---

[28] The verb translated "despise" (תעב) has the same root as the word often rendered "abomination" or "detestable thing" (Deut 7:26). It is sometimes rendered "abhor" (Deut 23:7; Amos 5:10) and should describe one's response to falsehood rather than to justice (Ps 119:163).

[29] Mays, *Micah*, 88.

[30] B. Vawter, *Amos, Hosea, Micah* (Wilmington: M. Glazier, 1981), 147.

[31] D. R. Hillers, *Micah*, Her (Philadelphia: Fortress, 1984), 48. Archaeology has confirmed the building activity, the expansion programs, and the tremendous population growth during this period in Judah and Jerusalem (see Introduction: Historical Setting, pp. 23–28).

worked hand in hand. The politicians got their way in the courts, and the judges were paid for their destruction of justice. The prophets also benefited from this arrangement and supported the government in turn.[32]

Yet the leaders claimed to "lean upon" (= trust in) the Lord because of their mistaken temple theology (cf. Jer 7:4,8,12–15). They reasoned that Jerusalem was inviolable because the Great King's earthly throne (the ark of the covenant) was located there in the temple (see Introduction, p. 27). It was inconceivable to them that Jerusalem and the Lord's temple would ever be destroyed. How wrong they were! Just such a "disaster" (see comments on 2:3) was predicted in the next verse—and fulfilled (though, thanks to godly King Hezekiah, Jerusalem did not fall until a little over one hundred years later). Allen asks a pertinent question: "If the most sacred institution was not serving its purpose but in the hands of religious perverts was acting as a barrier to God, of what further use could it be to him?"[33] Corrupt leaders who use their positions of power and influence for self-aggrandizement will be judged severely (v. 12).

3:12 "Therefore," because of the sins and disobedience of the leaders just delineated, Zion/Jerusalem and the temple would be devastated. The destruction occurred in 586 B.C. Micah 3:12 was quoted a century later in Jer 26:18. The next verse in Jeremiah indicates that Micah's preaching may have been instrumental in the revival under King Hezekiah (see 2 Kgs 18:1–6; 2 Chr 29–31).

Lamentations describes the awful fulfillment of this prophecy (see Introduction, p. 30).[34] It is ironic that those who thought they were the builders of Zion (v. 10) actually turned out to be, in a sense, its destroyers. The Lord, because of their breach of covenant, used King Nebuchadnezzar's Neo-Babylonian army to raze Jerusalem and its temple. They were reduced to a "mound of ruins" (translating the Hb. word *ʿîyyîn*[35]) similar to an archaeological tell and to Ai (see also comments on 1:6), foreshadowing the Roman destruction of A.D. 70. Jerusalem became a place suitable only for wild animals. And the temple mount that thronged with worshipers became as deserted as when Abraham almost offered Isaac there on Mount Moriah (Gen 22:2,14).

Since "justice" is a key word linking all three pericopes in chap. 3 (vv. 1,8–9), it is appropriate to conclude the comments on them with this practical word from Craigie, reminding us of the contemporary relevance of that theme:

---

[32] J. M. Boice, *The Minor Prophets*, 2 vols. complete in one edition (Grand Rapids: Kregel, 1996), 2:28.

[33] L. C. Allen, *The Books of Joel, Obadiah, Jonah and Micah*, NICOT (Grand Rapids: Eerdmans, 1976), 255.

[34] Cf. Lam 1:1,4,6,18–19; 2:2,6,9–10,20; 5:17–18, etc.

[35] Note the Aramaic plural ending on עִיִּין (*ʿiyyîn*) but the Hebrew plural on the parallel in Jer 26:18.

Addressing the House of Commons in 1871, [Benjamin Disraeli] said, "We have legalized confiscation, consecrated sacrilege, and condoned high treason." One suspects that he was familiar with Micah! But injustice was not peculiar to Micah's age; it is a disease which would permeate every age and every segment of human society, and which must by every means be eliminated.[36]

2. Future Hope (4:1–5:15)

(1) Zion's Future Exaltation (4:1–5)

[1]In the last days
the mountain of the LORD's temple will be established
as chief among the mountains;
it will be raised above the hills,
and peoples will stream to it.
[2]Many nations will come and say,
"Come, let us go up to the mountain of the LORD,
to the house of the God of Jacob.
He will teach us his ways,
so that we may walk in his paths."
The law will go out from Zion,
the word of the LORD from Jerusalem.
[3]He will judge between many peoples
and will settle disputes for strong nations far and wide.
They will beat their swords into plowshares
and their spears into pruning hooks.
Nation will not take up sword against nation,
nor will they train for war anymore.
[4]Every man will sit under his own vine
and under his own fig tree,
and no one will make them afraid,
for the LORD Almighty has spoken.
[5]All the nations may walk
in the name of their gods;
we will walk in the name of the LORD
our God for ever and ever.

The literary form is an eschatological oracle of salvation[37] that immediately follows the surprising announcement of Zion's fall and the temple's destruction (3:12). Far from being a contradiction of 3:12 (as some scholars believe), it probably was deliberately placed after the previous oracle of judgment to indicate that although the temple would be destroyed, in the eschato-

[36] Craigie, *Twelve Prophets*, 30.

[37] See Introduction (p. 41), as well as the introduction to 2:12–13 and note.

logical Zion it would be restored in even grander style to become the worship and learning center for all nations. "Zion will eventually be exalted from the deepest degradation to the highest glory."[38] Isaiah 2:2–4 is almost identical to Mic 4:1–3. Probably both Isaiah and Micah made use of a common source or tradition, but Archer believes that the same revelation may have been "granted to both prophets at about the same time; it is hardly likely that one would have copied from the other."[39]

4:1 In this salvation (or deliverance and restoration) oracle Micah announces the future glory of the temple mount and the ideal happiness and security of God's worshipers (both Jew and Gentile). Sailhamer, in his comments on the parallel in Isaiah 2, agrees: "From the very beginning the passage appears to have been understood as a picture of a future age when Jerusalem would be restored and would become the center of the worship of God among all nations."[40]

The time of the prophecy's fulfillment is set in "the last days." The phrase can refer to the general or undetermined future (e.g., Gen 49:1; Num 24:14; Deut 31:29, "in days to come"), but in contexts like this one it usually appears to have in view the Messianic age. "In a real sense the last days began with the first coming of Christ (see Acts 2:17; Heb 1:2) and will be fulfilled at his second coming."[41]

"The mountain of the LORD's temple" is equivalent to "the temple hill" (i.e., Mount Zion/Moriah) in 3:12. It was first exalted when David brought the ark of the covenant there (symbolizing the throne of King Yahweh among his kingdom people) and when Solomon built "the LORD's temple" there. But the time will come when it will be even more exalted as the most important mountain of all (cf. Ps 48:1–3,8).[42] Is "be raised above the hills" to be understood literally or figuratively? In view of the topographical changes prophesied in passages like Zech 14:4–5,10, Delitzsch argues for both. He insists that "it is not merely an exaltation of the temple mountain in the estimation of the nations that is predicted, but a physical and external elevation also."[43]

---

[38] COT, *Minor Prophets*, 1:455.

[39] G. L. Archer, Jr., "Micah," in *The New Bible Commentary Revised*, ed. D. Guthrie et al. (Grand Rapids: Eerdmans, 1970), 756; but see the discussion in J. N. Oswalt, *The Book of Isaiah Chapters 1–39*, NICOT (Grand Rapids: Eerdmans, 1986), 115–16.

[40] J. H. Sailhamer, "Evidence from Isaiah 2," in *A Case for Premillennialism*, ed. D. K. Campbell and J. L. Townsend (Chicago: Moody, 1992), 94–95.

[41] NIVSB, Isa 2:2 n. Hill adds, "According to some, the phrase connotes those 'latter days' when God fulfills the prophecies concerning the restoration of Israel, the judgment of the nations, and the establishment of the messianic kingdom" (A. E. Hill, "אַחֲרִית," in *NIDOTTE* 1:362).

[42] The "as" in "as chief" (בְּרֹאשׁ) represents *beth* of essence, identity, or equivalence in the Hebrew text (cf. *IBHS*, 198).

[43] F. Delitzsch, *Biblical Commentary on the Prophecies of Isaiah*, 2 vols., trans. J. Martin (1877; reprint, Grand Rapids: Eerdmans, 1965), 1:114.

Thus Mount Zion and its temple will be elevated probably both physically and in prominence. Finally, the verse indicates that "peoples will stream to it." Doubtless "peoples" is to be understood here in the same essential sense as the Isaiah parallel: "all nations." The Hebrew for the verb "stream" has the same root as the Hebrew word for "river." The picture is that of people from "many nations" (v. 2) rushing like a great river toward Jerusalem. This is elucidated further in the next verse.

4:2 The thought at the end of v. 1 continues here. People from many nations will exhort one another to join together in a great pilgrimage to the temple in Jerusalem. O. Kaiser observes, "Just as Israel once travelled in the desert to the mountain of God, in order to receive the law there (cf. Exod 19ff.), the nations now travel on pilgrimage to the sanctuary of the people of the twelve tribes, to the house of the God of Jacob."[44] Similar prophecies appear in Zech 8:20–23; 14:16–19.[45] Next the people state the purpose of their pilgrimage: The Lord "will teach us his ways." The Lord's "ways" are his "plans in the moral government of the world, and the way in which he would have men walk in order to please him."[46] The purpose of the instruction, in turn, is not merely to impart the knowledge of God's will but that the nations would live ("walk") in accordance with it. There is an implied rebuke here to Israel at the time of Micah (cf. Mal 1:11–14). Thus ends what the nations say—a fulfillment of God's promise to Abraham in Gen 12:3.

Micah introduces the reason for the nations' eagerness to go on pilgrimage to Jerusalem with a *kî* ("For") in the Hebrew text (the NIV lets juxtaposition carry the force). Alternatively, *kî* could be emphatic—"Indeed." In the context "law" (*tôrâ* without the article) probably means more generally "instruction" (it has the same Hb. root as the verb "teach"). Jerusalem may fall (3:12), but it will be fully restored as the world's religious capital and learning center. (For "word of the LORD" in the sense of "prophetic word of revelation," see comments on 1:1.) Some interpreters "spiritualize" this verse, so that Jerusalem no longer refers to the earthly city in Israel. But Sailhamer objects:

> In the book of Micah, the visions of destruction … have their reference in the literal city of Jerusalem. By the same token it seems reasonable to conclude that the visions of the restoration of that desolate city are also to be understood within the framework of a literal reference to Jerusalem. There is no reason to suppose that the prophets' description of Israel's future restoration was any less concrete than their description of Israel's destruction.[47]

Similarly, Delitzsch sees a future fulfillment, while allowing for some fulfillment already:

---

[44] O. Kaiser, *Isaiah 1–12: A Commentary*, OTL (Philadelphia: Westminster, 1972), 27.

[45] See my comments in "Zechariah," 654–55, 695–96.

[46] Deane et al., "Micah," 49.

[47] J. H. Sailhamer, "Evidence from Isaiah 2," 97.

> This was fulfilled on that day of Pentecost, when the disciples … proclaimed the … gospel, in the languages of all the world. It was fulfilled … in the fact that the word of the gospel … flowed through the whole of the known world. But these fulfillments were only preludes to a conclusion which is still to be looked for in the future. For what is promised in the following verse is still altogether unfulfilled.[48]

4:3 "The effect of this reception of true religion shall be universal peace."[49] Instead of nations going to war against one another, the Lord himself will judge between them and settle their differences (cf. Isa 11:3–4). Such judging was a royal function in the ancient Near East.[50] In view of the parallelism with "many peoples," "strong nations" should perhaps be rendered "numerous nations," as well as in v. 7 (see comments there). The Hebrew for "strong" can mean either and is translated "numerous" in Exod 1:9 and footnoted as an alternative rendering in Isa 53:12 (cf. also Num 32:1 and perhaps Pss 35:18; 135:10; Prov 7:26; Amos 5:12). Numerous Gentile nations will learn to live at peace with one another.

The result of the Lord's action in vv. 2–3a is next stated, so that the *waw* consecutive prefixed to the Hebrew perfect tense could be translated "So" or "Then": "So they will beat their swords into plowshares and their spears into pruning hooks." Because of the Lord's direct intervention, weapons of warfare will become useless. "Here is synecdoche where the abandonment of two weapons—swords and spears—stands picturesquely for total disarmament."[51] The arms race will be over. Precisely the opposite picture is portrayed in Joel 3:10.[52] "What is here called a plowshare was actually an iron point mounted on a wooden beam. Ancient plows did not have a plowshare proper."[53] The verse closes with the prophecy that one nation will not use its weapons ("sword") against another nation. People will not even train for war anymore. The "West Points" of the world will no longer be necessary. Instead of learning the art of war, the nations will learn the art of peace. When they all submit to "our Lord and his Christ" (Rev 11:15; cf. Ps 2:1–3,10–12), peace (Shalom) will break out.

This is a description of Messianic, and even millennial, conditions. Yet how different the situation will be until then, with wars and rumors of wars and nation rising against nation (Matt 24:6–7)! Although this vision of universal peace (v. 3b) is the United Nations motto, in a world of sin, fallenness, and depravity there can be no lasting external peace until the Prince of Peace

[48] Delitzsch, *Biblical Commentary on the Prophecies of Isaiah*, 116.

[49] Deane et al., "Micah," 49.

[50] Barker, "Zechariah," 664–65 (Excursus).

[51] A. B. Mickelsen, *Interpreting the Bible* (Grand Rapids: Eerdmans, 1963), 187.

[52] See D. A. Garrett (*Hosea, Joel,* NAC [Nashville: Broadman & Holman, 1997], 385), who interprets the expression there as "a proverbial call to arms."

[53] NIVSB, Isa 2:4 n.

returns to establish his Davidic kingdom fully and forever and rule it himself (cf. 2 Sam 7:12–16; Ps 89:3–4,19–29,33–37; Isa 9:6–7; Ezek 34:23–24; Dan 7:13–14,27; Zech 9:9–10; 14:9; 1 Cor 15:20–28; Eph 1:9–10; Heb 2:5–9; 10:12–13; Rev 19:11–20:6). Such rule rightfully belongs to him, and one day the obedience of the nations will be his (see Gen 49:10; Ezek 21:27). However, that does not mean that we should not do everything in our power in the meantime to bring about as much external peace (in addition to personal, internal peace) as is humanly possible (see Matt 5:9; Rom 12:18; 1 Tim 2:1–8; Jas 3:17–18).

4:4 The vine and the fig tree are intended to picture proverbially the security, prosperity, and contentment of God's peaceable kingdom (1 Kgs 4:25; Zech 3:10; cf. Isa 11:6–10; 35; 65:20–25). Fear will be a thing of the past (Zeph 3:13). "Fig trees were valued for their fruit and for their shade. Like the vine, fig trees became a symbol of security and of prosperity."[54] Embry adds "personal peace" to the symbolism.[55] And all this will happen because the Lord Almighty has spoken it. "The LORD Almighty" is a good rendering of Yahweh Sabaoth (traditionally "the LORD of hosts"). Equally good would be "the LORD who rules over all."[56]

When will the idyllic, utopian scenes depicted in vv. 1–4 be realized? Three answers have been given: (1) The passage is a hyperbolic idealization of the restored Jerusalem and Judah and the rebuilt temple that existed after the people's return from Babylonian exile (vv. 8–10); (2) the fulfillment has been inaugurated through the coming of the Messiah and the universal preaching of the gospel but will not be completed until the return of Christ; (3) it is solely a prophecy of conditions during a still future reign of Christ on earth (see comments on v. 3). Aside from the words "hyperbolic idealization" in (1) above, there could be some truth in all three positions if one accepts the principle of the progressive fulfillment of certain prophecies. Thus various elements could be partially fulfilled in the first two stages, climaxing in the third stage with a final, complete fulfillment in Christ's millennial kingdom.[57] Here is how three different, representative interpreters deal with the problem of fulfillment:

1. Justin Martyr (ca. A.D. 110–165) argued that a portion of 4:1–7 had already been fulfilled in Christians at Christ's first advent and that the rest would be fulfilled at his second advent.[58]

---

[54] R. Gower, *The New Manners and Customs of Bible Times* (Chicago: Moody, 1987), 118.

[55] E. M. Embry, "Tree, Plant, Root, Branch," in *NIDNTT* 3:865–66.

[56] See my chapter, "The Lord Almighty," in *The Making of the NIV*, ed. K. L. Barker (Grand Rapids: Baker, 1991), 107–8,161.

[57] See comments on 2:12 and n. 78 there.

[58] Justin Martyr, "Dialogue with Trypho, a Jew," in *Ante-Nicene Fathers*, ed. A. Roberts and J. Donaldson, rev. A. C. Coxe (1885; reprint, Peabody, Mass.: Hendrickson, 1995), 1:253–54.

2. Naegelsbach interprets that "the Prophet himself says that it shall follow in the last time."

> If it now began a long time ago; if especially the appearance of the Lord in the flesh, and the founding of His kingdom and the preaching of the gospel among all nations be an element of that fulfillment, yet it is by no means a closed up transaction. … If many, especially Jewish expositors have taken the words too coarsely, and outwardly, so on the other hand we must guard against a one-sided spiritualizing. Certainly the prophets do not think of heaven. Plows and pruning hooks have as little to do with heaven as swords and spears. And what has the high place of Mount Zion to do in heaven? Therefore our passage speaks for the view that one time, and that too here on this earth, the Lord shall appropriate the kingdom (lx. 21; Matt. v. 5), suppress the world kingdoms and bring about a condition of peace and glory.[59]

3. Sailhamer speaks of the parallel passage in Isaiah, but his words apply equally to Micah 4:

> Isaiah's visions of the future looked to a time when the Davidic kingship would be restored in Jerusalem and the Messiah would reign over that kingdom and rule all the nations of the world. In other words, they look to a time that fits remarkably well with John's vision of the earthly reign of Christ in Revelation 20. …
>
> Historically, it is hard to understand Israel's prophets any other way than that they longed for a physical, that is, earthly, reestablishment of the Davidic monarchy. The fact that prophetic books such as Isaiah continued as Scripture long after the postexilic period shows that their reference looked far beyond any temporal fulfillment within Israel's own immediate history. If our goal is to describe the reference of Isaiah's visions as he would have understood them, we can only hope to do so by paying close attention to the sense of those visions as they are given us in the book of Isaiah. That sense … fits best in the context of an earthly reign of Christ in Jerusalem as a precursor to the eternal state.[60]

4:5 Micah brings his hearers (and readers) back to present reality. "The nations which in the final days will seek to learn the ways of Yahweh now wander in the name of other gods."[61] "Walk in the name of" has been variously explained and/or translated: "trust in, worship, and obey" (NIrV), "be loyal to" (REB), "live by" (God's Word), "follow" (CEV), "live in conformity to the will and character of,"[62] "give allegiance to,"[63] "walk in the strength

[59] C. W. E. Naegelsbach, "Isaiah," in *Commentary on the Holy Scriptures*, ed. J. P. Lange and P. Schaff (Grand Rapids: Zondervan, n.d.), 57.

[60] Sailhamer, "Evidence from Isaiah 2," 101–2.

[61] Vawter, *Amos, Hosea, Micah*, 150.

[62] J. R. Riggs, *Micah*, BSC (Grand Rapids: Zondervan, 1987), 52.

[63] R. B. Chisholm, Jr., *Interpreting the Minor Prophets* (Grand Rapids: Zondervan, 1990), 145.

of."[64] In the second half of the verse Micah either quotes the faithful remnant of God's people or speaks for them ("we"). In contrast to the polytheistic, idolatrous, corrupt people of the pagan nations, God's chosen people are determined to worship and follow faithfully their covenant "LORD," the one true, living God—and to live such a life of faith, faithfulness, obedience, and complete commitment to him forever. That is how all God's people should live while awaiting the final, complete fulfillment of the glorious future promised in vv. 1–4, when God's irresistible kingdom will be ushered in on this earth by Christ the King and will continue eternally on the new earth. These momentous future events should provide an incentive for holy, faithful, fruitful service in the present (cf. 1 Thess 5:6,8,11; Titus 2:11–14; Heb 10:25; Jas 5:8–9; 1 Pet 4:7–11; 2 Pet 3:11–13; 1 John 2:28; 3:2–3).

(2) Restoration of a Remnant and Zion (4:6–8)

6"In that day," declares the LORD,
"I will gather the lame;
I will assemble the exiles
and those I have brought to grief.
7I will make the lame a remnant,
those driven away a strong nation.
The LORD will rule over them in Mount Zion
from that day and forever.
8As for you, O watchtower of the flock,
O stronghold of the Daughter of Zion,
the former dominion will be restored to you;
kingship will come to the Daughter of Jerusalem."

The genre of this literary subunit is an eschatological salvation oracle. "In that day" indicates that it is an eschatological oracle, in which the Shepherd-King is seen restoring his flock and reigning over them in Zion. Now they are weak; one day their covenant Lord and King will make them strong.

4:6 In context "In that day" probably is generally equivalent to "In the last days" (v. 1).[65] "Jerusalem," "mountain," and "Zion" are mentioned in both the preceding salvation oracle and this one, linking the two oracles quite closely in theme and motifs. Micah quotes the Lord directly in vv. 6–8, using "declares the LORD" to stress that the origin of his message is God himself, thus giving divine authority to the prophetic utterance. God's people are portrayed as weak, wounded, scattered sheep in exile among the nations without a shepherd. Although he is the one who, because of their sin, afflicted them and brought them to such grief (for the meaning of the Hb. root used here, see

[64] COT, *Minor Prophets*, 1:458 (cf. Prov 18:10; Zech 10:12).

[65] For a discussion of "In that day" see Barker, "Zechariah," 619–20 (on 2:11–12).

1:12; 2:3), as the good royal Shepherd he will rescue, gather, and restore them (cf. 2:12; Isa 40:10–11; 54:7; Jer 23:3–4; 31:7–14; Ezek 11:16–17; 20:34–44; 34:11–16,23–24; Zeph 3:19–20; Zech 10:8–12). Although the word "exiles" may reflect the Assyrian and Babylonian captivities as background, it has primarily in view the Diaspora (dispersion of the Jews) that followed the Roman destruction of Jerusalem in A.D. 70. Thus the restoration in view probably is the final, future one.[66] Fausset makes a contemporary application of the principle: "Affliction is the discipline appointed to train the believer for coming glory."[67] So the best is yet to come for the faithful remnant of Israel (Rom 11:26).

4:7 The Lord promises to make the "lame" of v. 6 into a faithful remnant (for "remnant" see comments on 2:12). Indeed, he will make them into a "strong nation," though "strong" also could mean "populous" (see comments on v. 3). The weakling of v. 6 will be able to say, "I am strong!" (Joel 3:10; cf. 1 Cor 1:26–31). Micah may be the speaker in the second half of the verse (note the change from first person to third), yet it is not uncommon for the Lord to refer to himself in the third person. The Lord will rule over the restored faithful remnant and strong (or populous) nation in Mount Zion, the site of the temple that contained the ark of the covenant, representing the Great Shepherd-King's earthly throne. According to Zech 14:9 he will reign not just over "them" but also over "the whole earth." The last colon of the verse indicates that his reign will never end (cf. Ps 146:7–10). So the Messiah (God's "Anointed" King) will rule over a universal and eternal kingdom (see also Isa 9:6–7; Dan 7:14,27; Luke 1:32–33; Rev 11:15).[68]

4:8 The Lord (or Micah) now addresses Jerusalem (and its inhabitants). The watchtower of God's flock is Jerusalem, the capital city of David, the shepherd-king. Jerusalem's strength gives security to the Lord's flock. The NIV provides "hill" as an alternative rendering of "stronghold." The Hebrew word is *ʿōpel*. "Ophel" was the name given to the southeastern slope of "the temple hill" (3:12). King David's palace was situated on it. The City of David and Zion were originally identified with it. Later, both terms came to be used of the entire city of Jerusalem. Both "Daughter of Zion" and "Daughter of Jerusalem" are personifications of the capital city. The "former dominion" refers to the glorious past under David (perhaps Solomon is also in view). The Davidic kingdom will be restored and will be even more glorious under the Messiah (Luke 1:32–33). "In Messiah the glory and power are restored to the throne of David."[69]

---

[66] Ibid., 672.

[67] Fausset, "Jeremiah–Malachi," 599.

[68] For "The LORD will rule" see comments on Zech 2:10 in Barker, "Zechariah," 619.

[69] Deane et al., "Micah," 51.

(3) From Distress to Deliverance (4:9–10)

[9]Why do you now cry aloud—
have you no king?
Has your counselor perished,
that pain seizes you like that of a woman in labor?
[10]Writhe in agony, O Daughter of Zion,
like a woman in labor,
for now you must leave the city
to camp in the open field.
You will go to Babylon;
there you will be rescued.
There the LORD will redeem you
out of the hand of your enemies.

The literary form of this section is a mixed type—an oracle of both judgment and salvation (or deliverance). Another label is "combined salvation-and-judgment-speech."[70] The next three pericopes (4:9–10; 4:11–13; 5:1–4) all begin with the word "now" (in the Hb. text) and end with an assertion that the present or anticipated bad situation will be changed for the better. For example, in vv. 9–10 Micah foresees the collapse of the Davidic monarchy and the impending exile in 586 B.C. as well as the restoration commencing in 538.

4:9 This verse can be understood in two ways (or even in one or two additional ways, according to a few commentators). First, anticipating the results of the prophesied Babylonian exile of v. 10, Micah asks rhetorical questions concerning the loss of a Davidic king in Jerusalem. He pictures its citizens as lamenting their forthcoming loss of the kingdom of Judah and its king. "The loss of the king was a much more painful thing for Israel than for any other nation, because such glorious promises were attached to the throne, the king being the visible representative of the grace of God, and his removal a sign of the wrath of God and of the abolition of all the blessings of salvation which were promised to the nation in his person."[71] (Cf. Lam 4:20.) King Jehoiachin would be taken prisoner to Babylon by Nebuchadnezzar, king of the Neo-Babylonian empire. Nebuchadnezzar would also have King Zedekiah's eyes put out. Zedekiah too would be taken captive to Babylon. "Counselor" here is simply another word for "king." In fact, counseling was one of the functions of ancient Near Eastern kingship. (See Isa 9:6–7 for the Messiah as both king and counselor par excellence.) The pain of Jerusalem's people over such deprivation will be so intense that it is compared to that of a woman in labor and about to give birth (cf. Jer 4:31; 6:22–24).

---

[70] Cf. C. Westermann, *Basic Forms of Prophetic Speech*, trans. H. C. White (London: Lutterworth, 1967), 81.

[71] Keil, *Minor Prophets*, 1:464–65.

Second, "king" and "counselor" can be taken as references to God (in that case, they should be capitalized). There is considerable support for this understanding. In v. 7 it is the Lord who is the King. In v. 12 he is presented as Counselor. In Jer 8:19 similar rhetorical questions are asked with God as the referent: "Is the LORD not in Zion? Is her King no longer there?" In this second interpretation of the verse, facing the Assyrian threat at that time, Micah is rebuking his people for their panic and failure to trust in God, their heavenly King. This second view is held by B. Waltke (who follows B. Renaud), H. Wolff, and E. Pusey.

The first view, on the other hand, is preferred by L. Allen, D. Hillers, W. Kaiser, C. Keil, J. Mays, T. McComiskey, C. Naegelsbach, J. Smith, and R. L. Smith (see the Bibliography for the bibliographical data on all these authors). Three primary reasons are usually cited for that preference: (1) If the second view is correct, it seems strange for Micah to rebuke the people's pain like a "woman in labor" (v. 9), then to command them to writhe in agony "like a woman in labor" in the next verse. (2) Again assuming the second interpretation, *ʾābad* ("perished," v. 9) appears to be inappropriate for deity. (3) The first view provides a more natural, unified reading of the text in the immediate context, for then the prophesied event and time frame would be the same in both verses. All things considered, the first understanding seems slightly favored. Incidentally, the contention of some that *melek* ("king") is not used in this book of a human king is demonstrably incorrect, since it is used of Balak in 6:5.

4:10 After portraying his people's wailing and lamenting because of what the Babylonians will do to them, Micah next commands them to writhe in agony "like a woman in labor" (see also v. 9). Then he provides the reason for such distress ("for"): they must leave their city (cf. 3:12). Since Micah is delivering this message shortly before 700 B.C. and is prophesying the Babylonian deportations that started in 605 B.C., "now" is equivalent to "in the near future." Their leaving Jerusalem to first "camp in the open field" must refer to their staying in deportation camps until being taken to Babylon. The prophecy of exile in Babylon ("You will go to Babylon") could have been known to Micah only by divine inspiration, particularly since Assyria was the dominant power at that time (similarly in the case of Isaiah's prophecy in Isa 39:5–7).

Even though the people of Judah would be thus exiled, the Lord would rescue and "redeem" them from the Babylonian captivity in a new exodus (cf. Isa 41:14; 48:17,20). So the deliverance would come not at Jerusalem but "there" (in Babylon), repeated for emphasis. The Hebrew verb for "redeem" here is *gāʾal.* It is familiar to many Christians in its participial form, commonly Anglicized as *goel* ("kinsman-redeemer"). The Old Testament picture of such a redeemer is that of an obligated family protector. The role of Yahweh as Goel (Redeemer) is one of the motifs of Micah's contemporary, Isaiah. The

Lord is portrayed in the Book of Isaiah as the perfect Family Protector of Israel. (1) He is related to Israel as Father (63:16; 64:8) and Husband (54:5). (2) He redeems their property, for he regathers them to their land (54:1–8). This function is applicable here in Mic 4:10. (3) He redeems their freedom (35:9; 43:1–4; 48:20; 52:11–12), also applicable here in Micah. (4) He avenges them against their tormentors (47:3–4; 49:25–26; 64:4), also applicable here (see the next pericope). (5) He secures their posterity for the future (61:8–9).[72] Judah's redemption and restoration to their land here would be effected through Cyrus the Great, king of Persia (Isa 44:24–45:7). The ultimate Goel, of course, is Christ the Redeemer.[73] Through his redemptive work people are brought from distress to an even greater deliverance.

(4) From Siege to Victory (4:11–13)

11But now many nations
are gathered against you.
They say, "Let her be defiled,
let our eyes gloat over Zion!"
12But they do not know
the thoughts of the LORD;
they do not understand his plan,
he who gathers them like sheaves to the threshing floor.

13"Rise and thresh, O Daughter of Zion,
for I will give you horns of iron;
I will give you hoofs of bronze
and you will break to pieces many nations."

You will devote their ill-gotten gains to the LORD,
their wealth to the Lord of all the earth.

This is another oracle of judgment and salvation—a mixed type. The judgment is against the gloating enemies of Jerusalem, who will lay siege to it. The Lord will deliver his suffering people and bring them from siege to victory by enabling them to decimate their enemies.

4:11 This is the second of three consecutive oracles of judgment and salvation introduced by *ʿattâ* ("Now"). Opinions are divided concerning the "many nations." Some refer them to mercenaries from many nations in King Sennacherib's Assyrian army (701 B.C.). Others argue for the same, but in King Nebuchadnezzar's Neo-Babylonian army (588–586). Still others support the period of the Maccabees. It is possible that all these could be typolog-

[72] For a complete study of Hebrew words for "salvation," see J. F. A. Sawyer, *Semantics in Biblical Research* (London: SCM, 1972), 28–88.

[73] See NIVSB, Introduction to Ruth: Theme and Theology; see also Ruth 2:20 n.

ical stages in the progressive fulfillment of the whole prophecy. The final, complete stage, however, seems to be what Micah had primarily in view, namely, an eschatological onslaught against the Jews akin to the apocalyptic scene depicted in such passages as Isa 29:5–8; Ezek 38–39; Joel 3:1–3,12–17; Zech 12:1–9; 14:1–5,12–15; Rev 16:12–21.[74] The intent of the hostile nations is to "defile," pollute, desecrate, or profane God's holy city ("you"), holy land, and holy people by trampling on them with pagan feet. Those who are unholy desire to render the holy also unholy, like themselves, then to gloat over it.[75] But those who devastate Zion and its people will in turn be devastated (vv. 12–13).

4:12 The nations that are enemies of both God and his people do not know or understand that he is in complete control of everything that is happening, carrying out his own sovereign purpose, plan, and will—including even the siege of Jerusalem. They also do not realize what he has in store for them, to gather them "like sheaves to the threshing floor" to be threshed. King explains the imagery:

> Sometimes threshing is to be understood metaphorically, meaning the cruel treatment meted out to a conquered enemy. …
>
> Micah utilizes … the figurative sense when describing the restoration of Jerusalem amidst threats from neighboring nations. … God is the harvester, and Jerusalem (Zion) the beast treading on the sheaves. The attacking nations bent on the conquest of Jerusalem would themselves be vanquished.[76]

4:13 Micah quotes God in the first part of the verse, then takes up the strain himself in the second part. The Lord portrays Daughter Zion (cf. vv. 2,7–8,10–11) as a threshing ox or great heifer (see Hos 10:11), which he summons to thresh (cf. Deut 25:4; Isa 41:15), continuing the imagery of threshing from v. 12. The Lord promises to turn Jerusalem's horns into iron and her hoofs into bronze. So Jerusalem is being pictured as an ox that is threshing. Horns are a proverbial symbol of strength and power in the Bible. Iron is used here as a symbol of endurance and hardness.[77] The "horns" may include the figure of the goring ox (Exod 21:28–32; cf. Deut 33:17; 1 Kgs 22:11). God would also give his people bronze (not brass) hoofs (as threshing bulls), with which to "break to pieces" the attacking nations. The Hebrew verb used here

---

[74] For more details see Barker, "Zechariah," 680–82, 688–91, 694.

[75] The verb rendered "gloat" is חזה, "see." It may express the act of gazing at something with enjoyment or disdain (Ps 27:4; Song 6:13[7:1]; J. A. Naudé, "חזה," *NIDOTTE* 2:57). The nations will enjoy the sight of defiled Jerusalem. For the use of the singular verb (וְתַחַז) with the dual subject (עֵינֵינוּ) cf. *GBH* § 150d.

[76] P. J. King, *Amos, Hosea, Micah—An Archaeological Commentary* (Philadelphia: Westminster, 1988), 111–12.

[77] J. G. Baldwin, "Gold, Silver, Bronze, Iron," in *NIDNTT* 2:98.

could be more literally rendered "pulverize,"[78] signifying a crushing defeat. Because of divine enablement, Zion will be invincible.

Micah next prophesies that his people will "devote"[79] to the Lord the nations' "ill-gotten gains." The latter doubtless includes booty or plunder taken in battle. "Wealth" (lit. "strength") may also refer to military might. In the Old Testament, when defeated people and things were to be devoted to the Lord, it usually meant that everything perishable or flammable should be totally destroyed (cf. Josh 6–7), while gold and silver and other precious metals should be brought to the Lord's temple and used in his service.[80] "Lord" in Hebrew is *ʾădôn*, a shortened form of *ʾădōnāy* ("Master, Sovereign").[81] The section closes with the reminder that the Lord's sovereignty extends to the whole earth (Zech 4:14; 6:5). So the victory will ultimately be his.

(5) From Helpless Ruler to Ideal King (5:1–4; MT 4:14–5:3)

1Marshal your troops, O city of troops,
for a siege is laid against us.
They will strike Israel's ruler
on the cheek with a rod.

2 "But you, Bethlehem Ephrathah,
though you are small among the clans of Judah,
out of you will come for me
one who will be ruler over Israel,
whose origins are from of old,
from ancient times."

3Therefore Israel will be abandoned
until the time when she who is in labor gives birth
and the rest of his brothers return
to join the Israelites.

4He will stand and shepherd his flock
in the strength of the LORD,
in the majesty of the name of the LORD his God.
And they will live securely, for then his greatness
will reach to the ends of the earth.

---

[78] *HALOT*, 229.

[79] וְהַחֲרַמְתִּי ("You will devote") is not first person singular but an archaic form of the second feminine singular (referring to Jerusalem), as confirmed by the LXX, Syr., and Vg. (see GKC § 44h and n. 1).

[80] For a full discussion see N. Lohfink, "חָרַם, *ḥāram*; חֵרֶם, *ḥērem*," in *TDOT* 5:180–99.

[81] See comments on 1:2; see also Barker, "Zechariah," 632 (n. on 4:14 and references given there).

This is also an oracle of judgment and salvation—a mixed type—and the last of the three consecutive "Now" oracles (see comments at 4:9–10). It is one of the most familiar passages in Micah and contains the promise of the birth of a new King in Bethlehem whose greatness will reach to the ends of the earth.

5:1 Micah, representing the people ("us"), continues to address Jerusalem (see 4:13b). The opening words of the Hebrew text are open to at least three readings. The first is in the main text of the NIV: "Marshal your troops, O city [lit. 'daughter'] of troops."[82] This analysis is defended by Waltke and others and is the view preferred here.[83] The second is in the NIV footnote as an alternative translation: "Strengthen your walls, O walled city." But this reading involves changing the Hebrew verb root from *gādad* to *gādar.*[84] Longman favors a third reading: "Now gash yourself, daughter of marauder!" (a common meaning of the Hb. verb *gdd*). He explains, "The act of cutting oneself was a well-known expression of mourning in the nations surrounding Israel. Israel, however, was forbidden to engage in this practice (Deut 14:1), thus giving the command a sarcastic tone."[85]

The "siege" against the citizens of Jerusalem could refer to that of King Sennacherib's Assyrian army in 701 B.C. But it more likely refers prophetically to that of King Nebuchadnezzar's Neo-Babylonian army 588–586 (cf. 4:9–10). If so, the ultimate reference of Israel's (i.e., Judah's) "ruler" probably would be to Zedekiah, the last king of Judah, whom Nebuchadnezzar blinded by having his soldiers quite literally "strike Israel's ruler on the cheek with a rod" (see 2 Kgs 25:7; Jer 39:6–7; 52:10–11). Although "some suggest this ruler was Christ because (a) Christ was struck on the head (Matt 27:30; Mark 15:19) and face (John 19:3) and (b) He is referred to in Micah 5:2," Martin argues that the ruler is Zedekiah:

> (1) The first part of verse 1 refers to the Babylonian attack on Jerusalem. (2) The word "ruler" translates *šōpeṭ* ("judge"), whereas the word for ruler in verse

---

[82] Note the assonance in the Hb. text between הִתְגֹּדְדִי, "marshal your troops," and גְּדוּד, "troops."

[83] See, e.g., B. K. Waltke, "Micah," in *The Minor Prophets*, 3 vols., ed. T. E. McComiskey (Grand Rapids: Baker, 1993), 2:701–2. He explains that although the *hit.* of גדד normally means "cut oneself," the meaning "throng together" is required by Ps 94:21 and Jer 5:7. *HALOT,* 177, treats this as a secondary root, a denominative of גְּדוּד, "band, troop." The syntactical use of the verb here is imperfect of injunction (*IBHS*, 509).

[84] The LXX has νύν ἐμφραχθήσεται θυγάτηρ Εφραιμ ἐν φραγμῷ, "Now the daughter of Ephraim will have been blocked by a wall."

[85] T. Longman III, "Micah," in *Evangelical Commentary on the Bible*, ed. W. A. Elwell (Grand Rapids: Baker, 1989), 655–56. *HALOT,* 177, likewise reads גדד, "make incisions upon oneself" but emends בַּת־גְּדוּד to הִתְגּוֹדֵד, the infinitive, yielding an emphatic construction. Waltke, "Micah," notes, however, that גְּדוּד occurs in Jer 48:37 with the meaning "cuttings upon the hands as a sign of mourning" and in Ps 65:11[10] as "furrows" (2:701). See also Clines, *DCH* 2:316–17.

> 2, which does clearly refer to Christ, is *mōšēl. Šōpeṭ* forms an interesting wordplay on the similar-sounding word for "rod," *šēbeṭ*.) (3) Christ was not smitten by troops of an enemy nation while Jerusalem was besieged. However, Nebuchadnezzar did capture Zedekiah and torture him (2 Kgs 25:1–7). (4) A soon-coming event, not a distant-future one, seems to be suggested by the Hebrew word for "but now" in Micah 5:1 (not trans. in the NIV). This is followed by the distant future in verses 2–6. This pattern of present crisis followed by future deliverance is also seen in 4:11–13 in which the present (4:11) is introduced by "but now" and the distant future is discussed in 4:12–13.[86]

The pattern just referred to (present or soon-coming distress followed by later deliverance) also is seen in 4:9–10 (see previous comments on those verses).

5:2 Micah next quotes the Lord directly. The conjunction at the beginning *(wĕ)* is adversative ("But"). A sharp contrast is drawn between the weak and helpless ruler of v. 1 and the strong, ideal, Messianic King/Ruler of this verse. The Lord announces his birthplace and his Davidic roots. There is a change in addressee from Jerusalem (v. 1) to Bethlehem ("you").[87] Ephrathah (meaning "fruitfulness") is either another name for Bethlehem ("house of food") or the district in which Bethlehem was located (see Gen 48:7; Ruth 4:11) or possibly a clan name. Since it is in the tribal territory of Judah, it also is called "Bethlehem Judah" (Judg 17:7) and "Bethlehem, Judah" (Ruth 1:2). Bethlehem was situated about five miles south-southwest of Jerusalem. These expanded names distinguish it from the Bethlehem to the north in the territory of Zebulun (Josh 19:15).

Compared to Jerusalem with its magnificent buildings (3:10), Bethlehem is characterized as "small" (cf. the Christmas carol "O Little Town of Bethlehem"). This probably applies to both size and significance. Yet in spite of its relative insignificance, this birthplace of David (1 Sam 16:1,18; 17:12) would also become the birthplace of his greatest descendant, the Messiah (Matt 2:1–8; cf. John 7:42). Perhaps the "low state of David's line when Messiah was born also is implied here."[88] "Out of seeming littleness and weakness God has perfected strength."[89] The apostle Paul expressed this principle in 1 Cor 1:27–29. Even though Bethlehem is small, it is "by no means least" (Matt 2:6). In fact, it was greatly honored through the birth of the Messiah there.

The singular of the Hebrew for "clans" *(ʾelep)* apparently developed semantically from an original nuance of a numeral ("thousand," Num 35:4;

---

[86] J. A. Martin, "Micah," in *The Bible Knowledge Commentary*, ed. J. F. Walvoord and R. B. Zuck (Wheaton: Victor, 1985), 1486.

[87] There is also assonance between אַתָּה ("you") and the previous occurrences of עַתָּה ("now"). Here אַתָּה is addressed to Bethlehem; in 4:8 it was addressed to Jerusalem. David, of course, had a vital connection to both.

[88] A. R. Fausset, "Jeremiah-Malachi," 599; cf. Isa 11:1; Amos 9:11.

[89] Ibid., 602.

Josh 7:3) to a "military company of 1,000" men (Exod 18:21,25; 1 Sam 8:12) to the approximate number of a "clan" (Judg 6:15; 1 Sam 10:19,21) to the "city" where a clan lived (here; Amos 5:3) to the "ruler" of a clan (cf. Matt 2:6). Here "cities" or "towns" (GNB reads "towns") seems to be the most appropriate sense contextually,[90] though "clans" also is satisfactory. "For me" is equivalent to something like "to bring praise and glory to me by serving me and doing my will" (cf. Ps 40:7–8; John 4:34).

From Bethlehem would come "one who will be ruler over Israel" (i.e., over the entire nation, north and south). At last Israel will have a completely fit ruler! Probably too much has been made of the fact that the Hebrew for "ruler" here is *môšēl* instead of *melek* ("king"). Certainly one cannot say that *melek* is reserved exclusively for God in this book, since it is used of the "king" of Moab in 6:5. The verb from which *môšēl* is derived *(māšal)* can be used to refer to the Lord's rule (Judg 8:23; Ps 89:9). The nouns *memšālâ* ("dominion," from *māšal*) and *mamleket* ("kingship," from *mālak*) occur parallel to each other in 4:8. It is possible to argue that perhaps the use of *môšēl* here implies that God himself (in Trinitarian terms, God the Father) will retain his regal powers as the Great "King" *(melek)* of the universe and that this ruler will rule for him in carrying out his plan for the earth.

But who is this ruler? There is a near consensus that he is none other than the Messiah. All the ancient Jewish interpreters regarded the ruler as the Messiah (cf. Matt 2:5; John 7:41–42). The testimony of the Targums also favors the Messianic interpretation of the prophecy.[91] Longenecker includes 5:2 among the passages accepted in Judaism as applying directly to the Messiah.[92]

The verse ends with "whose origins are from of old, from ancient times." NIV footnotes provide this alternative rendering: "whose goings out are from of old, from days of eternity." A few, preferring the alternative reading (especially "from days of eternity"), have charged that the translation in the text shows carelessness in handling Old Testament Messianic prophecies and other doctrines.[93] On the contrary, equally competent scholars differ on the contextual interpretation of certain biblical passages, and this happens to be one of them. Those who prefer the footnote alternative naturally use it to argue for the eternal existence of the Messiah. Those who prefer the main text believe that the expression *mîmê ʿôlām* refers to the ancient "origins" of the Messiah in the line of David (as indicated in the Davidic covenant of

[90] See Wolff, *Micah*, 144.

[91] P. J. Gloag, *The Messianic Prophecies* (Edinburgh: T & T Clark, 1879), 118.

[92] Longenecker, *Biblical Exegesis in the Apostolic Period* (Grand Rapids: Eerdmans, 1975), 89.

[93] E.g., E. D. Radmacher and Z. C. Hodges, *The NIV Reconsidered: A Fresh Look at a Popular Translation* (Dallas: Redención Viva, 1990), 56–58.

2 Sam 7:12–16) and in the tribe of Judah (Gen 49:10).

The immediate context appears to favor the main text: "*Bethlehem ... of Judah,* out of *you* [emphasis mine] will come for me one who will be ruler over Israel." God does not say "from *me* will come for *you* ..."[94] The stress is on the "origins"[95] of the future Davidic ruler in the Davidic town of Bethlehem. McComiskey maintains that in this passage "the Davidic roots of the coming ruler are emphasized by the prophet Micah."[96] Significantly, Jesus is introduced in Matt 1:1 as "the son of David, the son of Abraham"—no doubt, in part, to present him as the fulfiller of the Davidic and Abrahamic covenants. Certainly the deity and eternality of the Messiah (the Son of God) are still plainly taught in other passages, particularly in the New Testament (John 1:1–3; 8:58; cf. Isa 9:6, "Mighty God, Everlasting Father").[97]

It is instructive that a Hebrew expression equivalent to "from of old" here *(miqqedem)* occurs in 7:20 *(mîmê qedem,* "in days long ago"), and that one almost identical to "from ancient times" here *(mîmê ʿôlām)* occurs in 7:14 (*kîmê ʿôlām,* "as in days long ago"). (The latter phrase also is used in Amos 9:11 of the time of David.) In both cases the phrases are anchored in history, 7:14 probably in the golden age of David and Solomon, and 7:20 in the patriarchal period. This same historical sense for *mîmê ʿôlām* is applied by the major Hebrew lexicons to its use in Mic 5:2: "ancient time, days of old,"[98] "days of old,"[99] "ancient times,"[100] "remote antiquity."[101] For contextual reasons numerous commentators also prefer this semantic category for *ʿolām* here. So while either interpretation is possible, the context seems to favor the main text over the footnote alternative.

5:3 "Therefore"—because God has designed to punish his people before delivering them and because the Deliverer is to arise from the little town of Bethlehem, not the great city of Jerusalem—God will abandon Israel (Judah)

---

[94] G. Van Groningen also notes that although "Zion, Jerusalem, Judah, and Israel, indeed, will realize great benefit" from this ruler who will come from Bethlehem, it is *"for me"* that he will do his work (*Messianic Revelation in the Old Testament* [Grand Rapids: Baker, 1990], 502).

[95] וּמוֹצָאֹתָיו, lit. "and his goings forth."

[96] T. E. McComiskey, *The Covenants of Promise* (Grand Rapids: Baker, 1985), 28.

[97] See also NIVSB, Rom 9:5 n.; J. R. White, *The King James Only Crontroversy: Can You Trust the Modern Translations?* (Minneapolis: Bethany, 1995), 215–16; and numerous commentaries.

[98] BDB, 761.

[99] E. Jenni, "עוֹלָם *ʾōlām* eternity," *TLOT* 2:855. Jenni and C. Westermann, *Theological Lexicon of the Old Testament,* 3 vols., trans. M. E. Biddle (Peabody, Mass.: Hendrickson, 1997).

[100] A. Tomasino, "עוֹלָם," *NIDOTTE* 3:347. "The basic meaning of the nom. [noun] is farthest time, distant time. ... It does not seem to mean eternity in the philosophical sense of the word (i.e., neither unbounded time nor eternal timelessness), although there are a few vv. where the meaning of the nom. is very much like the idea of eternity. ...*ʾôlām* is usually used to describe events extended into the distant past or future. Such distant time is clearly relative: it can be a time in one's own life (Ps 77:5[6]), a life span (Exod 21:6), or the furthest conceivable time (15:18)" (p. 346).

[101] *NIDNTT* 3:828.

by handing them over to their enemies. That condition will last until the promised Ruler is born and begins his rule. "Therefore" also is explained as meaning "because such great and blessed events are coming, the surrender of Israel to affliction can only be temporary, lasting till the point of time when, after painful pangs, the glorious birth takes place. He who is born for the salvation of the nation is, according to the context, no other than the ruler from Bethlehem."[102]

"She who is in labor" has been interpreted in at least three ways: (1) It refers to the mother of the Messianic Ruler promised in v. 2 (Mary):

> In view of the fact that Bethlehem must eventually produce the glorious Ruler, it follows that the judgment threatened in 3:12; 4:10; and 5:1 must in some sense continue until the day of his appearing. The fact that Messiah would be born in Bethlehem and not in Jerusalem, the city of David, presupposes that the family of David would have lost the throne. Such could only be the case if Israel had been overrun by her enemies. ... God's abandonment of Israel would only be temporary. Israel's oppression would continue until the birth of Messiah. "She who is with child" must be the virgin who would conceive and bear a son called Immanuel (Isa 7:14). The Immanuel promise was uttered about thirty years prior to the present passage. Thus the future king's birth would signal the beginning of the end of the nation's oppression (5:3a).[103]

(2) It refers to Bethlehem, out of which Israel's Ruler would come (v. 2).[104] (3) Most commentators (including this one) construe it as a reference to Israel (Judah) or, more particularly, Zion (Jerusalem). Thus it would echo 4:9–10. God's chosen people (the covenant nation), then, would bring forth the Messianic Ruler. The Ruler's "brothers" (=his people) would return from exile to join the other Israelites in Judah and Jerusalem as a restored, reunified, complete covenant nation again. Probably the believing, faithful, righteous remnant is in view in the "brothers." Although such prophecies "receive a fulfillment in the immediate future, and in Messiah's first advent, they also look forward to their exhaustive fulfillment in the final consummation of all things at Messiah's second advent in glory."[105] The principle of progressive fulfillment is at work again. For the final, complete stage in the progressive fulfillment of the whole in the future, see Isa 11:10–16; Ezek

---

[102] C. von Orelli, *The Twelve Minor Prophets,* trans. J. S. Banks (1897; reprint, Minneapolis: Klock & Klock, 1977), 208.

[103] J. E. Smith, *The Minor Prophets* (Joplin, Mo.: College Press, 1994), 332.

[104] McComiskey, "Micah,"7:428.

[105] Fausset, "Jeremiah–Malachi," 603.

16:53–63; Hos 3:4–5; Zech 10:9–12.[106]

5:4 Virtually everyone agrees that the antecedent of "He" is the coming Ruler of v. 2, namely, the Messianic Son of David. After his people return to him (v. 3), here is what the Messiah will do for them. First, he will begin his rule over them ("will stand" probably meaning something like "will be installed as King"; cf. Ps 2:6 for the concept). Alternatively, the sense may be that his reign will endure or last forever. Second, he will be their Shepherd-King—feeding, leading, and protecting them—essentially taking good care of them (see 2:12 and 4:8 and comments; cf. 2 Sam 5:2; 7:8; Pss 23:1; 95:7; 100:3; Isa 40:11; Jer 23:2–6; 31:10; Ezek 34:11–16,23–24,31; Zech 10:3; Matt 2:6; John 10:11; Heb 13:20; 1 Pet 5:4). Such a shepherding ministry was a royal function in the ancient Near Eastern world.[107] Van Groningen makes this comparison between the Messianic King and his ancestor David:

> As David was a shepherd (Pss 23; 78:70–72), so his antitype, the royal Shepherd, will lead, feed, protect, and exercise authority over his own. As a Shepherd, he will be invincible: David protected his flock from the lions and bears; the ruling Shepherd will be endowed *bĕ ʿōz yhwh* (with the strength of Yahweh), exercising divine strength to protect the flock.[108]

The Lord himself will enable the Shepherd-King to do his work ("in the strength of the LORD"; cf. "Mighty God" in Isa 9:6 and "Spirit of … power" in Isa 11:2; see also Isa 61:1). The promised Ruler will carry out his ministry in the "majesty" (=regal authority and power) of the "name" (=the Lord himself or his manifested character) of the Lord "his God" (speaking of the special, intimate relationship between the two). The language here may echo that of the Shepherd-King's ancestor David, who also was a shepherd-king: "I come against you in the name of the LORD Almighty, the God of the armies of Israel, whom you have defied" (1 Sam 17:45; cf. Mic 4:5).

As a result of the above, the royal Shepherd's people ("flock") will live securely. The Hebrew for "live securely" means simply "live," "dwell," or "sit"; but the ultimate sense is doubtless what the NIV has (so it is a pregnant or elliptical construction). The picture evoked is that of 4:4, where the Hebrew for "sit" is the same verb used here. "For" further explains how all these accomplishments are possible. "Then" is literally "now," but it refers to the future time when all these things would come true. Finally, the Messianic

[106] For a final, complete restoration of elect Israel in the future, not only to their land but also to their Messiah, see Barker, "The Scope and Center of Old and New Testament Theology and Hope," in *Dispensationalism, Israel and the Church*, ed. C. A. Blaising and D. L. Bock (Grand Rapids: Zondervan, 1992), 304, 318–28; L. R. Helyer, *Yesterday, Today and Forever: The Continuing Relevance of the Old Testament* (Salem, Wis.: Sheffield, 1996), 324–44.

[107] J. A. Soggin, "רעה *rʿh* to tend," *TLOT* 3:1248.

[108] Van Groningen, *Messianic Revelation in the Old Testament*, 505.

Shepherd will be so great that his rule will be universal (cf. 4:1–5; Pss 2:8–9; 72:8–11; Zech 9:10; Luke 1:32–33). That is why he can accomplish all the preceding. Craigie concludes his treatment of this section with these practical words:

> Matthew's quotation of Micah's prophecy [Matt 2:6] has set it in a new perspective for the Christian reader of the Old Testament. The deliverer has come to this world in the person of Jesus; like David, Jesus is the new Shepherd of God's sheep, offering security from external enemies and a life of security. Jesus, of the Davidic line, is above all a gift of God to this world. To those who feel shut in on every side, like the besieged citizens of Jerusalem who first heard these words, Jesus brings the prospect of deliverance and security. And that is the essence of the Christmas message: God makes a gift to a besieged world through whom deliverance may come.[109]

(6) The Ideal King Will Deliver His People (5:5–6; MT 5:4–5)

5 And he will be their peace.

When the Assyrian invades our land
and marches through our fortresses,
we will raise against him seven shepherds,
even eight leaders of men.
6 They will rule the land of Assyria with the sword,
the land of Nimrod with drawn sword.
He will deliver us from the Assyrian
when he invades our land
and marches into our borders.

The literary form is a deliverance or salvation oracle (see introduction to 2:12–13). The NIV's sectional heading should be eliminated from v. 5, and the first poetic colon of the verse should be connected to this pericope instead of the previous one. It seems rather transparent—even more so in Hebrew—that the first three cola of v. 5 together with the last three cola of v. 6 mark off (i.e., as an inclusio) these verses as a unit. Furthermore, the pronoun "their," supplied in "their peace," should read "our" to agree with the following first-person plural pronouns (the Hb. is lit. "and this one will be peace"). Finally, v. 5 should be punctuated to correspond to the punctuation of v. 6, thus revealing the chiastic structure of the two verses:

a And he will be our peace [and security; see comments on 5:5]
  b when the Assyrian invades our land
    c and marches through our fortresses.

[109] Craigie, *Twelve Prophets*, 40.

d We will raise against him seven shepherds,
even eight leaders of men.
d′ They will rule the land of Assyria with the sword,
the land of Nimrod with drawn sword.
a′ He will deliver us from the Assyrian
b′ when he invades our land
c′ and marches into our borders.

Waltke elaborates:

> Lines a and a′ pertain to Messiah's peace and protection of his imperium [dominion]; lines b–c and b′–c′ to Assyria's threat against Israel's security; and lines d–d′ to Messiah's subordinate shepherds through whom he accomplishes his victory over Assyria. … The chiasmus functions to subordinate the sheik-shepherds to Messiah and to attribute victory to him.[110]

There are also links between vv. 5–6 and vv. 2–4: (1) the subject (the Messiah), (2) the root *rʿh* ("shepherd"), (3) the restored Israelites (v. 3), who are the antecedents of the first-person plural pronouns in vv. 5–6, and (4) the peace and security of the Messiah's kingdom: "they will live securely" (v. 4), and "he will be our peace [and security]" (v. 5).

5:5–6 The logical and most natural antecedent of "he" is the Messianic Shepherd-Ruler of vv. 2–4. The opening colon could be rendered, "And he will be the one of peace."[111] The Davidic Messiah would be "our peace" (cf. Eph 2:14). In Isa 9:6 he is called "Prince of Peace." In addition to denoting peace in the sense of the absence of war and hostility, *šālôm* also connotes security, prosperity, general well-being, and at times even internal, spiritual peace (Isa 53:5; 54:10; cf. Luke 2:14). I have attempted to bring out the fuller semantic range of the term here by translating it "peace and security" (see above).

Many interpreters agree that *Assyrian* here and *Assyria* (v. 6) are symbolic of all potential enemies of God's people in the present and future (as in 7:12; cf. Isa 11:11; Zech 10:10–11).[112] For example, Kaiser has written: "The 'Assyrian' of verse 5 is typical and representative of all of Israel's enemies in that future day when the nations shall attempt to deal once and for all with 'the Jewish question.'"[113] The scene is similar to that in 4:11–13 (see com-

---

[110] Waltke, "Micah," 708.

[111] *IBHS*, 337–38.

[112] Although J. L. Mays asserts that "in the present MT 'Assyria' stands outside any expected syntax" (*Micah,* OTL [Philadelphia: Westminster, 1976], 119), Hillers counters that "actually it is rather common for the subject of a temporal/conditional clause beginning [with] כִּי to precede the conjunction" (*Micah*, 68). Hillers translates, "As to Assyria, when they come into our land …"

[113] W. C. Kaiser, Jr., *Toward an Old Testament Theology* (Grand Rapids: Zondervan, 1978), 204. See also Mays, *Micah,* 119.

ments there). The principal point is that whenever God's people are threatened with extermination, God will enable them to raise up a superabundance of capable leaders against their enemies. "Seven … eight" is a conventional Hebrew way of indicating "many" or "more than enough."

Verse 6 basically reiterates the thought of v. 5, to which it is chiastically parallel (see above). "They" refers to the leaders just mentioned. "Rule" is literally "shepherd." The "land of Nimrod" may refer to Assyria or Babylonia (Gen 10:8–12): Babylonia was subordinate to Assyria at the time of Micah's ministry—but see comments on "Assyrian" in v. 5. The first "He" refers to the ruler of vv. 2,4a, while the second "he" refers to "the Assyrian." God will enable his people and their leaders to triumph over his and their enemies (cf. Matt 16:18).

(7) The Remnant among the Nations (5:7–9; MT 5:6–8)

7The remnant of Jacob will be
in the midst of many peoples
like dew from the LORD,
like showers on the grass,
which do not wait for man
or linger for mankind.
8The remnant of Jacob will be among the nations,
in the midst of many peoples,
like a lion among the beasts of the forest,
like a young lion among flocks of sheep,
which mauls and mangles as it goes,
and no one can rescue.
9Your hand will be lifted up in triumph over your enemies,
and all your foes will be destroyed.

The theme of Israel's (Judah's) faithful remnant triumphing over their enemies is continued in this pericope. It is an oracle of salvation or deliverance. Positively, God's people will be a blessing, bringing life and renewal to the nations. Negatively, the remnant will be a source of death and divine judgment to their oppressors, as the tables are turned and the victims become the victors (cf. Gen 12:3). God's kingdom will be victorious.

5:7 The survivors of persecution are called the "remnant of Jacob" because they will represent all twelve sons (tribes) of Jacob (see comments on 2:12; 4:6–8). "Peoples" is synonymous with "nations" (v. 8). The similes ("like dew … like showers") speak of life, renewal, refreshment, and fertility. Thus Israel will be a blessing to the other nations and people groups of the world, as her covenant Lord intended originally. Just as dew and showers do not depend on humankind to perform their refreshing influence, so Israel will trust in her Lord. The Lord himself will make his people such a blessing (cf.

Ps 72:6,16–19). It would be preferable to translate the Hebrew verb rendered "linger for" as "depend on" or "trust or hope in."[114] Mays and Wolff understand the similes differently, but the interpretation offered here seems more natural for this context.[115]

5:8 "Remnant of Jacob," "in the midst of many peoples," and the double simile are links to v. 7. The relationship, however, is one of contrast. The remnant's positive influence was emphasized in the previous verse. Here its negative effect is stressed: Israel will also be a source of death. Just as a lion mauls and mangles sheep and other animals, so Israel will overcome all her foes. (Judas Maccabeus is compared to a lion in 1 Macc. 3:4.) Her covenant Lord will enable her to be invincible, so that her ultimate victory is inevitable. No one will be able to withstand her. The Messiah's kingdom must triumph over all opposition. The principle of vv. 7–8 is essentially that of Zech 8:13 and 2 Cor 2:14–16. Perhaps there is also an implied warning here against anti-semitism.

5:9 In a bold apostrophe Micah now addresses the remnant directly. The opening words may be read as a wish ("May your hand be lifted up …") or as a promise ("Your hand will be lifted up …").[116] The latter seems more consonant with the preceding verses. "Hand" is symbolic of power. The current subjugation of the remnant will be reversed. When the Messiah's kingdom comes in its fullness, he will enable his people to be victorious over all foes. Clark illustrates: "So it has been down the centuries. The spiritual blessings given uniquely to Israel enabled her to outlast all the persecutions of her enemies from Nebuchadnezzar to Hitler and Nasser and to survive after they have been destroyed."[117]

(8) Obliteration of Military Power and Pagan Worship (5:10–15; MT 5:9–14)

10"In that day," declares the LORD,
"I will destroy your horses from among you
and demolish your chariots.
11I will destroy the cities of your land
and tear down all your strongholds.
12I will destroy your witchcraft
and you will no longer cast spells.
13I will destroy your carved images
and your sacred stones from among you;

[114] Waltke, "Micah," 713. For similar uses elsewhere cf. 1 Sam 10:8; 13:8; Pss 31:24; 33:18,22; Isa 42:4; 51:5; Mic 7:7.

[115] See Mays, *Micah*, 122–23; Wolff, *Micah*, 156.

[116] GKC § 109k.

[117] D. J. Clark, "Micah," in *The International Bible Commentary*, ed. F. F. Bruce et al. (Grand Rapids: Zondervan, 1986), 935.

you will no longer bow down
to the work of your hands.
14I will uproot from among you your Asherah poles
and demolish your cities.
15I will take vengeance in anger and wrath
upon the nations that have not obeyed me."

The form or genre is another oracle of deliverance—perhaps an eschatological salvation oracle (note "In that day"). God performs radical surgery to rid his people of the things that once caused them to stumble—ultimately a spiritual deliverance. In the second-advent stage of the Messianic era, God's people will not depend on weapons of war or pagan idols. The successes of his people are always achieved by dependence on him, not on military power and religious objects of faith (cf. Isa 2:6–8).

5:10–11 Now Micah quotes the Lord as speaking directly to his people. "In that day" has occurred previously in 2:4; 4:1,6. "Declares the LORD" is also used to announce God's word in 4:6. In v. 9 the promise was given that all Israel's enemies would be destroyed. The repetition of "I will destroy" identifies the ultimate agent of destruction as the Lord himself—Israel's covenant Lord; but here the destruction is directed against his own covenant nation. Israel had often trusted in horses and chariots, but the Lord will obliterate them so that his people will trust in him alone for success (see Deut 17:16; Ps 20:7; Isa 2:7; 31:1; Zech 9:10). The Lord will also destroy their cities (v. 11) and strongholds (probably referring to fortified cities; cf. Jer 5:17). So all military power will be removed (see the exposition of 1:13).

5:12–14 Next, all objects of pagan worship will be purged from God's people. His people will no longer be unfaithful by committing spiritual adultery with false gods, idols, cult objects, and the occult. As I have written elsewhere:

> Asherah was a Canaanite fertility or mother goddess and consort of El (cf. Ugaritic *ʾatrt, Athirat*), and also the wooden cult object or "sacred pole" by which she was represented. Apparently, the plurals *Asherim* and *Asheroth* refer only to her images or cult objects. The contexts show that Asherah was a goddess (or an object representing her) who was worshiped along with Baal (Judg 3:7; 2 Kgs 23:6).[118]

Such detestable practices were clearly prohibited in covenant law (Exod 20:3–6; 22:18; Lev 19:26; Deut 13:1–5; 18:9–14; Isa 8:16–20; cf. comments on Mic 1:7). So the covenant Lord (Yahweh) will destroy their witchcraft (the Hb. word, which is plural, could also be rendered "sorceries"). They will no longer cast spells ("cast spells" could also be translated "practice magic").

The Lord will likewise destroy their carved images (v. 13), referring to idols. And he will remove their sacred stones, referring to cult objects.

---

[118] Barker, "Grove," *ZPEB* 2:851.

Archaeologists have discovered such standing pillars in many parts of ancient Canaan. With all these purged from their land, they will no longer worship the work of their hands. Kelley makes this contemporary application:

> Micah condemned idolatry because it involved people in the worship of that which their own hands had made. ... The temptation to worship the work of our own hands is as real today as it was in the time of the prophet. Our forms of idolatry may be more sophisticated than those that Micah encountered, but they are basically the same. We trust in our own skill and ingenuity to lead us through our problems. We feel more secure trusting the works of our own hands rather than trusting God supremely. And this is what idolatry is all about.[119]

Since the word "cities" is a surprising parallel to "Asherah poles" and since "cities" have already been dealt with (v. 11), some scholars emend the Hebrew root used here *(ʿr)* to achieve a more suitable meaning. But it is probably best to retain the Hebrew text as it is and to regard "cities" as the centers of idolatrous and occult practices, which would yield an appropriate parallel thought. In any event, the Lord will eradicate all vestiges of pagan worship. God will take vengeance on the disobedient Gentile nations (see Deut 32:35; Rom 12:19; Heb 10:30).

5:15 Some are troubled by the concept of God's "vengeance." As R. L. Smith notes, "We often associate the idea of revenge, retaliation, vindictiveness, excessive punishment with the word 'vengeance.'" But God's "vengeance" is quite different.

> It is used of a judge or suzerain whose responsibility it was to determine the innocence or guilt of an accused, then to administer grace or punishment as the case demanded. Here Micah says that Yahweh acting as the Judge of the world will punish those nations who rebel against him.[120]

Some of these rebellious nations were the very ones from whom the Israelites had learned their corrupt and pagan ways. Now those nations must also be judged and brought under the Lord's reign. "Anger and wrath" are here equivalent to "righteous indignation."[121] "Obeyed" is a good example of the Hebrew verb *šāmaʿ* meaning more than simply "heard" or "listened to" (see comments on 1:2). A time is coming when "the obedience of the nations" (Gen 49:10) will be given to "the Lion of the tribe of Judah" (Rev 5:5; cf. Pss 2:8–9; 110:2,6; Rev 11:15). "Yahweh will be satisfied with nothing less than a world-wide kingdom."[122] He will be the omnipotent Sovereign over all.

---

[119] P. H. Kelley, "Micah ... Malachi," vol. 14, LBBC (Nashville: Broadman, 1984), 40.

[120] R. L. Smith, *Micah–Malachi*, WBC (Waco: Word, 1984), 49.

[121] For further discussion of anger on the part of God, see Barker, "Zechariah," 609 (n. on v. 2).

[122] J. M. P. Smith, *A Critical and Exegetical Commentary on the Books of Micah ...*, ICC (Edinburgh: T & T Clark, 1911), 117.

SECTION OUTLINE

IV. THIRD CYCLE (6:1–7:20)
  1. God's Charges against Judah Primarily (6:1–7:7)
    (1) A Divine Covenant Lawsuit (6:1–8)
    (2) Further Charges and the Sentence (6:9–16)
    (3) A Lament over a Decadent Society (7:1–7)
  2. The Ultimate Triumph of God's Kingdom (7:8–20)
    (1) A Psalm of Trust (7:8–10)
    (2) A Promise of Restoration (7:11–13)
    (3) A Prayer, the Lord's Answer, and the Response (7:14–17)
    (4) A Hymn of Praise to God (7:18–20)

IV. THIRD CYCLE (6:1–7:20)

This is now the third cycle of judgment and salvation (see Introduction, "Structure," p. 34). The judgment theme is presented in 6:1–7:7, the salvation or restoration theme in 7:8–20.

1. God's Charges against Judah Primarily (6:1–7:7)

(1) A Divine Covenant Lawsuit (6:1–8)

[1]Listen to what the LORD says:
"Stand up, plead your case before the mountains;
let the hills hear what you have to say.
[2]Hear, O mountains, the LORD's accusation;
listen, you everlasting foundations of the earth.
For the LORD has a case against his people;
he is lodging a charge against Israel.

[3]"My people, what have I done to you?
How have I burdened you? Answer me.
[4]I brought you up out of Egypt
and redeemed you from the land of slavery.
I sent Moses to lead you,
also Aaron and Miriam.
[5]My people, remember
what Balak king of Moab counseled
and what Balaam son of Beor answered.

Remember [your journey] from Shittim to Gilgal,
that you may know the righteous acts of the LORD."

6With what shall I come before the LORD
and bow down before the exalted God?
Shall I come before him with burnt offerings,
with calves a year old?
7Will the LORD be pleased with thousands of rams,
with ten thousand rivers of oil?
Shall I offer my firstborn for my transgression,
the fruit of my body for the sin of my soul?
8He has showed you, O man, what is good.
And what does the LORD require of you?
To act justly and to love mercy
and to walk humbly with your God.

The literary form is a divine covenant lawsuit (see introduction to 1:2–7), as confirmed by the Hebrew word *rîb* ("case") in vv. 1–2. This section is one of the most familiar passages in Micah and is one of the great summaries of true religion—particularly v. 8. J. K. West has given a helpful analysis of its structure: (1) summons (v. 1), (2) charge to witnesses (v. 2), (3) plaintiff's case (vv. 3–5), (4) defendant's response (vv. 6–7), (5) indictment or judgment: required amendment (v. 8).[1]

Stuart paraphrases vv. 1–8 like this:

6:1–2 The Lord launches a divine legal proceeding against Israel, with the mountains as a symbolic jury.

6:3–4 God declares his innocence. Their sin certainly cannot be blamed on him —he rescued, helped, and guided them.

6:5 Israel should reflect on its early history: how the king of Moab tried to get the false prophet Balaam to curse Israel and how Balaam ended up blessing them, or how God led Israel through the Jordan dry-shod, from one side (Shittim) to the other (Gilgal).

6:6–7 What then does God want from his people? Are sacrifices all he wants? Would even sacrificing one's oldest child be adequate to cover one's sins?

6:8 God has already told you what he wants: justice, loyalty to his covenant, and careful living.[2]

6:1–2 The pericope opens with the imperative *šimʿû,* Micah's call to the Israelites to "Listen to" or "Hear" what the Lord is saying (an active participle

[1] J. K. West, *Introduction to the Old Testament,* 2d ed. (New York: Macmillan, 1981), 339.
[2] D. Stuart, *Favorite Old Testament Passages* (Philadelphia: Westminster, 1985), 127.

in Hebrew) to his people (see comments on 1:2). The same Hebrew word, *šimᶜû,* marks the beginning of the first and second cycles of judgment and salvation (1:2; 3:1). Later in the verse the addressees in the Lord's speech are still his own chosen, covenant people, though this is disputed by some due to the change to the singular "you" in "what you have to say" (lit. "your voice"). The greatest internal consistency is achieved, however, when the Lord is construed as addressing his people in v. 1, the mountains (as witnesses) in v. 2, and his people again in vv. 3–5. The singular "you," employed in Micah's quotation of the Lord, is easily explained by the Lord's thinking of his people in terms of the collective noun *ᶜam* ("people"), as in v. 3 ("My people"), where the singular "you" also is used. So in v. 1 the covenant Lord summons the vassal people of his kingdom to appear in court and present their case or defense in the presence of the mountains as witnesses.

"Stand up" here means "Get ready to speak" or "Stand up to defend yourself in court." The people are told to "plead your case" or "make your defense" or "make your complaint" (see the comments on *rîb* in the introduction to 1:2–7).[3] And they are to do so "before the mountains" and "hills." "Inanimate objects were called on as third-party witnesses because of their enduring nature and because they were witnesses to his covenant (see Deut 32:1; Josh 24:27; Isa 1:2 and note)."[4] In v. 2 the Lord rhetorically charges them to function as witnesses. "Foundations of the earth," standing parallel to "mountains," probably refers to the bottoms of the mountains in the ocean depths. The Lord wants them to hear his accusation of his people, his case against them, and the charges he is bringing against Israel (referring primarily to Judah, though the term could include the Israelites who had fled from the Northern Kingdom to the Southern Kingdom). (When the Lord is speaking, it is not uncommon for him to refer to himself in the third person, as here.) Concerning the reference to Israel as "his people," "It is because Israel is God's people that her sin is so heinous, and that God condescends to plead with her."[5]

6:3–5 Now the Lord presents his case against his people. He uses language that speaks of covenantal relationship by referring to Israel as "My people" and to himself as "your God" (v. 8). This is indicative of tender rebuke. He begins by asking questions that are reminiscent of "What more could have been done for my vineyard than I have done for it?" (Isa 5:4) and "I have not

[3] For further discussion of ריב see G. Liedke's treatment in *TLOT* 3:1232–37, especially p. 1236.

[4] NIVSB, Mic 6:1–2 n. Also cf. Ezek 36:6. "The OT frequently associates mountains with what is permanent and unchangeable ... The mountains are also extremely resistant to destruction and will be the last thing to disappear if the earth ever suffers the ultimate catastrophe (Ps 46:2–3[3–4]; Isa 54:10)" (M. Selman, "הַר," *NIDOTTE* 1:1051).

[5] W. J. Deane et al., "Micah," in *The Pulpit Commentary*, 23 vols., reprint, ed. H. D. M. Spence and J. S. Exell (Grand Rapids: Eerdmans, 1983), 14:87.

burdened you … nor wearied you" (Isa 43:23) and ultimately "My yoke is easy and my burden is light" (Matt 11:30). He then tells his people to answer him, but since the questions are followed by embarrassing silence, he himself provides the answer by reminding them of what he has done for them. Far from "burdening" them, he has expressed his providential care for them at many times, in different ways, and through different leaders and mediators. He refers to these expressions as his "righteous acts" (v. 5).

First (v. 4), he redeemed them (i.e., their ancestors) from the bondage of slavery in Egypt.[6] There is a wordplay between *helʾētîkā* (v. 3, "have I burdened you") and *heʿĕlitîkā* (v. 4, "I brought you up"). Essentially the Lord is saying, "I have not weighted you down; instead, I have brought you up out of slavery into settlement in the promised land." The whole exodus event is often cited in the Old Testament as the supreme demonstration of the Great King's grace, love, power, and care for his people. Therefore they should respond with grateful love, faith, faithfulness, and obedience to the stipulations of their Suzerain's covenant with them. Such a function of their deliverance from Egypt began as early as the exodus event itself in conjunction with the giving of the law (the Sinaitic covenant) at Mount Sinai (Exod 20:2).

The law therefore was given to the redeemed people of God as a means of expressing their love to God as well as a means of governing their relationship to God and to each other. The law "was not a way of salvation but a way to enjoy an orderly life and God's fullest blessing within the covenantal, theocratic arrangement. Thus God's grace precedes the covenantal law he gave to his people and represents a use of salvation history to inspire grateful obedience."[7] Unfortunately the Lord's mighty saving acts did not "inspire grateful obedience" on the part of the majority of his covenant people, as the Book of Micah has clearly demonstrated up to this point. Rather, they have broken covenant, which is why the Lord registers a complaint against them.

Second, he gave them competent human leaders: Moses, the great lawgiver and human founder of Israel as a separate, recognized national entity; Aaron, the high priestly mediator; and Miriam, a prophetess and poet (Exod 15:20–21; cf. Num 12:2). Even in the eighth century B.C. God had provided gifted leaders for his people: a godly king like Hezekiah and good prophets such as

[6] For a good study of the Hebrew verb פָּדָה ("redeemed") see J. J. Stamm's article in *TLOT* 2:964–76, noting particularly the distinction he makes between the use of the verb in religious literature, where it concerns redemption by God that no longer involves the exchange of something of equivalent value, and its use in legal and cultic contexts, where the payment of some sort of price or ransom is required. In the case of the religious usage, only Yahweh is the subject of redemption; accordingly, he never offers a compensating price. So the emphasis is on the Lord as Redeemer-Savior-Liberator (as here).

[7] K. L. Barker, "The Scope and Center of Old and New Testament Theology and Hope," in *Dispensationalism, Israel and the Church*, ed. C. A. Blaising and D. L. Bock (Grand Rapids: Zondervan, 1992), 295.

Isaiah, Micah, and Hosea. But they rebelled against such spiritual leaders, both past and present.

Third (v. 5), the Lord turned their enemies' curses into blessings. He exhorted his people to remember what happened when King Balak wanted the false prophe Balaam to pronounce a curse on Israel (see Num 22–24). We now know even more about Balaam, thanks to archaeology:

> In 1975 about a dozen panels were discovered which had tumbled down from the walls of a temple at Deir Alla in Transjordan. The inscriptions are written in cursive Aramaic script. They date from the eighth or seventh century B.C. and contain a nonbiblical account about Balaam and his visions, prophecies, and acts. He is called "seer of the gods" and evidently came to have a prominent role in the religious traditions of the region east of the Jordan.[8]

"What Balak king of Moab counseled" was to call down a curse on Israel. "What Balaam son of Beor answered" was to pronounce a blessing instead. So the Lord frustrated Balak's plan by forcing Balaam to prophesy good for Israel (Deut 23:3–6).

Fourth, the Lord also exhorted his people to "remember" how he brought them from the plains of Moab into Canaan.[9] Shittim was Israel's last encampment east of the Jordan River (Josh 3:1); Gilgal was their first stop west of the Jordan (Josh 4:19). Of course, this is a reference to the miraculous crossing of the Jordan. So the Lord was faithful to fulfill his promise not only to bring Israel "up out of Egypt" but also to bring them into the promised land. His purpose in all this was that they would "know the righteous acts of the LORD." These saving deeds of the Lord demonstrated his righteous character. He was in the right; they were the ones who were in the wrong. In fact, in view of all that their Suzerain had done for them, the people of his kingdom should have rendered total allegiance and full commitment to him and to the terms of his covenant with them. Instead, they were unfaithful, rebellious covenant-breakers. The Great King, on the other hand, has been completely faithful: "All these instances of God's interposition prove how faithful he is to his promises, how he cares for his elect."[10] So the people's complaints are baseless.

6:6–7 The defendant, Israel (Judah), responds. Either they speak as a corporate personality ("I"), as occasionally in the Psalms, or a representative

---

[8] G. Baez-Camargo, *Archaeological Commentary on the Bible* (Garden City: Doubleday, 1984), 52; for a good commentary on Num 22–24 and the problems swirling around Balaam, see R. B. Allen, "Numbers," in EBC, 12 vols., ed. F. E. Gaebelein (Grand Rapids: Zondervan, 1990), 2:885–914; and see NIVSB, Num 22:8 n.

[9] The fourth line of v. 5 in Hebrew has only מִן־הַשִּׁטִּים֙ עַד־הַגִּלְגָּ֔ל, "from Shittim to Gilgal." The NIV fills out the meaning by repeating the assumed verb זְכָר, "remember," from the first line, and supplying the object, "journey."

[10] Deane et al., "Micah," 87.

(perhaps Micah?) speaks for them. Kaiser introduces his exposition of these verses like this:

> Two different and opposing kinds of false claims are made about this text. Some readers see the text refuting all external, ceremonial religion in favor of a totally internalized faith response to God. Others, reacting against more conservative theologies of the atonement, argue that essential religious acts focus solely on issues of justice, mercy and humility; all else is beyond what even God expects of the most devout. Unfortunately, both positions are extremes that fail to grasp the prophet Micah's point.[11]

The people begin by asking what they should bring[12] to the Lord to please him when they come to worship him. They correctly recognize that he is the "exalted God" (cf. Ps 46:10). Then they make some specific suggestions in reply to their opening question. Shall they bring burnt offerings? They think ritual alone is a solution when in reality it is part of the problem. No mere ceremony is ever sufficient. "False worshipers think God's favor, like theirs, can be bought" or earned. They "offer the Lord everything but what he asks for: their loving and obedient hearts."[13] "Offerings … are no substitute for obedience to God's will."[14] The burnt offering was wholly consumed and was intended to express one's devotion, commitment, and complete surrender to God. Yet such total commitment is the one thing the offerers were still withholding from the Lord. Calves a year old were regarded as the best sacrificial animals at the right age (Lev 9:3).

In v. 7 the worshipers "up the ante," so to speak, by wondering whether a greater quantity of offerings would please the Lord. "Thousands" and "ten thousand" are examples of hyperbole, though King Solomon did offer 22,000 cattle and 120,000 sheep and goats as fellowship (traditionally "peace") offerings at the dedication of the temple (1 Kgs 8:63)—obviously impossible for average Israelite worshipers. Rams were common sacrificial animals (Lev 5:15), and olive oil was a common sacrificial substance (Lev 2:1,4,15).

Finally, the worshipers hypothetically wonder whether sacrificing their firstborn children would atone for their sins (on "transgression" and "sin" see

---

[11] W. C. Kaiser, Jr., *Hard Sayings of the Old Testament* (Downers Grove: InterVarsity, 1988), 226–27.

[12] "Come before" translates קדם, a denominative verb related to קֶדֶם, "front, before, earlier, east." It refers to an act resulting in being in front of something, either spatially or temporally. It is often used in the negative sense of confronting (e.g., Ps 18:5[6],18[19]; 2 Kgs 19:32; Amos 9:10; Job 30:27). It can describe God bringing blessings to someone (Pss 21:3[4]; 59:10[11]; 79:8). It is also used of prayer and worship, as here (e.g., Pss 88:13; 95:2; 119:147). See also Deut 23:4[5]; Job 41:11.

[13] B. K. Waltke, "Theology of Micah," in *Evangelical Dictionary of Biblical Theology*, ed. W. A. Elwell (Grand Rapids: Baker, 1996), 527.

[14] H. Vorlander, "Gift, δῶρον," *NIDNTT* 2:42.

comments on 1:5). This, in fact, is what King Ahaz did (2 Kgs 16:3; 2 Chr 28:3). The Ammonites sacrificed their children to their God, Molech (Lev 20:2–5; 1 Kgs 11:5). The detestable practice spread to Phoenicia, Canaan, and even to the Israelites themselves on occasion. For God's people to engage in child sacrifice would only increase their sins because God expressly prohibited it (Lev 18:21; Deut 18:10). Jeremiah condemned such a horrible ritual (Jer 7:31; 19:5; 32:32; for the biblical teaching on redeeming the "firstborn" see Exod 13:2,13; 22:29; 34:20). Since the people of God's covenant community were willing to bring any of these sacrifices to the Lord, they doubtless believed that he was bringing unjust charges against them. What the Lord really wanted most of all, however, was not the offerings but the hearts, allegiance, and obedience of the offerers (cf. Rom 12:1; Heb 10:4). "They would offer everything (even what God forbade) excepting only what alone he asked for, their heart, its love and its obedience."[15] The truth taught in this passage is basically the same as that expressed in 1 Sam 15:22; Pss 40:6–8; 50:8–15,23; 51:16–19; Isa 1:11–15; Jer 6:19–20; 7:22–23; Hos 6:6; Amos 5:21–24; Zech 7:4–10.

6:8 "This verse stands as the motto of the alcove of religion in the reading room of the Congressional Library in Washington."[16] Politicians have quoted it often in their election campaigns (if only more would practice it!). Numerous accolades have been showered on it. For example, von Rad says, "This is the quintessence of the commandments as the prophets understood them."[17] J. M. P. Smith calls it "the finest summary of the content of practical religion to be found in the OT."[18] And Boadt observes, "The rabbis who commented on this verse in the early centuries of the Christian era called it a one-line summary of the whole Law."[19]

The Lord through Micah now announces to Israel (Judah) what he does require ("man" here represents corporate Israel). He does not desire ritual sacrifices divorced from a changed life—a life given over completely to the covenant Lord. Rather, his people must change their ways and actions (Jer 7:3,5–7). Furthermore, he had already revealed what he requires and "what is good." Where? In passages like Deut 10:12–13:

> And now, O Israel, what does the LORD your God ask of you but to fear the LORD your God, to walk in all his ways, to love him, to serve the LORD your

---

[15] E. B. Pusey, *The Minor Prophets: A Commentary*, 2 vols. (Grand Rapids: Baker, 1950), 2:82.

[16] G. L. Robinson, *The Twelve Minor Prophets* (1926; reprint, Grand Rapids: Baker, 1967), 100.

[17] G. von Rad, *Old Testament Theology*, trans. D. M. G. Stalker, 2 vols. (New York: Harper & Row, 1965), 2:186–87; also in his book, *The Message of the Prophets* (London: SCM, 1968), 155.

[18] J. M. P. Smith, *A Critical and Exegetical Commentary on the Books of Micah*, ICC (Edinburgh: T & T Clark, 1911), 123.

[19] L. Boadt, *Reading the Old Testament* (New York: Paulist, 1984), 336.

God with all your heart and with all your soul, and to observe the LORD's commands and decrees that I am giving you today for your own good.

Three requirements are specified in v. 8. First, they must "act justly" (see comments on 3:1). Boice points out, "To act justly is most important, for it does not mean merely to talk about justice or to get other people to act justly. It means to do the just thing yourself."[20] Second, they must "love mercy." The Hebrew for "mercy" is *ḥesed,* which essentially and primarily means "faithful covenant love."[21] Third, they must "walk humbly" with their God ("your God" is relational covenant terminology and is the counterpart to "my people" in v. 3). "Walk" means to "live" in a certain way, but the Hebrew for "humbly" is difficult because it is not the usual word for humility. It almost certainly does not mean "humbly." Probably the NIrV is as accurate as any version. Here is its rendering of the entire verse: "People of Israel, the LORD has shown you what is good. / He has told you what he requires of you. / You must treat people fairly. / You must love others faithfully. / And you must be very careful to live / the way your God wants you to." So "walk humbly" would be better rendered "walk carefully (with your God)," which ultimately means "be careful to live the way your God wants you to."[22]

The *Lion Encyclopedia* summarizes the meaning and application of this great text: "Micah is repelled by sacrifices and worship which are not matched by just dealing and real spirituality. His central concerns are for social justice and true religion."[23] So does A. R. Fausset: "Without love, holiness of heart, and righteousness of life, flowing from faith in Christ, all our church-goings, forms of prayer, and almsgivings profit us nothing."[24] J. P. Lewis adds: "Worship and morality cannot be divorced from each other. They are two sides of the same coin."[25] C. L. Feinberg provides this summary: "The piety that God approves consists of three elements: a strict adherence to that which is equitable in all dealings with our fellowmen; a heart determined to do them good; and diligent care to live in close and intimate fellowship with God.[26] And T. E.

[20] J. M. Boice, *The Minor Prophets*, 2 vols. (Grand Rapids: Kregel, 1996), 2:44.

[21] For further study of חֶסֶד see Barker, "False Dichotomies between the Testaments," *JETS* 25 (1982): 6–11; see also the references cited there, particularly N. H. Snaith, *The Distinctive Ideas of the Old Testament* (New York: Schocken, 1964), 94–142.

[22] The verb צנע occurs only here. The root occurs elsewhere only in Prov 11:2. W. J. Dumbrell notes that the word "has in recent commentaries been interpreted as 'walk wisely,' largely based on the Qumran Manual of Discipline rendering and the use of the root in Ecclesiasticus" ("צנע," *NIDOTTE* 3:822).

[23] P. Alexander et al., eds., *The Lion Encyclopedia of the Bible* (Batavia: Lion, 1978), 98.

[24] A. R. Fausset, "Jeremiah-Malachi," in *A Commentary Critical, Experimental and Practical on the Old and New Testaments*, 6 vols., by P. Jamieson, A. R. Fausset, and D. Brown (Grand Rapids: Eerdmans, 1967), 4:606.

[25] J. P. Lewis, *The Minor Prophets* (Grand Rapids: Baker, 1966), 36.

[26] C. L. Feinberg, *The Minor Prophets* (Chicago: Moody, 1976), 179.

McComiskey maintains: "The standards of this verse are for those who are members of the covenantal community and delineate the areas of ethical response that God wants to see in those who share the covenantal obligations. These standards have not been abrogated for Christians, for the New Testament affirms their continuing validity. We are still called to the exercise of true religion, to kindness, and to humility (1 Cor 13:4; 2 Cor 6:6; Col 3:12; Jas 1:26–27; 1 Pet 1:2; 5:5). Christians are in a covenant relationship with God in which the law *(torah)* has been placed within their hearts (Jer 31:33; cf. Heb 10:14–17), not abrogated."[27]

Jesus probably had this verse in mind when he said (Matt 23:23):

> Woe to you, teachers of the law and Pharisees, you hypocrites! You give a tenth of your spices—mint, dill and cummin. But you have neglected the more important matters of the law—justice, mercy and faithfulness. You should have practiced the latter, without neglecting the former.

Here he regards justice, mercy, and faithfulness as "the more important matters of the law."

What, then, is Micah's (and the Lord's) point? Here is how Kaiser concludes his study of vv. 6–8 (see above for his introduction):

> Thus this saying is not an invitation, in lieu of the gospel, to save oneself by kindly acts of equity and fairness. Nor is it an attack on the forms of sacrifices and cultic acts mentioned in the tabernacle and temple instructions. It was instead a call for the natural consequence of truly forgiven men and women to demonstrate the reality of their faith by living it out in the marketplace. Such living would be accompanied with acts and deeds of mercy, justice and giving of oneself for the orphan, the widow and the poor.[28]

As the Lord said to Shallum, King Josiah's son, "Did not your father have food and drink? He did what was right and just, so all went well with him. He defended the cause of the poor and needy, and so all went well. Is that not what it means to know me?" (Jer 22:15b–16). Two applications of this passage are offered by Stuart:

1. Faithful participation in worship is not enough. It must be accompanied by faithful, proper living.
2. A good look at the past reminds us of God's loyalty, and of our responsibility to be loyal to him in return.[29]

(2) Further Charges and the Sentence (6:9–16)

[9]Listen! The LORD is calling to the city—
and to fear your name is wisdom—

---

[27] McComiskey, "Micah," EBC 7:436–37.

[28] Kaiser, *Hard Sayings*, 228.

[29] Stuart, *Favorite Old Testament Passages*, 130.

"Heed the rod and the One who appointed it.
10 Am I still to forget, O wicked house,
your ill-gotten treasures
and the short ephah, which is accursed?
11 Shall I acquit a man with dishonest scales,
with a bag of false weights?
12 Her rich men are violent;
her people are liars
and their tongues speak deceitfully.
13 Therefore, I have begun to destroy you,
to ruin you because of your sins.
14 You will eat but not be satisfied;
your stomach will still be empty.
You will store up but save nothing,
because what you save I will give to the sword.
15 You will plant but not harvest;
you will press olives but not use the oil on yourselves,
you will crush grapes but not drink the wine.
16 You have observed the statutes of Omri
and all the practices of Ahab's house,
and you have followed their traditions.
Therefore I will give you over to ruin
and your people to derision;
you will bear the scorn of the nations."

The form is also a divine covenant lawsuit, containing the further charges (see 6:1–8) of dishonest business practices, lying, and acts of violence. The sentence is a life of futility, frustration, scorn, and destruction. Here is a possible outline of the section: (1) opening statement (v. 9), (2) catalog of commercial and social sins (vv. 10–12), (3) announcement of punishment from God (vv. 13–15), and (4) summary statement (v. 16).

6:9 Because God's people were very far from acting in the spirit of v. 8, he now begins to rebuke them sternly for their prevailing sins. The pericope begins with an "attention-getter": "Listen!"[30] However, *qôl* also could be rendered "voice": "The voice of the LORD is calling." "City" probably refers to Jerusalem (i.e., by metonymy, its people), though a few suggest Samaria. To arrive at the meaning "fear," one must make a minor vowel change in the Hebrew word. As it stands, the MT reads, "And whoever regards your name has wisdom (or sound judgment)." However, the concept of "fear" seems preferable (see Ps 86:11). "Your" is an apostrophe on the part of Micah in which he addresses God directly. To fear the Lord's name is tantamount to fearing the Lord himself, for "name" frequently is used as a surrogate for God or to signify his revealed character. To fear the Lord is to worship "Yahweh

[30] For this use of קוֹל see GKC § 146b.

with particular attention to the concept of faithfulness to him as the covenant God."[31] The fear of the Lord is often related to obedience to his covenantal commands (e.g., Ps 119:63). The clause in this verse is similar to the statement in Prov 9:10: "The fear of the LORD is the beginning of wisdom" (cf. 1:7; Job 28:28; Ps 111:10). The fear of the Lord has also been defined as a "loving reverence for God that includes submission to his lordship and to the commands of his word (Eccl 12:13)."[32]

As indicated in the NIV translators' textual note, the meaning of the Hebrew in Micah's quotation of God's words at the end of the verse is uncertain. By emending the text, one can translate "Heed, O tribe [of Judah] and the assembly of the city [of Jerusalem]." McComiskey, however, observes:

> NIV follows the Hebrew, which makes good sense as it stands. The "rod" *(maṭṭeh)* is the punishment that Israel will endure, and she is told to "heed" it.
>
> Isaiah uses the word *maṭṭeh* ("club") of the Assyrians (10:5,24). In Isaiah 10:5 the nation of Assyria is pictured as the instrument of God's wrath. If Micah used *maṭṭeh* in the same way here, there is then a logical connection with the cry of alarm in v. 9. That alarm would herald the coming of the Assyrians, and the one who "appointed" the rod would be God himself. The people were to "heed," i.e., attend to the fact that the invasion would come and that it was God who would effect it through the instrumentality of the Assyrians.[33]

6:10–12 Here begins a catalog of Jerusalem's (and Judah's) commercial and social sins, providing additional reasons for their coming judgment. "I" is the Lord (v. 9). He rhetorically asks whether he should forget or overlook the abuses of the wealthy wicked.[34] "Wicked house" could refer to the wicked city (= people—primarily the merchants and leaders) of Jerusalem or to the literal house of the wicked, where they store up their stolen treasures. There is a wordplay between *rāšāᶜ* ("wicked") and *rešaᶜ* ("ill-gotten"). They are condemned for using the short ephah (about half a bushel), which is accursed (by God). Cheating in weights and measures is prohibited in covenant law (Lev 19:35–36).

In v. 11 the Lord again rhetorically asks whether he should acquit a merchant or trader who uses dishonest scales and carries a bag of false weights, thus falsifying weights and measures (in his own favor, of course). These merchants and traders were using weights that weighed things heavier than they actually were or lighter than they really were, depending on whether they were buying or selling. They resorted to all the "tricks of the trade."

---

[31] H.-P. Stähli, "ירא *yr*ʾ to fear," *TLOT* 2:575.

[32] NIVSB, Prov 1:7 n.

[33] McComiskey, "Micah," 438.

[34] The rendering "forget" assumes that הַאִשׁ is defective for הַאֶשֶּׁ(ה), from נשׁה, "forget" (Deut 32:18; Lam 3:17; Hab 3:10). See BDB, 674.

Again such evil practices were condemned in Pentateuchal law, wisdom writings, and prophetic literature (Deut 25:13–16; Prov 11:1; 20:23; Hos 12:7; Amos 8:5).

The antecedent of "Her" (v. 12) is the city of Jerusalem and its inhabitants (v. 9). The unscrupulous rich are denounced for their violence *(ḥāmās)*. They had become wealthy through greed and fraud. Their evil, oppressive attitudes and actions had infected the general populace because Jerusalem's "people" are characterized as liars (see comments on 2:11). They were guilty of speaking deceitfully. Not one word they uttered could be trusted. They were ripe for divine judgment, and that is what now follows.

6:13–15 "Therefore"—because of all the crimes of vv. 10–12—God threatens punishment. The law of divine retribution is at work. Sin brings suffering. The principle also is expressed in the New Testament:

> Do not be deceived: God cannot be mocked. A man reaps what he sows. The one who sows to please his sinful nature, from that nature will reap destruction; the one who sows to please the Spirit, from the Spirit will reap eternal life. (Gal 6:7–8)

Hillers discusses these verses as an example of Old Testament "futility curses":

> that is, the guilty will undertake a course of action and inevitably be frustrated in it. The nearest biblical parallels are Deut 28:30–31 and 38–40, with briefer examples in Lev 26:26 and, in the prophets, Hos 4:10, "They shall eat but not be satisfied: they shall play the harlot but not increase," cf. 5:6; 8:7; 9:12; 9:16; and Amos 5:11: "You have planted pleasant vineyards, but you shall not drink their wine." Biblical curses of this pattern, and other prophetic threats, have parallels in the curses attached to Near Eastern treaties. It is clear that Micah, like other prophets, drew on a traditional stock of maledictions, and it is plausible to suppose that he meant to imply that just these evils were coming because the Israelites had broken their covenant with God.[35]

"You" refers to the people of Jerusalem and Judah, as "your" does in v. 10. God had already begun to destroy Jerusalem and Judah through the Assyrians in 722–721 B.C. and again in 701 B.C.[36] The process of destruction would be completed by the Babylonians in the period 605–586 B.C. All this would happen "because of your sins" (enumerated above).

In vv. 14–15 several "futility curses" will be fulfilled against them, frustrating their efforts. First, they will eat but not be satisfied (or full); their stomachs will still be empty. Because of war, locust plagues, blights, and/or

---

[35] D. R. Hillers, *Micah*, Her (Philadelphia: Fortress, 1984), 82.

[36] It is possible to render the first two lines of v. 13 as "So also I will make you ill and destroy you; / I will ruin you because of your sins." The NIV is supported by LXX, Aquila, Theodotion, Syr., and Vg. On reading וְגַם as "therefore" see *IBHS* § 39.3.4d.

famine, they will not have enough to eat; so they will still be hungry. Second, they will store up food (and perhaps other things) for the future, but they will save nothing because what little they do manage to save will be destroyed by enemies (ultimately God—"I"; cf. Lev 26:14–16; Deut 28:33,49–51). "Sword" speaks of violence and destruction in battle. It is possible to translate the last half of v. 14 like this: "You will press toward birth but not give birth, / and what you bring to birth I will give to the sword."

Third (v. 15), they will plant seeds but not harvest the crops (cf. Hag 1:6–11). Doubtless they will suffer all this because of an enemy invasion. What the enemies (Assyrians and, later, Babylonians) will not destroy, they will use for themselves. Fourth, the people will press or squeeze olives but not be able to use the resulting oil on themselves. The Hebrew for "press" is the verb (*dārak,* lit. "tread"). Since it is used only once here and serves for both olives and grapes, and since normally only grapes are trampled with bare feet, this may be a case where a verb is used that is appropriate for only one of the objects, namely, grapes.[37] The situation is similar in Exod 20:18, where in Hebrew only the verb "saw" is used for "thunder," "lightning," "trumpet," and "mountain." Obviously only lightning and mountain are seen, whereas thunder and trumpet are heard (most English versions supply "heard" as appropriate). Fifth, as just intimated, they will crush (lit. "tread" or "trample" or "stamp") grapes but not get to enjoy the wine. So God, in fulfillment of the covenant curses for disobedience, will turn all their blessings into curses (cf. Mal 2:2). "An economy based on fraud and violence will, like any modern-day pyramid scheme, eventually collapse under its own crushing weight, and the prophet does not even need to proclaim that God is behind it all (v. 13)."[38]

6:16 The pericope concludes with a summary statement, with v. 16a perhaps corresponding to vv. 10–12 and v. 16b to vv. 13–15. God's people are condemned for observing the statutes of Omri and all the practices of Ahab's family and for following their traditions (cf. Ps 94:20). Omri and his son Ahab were kings of the Northern Kingdom of Israel. Omri founded a dynasty as well as Israel's capital at Samaria (1:1,5–6; see 1 Kgs 16:23–24). "Samaria represented the policies of Omri and Ahab: political, economic, and religious dependency of the Northern Kingdom on the nations."[39] Kings Omri and Ahab did more evil than all the kings who preceded them (1 Kgs 16:25–26,30–33; 2 Kgs 8:18). Under the influence of his pagan wife Jezebel, Ahab introduced Baalism and the worship of Asherah into the Northern

[37] This literary feature is called *zeugma.* See Gen 4:20; Hos 1:2; Luke 1:64 (lit., "Immediately his mouth was opened and his tongue").

[38] W. P. Brown, *Obadiah through Malachi*, Westminster Bible Companion (Louisville: Westminster John Knox, 1996), 61.

[39] W. A. VanGemeren, *Interpreting the Prophetic Word* (Grand Rapids: Zondervan, 1990), 152–53.

Kingdom. Both kings abused their power (cf. the judicial murder of Naboth in 1 Kgs 21:1–26).[40]

In the last half of the verse, God announces that "therefore"—because the leaders and people of Jersualem and Judah are so much like their northern neighbors, Samaria and Israel (cf. chap. 1)—they too must suffer "ruin" (the same Hb. root as in v. 13). "The same sins which led to the demise of the Northern Kingdom will bring an end to Judah."[41] They must also be subject to derision (cf. 2:4). "Such scornful hooting is perhaps that same reaction that the secular world has to the church when the community that is supposed to be the body of Christ fails to live up to its covenant with its Lord or the degeneracy of one of its leaders is exposed."[42] Finally, they will have to bear the scorn of the nations.[43] Such a judgment would be another fulfillment of a covenant curse for disobedience (Deut 28:37). Disobedience brings disaster.

(3) A Lament over a Decadent Society (7:1–7)

1What misery is mine!
I am like one who gathers summer fruit
at the gleaning of the vineyard;
there is no cluster of grapes to eat,
none of the early figs that I crave.
2The godly have been swept from the land;
not one upright man remains.
All men lie in wait to shed blood;
each hunts his brother with a net.
3Both hands are skilled in doing evil;
the ruler demands gifts,
the judge accepts bribes,
the powerful dictate what they desire—
they all conspire together.
4The best of them is like a brier,
the most upright worse than a thorn hedge.
The day of your watchmen has come,
the day God visits you.

---

[40] The NIV's rendering of the third-person verb as second person ("You have observed") is explained in the Preface to the NIV: "And though the Hebrew writers often shifted back and forth between first, second, and third personal pronouns without change of antecedent, this translation often makes them uniform, in accordance with English style and without the use of footnotes."

[41] R. L. Smith, *Micah–Malachi*, WBC (Waco: Word, 1984), 53.

[42] E. Achtemeier, *Minor Prophets I*, NIBC (Peabody, Mass.: Hendrickson, 1996), 356.

[43] For "the scorn of the nations" the MT has וְחֶרְפַּת עַמִּי, "the scorn due my people." If this is the correct reading, then Fausset's comment would be apropos: "The greater was my grace to you, the greater shall be your punishment for having despised it." Most modern English versions, however, follow the LXX here, which has the plural λαῶν, "peoples" (i.e., "nations"), instead of the singular "my people."

Now is the time of their confusion.
[5]Do not trust a neighbor;
put no confidence in a friend.
Even with her who lies in your embrace
be careful of your words.
[6]For a son dishonors his father,
a daughter rises up against her mother,
a daughter-in-law against her mother-in-law—
a man's enemies are the members of his own household.
[7]But as for me, I watch in hope for the LORD,
I wait for God my Savior;
my God will hear me.

Here Micah expresses his complaint in vv. 1–6 and his confidence in v. 7. So the form is a lament (see introduction to 1:8–16), in which the prophet begins with a woe because he seems to be the only godly or righteous person left (vv. 1–2). He cannot trust anyone. Everyone may be setting a trap for someone else. People do evil with both hands. Even family members rise up against each other (v. 6). Jesus applied the words of this verse to his own times (Matt 10:21,34–36). But even though Micah cannot trust human beings, he can trust God, his Savior (v. 7).

7:1 Micah (perhaps speaking for a penitent and believing godly remnant of Jerusalem) responds to the Lord's threats of impending doom in the previous chapter with a lament over such a decadent society. He begins with a cry of personal distress: "What misery is mine!" The same words are translated "woe to me!" in Job 10:15. Next, the reason for the woe is provided (note the Hb. *kî*, "for"). Micah employs a simile to teach that looking for the godly at Jerusalem in his time (v. 2) is like looking for summer fruit after the harvest has ended (v. 1). He likens himself to someone who craves refreshing fruit and goes to a vineyard at the time for gleaning, only to be disappointed because not even one cluster of grapes is left. Similarly, the early figs have already been stripped. "The 'first-ripe fig,' the early green fig, is the most delicious of the fruit."[44] The vineyard probably is intended to represent Judah, while the fruit is meant to stand for the "godly" and "upright" of v. 2 (cf. Hos 9:10).

7:2 "Micah laments the disappearance of the righteous man (7:2), reminding us of Abraham's plea for Sodom (Gen 18:23ff.), of Jeremiah's search in Jerusalem for a man doing justice (Jer 5:1), or of Diogenes and his lantern looking in Athens for the honest man."[45] This verse explains the figurative language of v. 1. The fruit that was gone is now identified as the

[44] P. J. King, *Amos, Hosea, Micah—An Archaeological Commentary* (Philadelphia: Westminster, 1988), 115.
[45] Lewis, *The Minor Prophets*, 34.

"godly" or "upright man," who is equally difficult to find in Jerusalem and Judah.[46] The Hebrew for "godly" is *ḥāsîd* ("one who is faithful" or "one who practices faithful covenant love"). It has the same root as the word for "mercy" in 6:8 (see comments there). The "upright" are "those who maintain the moral rectitude of the covenant."[47]

"Just as nothing worth eating remained in the fields, even so nothing good or worthwhile remained in Judah."[48] The language of the text here is reminiscent of Rom 3:10–20. "All men," in context, should perhaps be limited to those in v. 3—rulers, judges, and the powerful—though corruption does spread from the top down. The corrupt lie in wait to shed blood by committing murder. Each hunts down his "brother" (a fellow Israelite) to trap him and catch him as in a hunter's net (cf. Ps 10:2,8–9). "If no one happened along, they would go out looking for the prey!"[49] Such is the description of a morally bankrupt society. Isaiah similarly characterized the people (especially the leaders) of his and Micah's generation:

> The vineyard of the LORD Almighty
> is the house of Judah
> and the men of Judah
> are the garden of his delight.
> And he looked for justice, but saw bloodshed;
> for righteousness, but heard cries of distress. (Isa 5:7)

7:3 As Chisholm notes, the phrase "both hands" means that the corrupt people of Israel "directed all their energies ... to evil deeds which they successfully carried out." He further explains that the phrase "are skilled" (*lĕhêṭîb,* lit. "to do well") "is dripping with sarcasm. Elsewhere this phrase is used in a moral/ethical sense ('to do what is right/proper') and stands in contrast to doing evil (Isa 1:16–17; Jer 4:22; 13:23). Here the phrase simply has a neutral sense ('to do diligently or thoroughly') and describes how these sinners efficiently carried out their evil plans and deeds."[50]

This verse may be compared to Jer 4:22: "They are skilled in doing evil; they know not how to do good." Such evil was done primarily by the leaders who were in control: the ruler, the judge, and the powerful (lit. "the great one"; for the sins committed here see comments on 3:11). "Demands" translates a Hebrew participle indicating that the ruler was constantly demanding gifts. The same is true of the Hebrew participle behind "dictate": The power-

[46] Note the repetition of the word אֵין / אָיִן, "there is not," in vv. 1–2.

[47] Waltke, *Micah: An Introduction and Commentary,* in *Obadiah, Jonah and Micah*, by D. W. Baker, T. D. Alexander, and B. K. Waltke, TOTC (Downers Grove: InterVarsity, 1988), 200.

[48] P. H. Kelley, "Micah … Malachi," vol. 14, LBBC (Nashville: Broadman, 1984), 47.

[49] J. E. Smith, *The Minor Prophets* (Joplin: College Press, 1994), 354.

[50] R. B. Chisholm, Jr., *Interpreting the Minor Prophets* (Grand Rapids: Zondervan, 1990), 156.

ful were always dictating what they desire—another illustration of the fact that power generally corrupts. As if their corruption was not bad enough individually, these power brokers would coordinate their efforts and "conspire" (lit. "weave") together to take advantage of others by requiring "payoffs" in order to "feather their own nests."

7:4 Even the best and most upright (see v. 2) of the corrupt leaders referred to in v. 3 are as harmful as briers and thorn hedges, which ensnare, wound, and tear their victims. "Any who expect goodness from them end up entangled in a thicket of intrigue and avarice."[51] In a bold apostrophe Micah switches from the third person to the second person in direct address. But who is the referent in "your" and "you"? The sentence has been interpreted in two ways: (1) The day for judging your (=the people's) watchmen (=their false prophets) has come (i.e., is imminent)—the day God visits (= judges) you (the people). (2) The day of judgment your (=the Lord's) watchmen (=his true prophets) warned about has come (i.e., is imminent; see "Now")—the day you (=God) visit (=judge). There are good arguments for both views, and scholars are divided. Of course, both would be true, though perhaps the second understanding is slightly favored.

Prophets are also referred to elsewhere as watchmen, lookouts, or guards (Jer 6:17; Ezek 3:17–21). The Lord can "visit" people either in blessing or in judgment. In this context the visitation is clearly one of judgment. The sooncoming judgment is further pictured as a time of their (=the people's, with special reference to the officials of v. 3) confusion (or chaos or disorder or panic) because of siege and battle. (There is assonance between "thorn hedge" *[mĕsûkâ]* and "confusion" *[mĕbûkâ]*.) "Has come" and "Now" may indicate that the prophesied punishment is not just imminent but had already begun. If so, the fall of Samaria and the reduction of Judah to a vassal state in 722–721 B.C. are certainly in view. If Sennacherib had already destroyed many cities in Judah and laid siege to Jerusalem in 701, that would also be included. But the process would be completed by the Neo-Babylonian king Nebuchadnezzar in 605–586 B.C.

7:5–6 In view of the complete disintegration of society in Micah's day, he counsels his contemporaries. The disintegration includes the breakdown of home and family (this happens when the principles of 6:8 are not followed). The result is that one cannot trust his neighbor or friend (cf. Ps 146:3). In fact, for fear of betrayal one must be careful of his words even with his wife ("with her who lies in your embrace"). Of course, one should always be careful about his words with anyone.

In v. 6 several illustrations of treachery and societal collapse are given, providing the reason for the advice in v. 5. A son "dishonors" his father by

[51] J. L. Mays, *Micah: A Commentary*, OTL (Philadelphia: Westminster, 1976), 152.

treating him like a "fool" (Hb. *mĕnabbēl*). A daughter rises up in rebellion against her mother, violating Exod 20:12: "Honor your father and your mother." To honor is to prize highly (Prov 4:8), care for (Ps 91:15), show respect for (Lev 19:3; 20:9), and obey (Deut 21:18–21; Eph 6:1). A daughter-in-law rises up against her mother-in-law. The classic example of a daughter-in-law doing precisely the opposite is Ruth's loving loyalty to Naomi (Ruth 1:15–18; 2:11–12,17–18; 3:5,17; 4:15). Finally, a man's enemies are the members (lit. "men") of his own household. According to J. Kühlewein, this refers to "residents of the same house."[52] In the extended families of those days, that would include sons-in-law and household servants and their families. (See introduction to 7:1–7 for the NT use of this passage.)

Tragically many within our own society today have fractured, fragmented, and hostile families that seem bent on self-destruction. Like the old Roman Empire, we are decaying from within. Our movies, television shows, and magazines are filled with sexual immorality, divorce, drugs, violence, filthy language, and rebellion against all authority in the name of unbridled freedom. We attempt to justify the old immorality by renaming it and calling it the new morality. We claim that there are no moral absolutes, that everything is relative. Paul prophesied such a time for the last days in which we are now living (note Heb 1:2, "these last days"):

> People will be lovers of themselves, lovers of money, boastful, proud, abusive, disobedient to their parents, ungrateful, unholy, without love, unforgiving, slanderous, without self-control, brutal, not lovers of the good, treacherous, rash, conceited, lovers of pleasure rather than lovers of God—having a form of godliness but denying its power. Have nothing to do with them. (2 Tim 3:2–5; cf. Rom 1:18–32)

How much more profitable and edifying it is to emulate the pattern of Mal 4:6: "[Elijah] will turn the hearts of the fathers to their children, and the hearts of the children to their fathers" (cf. Luke 1:17). As in the case of Micah and the people of his day, homes and churches and nations are usually no better than their leaders. We should join Micah in a lament over a decadent society.

7:7 The complaint (vv. 1–6) is now followed by confidence (v. 7). Just as the Book of Ruth illumines the otherwise unrelieved darkness of the period of the judges, so Micah—perhaps speaking for the righteous, faithful remnant—brings some relief to his own dark times by the light of his trust and hope in God. Such a hopeful element is actually quite common in laments.[53] Psalm 55 (a psalm of individual lament and/or petition) expresses it like this: "But I call to God, / and the LORD saves me. … I cry out in distress, / and he hears my voice" (Ps 55:16–17). So Micah 7:7 probably is best construed as belonging

---

52 "אכל *ʾkl* to eat," *TLOT* 1:101.

53 L. C. Allen, *The Books of Joel … Micah*, NICOT (Grand Rapids: Eerdmans, 1976), 384, 389.

to this pericope, though it also functions as an effective transition to the next section. The word "but" (a Hb. adversative *waw*) draws a sharp contrast between faithful Micah and his unfaithful contemporaries (cf. 3:8). "Watch" provides a link with v. 4 ("watchmen"), where the same Hebrew root occurs. There, however, the watching was for judgment; here it is for salvation.

In Hebrew terminology words like "hope" and "wait" belong to the semantic category of verbs like "trust," "believe," and "put one's faith in" (see comments on 5:7). "I wait" translates a Hebrew verb form (cohortative of resolve) meaning "I am resolved to wait for God my Savior to act." Mays says:

> He watches the future for an act of God (Ps 5:4) as besieged men watch the horizon for the appearance of relief. He does not give up and surrender to depression, but 'waits,' the most powerful form of action by the helpless ... who express in their waiting the knowledge that God comes to them in the form of salvation.[54]

"My Savior" and "my God" speak of the personal relationship between the Lord and his prophet and of Micah's trust in and commitment to his covenant God.[55] The names Joshua and Jesus have the same Hebrew root as "Savior" (lit. "salvation"), and they both mean "The LORD saves." That is why our Lord and Savior is named Jesus: "You are to give him the name Jesus, because he will save his people from their sins" (Matt 1:21). "God will hear me" includes the sense of "God will respond to me by helping me and saving/delivering me" (see comments on 1:2). Micah's great affirmation of faith is very much like that of Habakkuk: "Though the fig tree does not bud ..., / yet I will rejoice in the LORD, / I will be joyful in God my Savior" (Hab 3:18).

2. The Ultimate Triumph of God's Kingdom (7:8–20)

This completes the final salvation section in the three cycles of judgment and salvation (see Introduction: "Literary Forms," p. 34). There is a near consensus that this last pericope of the book is a prophetic liturgy. It is made up of four smaller subunits.

(1) A Psalm of Trust (7:8–10)

8 Do not gloat over me, my enemy!
Though I have fallen, I will rise.
Though I sit in darkness,
the LORD will be my light.

---

[54] Mays, *Micah,* 157.

[55] For "Savior" involving the Hebrew root (ישׁע) see Barker, "Deliver (Deliverance)," in *ZPEB* 2:89–90; for further study of Hebrew words for salvation see J. F. A. Sawyer, *Semantics in Biblical Research* (London: SCM, 1972), 28–88.

[9]Because I have sinned against him,
I will bear the LORD's wrath,
until he pleads my case
and establishes my right.
He will bring me out into the light;
I will see his righteousness.
[10]Then my enemy will see it
and will be covered with shame,
she who said to me,
"Where is the LORD your God?"
My eyes will see her downfall;
even now she will be trampled underfoot
like mire in the streets.

This little psalm has its greatest affinity with psalms of trust, such as Pss 11; 16; 23; 27; 125. In them the quality of trust is highlighted because faith shines through the darkness of danger and distressing situations:

In the LORD I take refuge …
When the foundations are being destroyed,
what can the righteous do?
The LORD is in his holy temple
the LORD is on his heavenly throne.
Ps 11:1,3–4

I have set the LORD always before me;
Because he is at my right hand,
I will not be shaken.
Ps 16:8

Even though I walk
through the valley of the shadow of death,
I will fear no evil,
for you are with me.
Ps 23:4

The LORD is my light and my salvation—
whom shall I fear?
The LORD is the stronghold of my life—
of whom shall I be afraid?
Ps 27:1

Those who trust in the LORD are like Mount Zion,
which cannot be shaken but endures forever.
As the mountains surround Jerusalem,
so the LORD surrounds his people
both now and forevermore.
Ps 125:1–2

Similarly and significantly, Micah expresses his (and the righteous remnant's) trust in their incomparable and faithful God during Judah's and Jerusalem's darkest hour.

7:8 Zion (or Jerusalem) is the speaker (confirmed by the Hb. feminine pronominal suffix in v. 10, "*your* God"). Its people rhetorically address their enemies ("enemy" is probably collective). They do not want their enemies to gloat over their fall, doubtless speaking of the fall of Jerusalem in 586 B.C. (see 3:12; 4:10; 6:13–15 and comments). This kind of prophetic or anticipatory perspective is not unparalleled: "In his message to the exiles of the sixth century B.C. [Isa 40–66], Isaiah was projected into the future, just as the apostle John was in Rev 4–22."[56] Compare Ezekiel's being transported by the prophetic Spirit to Jerusalem in visions of God and then back again to Babylonia (Ezek 8:3; 11:24).

If "enemy" is in fact collective, it probably includes Babylonia and Edom. If it is not collective, it most likely has Edom principally in view (Obad 11–14). In Ps 30:1 David thanked the Lord for not letting his enemies gloat over him (i.e., over his demise). In Mic 4:11 nations had said, "Let our eyes gloat over Zion!" Here Jerusalem's inhabitants tell their enemies (or enemy) not to gloat over them. The reason for the request is given next: Although the Jerusalemites (and Judahites) will fall (see above), by faith they declare that they will rise. This, in fact, happened in 538 B.C.—in the restoration from Babylonian exile. Even though they sit in the darkness of captivity, the Lord will be their light (cf. Isa 42:7; 49:9; 61:1). Light frequently symbolizes well-being, life, freedom, and salvation (deliverance). To confess "The LORD is my light" (Ps 27:1) is to express one's trust in him as the source of those benefits (cf. Ps 36:9).

7:9 God's people indicate that they are willing to bear the Lord's "wrath." This is a metonymy of cause for effect, in which wrath is put for punishment. "Because I have sinned" provides the reason for the divine discipline, showing that the judgment is deserved (on "sinned," *ḥāṭāʾ*, see comments on 1:5; on confession of sin see Prov 28:13; 1 John 1:9; on sin as the cause of God's anger and punishment see Zech 1:2–6). Jerusalem's people are also willing to bear God's punishment because they know it is only temporary ("until"). The Lord will plead their case,[57] that is, he will defend their cause (cf. 6:1 and comments there). He will also establish their right or, better, execute justice for them, that is, he will make things right for them (see 6:8 and comments there).

Their trust is further confirmed by their confident statement that the Lord will bring them out into the light (see comments on v. 8). Their return from Babylonian exile to the promised land will be like a new exodus. Finally, they confidently expect to see the Lord's righteousness displayed for their advantage. That is, they will experience God's saving acts, which will dem-

---

[56] NIVSB, Introduction to Isaiah: "Date."

[57] The cognate accusative naturally features assonance: *yārîb rîbî*, "he pleads my case."

onstrate his righteous character in that he keeps his covenant promises to them (see comments on 6:5).

7:10 It now becomes clear even in English translation that “enemy” is feminine: “she who said to me,” “her downfall,” and “she will be trampled.” Thus reference must be to a city or a country or—if the feminine noun “enemy” and the feminine pronouns are collective—to cities or, perhaps more likely, countries. So theoretically Babylon (representing Babylonia) or Edom—or both—could be the referent.

There is a correspondence between the “seeing” by the enemy here and the “seeing” by both later in this verse and in v. 9.[58] As the enemies did to Israel, so Israel will do to them (contrast Matt 7:12). Consequently they will be covered with shame (cf. Isa 50:7–8). One of the things they did was to hurl a rhetorical, scornful taunt at Judah, blaspheming even the Lord himself in the process (“Where is the LORD your God?”—cf. Ps 42:3,10; Joel 2:17). Such taunts, however, would cease. Why? Because the enemies will fall, and restored Jerusalem will see it with pleasure (see above). It is punishment in kind (cf. v. 8; 4:11; Obad 15: “As you have done, it will be done to you; / your deeds will return upon your own head”). The punishment-fits-the-crime principle is at work (see Gal 6:7–9). Perhaps a modern proverb would be appropriate at this point: “Curses are like young chickens; they always come home to roost.”[59] The enemies’ downfall will be so great that they will be walked on and trampled like mire or dust or dirt in the streets (cf. Isa 10:6; Zech 1:15).

(2) A Promise of Restoration (7:11–13)

11The day for building your walls will come,
the day for extending your boundaries.
12In that day people will come to you
from Assyria and the cities of Egypt,
even from Egypt to the Euphrates
and from sea to sea
and from mountain to mountain.
13The earth will become desolate because of its inhabitants,
as the result of their deeds.

This short subunit could also have been called an oracle of salvation (or deliverance or restoration).

[58] וְתֵרֶא, “Then he [my enemy] will see it,” is probably jussive in form only, not in actual syntactical function (see GKC § 109k). Instead of a wish, a confident statement (NIV) would seem to better fit the context here in a psalm of trust.

[59] R. Southey (1774–1843), *The Curse of Kehama*, motto; quoted by Bartlett, *Familiar Quotations*, ed. E. M. Beck, 14th ed. (Boston: Little, Brown and Co., 1968), 532.

7:11 As King explains, "the building of your walls" is "a metaphor for the reestablishment of the Jews in the promised land .... The prophet most likely has in mind the walls of Jerusalem, though *gādēr* is not the common term for city walls."[60] "Your" is feminine singular in Hebrew, so Zion or Jerusalem is being addressed. The unusual use of *gādēr* for "walls" may point toward a metaphorical use to speak of the restoration of the Jews to Judah and Jerusalem. The Hebrew word *gādēr* usually refers to the stone wall around a vineyard or field. If it does refer to Jerusalem's city walls in a literal sense, part of the fulfillment occurred about 445 B.C., when Nehemiah restored its walls. However, "In that day" (v. 12) seems to indicate an eschatological fulfillment as well. Perhaps vv. 11–13 are progressively fulfilled in at least two stages. According to Zech 2:4–5 ("Jerusalem will be a city without walls ...") "Jerusalem will become so large and prosperous that it will expand beyond its walls. Indeed, it will overflow so much that it will be as though it had no walls. Evidently many of its people and animals will have to live in the surrounding unwalled villages (cf. Ezek 38:11)."[61] As Boice explains, "as the book draws to a close, he [Micah] looks beyond the deportation to another deliverance and regathering into the Promised Land. In that day the enemies of the people will be defeated, Jerusalem will be rebuilt, and the borders of the nation will be extended as they were previously."[62]

7:12–13 Verse 12 further develops v. 11 (on the eschatological import of "In that day" see comments on 4:1,6). The word "day" is utilized to signal three developments in vv. 11–12. The NIV rightly supplies "people" as the subject of the Hebrew collective singular (or impersonal) verb. For "people" will come to Jerusalem from "Assyria … Egypt … Euphrates … sea … mountain." Allen applies these geographical terms literally to the areas from which Jewish exiles will return,[63] while McComiskey understands them symbolically or figuratively for the people of all nations coming to Jerusalem.[64] Parallel passages seem to support the latter view—that reference is to all believers from the whole world (4:1–5; Ps 72:8; Isa 2:1–5; Zech 9:10; 14:16–19; but cf. Isa 19:18–25).

As for the unbelievers of the world, the earth (i.e., the rest of it) will become a horrible desolation because of their evil deeds (v. 13; see Isa 24:1–6; Zeph 1:18; 3:8). Such will be the "fruit" (Hb. *pĕrî*) of their actions. They will bring the devastation on themselves. "In 6:16 Jerusalem was an island of ruin amidst a sea of scornful enemies. Here the picture is reversed, and it is

[60] P. J. King, *Amos, Hosea, Micah—An Archaeological Commentary*, 73.

[61] Barker, "Zechariah," 7:616–17.

[62] Boice, *The Minor Prophets*, 2:49.

[63] Allen, *The Books of Joel … Micah*, 397–98.

[64] McComiskey, "Micah," in EBC 7:443.

an island of blessing amidst a sea of desolation."[65] Jerusalem and the Holy Land will be like an oasis in the desert of the earth. Allen appropriately concludes this section:

> The oracle is the counterpart to the Christian doctrine of the Last Judgment. In traditional language which Israel could understand it expresses the assurance that deficits in the moral balance sheet of the world are eventually to be paid, while the kingdom of God is to be established in triumph.[66]

It will be a fulfillment of Gen 12:3: "I will bless those who bless you, / and whoever curses you I will curse."

(3) A Prayer, the Lord's Answer, and the Response (7:14–17)

14Shepherd your people with your staff,
the flock of your inheritance,
which lives by itself in a forest,
in fertile pasturelands.
Let them feed in Bashan and Gilead
as in days long ago.

15"As in the days when you came out of Egypt,
I will show them my wonders."

16Nations will see and be ashamed,
deprived of all their power.
They will lay their hands on their mouths
and their ears will become deaf.
17They will lick dust like a snake,
like creatures that crawl on the ground.
They will come trembling out of their dens;
they will turn in fear to the LORD our God
and will be afraid of you.

Undoubtedly speaking for the godly remnant in Jerusalem and Judah, Micah prays for the fulfillment of the promised salvation and restoration of vv. 11–13 (v. 14), and the Lord assures his people that his faithful covenant love will not fail (v. 15).

Then the Spirit leads Micah (perhaps still representing the righteous, faithful remnant) to prophesy that the hostile nations will be humbled (vv. 16–17). It is also possible that "these verses constitute a prayer that God will show his wonders again as in the exodus, that the nations will see and be ashamed, and that they will turn to the Lord in fear."[67]

---

[65] D. J. Clark and N. Mundhenk, *A Translator's Handbook on the Books of Obadiah and Micah* (New York: UBS, 1982), 185.

[66] Allen, *The Books of Joel ... Micah*, 398.

[67] NIVSB, 7:15–17n.

7:14 Using the imagery of the Lord as royal Shepherd, Micah (and/or the people of Zion) prays that he will shepherd his people with his staff or rod (cf. Ps 23:4). Gower explains, "The rod symbolized the protection of the people and was eventually stylized into a sceptre."[68] Since "Shepherd" is employed as a motif not only here but also in 2:12; 4:6–8; 5:4 (see comments on those passages), it indicates that the royal shepherd metaphor occurs in all three salvation or hope sections of the book. The Shepherd's people are called the flock of his inheritance (or possession—they belong to him; see v. 18; Pss 94:14; 95:6–7; 100:3). Furthermore that flock "lives by itself" (see Num 23:9; Deut 33:28) in a forest, in fertile pasturelands. This may refer to their restricted territory, since the Assyrians occupied and used the best land. The Hebrew for "forest" is given a negative nuance in 3:12 ("thickets"). So "in fertile pasturelands" may mean "in the midst of fertile pasturelands" (as in the Hebrew), i.e., with the best land all around them but in the hands of others. That same phrase could be rendered "in the midst of Carmel," but the parallelism with "forest" or "thickets" seems to favor the main NIV text.

Then Micah/Zion prays that their Shepherd will once again let them feed (=will provide their "daily bread," so to speak) in Bashan and Gilead. King comments on these two regions:

> Gilead, a highland region in Transjordan, is bounded on the north by the Yarmuk River and on the south by the city of Heshbon. The land of Gilead has always been famous for its fertile land; for that reason Micah was able to say, "Let them feed in Bashan [a fertile plateau adjacent to Gilead] and Gilead as in the days of old" (Micah 7:14). The King's Highway ("the royal way"), the well-known international caravan roadway in Transjordan extending from Damascus to the Gulf of Aqaba, passed through Gilead. Control over Gilead alternated between Israel and Aram, until it was taken by Tiglath-pileser III in 734 B.C.E.[69]

So this may also have been a prayer for the return of that rich and fertile land to the people of Zion (see Zech 10:10). "As in days long ago" could refer to the time of Moses and Joshua, under whom those regions were first occupied by the Israelites, or to the kingdoms of David and Solomon, when those areas were securely in their possession (cf. 4:8 and comments).

7:15 Micah now quotes the Lord's answer to the prayer of v. 14. God responds with "exodus theology" (see comments on 6:4). He refers to the time when his people came out of Egypt, and he showed them his "wonders" (=supernatural occurrences; see Ps 114 for the highlights of those miraculous wonders). His future mighty saving acts for them in a kind of new exodus and restoration will include numerous similar displays of his redemptive grace

[68] R. Gower, *The New Manners and Customs of Bible Times* (Chicago: Moody, 1987), 145.

[69] King, *Amos, Hosea, Micah*, 50.

and power in their behalf. "You" and "them" are both collective masculine singular pronouns in the Hebrew text, referring to God's people as a corporate solidarity (see comments on 6:6–7).[70]

7:16–17 These two verses are framed by a Hebrew wordplay involving *yirʾû* ("they will see") and *wĕyirĕʾû* ("they will be afraid"). Micah—probably again speaking for the believing community (see "our" in v. 17)—gives the response to the Lord's answer with a Spirit-inspired prophecy. In v. 15 God had said, "I will show them [lit. 'I will cause them to see'] my wonders." Now Micah prophesies, "Nations will see" those wonders. There is an obvious wordplay here between *ʾarʾennû* ("I will show them [lit. 'him,' a collective for God's people]") and *yirʾû* ("they will see"). When the nations see God's wonders, they will be "ashamed, deprived of all their power." This probably indicates that when they see the awesome display of divine omnipotence in behalf of God's people, they will be ashamed of their puny efforts to resist him. Their so-called power fades into insignificance. They also will lay their hands on their mouths in awe and amazement (contrast the taunt of v. 10). And their ears will become deaf, perhaps meaning that they will turn a deaf ear to all this. They do not want to hear anything more about the Lord's powerful redemptive acts for his people. To judge from the similarity in language, this verse and the next appear to be an echo of v. 10.

Verse 17 depicts further reactions by the nations. The expression "lick dust like a snake" may have as its background Gen 3:14 and may also be compared to the modern idiom "to bite the dust," symbolizing defeat (see Ps 72:9; Isa 65:25). The "creatures that crawl on the ground," King explains, "are hard to define, perhaps earthworms or a broader term. Whatever the specific reference, they are an effective symbol of the nations' humiliation."[71] Finally the nations will come trembling out of their dens, that is, out of their hiding places. And they will turn in fear to the Lord and will be afraid of him. ("Our God" shows that Micah speaks for the Lord's other true followers, and "you" is an apostrophe of direct address to God.) It is difficult to determine the nature of the "fear" here, and scholars are divided. Some take it as analogous to Ps 18:43–45, where the nations cringed in fear before David. This was a forced submission because they were literally afraid of him. Others, however, maintain that the nations of v. 17 sincerely turn to the Lord in holy fear, that is, in reverential trust and voluntary submission (cf. Hos 11:10–11). If this is the correct interpretation, Achtemeier's comments are pertinent:

> Israel has begun to realize here that its salvation by God will serve a greater purpose than simply its own exaltation and the restoration of its life. Its salva-

---

[70] For the change from second person ("you") to third person ("them") see comments on 6:16.

[71] King, *Amos, Hosea, Micah*, 133,135.

tion will have something to do with the salvation of all peoples, who will themselves finally turn to worship the one true God.[72]

Paul's word in Rom 11:11–15 would also be relevant, particularly vv. 12,15.

(4) A Hymn of Praise to God (7:18–20)

18 Who is a God like you,
who pardons sin and forgives the transgression
of the remnant of his inheritance?
You do not stay angry forever
but delight to show mercy.
19 You will again have compassion on us;
you will tread our sins underfoot
and hurl all our iniquities into the depths of the sea.
20 You will be true to Jacob,
and show mercy to Abraham,
as you pledged on oath to our fathers
in days long ago.

The prophetic liturgy closes with a hymn of praise to God.[73] It declares God to be incomparable in grace and truth, showing faithfulness to Jacob and unfailing covenant love to Abraham. Feinberg observes:

> The last three verses of this book are joined to the book of Jonah for reading in the synagogue on the afternoon of the Day of Atonement. Once a year on the afternoon of New Year, the orthodox Jew goes to a running stream or river and symbolically empties his pockets of his sins into the water, while he recites verses 18–20.[74]

Carlson suggests this outline of the subunit: Yahweh is the God of (1) forgiving love (v. 18), (2) redeeming power (v. 19), and (3) perpetual faithfulness (v. 20).[75]

7:18 The type of rhetorical question beginning this verse is used in order to express a "forcible denial."[76] So the reply is "No one." The question is a way of affirming God's incomparability.[77] Here he is incomparable particu-

---

72 Achtemeier, *Minor Prophets I*, 366.

73 For a study of the literary genre of praise see Barker, "Praise," in *Cracking Old Testament Codes*, ed. D. B. Sandy and R. L. Giese, Jr. (Nashville: Broadman & Holman, 1995), 217–32.

74 C. L. Feinberg, *The Minor Prophets* (Chicago: Moody, 1976), 186.

75 E. L. Carlson, "Micah," in *The Wycliffe Bible Commentary*, ed. C. F. Pfeiffer and E. F. Harrison (Chicago: Moody, 1962), 853.

76 GKC § 148c. For the relationship between Micah's name and "Who is a God like you?" see Introduction: "Author" (p. 31).

77 See C. J. Labuschagne, *The Incomparability of Yahweh in the Old Testament* (Leiden: Brill, 1966); also cf. Exod 15:11; Isa 40:18,25 and numerous passages in Isaiah, as well as in Psalms.

larly in his forgiving love and grace. Mays points out that this book, "which begins with a portrayal of YHWH's advent in wrath, concludes with praise of his mercy."[78] To emphasize the point, three different Hebrew words for sin are used and four verbs that indicate forgiveness ("pardons … forgives … tread … hurl"). More literal renderings of the verbs would yield "takes away … passes over (cf. Exod 12:12–13; 1 Cor 5:7) … subdue … hurl." "Sin" is the same Hebrew root that occurs in "iniquities" (v. 19) and should have been translated "iniquity" here for consistency within the same unit. The Hebrew term connotes what is twisted, crooked, or perverse. For "transgression" see comments on 1:5. Waltke notes: "The crucial vocabulary of Micah 7:18 is used in connection with the Suffering Servant of Yahweh in Isaiah 53: *nāśāʾ* (to bear) (v. 12), *ʿāwōn* (iniquity; vv. 6,11), *pešaʿ* (transgression; vv. 8,12)—all in connection with Yahweh's pleasure *(ḥāpēṣ;* v. 10)."[79]

The people he thus forgives are the "remnant of his inheritance."[80] Rather than staying angry forever (see Pss 30:5; 103:8–18) the Lord instead delights to show "mercy" (more lit. "faithful covenant love," Hb. *ḥesed*); see comments on 6:8 and note). Samuel Davies nicely captures the sentiments of this verse in his hymn, "Great God of Wonders":

Great God of wonders! all Thy ways
Are matchless, God-like and divine;
But the fair glories of Thy grace
More God-like and unrivaled shine.

In wonder lost, with trembling joy,
We take the pardon of our God:
Pardon for crimes of deepest dye,
A pardon bought with Jesus' blood.

O may this strange, this matchless grace,
This God-like miracle of love,
Fill the whole earth with grateful praise,
And all th'angelic choirs above.

Who is a pard'ning God like Thee?
Or who has grace so rich and free?

7:19 The Hebrew for "compassion" suggests a tender, maternal love such as a mother would have for her child. The Hebrew for "tread underfoot" also could be rendered "subdue." Sin is pictured as an enemy that God con-

---

[78] Mays, *Micah: A Commentary*, 166.

[79] Waltke, "Micah," in *The Minor Prophets*, 3 vols., ed. T. E. McComiskey (Grand Rapids: Baker, 1993), 2:762.

[80] For the believing "remnant" see comments on 2:12; 4:6–7; 5:7–8. For the change from second person to third person ("his") see comments on 6:16. For "inheritance" see comments on v. 14.

quers and liberates us from. "God overcomes sin and sets his people free."[81] Fausset adds, "When God takes away the guilt of sin, that it may not condemn us, He takes away also the power of sin, that it may not rule us."[82]

Finally, just as the Lord hurled Pharaoh's chariots and his army into the sea and they sank to the depths like a stone (Exod 15:4–5), so he will hurl all "our" sins into the depths of the sea. This, of course, speaks of the complete forgiveness of sin and the removal of its guilt forever (see Jer 50:20). "God not only puts our sins out of sight [Isa 38:17]; he also puts them out of reach (Mic 7:19; Ps 103:12), out of mind (Jer 31:34), and out of existence (Isa 43:25; 44:22; Ps 51:1,9; Acts 3:19)."[83] Most Hebrew manuscripts of the MT actually read "*their* iniquities (better, 'sins')" instead of "*our* iniquities." However, "our" is supported by some Hebrew manuscripts and the versions (LXX, Syr., and Vg.), as well as by perhaps the context. A few commentators prefer to retain "their" and refer it to the nations of vv. 16–17. Then the forgiveness spoken of here would include both Jews and Gentiles. Of course, this is ultimately true anyway, whether or not the text explicitly states it here. In a more practical vein, Boice writes, "A stanza from a hymn by Martin Luther aptly summarizes the entire last chapter of Micah's prophecy. If we have understood and responded to the prophecy, we should be able to join in his sentiments.

> Though great our sins and sore our wounds
> and deep and dark our fall,
> His helping mercy hath no bounds,
> his love surpassing all.
> Our trusty living Shepherd he,
> Who shall at last set Israel free
> from all their sin and sorrow."[84]

7:20 Much of the theology dealing with the Lord's attributes and actions in vv. 18–20 is ultimately derived from the great confession of faith (as part of a covenant renewal ceremony) in Exod 34:6–7. The Hebrew words for "true" *(ʾĕmet)* and "mercy" *(ḥesed)* are sometimes rendered "truth" or "faithfulness" and "grace" respectively, reminding the reader of John 1:17: "For the law was given through Moses; grace and truth came through Jesus Christ." Of "mercy" Snaith has said, "This is typical of a large number of cases where the word *[ḥesed]* is used of [God's] persistent, sure covenant-love for Israel all through the years."[85] Hillers adds, "The terms in parallel in v. 20 ('loyalty' [*ʾĕmet*]

---

[81] Kelley, "*Micah ... Malachi,*" 52.

[82] Fausset, "Jeremiah–Malachi," 610. To be closer to the Hebrew text, "sins" and "iniquities" should be reversed in the NIV. For "iniquities" (better, "sins") see comments on 1:5. For "sins" (better, "iniquities") see comments on v. 18.

[83] NIVSB, Isa 38:17n.

[84] Boice, *The Minor Prophets*, 2:53.

[85] Snaith, *The Distinctive Ideas of the Old Testament*, 104.

and 'love' [*ḥesed*]), with the following reference to God's oath, must be understood specifically as the loyalty and fidelity to be displayed to a covenant partner."[86] All this is in keeping with promises the covenant Lord swore on oath to the fathers of Israel "in days long ago" (see comments on 5:2). God had sworn to Abraham (Gen 22:17) and Jacob (Gen 28:14) that their descendants would be as numerous as the stars in the sky, the dust of the earth, and the sand on the seashore; and he had promised Abraham that he would be the father of many nations (Gen 17:5; cf. Luke 1:54–55). All believers are ultimately included in this promise (Rom 4; Gal 3:6–29; Heb 11:12).

What a wonderful note on which to end the prophecies of this very relevant book! At the conclusion of his exposition of Micah, Martin Luther quotes a prayer with which Jerome ended his commentary on this exquisite book:

> O God, who is a God like unto Thee? Who pardonest iniquity, passest by the transgression of the remnant of Thy people; who retainest not Thine anger forever because Thou delightest in mercy! Thou hast turned to us again and hast had compassion upon us. Thou hast subdued our iniquities and hast cast all our sins into the depths of the sea. Oh, preserve unto us this Thy mercy forever and ever, so that we may walk in the light of Thy Word and escape all dangers threatening us from Satan and the world, through Jesus Christ, Thy Son and our Redeemer. Amen. Amen. Amen. (Luther's Saemmtl. Schriften, St. Louis, XIV, 1169)[87]

Perhaps it would not be amiss to append our own prayer to Jerome's:

> God of the written Word, grant us such an appreciation for this portion of your holy and inspired Word that we will study it, teach it, and put it into practice. And may our Sovereign Lord and incomparable God be praised, worshiped, and glorified. In the name of the Divine Word, your Son and our Lord and Savior, Jesus Christ. Amen.

There probably is no more appropriate way to close our study of this major message of the minor prophet Micah than with these words of Frederick W. Faber in his hymn "There's a Wideness in God's Mercy":

> There's a wideness in God's mercy
> Like the wideness of the sea;
> There's a kindness in His justice
> Which is more than liberty.
>
> For the love of God is broader
> Than the measure of man's mind,
> And the heart of the Eternal
> Is most wonderfully kind.

---

[86] Hillers, *Micah*, 91.

[87] Quoted by T. Laetsch, *Bible Commentary: The Minor Prophets* (Saint Louis: Concordia, 1956), 292.

Nahum

INTRODUCTION OUTLINE

1. The Date of the Book
2. The Historical Setting
3. Nahum, the Man
4. Nahum, the Book
5. The Message of Nahum
   (1) The Sovereignty of the Lord
   (2) The Nature of God
   (3) The Nature of Sin
   (4) Hope for God's People

INTRODUCTION

"We often wish Nahum were not in the canon, and the book has been almost totally ignored in the modern church."[1] Its message of judgment does not fit the picture we want to have of a loving, forgiving God. Nahum centers attention entirely on the impending fall of Nineveh resulting in the delivery of the people of Judah. This central focus produced a message of hope to the people of Judah in a most unusual literary form, sometimes called a hymn of hate. Nahum's message has become the prototype of the destruction of all evil—from that of Nineveh to Nazi Germany to the final end of all evil like that of Babylon in Revelation 18. Nahum's message is essential and timeless: the Lord reigns and will have the final word against evil. This means hope and deliverance by God for God's people.

3. The Date of the Book

The few historical references in the Book of Nahum give us a *terminus post quem* and a *terminus ad quem* for the book, that is the earliest possible and latest possible dates. The "book" of Nahum (1:1) must have been composed after the fall of Thebes (No-Amon) to the Assyrian army in 663 B.C., since that event is

[1] E. Achtemeier, *Nahum–Malachi,* INT (Atlanta: John Knox, 1986), 5.

placed in the recent past in 3:8–10. The conquest of Thebes, the capital of Egypt, constituted one of the great feats in ancient times. Located deep in Egypt, protected by the Nile River and hazardous terrain, it seemed impregnable.

The fall of Nineveh in 612 B.C. to a coalition of Medes and Babylonians serves as the latest possible date of the book,[2] since Nahum speaks of Nineveh's fall as a future event.[3] Its fall would be a significant historical turning point, presaging the eventual fall of the Assyrian Empire and introducing ambitious new leaders in Babylon as the next empire to dominate the world. Most commentators place the time of writing shortly before the fall of Nineveh in 612 B.C.,[4] though the date 625, when the Medes besieged the city, is also given as a possibility.[5] G. Fohrer regarded the "wicked" in 1:15 to be Ashurbanipal (668–627 B.C.), with the verse presupposing his death in 627 B.C. He also assumed that Josiah had not yet attempted to reunite the remnant of the Northern Kingdom with the Southern Kingdom since 2:2 indicates that that event still lay in the future. He concluded that the time of Ashurbanipal's death gave a plausible time for the date of the book.[6]

Since the message was received from God, it may have been written at an earlier time when Nineveh's demise seemed highly unlikely.[7] W. A. Meier

---

[2] Some have tried to maintain that Nineveh had already fallen when the book was written and that the event is placed in the future for liturgical purposes. For reaction against this view see G. Fohrer, *Introduction to the Old Testament* (London: SPCK, 1970), 448; O. Eissfeldt, *The Old Testament: An Introduction,* trans. P. R. Ackroyd (New York: Harper & Row, 1965), 415; A. Weiser, *The Old Testament: Its Formation and Development,* trans. D. M. Barton (New York: Association, 1961), 258. See further under "Nahum, the Book."

[3] M. A. Sweeney argues that the refutation pattern he has established for the book "presupposes the fall of Nineveh as an established fact" ("Concerning the Structure and Generic Character of the Book of Nahum," *ZAW* 104 [1992]: 375). It is either a past fact of history or a foregone conclusion. He would place the date of the book precisely at 612 either shortly before or after Nineveh's fall.

[4] E.g., Achtemeier, *Nahum–Malachi,* 7.

[5] J. A. Soggin, *Introduction to the Old Testament,* 3d ed. (Philadelphia: Westminster, 1980), 326. W. C. Kaiser, Jr., narrowed the time frame between the death of Ashurbanipal in 627 B.C. and the collapse of Nineveh in 612 B.C. (*A History of Israel* [Nashville: Broadman & Holman, 1998], 232). K. Cathcart sees two possible dates, either about 625 or shortly before 612 (*ABD* 4:999). J. J. M. Roberts says Nahum's message could have been a major support to Manasseh's brief revolt about 652–648, but it is also possible to choose a slightly later date (*Nahum, Habakkuk, and Zephaniah: A Commentary,* OTL [Louisville: Westminster/John Knox, 1991], 39). Opting for the latter, Roberts places Nahum between 640 and 630.

[6] Fohrer, *Introduction to the Old Testament,* 448–49.

[7] W. A. Maier, *The Book of Nahum: A Commentary* (St. Louis: Concordia, 1959), 34; T. Longman III, "Nahum," in *The Minor Prophets: An Exegetical and Expository Commentary,* ed. T. E. McComiskey (Grand Rapids: Baker, 1993), 2:766. W. Rudolph says that Maier's concern to date the material prior to Thebes' revival is without import because the new Egyptian regime paid no attention to Thebes and never rebuilt it (*Micha, Nahum, Habakuk, Zephanja,* 143–44). Rudolph opts for a date around the middle of the seventh century or about 650 B.C., but he sees Nahum as remaining underground with his material only "published" after the death of Ashurbanipal (pp. 144–45). Note Soggin's statement: "The situation is such that the prophet can announce its fall any minute" (*Introduction to the Old Testament,* 326).

argues that the book's indictments of Assyria (e.g., 3:1–4,16) point to a time before Assyrian power began to wane, as it did after the death of Ashurbanipal or even somewhat before.[8] Nahum's purpose was to comfort Judah and to encourage Josiah. The young Josiah would have taken great comfort in hearing of the coming destruction of Nineveh whether imminent or in the near future.

We must conclude that the slight amount of evidence available gives little help in situating the book between 663 and 612 B.C. Perhaps the weakness of Israel and the overwhelming strength of Assyria assumed in the book points to a time before 627.

4. The Historical Setting

Every person and every event is set within a historical context without which neither the person nor the event can be understood. This was especially true of the man Nahum and the book that bears his name since all we know of them is the absolute concentration on Nineveh and Assyria. To understand the book we must understand the history of the Assyrian Empire, whose impending doom Nahum so eloquently announced.

Since the time of Tiglath-pileser III (745–727 B.C.),[9] Assyria had dominated the ancient Near East. Its dominance and influence extended beyond the merely political requirements of allegiance and taxation to the practices of worship of the vassal nations. Second Kings describes the practices of both Menahem of Israel and Ahaz of Judah in regard to Tiglath-pileser. Menahem gave Pul a thousand talents of silver "to gain his support and strengthen his own hold on the kingdom" (2 Kgs 15:19). This statement probably meant that Pul had besieged the city of Samaria and demanded the payment to remove his troops. The text states that Pul then withdrew from the land of Israel.

Ahaz entreated Tiglath-pileser to aid him in resisting Rezin of Syria and

---

[8] Maier, *The Book of Nahum*, 30–31. He goes on to argue for a date shortly before 654 B.C. since the book assumes the destruction of Thebes but not its restoration. This also would explain the failure to mention the Medes, Scythians, and Babylonians (pp. 31–37). O. P. Robertson agrees that the view presented of Assyria assumes a time prior to Ashurbanipal's death. He also suggests the lack of reference to Judah's sins would fit the time of reform at the end of Manasseh's reign, ca. 650–642 (2 Chr 33:10–17) or the beginning of Josiah's (*The Books of Nahum, Habakkuk, and Zephaniah* [Grand Rapids: Eerdmans, 1990], 31). R. B. Dillard and T. Longman III tentatively suggest a date between 652 and 626 B.C. (*An Introduction to the Old Testament* [Grand Rapids: Zondervan, 1994], 405). R. D. Patterson favors a date between 660 and 654 B.C. (*Nahum, Habakkuk, Zephaniah,* WEC [Chicago: Moody, 1991], 6–7). D. W. Baker suggests it may have been Nahum's prophecy that sparked Manasseh's rebellion in 652–648 B.C. (*Nahum, Habakkuk, Zephaniah,* TOTC [Downers Grove: InterVarsity, 1988], 20).

[9] In the biblical accounts Tiglath-pileser (2 Kgs 16:7) also is known as Pul (2 Kgs 15:19). For more details regarding his involvement with Israel and Judah see E. H. Merrill, *Kingdom of Priests: A History of Old Testament Israel* (Grand Rapids: Baker, 1987), 393–98.

Pekah of Israel in their attempts to revolt against Assyria. Tiglath-pileser rescued Ahaz from his rivals but exacted a terrible toll on Judah—a toll that continued to the time of Nahum. Ahaz, perhaps as a demand of Tiglath-pileser, set up an altar in Jerusalem on which he sacrificed (2 Kgs 16:10–16).[10]

For the next one hundred years, Judah remained as a vassal of Assyria. Assyria's dominance, reinforced by ruthless military might, must have seemed to most people of the day to be an eternal fixture on the world scene. The power and permanence of Assyria made Nahum's message even more significant.

Assyrian power centered in its capital city: Nineveh. The Khoser River separated the city into two parts, a northern mound called Kuyunjik, twice the size of the southern mound called Tell Nebi Yunus. An eight-mile-long wall encircled the city, enclosing eighteen hundred acres. The Bible credits Nimrod, the great hunter, with founding Nineveh (Gen 10:11). Archaeologists date the earliest remains of the city back to about 5000 B.C. After 3000 B.C. a temple was built there for Ishtar, the goddess of love and war. From 1400 to 1200 B.C. Shalmaneser I and Tiglath-pileser I conducted extensive building campaigns. The glory era of Nineveh came, however, around 700 B.C. Sennacherib built a new palace and made Nineveh the capital of Assyria, replacing Ashur. He built magnificent public gardens. He built an extensive thirty-mile-long aqueduct and water system. Esarhaddon and Ashurbanipal continued the building program, a major feature being Ashurbanipal's massive library which has yielded thousands of tablets for archaeologists and historians to study. Nineveh's King Sennacherib attacked Jerusalem and set the stage for God's great miracles with Isaiah and Hezekiah (Isa 36–39).[11]

By the time of Manasseh (696–641 B.C.), Assyrian dominance over Judah seemed to be institutionalized. Manasseh erected altars for Baal, made an Asherah, and worshiped the host of heaven (2 Kgs 21:3). Manasseh's evil provoked God to anger and led to the eventual downfall of the Southern Kingdom (2 Kgs 21:10–15). His fifty-five year reign proved too difficult to overcome and sealed the doom of Judah.

After Manasseh's death (641 B.C.), Amon, his son, reigned two years in Jerusalem and continued the practices of his father. Amon seemed even more evil than his father and died at the hands of his own servants (2 Kgs 21:23). Malamat suspected that an anti-Assyrian party engineered the plot against Amon as a means of striking for a change in national policy.[12] By the time

[10] Cf. A. T. Olmstead, *History of Assyria* (Chicago: University of Chicago Press, 1923), 198, 632–34. P. R. House, however, argues that Ahaz acted on his own for the advantage of himself and his country (*1, 2 Kings,* NAC [Nashville: Broadman & Holman, 1995], 337).

[11] For Nineveh see L. F. DeVries, *Cities of the Biblical World* (Peabody, Mass.: Hendrickson, 1997), 31–34, with bibliography; Maier, *The Book of Nahum*, 87–108.

[12] A. Malamat, "The Historical Background of the Assassination of Amon King of Judah," *IEJ* 3 (1953): 26–29.

Amon's son, Josiah, came to the throne (639 B.C.), Assyria had dominated Judah for over a century. During that time Assyria demonstrated its cruelty and barbarism by subjugating the city states of Syria-Palestine.

Though little is known of the early years of Josiah's reign or of those leaders who ruled for the boy-king, he must have been influenced by people who longed for the return of Judah to a political and religious revival. When Ashurbanipal, Assyria's last strong leader, died in 627 B.C., Josiah acted swiftly to begin a prolonged period of religious reform. The writer of Chronicles informs us that Josiah took the first steps toward reform in the eighth year of his reign, "while he was still young" (2 Chr 34:3). By 627 in his twelfth year he moved to purge Jerusalem of its foreign religious influences. Josiah had the altars of the Baals broken in his presence along with the Asherim and the graven and molten images (2 Chr 34:3–7).[13] J. Bright saw this as an indication that Josiah had renounced the gods of Assyria and rejected completely the syncretistic policies of Manasseh.[14]

The year 627 B.C. must have been a momentous one in history. Several events converged that changed the course of history. Along with the opportunity that Ashurbanipal's death provided Josiah, God began speaking through two prophets who severely reproached those who turned from following the Lord to bow down before the host of heaven (Zeph 1:4–6). Both Jeremiah and Zephaniah spoke of renewing the nation's allegiance to the Lord.

Nahum's message fits well into this historical context. Even more than Jeremiah and Zephaniah, Nahum encouraged those who instituted the process of reform in Jerusalem. Nineveh would soon fall; Judah would be free to practice its religion and chart its own course. The Lord would act on Judah's behalf.

In 621 B.C., probably as a result of the reforms already begun by Josiah, Hilkiah found the book of the law in the house of the Lord. The book called for the destruction of the high places and the institution of Jerusalem as the center of worship. The nature of the reforms instituted indicates that the "book of the law" was some form of the Book of Deuteronomy.[15]

Finding the book of the law added to the impetus for religious reform. The people kept the Passover, and Josiah put away the mediums and the wizards out of the land. The author of Kings judged Josiah to be one of Judah's greatest leaders: "Neither before nor after Josiah was there a king like him who turned to the Lord as he did—with all his heart and with all his soul and with all his strength, in accordance with all the Law of Moses" (2 Kgs 23:25).

---

[13] Cf. J. A. Thompson, *1, 2 Chronicles,* NAC (Nashville: Broadman & Holman, 1994), 374–75.

[14] J. Bright, *A History of Israel,* 3d ed. (Philadelphia: Westminster, 1981), 319–22. See 2 Kgs 21:24.

[15] W. F. Albright, "The Biblical Period," in *The Jews: Their History,* ed. L. Finkelstein (New York: Schocken, 1949), 47. Also see the recent summary of the debate regarding "the book of the law" in House, *1, 2 Kings,* 382–84.

History soon played out the threats Nahum so vigorously offered. Ashurbanipal's death brought weakness and civil strife. Seminomadic groups including Cimmerians, Scythians, and Medes exerted pressure. Nabopolassar gained control in Babylon and wrested its independence by 623. In 614 Ashur fell to the Medes. Finally, in 612 Nabopolassar united with the Medes to attack and take Nineveh. They then took Haran about 610 and Carchemish in 605.[16]

5. Nahum, the Man

Except for the book by his name, we know almost nothing about Nahum,[17] though he may well have been the prophet who broke a half century of prophetic silence.[18] Rudolph sees the double title giving the situation of the prophecy prior to information about the prophet as indicating that the content of the message was more important than the person of the prophet.[19] Watts builds on his theory of oracles against foreign nations as part of a royal Zion festival to imply that prophets like Nahum were temple prophets who sought answers from God for God's people about the current issues of life.[20] Such a sweeping explanation goes far beyond anything in the text.

The name itself comes from the root *nḥm,* meaning "to comfort." This is the word used in the divine call of Isa 40:1, "Comfort, comfort my people." The exact meaning of the name is unclear. It may be either a shortened form of something like "Nehemiah," meaning "Yahweh has comforted," or a form that perhaps means "comforter."[21] The idea of comfort fits the book perfectly. Nahum comforted the people of Judah by telling of Nineveh's coming destruction.

---

[16] See W. C. Kaiser, Jr., *A History of Israel* (Nashville: Broadman & Holman, 1998), 385–94; Patterson, *Nahum, Habakkuk, Zephaniah,* 3–7; to see traditional accounts of the fall of Nineveh compared to Nahum's prophecy of it, see Maier, who concludes, "The harmony between prediction and fulfillment is so clear and startling that some recent writers have declared the book to be a *post eventum* record of the fall. ... It constitutes one of the most dramatic and electrifying instances of divine prophecy in the OT" (*The Book of Nahum,* 108–39).

[17] Note that Maier shows how pictures of Nahum as a provincial prophet of the rural hinterland with a farmer's lack of delicacy cannot be established from the evidence of the text (*The Book of Nahum,* 18–19).

[18] Robertson, *The Books of Nahum, Habakkuk, and Zephaniah,* 30.

[19] Rudolph, *Micha, Nahum, Habakuk, Zephanja,* 148.

[20] J. D. W. Watts, "The Books of Joel, Obadiah, Jonah, Nahum, Habakkuk and Zephaniah," in *The Cambridge Bible Commentary on the New English Bible* (Cambridge: University Press, 1975), 5–8. R. L. Smith says such a hypothesis as Watts' would "provide an excellent *Sitz im Leben* for chap. 1" (*Micah–Malachi,* WBC 32 [Waco: Word, 1984], 32, 67).

[21] *HALOT,* 685, 689. Also note נִחֻמִים ("comfort") in Isa 57:18; Zech 1:13. The meaning "comforted by Yahweh" assumes an original longer form like *nĕḥumyah* (W. S. LaSor, D. A. Hubbard, and F. W. Bush, *Old Testament Survey: The Message, Form, and Background of the Old Testament* [Grand Rapids: Eerdmans, 1982], 445; cf. Soggin, *Introduction to the Old Testament,* 325).

Maier uses Nahum's message to characterize him as a person with the "qualities of true greatness."[22] Patterson sees him as a person with "a high view of God and his Word … a perceptive man, one who noted the courses of nature, society, and history."[23] Heflin points to the historical setting showing that the prophet spent his entire life under Assyrian domination and so was a man of abiding faith with the "overwhelming belief that evil could not stand forever. … Nahum was a man of righteous indignation … incensed by Assyria's inhumanity to people."[24]

J. M. P. Smith follows German commentators like Jepsen and Marti in identifying Nahum as a false prophet, but Maier adequately refutes such claims—if the people of God have not already refuted them by following the leadership of the Spirit to include the book in inspired canon. Maier says, "Every statement in this code of false-prophet principles which higher criticism has ascribed to Nahum is contradicted by the book itself."[25] Later Maier contends: "Nothing in Nahum's oracles would lull his own people into carnal security, a characteristic of the false prophets (Jer 6:14; 8:11), nor confirm Israel in its sins, causing it to forget Yahweh's name (Isa 56:10; Jer 23:27). … The small book is treated as though it were a compendium of theology, and without any basis in the prophet's own utterances detailed theological opinion is ascribed to him on subjects on which he has not expressed himself."[26]

Patterson devotes a long discussion to the satire and woe of Nahum's message that seems to indicate a vengeful attitude unlike that of the New Testament, outlining the various solutions to the issue. He concludes by showing that in these prayers, God is at work. "Essentially it is God's sovereign authority and reputation for righteousness that are at stake in Judah's controversy with Nineveh. … If Nahum's words seem harsh, then it is because he must use appropriate literary convention to express the seriousness of the situation. As one who understands the divine perspective and senses the issues in God's teleology that are at stake, he cannot do otherwise."[27]

Likewise uncertain is the location of Nahum's hometown, Elkosh. Sites in Assyria (at Al-Qush near Nineveh), Galilee (at El-Kauzeh or even Caper-

---

[22] Maier, *The Book of Nahum*, 20. Qualities include reverence for the Almighty, trust in divine justice and goodness, condemnation of national iniquity, positive conviction that God will keep His word, mighty intellect, patriotism and courage, almost unequaled gift of vivid presentation.

[23] Patterson, *Nahum, Habakkuk, Zephaniah,* 8.

[24] J. N. B. Heflin, *Nahum, Habakkuk, Zephaniah, and Haggai,* BSC (Grand Rapids: Zondervan, 1985).

[25] Maier, *The Book of Nahum*, 5.

[26] Ibid., 77.

[27] Patterson, *Nahum, Habakkuk, Zephaniah,* 15–16.

naum, which may mean "Village of Nahum," *kĕpar naḥûm*), and Judah (at Betogabris/Beth-Govrin) have been suggested without consensus.[28]

6. Nahum, the Book

The Book of Nahum dramatically portrays God overwhelming Assyria to relieve his oppressed people. No eyewitness could have described the panic in Nineveh more vividly. Von Rad noted that Nahum's poetic ability is unexcelled among Old Testament poets.[29] Lowth wrote, "None of the minor prophets … seem to equal Nahum in boldness, ardor, and sublimity. His prophecy, too, forms a regular and perfect poem: the exordium is not merely magnificent, it is truly majestic; the preparation for the destruction of Nineveh, and the description of its downfall and desolation, are expressed in the most vivid colours, and are bold and luminous in the highest degree."[30]

To create such majestic poetry, the prophet employed several poetic and stylistic devices. Maier lists the following: originality and independence from other poets, unique vocabulary and syntactical constructions, grammatical and syntactical purity, power of description, use of stylistic devices such as the rhetorical question (1:6,9; 2:12; 3:7–8,19), the elliptical sentence (3:2), apostrophe (2:1ff.), metaphors and similes (1:10; 2:12; 3:4,12,17), assonance and alliteration (2:11), abrupt change of person and number (1:9,11–12,15; 2:2,8–10,13; 3:1,5,18), repetition (1:2), and use of synonyms (1:6).[31]

Patterson extends the list of poetic elements: book ending/enveloping of sections ("scattering" 2:1; 3:18–19), subsections (*bĕlîyāʿal,* "wickedness" 1:11,15), and individual cola (Yahweh, 1:3); hooking/stitching to link units of the book with catchwords and themes such as "LORD" in 1:2 and "wrath" (1:2 with 1:3–10), plotting (1:3–10 with 1:11–15), attacking (2:1–2 with 2:3–10), plundering (2:3–10 with 2:11–13), chariots and "I am against you" (2:11–13 with 3:1–7), and death and destruction (3:1–7 with 3:8–19). Refrain and repetition signal either the beginning or ending of a smaller unit: "not again/no one" [1:15; 2:9,13; 3:3,7(?),19]; "look" (1:15; 2:13; 3:5,13); fire that consumes (1:6,10; 2:3,13; 3:13,15); and the use of rhetorical questions (1:6; 2:11; 3:8,19). Patterson extends the list of similes and metaphors to include 1:3b,6,13; 2:4,7–8,11–13, 3:4–6,12–13,15,17–18. He sees synec-

---

[28] Y. Kobayashi, "Elkosh," *ABD* 2:476. Also see the discussion in Maier, *The Book of Nahum,* 21–26.

[29] G. von Rad, *Old Testament Theology,* trans. D. M. G. Stalker (New York: Harper & Row, 1965), 2:188.

[30] R. Lowth, *Lectures on the Sacred Poetry of the Hebrews,* trans. G. Gregory (London: Tegg, 1839), 234. Also see S. R. Driver, *An Introduction to the Literature of the Old Testament,* 11th ed. (Edinburgh: T & T Clark, 1913), 336; Maier, *The Book of Nahum,* 40–42.

[31] Maier, *The Book of Nahum*, 40–42.

doche (2:4,10,13; 3:13), picturesque brevity (2:1,9–10b; 3:2–3), irony (2:1,8; 3:14–15), satire (2:11–13; 3:8–13,14–19), woe (3:1–7), enjambment (2:12; 3:7), chiasm (1:2; 3:1–7), staircase parallelism (3:15), terraced parallelism (1:2), pivot-pattern parallelism (2:4), an acrostic poem (1:2–10), alliteration and assonance (1:2–3a,4b,5; 2:1–2,6–7,9,11–13; 3:4,7,10,18). Thus he calls Nahum "the poet laureate among the Minor Prophets."[32]

How the book was used in worship has been a major topic of discussion. O. Kaiser and others considered the book to have been a single, unified composition for use during a celebration after the fall of Nineveh. This liturgy was then recited in the temple in Jerusalem on the following New Year festival.[33] B. S. Childs, however, notes that "the cultic interpretation has been sharply rejected by many scholars ... and shows little signs of winning a majority."[34] R. K. Harrison, for example, states: "Quite aside from the gratuitous nature of the assumptions relating to the New Year festival, this theory breaks down because the denunciations of Nineveh in Nah 2:4–3:17 look forward in a genuine fashion to future events and do not recall what has already happened. ... While Judah was warned to 'keep her solemn feasts' [1:15], there is nothing specifically cultic about this composition, and no grounds exist for assuming that it was compiled under the auspices of the cultus."[35] Maier agrees: "The whole idea of a New Year's service with such antiphonal readings is absolutely without foundation. We have no evidence whatever that a celebration of this kind was actually held in Jerusalem."[36]

---

[32] Patterson, *Nahum, Habakkuk, Zephaniah,* 10–11, which builds on the article he wrote with M. E. Travers, "Literary Analysis and the Unity of Nahum," *GTJ* 9 (1988): 45–58.

[33] The hymn at the beginning (1:2–9) and the reference to the "festivals" in 1:15 is considered evidence of this. O. Kaiser, *Introduction to the Old Testament: A Presentation of Its Results and Problems* (Minneapolis: Augsburg, 1975), 231–32. R. K. Harrison (*Introduction to the Old Testament* [Grand Rapids: Eerdmans, 1969], 929) points out that the view of Nahum as liturgy began with P. Haupt (1907) and was taken up by P. Humbert (1926) and E. Sellin (1929). Watts ("Joel, Obadiah, Jonah, Nahum, Habakkuk and Zephaniah," 5) sees all oracles against the nations fitting into the royal Zion festival and thus sees Obadiah, Nahum, and Habakkuk as "liturgical expansions" of such foreign oracles and thus "part of the festival's celebration of the 'day of the Lord.'" Maier (*The Book of Nahum*, 42) critiques such analysis as denying "the force of biblical prophecy and its harmonious agreement with the facts of fulfillment." He contends that "no decisive facts support this theory, whereas it is invalidated by several specific facts. ... It is built on a radical mutilation of the text. To secure address and reply, questions and answers, Nahum's words are arbitrarily altered to read as required" (p. 44).

[34] B. S. Childs, *Introduction to the Old Testament as Scripture* (Philadelphia: Fortress, 1979), 442.

[35] Ibid., 929. Maier also provides a helpful summary of Humbert's arguments and a refutation (*The Book of Nahum,* 42–44).

[36] Meier, *The Book of Nahum,* 45; Rudolph claims that purely secular pieces as large as 2:4–13 and 3:8–17 do not fit in a worship celebration and that 3:18–19 is impossible to conceive as the concluding response of the worshiping community since it gives no thanks to Yahweh and does not even mention his name (*Micha, Nahum, Habakuk, Zephanja*, 145).

G. Fohrer contended for a series of independent sayings that presuppose and continue the thought of one another, "thereby constituting a whole with an objective unity."[37] He felt that the lack of dialogue between God and the people meant that the work had not been intended for cultic recitation. "What we probably have in the book is an artfully assembled series of utterances belonging to various literary types, what might be termed a 'cantata' to be

THEME	NAHUM	ISAIAH
Messenger coming	1:15 (cf. 12)	52:7
No more invasion	1:15	52:1 (51:22–23)
Liberation from shackles	1:13	52:2
Liberation from affliction	1:12	51:21
Sold into slavery	3:4	52:3
Messenger formula	1:12	52:3
Drunk	3:11	51:21
Ruin	3:7	51:19
Destruction	3:19	51:19
Sword	2:13; 3:3,15	51:19
Wrath of God	1:2,6	51:17,20,22
Comfort, mourn for	3:7	51:19
Console, comfort	3:7	51:19
Drying the sea	1:4	50:2
Lebanon, Bashan, Carmel	1:4	33:9
Vengeance	1:2	59:17–19
Storm and earthquake	1:3–6	29:6
Withering vegetation	1:4	33:9; 50:2
Waters dried up	1:4–5	42:15

[37] Fohrer, *Introduction to the Old Testament,* 450.

THEME	NAHUM	ISAIAH
Feet of good news	1:15	52:1,7
Plunder	2:9–10	24:1,3
Trembling	2:10	21:3–4
Shame of nakedness	3:5–7	47:2–3
Who can comfort?	3:7	51:19
Whirlwind and fire	1:3,6	66:15–16

recited in the cult by the prophets."[38]

Armerding says that the material in Nahum comes not from worship but from Israel's historic and prophetic traditions. The Sinai revelation is "echoed" in 1:2–6 and then applied in the remainder of the book. Particularly the legacy of Isaiah finds reflection in Nahum, especially in 1:15 (see Isa 52:7). The chart above shows literary links Armerding finds between the two books.[39]

Longman and Dillard point out that the first verse calls Nahum's work a *sēper,* "book." This is significant since Nahum is the only one of the prophetic works thus named. Whereas most of the other prophets were at least initially preachers and their books were composed after their sermons, "Nahum, it appears, wrote a book." This suggestion is believed to be confirmed by the observation that some of Nahum's poetic devices, such as the partial acrostic in 1:2–8, are more visual than auditory.[40]

While arguing for the unity of the book, Maier notes that "almost every one of the forty-seven verses has been said by one critic or another to contain a subsequent addition."[41] As with most prophetic books, critics have created a

---

[38] Ibid.

[39] Armerding, "Habakkuk," 453–56.

[40] Dillard and Longman, *An Introduction to the Old Testament,* 406; Longman ("Nahum," 2:769) notes, however, voices such as Achtemeier (*Nahum–Malachi,* 7), who argues the label "book … does not imply that it was originally written and not spoken."

[41] Maier, *The Book of Nahum,* 50. Patterson says all of this "rests on the shakiest of premises. The rejection of part of the superscription because it is a double title flies in the face of the same phenomenon elsewhere (e.g., Hos 1:1–2; Amos 1:1; Mic 1:1; cf. Isa 13:1). The supposedly interpolated acrostic hymn of praise can be seen as part and parcel of the message and development of the entire book. … Rejecting the genuineness of the 'hopeful sayings' would necessitate doing so in virtually every prophetic book, for the prophets uniformly combine condemnation and comfort in their messages. … To deny the closing dirge to Nahum is subjective at best and erroneous in fact, for it forms a proper ending refrain not only to the previous taunt song (3:8ff.) but also to the entire second half of the book (2:1–3:19)" (*Nahum, Habakkuk, Zephaniah,* 12).

long literary history of editorial additions and rearrangements.[42] Nogalski summarizes these and then adds his own theory about how redaction incorporated Nahum into the book of the twelve.[43] He argues that the acrostic hymn and the literary transition in 1:9–10 were "redactionally incorporated into a preexisting Nahum corpus."[44] Such weaving also involved transition elements in 1:12b–13; 2:1–3.[45] This corpus can be structured as:

1:11–12	Nineveh's numerical strength will not deliver it from destruction
1:14	The preparation of the grave of the king of Assyria
2:3–13	First description of Nineveh's destruction
3:1–15	Second description of Nineveh's destruction
3:16–17	Nineveh's numerical strength will not deliver it from destruction
3:18–19	Mocking funeral dirge at the grave of the king of Assyria.[46]

The redactional element was postexilic and included the incorporation of materials from "Deutero-Isaiah" into Nahum. He also sees a "creeping locust" layer in 3:15ac,16b interpreting Assyria as one of the locusts of Joel.[47] A sure sign of an original literary work would be a significant literary structure. A book with such poetic mastery should evidence a progression of thought built around some theme or logical scheme. So scholars have sought to demonstrate the logical argument of the book. Maier suggested 1:1 Title; 1:2–8 Introductory Ode; 1:9–2:1 Prediction of Nineveh's End; 2:2–14 Dire Picture of Nineveh's End; 3:1–19 Prophetic Denunciation of Nineveh, thus seeing one focus and theme presented four different ways.[48]

D. Baker sees 1:12–2:2 as a court scene with alternating verdicts of judgment and acquittal for Assyria and Judah. He views 2:3–10; 3:2–3 as a vivid

---

[42] Several studies explain textual difficulties as the result of postexilic redaction in light of eschatological thought in the early Persian period. See J. Jeremias, *Kultprophetie und Gerichtsverkündigung in der späten Königszeit Israels*, WMANT 35 (1970); H. Schulz, *Das Buch Nahum: Eine redaktionskritische Untersuchung*, BZAW 129 (1973); B. Renaud, "La composition du livre de Nahum: Une proposition," *ZAW* 99 (1987): 198–219; K. Seybold, "Vormasoretische Randnotizen in Nahum 1," *ZAW* 101 (1989): 71–85; and *Profane Prophetie: Studien zum Buch Nahum*, SBS 135 (1989). A critique of such theories forms the basis of the study by Sweeney, "Concerning the Structure and Generic Character of the Book of Nahum," 364–77.

[43] J. Nogalski, *Redactional Processes in the Book of the Twelve*, BZAW 218 (New York/Berlin: Walter de Gruyter, 1993), 93–128. He sees changes in the opening acrostic (1:2–8) resulting from editorial desire (p. 105) "to attach the theophany (and the book of Nahum) to Micah 7." In so doing Nogalski argues (p. 116) that "the redaction of Nah 1 was cognizant not only of its position adjacent to Micah 7, but that it was aware of a larger corpus including Hosea, Joel, Amos, and Micah" as seen in use of language and images related to Amos 1:2; Mic 1:2–7; Hos 14; Joel 1:5; 2:13,20; 4:21; Jonah 4:2.

[44] Ibid., 115.

[45] Ibid., 275

[46] Ibid., 114.

[47] Ibid., 276.

[48] Maier, *The Book of Nahum*, 14–16.

description of siege and battle created around the dirge of 3:1.[49]

Patterson sees a tight structure for the book, one so tight that the structure often is used as an argument for the authenticity of text, supposed editorial editions, and interpretations. A repeating structure shows theme (1:2; 2:1–2), development (1:2–10; 2:3–10; 3:1–7), and application (1:11–15; 2:11–13; 3:8–19). "Nahum closes each major section (1:15; 3:18–19) as well as two subsections (2:13; 3:7) with a refrain concerning the activity/inactivity of a messenger."[50]

Achtemeier sees an opening hymn (1:2–11) and a final judgment oracle in the form of a dirge (3:14–19) forming an inclusio through the use of the Hebrew word *rāʿâ,* "evil." These are sandwiched around four judgment oracles (1:12–15; 2:1–13; 3:1–7,8–13), each of which concludes with a divine word introduced by "behold" (1:15; 2:13; 3:5,13).

Sweeney uses form critical markers to see the disputation speech as the primary form behind the book and to divide the book into three basic subunits:

1:2–10 Theophanic hymn addressing Judah and Nineveh followed by a rhetorical question of their estimation of Yahweh's power;
1:11–2:1 Address to Judah indicating reasons for a change in attitude since in ending Assyrian pressure Yahweh has shown his power;
2:2–3:19 Address to Nineveh and the Assyrian king indicating reason for a change of attitude since Yahweh has demonstrated his power.[51]

K. Spronk shows the weakness of Sweeney's argument in building too much on the centrality of 1:9 and inability to deal with the change of address in 1:14.[52] Armerding lists ten elements (five dealing with the causes and five

[49] Baker, *Nahum, Habakkuk, Zephaniah,* TOTC 23b (Downers Grove: InterVarsity, 1988), 23.

[50] Patterson, *Nahum, Habakkuk, Zephaniah,* 9.

[51] Sweeney, "Concerning the Structure and Generic Character of the Book of Nahum," 374. He bases his work on study of the second masculine and second feminine address forms by B. Becking, "Is het boek Nahum een literaire eenheid," *NTT* 32 (1978): 107–24. He follows A. Graffy in describing the disputation genre as a quotation of the people's opinion to be disputed and the refutation that corrects the people's opinion (*A Prophet Confronts His People: The Disputation Speech in the Prophets,* AnBib 104 [1984]: 105). Because 1:2–10 does not quote the people's opinion directly but does use the form of a rhetorical question, Sweeney is forced to admit that the "three elements of Nah 1:2–3:19 do not constitute a prophetic disputation speech per se, but a prophet refutation speech that is derived from the basic disputation pattern ("Concerning the Structure and Generic Character of the Book of Nahum," 375). He points with agreement to the less rigid structure championed by D. F. Murray ("The Rhetoric of Disputation: Reexamination of a Prophetic Genre," *JSOT* 38 [1987]: 95–121), who sees three elements in the genre: thesis, counterthesis, and dispute, which Sweeney says correspond to Nahum in that the thesis of Yahweh's impotence is held by the prophet's dual audience but not stated explicitly by the prophet; the counterthesis appears in 1:2–10; the dispute on two fronts appears in 1:11–2:1 and 2:2–3:19.

[52] K. Spronk, "Synchronic and Diachronic Approaches to the Book of Nahum."

with the manner of Nineveh's fall) as uniting the various sections of the book. He then sees a simple structure: judicial decree against Nineveh (chap. 1) and its precise execution (chaps. 2–3). The book with its "contrast of interlocked, conflicting destinies … is constructed on a clear-cut dialectic of 'good' (1:7; cf. vv. 3,12–13,15; 2:2) and 'evil' (1:11; cf. vv. 3–6,8–11,12,14–15; 2:1–10)."[53]

Armerding outlines a detailed structure for the book built around a judgment, sentence, response pattern repeated in chap. 1 and chaps. 2–3:[54]

THEME	CHAPTER 1	CHAPTERS 2–3
	JUDGMENT A	JUDGMENT A′
Executed on evil	1:11	3:19
By flood	1:8	2:6,8
By fire	1:6	2:4; 3:13,15
That consumes	1:10	3:13,15
By drunkenness	1:10	3:11
Exception	1:7 (those who trust)	2:2 (Jacob/Israel)
	SENTENCE B	SENTENCE B′
Messenger Formula	1:12	2:13; 3:5
Against	1:14	3:13; 3:5
Result: cut off	1:14–15	2:13; 3:16
No more	1:14–15	2:13
End: vileness, shame	1:14	3:5
	RESPONSE C	RESPONSE C′
On the mountains	1:15	3:18
Proclaim	1:15	3:13; 3:19

Spronk[55] says the lack of agreement on the basic structure of the prophecy

[53] C. Armerding, "Habakkuk," EBC 7:451–52.
[54] Armerding, "Habakkuk," 453.
[55] Spronk, "Synchronic and Diachronic Approaches to the Book of Nahum," 165.

makes one question its unity: "Every new study seems to result in a new division of the text." The disagreement may not be as strong as Spronk intimates. Students of Nahum's book easily isolate certain structural features of the book:

Opening hymn in 1:2–8
Interpretation of the hymn in 1:9–11
Messenger speech opening a new section in 1:12
Announcement speech setting opening new section 1:15
Battle description in 2:3–12
Divine announcement opening in 2:13
Woe oracle beginning in 3:1
Divine announcement opening repeating 2:13 in 3:5
Historical comparison beginning in 3:8
Direct address to doomed king of Assyria in 3:18.

The question is how one interprets these structural markers and whether one breaks them up into larger or smaller units. The present commentary follows the chapter division of the English text to isolate three major divisions in the text. Chapter 1 uses hymnic and oracular language to describe the character of God. Chapter 2 uses oracular and battle description language to announce the Lord's judgment on Nineveh. Chapter 3 uses the language of funeral woes and dirges along with historical comparison to pronounce death on Assyria.

The text of Nahum "is especially well preserved, with possible corruptions being cited in few places (e.g., 1:4b; 3:18)."[56] This has led to the conclusion that "recently discovered witnesses of the text of Nahum in modern times include the Pesher of Nahum (4QpNah) found at Qumran, the Hebrew Scroll of the Minor Prophets from Wadi Murabaat (Mur 88), and fragments of the Greek text of the Minor Prophets from Nahal Hever (8 Hev XIIgr). There are no significant variants in the text of Nahum in these scrolls, and the student of the text probably should pay more attention to linguistic investigation than to dubious textual reconstruction."[57] English readers do need to know that the English textual tradition has followed the Septuagint and included fifteen verses instead of the Hebrew text's fourteen. Thus Hebrew 2:1 becomes English 1:15, and each verse in chap. 2 in English is one number behind its Hebrew counterpart. English 2:1 equals Hebrew 2:2.

---

[56] Patterson, *Nahum, Habakkuk, Zephaniah,* 13; Rudolph (*Micha, Nahum, Habakuk, Zephanja,* 144) says the only editorial additions are phrases in 2:3 and 3:8.

[57] *ABD* 4:998. Roberts (*Nahum, Habakkuk, and Zephaniah,* 37) does see "a number of textual problems in the book, but the only clear gloss is the awkwardly placed comment in 2:2."

7. The Message of Nahum

Nahum often is judged to be a false prophet with only a hymn of hate (see "Nahum, the Book"). G. A. Smith noted how Zephaniah also dealt with the doom of the Assyrian capital but with the added concern for the wickedness of the people of Judah: "For this Nahum has no thought. His heart, for all its bigness, holds room only for the bitter memories, the baffled hopes, the unappeased hatreds of a hundred years."[58] Closer examination of Nahum's book finds an awesome view of a sovereign, just God who enforces international justice and absolute moral standards while offering hope to a downtrodden, depressed people. "Nahum is not primarily a book about human beings, however—not about human vengeance and hatred and military conquest—but a book about God.[59] "Nineveh will be judged not because it is Judah's enemy but because it is God's enemy. Anyone who flaunts self in proud rebellion against God—Judah as well as Nineveh—will eventually face divine judgment."[60] Harrison points out that Nahum is concerned for "the power and justice of God in history in the same way as the eighth-century prophets." Nahum is no "narrow-minded patriot obsessed by fanatical nationalistic tendencies."[61] "The author is not expressing some personal feeling of vindication over some hurt by the oppressor, nor even a nationalistic chauvinism that pagan nations must be punished. Rather, Yahweh is applying his universal standard against evil, no matter who is responsible."[62] In fact, Nahum's is one of the most sublime messages of the Old Testament. T. Longman observes that only later in the book is Nahum's message of Yahweh as Warrior applied explicitly to Assyria and Judah. "The psalm that occurs at the beginning of the book presents a picture of God applicable for all times—he is the Warrior who judges evil."[63] Although like the other prophets the message of Nahum is historically conditioned, it applies to any

---

[58] G. A. Smith, *The Book of the Twelve Prophets* (London: Hodder & Stoughton, 1898), 90. Note, however, Nah 1:12. Others have attacked the message of Nahum by comparing it to that of the great eighth-century prophets who dealt with social and ethical issues of the day. J. M. P. Smith, e.g., characterized Nahum as a "representative of the old, narrow and shallow prophetism" (*A Critical and Exegetical Commentary on Nahum,* ICC [Edinburgh: T & T Clark, 1965], 281). Childs has reminded the biblical student that "to criticize Nahum from the perspective of Amos's theology fails to reckon seriously with the function of a collection of writings which together exercised its authority upon a community of faith" (*Introduction to the Old Testament as Scripture*, 446). Maier, *The Book of Nahum*, 70–87, catalogs the complaints against Nahum's message and shows how such complaints are not justified.

[59] Achtemeier, *Nahum–Malachi,* 5.

[60] Heflin, *Nahum, Habakkuk, Zephaniah, and Haggai,* 21.

[61] Harrison, *Introduction to the Old Testament*, 930.

[62] Baker, *Nahum, Habakkuk, Zephaniah,* 23.

[63] Longman, "Nahum," 2:776. The NIV has added references to Nineveh in 1:11,14; and 2:1. It also added "O Judah" in 1:12 and "the city" in 2:7.

circumstances in which evil appears to be overwhelming the good. The message of the prophet Nahum is a message of the power of God to overcome the power of evil. As M. Luther wrote: "[Nahum] teaches us to trust God and to believe, especially when we despair of all human help, human powers, and counsel, that the Lord stands by those who are His, shields His own against all attacks of the enemy, be they ever so powerful."[64]

(1) The Sovereignty of the Lord

Yahweh, the God of Israel, is the Sovereign Lord of the universe. Like the prophets who came before him, Nahum saw the Lord exercising his authority over all the nations. Nahum had an uphill battle convincing his Judean audience with such a message. "To the suffering remnant, there was little question that God would and did punish his own covenant people; but whether he was equally able and willing to impart justice to the powerful heathen nations surrounding Israel was untested. ... The severity and kindness of God were both under scrutiny: the former as to whether it applied only selectively to his own people, and the latter in the context of God's ability and desire to bring about ultimate salvation for those who were faithful to him."[65]

Nahum's message follows the theme of Isaiah, who saw Yahweh as the Lord of history. Like Isaiah, Nahum knew that the Lord works in history to accomplish his purpose. The same God who could use Assyria as the "rod of my anger" (Isa 10:5) also could punish "the king of Assyria for the willful pride of his heart and the haughty look in his eyes" (Isa 10:12). Nahum powerfully portrays the pride, greed, self-centeredness, idolatry, violence, lack of mercy, and false security of Nineveh. All nations condemn such characteristics and crave the destruction of such an all-powerful and all-sinful world dominator. No nation by itself has power to bring such dreams to actuality. Nahum introduced to the scene the One who could destroy the destroyer. The Sovereign Lord of history rules all nations, even those who do not acknowledge him. He would accomplish what no other gods and no other nations could. Assyria would fall!

This sovereign Lord rules nature (1:4–6,8) and the world's nations (1:3,6–10,15; 2:1,3–7). All history stands under his control (1:12; 2:13: 3:5–7). He waits in patience (1:3a) but eventually brings his justified judgment on the sin of every greedy, prideful nation (1:2–3,8–10,14; 2:13; 3:5–7,11–19) because of his zealous jealousy to maintain the loyalty of his own people (1:2). His word is not entirely one of judgment. He gives hope to those who trust him (1:7–

[64] Quoted in Maier, *The Book of Nahum,* 85–86.

[65] Armerding, "Habakkuk," 456.

8;12–13,15; 2:2). "When the forces opposing God are so firmly ensconced and the flickering lamp of God's people is at the point of extinction, however, it is easy for the remnant to forget. Nahum reminds us, as do the ruins of ancient Nineveh, that God himself is the ultimate Ruler. He will have the final word."[66]

(2) The Nature of God

"Nahum is based on the monolithic concept of God's sovereign justice, whose working in salvation history eludes the sociologist and philosopher and is perceived by prophetic eyes alone."[67] Nahum described God as jealous, avenging, and good. Though these attributes seem contradictory, Nahum showed the righteousness of a caring God, a God who is zealous for the well-being of his people. After all, what truly good human being could sit idly by in the face of cruel oppression such as that meted out by Assyria? How much less could God allow such wickedness to continue? "At the heart of his message is a recognition of Yahweh as a God of justice who will not let injustice and oppression go unpunished."[68]

According to Maier, Nahum speaks "with eloquent beauty" of Yahweh in his universality (1:12–14; 2:14; 3:5), his justice (1:2–3), his omnipotence (1:4,9), and his majesty (1:3,5), but also in his mercy (1:3,7,12) and in his faithfulness (1:7).[69] Nahum showed that ending oppression requires the removal of the oppressor. He showed the compassion of the one who fights against evil. A man who is deeply and truly religious is always a man of wrath. Because he loves God and his fellow men, he hates and despises inhumanity, cruelty, and wickedness. Every good man sometimes echoes the words of Nahum.[70]

Far from presenting a one-sided view of God, Nahum pictured God as faithful (1:7), merciful (1:3), good, (1:7), and just (1:2–3).

(3) The Nature of Sin

Nahum concentrated on human sin as well as on the sovereignty and nature of God. "Evil introduced and evil done away form the inclusio of the thought of the book."[71] Judah had been afflicted for their sins (1:12 and perhaps in 2:3). Such sin, whoever commits it, rouses God's burning fury (1:6). More importantly for Nahum, Nineveh, the head of the Assyrian world-dominating empire, had gone far beyond any moral boundaries acceptable in international

---

[66] Ibid., 457.

[67] Ibid., 452.

[68] Roberts, *Nahum, Habakkuk, and Zephaniah,* 39.

[69] Maier, *The Book of Nahum,* 84–85.

[70] R. Calkins, *The Modern Message of the Minor Prophets* (New York: Harper & Brothers, 1947), 86.

[71] Achtemeier, *Nahum–Malachi,* 6.

diplomacy much less by the Holy God. She treated nations as objects of commerce to be bought and sold or as harlots to be paid for their love and loyalty and then discarded at will (3:4,19). Nahum is a "seer of God who declares that the haughty city has decreed its own destruction because of its moral corruption, its oppression of Judah and other nations, its violence, bloodshed, lies, deceits, and, above all, its rejection of God."[72] Nahum shows that when the military might of a nation becomes its security and its god, then sin has conquered the nation, and it will fall. Sin is not limited to those with specific instructions from God's book about it. Every person knows basic human rights and values. Any person or nation who refuses to follow these rights and values is condemned as a sinner and faces God's judgment. Such basic understanding of sin informed Paul as he wrote the magisterial description of sin and punishment in Romans 1–3.

(4) Hope for God's People

Nahum's "concern to reassure Judah of Yahweh's ability and will to destroy Nineveh runs throughout the book."[73] Nahum's message was ultimately proclaimed to God's people, not to Nineveh. He promised a day they would again celebrate their feasts and complete the vows they had made during times of hardship and oppression (1:15). "The message of God through Nahum was to encourage God's people. Oppressed by a seemingly invincible foe who had overwhelmed the entire region from the Nile to the Tigris, Israel could not look to her own power, but only to God for deliverance. Yet within a few years, the invincible was no more, vanquished by the hand of God, before whom no nation can stand."[74] The message once fulfilled became a beacon of hope through the ages. Its light continues to shine brightly as God's people endure a world ruled by materialistic godlessness. God did it once for Israel against ugly Nineveh. He showed us in Jesus Christ and his cross and resurrection that the battle has been won. We know God can and will win the battles we face today. He will also win the ultimate battle against all the forces of darkness until his glory and splendor are recognized and praised in all the ends of the earth. As Watts concludes: "Nineveh is no ordinary city for the prophet, nor is Assyria just another degenerating civilization. They stand for the ultimate supernatural evil that frustrates and suppresses the purposes and people of God. Their defeat is a sign of the victory of God and the basis for hope that this power and justice will ultimately conquer all evil."[75]

---

[72] Maier, *The Book of Nahum*, 74.

[73] Roberts, *Nahum, Habakkuk, and Zephaniah,* 38.

[74] Baker, *Nahum, Habakkuk, Zephaniah,* 24.

[75] Watts, "Joel, Obadiah, Jonah, Nahum, Habakkuk and Zephaniah," 120.

Christians normally speak of Old Testament hope in terms of messianism. Patterson shows how Nah 1:15 has been used for messianic import in the church.[76] Robertson notes, however, "the most distinctive thing about the messianism of Nahum, Habakkuk, and Zephaniah is the absence of virtually a trace of messianism." He explains this as a "delusion with the historical experience of kingship in Israel. … All three of these prophets labored after the depravities of Manasseh had sealed the fate of the nation's future. No repentance could remove the stench of the abominations that had been practiced by Israel for over fifty years (cf. 2 Kgs 21:10–15; 22:14–20).[77] Those very functions that once had been assigned to the scion of the line of David now revert to the person of God the Lord himself. … In the last hours before the Exile it is as though the Lord interrupts the movement toward messiah to declare clearly that he alone can be king in Israel. … It may well be that Nahum, Habakkuk, and Zephaniah did not have the complete picture of the Way and the One who would redeem his people Israel. But their unique ministry, even in the absence of 'messianism' as it is commonly perceived, supplied a vital contribution to the ongoing revelation of the God-man who would be Savior and king, even the Lord, Jesus the Christ."[78]

---

[76] Patterson, *Nahum, Habakkuk, Zephaniah,* 15.

[77] Robertson, *The Books of Nahum, Habakkuk, Zephaniah,* 17.

[78] Ibid., 19–20.

OUTLINE OF NAHUM

Title Verse (1:1)

I. The Character of God (1:2–15)
   1. The Revelation of God (1:2–6)
   2. The Lord's Care for Judah (1:7–11)
   3. The Lord's Word for Judah (1:12–13)
   4. The Lord's Word to Nineveh (1:14)
   5. The Joy of Deliverance (1:15)

II. The Lord's Judgment of Nineveh (2:1–13)
   1. Warning to Nineveh (2:1)
   2. Comfort to Judah (2:2)
   3. Description of Nineveh's Attackers (2:3–5)
   4. Description of Nineveh's Defeat (2:6–10)
   5. The Hopelessness of Nineveh (2:11–12)
   6. The Lord Fights against Nineveh (2:13)

III. The Woe over Nineveh (3:1–19)
   1. The Destruction of Nineveh (3:1–4)
   2. The Humiliation of Nineveh (3:5–7)
   3. The Weakness of Nineveh (3:8–13)
   4. The Hopelessness of Defense (3:14–19a)
   5. The Joy in Justice (3:19b)

SECTION OUTLINE

TITLE VERSE (1:1)

I. THE CHARACTER OF GOD (1:2–15)
   1. The Revelation of God (1:2–6)
      (1) The Description of God's Being (1:2–3)
      (2) The Description of God's Actions (1:4–6)
   2. The Lord's Care for Judah (1:7–11)
   3. The Lord's Word for Judah (1:12–13)
   4. The Lord's Word to Nineveh (1:14)
   5. The Joy of Deliverance (1:15)

TITLE VERSE (1:1)

In historical contexts some years mean more than others. The years 1776, 1789, and 1989 proved to be watershed years in world history. The American Revolution, the French Revolution, and the "Velvet" Revolution in Eastern Europe brought on significant changes in the world.

The last quarter of the seventh century B.C. and the first quarter of the sixth century B.C. proved to be as meaningful for the inhabitants of the ancient Near East. The year 612 B.C. changed the complexion of that part of the world. Nineveh, the city that represented the cruel and barbaric Assyrian Empire, fell to a coalition of Medes and Babylonians in 612 B.C. Although the full impact of the destruction of Nineveh waited to be revealed, the fall of the city signaled that the ancient Near East faced many changes.

Sometime before the fall of Nineveh,[1] Nahum preached a message that sounds much like hate to the ears of people familiar with Jesus' words to love our enemies. To the people of Nahum's day, his message was one of comfort and deliverance of oppressed people. For the oppressed to be freed, the oppressor had to be removed. Nahum spoke about the end of the oppressor, Nineveh.

[1]An oracle concerning Nineveh. The book of the vision of Nahum the Elkoshite.

1:1 For the most part each prophetic book of the Old Testament contains a title verse that gives the name of the prophet, a brief description of the time period involved, and the subject of the prophet's message (e.g., Amos 1:1; Zeph 1:1). The Book of Jonah lacks this title, probably because it tells the story of Jonah rather than recording the preaching of Jonah.

[1] See Introduction: "The Date of the Book."

The title verse of Nahum identifies its contents as an "oracle," a "book," and a "vision." It also identifies the general topic as "Assyria" and gives in the briefest terms an identification of the prophet.

The name "Nahum" speaks of comfort and fits appropriately the message of the prophet (see Introduction). His message of the coming destruction of the oppressor, Nineveh, provided comfort for the oppressed people of the ancient Near East suffering under a heavy yoke of tyranny and barbarism.

Apart from his name and his hometown (see Introduction for suggested locations of Elkosh), we know nothing about the prophet Nahum. He is mentioned only in this verse and in Luke 3:25, though names from the same root word are common in the Bible (e.g., Nehemiah and Menahem). The word also is common in Northwest Semitic inscriptions.[2]

Nahum's message is called a *maśśāʾ*, usually translated "burden" or "oracle."[3] The term can refer to wisdom sayings (Prov 30:1; 31:1) but usually is found in prophetic material, referring to a divine word regarding the foreign nations as it does in this instance. Isaiah used the term repeatedly in the section of his book concerning the foreign nations (Isa 13:1; 14:28; 15:1; 17:1; 19:1; 21:1,11,13; 23:1; 30:6). Habakkuk's message bore the same terminology, though he spoke about the destruction of the tyrant rather than directly to the foreign nation (Hab 1:1; cp. Jer 23:33; Ezek 12:10). The prophetic speech may be directed against individuals (2 Kgs 9:25; Isa 22:1; 2 Chr 24:27). The word may also be used for oracles of salvation (Zech 9:1; 12:1; Mal 1:1). The basic meaning of the term is thus "oracle" or "prophetic saying"[4] and not "burden,"[5] but the underlying connotation of "burden" may

---

[2] See J. J. M. Roberts, *Nahum, Habakkuk, and Zephaniah: A Commentary,* OTL (Louisville: Westminster/John Knox, 1991), 41, for examples and bibliography.

[3] The meanings come from two usages of the Hb. נשׂא, "to lift, raise." To raise one's voice gives rise to the meaning "pronouncement or oracle." To lift a load suggests "burden." See *HALOT* 2:638–39 for the two meanings: "load, burden" in Exod 23:5; 2 Kgs 5:17; Isa 22:25; "pronouncement" in 2 Kgs 9:25; Lam 2:14; Prov 30:1. H. P. Müller gives the arguments and literature for one or two sources for this term (*TWAT* 5:20–21). Some suggest the translation "oracle" is too general. J. A. Soggin prefers "charge" (*Introduction to the Old Testament* [Louisville: Westminster/John Knox, 1989], 303, 325). For a defense of "oracle" see R. D. Patterson, *Nahum, Habakkuk, Zephaniah,* WEC (Chicago: Moody, 1991), 19.

[4] See W. Rudolph, *Micha-Nahum-Habakuk-Zephanja*, 148; J. D. W. Watts, "The Books of Joel, Obadiah, Jonah, Nahum, Habakkuk and Zephaniah," in *The Cambridge Bible Commentary on the New English Bible* (Cambridge: University Press, 1975), 98; Patterson, *Nahum, Habakkuk, Zephaniah,* 19–20; D. W. Baker, *Nahum, Habakkuk, Zephaniah,* TOTC (Downers Grove: InterVarsity, 1988), 21.

[5] F. Stolz ("נשׂא *nśʾ* to lift, bear," *TLOT* 2:773–74), O. P. Robertson (*The Books of Nahum, Habakkuk, and Zephaniah,* NICOT [Grand Rapids: Eerdmans, 1990], 55), and W. A. Maier (*The Book of Nahum: A Commentary* [St. Louis: Concordia, 1959], 145–47) argue for "burden" following P. A. H. de Boer (*OTS* 5 [1948]: 197–214) and J. N. B. Heflin (*Nahum, Habakkuk, Zephaniah, and Haggai,* BSC [Grand Rapids: Zondervan, 1985], 33–34). Despite Jeremiah's play on the word (Jer 23:33–38), the term does not automatically designate a prophecy as coming from a false cultic prophet; see Roberts, *Nahum, Habakkuk, and Zephaniah,* 40.

well have commended itself to any native speaker of Hebrew.[6]

Of all the prophetic works only Nahum is described as a "book" in the title verse.[7] As mentioned in the Introduction, this suggests that rather than originating as sermons preached by the prophet, this work may have been produced initially as literature. This most likely took the form of a scroll that may have been circulated as an underground pamphlet during times of Assyrian persecution.[8]

Nahum's message came to him by means of a "vision." That is, "the prophet perceived God's revelation with the mind's eye."[9] "A vision is an event through which the Lord spoke to a prophet. ... On the one hand, it refers to the thing seen, the vision or the appearance of the vision (Dan 7:1). On the other hand, it shows the effect on the seer: He is encouraged, chosen, shocked, pardoned, et cetera. Not a visual image but a word from God is received. ... The prophetic vision primarily involved a revelation of God and his word, and only then a visual impact: God let it be known what he wanted or what he was going to do and showed it to someone whom he had chosen for this purpose."[10] Watts says,

[6] R. J. Coggins and S. P. Re'emi speak of the "implicit idea of judgment" (*Israel among the Nations,* ITC [Grand Rapids: Eerdmans, 1985], 16).

[7] Watts ("Joel, Obadiah, Jonah, Nahum, Habakkuk and Zephaniah," 100) sees the original use of the written "book" as that of a sermon text intended to be preached or a play script. Heflin contends that "committing Nahum's prophecy to writing was merely another step in its eventual placement in the Old Testament canon. It was obviously a step taken for all of the canonical prophetic books, despite the omission of the precise word from their titles" (*Nahum, Habakkuk, Zephaniah, and Haggai,* 35–36).

[8] C. F. Keil, "Nahum," in *The Twelve Minor Prophets 2,* trans. J. Martin (Grand Rapids: Eerdmans, 1949), 9; T. Longman III, "Nahum," in *The Minor Prophets: An Exegetical and Expository Commentary,* ed. T. E. McComiskey (Grand Rapids: Baker, 1993), 786. Rudolph (*Micha-Nahum-Habakuk-Zephanja,* 150) appears to follow the commentary of A. H. Edelkoort that Nahum's book was an underground "Flugschrift" or pamphlet of those in flight, passed from hand to hand because Manasseh's support of Assyria made any word against Assyria dangerous (*Nahum, Habakuk Zephanja* [Amsterdam: 1937], 39–45). E. Achtemeier (*Nahum–Malachi,* INT [Atlanta: John Knox, 1986], 7), Patterson (*Nahum, Habakkuk, Zephaniah,* 21); Maier (*The Book of Nahum,* 144), Heflin (*Nahum, Habakkuk, Zephaniah, and Haggai,* 35–36), and Roberts (*Nahum, Habakkuk, and Zephaniah,* 41) see no reason to assume that "book" means the material was originally written and not spoken. Patterson writes: "The use of the term may simply suggest that Nahum's burdensome vision, whether delivered orally or not, has now under divine inspiration been committed to a permanent record that all may read (cf. Hab. 2:2)."

[9] Heflin, *Nahum, Habakkuk, Zephaniah, and Haggai,* 36.

[10] J. G. McConville, "חזה," *NIDOTTE* 2:58–59. For the word content of vision he refers to 1 Sam 3:1; Ps 89:19. People could seek a vision (Ezek 7:26), but God could prevent prophets from having visions (Lam 2:9; Mic 3:6), and false prophets might have false visions (Jer 14:14; 23:16). Dreams and theophanies are distinct from visions, often related to the nighttime. A. Jepsen notes that of 115 occurrences of the root *chazah,* eighty-six are tied to prophecy (*TWAT* 2:824–25). He agrees that the root refers to word reception and not images as seen in Gen 15:1; 2 Sam 7:4,17; Job 4:13; 33:14–16; Hos 12:11; Jer 14:14; 23:16; Ezek 12:23. This is true in what may be the oldest reference, Num 24:3–4,14–15. Jepsen summarizes his conclusions: It signifies a revelation of God's word received at night during a deep sleep and frequently associated with agitated circumstances. In this visual appearances play no or at best a small role (p. 827).

"In a vision the usual restrictions of reason, time and space recede and the prophet is seized by a compulsion to see and speak in a heightened consciousness what he recognizes to be from God. The excellent poetic form of the book was understood to be a direct result of 'inspiration.'"[11] This word *ḥazôn* is also found in the opening verse of Isaiah and Obadiah (see also Hab 2:2). We are not told how the vision occurred. The prophets described various ways the word of the Lord came to them. The opening verses of Amos and Micah say the prophet "saw" it, using the related verb *ḥāzâ*.

> "This vb. in the context of prophetic perception refers to a revelation of the divine word, usually at night during a deep sleep and sometimes associated with emotional agitations. Prophetic seeing assumes the character of a vision (Ezek 12:27; 13:16). ... Visual manifestation, however, played, at most, a minor role. The emphasis in the revelatory vision was on the revelation of the divine word, which endowed the prophet with special knowledge of divine things, which he had to proclaim (Isa 1:1; 2:1; 13:1; Amos 1:1; Mic 1:1; Hab 1:1)."[12]

The point is that the message was revealed to them by the Lord and was no human invention or imagination (cf. Jer 14:14; 23:16).[13] "This prophetic material is not presented as the product of an ecstatic dervish whose mind swirled with frenzied irrationalities. His *vision* could be laid out as an objective, rational piece of literature with a unified theme embodying elaborate poetic structures."[14]

In Nahum's day Nineveh served as the capital of Assyria, which had dominated the ancient Near East for a century. The armies of Assyria, with their ruthless methods, struck fear in the lives of the people of the time. Nineveh's destruction would make the people of the world clap their hands (Nah 3:19). The people of Israel and Judah especially suffered from the onslaughts of the Assyrians. For this reason Jonah rebelled against going to Nineveh to preach repentance. He and many others wanted Nineveh judged instead of forgiven.

In 732 B.C. Tiglath-pileser's armies had ravaged the northern tribes of Israel. In 722 B.C. Assyria besieged and captured Samaria. The cruel Assyrian policy of exile wreaked social havoc on the Northern Kingdom. The Assyri-

---

[11] Watts, "Joel, Obadiah, Jonah, Nahum, Habakkuk and Zephaniah," 100.

[12] McConville (*NIDOTTE* 2:58), who also notes that a false prophet could have a vision (Zech 10:2; Isa 30:10; Lam 2:14; Ezek 13:6–9,23; 21:34; 22:28). The nighttime reception of the vision that might lead one to think of dreams or images also apparently referred to reception of God's word as Jepsen (*TWAT* 2:826) shows, referring to Job 4:12–16; Mic 3:6; 1 Sam 7:4,17; Gen 15:1; Job 20:8; 33:15; Isa 29:10. Roberts notes that though it originally designated the manner of reception of revelation, it may have come to mean little more than "prophecy" (*Nahum, Habakkuk, and Zephaniah,* 41).

[13] See Patterson, *Nahum, Habakkuk, Zephaniah,* 19.

[14] Robertson, *Nahum, Habakkuk, and Zephaniah,* 55.

ans removed many people from Samaria and exiled them to foreign lands while bringing other captured peoples to settle in the Northern Kingdom. The action effectively ended the possibility of revolt.

During the reign of Manasseh (698/97–642 B.C.) in the Southern Kingdom, Assyria exercised effective control over Judah. Assyrian images filled the temple. Manasseh encouraged worship of Assyrian deities and acquiesced to Assyrian policy. In 663 B.C. Assyria accomplished the unthinkable, conquering and destroying the great Egyptian city of Thebes (No-Amon; Nah 3:8). Assyria seemed invincible. But the defeat of Nineveh in 612 B.C., in fulfillment of Nahum's prophecy, would signal the beginning of the end for Assyria.

Nahum prophesied at the crossroads of history. He proclaimed a word that came to pass, and he called the people to authentic faith in God (cf. Deuteronomy's assessment of a true prophet, Deut 13:1–5; 18:21–22). Nahum demonstrated that he knew the Lord God of Israel. He described God as one who judges the guilty and gives respite to the oppressed. "He fulfilled the highest calling of prophecy in looking beyond the 'facts' of the news to discern and proclaim the intentions of God."[15]

Nahum's "book" encouraged Judah. God delivers the oppressed; he punishes the oppressor. Nahum's message brought hope to a people without hope, announcing the victory of the Lord over the wicked ones. G. A. Smith called the message of Nahum "one great At Last!"[16] Nahum's message demonstrates that the LORD is the Lord of history. He works his will in the world in his own way and according to his own time. For our world the message of Nahum is timely. God is at work. The forces of evil will not conquer all.

I. THE CHARACTER OF GOD (1:2–14)

The greatest question of human history involves knowing God. Who is God? What is he like? In various ways the prophets sought to answer these questions. Isaiah spoke of the Lord as the sovereign Lord of the universe, the holy Creator God who is incomparable in the heavens (Isa 40:9–26). Nahum described God in classic Hebrew terms. He is slow to anger yet judges the guilty. He avenges the oppressed and comforts the powerless.[17]

---

[15] Watts, "Joel, Obadiah, Jonah, Nahum, Habakkuk and Zephaniah," 101.

[16] G. A. Smith, *The Book of the Twelve Prophets,* EBC (London: Hodder & Stoughton, 1898), 2:91.

[17] Maier (*The Book of Nahum,* 60–61) sees the prophet answering three questions uppermost in the minds of his audience: Why will God destroy Nineveh? Can God destroy powerful Nineveh? What will happen to God's children when this consuming wrath flares high? Divine justice makes God destroy (vv. 2–3). His omnipotence shows he can destroy (vv. 4–6). God has promised to prove himself a stronghold for his people (v. 7).

Nahum 1:2–8 is an incomplete acrostic in Hebrew, employing nine of the first eleven letters of the Hebrew alphabet.[18] In a complete acrostic each line, couplet, or stanza begins with the succeeding letter of the alphabet (e.g., Pss 111; 119; 145; Lam 1–4). But the acrostic here is irregular. The first line of v. 2 begins with *aleph,* but the letter *beth* is found only in the second line of v. 3. The fourth, seventh, and tenth letters, *daleth*, *zayin*, and *yod,* are missing. Verse 5a and v. 5b begin with *heh* and *waw*; the second line of v. 6 begins with *heth;* v. 7a, with *tet;* v. 7b, with the conjunctive *waw* followed by *yod;* and v. 8, with *kaph.* It can be argued that v. 9 contains the next two letters *lamedh* and *mem* but in reverse order. Various scholars have attempted to reconstruct the text on the assumption that an original complete acrostic has been corrupted.[19] But the unsatisfying results would suggest that this assumption probably is incorrect and that the text exists essentially as it was written.[20]

---

[18] For a history of study of the acrostic issues, see Maier, *The Book of Nahum,* 52–62, who somewhat overplays the case against an original acrostic as he concludes (p. 57): "This *tour de force* is so arbitrary and the procedures followed by other advocates of acrosticism so divergent that the claim for an original alphabetical arrangement should be completely rejected." Heflin says of the acrostic: "Its presence has not been demonstrated with any assurance. It is quite unlikely that it will ever be reconstructed with certainty—if it exists at all" (*Nahum, Habakkuk, Zephaniah, and Haggai,* 27). Robertson echoes the sentiment: "When five of the eleven proposed instances of alphabetic succession manifest an irregularity, a certain self-restraint in assertions concerning the presence of an acrostic poem seems well-advised. Theories about the possible corruptions of an original acrostic have a great deal to overcome, particularly in view of the solid structures of parallelism within the text as it now stands" (*Nahum, Habakkuk, and Zephaniah,* 58). Baker complains that the "only motivation for change is for the text to fit to a pattern which theoretically arose from the text, making the argumentation circular" (*Nahum, Habakkuk, Zephaniah,* 22).

[19] Longman lists three approaches to the problem: (1) assume a text made corrupt through manuscript copying and transmission and so feel free to emend the text to restore the original acrostic ("Nahum," 2:773). H. Gunkel went so far as to restore an acrostic using all the letters of the Hebrew alphabet and reaching to 2:1,3 ("Nahum 1," *ZAW* 13 [1893]: 223–44); already in 1898 J. Wellhausen showed that the acrostic could not extend beyond 1:8 (*Die kleinen Propheten übersetzt und erkl ärt,* Vol. 5 in *Skizzen und Vorarbeiten,* 3d ed. [1898]). (2) Assume an acrostic never occurred. (3) Recognize a partial acrostic. Longman opts for the last solution.

[20] Recent studies have shown the unity of the acrostic as well as the unity of the Book of Nahum. Cf. S. J. DeVries, "The Acrostic of Nahum in the Jerusalem Liturgy," *VT* 16 (1966): 476–81; D. L. Christensen, "The Acrostic of Nahum Reconsidered," *ZAW* 87 (1975): 17–30; idem, "The Acrostic of Nahum Once Again," *ZAW* 99 [1987]: 409–15; Patterson (*Nahum, Habakkuk, Zephaniah,* 18); and M. E. Travers, "Literary Analysis and the Unity of Nahum," *GTJ* 9 (1988): 45–58. Patterson warns conservative scholars not to reject the acrostic theory altogether. He sees an *aleph* to *kaph* acrostic in vv. 1–10 with two lines for the title, six for *aleph,* two for each of the succeeding letters, and eight lines for *kaph* to balance the opening title and *aleph* section, the weighted lines forming a frame for the psalm. He lets the prescribed letter occur within the line, not necessarily as the first letter of the line. He thus emends the *daleth* line and lets *yodh* be the second letter of its line and *zayin* be the second word of its line.

An acrostic often presents a message of completeness.[21] The proverb concerning the virtuous woman also is an acrostic, probably demonstrating the ideal woman (Prov 31:10–31). An acrostic concerning God might demonstrate the perfection of the Lord who meets the needs of those who call on him. This may have been the prophet's intention. On the other hand, Christensen suggests: "If an entire acrostic conveys completeness, half an acrostic may well be a prophetic way of indicating incompleteness with still more to come. Assyria faces imminent judgment, but only half of what is eventually in store for her."[22] Longman suggests that the chaotic acrostic points to the cosmic upheaval resulting from the appearance of the Divine Warrior.[23]

The chapter takes the form of a descriptive hymn of praise, testifying of the power of the Lord to deliver his people.[24] Somewhat ironically, the hymn praises God for his judgment, for judgment on the enemy brings salvation to God's people. Unlike most hymns, it does not begin with an imperative call to praise, but it does have the cluster of hymnic participles.[25] Like most psalms, the psalm of Nahum could fit most any situation in which the Lord is praised and glorified. Similar statements concerning the Lord are found in Pss 29; 33; 103; 104.

---

[21] W. G. E. Watson, *Classical Hebrew Poetry: A Guide to Its Techniques,* JSOTSup 26 (Sheffield: JSOT, 1986), 198.

[22] D. L. Christensen, "The Acrostic of Nahum Reconsidered," 25. Coggins and Re'emi shrug this argument off: "Not all will find this argument convincing. It is probably better to admit freely that we do not know the circumstances which led to this poem being left in this apparently incomplete state, either by Nahum himself or by the redactors of the material. Certainly at some point the very existence of an acrostic seems to have become obscured, for even to achieve the eleven-line pattern requires some minor textual adjustment" (*Israel among the Nations,* 19). They do see this as the first of several examples of Nahum being willing to adopt cultic forms. Roberts suggests that the prophet borrowed part of a preexisting acrostic he had learned in cultic hymnody (*Nahum, Habakkuk, and Zephaniah,* 48).

[23] Longman, "Nahum," 2:775.

[24] Baker, *Nahum, Habakkuk, Zephaniah,* 26.

[25] R. Smith: "It is a descriptive psalm, not concerned with the attributes of Yahweh, but with his actions. The praise they illicit from his worshipers is response to his intervention in their history" (*Micah–Malachi,* WBC 32 [Waco: Word, 1984], 73). Smith should emphasize that depiction of God's attributes lends to description of action in Nahum 1. He does point to a parallel structure in Psalm 113. Smith goes on to locate the hymn in a New Year festival liturgy. This goes far beyond the evidence of our knowledge of Hebrew worship and does not call on the specific elements of this hymn but on a supposed background for several elements of the hymn in ancient creation and battle of the gods language. Longman compares this hymn to victory hymns such as Psalm 98, whose original function was "to sing the praises of Israel's Warrior in the aftermath of a victory," noting that here "the victory is celebrated before the battle is actually waged. … The prophet could utter the victory shout years before the battle" ("Nahum," 2:788).

1. The Revelation of God (1:2–6)

Although spoken against Nineveh, the message of Nahum does not specifically mention Nineveh until Nah 2:8 (Heb 2:9), although the NIV adds the name Nineveh in several places (1:8,11; 2:1). From the context of the book and from internal considerations, these probably are correct additions, but adding the name (Judah also is added to the text in Nah 1:12) detracts from the force of the description of the Lord. In every age and against every oppressor, the Lord is a jealous and avenging God. All those who oppose the Lord receive the brunt of his wrath.

Much of Nahum's message in this section fits the description of the Lord throughout Israel's history. The description of the Lord as slow to anger and not leaving the guilty unpunished occurred with regularity in the Old Testament. This description apparently formed part of a confessional formula to describe the Lord. The formula with some fuller descriptions added are found in Exod 34:6–7; Num 14:18; Pss 103:8; 86:15; 145:8; Neh 9:17; Joel 2:13; Jonah 4:2.

(1) The Description of God's Being (1:2–3)

2The LORD is a jealous and avenging God;
the LORD takes vengeance and is filled with wrath.
The LORD takes vengeance on his foes
and maintains his wrath against his enemies.
3The LORD is slow to anger and great in power;
the LORD will not leave the guilty unpunished.
His way is in the whirlwind and the storm,
and clouds are the dust of his feet.

1:2 The first two verses of Nahum's message set the tone for the entire book. The book emphasizes the destruction of Nineveh, but it also stresses hope for God's people. Nahum based his hope on the presence of God in the world. The oppressing nation would be removed because of the sovereignty of God. Nahum does not contain a pollyanna-type religion. The prophet was not an unabashed optimist; rather his optimism came because of the character of God. The God who is slow to anger and great in power will not leave his people. He will provide for their needs.

For God not to have overthrown the Assyrians would have meant that he was not true to himself. The character of God means that evil cannot triumph in the world.

> For if God does not destroy the evil human beings have brought into God's good creation, the world can never return to the wholeness he intended for it in the beginning. To divest God of his function as destroyer of wrong is to acquiesce to the present corrupt state of the world—to accept the sinful status quo

and simply to put up with whatever is done by selfish and prideful and corrupted men and women.[26]

In the Hebrew text the participle *nōqēm,* "avenging," is used three times in this verse, once as an adjective and twice as the verb of its clause, "takes vengeance." The participle carries the idea of continuous activity. In West Semitic languages the word group *nqm* "seems to have been preferred for its legal connotations and should, therefore, be associated with the maintenance of justice."[27] This gives a positive connotation to the word, connecting it to lawfulness, justice, and salvation. It is normally God's prerogative at times given to people used as his instruments. To carry out the vengeance inherent in *nqm* one must have proper authority or legitimacy. The use of *nqm* suggests that God is King. Nineveh had failed to acknowledge this and had taken vengeance against the nations into their own hands without proper authority from God.[28] "God's 'vengeance' in the OT can be described as the punitive retribution of God, who, as the sovereign King—faithful to his covenant—stands up for the vindication of his glorious name in a judging and fighting mode, while watching over the maintenance of his justice and acting to save his people."[29] It is never used for blood revenge.[30] Nahum emphasized the work of God to defeat his enemies. "The notion of 'vengeance' is no foreign element in the OT revelation of God, but is a consequence of his holiness (Jer 50:28–29); zeal (Isa 59:18), coupled with his wrath (Mic 5:14), is subordinate to his justice (Isa 63:1,4). Yahweh is the *'el neqamot,* God of vengeance (Ps 94:1)."[31] Patterson points out that "because God is holy, He cannot let sin go unpunished; because only God is perfectly holy and just, as well as all-wise, only He can extract the proper punishment (Ps 94)."[32]

In vengeance God disciplines his people Israel (Lev 26:15; Jer 5:9,29; Isa 1:24–26; 59:17–18). Most often his vengeance is turned against foreign nations who "attempt to reach out for world power in their unlimited lust of power (Isa 47:3; Jer 46:10; 50–51). Such nations injure God's honor (Deut

[26] Achtemeier, *Nahum–Malachi,* 10.

[27] H. G. L. Peels, "נקם," *NIDOTTE* 3:154. The following discussion is based on this work, pp. 154ff., without being repeatedly footnoted.

[28] See C. Armerding, "Habakkuk," EBC 7:461–62.

[29] Peels, *NIDOTTE* 3:154–55.

[30] Here Peels opposes the view of E. Lipinski (*TWAT* 5:602–12), who devotes the greater part of his article to blood revenge. Peels' argument is echoed by Coggins, Re'emi, *Israel among the Nations,* 20.

[31] Peels, *NIDOTTE* 3:155.

[32] Patterson, *Nahum, Habakkuk, Zephaniah,* 25. Maier adds: "Since He is Righteousness in its perfect essence, He must arise to rebuke every violation of His will, especially the abhorrent, deep-rooted evils with which Nineveh has long increased its guilt. … This execution of justice is … the predetermined payment which the Almighty demands for every unforgiven infraction of His Law" (*The Book of Nahum,* 150).

32:26; Mic 5:14) as they seek to destroy his people (Num 31:2; Deut 32:35; Ps 79:10). Vengeance over the enemy is often salvation for God's people (Isa 34:8; 35:4; 59:18; 61:2; 63:4; Jer 51:36). Nahum repeats the root *nqm* three times, perhaps using a Hebrew manner of expressing the superlative to show that "God is the greatest avenger of all; He is the avenger of avengers."[33] Divine vengeance can bring great joy (Ps 58:11; Deut 32:43). The God of vengeance "is a threatening picture only to those who want to be their own gods and rule the earth in their own ways, but to those who trust God it is a comfort and an affirmation that he is truly sovereign."[34] This all means that prayer for vengeance in the Psalms is prayer for the victory of lawfulness and the revelation of God. "The imprecation, in its deepest intention, is a cry for the breakthrough of God's kingdom in liberation and vengeance. Without God's vengeance there is no justice (Ps 58:12) and no future (Deut 32:43; Ps 149:7–9). Thus the New Testament also takes up the call for God's vengeance to replace human vengeance (Rom 12:19; Heb 10:30)."[35]

In Nahum's day the fertility religions held significant influence in Judah. Worshiping the Canaanite gods or worshiping the Lord alongside the Canaanite gods remained a strong possibility. Both Zephaniah and Jeremiah, Nahum's contemporaries, condemned the worship of the fertility gods. So Nahum used three names for the holy God.[36] "El," used in place of the normal generic divine designation Elohim, was the ancient Father of the gods in Canaanite religion. "Baal," a name associated with the Canaanite fertility gods, was often used for the Lord and indicated the Lord's power. The covenant name is Yahweh (The LORD), which alone appears after v. 2. El and Baal are found only in v. 2. "The juxtaposition of these three divine names in one line of poetry is surely a deliberate dramatic device."[37] Nahum is showing that Yahweh functions in any role that someone might be tempted to attribute to one of the Canaanite gods or to any other god.[38] God is jealous and avenges himself against anyone who would occupy his place as God. The fer-

[33] Heflin, *Nahum, Habakkuk, Zephaniah, and Haggai,* 39.

[34] Achtemeier, *Nahum–Malachi,* 8.

[35] Roberts reminds that vengeance "does imply harsh punitive retribution in retaliation for wrongs committed against one. … God will not let injustice win out. … One should beware of any bogus morality that dismisses vengeance as both inappropriate to humans and unworthy of God. … vengeance cannot be discarded without discarding the concern for justice as well" (*Nahum, Habakkuk, and Zephaniah,* 49).

[36] Verse 2 can be translated literally, "El is a jealous and avenging Yahweh; / An avenging Yahweh and Baal of wrath. / An avenging Yahweh to his foes and preserving [wrath] to his enemies." In this context Baal may bring to mind the Canaanite god, but its function in the sentence is as a common noun meaning "lord, master, or husband of."

[37] Coggins and Re'emi, *Israel among the Nations,* 21.

[38] Patterson suggests that the use of Baal, the Canaanite storm god, may be a veiled reference to the Assyrian storm god Hadad (*Nahum, Habakkuk, Zephaniah,* 26).

tility gods, whose worshipers ascribed to them the power of rain and storm, remained powerless while the Lord is great in power.

"*Vengeance* describes the action that emerges from that jealousy," which is "God's attitude toward all rivals."[39] The Lord is a jealous God. Eichrodt went so far as to call jealousy "the basic element in the whole Old Testament idea of God."[40] God's jealousy is "a statement about God's self-respect; he will not be treated as merely one among many, nor will he allow his demands to be ignored; he is God, and he will be acknowledged as God or else."[41] "The image of God's 'jealousy' is of his zealous will driving forward toward his goal of salvation for his earth."[42] Jealousy distinguishes God from all other gods, for he "is not silent or passive in matters of righteousness and truth."[43] In modern society jealousy connotes only an evil idea. One can hardly get away from the image of a crazed person whose jealousy takes the life of another person. The Lord is jealous in the sense that he demands an exclusive relationship, zealously protects that relationship, and desires the worship that belongs to him alone. He cannot be worshiped alongside any other.

Hebrew *qana'* denotes both "jealous" and "zealous," having both "a positive sense (advocate zealously for the benefit of someone else) and a negative sense (bear a grudge against, resent). The various usages share the notion of an intense, energetic state of mind, urging towards action."[44] Zealous jealousy is an essential element in God's personal nature. He expresses it in action against Israel's idolatry, Israel's basic infringement of their covenant with God (Exod 20:5; 34:14; Deut 4:24; 6:15; Josh 24:19; 1 Kgs 14:22; Ps 78:58; Isa 42:8; 48:10; Ezek 8:3–4). Contrary to human jealousy, God does not react immediately against the rival who has taken away his beloved people but against the disloyal covenant partner. "The *qin'a* of God, therefore, differs radically from the envy of gods known from the surrounding areas, which can be aimed at fellow gods or at worshipers."

God's jealousy implies punishment because it is "the self-preservation of the sovereign, unapproachable, holy God." This punishment is not only directed against the beloved Israel. The prophets, including Nahum, direct it

---

[39] Robertson, *Nahum, Habakkuk, and Zephaniah,* 61. Longman notes that relationships with God and with a marriage partner are the only ones in which a person is bound by an exclusive tie and thus the only ones in which jealousy is considered proper ("Nahum," 2:788). Patterson details the biblical use of marriage as an image of God's relationship with his people (*Nahum, Habakkuk, Zephaniah,* 22–24).

[40] W. Eichrodt, *Theology of the Old Testament*, trans. J. A. Baker (Philadelphia: Westminster, 1961), 210, n. 1. For further discussion of this see T. C. Butler, *Joshua,* WBC 7 (Waco: Word, 1983), 275.

[41] Roberts, *Nahum, Habakkuk, and Zephaniah,* 49.

[42] Achtemeier, *Nahum–Malachi,* 8.

[43] Maier, *The Book of Nahum,* 150.

[44] Peels, *NIDOTTE* 3:938. The following discussion of קנא is based on Peels' work.

against the nations that threaten Israel's obedience to the covenant (Isa 42:13; Ezek 36:5–6; 38:19; cp. Zeph 1:18; 3:8). His caring jealousy also becomes "the stimulating force behind the decisive turn in redemptive history: the 'small remnant' and the coming of the Messiah are the result of God's burning love (=*qin'a*) for Israel." Robertson reminds us that "God's jealousy consumes, but it also redeems. Because he is jealous, he cares enough to redeem human beings out of their recalcitrant state."[45]

This vengeful, jealous God is also "wrathful," literally, "a baal of wrath," that is, a master, lord, or husband of wrath. Hebrew has several ways of expressing God's anger or ire.[46] "The Bible speaks unashamedly of Yahweh's passion, presenting him as an intense and passionate Being, fervently interested in the world of humans."[47] Nahum used the term *ḥēmâ,* which can refer to heat or poison. It "emphasizes the inner emotion, the inner fire of anger."[48] God's wrath is always raised by human disobedience.[49] Justice and rationality are the motives for his wrath. God can be angry at human cruelty (Exod 15:1–18; Mic 6:10–16), for "God is passionately concerned about the lives of human beings and whether justice takes place among them."[50] God also takes himself seriously and makes it dangerous for humans not to do so (Exod 32:7–14; Num 22:21–30; cp. Josh 24:19). He shows the rational reasons for his wrath, often in the form of the presentation of legal evidence, so that the people can learn from experience, know what causes God's anger, and avoid such action. God's anger is not the result of frustration or impatience. It has rational causes and results in visible consequences: military defeat, death, sickness, famine, captivity, earthquakes. Such actuality of wrath demonstrated God's power both to his people in their need and to the enemies in their pride and self-sufficiency. It called for faith from God's people. Wrath did not automatically bring destruction and judgment. Human repentance and divine mercy often acted to turn God from his wrath. Such understanding led Israel to pray for God's mercy and to live out God's righteousness.

Nahum does not simply picture God as a being of wrath; he is also master of that wrath, one who reserves it for his enemies. God holds his anger in reserve for the proper occasion to display it to his enemies. "God's government, including His judicial processes, is on schedule, even though to an

---

[45] Robertson, *Nahum, Habakkuk, and Zephaniah,* 61.

[46] B. Baloian counts 518 references to God as the subject of anger in the OT ("Anger," *NIDOTTE* 4:380).

[47] Ibid. Baloian notes that Yahweh's anger can even be celebrated (2 Sam 22:8,9,16; Ps 145:8).

[48] G. Sauer, "חֵמָה *ḥēmâ* excitement," *TLOT* 1:435.

[49] K.-D. Schunck, "חֵמָה *chēmāh,*" *TDOT* 4:464, who notes that Scripture views human wrath negatively but divine wrath positively.

[50] Baloian, *NIDOTTE* 4:381. The following discussion of anger is built on this article.

awaiting mankind His timing may seem to lag."[51] "He displays a calculated control in his dispensing of vengeance. He never gives way to passions, he never exceeds propriety, he never compromises his ultimate goals because of a reactionary response to current provocations. … God's mastery of his wrath is seen most clearly in the endurance by Father and Son in the hour of Christ's crucifixion."[52]

The hymn's opening verse starkly characterizes the God who will show Assyria who truly rules the world. "The three ideas (jealousy, wrath, vengeance) bound together in these opening lines form the groundwork for all of Nahum's prophecy. As a jealous God, Yahweh demands the absolute devotion that the only true and sovereign God deserves; in His righteous wrath, Yahweh alone can and will deal justly with all who sin, even as His justice dictates; and as an avenging God, Yahweh will discipline, defend, or deliver according to the demands of His holiness."[53]

Neither in Nahum's day nor in the modern age will the Lord accept syncretistic worship. God is zealous for the worship that should be directed toward him alone. The holy and avenging God is the Lord of all the earth. Both the people of Judah and the people of Assyria are his people. He maintains sovereignty over the earth. Therefore God brings judgment over the oppressor whether in Israel (Amos 2:6–8) or in Assyria.

1:3 Having opened with the characteristics of God that would dominate his book, Nahum turned to the other side of God. Yes, he was jealous, vengeful, angry. He controlled these, however, for the Lord is slow to anger, literally "long of nose." The expression repeatedly appears in Israel's credos or confessions of faith (Exod 34:6; Num 14:18; Neh 9:17; Joel 2:13; Jon 4:2). The psalmists praise this attribute of God (Pss 86:15; 103:8; 145:8). Peter referred to the same divine characteristic (1 Pet 3:20; 2 Pet 3:15). Such long-suffering patience becomes a fruit of the Spirit characterizing the Christian life (Gal 5:22; cp. 1 Thess 5:14).[54] Though Nahum did not expand on the idea of the Lord's patience, anyone hearing the prophet's words would know of the long-suffering God. Many people mistake the Lord's patience for impotence. Though he is patient, he is not weak. God's hot anger burns against the evildoer, but he is neither fickle nor capricious. He is slow to anger because he is great. He is unthreatened by the bully. Thus he can be slow to respond and patient even with the tyrant. This is good news to God's enemy, not so good news to the one suffering under the enemy's domination. Nahum uses the tra-

---

[51] Patterson, *Nahum, Habakkuk, Zephaniah,* 25. Note his discussion of the meaning of נטר, "reserve, keep, maintain" and *HALOT*'s mention of a possible second root for the verb meaning "to rage" without giving any passages for it. Cf. Longman, "Nahum," 788–89.

[52] Robertson, *Nahum, Habakkuk, and Zephaniah,* 62.

[53] Patterson, *Nahum, Habakkuk, Zephaniah,* 24.

[54] See Patterson, *Nahum, Habakkuk, Zephaniah,* 31.

ditional confession of faith to let Israel know that not only is God slow to anger against their sins but that he is also slow to anger against their enemy's sins. Just as Israel finally saw the Northern Kingdom destroyed by God's anger, so they will ultimately see Assyria destroyed.

God is great in power. Here Nahum creates his own version of Israel's credo statement.[55] In all the passages just listed, "slow to anger" is followed by "abounding in love."[56] Usually a statement about forgiveness is also attached. Nahum points neither to the love nor to the forgiveness of God. Instead, he points to God's power and his reliability in punishing sin. Power (Hb., *kōaḥ*) refers to brute physical power as that which Caleb claimed for himself as he sought to participate in the conquest (Josh 14:11; cp. 17:17; Judg 6:14; 16:5–6,9,15,17,19; Prov 20:29). Israel knew of a time when they had had no strength to face the enemy (Ps 22:15; 2 Chr 20:12; 2 Kgs 19:3; Hos 7:9). They also knew that God was the source of all strength (Deut 8:18; 1 Chr 29:12; Isa 40:29). Isaiah reported how the Assyrian king had boasted of his strength (Isa 10:13).

Nahum had news for the Assyrians and for Judah as they endured Assyrian domination: strength belongs to God and to no one else. God had often displayed that power: in creating the earth (Jer 10:12) and all its inhabitants (Jer 27:5),[57] forming the mountains (Ps 65:6), and calming the sea (Job 26:12). His power redeemed and delivered his people (Exod 32:11; Num 14:13; 2 Kgs 17:36; Isa 50:2; Neh 1:10). No one can stand against God's power (2 Chr 20:6; cp. Job 9:4,19; Ps 33:16). In the plagues God proved that to Pharaoh (Exod 9:16). Now Nahum says that God is going to prove that to Assyria. In so doing he will also prove it to his own people one more time.[58] "God is not only just (Rom 3:26), but as an omnipotent sovereign He has the inherent strength to effect His justice."[59]

The Lord is just. God does not leave the guilty unpunished. Here Nahum employs a legal term, not a ritual one. Again he apparently takes it from an established confessional statement (Exod 34:7; Num 14:18; cp. Jer 30:11; 46:28), perhaps first used to protect the divine name from misuse (Exod 20:7; Deut 5:11). *Nqh* refers to a court decision to let an accused person go free

---

[55] Robertson notes that Nahum wishes to stress the reality of judgment that must arise out of the nature of God (*Nahum, Habakkuk, and Zephaniah,* 63). The Lord may be forgiving and merciful. But the point of no return has been passed by Nineveh, and the only thing left is waiting for the judgment that is sure to come"; cp. Roberts, *Nahum, Habakkuk, and Zephaniah,* 50.

[56] This has caused several commentators to change the Hb. text to חסד without any manuscript warrant (see BHS). Maier (*The Book of Nahum,* 160–61) argues strongly for the present Hb. text.

[57] Thus H. Ringgren (*TWAT* 4:132) can give the basic meaning as "Lebenskraft," "the power of life or living"; A. S. van der Woude ("כֹּחַ *kōaḥ* power," *TLOT* 2:610) gives the similar basic meaning which the translator renders as "vital power."

[58] See R. Wakely, "כֹּחַ," *NIDOTTE* 2:621–31.

[59] Patterson, *Nahum, Habakkuk, Zephaniah,* 29.

unpunished (Exod 21:19; cp. Jer 25:29; 49:12) and often involved divine decision or participation (Num 5:31; 32:22–23; Josh 2:19; 1 Sam 26:9; 2 Sam 3:28). The psalmist can ask God to let him be innocent (Ps 19:13).[60] Whereas Jeremiah has used the confessional statement to remind Israel that they faced punishment for their sins, Nahum used it to reassure Israel that the nations too would have to stand before his bench, let him assume the role of Judge, and watch as he pronounced them guilty and assessed the punishment. Perhaps slow in acting from a human standpoint, God could still be counted on to know the enemy's sin, to bring the enemy to justice, and to exact just punishment.

Nahum goes beyond describing God's characteristics, at least those characteristics that relate to his decision about Nineveh. Nahum also describes God in action. Rudolph sees the central portion of Nahum's psalm (vv. 3b–6) as unfolding the meaning of God as "great in power."[61] He pulls from familiar biblical language and traditions to remind Israel that their God has always been a God who acts as well as a God who is.[62] The LORD is the Lord of nature. "He sweeps down upon the transgressors with the irresistible, unrestrained fury of a death-dealing tornado."[63] The Canaanites ascribed the power of fertility to the Baal gods (Hos 2:5,8) and saw Baal as the rider of the clouds. Israel often pictured Yahweh as the Divine Warrior who rode the clouds to battle (Pss 18:7–15; 68:4–6; cp. Matt 24:30).[64] Nahum indicates that the Lord brings the rain and provides for the revitalizing of the earth. The whirlwind, storm, and the clouds are not gods; they are the willing and obedient servants of the Lord who reigns supreme over nature.[65] "For all their grandeur, however, these mighty forces are dwarfed in the presence of the Lord, whom the highest heavens cannot contain; the tempest is but the disturbance caused as he marches by, and the dark storm clouds are merely dust stirred up by his feet (cf. 1 Kgs 19:11–13; Hab 3:8).[66] Often they symbolize God's judgment (Ps 83:15; Isa 29:6).[67] Robertson reminds us: When the NT depicts the Christ ascending in the clouds and promises his return in the same manner

[60] See C. van Leeuwen, "נצר *nṣr* to guard," *TLOT* 2:763–67.

[61] Rudolph, *Micha, Nahum, Habakuk, Zephanja*, 155.

[62] Cp. Robertson, *Nahum, Habakkuk, and Zephaniah,* 64–65, who concludes: "Yet time and experience ultimately establish the awesome power of God both in nature and history."

[63] Maier, *The Book of Nahum,* 157.

[64] See Longman, "Nahum," 2:789; R. L. Smith, *Micah–Malachi,* 74. Patterson lists the numerous OT passages that have some parallel thought to this depiction of Yahweh, the God of the storms (*Nahum, Habakkuk, Zephaniah,* 30).

[65] W. G. E. Watson, noting the frequency of *hendiadys* in acrostics, suggests translating v. 3d, בְּסוּפָה וּבִשְׂעָרָה דַּרְכּוֹ, "in the tempestuous whirlwind his road" (*Classical Hebrew Poetry: A Guide to Its Techniques,* JSOTSup 26 [Sheffield: JSOT, 1986]).

[66] Armerding, "Habakkuk," 7:462.

[67] Ibid.

(Acts 1:9,11), this picture of the prophet has reached its highest level of fulfillment. Every eye shall be drawn inevitably to him as he comes in glory, bringing destructive judgment on his enemies and blessing to his people."[68]

Robertson points to the combination of contrasting elements in God's character: "He is jealous, full of wrath, and by no means will clear the guilty; yet simultaneously he is good, longsuffering, merciful and gracious, slow to anger, abundant in lovingkindness, and forgiving iniquity, transgression, and sin (Exod 34:6,14; cf. Nah 1:2–3). This combination of elements inherently provides a framework for understanding such comprehensive doctrines as the love of God in providing atonement for sin, the sovereignty of God in working salvation, and the inevitability of the final destruction of sinners."[69]

(2) The Description of God's Actions (1:4–6)

4He rebukes the sea and dries it up;
he makes all the rivers run dry.
Bashan and Carmel wither
and the blossoms of Lebanon fade.
5The mountains quake before him
and the hills melt away.
The earth trembles at his presence,
the world and all who live in it.
6Who can withstand his indignation?
Who can endure his fierce anger?
His wrath is poured out like fire;
the rocks are shattered before him.

1:4 Nahum moves from who God is to what God does. As he does, he mixes the miracles of the past with the events of the present.[70] God subdues to himself all forms of creation. The jealous God can allow no rivals; the all-powerful God triumphs over all creation.

Did Nahum seek to remind us of the work of God in drying up the sea at the time of the exodus (Exod 14:21–22)?[71] "It is characteristic of the whole Bible to be deeply suspicious of the sea; thus, in the Revelation to John part of the promise was that there should be no more sea (Rev 21:1)."[72] Psalm 106:9 uses the word "rebuke" in reference to the crossing of the sea at the

---

[68] Robertson, *Nahum, Habakkuk, and Zephaniah,* 65.

[69] Ibid., 61.

[70] Rudolph, *Micha, Nahum, Habakuk, Zephanja,* 155.

[71] Roberts puts all the weight here on the Canaanite mythological background with the sweeping statement that "there is no clear reference to the exodus in Nahum's use of this mythological language" (*Nahum, Habakkuk, and Zephaniah,* 50). One must ask what would constitute "clear reference"?

[72] Coggins and Re'emi, *Israel among the Nations,* 22.

time of the exodus. Nahum here described God's absolute mastery of the created order (cp. Isa 50:2; 51:10; Ps 66:6). Just as God brought order into the world, he may reverse the order of creation. Rivers and seas were created to hold water. If the omnipotent God so chooses, he may dry up the sea and the rivers. Nineveh was especially vulnerable at this point. Assyria represented a major part of Mesopotamia, the land between the Tigris and Euphrates Rivers. Nineveh was proud that they had harnessed the Khoser River. If God can do these things, what will the wicked do in the day of judgment?

Bashan, Carmel, and Lebanon represented the most luxuriant, fertile areas of Palestine.[73] They were the least likely areas of all of Israel to show the effects of drought, but "in the presence of the terrifying God, these places would quickly wither and fade."[74] These areas contained most of the timber of Palestine. If Lebanon withered,[75] what would happen to the drier areas? Bashan is the northern Transjordan plateau; Carmel is the mountain range running northwestward until it juts into the Mediterranean Sea at Haifa; and Lebanon is the north-south mountain range to the north of Galilee. All these areas would withstand the most devastating drought, but none could stand before the Lord God. Everything comes under subjection to the power of God. "When Yahweh makes war, nature and the very structure of the earth fade and crumble before him."[76]

1:5 Verse 5 may refer to the presence of the Lord in a theophany. Mountains quaking and the earth trembling[77] occur frequently in the theophanies.[78] Both parallel parts of the verse speak of the presence of the Lord.

---

[73] Coggins and Re'emi (ibid., 23–24) point to the three mountains as standing elsewhere in opposition to God and Mount Zion (Bashan, Ps 68:16–16; Carmel, Amos 1:2; Lebanon, Ps 29:5–6). All three mountains appear in Isa 33:9. Longman ("Nahum," 2:790) notes the use of synecdoche here, the three geographical entities standing for the whole earth.

[74] See Heflin, *Nahum, Habakkuk, Zephaniah, and Haggai,* 41; and Maier, *The Book of Nahum,* 163–65, who gives extensive description and biblical references to each place.

[75] Many scholars, including Roberts (*Nahum, Habakkuk, and Zephaniah,* 44) and apparently even Patterson (*Nahum, Habakkuk, Zephaniah,* 18, 34) find ways to change Hb. אמלל, the first word of the second line of v. 4 in Hb., into a form of דלל to create a *daleth* line in the "acrostic." Maier argues vehemently against such a change (*The Book of Nahum,* 165–67).

[76] Longman, "Nahum," 2:790.

[77] Nahum also refers to the earth "melting," the normal meaning of Hb. מוג. Many interpreters use the needs of the context, the translations of the early versions, and parallels like Jer 4:24; Hab 3:6; Ps 18:7 to find a homonym meaning "sway, shake, or surge." See the discussion by Patterson, *Nahum, Habakkuk, Zephaniah,* 35, who sees a final decision being "elusive." Roberts defends "melt" on basis of parallels in Amos 9:13; Pss 65:11; 97:5; Mic 1:4 *(Nahum, Habakkuk, and Zephaniah).*

[78] See also Judg 5:4; Hab 3:6; Mic 1:3–4; Amos 9:5 for apparent theophanies with similar manifestations; Roberts shows mythological backgrounds for the images here (*Nahum, Habakkuk, and Zephaniah,* 51).

Mountains quake "from him." The earth trembles[79] "at his presence." This image of the earthquake is the most terrifying sign of divine power because the most firmly established thing in our experience is suddenly and unexpectedly shaken from its moorings, changing the landscape in a second.[80]

1:6 Verses 4–5 prepare the reader for the rhetorical questions of v. 6,[81] where four Hebrew words[82] express his wrath,[83] which pours out like fire and shatters rocks. "Together with other OT writers (Deut 4:24; 9:3; 32:22; Jer 7:20; 42:18; 44:6; Ezek 22:21; Amos 7:4) Nahum makes the red flames an apt picture of God's consuming wrath. ... even the rocks, typical of that which is hardest and strongest, crack into pieces."[84] Roberts is correct in seeing "the function of all this theophanic imagery is to underscore the awesomeness of Yahweh in order to prepare the way for the prophet's announcement of judgment on the Assyrian enemy."[85] Who indeed can stand before the wrath of the Lord? If the Lord rebukes the sea, dries up Carmel, and strikes fear into all the world, what can the wicked do? His very presence makes the mountains quake and the hills melt away. Those who have seen the power of God know that no one can stand before this awesome God. "If oceans, torrents, plateau countries, and mountain ranges can be wiped out, should Yahweh choose to remove them, what coalition of conquerors, even Assyria itself, can hope to thwart His purposes?"[86]

These verses remind the modern reader of the Book of Nahum that nothing

---

[79] "Trembles" comes from a common Hb. verb נָשָׂא, "lift up, raise up." Interpreters debate its meaning here because it does not have a direct object as is normal with this verb. Thus Longman makes the simple change to the Hb. root נשׁא, "to lay waste, to devastate" ("Nahum," 2:791). Maier summarizes the argument and pleads for the MT, pointing to intransitive uses of the verb in Hos 13:1; Ps 89:10; Hab 1:3 (*The Book of Nahum,* 170–71). Patterson (*Nahum, Habakkuk, Zephaniah,* 35) and Roberts (*Nahum, Habakkuk, and Zephaniah,* 44) likewise defend the MT.

[80] Rudolph, *Micha, Nahum, Habakuk, Zephanja,* 156.

[81] Longman says, "The effect of the rhetorical questions is to make the reader answer the question unconsciously. These questions also add a sarcastic, taunting note to the discussion" ("Nahum," 2:791).

[82] Longman says זַעַם, "indignation," is best translated "curse," reflecting the judicial context here ("Nahum," 2:91).

[83] Many scholars, including Roberts (*Nahum, Habakkuk, and Zephaniah,* 44), make a rather radical textual emendation to gain a *zayin* line in the "acrostic," transposing the first and second words of the line. Maier argues strongly against this: "How could an editor be so stupid or perverse either carelessly or willfully to change the word sequence and to destroy the alphabetical order?" (*The Book of Nahum,* 173–74). Patterson (*Nahum, Habakkuk, Zephaniah,* 18, 36) and Longman ("Nahum," 2:773–75, 791) argue for the MT. Roberts argues: "The corruption in the present form of the text reflects the tendency in textual transmission for unusual word order in poetic texts to be reverted back to more common patterns over the course of time" (*Nahum, Habakkuk, and Zephaniah,* 44).

[84] Patterson, *Nahum, Habakkuk, Zephaniah,* 172–73.

[85] Roberts, *Nahum, Habakkuk, and Zephaniah,* 51.

[86] Maier, *The Book of Nahum,* 165.

can stand before the Lord. We tend to think that our technology can save us and that our scientific research will deliver us from our evil. Nahum knew that the mighty army of Assyria could not stand before God. Our progress and technology stand impotent before the presence of God.

2. The Lord's Care for Judah (1:7–11)

7The LORD is good,
a refuge in times of trouble.
He cares for those who trust in him,
8 but with an overwhelming flood
he will make an end of [Nineveh];
he will pursue his foes into darkness.

9Whatever they plot against the LORD
he will bring to an end;
trouble will not come a second time.
10They will be entangled among thorns
and drunk from their wine;
they will be consumed like dry stubble.
11From you, [O Nineveh,] has one come forth
who plots evil against the LORD
and counsels wickedness.

1:7 "Nahum's text is brutally frank, even terrifying, through the first six verses."[87] God is jealous and avenging; he is slow to anger and great in power. God does command the clouds and the rain; he rebukes the sea and makes the rivers run dry. Who wants to serve such an awesome God? Can you do anything but stand in absolute terror before him? Nahum stops to calm such fears by setting forth "the positive function of God's warring activities."[88] He does so with the same confessional language with which he began (see vv. 2–3). With such confessional language an individual expresses trust in God and pledges obedience to him (Ezra 8:18,22; Pss 34:8; 73:1; 100:4–5; 106:1–3; 107:1–2; 109:21; Lam 3:25).

"The goodness of God forms a basic tenet of Israel's faith" (e.g., 2 Chr 5:13; Pss 25:7–8; 69:16; 118:1,29; 135:3; 136:1; 145:7–9; Jer 33:11)."[89] Such goodness is not abstract but "appears most clearly in his dealings with people"[90] Original sin was doubting the goodness of God (Gen 3:1–7; cp.

[87] Heflin, *Nahum, Habakkuk, Zephaniah, and Haggai,* 43.

[88] Longman, "Nahum," 2:792.

[89] Armerding, "Habakkuk," 7:464. Robertson (*Nahum, Habakkuk, and Zephaniah,* 70) ties "goodness" to God's covenant faithfulness.

[90] C. B. Bridges, Jr. "Good, Goodness," *EDBT,* ed. W. A. Elwell, 305.

Num 14:3,27). The God who brings judgment does so as a part of his goodness.[91] Yes, the same powerful God who does these things is good toward those who fear him.[92] He cares for his people who suffer from the hands of any enemy. Believers in Christ have already "tasted that the Lord is good" (1 Pet 2:3).

"These verses have the menacing ring of a judicial indictment, citing the evidence against the accused. It reveals a conspiracy against the Judge himself, the Lord whose justice and supreme authority have been announced in the preliminary proceedings of vv. 2–6; the outcome of the trial is therefore in no doubt, and the sentence is already anticipated in the charge developed here."[93]

Though vv. 8,11 speak of Nineveh in the NIV text, the Hebrew omits any specific reference to the oppressor, maintaining the mystery of the identity until the proper moment.[94] The NIV obviously is correct in its identification, but the Hebrew text reflects the tenor of the entire passage. The Lord moves against all foes, whether Assyrian, Babylonian, or any of the myriad enemies of the Lord and of his people.

Notice that the Lord's goodness does not preclude his pursuing his foes. He intends to care for his people. The Hebrew term *yd*ʿ (NIV "cares for") means literally "to know." God wants a personal relationship with his people in which they know him as a person, and he knows everything about them. Such knowledge is the basis of a relationship in which he can truly show care and concern (Exod 33:12; Pss 31:7; 91:14; Jer 1:5; 12:3). "This 'knowing' of the Lord must be understood in the full biblical sense of 'loving' with the most intense care (cf. Amos 3:2)."[95] Whatever his foes plot, the Lord will bring to a full end. The day of distress comes to all people, and the Lord is good to all who trust in him. His trusting people need not fear when God comes in the storms and clouds to wreak his vengeance and wrath on

[91] Heflin sees God is good to mean: he does not sin; he is faithful and trustworthy; he keeps his promises. His goodness is often demonstrated in his mercy.

[92] Roberts explains: "God's wrath is simply the reverse side of his goodness, because, as the continuation in v. 8 indicates, it is precisely Yahweh's violent judgment on his enemies that effects the salvation of his friends" (*Nahum, Habakkuk, and Zephaniah,* 52). Achtemeier concludes that "God will be king over us, and it is for us to decide whether he will exercise his kingship in love toward us or in wrath" (*Nahum–Malachi,* 15).

[93] Armerding, "Habakkuk," 7:464.

[94] Longman says the delay in mentioning Nineveh until 2:8 and Judah until 1:15 "gives interest to the story and opens up the book to much broader application" ("Nahum," 2:795). Similarly the indefiniteness of the pronouns builds suspense for the reader.

[95] Robertson, *Nahum, Habakkuk, and Zephaniah,* 70.

Assyria. The Lord is a refuge, literally a "stronghold in the day of distress."[96] The Lord himself is the fortified place where people flee in times of danger (see Neh 8:10; Pss 27:1; 31:2,4; 37:39; Prov 10:29; Isa 25:4; Jer 16:19). Freedom from danger is never part of God's agenda for his people. Protection and security in the midst of danger always is.[97]

The first two words of the last phrase in v. 7 are participles, indicating continual activity. The Lord keeps on knowing the ones who keep on seeking refuge in him.

1:8 The first two words of v. 8 could be connected with v. 7 or v. 8. Translations differ, but no strong reason exists to vary from the NIV translation.[98] This translation indicates the type judgment that will come for those who oppose the Lord and his people. The flood might remind those who read and hear Nahum's message of the destruction of the wicked at the time of Noah's flood. This phrase connects the passage with the earlier reference to God's drying up the sea (Nah 1:4).[99] "The great waters are now seen as God's instrument rather than his enemy."[100] All nature comes under his sovereignty. Maier represents many commentators in taking the flood reference literally and connecting it to other traditions that say floodwaters from the rivers were part of the destruction of Nineveh.[101]

God promised to make a "full end" of his enemies. The Hebrew word for "full end" is found in v. 8 and v. 9. In v. 8 the "full end" refers to "her place," a possible reference to Nineveh.[102] In v. 9 the "full end" indicates that the plots of the enemy will not come to fruition. In both cases the language magnifies the

---

[96] Longman ("Nahum," 2:792) emends the text with the LXX and J. D. Levenson ("Textual and Semantic Notes on Nah. 1:7–8," *VT* 25 [1975]: 792–95), reading לְקוָיו "to those who wait on him" instead of לְמָעוֹז, "refuge." Patterson translates: "Good (better) is Yahweh as (than) a fortress in the day of distress" (*Nahum, Habakkuk, Zephaniah,* 36). He defends the translation on p. 39. Roberts describes an even more complicated textual process with words falling from the Hb. text tradition underlying the MT and other words from the Hb. text tradition underlying the LXX (*Nahum, Habakkuk, and Zephaniah,* 44–45). Thus he restores: *ṭôb yhwh limḥakkāyw māʾôz bĕyôm ṣārāh*. Maier defends the MT (*The Book of Nahum,* 177–78).

[97] See Heflin, *Nahum, Habakkuk, Zephaniah, and Haggai,* 43–44.

[98] Longman argues that the phrase does double duty and should be read with both verses: "God will use the torrents to destroy those who resist him, but he will provide a safe haven for his people so they are not overwhelmed by the waters" ("Nahum," 2:792). Roberts insists that something has dropped from the text, but he makes no firm suggestion as to what dropped (*Nahum, Habakkuk, and Zephaniah,* 45). Maier sees the attempt to restore the *kaph* line of the "acrostic" as the only reason for such a change and concludes that all departures here from the MT are "without cause or benefit" (*The Book of Nahum,* 179).

[99] Longman recalls that עבר "is almost a technical term for God's leading the Israelites across dangerous waters" ("Nahum," 2:793).

[100] Heflin, *Nahum, Habakkuk, Zephaniah, and Haggai,* 105.

[101] Maier, *The Book of Nahum,* 180.

[102] Heflin notes that the subtle "her place" begins specific application of the general theological truth of God as an avenging, wrathful God (*Nahum, Habakkuk, Zephaniah, and Haggai,* 45).

sovereignty of the Lord. He and he alone controls history. "His judgment is an inevitable expression of his goodness on behalf of the victims of evil."[103]

The NIV interprets the Hebrew "her place" to be a reference to Nineveh. In its overall interpretation, this probably is correct.[104] The LXX, followed by the RSV and the GNB, uses "adversaries" or "enemies," a reading that better fits the theological significance of the passage.[105] God moves to overthrow his enemies, whoever they may be and in whatever time period.[106]

The second half of v. 8 repeats the meaning of the first half, a characteristic of Hebrew poetry called parallelism. "Darkness" stands for death (1 Sam 2:9; Job 20:21; Ps 88:12) as well as for the ninth plague (Exod 10:21–22).[107]

1:9 Apparently hymnic language ends here, and prophetic interpretation begins. The following section through 2:2 interweaves judgment against Assyria and salvation for Judah.[108] The prophet continued the thought in the previous verse—God will make a full end of his adversaries. "The crime of these enemies is identified here as settled, premeditated antagonism: they do not stumble into sin but actively 'plot' against the Lord."[109] Is this addressed to Judah or to the enemy?[110] Though the NIV uses "they," the Hebrew indi-

---

[103] Armerding, "Habakkuk," 7:465.

[104] Maier discusses all alternatives and defends the MT (*The Book of Nahum,* 182–83).

[105] Patterson (*Nahum, Habakkuk, Zephaniah,* 40) follows the LXX (τοὺς ἐπεγειρομένους) and emends the Hebrew text, as do Roberts (*Nahum, Habakkuk, and Zephaniah,* 45) and Rudolph (*Micha, Nahum, Habakuk, Zephanja,* 152).

[106] Again Longman argues for a double meaning of the phrase, classifying it as a "Janus parallelism, a word with two entirely different meanings, one suitable for the preceding line, one for the following line" ("Nahum," 2:793). See G. Rendsburg, "Janus Parallelism in Gen 49:26," *JBL* 99 (1980): 291–93; D. T. Tsumura, "Janus Parallelism in Nah 1:8," *JBL* 102 (1983): 109–11.

[107] Patterson sees "darkness" here "as an idiom for God's relentless pursuit that brings punishment in a final extermination of his foes (Isa 8:22; Zeph 1:15)" (*Nahum, Habakkuk, Zephaniah).* Maier sees the darkness as the final days of the Assyrian remnant holding out in Haran (*The Book of Nahum,* 181). Longman wants to make "enemies," not God, the subject, reading, "His enemies chase darkness," a sarcastic taunt of the enemies: "God does not impose judgment upon these people; they are in headlong pursuit of it" ("Nahum," 2:787, 793). Longman speaks of a quantitative balance: judgment (1:9–11); salvation (1:12–13); judgment (1:14); salvation (1:15); judgment (2:1); salvation (2:2). Roberts says parallelism argues against "enemies" as the subject, making it instead an adverbial accusative (*Nahum, Habakkuk, and Zephaniah,* 45).

[108] Longman says the two types of oracles are integrated better here than anywhere else in prophetic literature ("Nahum," 2:795). Roberts says the idiom חשב אל means "plot against" when used with an accusative רע, "evil" (*Nahum, Habakkuk, and Zephaniah,* 46). Since רע does not occur here, the meaning is "to meditate on, reflect on," with no necessary implication of hostile, active plotting against God. Maier takes the argument a step further in saying that Judah is meditating on doubts about God's ability to destroy Assyria (*The Book of Nahum,* 186–88).

[109] Armerding, "Haabakkuk," 7:465.

[110] Roberts (*Nahum, Habakkuk, and Zephaniah,* 52), along with Robertson (*Nahum, Habakkuk, and Zephaniah,* 71–73) and Maier (*The Book of Nahum,* 184, 186–88), suggests that v. 9 speaks to a Judahite audience. He sees the feminine singular in vv. 11–13 as referring to Judah or Jerusalem as a collective, while the masculine plural in v. 9 is the same audience referred to as the citizens of that same city or state.

cates "you" as the best translation. This translation also fits the context (see v. 11) and continues the theme of punishment from the preceding verse.[111] The meaning of the last phrase of the verse is clear. "Oppression will not arise a second time" because the Lord's destruction is complete. God needs only one battle to destroy Nineveh and their hopes. Nineveh will not live to fight another day. They face the end.

1:10 This verse presents major problems for translators,[112] but for the person seeking to focus on the theological message, the idea is clear. "They will be consumed" fits the same theological idea as "he will bring to an end" in the preceding verse. The verse describes a fire destroying dry thorn bushes or the stubble left in the fields after the harvest. The entangled thorn bushes allow the fire to spread over the land until they are all consumed.[113] Those who set themselves against the Lord cannot stand. God will bring total destruction against his enemies.[114] Armerding points out that the keynote of both lines is "helplessness,"[115] while Patterson finds the "point of the comparison in all three seemingly unrelated cases is that of total consumption: the bush by its thorns, the drunkard by his drink, the stubble by fire."[116] God will entirely consume his enemy. Roberts describes the double metaphor here: "Though God's enemies present a formidable front like a thicket of

---

[111] R. L. Smith sees the judgment oracle here addressed to Nineveh and to her patron goddess (*Micah–Malachi,* 77).

[112] W. R. Arnold said: "No man in his senses ever composed it" ("The Composition of Nahum 1:1–2:3," *ZAW* 21 [1901]: 225–65). The problem arises with the two Hebrew words translated in the NIV as "and drunk from their wine" (וּכְסָבְאָם סְבוּאִים). These words have no apparent connection with the remainder of the verse. A literal translation of the verse reads: "For though they be like tangled (*qal* passive participle) thorns, and be drenched (*qal* passive participle) in their drink, they will be wholly consumed as stubble fully dry." The footnotes in BHS illustrate the difficulty of the verse. Many commentators assume dittography with the similar sounding preceding words in the Hebrew text and thus omit the reference to those drenched in their drink. For an example of this see the RSV. The NIV footnote acknowledges the difficulty of the verse. Maier describes the emendations scholars have offered through the years (*The Book of Nahum,* 192–95). Longman expresses the feelings of most exegetes: "For lack of a better alternative it is best to stay with the Masoretic Text" ("Nahum," 2:796). Patterson (*Nahum, Habakkuk, Zephaniah,* 41) and Roberts (*Nahum, Habakkuk, and Zephaniah,* 46) echo the same sentiments. Coggins and Re'emi decide, "These words … seem to have been chosen more on grounds of assonance than to convey a precisely definable message" (*Israel among the Nations,* 28).

[113] Roberts sees the image saying, "Even if God's enemies present a formidable, unapproachable front like a thicket of interwoven thorns, God's destruction of them is still certain" (*Nahum, Habakkuk, and Zephaniah,* 46).

[114] Christensen concluded that the hymn is a "literary masterpiece," containing among other elements "highly developed assonance, repetitive parallelism (v. 2), eight instances of poetic chiasm, poetic inclusion, near perfect metrical balance between cola, and a studied internal balance within the poem" ("The Acrostic of Nahum Reconsidered," 23).

[115] Armerding, "Habakkuk," 7:466.

[116] Patterson, *Nahum, Habakkuk, Zephaniah,* 42.

interwoven thorns, and though their warriors are stout, well-provisioned, and well-liquored—this is not a dried up thicket, but a green one—they will still be devoured like dried-out stubble."[117]

1:11 The prophet addressed the oppressor: "From you has gone out one devising evil." The NIV again identifies the one devising evil as Nineveh, even though the Hebrew omits any such identification. Others interpret this to refer to the Assyrian king Sennacherib (705–681 B.C.), who moved against Jerusalem in 701 B.C. when Hezekiah reigned over Judah (2 Kgs 18:13–19:37).[118]

The prophet considered action against Jerusalem as against the Lord himself. Those who make themselves the enemies of God's people become the enemies of the Lord. This is why our actions toward the needy and oppressed are so important. Selfish actions that take advantage of the weak are a direct attack on the Lord of history. When we devise wicked schemes because it is in our power to do so, we oppose God himself.

The words translated "counsels wickedness" are found in several places in the Old Testament. As Patterson notes: "'One who counsels wickedness' stands in stark contrast to the coming Messiah, who will be a 'wonder of a counselor' (Isa 9:6)."[119] In some places the KJV transliterates the word for "wickedness" *(bĕlîyāʿal)* as "Belial." The sons of Eli were "sons of Belial," a phrase emphasizing their wickedness or worthlessness (1 Sam 2:12). Two "sons of Belial" carried out Jezebel's wicked plan to murder Naboth and to defraud him of his vineyard (2 Kgs 21:10). Later the phrase came to be associated with the wickedness of Satan (2 Cor 6:15).[120] "The context in Scripture for the usage of the term points consistently to a person who is depraved, despicable."[121] Usually this is taken as a reference to Sennach-

---

[117] Roberts, *Nahum, Habakkuk, and Zephaniah,* 46, 53. Maier summarizes: "Entangled thorns are easily destroyed, drunken warriors readily overcome. Therefore the fate of Nineveh is foretold" (*The Book of Nahum*).

[118] Longman sees the participial phrases as referring to "you" and the "he" to God, thus speaking "of God's departure from the sinful city of Nineveh" ("Nahum," 2:797).

[119] Patterson, *Nahum, Habakkuk, Zephaniah,* 47. The same Hebrew participle for "counseling, counselor" appears in both passages—יֹעֵץ.

[120] R. L. Smith notes that בליעל has recently been taken as a proper name for Belial, a demon comparable to Satan in Christian teaching (*Micah–Malachi,* 76). Roberts warns that "there is no clear evidence for this usage (of Belial as a proper name) in the OT" (*Nahum, Habakkuk, and Zephaniah,* 47–48). Smith insists that Belial suggests that "the human enemy, whoever he was, represented the Assyrian goddess."

[121] Robertson, *Nahum, Habakkuk, and Zephaniah,* 74, who points to Deut 13:13; Judg 19:22; 20:13; 1 Sam 2:12ff.; 15:17; 2 Sam 20:1; 1 Kgs 21:10,13; 2 Chr 13:7; Ps 41:8–9. P. D. Wegner says the term "generally refers to a person who has become so wicked and corrupt that he/she is a detriment to society" ("בלה," *NIDOTTE* 1:662). Belial (or Beliar) is used as a proper name in intertestamental literature: *Testament of the Twelve Patriarchs, Jubilees, Ascension of Isaiah, Sybilline Oracles,* and some Qumran documents.

erib,[122] but Robertson is correct in seeing Nahum's usage as broader: "All those wicked kings and leaders of the enemies of God's people who have come forth from Assyria manifest the characteristics of that brutal figure."[123] As Achtemeier says, "It certainly is the title which Nahum gives to evil incarnate in the form of Assyria."[124]

3. The Lord's Word to Judah (1:12–13)

12This is what the LORD says:

"Although they have allies and are numerous,
they will be cut off and pass away.
Although I have afflicted you, [O Judah,]
I will afflict you no more.
13Now I will break their yoke from your neck
and tear your shackles away."

1:12 The "hymn of hate" (vv. 2–8) set the mood by focusing on the all-powerful and all-good God, climaxing in the announcement of the end. The prophetic application of the hymn (vv. 9–11) characterized mysteriously the one whose end (v. 9b) was coming as the wicked, worthless *belial*-type character. Then suddenly the prophet shifts to traditional prophetic language, the true messenger speech announcing judgment (vv. 12–14), before concluding with the victory announcement in v. 15.

"This is what the LORD says" is the messenger formula so often used by prophets to introduce their oracles. This is an oracle of salvation giving Yahweh's intervention, its consequences, and its purpose.[125] It seems to indicate that the prophet saw himself as a messenger sent by the heavenly King with an authoritative message to his subjects.[126] This phrase, particularly associated with the prophets, identifies the Lord as the speaker for the first and only time in Nahum. This is "the prophet's guarantee that the predictions that follow are not merely human conjecture but the *dicta* of the infallible God Himself … the prophet's open declaration that his utterances are inspired, that he, as God's mouthpiece, speaks the message of divine, unchangeable truth."[127]

---

[122] See Maier's detailed application of the verses to Sennacherib's career (*The Book of Nahum,* 196–97).

[123] Robertson, *Nahum, Habakkuk, and Zephaniah,* 75. Heflin sees Belial as "a demonic representative of Ishtar/Nineveh plotting evil against the Lord" (*Nahum, Habakkuk, Zephaniah, and Haggai,* 106).

[124] Achtemeier, *Nahum–Malachi,* 16.

[125] R. L. Smith, *Micah–Malachi,* 78.

[126] See R. M. Hals, *Ezekiel*, FOTL XIX, 361; M. A. Sweeney, *Isaiah 1–39,* FOTL XVI, 546, with bibliography.

[127] Maier, *The Book of Nahum,* 200.

Nahum 1:1–11 speaks about the Lord in the third person. Now the Lord himself speaks first to Judah (vv. 12–13) and then to Nineveh (v. 14).

The Lord spoke to Judah in the second-person feminine singular. In v. 14 the Lord spoke to Nineveh in the same fashion. In v. 15 the Lord addressed Judah by name while referring to Nineveh in the second person in 2:1 (Eng.).[128] Though the NIV identifies Judah as the recipient of the word of the Lord in v. 12 and Nineveh as the recipient in v. 14, the Hebrew text omits both names.

The NIV probably is correct in its identification.[129] The title verse and the text itself indicate that the translators are correct in identifying Nineveh as the oppressor and Judah as the oppressed, but such an identification detracts from the theological message. The Lord marches against all oppressors of the earth. Is Nineveh the only enemy of God? Of course not, but in Nahum, Nineveh is the current enemy. "God will not wait until the enemy degenerates into a weakened state before initiating calamity. Even while they are undiminished in strength, full of arrogant self-confidence, God shall level them to the ground."[130]

Any person or nation aligned against justice and righteousness is the enemy of God. Thus Christian preachers have been correct in using the Book of Nahum to remind tyrants such as Adolf Hitler, Joseph Stalin, and Idi Amin of the Lord's judgment against the oppressor. Believers in every age are heartened to know that "the LORD is good, a refuge in times of trouble" (Nah 1:7).

Any person who uses power, status, or material wealth against the weak in society plants himself as opposed to God. God cares for the widow, the orphan, and the stranger in the land. These three groups, lacking a native-born adult male to stand in the gate, could be disadvantaged. For this reason God commanded his people to stretch out their hands to the poor (Deut 15:9–11) and to protect the weak in society. Can the people of God do any less today? To line up with the power brokers who pummel the weak is to oppose the Lord God.

Verse 12 is difficult to translate. The main question involves the meaning of the phrase following "this is what the LORD says." Whether the meaning is "unscathed" (NIV) or "strong" (RSV, GNB), the basic meaning comes through.[131] In the past Assyria used its force to intimidate and to bully. God

---

[128] The frequent interchange of persons is unusual in Hebrew, prompting A. B. Davidson to question whether v. 13 might not be an interpolation or marginal note (*Nahum, Habakkuk, and Zephaniah,* 29).

[129] See the argument of Maier, *The Book of Nahum,* 207.

[130] Robertson, *Nahum, Habakkuk, and Zephaniah,* 76.

[131] Maier lists thirteen different scholarly readings of the text (*The Book of Nahum,* 203–5). See also the discussion of Patterson, showing the various possibilities of meaning for שלמים: health, completeness, safety, prosperity, be strong, allies (*Nahum, Habakkuk, Zephaniah*). Patterson agrees with the NIV and D. J. Wiseman in reading "allies" ("'Is It Peace?' Covenant and Diplomacy," *VT* 32 [1982]: 311–26).

would not allow such intimidation in the future.[132] The Hebrew term for "cut off"[133] is a term used for the shearing of sheep, making the literal rendering "they shall be mown down" quite appropriate.[134]

"Pass away" reflects the same Hebrew root as the second word in v. 8, translated by NIV there as "overwhelming" but noted as a technical term for God's saving deeds in causing Israel to pass over the sea and the river. Here the verb is singular, whereas the previous verb is plural.[135] Maier interprets this as referring to the wicked counselor or Belial of v. 11.[136] Robertson, in continuity with the salvation history association of the term, sees God as the subject of "pass over." "In the very way in which he 'passed over' in the land of Egypt, so now again he through his agent the death angel shall smite Assyria."[137]

"This verse is the clearest indication that Nahum lived and worked before the decline of Assyria as a military and political state."[138] For more than one hundred years, Nineveh escaped unscathed. In Palestine itself Nineveh marched almost unopposed in 732 B.C. as the Assyrians took Damascus and ravaged the Northern Kingdom (Isa 7:1–17; 9:1–7). In 722 B.C. Assyria took Samaria after a three-year siege. In 701 B.C. Sennacherib boasted of having shut up Hezekiah like a bird in a cage.[139] In 663 B.C. the Assyrians accomplished the unthinkable by driving deep into Egypt to overrun Thebes (Nah 3:8). Could anyone ever stop Assyria? Only the Lord. He promised that the oppressor would cease from his troubling.

The Lord is sovereign over the ends of the earth. Had Nineveh simply

---

[132] BHS also gives the reading of the LXX, "ruler of many waters," and the Syr, "unto the rulers of waters." The problem arises with the proper division of the letters into Hebrew words.

[133] Maier lists seven radical solutions to the problem (*The Book of Nahum,* 205–6). He then equates Hebrew גזז with קשׂשׂ through an "interchange of related consonants." He translates "protected" or "mailed," i.e., covered with mail, or armor. The NASB reading of the text retains the MT as Maier always wants to do and claims to do here, without the consonantal interchange that is as arbitrary as the readings he so designates. Longman ("Nahum," 2:798) calls Maier's suggestion "a very unlikely possibility" (*The Book of Nahum*).

[134] Clark and Hatton, *A Handbook on the Books of Nahum, Habakkuk, and Zephaniah* (New York: United Bible Societies, 1989), 18. The Hebrew term for "pass away" is singular in contrast to the plural verb for "cut down." This has prompted some commentators to refer the verb "pass away" to the man who plotted evil against the Lord in v. 11.

[135] Patterson sees this as intentional, "a change in emphasis from the cutting off of the individual soldiers/units to the resultant demise of the entire army" (*Nahum, Habakkuk, Zephaniah,* 48–49).

[136] Maier, *The Book of Nahum,* 206, but he then argues that the *waw* introducing the next line should be redivided and placed on the preceding עבר, making the verb plural rather than singular. Roberts gives reasons for redividing the Hebrew to make עבר plural (*Nahum, Habakkuk, and Zephaniah,* 47).

[137] Robertson, *Nahum, Habakkuk, and Zephaniah,* 77.

[138] Longman, "Nahum," 2:798.

[139] *ANET.*

imposed its will over Israel and Judah? According to the prophets, Assyria had been allowed to follow its own inclinations to pillage and to plunder the earth. Isaiah knew that the Lord God raised Assyria to punish Israel and Judah (Isa 10:5–15). Because of the sin of Israel and Judah, God allowed the oppressor to use its might against a nation more righteous than itself. To be sure, this concept raised serious theological questions. How could any nation such as Assyria or Babylon be used of God in such a fashion (Hab 1:12–17)? Even though the Lord allowed Assyria to bring judgment on Israel and Judah, the Lord would judge Assyria for its arrogance and blasphemy (Isa 10:12–15).

Although the first half of v. 12 referred to Assyria in the third person, the Lord spoke directly to Judah in the second half of the verse. The Lord had afflicted Judah in the past, but he would afflict them no more.[140] One must not overlook the first part of this statement in a hurry to hear the good news of the second part. God is the afflictor as well as the deliverer from affliction. Assyria had not had a free hand in gaining control of Judah. God had made them his rod of oppression and discipline. Now Assyria would not have a free hand in maintaining control of Judah. God would intervene and deliver his people from affliction by afflicting Assyria. In the place of Judah's judgment would be the demise of the oppressor. "God never is insensitive to the sufferings of his people, although they may think he has forgotten them (Ps 119:6,71)."[141]

1:13 The strong Hebrew word *wĕᶜatâ,* literally "and now," introduces this verse. It "is used in cases of rhetorical analysis to introduce the next point in consequence."[142] Longman notes that it lends "a note of immediacy to it. We should note that the phrase plays an important part in the covenant texts, where it serves as a transition from historical review to the 'statement of substance' (Josh 24:14; 1 Sam 12:13)."[143]

The yoke commonly referred to oppression and forced devotion.[144] Breaking the yoke indicated a freedom from bondage and servitude.[145] People in

---

[140] ענה, "afflict," is found characteristically in the *piel,* a verb stem sometimes indicating intensification. Another meaning for the phrase could make the affliction refer to Nineveh, indicating finality. God would put a full and final end to Assyria (Davidson, *Nahum, Habakkuk, and Zephaniah,* 29).

[141] Robertson, *Nahum, Habakkuk, and Zephaniah,* 77.

[142] Patterson, *Nahum, Habakkuk, Zephaniah,* 49. Waltke and O'Connor (*IBHS* § 39.3.4f) call ועתה a temporal adverb with a logical or emphatic use, "introducing a shift in argumentative tack with a continuity in subject and reference."

[143] Longman, "Nahum," 799.

[144] Maier (*The Book of Nahum,* 208–10) sees a "rod" here rather than a "yoke," this being a picture of the taskmaster raising a rod over the head of a slave (Isa 9:4; 10:5,24; 30:31; Ps 2:9).

[145] In the same general time period as Nahum, the false prophet Hananiah broke Jeremiah's yoke bars to indicate an early return from the Babylonian exile (Jer 28:10–11). See also Isa 10:27 and Ezek 24:27 for similar uses of this idea.

ancient societies unambiguously understood the pictorial language and the meaning of the verse. The yoke referred to the wooden bar placed over the neck of the ox, and the bonds (shackles) indicated the leather straps used to attach the yoke to the ox's neck. (See Isa 52:2; Jer 2:20; 5:5; 30:8; Pss 2:3; 107:14; 116:16.)[146] Breaking the yoke bar and snapping the bonds allowed the animal to go free.[147] God intended to break the yoke and snap the bonds, ending the oppression of Judah. "The heavy weight of slaving long hours with excessive burdens will give way to the glorious liberty of the children of God, each person living in freedom to pursue his own labors to the glory of God."[148]

4. The Lord's Word to Nineveh (1:14)

14The LORD has given a command concerning you, [Nineveh]:
"You will have no descendants to bear your name.
I will destroy the carved images and cast idols
that are in the temple of your gods.
I will prepare your grave,
for you are vile."

1:14 A brief judgment oracle pronounces doom upon the king of Assyria who lived in Nineveh. Again the prophet emphasizes his authority in speaking for God. "The predictions are not the mere expressions of fallible men; they are rather the immovable decrees of the Eternal."[149] Though Nineveh is not mentioned specifically in the Hebrew text, the NIV is obviously correct in identifying it as the immediate oppressor. The use of the singular "you" indicates either the Assyrian king or the nation as a whole.[150]

Nineveh appeared invincible. Its gods appeared able to defeat the gods of the surrounding neighbors. Even the "gods" of Samaria and Jerusalem appeared unable to stand up to the might of the Assyrians. Assyria's arrogance knew no bounds. Isaiah 10:10–11 demonstrates the power and arrogance of the Assyrian leaders: "As my hand has reached to the kingdoms of the idols whose graven images were greater than those of Jerusalem and Samaria, shall I not do to Jerusalem and her idols as I have done to Samaria and her images?" (RSV). "Nahum does not have to prove to anyone that Assyria is worthy of punishment. Its oppressive policies were well known throughout

[146] See Longman, "Nahum," 2:799.

[147] Notice the use of the pronouns in v. 13: "And now I will break his yoke from upon you, and your shackles I will break away."

[148] Robertson, *Nahum, Habakkuk, and Zephaniah,* 78.

[149] Maier, *The Book of Nahum,* 211.

[150] For a fuller discussion of the names "Nineveh" and "Judah" supplied by the NIV text, see the previous discussion under Nah 1:12–13.

the ancient world."[151] Assyria saw itself as invincible. The people of Judah thought of Assyria in the same way, but the Lord commanded that the oppressing nation would die.

This leads to an important discussion of the date of the prophecy of Nahum. Most biblical scholarship has dated Nahum's message shortly before or after 612 B.C., when Nineveh actually fell. From the internal evidence of Nahum, an earlier date seems preferable.[152] The Book of Nahum describes Nineveh as strong and vigorous. Nahum 1:12 describes Nineveh as "unscathed and numerous," while 1:13 describes the yoke of Nineveh as remaining on Judah's neck. Nahum 1:14 pictures Nineveh as a powerful nation that faces an unexpected end from the hand of the Lord.[153] The best date would then be sometime before the eventual fall of Nineveh became apparent. At the zenith of Nineveh's power, Nahum received a message of consolation. God would do his great work. Even the might of Assyria could not stand before the awesome power of the Lord. Nineveh's end would come as a result of the decree of the Lord. Nahum did not describe coincidences; he described the deliberate plan of God to liberate his people and crush the barbaric oppressor.

The command of the Lord is given in three parts. Part one involved the future of the people of Nineveh. One of the most sorrowful tragedies of ancient peoples involved not producing offspring who would carry on the family name (see Deut 7:24; 29:20; 1 Sam 24:21). Even contemporary people feel the sorrow of the end of the family name. God commanded that the Assyrian destruction would be of such magnitude that the nation would have no offspring (lit., "seed") to carry on its name.[154] The memory of one's name was very important to Near Eastern royalty. "Ashurbanipal (669–627 B.C.), the last great king of Assyria, prays that the son who follows him would honor and preserve his name on the building inscriptions he had carved as his own memorial. But the decree of God declares that no one shall survive to maintain his name."[155]

The second part of God's command involved Assyria's worship and its power. God vowed to cut off the idols of Assyria. The NIV adequately distinguishes between the two kinds of idols to be overthrown. The first describes

---

[151] Longman, "Nahum," 2:799.

[152] Maier (*The Book of Nahum,* 209) asks when Judah was truly suffering under Assyria's yoke and finds the answer to be in Manasseh's reign (698–642 B.C.).

[153] For additional discussion of the dating of Nahum's message, see the Introduction.

[154] In the Hebrew text "descendants" is a verb (זרע in the *niphal*) that should be translated, "It shall not be sown from your name any more." BHS suggests a reading based on the Tg. using the verb זכר, "to remember": "Your name will not be remembered again." This change seems unnecessary and may even detract from the force of God's commandment concerning Nineveh.

[155] Robertson, *Nahum, Habakkuk, and Zephaniah,* 79, referring to D. D. Luckenbill, *Ancient Records of Assyria and Babylonia* (New York: Greenwood, 1927), 2:323, no. 838.

images carved from wood or stone while the second indicates metal that is melted and cast into a mold. By using the two words, Nahum referred to all kinds of images or idols. Habakkuk 2:18 also uses the words to refer to idols in general. The Assyrians worshiped a multitude of gods. Ishtar, the goddess of war, and many other deities, including Asshur, Anu, and Shamash, encouraged the Assyrians in their military adventures. Thus the gods of the Assyrians must fall with them. "The judgment of Nineveh's king demanded the destruction of the idolatrous religion on which his authority was founded."[156]

When Assyrian generals overran a city, they often looted the temples of the subjugated peoples, removing the images to Assyria. By doing so they demonstrated the superiority of Assyrian gods over the gods of the vanquished nation. The Lord determined to reverse the process. Removing the images and idols of Assyria powerfully communicated the sovereignty of the Lord God.[157] He alone reigns. Assyrian might would be short-lived. Assyria's power came only by the Lord's decree (see Isa 10:5–15).

The house of Assyria's gods would be stripped of its idols. The last part of the decree indicates the coming death of the Assyrian people. God himself decreed the destruction of Assyria. He would make their grave. The whole people would be killed and buried together because they were "vile." The word for "vile" is a verb indicating lightness or being of no account.[158] "The term "is used of a person's slighted reputation (2 Sam 6:22) and also of actively treating someone contemptuously (2 Sam 19:44; Isa 23:9), hence of cursing (Gen 12:3; 1 Sam 17:43; 2 Sam 16:5)."[159] Some commentators and translations change the Hebrew word to indicate shame or contempt.[160] "Because he [the Assyrian king], in contrast to his self-estimate, is actually of little consequence, God will provide a grave suitable for his true importance."[161] "So poor and wretched will she (Assyria) be that only God who planned her doom will be there to mark out her lowly grave in the ruins of

[156] Armerding, "Habakkuk," 7:468.

[157] Cp. Patterson, *Nahum, Habakkuk, Zephaniah,* 45. Maier notes that the temple of Ishtar in Nineveh looked back on fifteen hundred years of history whose destruction would be a "body blow to Assyrian pride and ancient tradition" (*The Book of Nahum,* 212). Armerding notes that "the statue of Ishtar was discovered, prostrate and headless, amid the ruins of her temple" ("Habakkuk," 7:469).

[158] Watts ("Joel, Obadiah, Jonah, Nahum, Habakkuk and Zephaniah," 108) interprets "light" to mean "too weak," saying the king of Assyria will have "neither time nor strength to build his own tomb, as was the custom of great rulers." Heflin sees "light" as meaning morally deficient (*Nahum, Habakkuk, Zephaniah, and Haggai,* 49).

[159] Patterson, *Nahum, Habakkuk, Zephaniah,* 51.

[160] Note that the NASB uses the word "contemptible." If the reader feels compelled to change the Hebrew to a stronger denunciation, the word "dunghill" is a better alternative. This translation describes the total and final end of those who oppose God. Not only will they die, but the Lord will make their grave a dunghill. This is the ultimate word of destruction.

[161] Smith, *Micah–Malachi,* 79.

the once proud city."[162]

The point of the passage seems to be the complete repudiation of a life opposed to the living Lord. All of the things that make life meaningful would be touched by the power of God. Religion, family, power, and life itself are lost to those who rebel against God. Assyria's false value system eventually brought about its destruction.[163] This important point should not be lost on the modern reader of Nahum. Any nation that lives by its might and opposes God cannot endure. Our emphasis on economics as the salvation of human beings and our belief in political solutions may stand judged as deficient before the Lord God.

5. The Joy of Deliverance (1:15)[164]

15Look, there on the mountains,
the feet of one who brings good news,
who proclaims peace!
Celebrate your festivals, O Judah,
and fulfill your vows.
No more will the wicked invade you;
they will be completely destroyed.

1:15 "In many ways Nahum 1:15 is the book's key verse."[165] The victory announcement comes at last. Having told of the Lord's goodness and his awesome power, Nahum then told of the Lord's ultimate deliverance of the people of Judah. The messenger returns from battle to inform God's people that the Divine Warrior is victorious. Life as usual can return, but not really life as usual—rather, life as usual was supposed to be under God.

The time period of Nahum's prophecy is crucial to the interpretation of the verse. In one sense the meaning is universal. God works. He is the Lord of history who delivers the oppressed and judges the oppressor. In that sense the message of Nahum is timeless. Isaiah 52:7 uses the first part of the verse to announce the return of the captive exiles from Babylon to Jerusalem.[166] For "one who brings good news" the ancient Greek translation (Septuagint) used a participle from *euangelizō,* from which English derived "evangelist." Chris-

[162] Patterson, *Nahum, Habakkuk, Zephaniah,* 45.

[163] J. H. Gailey, Jr., "The Book of Nahum," LBC (Richmond: John Knox, 1962), 45.

[164] Nah 2:1 in Hebrew.

[165] Heflin, *Nahum, Habakkuk, Zephaniah, and Haggai,* 49.

[166] Scholars debate how the two prophets used the same material. Did one borrow from the other, or did each take the material from a common source? Coggins and Re'emi *(Israel among the Nations)* suggest that "speculation whether one prophetic collection may have borrowed from the other is not very profitable, and such a purely mechanical relation in any case seems inherently unlikely. Rather it is more probable that there was a stock of oracular material which might be used as appropriate in the particular circumstances of each collection."

tians understand the powerful spiritual message involved in this passage. God's work has been to proclaim peace *(šālōm)* to all people of all ages. In the Messianic Age, God proclaims the greatest message of peace, that there is the possibility of peace in the restless human spirit.

At the same time the timing of Nahum's message determines the way the book is understood. Did Nahum proclaim this when the word of Nineveh's fall reached the city of Jerusalem? Shortly after the fall of Nineveh, the message would have gone out to the nations that the end of Assyria's dominance was in sight. If this is the case, then shortly before or after Nineveh's fall in 612 B.C. Nahum preached his words of joy to the people.

Would an earlier date be a better alternative? If Nahum's message fits better into an earlier time when Assyria continued to dominate the region, then the death of Ashurbanipal in 627 B.C. might have been the occasion for Nahum's joy.[167] Or Nahum may have readied the people for the good news that would soon come at some unspecified time in the future.

The verse begins with a Hebrew particle *hinnê,* "look." Patterson sees this as calling attention "to key descriptive statements. ... Here it introduces the close of the first portion of the book."[168] Longman says, "It signals a sudden transition from judgment to salvation."[169] Nahum used the entire verse to announce the good news of God's work.[170] The language here describes "God's solemn entry into his sanctuary, an ancient hymnic motif that was clearly of direct relevance to a time of historical threat."[171] In Hebrew thinking, the feet emphasized the messenger. In the Isaiah passage (52:7) the prophet described the feet as lovely, thus indicating the joy and happiness the messenger brought. The mountains surrounded Jerusalem. Anyone bringing a message would necessarily travel over the mountains to deliver the good news. The messenger brought good tidings and proclaimed peace. These are parallel statements that essentially mean the same.[172]

"The Hebrew word for 'peace' is one of the most remarkable words in that ancient biblical language. Its meaning is much more profound than simply the cessation of war. It refers to wholeness, completeness, total well-being."[173] In most cases peace means a quality of life. Peace is that which

---

[167] Armerding points out that the reigns of Amon and Manasseh involved suppression of true Israelite religion. "This provides further evidence for dating Nahum's prophecy toward the middle of the seventh century" ("Habakkuk," 7:469).

[168] Patterson, *Nahum, Habakkuk, Zephaniah,* 51.

[169] Longman, "Nahum," 800.

[170] Good news often includes peace (Isa 52:7; Luke 2:10,14; Acts 10:36).

[171] Coggins and Re'emi, *Israel among the Nations,* 33.

[172] In the Hebrew "one who brings good news, who proclaims peace" is מְבַשֵּׂר מַשְׁמִיעַ שָׁלוֹם. Both verbs are participles, indicating continuous action. מְבַשֵּׂר is *piel* from בשׂר, "bring good news, herald good tidings"; מַשְׁמִיעַ is *hiphil* from שׁמע, "hear," and so "cause to hear."

[173] Heflin, *Nahum, Habakkuk, Zephaniah, and Haggai,* 49.

you wish for a bride and groom on their wedding day. When you offer "all the good things of life" to a young couple, you are offering the Hebrew idea of *shalom*. In the present verse peace is the cessation of the oppressor. Judah had been at peace for a long time. That peace was the problem rather than the solution. Peace had been imposed by the Assyrians. As long as Judah paid its tribute, swore allegiance to the king of Assyria, and did not instigate rebellion (as would be the case with the removal of Assyrian images from the temple in Jerusalem), Judah could live in peace. God offered something far more meaningful to the people of Judah. He promised to bring peace with justice. God's peace meant that a wholeness would be returned to the land.

But how would Jerusalem respond to this messenger and the unexpected news of victory over invincible Assyria? The messenger's announcement leaves the decision in the people's hands. Can they possibly believe the news they so desperately want to hear, news that so long has remained in the realm of daydreams? Paul took up the message in Rom 10:14–15, probably using Isaiah's version. He reminded us of the heart of the gospel: "God's people are not charged with the responsibility of accomplishing their own deliverance. Instead, they are informed they must *believe* what has been reported to them as an act of God on their behalf."[174]

"As Nineveh's flourishing religion was to be buried, so the worship of oppressed Judah would be resurrected."[175] Nahum called Israel to celebration, a celebration based on the belief that the announced victory had actually occurred. Celebration was not a wild victory party. Celebration was a return to God's house to keep God's worship festivals in the way God commanded. "Neglect of the festivals and the vows was the same as neglecting Yahweh."[176] In this way "they shall respond to redemption by renewed consecration to the Lord. This celebration shall have no hangovers or sober regrets."[177]

Keeping their feasts may indicate that the people could now return to the practice of their religion. "Judah now had religious freedom, and Nahum wanted that freedom exercised responsibly."[178] Fulfilling their vows meant that their pleas for mercy had been heard. As Maier says, "The deliverance comes from God; He must be thanked."[179] Why is it easier to beg for mercy than to offer sincere thanksgiving to God? In every age the people of God must be reminded to "remember the LORD your God, for it is he who gives you the ability to produce wealth" (Deut 8:18).

---

[174] Robertson, *Nahum, Habakkuk, and Zephaniah,* 83.

[175] Armerding, "Habakkuk," 7:469.

[176] Longman, "Nahum," 2:800.

[177] Robertson, *Nahum, Habakkuk, and Zephaniah,* 84–85.

[178] Heflin, *Nahum, Habakkuk, Zephaniah, and Haggai,* 50.

[179] Maier, *The Book of Nahum,* 218.

God promised the cessation of hostility and the restoration of autonomy to the people of Judah. No more would the wicked invade the people of Judah. They would be completely cut off, a word of assurance that Judah's subservience to Assyria would soon end. Literally, the Hebrew reads, "For not again still to pass over you Belial.[180] "The tyrannical tool of Satan situated on Assyria's throne never shall be seen again. His overthrow is absolutely permanent."[181] Yes, Assyria did fall, and Assyria did not trouble Judah again.

The verse is a powerful reminder of the goodness of God in all ages. The Christian cannot help but be reminded of the beauty of the messenger who proclaims the newness of life in Christ. The message had an urgency about it because it proclaimed the timeless message of peace and good tidings. Yet the message referred to historical events that were fulfilled soon after the message of Nahum.

---

[180] Hebrew root עבר, which has appeared in vv. 7, 12 to recall God's saving acts: the death angel passing over, the people passing over the Red Sea and the Jordan River. On Belial see the comments and notes on v. 11.

[181] Robertson, *Nahum, Habakkuk, and Zephaniah,* 85.

II. THE LORD'S JUDGMENT OF NINEVEH (2:1–13)
1. Warning to Nineveh (2:1)
2. Comfort to Judah (2:2)
3. Description of Nineveh's Attackers (2:3–5)
4. Description of Nineveh's Defeat (2:6–10)
5. The Hopelessness of Nineveh (2:11–12)
6. The Lord Fights against Nineveh (2:13)

II. THE LORD'S JUDGMENT OF NINEVEH (2:1–13)

Chapters 2 and 3 bring us extraordinary poetic images of battle preparations, battle engagement, and battle defeat. Bible students looking for deeper theological secrets and intricate theological messages face disappointment. In these chapters Nahum offers basically one truth: "I am against you" (2:13; 3:5). Much of the rest is poetic description, but badly needed poetic description. The beauty of the poetry combines with the clarity of the brutal imagery to impress as no other form of language could the message of doom for Assyria and hope for Judah. "The form of the writing was just the kind of material which might have functioned well in stirring up the faith of an oppressed people."[1]

For more than a hundred years (since the time of Tiglath-pileser) Nineveh and the entire Assyrian civilization lived on the plundering of the nations by its armies.[2] Though Nineveh had lived in relative security and wealth (Nah 2:11–12), God vowed to end the reign of the oppressor.

The chapter envisions the attack against Nineveh and its defeat, but the prophet spoke not to Nineveh but for the benefit of Jerusalem. Although we cannot rule out Nahum's message reaching Nineveh, the primary audience for his preaching was the oppressed peoples who suffered under the domination of Assyria. The defeat of Nineveh meant the restoration of Jacob (Nah 2:2). Nahum spoke primarily to the people of Jerusalem and Judah, but he had a message for anyone who would heed the word of the Lord God of Israel. Nahum 2 functions as a vivid and effective picture of the coming destruction. The chapter underscores the message of hope and redemption given in the

[1] O. P. Robertson, *The Books of Nahum, Habakkuk, and Zephaniah,* NICOT (Grand Rapids: Eerdmans, 1990), 86.

[2] See Introduction.

preceding chapter.

Nahum 2 depicts the coming siege and fall of Nineveh. The prophet spoke as if the attacker was at the gates of the city, waiting for the command to advance and attack. The prophet also spoke of the frantic attempts by the king and the people to protect themselves, attempts doomed to failure. Though they had been handpicked, the troops would stumble and fall. Why? "I am against you."

Chapters 2–3 paint the same picture of destruction with different literary forms on its linguistic palette. Chapter 2 begins with a contrast between the fate of Nineveh (v. 1) and the fate of Israel (v. 2). Then in brief, staccato form battle preparations, battle technique, and battle dismay pour out (vv. 3–10). A rhetorical question raises a familiar metaphor of lions (vv. 11–12) to prepare for the concluding divine pronouncement of doom (v. 13). A woe oracle (3:1) reinforces the preceding pronouncement of doom and introduces another poetic narrative filled with the sights and sounds of battle (3:2–3) and concludes with an explanation of the cause of battle (v. 4). A repeated, extended pronouncement of doom (vv. 5–7) leads to a rhetorical question (vv. 8–9). This serves to introduce the historical example (v. 10) that makes believable the following prophecy of judgment (vv. 11–17). The prophecy concludes with a direct address to the Assyrian king pronouncing his final defeat and the international joy it brings.

1. Warning to Nineveh (2:1)

[1]An attacker advances against you, [Nineveh].
Guard the fortress,
watch the road,
brace yourselves,
marshal all your strength!

2:1 In this chapter the prophet warned the city of the coming destruction "with biting irony. ... In v. 2 Judah has been plundered; but in v. 9 Nineveh suffers that fate. In v. 2 the 'majesty' of Judah has been lost; but in v. 9 Nineveh's glory (Hb.: her treasure from booty and tribute) is stripped away. In v. 9 there is no end of Nineveh's treasures; but in v. 10 she is 'emptiness,' desolated and wasted' (Hb.). In v. 12 the lion has filled his cave with prey; but in v. 13 the prey is cut off. And finally, the end of the oracle contrasts with the end of the preceding one. ... God will bring about a complete reversal of the fortunes of Nineveh, for God is Lord over her and shatterer of her pride and life."[3]

---

[3]E. Achtemeier, *Nahum–Malachi, INT* (Atlanta: John Knox, 1986), 21–22. R. J. Coggins and S. P. Re'emi also trace the irony in the chapter (*Israel among the Nations,* ITC [Grand Rapids: Eerdmans, 1985)], 35–37).

At least two points should be made about this verse. First, Nahum did not want to warn Nineveh. Like almost everyone in Judah, he looked and hoped for the destruction of Nineveh. Second, although the verse is addressed to the oppressor (Nineveh was not named by the prophet until 2:8), the prophet intended the main idea of the message to be received by Judah rather than Assyria. These points fit much of what we know about Hebrew prophecy. The prophets of Israel spoke God's word to God's people. Although they often spoke about the foreign nations,[4] the force of their message was directed toward Israel.

The verse demonstrates the certainty of Nineveh's destruction. If Nahum actually proclaimed this message several years prior to Nineveh's fall in 612 B.C.,[5] then the form of this verse and succeeding verses in chap. 2 underscore the prophet's conviction that God indeed intended to defeat Nineveh and comfort Judah.

The verse consists of an opening phrase dominated by a participle in Hebrew, followed by four verb forms with the force of imperatives.[6] The "you" in the first line of the verse is feminine. The word for "city" in Hebrew is feminine. Nahum does not identify the "attacker" (or "one scattering/shattering").[7] The participle may refer to the use of battering rams to attack the gates of the city. A similar use of the battering ram may lie at the background of v. 5. But, as Heflin notes, the Hebrew word for "attacker" or "shatterer" as a noun and as a verb almost always refers to God in the Old Testament."[8] "The implication is that the human army soon to attack Nineveh is in Yahweh's employ."[9]

When Nineveh fell in 612 B.C., the shatterer was a coalition of Medes and

---

[4] Note the oracles against the foreign nations in Isaiah, Jeremiah, and Ezekiel.

[5] See Introduction.

[6] The first phrase is actually a *qal* infinitive absolute that functions as a command. The last three phrases contain verbs that are *piel* imperatives. For grammatical explanations see C. E. Armerding, "Habakkuk," EBC 7:473.

[7] Armerding ("Habakkuk," 7:472) points out that this is a common figure for a victorious king (Ps 68:1; Isa 24:1; Jer 52:8). T. Longman III says we know from history that the attacker or scatterer proved to be the armies of the Medes and Babylonians. He modifies this to say: "We must leave open the possibility, however, that the 'scatterer' refers not to these nations, but to God himself, who is the Divine Warrior. Behind the battles of the nations it is he who will destroy Nineveh (Ezek 29:12)" ("Nahum," in *The Minor Prophets: An Exegetical and Expository Commentary,* ed. T. E. McComiskey [Grand Rapids: Baker, 1993], 801). R. D. Patterson says: "Because the Assyrians would survive to fight two still later campaigns (Haran, 609 B.C.; Carchemish, 605 B.C.), 'scatterer' (cf. 3:18) is an appropriate designation for Nineveh's attackers" (*Nahum, Habakkuk, Zephaniah,* WEC [Chicago: Moody, 1991], 54).

[8] J. N. B. Heflin, *Nahum, Habakkuk, Zephaniah, and Haggai,* BSC (Grand Rapids: Zondervan, 1985), 52.

[9] J. J. M. Roberts, *Nahum, Habakkuk, and Zephaniah: A Commentary,* OTL (Louisville: Westminster/John Knox, 1991), 64.

Babylonians under Cyaxeres and Nebuchadnezzar. We do not know whether or not Nahum knew this. For Nahum the ultimate shatterer was God himself. No matter who the human agent of destruction might be, God rendered the Assyrians powerless. He planned to rescue the peoples of the world and particularly to rescue his chosen people from the iron hand of the oppressor.

God had decreed the destruction of Nineveh. The only thing the people of Nineveh could do was attempt to defend themselves. Human nature demands that citizens fight to defend their lives and their property even when the cause is hopeless.

"Nahum's admonitions are probably to be understood as irony, perhaps with a touch of sarcasm."[10] The people should defend themselves. "Guard the fortress" referred to the practice of placing men on the city walls to defend the city. Some translations use the word "ramparts," a possible meaning in Hebrew. The ramparts described the top of the walls of the city.

Nahum also counseled the leaders of Nineveh to "watch the road" for the coming attackers.[11] Nahum knew that the attack would be quick and decisive. "Brace yourselves" in the NIV means "to gird the loins," a phrase used often in the Bible to indicate physical activity. Girding the loins meant to tie the long robes around the thigh or waist in order to run, to work, or in this case to fight. The forcefulness of the attack and the might of the enemy meant that the people of Nineveh would have to "marshal all your strength!"

"Like a sentinel calling from a watchtower, Nahum warns the Ninevites to prepare for battle. He knows, however, that the warning is of no avail. No human force can stand against the power of God."[12]

2. Comfort to Judah (2:2)

[2]The LORD will restore the splendor of Jacob
like the splendor of Israel,
though destroyers have laid them waste
and have ruined their vines.

2:2 Here is Nahum's final word directed overtly to Judah. From this verse all else flows. Because God has decided to restore Judah's splendor, the battle must be engaged. Nineveh's splendor must vanish from the earth. Destruction for Nineveh meant comfort for Judah.

Some commentators question the significance of this verse in a section dealing with a warning to Nineveh of the impending doom. The verse is often

[10] Patterson, *Nahum, Habakkuk, Zephaniah,* 55.

[11] Longman notes the contrast with 1:15, where Judah is to look for the messenger of victory and peace, whereas here Assyria must look for the enemy coming to destroy ("Nahum," 801).

[12] Ibid., 802.

seen as an aside or as possibly being out of place in the text.[13] Though the verse does interrupt the flow of the imminent attack on Nineveh, it does not interrupt the theological message of the book or the chapter. "The pause seems to heighten the tension for Nineveh."[14] The message of the book is one of comfort to Judah by ending the oppression of Nineveh. Jacob will be restored because Nineveh's oppression will end. In fact, all the peoples will feel restoration at the fall of the oppressor. When the peoples hear the word of Assyria's demise, they will clap their hands, for all had felt the cruelty of the Assyrian power (Nah 3:19).

The NIV interprets (correctly) the first phrase of the verse as a future event the Lord was about to effect. However, the Hebrew verb "restore" is a prophetic perfect, a grammatical form the prophets often used to show that the prophet felt so sure of the coming restoration that he spoke of it as already having occurred. The prophets knew that the Lord does his work among his people. If God purposed to restore Israel, then the people could count the act as an accomplished fact. Though the work of God might occur far in the future, God would do his work of restoration as he determined to do.

Of whom did the prophet speak as he named Jacob and Israel?[15] Should we understand these names as synonymous parallelism, thus equating the names? Or do they refer to the north and south or south and north or only to the south?[16] Each way is possible, but the latter interpretation appears to fit

---

[13] BHS and many commentators suggest that Nah 2:3 be inserted at the end of chap. 1. Many commentators feel that moving the verse better fits the nature of chap. 1 and therefore does not interrupt the flow of chap. 2. For a fuller discussion of the merits of transposing the verse, see Roberts, *Nahum, Habakkuk, and Zephaniah,* 64–65.

[14] Heflin, *Nahum, Habakkuk, Zephaniah, and Haggai,* 51.

[15] These three options seem possible, with each having biblical warrant for the interpretation. (1) The two terms may refer to the entire nation. The GNB seems to take this interpretation with the translation, "The Lord is about to restore the glory of Israel, as it was before her enemies plundered her." The GNB refers only to Israel, implying that the entire nation will be restored. (2) Jacob may refer to the north and Israel to the south. This interpretation is supported by passages such as Amos 6:8; 8:7. The interpretation apparently would see the promise as referring to the Northern Kingdom destroyed by the Assyrians in 722 B.C. If this is correct, to whom would the promise be given? Nahum spoke to the people of about 627 B.C. Prophets normally spoke messages intensely relevant to the people of the day. (3) The third interpretation seems to fit the passage as well as the message of Nahum. Jacob referred to the south, while Israel referred to the north. A number of biblical references support this usage: Isa 43:1; 44:1; 46:3; Obad 18. God spoke to the Southern Kingdom. He promised to restore the Southern Kingdom as he had previously promised to restore the Northern Kingdom. See D. J. Clark and H. A. Hatton, *A Handbook on the Books of Nahum, Habakkuk, and Zephaniah* (New York: United Bible Societies, 1989), 27.

[16] Armerding thinks "evidently 'Judah' is envisaged here (cf. 1:2–13,15), though it is possible that the resurrection of Israel as a whole is promised (cf. Isa 9:1–8; 11:10–16)" ("Habakkuk," 7:472). Longman sees "Jacob" and "Israel" as "honorific titles of Judah" ("Nahum," 802). Patterson points this forward to the final eschatological victory of all Israel (*Nahum, Habakkuk, Zephaniah,* 55).

the context of the chapter as well as the theological message of the Book of Nahum. Nahum addressed the Southern Kingdom ca. 627 B.C. with the hopeful words for the people to whom he spoke. As God promised to deliver the now-defunct Northern Kingdom (Hos 14:5–7), he also promised to deliver the viable but weak Southern Kingdom.[17]

The word "splendor" *(gĕʾôn)* refers to the former majesty of the nation Israel. The Hebrew word means "height" (Job 38:11) and thus eminence either as pride (Exod 15:7; Isa 24:14; Mic 5:3) or as presumption (Jer 13:9; Ezek 16:56; Hos 5:7; 7:10).[18] By 627 B.C. Israel had fallen to the Assyrians almost a century earlier, and Judah consisted of a small area surrounding Jerusalem. The former splendor of the nation now consisted only of ancient memories. With the ascendance of Josiah to the throne of Judah in 627 B.C. and the corresponding death of Ashurbanipal of Assyria, a series of events began that saw the literal return of much of the glory of Israel.

Some translations use the word "vine" in place of the word "splendor."[19] The two words are the same except for one Hebrew letter. Hebrew parallelism would normally call for "vine" since the last phrase literally reads "and they have ruined their branches." "Branches" and "vines" would be parallel. The NIV attempts to follow the Hebrew but also to emphasize the importance of the imagery of the vine by translating "and have ruined their vines."[20]

The imagery of the vine is present in the use of the word "branches" in the last section of the verse. In the Old Testament the vine often indicated the nation Israel (Gen 49:22; Isa 5:1–7; Jer 2:21; 12:10; Ps 80:8–16). "The overall theme of this verse is not really changed whichever wording is followed" since the difference is between a figurative expression ("vine") or a literal one ("splendor").[21]

3. Description of Nineveh's Attackers (2:3–5)

[3]The shields of his soldiers are red;
the warriors are clad in scarlet.

---

[17] Heflin prefers to see a picture of the historical Jacob being played on here. "Jacob the patriarch was a deceiver; when converted, he became Israel. … What God may be saying here is that through the Assyrian crisis He has been working to bring Judah (living as Jacob the sinner) back to the status of Israel (one in right relationship with God)" (*Nahum, Habakkuk, Zephaniah, and Haggai,* 53).

[18] *HALOT* 1:169. *DCH* (2:293) includes "magnificence" among the definitions. It is especially used of the "splendor of the southern region of the Jordan with its lush vegetation, where lions lurked" (I. Cornelius, "גָּאוֹן," *NIDOTTE* 1:789).

[19] See especially the JB and Moffatt. This involves an unsupported textual emendation of גאון to גפן. Against this see Patterson, *Nahum, Habakkuk, Zephaniah,* 58.

[20] Longman sees "songs" as another possible translation, indicating the cessation of singing during battle. He compares Isa 24 ("Nahum," 802).

[21] Clark and Hatton, *Nahum, Habakkuk, and Zephaniah,* 27.

The metal on the chariots flashes
on the day they are made ready;
the spears of pine are brandished.
[4]The chariots storm through the streets,
rushing back and forth through the squares.
They look like flaming torches;
they dart about like lightning.

[5]He summons his picked troops,
yet they stumble on their way.
They dash to the city wall;
the protective shield is put in place.

2:3 After the section dealing with the comforting of Judah as the promised comforting of Israel, the prophet returned to the theme of the destruction of Nineveh. In graphic terms Nahum described the swiftness of the attack and the decisive defeat of Nineveh.[22] The attackers "display total utilization of the most modern, most sophisticated strategies of warfare."[23]

Details given by the prophet have led some commentators to deduce that Nahum's words must have come from a time after the fall of Nineveh in 612 B.C. How could someone describe the battle in such a vivid way?[24] The view of this commentary is that Nahum spoke the words of Nineveh's demise long before the actual fall of the city. No doubt Nahum knew of warfare and the swiftness of the armies of the world. In fact, Nahum describes the battle scene in more graphic detail than even the actual account given by the Babylonians.[25] Poetry generally allows for greater imagination and more graphic detail than prose. One would expect the prophet to use his poetic ability and the people's imagination to drive home the decisive nature of the Assyrian defeat and the ultimate deliverance of the people of Israel. Nahum even described the shouts of the attackers as they plundered the city. By vividly describing the attack on Nineveh, Nahum struck a decisive blow against the idea of Assyrian invincibility. Until Nahum, few people in Jerusalem dared believe that God might finally deliver Israel.

Parts or all of this section could refer to either the attackers or to the defenders of the city.[26] The KJV appears to assume that the first verses (2:3–

---

[22] For poetic, thematic, and linguistic features holding 2:3–3:7 together as a unit, see Armerding, "Habakkuk," 7:473–74.

[23] Robertson, *Nahum, Habakkuk, and Zephaniah,* 88, who calls this "total domination of the terrain."

[24] Coggins and Re'emi note that the poet may well be using conventional poetic language for enemy armies rather than describing the appearance and tactics of a particular one (*Israel among the Nations,* 37). They point to Ezek 23:6 for comparison.

[25] *ANET,* 303–6. See also R. L. Smith, *Micah–Malachi,* 83.

[26] Patterson (*Nahum, Habakkuk, Zephaniah,* 61–62) notes rhetorical tools used to show v. 4 is a hinge binding v. 3 with what follows and analyzes the section as "the enemy's assembling of his forces (v. 3), the initial advance (v. 4), and the all-out attack (vv. 5–6) and its aftermath (vv. 7–10)."

4) refer to the attackers while v. 5 implies the defense of the city (see "defence" in KJV for "protective shield" in NIV). Each verse should be examined to determine the best way to interpret the attack on the city.

Verses 3–4 describe the frightening appearance of the enemy attackers. Both verses seem to refer to those attacking the city rather than those defending the city. The Hebrew text seems definitely to identify the army of v. 3 with those attacking the city. "His soldiers" does not have an antecedent unless "his" refers back to v. 1, where the attacker advances against the city.

The city's attackers wore red uniforms and carried red shields. The two words for red are different, as indicated in the NIV. Both the Medes and the Babylonians were associated with red (Ezek 23:14). Whether the shields looked red because they were covered with dyed leather or because the shields were made of copper and reflected the sun is unknown.[27] The point is that the attackers looked powerful and invincible. Nahum probably foretold of the attack by using images that were known by the people of Judah. In their minds they could see the attackers besieging the city of Nineveh and finally overcoming the Assyrians. Nahum wanted to convey the certainty of God's deliverance to the people of Judah.

Nahum continued the thought of the coming destruction by describing the chariots' swift and relentless advance. The meaning of the chariot's advance is without doubt, but the precise meaning of the phrase is unclear. The word for "metal" is used only one time in the Hebrew Bible, making its exact meaning difficult to discern. The NIV translators and others think the word referred to the material from which the chariots were made. Others think of a word meaning "flash." Compare the RSV: "The chariots flash like flame when mustered in array."[28]

Chariots referred to light two-wheeled carts used in battle and pulled by horses. They usually carried two or three soldiers, one to drive and the others to fight. They proved to be effective in relatively flat terrain but ineffective in the hills of Judah. They nevertheless proved frightening to people because of their swiftness. "On the day they are made ready" refers to the attackers pulling the chariots into line (NEB) or generally preparing for attack.[29]

---

[27] J. D. Charles adds two additional solutions to the meaning of red shields: the color of victorious might and blood dripping ("Plundering the Lion's Den—A Portrait of Divine Fury (Nahum 2:3–11)," *GTJ* 10 [1989]: 190–91). From the context he concluded that the latter explanation is insufficient.

[28] Patterson outlines the various proposals: metal, torches or flashes, flickering, or coverings or caparisons of horses or chariots (*Nahum, Habakkuk, Zephaniah,* 65). He joins K. J. Cathcart in following a Ugaritic lead and choosing the latter, translating "the coverings on the chariot are like fire" (*Nahum in the Light of Northwest Semitic* [Rome: Biblical Institute Press, 1973], 87–88). Longman agrees ("Nahum," 804).

[29] The Hb. reads בְּיוֹם הֲכִינוֹ, "in the day of his preparation," an apparent reference to preparation for battle such as forming a line.

The phrase "the spears of pine are brandished" may be the correct translation. The Hebrew line refers to a kind of tree, which apparently is the material from which weapons were made.[30] According to Roberts, "The image seems to be that of a rippling or quivering effect in the sea of spears held aloft by the advancing spearmen of the attacking army."[31] The effect of the phrase and all of v. 3 is to picture for the people of Judah the power of the attackers. "The effect of the whole spectacle was designed to strike terror into the stoutest of hearts."[32] God decreed the destruction of Nineveh. Nahum wanted the people to know that God had the power on hand to ensure the end of Nineveh. By vividly describing the attackers, the prophet assured the people that God would do just as he had said. "For the prophet the armies are also the forces of the Lord who appear as chariots of fire, coming with the force of the storm and with the devastation of the earthquake. They work within the processes of history. But they are also the armies of the great day of judgment which subdue the chaotic powers of evil (cp. Ps 68:17; Josh 5:13–15; Joel 2:1–11)."[33]

2:4 Verse 4 continues the advance of the attackers. The text indicates the mad dash of the chariots as they moved through the suburbs and outlying areas of Nineveh toward the city walls.[34] "The imagery intends to depict the intermediate step of the approach of the assault force. Having been dreaded at a distance when the approaching hoard's brilliant uniforms first came into view, they can now be observed more closely. They have laid claim to all the territory immediately outside the city walls. … The last resistance has retreated behind the safety of the city's walls, and the fearful chariotry of the enemy rushes about securing every possible escape route."[35] The Hebrew word for "storm" means "to act wildly as a madman." The NIV translation captures the meaning of the Hebrew as the chariots "stormed" through the streets. We speak of jet fighters that "scream" overhead. Nahum wanted to convey the idea of panic and fear in Nineveh as they watched the powerful army arrayed against them. The swift movement of the chariots reflecting the

---

[30] The LXX uses the term ἱππεῖς, "horsemen." In the Hb. text the change from וְהַבְּרֹשִׁים ("pine" or "cypress," NASB) to וְהַפָּרָשִׁים ("horsemen") would be minor. Either term fits the context and helps describe the power of the attacker. The same word for horsemen is found in Nah 3:3.

[31] Roberts, *Nahum, Habakkuk, and Zephaniah,* 58

[32] Patterson, *Nahum, Habakkuk, Zephaniah,* 61.

[33] J. D. W. Watts, "The Books of Joel, Obadiah, Jonah, Nahum, Habakkuk and Zephaniah," in *The Cambridge Bible Commentary on the New English Bible* (Cambridge: University Press, 1975), 112.

[34] Patterson contends that the "flow of thought in the passage appears to demand a location outside Nineveh proper. Therefore, 'streets/squares' should probably be understood of the surrounding villages that made up Nineveh's suburbs" (*Nahum, Habakkuk, and Zephaniah,* 66). Longman says that here "the scene now shifts to the reaction within the city. … Utter confusion and panic grip the city as the blood-red army approaches its walls" ("Nahum," 805).

[35] Robertson, *Nahum, Habakkuk, and Zephaniah,* 89.

sun appeared like flaming torches. The speed of the chariots could be compared with lightning.

2:5 Who is the subject of the verse, attackers or defenders? The stumbling of the officers would appear to refer to the defenders of the city who fall in panic and stumble in disarray. A well-organized attack probably would not be characterized by stumbling (cp. Isa 5:27). The Hebrew text, however, appears to refer to the attackers. "He summons" is a singular verb whose closest singular antecedent would be the attacker of v. 1.[36] Why the attackers would stumble is unclear unless one thinks of the haste of the attackers as they throw up the protective shield and prepare to storm the city wall. In this context "stumble" is parallel with "dash," which would indicate that the haste of the attackers or the weight of the protective shield caused their stumbling.[37] Attackers used the mantelet or "protective shield" to guard against defenders of the city from counterattacking from the superior high ground or even from dropping objects from above (2 Sam 11:20–22). The mantelet protected the soldiers[38] who attempted to break down the city gates with a battering ram.

4. Description of Nineveh's Defeat (2:6–10)

[6]The river gates are thrown open
and the palace collapses.
[7]It is decreed that [the city]
be exiled and carried away.
Its slave girls moan like doves
and beat upon their breasts.
[8]Nineveh is like a pool,
and its water is draining away.
"Stop! Stop!" they cry,

---

[36] Longman ("Nahum," 805) reviews scholarly problems with זכור, lit., "remember." The NIV renders "summons." Longman suggests retaining the MT and the basic meaning of the verb. Patterson (*Nahum, Habakkuk, Zephaniah,* 67) looks to an Akk. cognate to come up with the meaning "give orders to."

[37] Interpreters use a variety of means to attempt to resolve the problem. The easiest may be the suggestion in BHS to add the word "not" before stumble. By changing one Hebrew letter, J. M. P. Smith translates instead of stumbling, "They take command of their companies" (*A Critical and Exegetical Commentary on Nahum,* ICC [Edinburgh: T & T Clark, 1965], 330). Armerding ("Habakkuk," 7:475) suggests the attackers were so successful they stumbled over the corpses of the slain enemy as they advanced on the city. Longman ("Nahum") says the picture is "that of soldiers stumbling in their overwhelming rush to the city wall." Likewise, Patterson (*Nahum, Habakkuk, Zephaniah*) speaks of an "overzealous response."

[38] Patterson suggests that the "picked troops" of NIV "probably refers to the magnificently attired (v. 3) general soldiery, here designated according to their established reputation" (*Nahum, Habakkuk, Zephaniah,* 68).

but no one turns back.
[9]Plunder the silver!
Plunder the gold!
The supply is endless,
the wealth from all its treasures!
[10]She is pillaged, plundered, stripped!
Hearts melt, knees give way,
bodies tremble, every face grows pale.

2:6 Nahum continued to describe the attack upon Nineveh by describing the physical surroundings and protection of Nineveh.[39] Any attacker would be forced to contend with the Tigris River. Nineveh was situated on the east bank of the Tigris River, and the river Husur (Khosr) ran through the city. Rivers provided natural protection for Nineveh but also proved to be the downfall of the city. Any conqueror would be defeated partly by the river or would harness the river's power to undermine the city of Nineveh. But now "her very means of protection have become the instruments of her destruction."[40]

Nahum described the "river gates," which apparently controlled the flow of water through a system of moats and channels that protected the city in times of trouble and harnessed the river's power in more peaceful times. Exactly how the attackers used the river to their advantage is unknown. Either of two possibilities is plausible. The attackers may have captured the river gates, thus controlling the flow of the water and allowing the attackers to move closer to the walls of the city. Or the river gates may have been used to flood the city. The NIV implies the latter idea by describing the palace as having collapsed.[41] The Hebrew text pictures the palace as "melting away" or "being dissolved," which may be a reference to the effects of flooding in the city.[42]

A Greek story attributes the fall of Nineveh to floodwaters that destroyed part of the defenses,[43] but the *Babylonian Chronicle* breaks off without

---

[39] Coggins and Re'emi (*Israel among the Nations,* 40–41) reemphasize the poetic nature of the account and warn against expecting the prophet to have had much detailed knowledge of Nineveh.

[40] Achtemeier, *Nahum–Malachi,* 21.

[41] Note the discussion by Charles ("Plundering the Lion's Den—A Portrait of Divine Fury [Nah 2:3–11]," *GTJ* 10:194–95) following D. J. Wiseman and others about the possibility of a high tide that may have swept away a large section of the city wall.

[42] Some translations take the word for "dissolved" (נָמוֹג *niphal* from מוג) to refer to the psychological effects of the people in the palace (see RSV and JB) by describing the palace as being in panic or "dismay" (RSV). The verb is used metaphorically in Isa 14:31 and Ezek 21:15 (D. W. Baker, *Nahum, Habakkuk, Zephaniah,* TOTC [Downers Grove: InterVarsity, 1988], 35). This is the normal usage in the *niphal,* but the *qal, polel,* and *hithpolel* refer to actual melting or dissolving (Roberts, *Nahum, Habakkuk, and Zephaniah,* 60).

[43] Diodorus Siculus, *History,* 2.26–27; Xenophon, *Anabasis,* 3.4.12.

describing the manner of the city's destruction.[44] Roberts pointed out that the language could be interpreted either literally or metaphorically. "On a literal level, one can think of the floodwater washing the palace away; on the metaphorical level, the language refers to the collapse of the will to resist."[45] Watts points further to the cosmic implications of the floods and rivers in relationship to Ancient Near Eastern stories of creation and flood.[46]

2:7 Nahum described the effects of the fall of the city (2:7) once the resistance from the palace collapsed (2:6). Although the effects are certain—people taken into exile, humiliated, and downtrodden—the exact language and meaning is unclear.[47] The interpretation hinges on two questions. (1) Should the first Hebrew word in v. 7 be understood as a verb (NIV, "it is decreed")[48] or as the name of the queen or princess of the city of Nineveh? (2) If the word meant a person, does this mean a literal person such as the queen?[49]

---

[44] *ANET,* 304–5.

[45] Roberts, *Nahum, Habakkuk, and Zephaniah,* 66. Roberts reminds the reader that since Nahum's prophecy dates from several years prior to the fall of Nineveh, it is unlikely the prophet attempted to give the specifics of the fall of Nineveh. "His description of the attack on the city is in the nature of a prophetic vision composed well before the event it envisions; thus one should be very hesitant in drawing too close a correspondence between his vision and the actual course of the final siege of Nineveh" (ibid.). Patterson argues for historical literal fulfillment of the prophecy, saying, "Biblical evidence and historical tradition combine to indicate that neither wall nor water would deliver the seemingly impregnable city" (*Nahum, Habakkuk, Zephaniah,* 63).

[46] Watts, "Joel, Obadiah, Jonah, Nahum, Habakkuk and Zephaniah," 113.

[47] Roberts (*Nahum, Habakkuk, and Zephaniah,* 60) says the first word of the sentence "has given rise to a host of interpretations, but none of them is convincing."

[48] Armerding ("Habakkuk," 7:477) shows linguistic parallels strongly supporting NIV translation, but Longman ("Nahum," 806) says this involves an extension of meaning of the verb and is "speculative" and "awkward." To take it as the name of the Assyrian queen is an option that Longman says has been "properly ridiculed" by G. R. Driver, "Farewell to Queen Huzzab [Nah 2:8]!" *JTS* 16 (1964), 296–98, and by H. W. F. Saggs, "Nahum and the Fall of Nineveh," *JTS* 20 (1969): 220–25. Longman uses background studies of actions accompanying military defeat to defend the "consensus" that has grown that sees the image of a statue of a defeated goddess being stripped, desecrated, and taken away to the enemy's temple, followed by devotees beating their breasts in mourning. A *yodh* must be added to the Hebrew text to get the word הבצי, "beauty," for the image of the goddess. How such a proposal is any less awkward and speculative than the NIV text may be questioned. Roberts (*Nahum, Habakkuk, and Zephaniah,* 60) says no attempt to read this as "beauty," or "gazelle," or "the lizard" "seems very convincing." So he favors an emended text with no textual support, relying on a word found only in Akk.: העתלה *(hāʿătallâ),* cognate with Akk. *etelletu,* "princess."

[49] Robertson argues: "The context in no way prepares for the mention of an otherwise unknown Assyrian queen" (*Nahum, Habakkuk, and Zephaniah,* 91). He prefers the verbal interpretation, translating, "It is settled." Roberts agrees the queen interpretation "is a relatively late proposal, and there is no historical or inscriptional basis for it" (*Nahum, Habakkuk, and Zephaniah,* 60).

Or does it refer to the city itself or to a goddess of the city?[50] If the NIV is correct, the meaning is clear. The city of Nineveh would be stripped and the spoil carried off. The women of Nineveh would go into exile[51] as slaves.

Taking the word as a proper name graphically describes the fate of the city. "Huzzab," the queen of the city, faced humiliation and exile. Among the Hebrews nakedness indicated extreme humiliation, even as it would in modern society. If the queen so suffered, could the ordinary citizens of the city fare any better? The queen's attendants sorrowfully follow her into exile.[52]

Another interpretation also deserves consideration. Could the proper name indicate the goddess Ishtar? If so, the idol would be stripped of its valuable decorations and be carried into exile with those who worshiped the goddess. Those sacred prostitutes who served in the temple of Ishtar would go into slavery with their mistress. Meier notes that the Hebrew term for "carried away" carries with it the meaning "to be led up for sacrifice."[53] Such a meaning is certainly appropriate for a defeated nation whose inhabitants are being carried away to serve the victor's God.

Nahum sought to portray the effects of God's fighting against the city of Nineveh. The destruction would be complete. No thing and no one could with-

---

[50] The problem arises with the Hb. word וְהֻצַּב, found only here in the Hebrew Bible. Maier (*The Book of Nahum,* 256) gives up: "It seems impossible to establish its meaning precisely and definitely," but then he chooses Huzzab, the Assyrian queen. He lists twelve proposed solutions to the problem and then decides the Hebrew term is written defectively without the final *yodh* and means "gazelle," an image of beauty for Israel and thus a poetic reference to the Assyrian queen or to the city (pp. 259–63). Without other references such words are only tenuously translated. The NIV follows the Hb. text, where the word could be translated as a *hophal* perfect meaning "it is fixed" or "it is decreed" (BDB, 662). Other translations take the word as a proper name, "Huzzab" (see KJV and RSV), which referred to the queen of Assyria or to the statue of the goddess Ishtar (for a discussion of the problems of translations see Clark and Hatton, *Nahum, Habakkuk, and Zephaniah,* 32–33). G. R. Driver surveyed the various options and based on Greek and Aramaic vocabulary translated the verse to read "the [captive] train goes into exile, they and their slave-girls are carried away" ("Farewell to Queen Huzzab!" *JTS* 15 [1964]: 296–98). Watts sees here something from the temple, perhaps the idol's pedestal ("Joel, Obadiah, Jonah, Nahum, Habakkuk and Zephaniah," 113). Patterson (*Nahum, Habakkuk, Zephaniah,* 69–70) says the solutions follow three patterns: (1) noun meaning "beauty," or "lady," or "mistress," referring either to the city of Nineveh or to the statue of the goddess Ishtar; (2) verb meaning "decreed" or "dissolved"; (3) some emendation of the text. Patterson follows NASB in seeing the word as a passive verb meaning "dissolved or crumbled," but he then attaches it to v. 6: "the palace collapses and crumbles."

[51] "Be exiled" (NIV) represents Hb. גֻּלְּתָה, literally, she was stripped. Patterson (*Nahum, Habakkuk, Zephaniah,* 70) wants to repoint the Hebrew text and read "her exiles, or her captives," relating it to 3:10 and providing meaning to 2:7 once he has taken the opening word of the Hebrew text and attached it to the previous verse.

[52] Women beating on their breasts is a common rite of lamentation in the ancient Near East; see S. N. Kramer, "The Curse of Agade," *ANETS,* 214. Coggins and Re'emi (*Israel among the Nations,* 42) point out that the normal meaning of the Hb. verb used here—נהג—usually means "to drive" and could refer to the delicate women of the court being herded like animals and driven off to captivity.

[53] Maier, *The Book of Nahum,* 262.

stand the onslaught of the attacking forces. The palace would collapse under the attack, and the leaders of Nineveh would go into exile in humiliation.

These words must have made a profound impression on the people of Jerusalem. For over a century the people of Israel and Judah suffered under the ruthlessness and oppression of Assyria. Now those leaders who most benefited from the cruel policies of exile, humiliation, and plunder would suffer exile, humiliation, and plunder.

2:8 For the first time since 1:1, the Hebrew text in 2:8 explicitly mentions Nineveh. Nahum probably used this for effect. He described terrible destruction from which no one could escape. He then identified the desolate city as the oppressor Nineveh. Those who first heard or read these words could not help but become excited at the thoughts of God's deliverance. They would clap their hands at the announcement of the defeat of Assyria (3:19).

Nahum apparently used Nineveh's geographical characteristics as a metaphor for the troops. Isaiah used the metaphor of water to refer to the inundation caused by the king of Assyria (Isa 8:7–8). Those who flowed over Israel and Judah could now be compared to a pool of water whose dam had broken, allowing its waters to flow away. Like waters flowing over a dam, Nineveh's defenders could not be stopped. Did Nahum mean that the waters protecting the city (2:7) had been drained away? If so, the prophet may here have meant that as the enemies drained away the water, so the people also would flee.

Nineveh is described as a leaking pool[54] whose major resource—water—is leaking away, leaving the pool empty. "The mighty waters of Assyria are no longer a threat to anyone. The tide has turned, Assyria's hosts have fled, and Nineveh is left high and dry."[55] As people flee in panic, authorities cry for them to stop, but no one pays attention. Panic reigns. Order is dissolved.[56] As

---

[54] Robertson (*Nahum, Habakkuk, and Zephaniah,* 93) says the pool could be seen as leaking, flourishing, or flooding (the verb for "draining away" is נָסִים, *qal* participle from נוּס, "flee"). He sees the image as describing Assyria's past glory as a flourishing pool. Maier (*The Book of Nahum,* 263–64) outlines the various interpretations of the pool and then concludes: "It appears more acceptable to assume that actually Nineveh has the appearance of an inundated area. It has been flooded (v. 7); its palace sways (and falls); the captured city looks like a pool. This translation is in harmony with the context and builds a gradual, logical development from v. 7" (p. 264).

[55] Roberts, *Nahum, Habakkuk, and Zephaniah,* 62.

[56] וְנִינְוֵה כִבְרֵכַת־מַיִם מִימֵי הִיא וְהֵמָּה נָסִים is the reading of the first line of v. 7[Eng. 8]. Patterson (*Nahum, Habakkuk, Zephaniah,* 70–71) gives grammatical reasons for reading the difficult Hb. text as: "As for Nineveh, her waters are like a pool of water, and they (her citizens) are fleeing away." Whether this is the exact translation of the Hebrew text may be debated, but it gives the meaning of the context. See the explicit description of the difficulties of the text by Armerding, "Habakkuk," 7:477–78, who gives the literal Hebrew of the first line as: "Nineveh (is) as a pool of water, since the days of it (existing), and/but they are fleeing." Robertson (*Nahum, Habakkuk, and Zephaniah,* 92) retains the MT to read: "Nineveh (has been) as a pool of water from her (ancient) days. Yet they are fleeing." Maier (*The Book of Nahum,* 265–66) lists the multiple emendations and interpretations of the text. Then he reads the personal pronoun הִיא as equivalent to הִי, "lamentation," found in Ezek 2:10. Thus Maier translates: "And (thus) Nineveh is like a pool of water from (the) days of lamentation; / And they are in flight" (p. 263).

Armerding describes it: “The image of water defines Nineveh’s fate with vivid irony. Nineveh was a place of watered parks and orchards. As at the Flood, however, ‘water’ became a source of death, overflowing its boundaries and bringing chaos to the inundated city.”[57]

The effect of hearing of Nineveh’s demise would bring joy and praise to the temple area. If God could bring an end to the most powerful nation in the ancient Near East, then the Lord God must truly be the Lord of history. Nahum’s message contains a number of underlying theological messages: the Lord God of Israel reigns over history, requiting the oppressor and delivering the oppressed. The Lord is a mighty warrior who is slow to anger and plenteous in mercy (1:2–3).

This verse contains several difficulties for the translator. The NIV follows most modern translations by accepting the ancient Greek text (the Septuagint) in the first line of the verse. The Hebrew text reads, “And Nineveh [is] like a pool of waters from earliest days,” meaning that though Nineveh has been like a pool of placid water from earliest times, now they flee.[58]

Though the Hebrew text omits the words “they cry,” the NIV and other translations (RSV and NEB) are obviously correct to add the words to aid understanding and to show direct speech. The officers and leaders of the people would command the defending troops to stop and to fight, but their commands would fall on deaf ears. “The desertion of the soldiers leaves the city open to the plundering that the next verse describes.”[59]

2:9 For two hundred years the kings of Assyria boasted of the treasures its troops confiscated from its neighbors. Now Nahum pictured the attackers plundering the silver and gold of Assyria. Nineveh’s treasures came from two sources: its powerful military, which brought the wealth of the nations to Nineveh, and the tribute Assyria required of its vassals. Normally the vassal nation fulfilled its duties to Assyria by vowing allegiance and by paying annual tribute. From these sources Assyria seemed to have an endless supply of wealth and treasure rooms stocked to capacity.

Apparently the prophet is the speaker in v. 9. “Nahum becomes so excited about the end of the evil city that he directs its looting in his imagination.”[60] Nahum encouraged those whom he saw taking the city to take the city’s wealth by force. Nabopolasser’s annals describe the capture of Nineveh by a

---

[57] Armerding, “Habakkuk,” 7:476.

[58] For discussion of the problems of translation see Clark and Hatton, *Nahum, Habakkuk, and Zephaniah,* 33. The differences in the Hb. and Gk. texts are minimal. In an unpointed Hb. text, one can easily see the possible confusion. The NIV and RSV follow the LXX (καὶ Νινευη ὡs κολυμβήθρα ὕδατος τὰ ὕδατα αὐτῆs καὶ αὐτοὶ φεύγοντεs) while the KJV and NASB continue with the MT.

[59] Longman, “Nahum,” 807.

[60] Ibid. Longman notes that the speaker could be taken to be one of the soldiers participating in the plundering or the prophet.

coalition of Medes and Babylonians and the plunder of the city's wealth: "They marched [upstream] on the embankment of the Tigris … they made a great attack against the city. In the month Abu, … he inflicted [upon the] entire [population]. On that day, … many prisoners of the city, beyond counting, they carried away. The city [they turned] into ruin-hills."[61]

"The treasures of the world may change hands from conqueror to conqueror. But ultimately they shall flow to him alone. All the glory of all the wealth of all the nations shall be consecrated to him."[62]

2:10 Nahum continued to impress his hearers and readers with the coming reality of Nineveh's demise. He used vivid language to drive home the certainty of the future events. One aspect of his language involved the use of words which are similar in both meaning and sound. This use of language "effectively conveys the pounding rhythm of devastation."[63]

"Pillaged, plundered, and stripped" all sound alike in Hebrew and have similar meanings *(bûqâ ûmĕbûqâ ûmĕbullāqâ).*[64] Though different translations attempt to duplicate the paronomasia into English (e.g., GNB uses "Nineveh is destroyed, deserted, desolate!"), the power of Nahum's message comes through without the duplication of the Hebrew verse. Nahum's pictorial language vividly describes the fear of the people of Nineveh. "The sight would send such a shudder through the strongest people that uncontrollable trembling would seize the entire body and their faces blanch. The portrayal is one of abject terror, painted again in synecdoche and picturesque brevity: melting hearts, knees knocking together, bodies writhing, faces made colorless with fright."[65] Nineveh's reign of terror would end. In Nineveh the people faint before the sure end of Assyria's dominance.

How could the people of Judah now fear? Should they not rejoice before the judgment of God? Should they not take heart at the word of King Josiah and his attempts to reform the kingdom?

We do not know how Nahum's prophecy fit into the situation in Judah. Nor do we know of Nahum's relationship to the Josianic reform movement. The Bible itself—and particularly the Book of Nahum—is silent concerning these questions, but we should question what effect Nahum's message had on Josiah and the people of Judah concerning the removal of Assyrian religious articles from the temple in Jerusalem (2 Kgs 22:1–23:30).

---

[61] *ANET,* 304–5.

[62] Robertson, *Nahum, Habakkuk, and Zephaniah,* 94.

[63] Ibid.

[64] Robertson notes the rhythmic effect of Nahum's language. "Each successive word is slightly longer than the former, so that a rhythmic buildup reinforces the message. The first two terms occur only here in the OT, and the third appears elsewhere only in Isa 24:1, where it is connected again with the verb *bāqaq*" (Robertson, *Nahum, Habakkuk, and Zephaniah,* 94).

[65] Patterson, *Nahum, Habakkuk, Zephaniah,* 64.

Nahum's message would serve to embolden anyone who wanted to remove Assyrian dominance over Judah. Anyone who loved the Lord alone would welcome the opportunity to reject the influence of Assyria and its gods. The language of Nahum would serve such a purpose. He told of the people of Nineveh fainting before the troops attacking the city. The prophet wanted to portray a people overcome with fear and without hope. In Hebrew thought the heart indicated emotion, thought, or will.[66] Nahum may have wanted to convey people whose courage failed and who no longer had the will to stand in the face of certain defeat. Trembling knees indicated the inability to stand up to the enemy or to run away. Belteshazzar reacted much the same way when he saw the handwriting on the wall as recorded in the Book of Daniel (Dan 5:6).

Who could stand against overwhelming odds? But remember that the enemy of Nineveh was the Lord. He would restore the splendor of Jacob. For this reason "bodies tremble."[67] The Hebrew word translated "bodies" *(mātĕnayim)* actually means "loins," a term often referring to physical strength (Job 40:16). The phrase is so constructed as to say that "anguish is on all loins," which could also refer to a woman undergoing labor pains (Isa 21:3).

The end of v. 10 could be translated more literally, "And the faces of all of them gather paleness." The last word in the verse is uncertain in meaning, but the sense seems to be that fear could be seen in their faces. We see "the absolute terror that Nineveh's destruction evoked in those who witnessed it."[68] For the final word *pā᾿rûr* the NIV and many other translations (e.g., RSV, GNB, JB) use "pale," a word that seems most natural in the context, or expressions of similar meaning such as "drained of colour" (NEB). Other choices are "black" or "crimson."[69]

All of the human qualities that made Assyria a great nation—courage, stamina, and drive—would be lost. Without these qualities, Assyria would suffer the fate of all other once proud nations. How ironic that the one who used fear and intimidation to subjugate its neighbors would suffer from fear and intimidation.

5. The Hopelessness of Nineveh (2:11–12)

[11]Where now is the lions' den,
the place where they fed their young,

---

[66] H. W. Wolff, *Anthropology of the Old Testament* (Philadelphia: Fortress, 1974), 40–58.

[67] Coggins and Re'emi (*Israel among the Nations,* 44) note that "the vivid description continues by fastening on those parts of the body which were thought to react especially to disaster: heart, knees, loins, face. The picture is of the whole being thrown into disarray as the extent of the desolation is revealed."

[68] Longman, "Nahum," 807.

[69] Note the reminders of Longman ("Nahum," 807–8) about the problems of how to translate facial expressions of emotions from and into different cultures.

where the lion and lioness went,
and the cubs, with nothing to fear?
12 The lion killed enough for his cubs
and strangled the prey for his mate,
filling his lairs with the kill
and his dens with the prey.

2:11 These verses sound as if Assyria no longer existed. Where now was the scourge of the earth? In fact, Assyria appeared to be as strong as ever. Nahum used sarcasm to show the certainty of Nineveh's fall. After the destruction of the attacking forces, where now would the lion bring its prey? Throughout its history Assyria referred to itself as the lion and used the lion's tactics as its own. The armies of Assyria ruthlessly attacked its prey, strangling its enemies' cities and bringing its prey to its lair. But "the lion symbolized strength, cunning, and lordship, and, to the nations conquered by Assyria, the lion symbolized ruthlessness."[70]

Assyrian chronicles and sculpture repeatedly referred to the lion. Assyrian kings often presented themselves in terms that resembled the behavior of lions,[71] and the Assyrians boasted of their cruelty toward their enemies. Ishtar, the Assyrian goddess, was often represented as a lioness or as mounted on a lion's back.[72] Nahum thus mocked Assyria's tactics and its success. To the people of Judah the effect was: How the mighty have fallen!

Nahum asked two rhetorical questions. The effect was to ask, Where now was the lion's den where he fed his cubs and dwelt in safety? What had happened to mighty Nineveh? God's judgment had come even to the lion's den—to Nineveh. The people of Judah no longer would fear the savagery of the lion of Assyria. Coggins and Re'emi point out that on another level "Yahweh himself can be alluded to in the prophetic tradition as a lion (cf. the picture of his roaring in Amos 1:2 and the direct comparison made in Amos 3:8), and that tradition appears to have been in our prophet's mind in this poem." They recognize, however, that the more prominent reference here is to the Assyrian rulers as lions.[73]

Nahum used several words meaning lion, thus driving home the point of Nineveh's demise.[74] In a sense Nahum spoke of the entire Assyrian society. Kings, queens, and princes manifested the beastly traits of lions. All suffered

---

[70] Longman, "Nahum," 807–8, referring to P. Machinist, "Assyria and Its Image in the First Isaiah," *JAOS* 103 (1983): 719–37. R. L. Smith (*Micah–Malachi,* 84) says the taunt song could have been used in cultic celebration.

[71] Robertson, *Nahum, Habakkuk, and Zephaniah,* 95.

[72] J. D. W. Watts, "Joel, Obadiah, Jonah, Nahum, Habakkuk and Zephaniah," 114.

[73] Coggins and Re'emi, *Israel among the Nations,* 44. See Isa 5:29.

[74] Nahum spoke of the full-grown male lion (אַרְיֵה), the lioness or possibly Asiatic lion (לָבִיא), the young lion (כְּפִיר), and the whelp (גּוּר).

the fate of ruin of destruction. They no longer could enjoy the spoil of the nations. They no longer could dwell in safety. Most importantly, they no longer could command fear from the peoples of the world.

The "lion's den" is a metaphor for Nineveh, a place of safety and rejoicing over the prey. "The place where they fed their young" usually refers to a pasture in Hebrew but may here be understood as "feeding place."[75] The place "where the lion and lioness went" is another metaphor for Nineveh.[76] In this place the lion, lioness, and the whelps could roam in safety, oblivious to the dangers of the outside world. All such safety ended for Nineveh.

2:12 Verse 12 continues the metaphor of Nineveh as the lion's den and the leaders of Nineveh as the lions. Both halves of the verse are parallel constructions. In this case the second part of each half of the verse echoes the meaning of the first part but in slightly different words.

Lions actually do "strangle" their prey by biting into the throat to cut off the supply of air. This manner of killing is especially effective when the lion attacks a larger animal. The ferocity of the lion filled his lair with food for the lioness and the cubs. Thus the image here is one of "brutality. … Assyrian cruelty stands almost unparalleled in the record of human history. With due allowances for the exaggerations characteristic of the cuneiform chronicles, the extent of the violence and bloodshed to which the Nineveh conquerors resorted is almost incredible."[77]

For years Nineveh lived by force. The wealth of the nations flowed to Assyria as its armies subjugated the peoples of the ancient Near East. The annual tribute of vassal nations continually provided food and valuables for the people of Assyria. But where now was mighty Nineveh? Where now were the sculptures of lions? Where now was Ishtar the lioness?

Nahum's message provided hope for Jerusalem. The ferocity of Nineveh would end. The Lord himself would deliver the people of Judah by destroying the lion of Assyria.

---

[75] BHS suggests transposing two Hb. letters, resulting in "cave" rather than "pasture" or "feeding place." While the transposition better fits the parallelism, the sense of the passage is not unduly affected by "feeding place," and no manuscript of versional evidence exists to strengthen the transposition. Maier (*The Book of Nahum,* 278–79) says the emphasis is not on a pasture as a locality but on the food provided by the pasture. Thus he translates "fodder," which he sees as a figure for "booty." Patterson (*Nahum, Habakkuk, Zephaniah,* 77) argues that the term refers to "open country" and "may intend simply the district where the lion's cave was found."

[76] The LXX uses εἰσελθεῖν, "to enter," which in Hb. (לָבוֹא) would be only slightly different from lioness (לָבִיא). Those who follow the LXX understand this as a reference to the lion's return to his den after hunting.

[77] Maier, *The Book of Nahum,* 281, who supplies excerpts from the Assyrian chronicles.

6. The Lord Fights against Nineveh (2:13)

[13]"I am against you,"
declares the LORD Almighty.
"I will burn up your chariots in smoke,
and the sword will devour your young lions.
I will leave you no prey on the earth.
The voices of your messengers
will no longer be heard."

2:13 Where does this verse belong? Some commentators and translators connect it with what comes before while others believe it should be part of the final chapter of Nahum. Evidence for the latter case can be found in Nah 3:5. Both 2:13 and 3:5 begin with exactly the same words (lit.): "Behold, I am against you, oracle of the LORD of hosts," suggesting that each verse begins a new section. Thus 2:13–3:4 would be connected. The reference to lions in 2:13, however, seems to support the traditional chapter division. The content of the verse also seems to point to 2:13 as the conclusion of the theme of the Lord's judgment of Nineveh as found throughout chap. 2.

"Behold, I am against you'; that is the determinative word (v. 13; cf. 1:14; 2:7 Hb.; 3:5), for how we as nations and individuals stand in the eyes of God finally determines our death or life."[78] The formula is called the "challenge to a duel formula" …, originally set in the report of a duel (1 Sam 17:45–49). In prophetic usage it serves simply to introduce a prophetic announcement of punishment."[79]

"Behold" or "look" *(hinnê)* figures prominently in the Hebrew text even though it is omitted by the NIV. The word catches the attention of the hearer and the reader. In modern English it has the force of "think carefully" or "listen to this."[80] "Nahum uses the particle several times at strategic points as a transitional device (cf. 1:15; 3:5,13). This particle is often used to introduce divine pronouncements and to authenticate a prophet's words."[81]

The phrase "declares the LORD Almighty" (lit., "oracle of Yahweh of hosts")[82] demonstrates the power of the Lord. The one against Nineveh is no one less than the Lord himself. Since the message of Nahum is primarily

---

[78] Achtemeier, *Nahum–Malachi,* 22.

[79] R. M. Hals, *Ezekiel*, FOTL XIX, 32. Of the twenty occurrences, fourteen appear in Ezekiel. See Jer 21:13; 23:30; 50:31; 51:25; Ezek 5:8; 13:8,20; 21:8; 26:3; 28:22; 39:1.

[80] Clark and Hatton, *Nahum, Habakkuk, and Zephaniah,* 38.

[81] Patterson, *Nahum, Habakkuk, Zephaniah,* 78, referring to D. Vetter, *THAT* 1:505–7.

[82] Hals (*Ezekiel*, 361 362) calls this "the prophetic utterance formula. It labels a prophetic speech as the word of Israel's God, usually being placed at the end of a unit or a major section within a unit. The original setting may well have been the vision report of a seer (Num 24:3)." See S. Meier, *Speaking of Speaking: Marking Direct Discourse in the Hebrew Bible,* VTSup 46 (Leiden: Brill, 1992), 289–314. The formula occurs 364 times in the Old Testament.

addressed to the people of Judah and Jerusalem, declaring the Lord's personal intention to destroy Nineveh conveyed the certainty of Nineveh's demise.

The Lord of hosts referred to the power of the Lord and is found often in the Old Testament in military contexts.[83] This may refer to the armies of the Lord or to the host of the heavens—either stars or angels. In either case (or it may have been used in both ways) the phrase describes the Lord as powerful to defeat the armies of Nineveh. "Hosts has reference to any group, human or divine, called upon by God to mediate a divine objective, which may or may not be military in nature. The fact that the phrase occurs 251 times in the Prophets may reflect the prophet as a member of the divine council (Jer 23:18,22), and the word of God thus becomes a divine instrument, often for purposes of judgment" (23:29).[84] Martens notes that as "a military title, it signifies that God is equal to any adversary and well able to achieve victory."[85]

"Chariots," "lions," "prey," and "messengers" referred to the strength of the Assyrians. The Lord himself intended to reduce Nineveh's strength to rubble. Chariots intimidated opposing warriors. At times the chariot contained three soldiers: a driver, a shield bearer, and a warrior. The swift movement of the chariot with the power of its horses and the ferocity of the warrior struck terror in ancient people.[86] Again the Lord used Nineveh's methods to punish them. Nineveh used the chariot to intimidate and to destroy. The warriors of Nineveh left the ruins of its enemies in smoke. God would use the same means to bring an end to Nineveh and to deliver the people of Judah.

The "young lions" connects this verse with the preceding verses, where the lions referred to the power of Nineveh. Though the phrase does not mean much to people unaccustomed to warfare using the sword, the Hebrew text expresses the horror of the sword, "And your young lions will be eaten with the sword."

The picture of the young lions continues in the next clause: "I will leave

---

[83] Note the repeated use of the phrase in the Books of Samuel, particularly in military contexts (1 Sam 4:4; 17:45; 2 Sam 5:10).

[84] T. Fretheim, "Yahweh," *NIDOTTE* 4:1297–98. A. S. van der Woude ("צָבָא *ṣābāʾ* army," *TLOT* 2:1045) defends the "plural of extension" interpretation and thus the NIV translation as Lord Almighty.

[85] E. A. Martens, "God, Names of," *EDBT,* 299. It also "designates God as the regnant God (Ps 103:19–21), the enthroned God whose royal decrees will carry the day (Isa 14:24; Jer 25:27). … God retains exclusive prerogative as deity. Any competing ideology is idolatry, whether that be the ancient worship of Baal or the modern preoccupation with technique, nationalism, or militarism."

[86] The Hb. text seems strange at this point, reading lit., "I will burn in the smoke her chariot." The remainder of the verse uses "your" to refer to the Assyrians, and the entire verse is a direct address of the Lord to the Assyrians. For these reasons many translations follow the LXX, which declares God's intention to burn πλῆθός σου, "your multitude." BHS proposes "your chariot," which is followed by the NIV. Other proposals in BHS include "your resting place" and "your thicket." Each of the proposals has some merit, but the point is clear in all of the ideas: the Lord is against Nineveh and will destroy the power of Nineveh.

you no prey on the earth" (lit., "I will cut off from the earth your prey"). Nineveh had prospered at the expense of its subjugated people. If Nineveh's armies could not bring back its prey, Nineveh itself would suffer and ultimately fall prey to a greater force.

Nineveh sent its messengers[87] and envoys throughout its sphere of influence. Now "the haughty city will have no more representative heralds, for no nation remains to be represented."[88] In Rabshakeh's negotiations with Hezekiah's messengers, Rabshakeh's messengers spoke with the authority of the king and sought to undermine the resistance of the besieged peoples (1 Kgs 18:19–21,26–27). This shows that "messengers from the Assyrian king were not simply bringers of information; rather, they symbolized the threat that failure to conform to the demand implicit in their message would bring swift and disastrous punishment from the great king of Assyria."[89] Now such messengers were silenced. No one faced their demands anymore. God had spoken the final word.

Verse 13 contains four evidences of the coming end of Nineveh. Because the awesome Lord of the universe is against Nineveh, (1) Nineveh's chariots would be burned, (2) the sword would devour its soldiers, (3) no prey would be brought back to Nineveh, and (4) the voice of its messengers would be stilled. With vivid words and powerful metaphors, Nahum described the coming destruction of Nineveh as if it had already taken place. The Lord reigns. No nation can long endure that turns its back on God. Israel's apostasy and Nineveh's arrogance would both be punished.

Thus "this verse draws together the major motifs and vocabulary of Nahum's prophecy: the Lord's inexorable opposition to Nineveh; the destruction of its military resources; the role of 'sword' and 'fire' that 'consume' the enemy; the cutting off of Nineveh and its 'prey'; the termination of its cruelty, symbolized by the 'young lions'; and the reversal of fortunes that awaits Assyria and Judah, exemplified in the fate of the 'heralds.'"[90]

Through these verses the Lord showed himself to be the Lord of the universe, working through history to accomplish his righteous purpose in the world. Nahum declared the Lord's compassion for Judah by indicating the Lord's removal of the oppressor.

---

[87] For "your messengers" the MT has מַלְאָכֵכֵה, a "wholly abnormal" form for the second person suffix. GKC (§ 91l) suggests this is a case of dittography with the following ה and recommends reading מַלְאָכַיִךְ.

[88] Maier, *The Book of Nahum,* 286.

[89] Coggins and Re'emi, *Israel among the Nations,* 46.

[90] Armerding, "Habakkuk," 7:479.

SECTION OUTLINE

III. THE LAMENT FOR NINEVEH (3:1–19)
   1. The Destruction of Nineveh (3:1–4)
   2. The Humiliation of Nineveh (3:5–7)
   3. The Weakness of Nineveh (3:8–13)
   4. The Hopelessness of Defense (3:14–19a)
   5. The Joy in Justice (3:19b)

III. THE LAMENT FOR NINEVEH (3:1–19)

Nahum closes on a gruesome note. "Blood, lies, plunder, harlotries, corpses, filth, and sorceries characterize this section."[1] The third chapter of Nahum continues the theme of the certainty of Nineveh's destruction. As in the preceding chapter, the prophet described Nineveh's destruction as a fact accomplished or as in progress. In chap. 3 the prophet described Nineveh's end and lamented for the lost city, but all who heard the joyous words of Nineveh's downfall would clap their hands in glee.

From the beginning of this brief message, the prophet skillfully progressed from a description of the greatness of God to the full and final end of Assyria. No one can stand against the greatness of God. Many people assumed that Nineveh would go on forever. After all, for more than a hundred years Nineveh reigned almost without challenge. Assyria accomplished the unthinkable task of penetrating deep into Egypt and taking Thebes. In the minds of most people of that part of the world, a nation that could conquer Thebes must be invincible and impregnable. But Nahum's message used Assyria's history against itself. If Thebes could be destroyed, Nineveh could suffer defeat and disgrace as well. Nineveh must face the awesome God. God would bring a final end to Nineveh, and he would restore the oppressed peoples. The time of Nineveh's fall would be a time for the peoples of the world to rejoice.

As in chap. 2 the text uses the wide range of emotions available only in poetic imagery to drill into the readers' hearts and minds the power and surprise of the fall of invincible Nineveh. From this imagery and emotion, theological conclusions can be drawn. Such conclusions represent the central message that Nahum has spoken from chap. 1 on: God is sovereign over all creation and especially over any imitators who would claim universal power for themselves and ignore God.

[1] R. L. Smith, *Micah–Malachi,* WBC 32 (Waco: Word, 1984), 85.

1. The Destruction of Nineveh (3:1–4)

[1]Woe to the city of blood,
full of lies,
full of plunder,
never without victims!
[2]The crack of whips,
the clatter of wheels,
galloping horses
and jolting chariots!
[3]Charging cavalry,
flashing swords
and glittering spears!
Many casualties,
piles of dead,
bodies without number,
people stumbling over the corpses—
[4]all because of the wanton lust of a harlot,
alluring, the mistress of sorceries,
who enslaved nations by her prostitution
and peoples by her witchcraft.

The first three verses of the chapter consist of a series of staccato-like phrases that illustrate the panic and confusion in the city during the attack. People under attack do not take the time to speak in complete sentences. Under stress, commands and cries of distress fly out of people's mouths. The prophet effectively demonstrated the disarray in the city. The fourth verse turns to a longer poetic line and introduces the analogy of a harlot. Because of similar vocabulary and style,[2] commentators often want to connect 3:1–3 with the last section of chap. 2 rather than with v. 4. However, 2:13 opens with a standard formula that marks it as a unit unto itself or as a unit closing what preceded. The woe formula beginning 3:1 likewise introduces a new section of its own, as does the opening formula of 3:5. The commonalities between 3:1–3 and 2:13 may indicate the skill of the writer in producing the entire written document rather than linking an independent unit together.

3:1 "Woe" is a word characteristic of the prophets. Translators use several different words to communicate the distinctive meaning of the Hebrew word *(hôy)*. "Ho," "Ah," "Alas," and "Shame on you" all describe the meaning of the Hebrew term. The word usually announces a theme of judgment.

Though the term "woe" is found in many books of the Old Testament, the prophets used it most often and in relationship to God's divine judgment. In the present context the word is a statement rather than a wish. In this sense the

---

[2] For similarities see C. E. Armerding, "Habakkuk," EBC 7:479–80.

usage runs parallel to Nahum's certainty of the destruction of Nineveh. The GNB catches the inevitable judgment against Nineveh: "Doomed is the lying, murderous city." Of the fifty-three occurrences in the Old Testament, R. J. Clifford listed three possible uses for *hôy*: (1) to describe funeral laments (eight times), usually translated "alas"; (2) a cry to get attention (four times), usually translated "ho" or "ah"; (3) and announcement of doom (forty-one times and used only by the prophets), usually translated "woe to."[3]

The use of "woe" can be understood as a curse or as a lament. The prophets used the term in both ways.[4] As a curse the prophet used the term to indicate the certainty of judgment. In Israel and among other nations, the spoken word possessed the ability to bring its own result. No wonder kings kept scores of loyal prophets always ready to pronounce good things for the king.

Many times the term "woe" is used as a lament (Jer 22:18; 34:5), but this does not seem to be the force of Nahum.[5] Nahum confidently predicted the downfall of Nineveh. Any lament would be for effect, not sorrow.[6]

The following three phrases graphically depict the sin of Nineveh and its inevitable judgment. "The description depicts the Assyrians' use of treachery and alluring platitudes to gain others' loyalty."[7] First, Nahum described Nineveh as the bloody city. Throughout its history, Assyria relished its militarism.

---

[3] R. J. Clifford, "The Use of *Hôy* in the Prophets," *CBQ* 28 (1966): 458–64.

[4] O. P. Robertson insists the woe exclamation (הוֹי) "does not precisely communicate a curse, a woe. Instead, it gives expression to an agony, a pain at an offense being witnessed. It hurts to watch people being slowly crushed by a system calculated to squeeze the last breath from the defenseless" (*The Books of Nahum, Habakkuk, and Zephaniah,* NICOT [Grand Rapids: Eerdmans, 1990], 100).

[5] R. D. Patterson sees "woe" as a "word drawn from a lamentation liturgy for the dead" (*Nahum, Habakkuk, Zephaniah,* WEC, ed. K. Barker [Chicago: Moody, 1991], 81). He finds three parts to the woe oracle: invective (vv. 1,7), threat (vv. 2–3,5–6), criticism (v. 4). T. Longman III likewise sees funeral processions in the background, saying: "The association of the word with death probably led the prophets to use it as they foresaw destruction coming" ("Nahum," in *The Minor Prophets: An Exegetical and Expository Commentary,* ed. T. E. McComiskey [Grand Rapids: Baker, 1993], 812). He then continues, however, in the opposite direction in applying this to Nahum: "In many of the prophetic uses, and certainly in the use here in Nahum, *hôy* no longer marks an expression of lamentation for the dead. On the contrary, Nahum is far from lamenting the coming destruction of vicious Nineveh. Indeed he can hardly restrain his joy at the prospect. *Hôy* has become a threat or a curse directed against the enemies of God."

[6] Note the discussion of "woe" by E. R. Dalglish, "Nahum," in *Hosea–Malachi,* BBC (Nashville: Broadman, 1972), 7:242; and R. Smith, *Micah–Malachi,* 86, and E. Gerstenberger, "The Woe Oracles of the Prophets," *JBL* 81 (1962): 249–63. Dalglish sees the present verse as an oracle of woe rather than lament and numbers thirty-six or fifty-one occurrences of "woe" as a curse, but Gerstenberger argues against this assessment. R. J. Clifford felt certain that Nahum spoke a word of judgment (*CBQ* 28 [1996]: 462). D. W. Baker correctly notes that the use of the woe form here is ironic, since the demise of the tyrant would be welcomed, not mourned" (*Nahum, Habakkuk, Zephaniah,* TOTC [Downers Grove: InterVarsity, 1988], 23b, 36).

[7] Patterson, *Nahum, Habakkuk, Zephaniah,* 83.

The atrocities of the armies of Assyria are legendary. Shalmaneser III (858–824) represented well the character of the city and its practices:

> I slew their warriors with the sword, descending upon them like Adad when he makes a rainstorm pour down. In the moat (of the town) I piled them up, I covered the wide plain with the corpses of their fighting men, I dyed the mountains with their blood like red wool. I took away from him many chariots (and) horses broken to the yoke. I erected pillars of skulls in front of his town, destroyed his (other) towns, tore down (their walls) and burnt (them) down.[8]

For all these things Shalmaneser III and the other kings of Assyria gave praise to the gods of Assyria and to their own heroic behavior. Shalmaneser III erected a stela that chronicled his "heroic behavior" and his "deeds in combat."[9]

Nineveh lived by bloodshed and seemed to relish the opportunity to inflict more destruction on others. "All warfare, modern as well as ancient, is violent, but Assyria surpassed the ancient Near Eastern world in terms of violence and bloodshed."[10] The shedding of blood ensured the continued plunder the armies of Assyria brought to the country. Nahum concluded that a nation built on bloodshed could not endure. Maier appropriately concluded:

> The atrocious practice of cutting off hands and feet, ears and noses, gouging out eyes, lopping off heads and then binding them to vines or heaping them up before city gates; the utter fiendishness by which captives could be impaled or flayed alive through a process in which their skin was gradually and completely removed—this planned frightfulness systematically enforced by the "bloody city" was now to be avenged.[11]

God's prophets announced the doom of any city built on blood (Mic 3:9–12). Neither Jerusalem nor Nineveh could stand on bloodshed, but the city built on the Lord would endure forever (Mic 4:1–4).

Second, Nahum assailed Nineveh for its deceit. He described the city as full of lies. For years Assyria lied to its vassals and to those with whom the nation negotiated. Whether through self-interest or blatant deceit, Assyria lied to the nations. The Hebrew presents the stark reality of Nineveh: "All of it [is] a lie."

The Hebrew word for "lie" *(keḥaš)* can also mean "that which fails," such as the olive tree (Hab 3:17). Promising prosperity with its luxuriant foliage, the tree fails (or "lies"). Nineveh lied to the nations. The Rabshakeh, the messenger of Sennacherib, promised prosperity but delivered destruction (2 Kgs 18:31–32).

---

[8] *ANET,* 277.

[9] Ibid.

[10] Longman, "Nahum," 812.

[11] W. A. Maier, *The Book of Nahum: A Commentary* (St. Louis: Concordia, 1959), 292.

> Do not listen to Hezekiah; for thus says the king of Assyria: "Make your peace with me and come out to me; then every one of you will eat of his own vine, and every one of his own fig tree, and every one of you will drink the water of his own cistern; until I come and take you away to a land like your own land, a land of grain and wine, a land of bread and vineyards, a land of olive trees and honey, that you may live, and not die. And do not listen to Hezekiah when he misleads you by saying, the Lord will deliver us."

Nineveh's prosperity, brought about by oppression and injustice, seemed to promise material success to the nations as well. Its promises were lies. The entire city was a lie. Like the harlot (Nah 3:4), Nineveh had seduced the nations. The result would be her destruction.

Third, Nahum described the city as full of plunder. "The prophet here presents a one-sentence synopsis of Assyria's history."[12] From the standpoint of translation and interpretation, the phrase can refer both to the wealth amassed as well as the wealth to be plundered by the invaders of Nineveh. In either case the point is the same: this city built on blood and lies and filled with the wealth of the nations would be plundered itself.[13]

3:2 Verses 2–3 propel the reader and hearer into the streets of Nineveh with its chaos and panic. The phrases are brief but descriptive of the events that one day would occur in the heart of Assyria itself. "There is no transitional statement between the woe oracle and the short vision connected to it. … God has allowed Nahum to witness the fall of Nineveh even though it is years, perhaps even decades, away."[14]

Nahum's use of language reached its height in these brief verses (2–3). He described the sights and sounds of people who would live a lifetime during the space of a few hours. Nahum used the word "voice" or "sound" twice in v. 2. The NIV translates these as "crack" and "clatter." The Hebrew word *qôl* describes diverse sounds, from "voice" to "sound" to "thunder." In the Hebrew text all the nouns are grammatically singular, but they probably function as collectives. Thus the NIV follows the rendering by making all of the nouns plural.

The word translated "galloping" is found only here in the Hebrew text, making definitive translation almost impossible. Most English translations use some form of the word "gallop." The Hebrew word is a participle, thus calling for some idea of present, continuous activity.

Chariots traveling swiftly bounced along uneven streets. All of these phrases emphasized the sights and sounds of warfare in the very streets of the

---

[12] Maier, *The Book of Nahum*, 293.

[13] The positioning of the two Hb. words, פרק ("plunder") at the beginning of the line and טרף ("prey") at the end, suggests a chiasmus. For a fuller discussion see K. J. Cathcart, *Nahum in the Light of Northwest Semitic* (Rome: Biblical Institute Press, 1973), 17.

[14] Longman, "Nahum," 813.

city. Those who relished the terror[15] struck in the hearts of others now would experience the fear arising from chariots bounding through their own streets. People on foot would panic at the swiftness of the chariot in the streets of the city.

The two Hebrew words for "jolting chariots" begin with the same letter and have similar sounds *(merkābâ mĕraqqēdâ)*. A possible translation that preserves the idea of the Hebrew is "the rattling sound of racing chariots."[16]

Why did the prophet speak in such vivid language? Nahum's message centered around the destruction of Nineveh, but he directed his message to the people of Judah and Jerusalem. By allowing the people of Jerusalem to "see" what would happen in Nineveh, Nahum inspired faith and encouraged them to expect the deliverance of God. If this occurred in 627 B.C., Nahum's words encouraged and emboldened those calling for reform of Judah's political and religious institutions. These words should encourage all people who waste away under oppression. The last word of this world is not from the lips of those who control the sword but from the living God.

3:3 "The survey of the jolting chariots gives way to swift-moving flashes of battle and to a multipicture montage of the defeat which Nineveh suffers. ... During the siege the infantry played the important role; now that the walls have fallen, the charging cavalry comes into prominent action."[17] Nations that live by the sword die by the sword. Nineveh would experience a punishment in kind. It lived by intimidation, lies, and bloodshed. Its streets would be filled with the corpses of its inhabitants.

Nahum described the army surging through the streets of Nineveh. Everywhere one looked, he saw only cavalry, swords, and spears. No one could escape. Such movement through the heart of the city resulted in innumerable casualties. "Nahum's readers are thus presented with a somber view of a ghastly sight."[18] Nahum used three different terms for dead bodies, each with slightly different meaning. "Casualties" indicated people who had been fatally pierced, while "dead" refers to a person who has collapsed. The final word is used twice to refer to "bodies" or "corpses," a word indicating a body lying face down.[19] As attacking soldiers stumbled in their haste to attack the

---

[15] Patterson notes that "the Assyrian battle chariot was feared far and wide. Sennacherib called his private war chariot, 'The Vanquisher of the Wicked and Evil' and also 'The Vanquisher of the Enemy" (*Nahum, Habakkuk, Zephaniah,* 88).

[16] D. J. Clark and H. A. Hatton, *A Handbook on the Books of Nahum, Habakkuk, and Zephaniah* (New York: United Bible Societies, 1989), 42.

[17] Maier, *The Book of Nahum,* 297.

[18] Patterson, *Nahum, Habakkuk, Zephaniah,* 89.

[19] Robertson, *Nahum, Habakkuk, and Zephaniah,* 106. See also Patterson, *Nahum, Habakkuk, Zephaniah,* 89. BHS and some commentators remove the last phrase for metrical reasons, probably because of the use of a verb in a context without verbs. The verb "stumbling" connects the passage to Nah 2:5, where the attackers stumble at the charge against the city.

city (2:5), now citizens and soldiers of the city stumble over dead compatriots in their panic to flee the city.

The beginning of v. 2 and the ending of v. 3 are in contrast. The section begins with the din of battle but ends with the silence of the dead. From cracking whips to flashing swords the scene shifts to piles of bodies that seem to be the only way of slowing down the attack.

3:4 This is a "hinge" verse binding what precedes and what follows "with vividness and smoothness of succession."[20] Why did this kind of carnage take place? "All because of the wanton lust of a harlot." Nineveh's destruction came from its seduction of the nations. Alluring promises of prosperity and protection turned out to be curses that entrapped the other nations like Judah in a demoralizing cycle of dependency and oppression."[21] It had behaved as a prostitute; now it would suffer the humiliation of a prostitute.

The theme of Nineveh as a prostitute who enticed the nations continues through v. 7 and is a fairly common theme in Scripture.[22] Revelation 17–18 also describe the enemies of God in terms of the harlot. The most common use of the metaphor is found with the people of God. The adultery motif vividly describes the seriousness of the people's turning away from God. This is not, however, the meaning of the current metaphor. Assyria had not worshiped the Lord. Nahum's use of the prostitution metaphor stemmed from two sources.

First, Nineveh's political leadership behaved as a prostitute, enticing poorer and weaker nations with its wealth and charms. "As a harlot dispenses her favors 'for hire' ..., so Nineveh, like a scheming prostitute, has cunningly sold her military aid to other countries."[23] The weaker nations fell victim to the allure of Assyria's wealth and power. They looked to Assyria for protection and material wealth, but they soon learned that, like the prostitute, the promises of Assyria only led to destruction. Nineveh "sacrificed any semblance of morality to personal interest."[24]

A prime example of the allure of Assyria was the enticement of Ahaz of Judah. During the Syro-Ephraimitic crisis, Ahaz refused to listen to the words of Isaiah the prophet, choosing rather to accept the protection of the Assyrian king (Isa 7:1–8:8). Ahaz rejected the Lord's protection and aligned himself with Assyria.

---

[20] Patterson, *Nahum, Habakkuk, Zephaniah,* 84.

[21] W. P. Brown, *Obadiah through Malachi*, Westminster Bible Companion, ed. P. D. Miller and D. L. Bartlett (Louisville: Westminster/John Knox), 78.

[22] Longman notes that "from the Israelite perspective, the most wicked types of females were prostitutes and sorceresses. These women sought money and domination beyond acceptable social and religious norms" ("Nahum," 815).

[23] Maier, *The Book of Nahum*, 302.

[24] Armerding, "Habakkuk," 7:481.

Tiglath-pileser III of Assyria happily came to the aid of Ahaz. In the pattern of many other despots, he used the protection of his friend Ahaz as an excuse to take Damascus and to ravage the northern tribes of Israel in 732 B.C. This action set in place the eventual capture of Samaria by the Assyrians in 722 B.C. and began a century of Assyrian domination of Judah. Objects of Assyrian worship were set up in the temple, and Judah followed the path of idolatry championed by Assyria (2 Kgs 16:10–16). During the long reign of Manasseh (696–641 B.C.), Judah prostituted itself by following the harlot Assyria (2 Kgs 21:1–26).

Second, sacred prostitution played a large part in the worship of the chief deity of the Assyrians, Ishtar. Worshipers of Ishtar often referred to her as a prostitute.[25] "Nahum's chief complaint against Nineveh is for its spiritual atrocities."[26] "All because of the wanton lust of a harlot" indicates that Assyria's destruction (Nah 3:1–3) came because of its evil deeds. The Lord God is the righteous judge of the universe. Evil cannot go unpunished. God will end oppression.

Much like the writer of Proverbs, Nahum described the wiles of the harlot. "For the lips of an adulteress drip honey, and her speech is smoother than oil; but in the end she is bitter as gall, sharp as a double-edged sword" (Prov 5:3–4). She is "fair and graceful, a mistress of witchcraft." In this instance "sorceries," or "witchcraft," refers to her spells and charms.[27] "Assyrians were utterly superstitious and wholly dedicated to sorcery."[28] The nations had been spellbound to the power of Assyria only ultimately to regret her allure.

Lines three and four in the Hebrew text use important words (*zĕnûnîm*, "lust/prostitution," and *kĕšāpîm*, "sorceries/witchcraft") from lines one and two. Assyria the harlot "enslaved" nations by its prostitution. The Hebrew text uses the word "sold" *(mākar)*, thus leading to the idea in the NIV of being sold into slavery. "The corrupt capital sold nations, so that their people individually became slaves to the Assyrians and others."[29] Assyria also enslaved nations by witchcraft. "By unholy means, dark, treacherous dealings, she relegates 'peoples' (smaller nations or racial groups, Jer 25:9; Ezek 20:32; Amos 3:2) into slavery."[30] This probably is a correct association. Assyria's attraction

---

[25] Clark and Hatton, *Nahum, Habakkuk, and Zephaniah,* 44.

[26] Patterson, *Nahum, Habakkuk, Zephaniah,* 90.

[27] Robertson describes Assyria's sorcery: "The city is no amateur in the art of sorcery. She is a master at black magic. Rather than doing what is right and leaving the future to God, this entire community sets to itself the task of determining the course of the future so that it will result in its own benefit. Employing every means—even resorting to the trade of the wizard—the inhabitants of Nineveh deny the sovereignty of God over the affairs of men" (*Nahum, Habakkuk, and Zephaniah,* 103).

[28] Maier, *The Book of Nahum*, 302.

[29] Ibid., 304.

[30] Ibid.

lured nations into league with Assyria only to learn too late that association with Assyria often led to loss of land and loss of life. This is what happened to Samaria and to many other states in Palestine.

E. Achtemeier points out that this passage describes the nature of Assyria to deceive and the nature of human beings to be "fooled by the attractions of the world." We are allured by status, power, wealth, or by those who seem to have solutions to our problems. "And so we take refuge in the petty powers of this world and 'do not look to the Holy One of Israel' (Isa 31:1)."[31]

2. The Humiliation of Nineveh (3:5–7)

5"I am against you," declares the LORD Almighty.
"I will lift your skirts over your face.
I will show the nations your nakedness
and the kingdoms your shame.
6I will pelt you with filth,
I will treat you with contempt
and make you a spectacle.
7All who see you will flee from you and say,
'Nineveh is in ruins—who will mourn for her?'
Where can I find anyone to comfort you?"

3:5 For the second time Nahum declared the Lord's opposition to Nineveh: " 'I am against you,' declares the Lord Almighty." The same words are found in Nah 2:13, suggesting to some that Nah 2:13 begins a new section that continues through chap. 3.[32] On several occasions Nahum returned to a theme he had discussed previously. Maier decides that "since the Almighty has spoken twice, Nineveh is doubly doomed."[33]

In both verses the NIV ignores the introductory participle *hinnê,* a word that has the force of "look" or "take notice." In the Hebrew text the word demands action on the part of the reader. The phrase "declares the LORD Almighty" is literally "oracle of the LORD of hosts," calling attention to the Lord as the speaker and indicating the military aspects of the following message. Longman sees in the military reference a picture of "the vast forces under Yahweh's control … the cosmic powers that God uses to effect his will in history."[34]

---

[31] E. Achtemeier, *Nahum–Malachi,* IBC (Atlanta: John Knox, 1986), 24.

[32] Clark and Hatton argue for the preceding verse to be included in the section because of the subject matter. The theme of the prostitute begins in 3:4 and continues through 3:7. Nah 2:13 also continues a metaphor (that of Nineveh as a lion) begun in the previous verse. Several translations treat Nah 3:4–7 as a paragraph, including the JB and the NEB.

[33] Maier, *The Book of Nahum*, 306.

[34] Longman, "Nahum," 816.

Nahum gives five consequences of the Lord's being against Nineveh. Each consequence begins with the verb in the first person, though most translations do not show the personal use of the first-person singular. By speaking in the first person rather than using an intermediary or chosen servant, God shows his explicit contempt for the tactics of Assyria. The Lord of history would bring the utter humiliation of the oppressor.

In this section God addressed Nineveh in the second-person singular, a device that shows God's utter opposition to oppression and to the use of force. The message of God combats all forms of evil that seek to take advantage of others. God spoke to Nineveh directly to show the importance of right actions toward others.

The first consequence reflects the analogy of Nineveh as a harlot. Nineveh had behaved as a harlot to the nations, and Nineveh would be treated as a harlot. During her seduction of the nations, Nineveh eagerly exposed her nakedness. Now God promised to expose Nineveh's nakedness to the nations and to show what she had been. Ezekiel described this exact punishment for Jerusalem because she had acted as a harlot (Ezek 16:35–37; see also Jer 13:26). Lifting up the skirt and exposing the woman's nakedness was a customary punishment for women guilty of adultery (Hos 2:10).

The second consequence results from the first. God promised to show the nations and the kingdoms Assyria's nakedness and her shame. "Nations" and "kingdoms" are parallel terms as are "nakedness" and "shame." The parallel terms help the reader understand the significance of the verse. Nakedness implied shame. As used here, nakedness is a euphemism for the sexual organs. Nineveh had shamed others; now Nineveh would be shamed. The bully of the region would be shamed by its plight. Nations and kingdoms had been intimidated by Nineveh's power and seduced by Nineveh's wealth. When the Lord exposed Nineveh's shame, the nations would understand the complete downfall of Assyria. The Lord's words through Nahum show that sin always brings consequences.

Modern society has problems with both sin and consequences. We make "mistakes" and assume that our mistakes can be covered over. Many religious people expect the indulgent grandfather of the universe to remove the consequences of our actions. Even committed Christians often confuse the relationship between sins and consequences, wondering why God does not do something about the things that occur in the world.

We often seem to worship God because he keeps us from evil rather than for the sake of knowing him. Nahum reminds us that consequences always follow sin. Reflecting on passages such as these also calls us to worship God for who he is rather than for what he can do for us. While we reflect on these truths, we also remember that worshiping God brings the greatest blessings in life.

3:6 The third consequence intensified Nineveh's public humiliation. "Just as Nineveh has abused its captives, exposing them to public ridicule, so he shall make Nineveh a spectacle of shame that the nations will never forget. Everyone will come and stare at Nineveh the gazingstock. International shame and disgrace shall replace pomp and pride."[35] Nineveh would be pelted with detestable things. "Filth" might include all kinds of household garbage. It "may connote anything that God thinks is detestable."[36] Though this treatment of a harlot is not found in the Old Testament, this may have been the spontaneous response to prostitution and to those who sought to profit by the misfortunes of others. The nation that had publicly humiliated others would be publicly humiliated.[37]

The translators of the Septuagint used the same word for "filth" *(bdelugma)* as they used to describe the "*abomination* of desolation" in Matt 24:15. The "abomination of desolation" described that which was most repulsive. So Nineveh would be repulsive to those it had formerly seduced (2 Sam 13:15).

Those who first heard Nahum's message could not have missed the significance of God's intention. He would bring a matching punishment against Nineveh. How ironic that the nation that used these tactics of intimidation and humiliation to its advantage would suffer its own kind of treatment.

The fourth consequence naturally followed after being pelted with filth. God would treat Nineveh with contempt. Literally, the Hebrew says that God would treat Nineveh as a fool.[38] Was this really the city and the nation that so many people feared? Could this nation covered in rubbish really command the obedience of the nations and the people of Judah?

Nahum's words provided hope for the people of Jerusalem. Jerusalem could not suffer much longer under the yoke of such a contemptible nation. Soon Jerusalem would be free, the Assyrian images would be removed from the temple, and the people would know of the goodness and protection of God.

As a final consequence God would make Nineveh a spectacle.[39] "The pic-

---

[35] Robertson, *Nahum, Habakkuk, and Zephaniah,* 110; cf. also Baker, who cites Isa 47:3; Jer 13:22,26; Ezek 16:37–39; Hos 2:3,9 (*Nahum, Habakkuk, Zephaniah,* 23b, 37).

[36] Longman, "Nahum," 816.

[37] Patterson paints the picture: "Despoiled Nineveh will be treated as a detested and abominable thing. Condemned for her abhorrent idolatrous worship, a thing of incredible filth in God's sight, she is treated as an object of revulsion by having dirt heaped upon her. It is an action denoting intense disrespect (2 Sam 16:13; cf. Mal 2:3)" (*Nahum, Habakkuk, Zephaniah,* 86).

[38] *HALOT,* 663. The phrase in the NIV, "I will treat you with contempt," is one word in the Hebrew (וְנִבַּלְתִּיךְ).

[39] The translation has occasioned some controversy. The translation in the NIV represents the most common view. God declared that he would treat the people as a spectacle or as a gazingstock (RSV). Patterson proposes a hendiadys for the last line of v. 6, thus combining the last two consequencs into a "contemptible spectacle" *(Nahum, Habakkuk, Zephaniah,* 92). Some translators think "spectacle" (כראי) should be "feces" or "excrement," thus making the last phrase of v. 6 parallel to the first one, "I will pelt you with filth." In vv. 5–7 Nahum repeated the use of the verb "to see" (ראה): "I will show [וְהַרְאֵיתִי] the nations your nakedness" (v. 5) "and make you as a spectacle [כְּרֹאִי]" (v. 6); and "all who see [רֹאַיִךְ] you will flee from you" (v. 7).

ture of Nineveh, naked and besmirched, will be revolting in the extreme."[40] Nations would look on the harlot with contempt and scorn rather than desire. Nineveh's kings apparently delighted in making subjugated kings public spectacles. In their inscriptions Assyrian kings boasted of making captured kings wear a dog's collar and watch the bar of the city gate.[41]

God promised to make Nineveh the same kind of spectacle and worse. Assyria's demise could not be mistaken. God would destroy Nineveh and thus free all the captive peoples of the allure of the harlot, Nineveh. "Justice must be done even from a new covenant perspective (Rom 12:19)."[42]

3:7 What can you do when you look on sights that are repulsive? All who see such sights must turn their heads in revulsion. Nahum described those who looked on Nineveh in just this way. Everyone who saw Nineveh the harlot would experience disgust. They would turn away in horror.

The onlookers speak:[43] "Nineveh is in ruins." The metaphor appears to change in the first part of this verse from that of the prostitute to the actual destruction of the city by the invading army. From Nahum's perspective the city lay in ruins. The city with all its finery and buildings was wasted. Nineveh, which had wasted so many cities, was only a pile of rubble. Its buildings had been reduced to bricks, wood, and rubble.

Who would mourn for Nineveh? The last two questions of v. 7 are rhetorical. No one laments over Nineveh. In contrast, all who heard of the fall of Nineveh would clap their hands in joy.[44] Assyria "drops out of history, friendless and unwept, because her calculated cruelties had irreconcilably estranged her victims."[45] Even the Lord could not find comforters[46] for the wicked city: "Where can I find anyone to comfort you?" Is there a note of caring and con-

---

[40] Maier, *The Book of Nahum,* 312.

[41] *ANET,* 298.

[42] Robertson, *Nahum, Habakkuk, and Zephaniah,* 110.

[43] Patterson sees the speakers here as those fleeing the city and discerns therein a "messenger" motif ending a subsection as in 1:15; 2:13; 3:18–19 (*Nahum, Habakkuk, Zephaniah,* 86).

[44] The questions for Nah 3:7 are twofold: Where does the quotation end, and should "you" in the last question be "her"? The last question in the verse, "Where can I find anyone to comfort you?" probably answers both questions. The beginning of the verse suggests that many people would look on Nineveh in revulsion and say that Nineveh is wasted. Who would mourn for her? Since the next question is in the first person and Nineveh is referred to in the second person, the quotation appears to end before the second question concerning who would lament for Nineveh. The placing of the major accent *(athnach)* also argues for this end to the quotation. In order for the quotation to continue to the end of the verse, "you" must become "her" as in the LXX, a change easily made in an unpointed Hb. text. The best conclusion probably follows the NIV. God asks the last question and speaks directly to Nineveh ("you"). Not even God can find anyone to lament for the fallen Nineveh.

[45] Maier, *The Book of Nahum*, 312.

[46] Comforters (מְנַחֲמִים) is built off the same root as the prophet's name and is often seen as a wordplay on that name. The comfortless message for Nineveh brings hope and comfort to Mr. Comfort's real audience: Judah and Jerusalem.

cern on the prophet's part here? Does the prophet have a compassionate side as Heflin wants him to?[47]

3. The Weakness of Nineveh (3:8–13)

8Are you better than Thebes,
situated on the Nile,
with water around her?
The river was her defense,
the waters her wall.
9Cush and Egypt were her boundless strength;
Put and Libya were among her allies.
10Yet she was taken captive
and went into exile.
Her infants were dashed to pieces
at the head of every street.
Lots were cast for her nobles,
and all her great men were put in chains.
11You too will become drunk;
you will go into hiding
and seek refuge from the enemy.

12All your fortresses are like fig trees
with their first ripe fruit;
when they are shaken,
the figs fall into the mouth of the eater.
13Look at your troops—
they are all women!
The gates of your land
are wide open to your enemies;
fire has consumed their bars.

3:8 "The point of this taunt song is not to compare the relative strengths of the Assyrian and Egyptian empires, but to announce that human might is as nothing before the wrath of God."[48] People who thought of the power of Nineveh in legendary ways had difficulty understanding that Assyria could crumble. After all, those who heard Nahum's message had only known of one power in the world—Assyria. From the time of Tiglath-pileser in 745 B.C., Assyria exerted influence over the ancient Near East. As a result, other people of the world thought of Assyria in epic proportions and assumed that no one could defeat the Assyrian power.

---

[47] J. N. B. Heflin, *Nahum, Habakkuk, Zephaniah, and Haggai,* BSC (Grand Rapids: Zondervan, 1985), 61.

[48] Achtemeier, *Nahum–Malachi,* 26.

Nahum wanted to show that Nineveh could be defeated. Was Nineveh any better than Thebes? Thebes "was the first great city of the Orient, and it remained one of the world's leading cities for over fourteen hundred years."[49] Thebes, too, appeared invincible. Both cities depended on water for protection, and both survived for centuries. Nahum asserted that as Thebes fell so also Nineveh would fall. He addressed the people of Nineveh by asking the rhetorical question, "Are you better than No-Amon?" Of course not! As No-Amon (Thebes) fell to Assyria in 663 B.C., so Nineveh would also fall. Reputation, intimidation, and fortifications could not stand before the mighty God.

Assyria's drive deep into Egypt to conquer Thebes proved to be one of the military wonders of the ancient world. Egypt relied on its geography to protect itself. Protected by deserts to the south and west and the Nile and the Red Sea to the east and the Mediterranean Sea to the north, Egypt seemed impenetrable.[50] Only the marshy area in the land of Goshen where the Suez Canal now lies gave Egypt any sense of vulnerability. During the time preceding the exodus of the people of Israel from Egypt, the pharaoh worried about the large number of slaves in that area of Egypt and what would happen should an invader convert these slaves to help raid Egypt. This formed part of the background for the pharaoh's attempt to limit the Hebrew population by killing male children born to the Hebrews (Exod 2).

Because of its location and fortifications, Nineveh thought of itself as similarly protected from invaders. A series of canals protected Nineveh from outside attack. The Nile, a half-mile wide at Thebes, protected this capital of Egypt. Thebes, the Greek name for the city, lay on the east bank of the Nile about four hundred miles (650 km) south of Cairo. In the Hebrew text the name for the city is No-Amon, meaning "the city under the care of the god Amon."[51] The ruins of Luxor and Karnak testify of the greatness of the city,

---

[49] Ibid., 25.

[50] Robertson describes the situation: "The wall of water that surrounded Thebes provided a year-round buffer difficult for any invader to overcome (v. 8). The coterie of kindred nations that encompassed the capital city of Thebes added military and political difficulties for any potential enemy (v. 9)" (*Nahum, Habakkuk, and Zephaniah,* 112). R. J. Coggins and S. P. Re'emi warn against searching Nahum's descriptions for absolutely accurate details of geography and history. "Themes which cannot be accurate historically or geographically are juxtaposed for literary effect. Thus the expression 'her rampart a sea' cannot be taken literally, for Thebes is almost 645 km (400 mi.) from the nearest sea, but it summons up the idea of Yam, the primordial sea whose power is overthrown by Yahweh" (*Israel among the Nations,* ITC [Grand Rapids: Eerdmans, 1985], 52). On the other side Maier argues: "It should be evident from Nahum's presentation, however, that he was well informed regarding the major factors in No-Amon's situation. His words contain nothing fantastic" (*The Book of Nahum,* 316–17).

[51] The name "populous No" of the KJV comes from the identification by Jerome. Thebes is often called No (נֹא) from the Egyptian word "city" (Jer 46:25; Ezek 30:14–16). Jerome apparently used a rabbinic interpretation for his usage of the name. Jerome, in fact, later identified No with Alexandria, a clear misidentification. No-Amon or Thebes serves the translator better for its accuracy. Note R. L. Smith (*Micah–Malachi,* 87–88) for further discussion of the use of the name.

often called the greatest city of the ancient world.[52]

When Nahum spoke of the water surrounding the city, he probably wanted to convey the similarities between Thebes and Nineveh. Both cities were situated by great rivers of the world, and both derived from those rivers protection as well as secure sources of water during attack. Although as far as we know Thebes did not have the system of canals that Nineveh used for its protection, the cities were similar in their dependence on water.

For Thebes, like Nineveh, "the river was her defense, the waters her wall."[53] The words for "defense" and "wall" both refer to fortifications of a city. "Defense" conveys the idea of protection against the enemy, but the word misses the significance of the Hebrew term, which refers to a "rampart" or an outer wall of fortification as found in 2 Sam 20:15. The Hebrews often called the rampart a "son of a wall," meaning a smaller wall than the main defensive area of the city. "At Thebes, Nahum declares, the first defense before the walls of the city was 'the sea.'"[54]

The context shows Nahum's point. "He does not stress moral or political superiority but the advantages of strategic location."[55] Nahum intended to convey the idea that Nineveh, like Thebes, depended on the waters as both the outer fortification and the main defense. After all, what could be a better defense than a half-mile wide river? Who could hope to penetrate such a natural barrier? Yet Assyrian force accomplished just such a mission.[56] Nahum made his point quite clear. If Thebes could fall, Nineveh could be overrun as well.

3:9 In the time of the destruction of Thebes, Egypt could have been described as "Greater Egypt." The twenty-fifth Egyptian dynasty (715–663 B.C.) consisted of kings who were Sudanese in origin and who ruled an area

---

[52] Clark and Hatton, *Nahum, Habakkuk, and Zephaniah,* 49.

[53] J. D. W. Watts claims that "the elaborate references to *streams* and *water* seem to go beyond a factual description of the city's position. The Egyptians thought of Thebes as a sacred city, built on the first dry land to emerge from the primeval waters. They considered the river Nile to be the supreme manifestation of creation's blessings, and based their faith and security on its powers. Nahum sees it, rather, as a symbol of their arrogant and heathen attitude against the Lord" ("The Books of Joel, Obadiah, Jonah, Nahum, Habakkuk and Zephaniah," in *The Cambridge Bible Commentary on the New English Bible* [Cambridge: University Press, 1975], 118–19).

[54] Maier, *The Book of Nahum,* 317.

[55] Ibid., 314. See his comparison between Thebes and Nineveh (p. 319).

[56] Nahum described the rampart as a "sea" (יָם). Of course, the Nile was not a sea in the technical sense, just as the Sea of Galilee and the Dead Sea are anot really seas. But in its significance the Nile served as the "sea" and outer defense for Thebes. No one should think that it could be overcome. The last phrase of Nah 3:8 (מִיָּם חוֹמָתָהּ) literally reads "from a sea her wall," which seems to take away the smoothness of the message as well as the parallelism of the verse. The NIV thus follows the versions in reading "waters." In an unpointed Hebrew text (the way Hebrew was written in ancient times) the word could be read as either "sea" or "waters." The NIV agrees with many other translations in changing the pointing of the text.

much larger than Egypt itself. Thebes served as the center of this empire. Egypt, the nation that prided itself in its defenses and its alliances, fell. For Nineveh and for those receiving Nahum's message in Jerusalem, the message must be clear: Nineveh too would fall! The Lord would end oppression by removing the oppressor. Nineveh would go the way of Thebes and all other empires before it.

"Cush" in the Hebrew text refers to the country of Ethiopia, which lay to the south of Egypt and included most of modern Sudan and parts of modern Ethiopia. In addition to controlling such a large territory, Egypt counted on alliances with surrounding nations to help defend it in times of distress. These alliances, well known in the ancient world, probably obligated the people of Put and Libya to come to Egypt's defense in case of attack and to deny access to armies that might invade from the area of those nations.[57] The alliances gave Thebes what appeared to be an endless supply of troops, but "from the divine perspective those measurements of relative strength had little significance."[58] Robertson reminds that "no neighbors loved and supported Nineveh out of a natural bond such as these nations felt toward Thebes."[59]

Commentators and translators are divided about the location of "Put." The NIV seems to take the more natural solution of separating "Put" from "Libya," though others see the two nations as nearly synonymous.[60] The Masoretic Text gives two different words and apparently refers to two different places.

Libya lay to the west of Egypt as it does to this day. Put is more difficult to identify. Many interpreters think "Put" refers to the area to the south of Egypt along the coast and near the southern end of the Red Sea, probably to be identified with the country of Somalia. This identification would be consistent with the foreign policy of Egypt and its defense needs. By making alliances with Libya to the west and Put to the south, Egypt assured itself of protection.[61] Armies could not invade Egypt from those directions. The Mediterranean Sea defended Egypt to the north. Only Egypt's border adjoining the Sinai proved vulnerable. Egypt could amass its defenses in this area and protect itself from all outside harm.

3:10 Nahum's point was that if Thebes, with all its defenses, could fall,

---

[57] Coggins and Re'emi compare this to Ps 68:31, "where 'Egypt' and 'Ethiopia' are again used—not so much as geographical designations but as symbolizing former enemies now rendered harmless by the power of God. ... The names should be regarded as evocative of distant and alien powers, rather than as precise geographical designations" (*Israel among the Nations,* 53).

[58] Robertson, *Nahum, Habakkuk, and Zephaniah,* 115.

[59] Ibid., 114.

[60] The GNB translates, "Libya was her ally," equating "Put" with Libya. The NIV agrees with the RSV.

[61] Longman feels that "in effect, these allies represent the whole northwestern corner of Africa" ("Nahum," 819).

how could Nineveh consider itself impregnable? As surely as Thebes fell to Assyria, Nineveh would fall at the judgment of the great God. Though well-positioned with natural defenses and allied with its immediate neighbors, Thebes went into captivity. The same would happen to Nineveh. Nineveh knew the example well. Its armies, under the ultimate command of Ashurbanipal the king, took Thebes in 663 B.C. The policies of exile, slave trading, and slaughter of infants were the ruthless policies of Nineveh as carried out by the most efficient and barbaric army of the time.

Assyria practiced a cruel system of exile for captured nations. Samaria serves as the prime example. When Samaria fell to Assyria under Tiglath-pileser III in 722 B.C., Assyria carried off many of the citizens of the Northern Kingdom to distant nations. Many of the citizens of those and other nations suffered exile to Samaria. The Old Testament indicates that the Samaritans, with their distinctive theological views and enmity with the people of Judea, came from the exile imposed by the Assyrians (2 Kgs 17:1–41).

Four events occurred even though Thebes benefited from its superior geographical defenses and its military alliances. First, the people of Thebes were taken captive and went into exile.

Second, the attackers cruelly destroyed even the infants of Thebes. The picture of dashing in pieces conveys the most barbaric treatment imaginable. The invaders crushed the infants against the stones and buildings of the city. Such cruelty abounded in ancient times. At a later time the psalmist declared the joy of the one who could dash the heads of the infants of Babylon against the rock (Ps 137:9). The whole point of Nahum's message was that Nineveh would suffer the same fate as the people of Thebes. "At the head of every street" refers to the fact that these atrocities occurred in public places in full view of everyone. All over the city and without shame or remorse the invaders cruelly destroyed the innocent children of Thebes.

Third, the noble men of Thebes became slaves to the attackers.[62] The invaders cast lots to determine who would obtain which slave. Those who ruled the city became the object of gamblers. Casting lots for the inhabitants of the city is found often in the Old Testament (Obad 11; Joel 3:3). Clark and Hatton described the casting of lots as possibly referring to writing the names of persons on stones with the stones placed in some kind of container before being cast to the ground. The first stone hitting the ground indicated the person chosen.[63]

Fourth, the leading men of Thebes tramped off to exile in chains, a com-

---

[62] Coggins and Re'emi point to similar language in Isa 3:5; 13:16; 20:4; 23:8; and particularly Ps 149:8 to conclude that "the parallel is so close as to suggest either that this language was regularly used in oracles against foreign nations or perhaps, more specifically, that it may have been part of some liturgy associated with holy war" (*Israel among the Nations,* 53).

[63] Clark and Hatton, *Nahum, Habakkuk, and Zephaniah,* 52.

mon practice in ancient times (2 Kgs 25:7; Isa 45:14; Jer 40:1,4). The great men who decided the lives of others and determined the direction of the nation felt the helplessness of going bound hand and foot into exile. "The fate of Thebes would lead Assyria to expect that its punishment might follow the same lines."[64]

3:11 "The violent victor will become the violated victim."[65] Like Thebes before it, Nineveh too would fall to an invading army. Verses 11–13 heighten the tension and leave no room for doubt about the fate of the city and nation. "The prophet … uses five different images to vivify the helplessness of the city that by unrighteousness and brutality has made itself God's enemy. Nineveh is described as a nation that has become:

like a staggering drunk
like a panicked fugitive
like a trembling fig tree
like a feeble woman
like a city with gates thrown open."[66]

As Achtemeier emphasizes, "Nahum is a master of metaphor. … In 2:1–13 Nineveh was a lion deprived of its prey, in 3:1–7 a harlot shamed and exposed. Now, in this taunt song, Nineveh becomes a drunk, weak and dazed."[67]

The "you" of v. 11 is emphasized in the Hebrew text. The effect is that "you" as well as Thebes would go into exile.[68] Drunkenness often portrayed a sense of helplessness, particularly before the wrath of God. "Nineveh will become senseless and oblivious to the events that will spell its defeat."[69] Like the nations before, Nineveh must drink the cup of God's wrath (Isa 51:17; Jer 25:15–17; Ezek 23:31–34). Like all those who oppose God, Nineveh would stagger under the judgment of God for its ungodly actions.[70]

How Nineveh would go into hiding is unclear.[71] Could they hide from the

---

[64] Baker, "Nahum, Habakkuk, Zephaniah," 38.

[65] Brown, *Obadiah through Malachi,* 79.

[66] Robertson, *Nahum, Habakkuk, and Zephaniah,* 118. Longman calls these a "a litany of misfortunes that will befall Nineveh" ("Nahum," 822).

[67] Achtemeier, *Nahum–Malachi,* 25.

[68] The Hb. text heightens the tension against Nineveh. Nah 3:10 emphasizes Thebes: "Even she to the exile." Nah 3:11a and Nah 3:11b emphasize Nineveh: "Even you will be drunk; … even you will seek refuge." Each phrase begins with the Hb. (גַּם).

[69] Longman, "Nahum," 822.

[70] Baker says, "Assyria's state will be that of staggering inebriation from the wine of God's wrath (Jer 25:15–17; Obad 16; Hab 2:16), and a cowering fear of the enemy" (*Nahum, Habakkuk, Zephaniah,* 23b, 38).

[71] W. Rudolph sees the *niphal* of עלם as reflexive, thus meaning "to be hidden in oneself, to pass out" (*Micha, Nahum, Habakuk, Zephanja,* KAT XIII 3 [Gutersloh: Gütersloher, 1975]). He is followed by Longman, "Nahum," 822.

wrath of God? Could anyone escape the day of God's judgment? The difficulty has led many translators, including BHS, to look for a word meaning "faint" or "dazed." By changing one Hebrew letter, the change can be effected. In defense of the Masoretic Text, the second part of the verse indeed speaks of hiding in the day of trouble. The people of Nineveh would seek a refuge from the enemy.[72] Try as they might to escape the wrath to come, Nineveh could not escape. It must drink the cup of the Lord's wrath.

3:12 Nineveh had no way to find refuge from the enemy. The fortresses of Nineveh probably guarded mountain passes or other strategic entrances to Assyria. These cities had especially fortified walls to help repel the enemy and to give Nineveh and the other cities of Assyria time to prepare its defenses.

These cities would be like trees full of ripe fruit. "This stresses the ease and speed with which the Ninevite strongholds will fall. Those who gather the first-ripe figs need not laboriously climb high trees and then carefully pick a few figs from each branch; when the trunk of the tree is merely shaken, the fruit falls, as it were, into the mouth of the eater, with a minimum of exertion. … In the same easy way, at the final attack on Nineveh, the invaders, particularly in attacking the fortresses before the city, will not be forced to wage long, wearisome campaigns at the cost of much labor and blood. When the last assault begins, these defenses will fall quickly."[73] In modern idiom the expression meant that the fortresses of Assyria would be "like taking candy from a baby." Fig trees filled the land of Israel. The people of Israel considered the first-ripe figs a delicacy. Nineveh faced certain defeat. The fortresses would be like the first-ripe fruit of the fig tree, juicy and ready for the eating. John took up the figures of Nahum to describe events of the final judgment (Rev 6:13–17). "The readiness for judgment which ripened for Nineveh in Nahum's day soon shall characterize the whole of the earth."[74]

3:13 Nineveh's troops had lost the ability to fight and to defend the city. The Hebrew text refers to the people as "women,"[75] but the idea must have

---

[72] Another way is to take the verb נַעֲלָמָה as a *niphal* meaning "to be hidden." This would emphasize the result of Nineveh's being drunk after drinking the cup of God's wrath. Cp. J. J. M. Roberts, *Nahum, Habakkuk, and Zephaniah: A Commentary,* OTL (Louisville: Westminster/John Knox, 1991), 71, and Robertson, *Nahum, Habakkuk, and Zephaniah,* 118. Robertson understands Nineveh being hidden as the result of the Lord's judgment and reminds the reader that although Thebes' ruins remain until the present, the ruins of Nineveh were hidden for centuries. But does this understanding reject the sequence of the verse? Nineveh would be drunk, hidden, and would seek refuge. Robertson's interpretation would need to change the sequence so that being hidden comes at the end of the verse.

[73] Maier, *The Book of Nahum,* 332–33.

[74] Robertson, *Nahum, Habakkuk, and Zephaniah,* 119.

[75] D. Hillers shows parallels to the language of troops acting like women in ancient Near Eastern treaties (*Treaty Curses and the Old Testament Prophets,* BibOr 16 [Rome: Pontifical Biblical Institute Press, 1964], 66–68).

been that the "troops" of the city could not defend it from the advancing enemy.[76] The crack troops of Assyria would fail in the time of attack.

Assyria's "gates" probably referred to the fortresses. The enemy had flung the mountain passes wide open for the attackers to flow through.[77] The bars of the city protected the city gates from unwanted entry. They had been devoured by the fire.

The gates and bars could be figurative, describing the fortresses on the borders of Assyria,[78] or the terms could be literal, describing the enemy who enters the city without resistance. Since the verse describes your "land," the figurative description seems to fit the verse. Nothing stood in the way of the enemies of Assyria.

"It is a twist of divine inspiration. The prophetic voice informs the sinner that his triumphs confirm his fate. His victories must be viewed as the harbingers of his own final defeat."[79] Nineveh and the nation Assyria stood wide open to attack. Nothing could prevent its destruction. Assyria relied on its geographic location (3:8), its allies (3:9), its fortresses guarding the nation (3:12), and its well-trained army (3:13) for protection. None of these could defend the nation from the wrath of God to come. "In the hand of the Lord there is a cup, with foaming wine, well mixed; and he will pour a draught from it, and all the wicked of the earth shall drain it down to the dregs" (Ps 78:5, RSV).

4. The Hopelessness of Defense (3:14–19a)

14Draw water for the siege,
strengthen your defenses!
Work the clay,
tread the mortar,
repair the brickwork!
15There the fire will devour you;
the sword will cut you down
and, like grasshoppers, consume you.
Multiply like grasshoppers,
multiply like locusts!

---

[76] Maier goes so far as to refer to a Latin source for a picture of Ashurbanipal dressed and made up like a woman to say, "Overlooked in this connection have been the traditions of the effeminate degeneracy in Assyria shortly before its fall" (*The Book of Nahum,* 335).

[77] The verbs in the last two clauses are both prophetic perfects, portraying the events as certain, though they would take place in the future. "Are wide open" translates the emphasis added by the infinitive absolute (פָּתֹוחַ נִפְתְּחוּ).

[78] Maier concludes that "the outlying fortresses and barriers will be captured and then destroyed by fire, the usual climax to Assyrian conquest and victory" (*The Book of Nahum,* 336).

[79] Robertson, *Nahum, Habakkuk, and Zephaniah,* 120.

[16]You have increased the number of your merchants
till they are more than the stars of the sky,
but like locusts they strip the land
and then fly away.
[17]Your guards are like locusts,
your officials like swarms of locusts
that settle in the walls on a cold day—
but when the sun appears they fly away,
and no one knows where.

[18]O king of Assyria, your shepherds slumber;
your nobles lie down to rest.
Your people are scattered on the mountains
with no one to gather them.
[19]Nothing can heal your wound;
your injury is fatal.

Nahum's closing oracle "forms the complementary piece to 1:2–11 and ends, as did that introductory hymn, with the word 'evil' *(ra*ᶜ*ah).*"[80] Nahum sings an ironic taunt song inviting Nineveh to shore up their defenses (vv. 14–17), then launches into a direct attack on the king of Nineveh announcing his immediate demise (vv. 18–19). Nahum counseled the Assyrians to prepare for attack even though he knew that the fire would devour them and the sword would cut them off (3:15).

3:14 "The scene now shifts from the outlying fortresses to Nineveh itself."[81] Through a series of imperatives, Nahum issued a "formal call to battle,"[82] commanding the people of Nineveh to prepare for the coming siege. The first matter of preparation involved the water supply. Sennacherib boasted of improving the water supply of Nineveh dramatically when it had been woefully inadequate.[83] Ancient armies did not as much overwhelm the enemy city as starve the besieged city. Water meant more than anything else. Did the people of Nineveh need to worry about water? After all, the river and canals surrounded the city. Some commentators see the process as that of filling the moats that helped make up the city's defenses, but Maier insists that "the Hebrew word here employed for 'to draw' is never used for such tactical operations but always denotes the drawing of water (usually from a well) to satisfy the thirst of men and animals."[84]

Nahum encouraged the people to inspect the fortresses along the wall of

[80] Achtemeier, *Nahum–Malachi,* 27.

[81] Maier, *The Book of Nahum,* 339.

[82] Longman, "Nahum," 823.

[83] See Maier, *The Book of Nahum,* 339.

[84] Ibid., 340. H. Schmoldt confirms this: "Das Verb wird ausschliesslich für das Schöpfen von Wasser verwendet" (*TWAT* 7:892). "The verb is exclusively used for drawing water."

the city to reinforce the walls and to prepare for the battle to come. "Here, unlike the emphasis on outlying strongholds in v. 12, the text refers to the fortified positions in Nineveh itself, the gates and the other strategic localities within the city. These must now be strengthened to resist the brunt of repeated attacks."[85] In Nineveh the people primarily used brick for building, and they would use bricks to bring the fortifications to battle ready.[86]

Strengthening the walls would depend on the making of an adequate number of bricks. The remainder of v. 14 reflects the process of making bricks. God has called Nineveh to a "superhuman effort" in defense preparations, "and all of it will be to no avail."[87] Bricks were made by people going into the clay and trampling the mortar to make it possible to be shaped. At this point the workers placed the clay into a wooden brick mold that would ensure uniform size for the bricks. When the bricks dried, they would be ready for repairing the weakened portion of the walls. The ironic nature of these exhortations is made apparent by the context.

As Patterson explains: "The force of the irony becomes immediately apparent. In those matters where the most extensive preparations are urged to be taken—water and walls—the city was to meet its demise (see 2:6–7)."[88] Robertson likewise explains that God "mocks them by urging them to consider the most extreme measures they might take to avoid the coming calamities. All their efforts will prove to be utterly futile. Their diligence, discipline, and self-denial will be of no use."[89]

3:15 Nahum's satire and irony rise to new heights. Having called Nineveh to battle, he immediately describes the depth of their defeat. "The walls of the city of Nineveh will become the borders of their tomb, not their defense."[90] As if to emphasize the futility of their preparations, Nahum told them that the fire would devour and the sword would cut them off. No matter what they did, destruction was inevitable. "The possessions and powers of this world do not avail against the Lord of Hosts."[91]

Nahum and other prophets used fire as a symbol of defeat and destruction of any kind (Amos 1–2). The prophet used the verb "to eat" with the fire, as if the flames would "lick" the people. The sword and fire both represented the instruments of warfare generally and indicated the coming destruction for Nineveh. After the capture of a city, the enemy often burned it, possibly as punishment for its resisting capture. The resulting charred remains continue to

[85] Maier, *The Book of Nahum,* 340.

[86] Clark and Hatton, *Nahum, Habakkuk, and Zephaniah,* 55.

[87] Robertson, *Nahum, Habakkuk, and Zephaniah,* 123.

[88] Patterson, *Nahum, Habakkuk, Zephaniah,* 103.

[89] Robertson, *Nahum, Habakkuk, and Zephaniah,* 122.

[90] Longman, "Nahum," 823.

[91] Achtemeier, *Nahum–Malachi,* 28.

aid archaeological research by helping to date the destruction of the cities.

A literal translation of the third line reads, "It will consume you like the locust" (Nah 3:15). Several problems come from this translation. (1) To what does "it" refer? The nearest noun is the "sword," but the "fire" seems to be most natural. The sword could not be used to destroy the locust, but farmers often used fire to rid themselves of the locust. (2) Does "like the locust" refer to the fire or sword consuming or to the way the locust consumes crops?[92] (3) Four different Hebrew words for "locust" occur in Nah 3:15–17. What did Nahum intend to convey by these words? The first word in the text, translated "grasshoppers" in the NIV, probably refers to the young locust, which has a more voracious and destructive appetite than the mature locust. Nahum's meaning then would be that like the destructive young locust, the attackers of Nineveh would consume the populace of Nineveh.[93]

The second word for "locust" is translated "locust" in the NIV and apparently refers to the mature locust. The remaining two words (in v. 17) indicate swarms of locusts. The use of swarms probably indicates the large number of Assyrian officials.[94] "The devouring of an entire metropolitan area by a small creature like the locust underscores the futility of man's grandiose plans. The most obscure and seemingly defenseless of God's creatures brings to their knees the most powerful of God's adversaries."[95]

The last two lines of v. 15 begin a new section that describes the leading men of Nineveh in terms of the locusts. The words are filled with irony. Nahum commanded (an imperative) the people to multiply as the young locust and to multiply as the mature locust. Nineveh had multiplied its mer-

---

[92] Taking these problems into account, Clark and Hatton (*Nahum, Habakkuk, and Zephaniah,* 56) provide four possible meanings for the phrase:

1. The sword will devour you as it devours the locust;
2. The sword will devour you as the locust devours the crops;
3. The fire will devour you as it devours the locust;
4. The fire will devour you as the locust devours crops.

Clark and Hatton, as well as the translators of the NIV, take the second alternative as being the most likely since the antecedent to "it" is the nearest noun "sword," and the sword could not be used to remove locusts. This leaves the second suggestion as the only reasonable alternative. Other translations remove the line completely as being a duplication of material found later in vv. 15–16 (see BHS). Maier translates: "It [the fire] shall devour thee as it [the fire] devours the locust," arguing that "here neither 'the sword' nor 'the locust' is the subject, but 'the fire.' The fact that the verb תֹּאכְלֵךְ has been used at the beginning of this verse with fire speaks for its association here with the same verb" (*The Book of Nahum,* 346).

[93] The word for "locust" or "grasshopper" (יֶלֶק) means "to strip off the skin," an apparent reference to the young locust, which sheds its skin and then has usable wings. See J. A. Thompson, *BT* (1974): 25:405–11.

[94] Maier wants to interpret the passage so that every reference to locusts in 3:15–17 refers to Nineveh (*The Book of Nahum,* 346).

[95] Robertson, *Nahum, Habakkuk, and Zephaniah,* 124.

chants at the expense of the nations. Now those merchants would not save the nation. As locusts on a sunny day, they would fly away.

3:16 Nineveh had increased its wealth by plundering the nations. "With the vast territory of the empire under one central government, commerce could flourish throughout this area as never before. … For centuries the traders left Nineveh for all parts of the empire, and the riches of a booty-heavy people necessarily produced much internal commerce."[96] The city and the nation had multiplied its wealth and the number of its merchants. Like locusts that strip the land and then fly away to more productive regions, the merchants would leave the city, fleeing for their lives and looking for greener pastures where they could resume their merchandising. "The wealth and foreign connections produced by Nineveh's commerce have not been able to restrain the flight of its people."[97]

3:17 The twin themes of hopelessness and locusts continue in v. 17. As in the preceding verse, those people most likely to defend the city would depart like the locust. The words for "guards" and "officials" are Assyrian loan words that Nahum used to heighten the effect. Though the words are difficult to translate, the idea of guards and officials indicates the nature of those fleeing the city like locusts. "Their leaders may be vast in numbers, but they are inept, ineffective, and essentially looking after their own interests."[98] How could Nineveh stand if those with the most to lose deserted the city? How could Nineveh stand with leaders they cannot trust? This theme of false trust permeates prophetic literature. Usually, such condemnation attacks Israel and its failure to trust God. Nahum shows it can be used "against any who dared to make claims concerning their own power."[99]

Cold weather affected the locust. On cold days the locusts barely moved, preferring to hide in the crevices provided by stone fences that surrounded the fields of Assyria. When the weather warmed, the locusts began to move again and flew away. Who knows where locusts fly? Can you keep up with a swarm of locusts? If you can find the locusts who fly away, you can also find the leading officials of Nineveh on the day of attack. Longman shows how Nahum has satirically taken a common image using locusts to describe "unstoppable armies" and used it instead to describe armies and nations characterized by weakness and disloyalty.[100]

"The Assyrians had based their empire on expediency and self-interest, multiplying power, wealth, and personnel like locusts for their own gratification. Now their empire was to succumb as a victim of the self-interest it had

[96] Maier, *The Book of Nahum,* 348.
[97] Ibid., *The Book of Nahum,* 349.
[98] Robertson, *Nahum, Habakkuk, and Zephaniah,* 126.
[99] Coggins and Re'emi, *Israel among the Nations,* 57.
[100] Longman, "Nahum," 826.

promoted—eaten away from within no less than it was devoured by the sword from without."[101]

3:18 "Although most of the Book of Nahum pulses with energy as it reflects the visionary battle, the last section is composed of quiet, dirgelike cadences."[102] The next two verses continue the theme of the hopelessness of Nineveh's defense but also begin to indicate the joy of the defeat of Nineveh. The verses are addressed to the king of Assyria.[103] "The irony is that the king of all people is the *last* person to know that his power has been pulled out from under him."[104]

Assyria's shepherds (rulers) and nobles slumbered through the battle. No one watched over the city and the nation. "The collapse of effective loyalty penetrated even Assyria's aristocracy."[105] "Sleep" may also be a metaphor for death, a poignant description of Assyria's certain destruction. All who would defend the bloody city have been killed. "As the Assyrian ruler surveys the ranks of his 'shepherds,' he learns that his warriors, administrators, and counselors are silent in eternal sleep. … Their leaders silent in death, the people are without guidance and direction. Consequently they are dispersed. The shepherds dead, the flock is scattered."[106]

The resultant lack of leadership meant that the people would be scattered over the countryside with no one to assemble the people. Since the leaders are compared with "shepherds," the people are compared with sheep with the inevitable results when there is no shepherd to lead them.

"The people of the king of Assyria had been scattered on the mountains and not one of his appointees had an inclination to gather them. Much less had the king himself any inclination to gather the sheep. What a contrast with the King of Kings and Lord of Lords, the Son of God who as the good shepherd laid down his life for the sheep (John 10:11)."[107]

3:19a "In the final lines of his oracle the prophet precludes all hope for a restored Nineveh. The proud city will be destroyed irreparably, the Assyrian kingship is inescapably doomed."[108] Nahum emphasized the fatal wounds of the king of Assyria and his subjects. God had assured Nineveh's destruction; Judah's deliverance would be complete.

---

[101] Armerding, "Habakkuk," 7:488–89.

[102] Longman, "Nahum," 828.

[103] Most of Nahum's prophecy is addressed to the city of Nineveh as a feminine figure. Beginning in 3:18, the prophet addressed the king of Assyria, though BHS suggests that "shepherds" and "nobles" be read as feminine with the Syr and that the phrase "king of Assyria" may be an addition.

[104] Brown, *Obadiah through Malachi*, 79.

[105] Armerding, "Habakkuk," 7:489.

[106] Maier, *The Book of Nahum*, 357–58.

[107] Robertson, *Nahum, Habakkuk, and Zephaniah*, 128.

[108] Maier, *The Book of Nahum*, 361.

5. The Joy in Justice (3:19b)

Everyone who hears the news about you
claps his hands at your fall,
for who has not felt
your endless cruelty?

3:19b In early days Nahum's prophecy received considerable criticism for its joy at the destruction of Nineveh. The argument went something like this: Since God loves all people, how could the canon contain such blatant joy over the destruction of the enemy?

Although this idea certainly presents a concern for the interpreter, the question appears to miss the theological point of the book. As surely as the sovereign God judges his own people, thrusting them into exile in Babylon, God may also bring deliverance for his people. In each instance he worked according to his divine purpose for the world. "Human beings can be justly glad when tyrants meet their due and the earth is once again delivered from the corruptions of human power and rule. Such deliverance is a witness to the righteous lordship of God."[109]

"Everyone who hears the news about you" included all the smaller states of Western Asia. All would rejoice in Nineveh's demise because all had come under Nineveh's endless cruelty.[110] God's judgment of Nineveh aided Judah and the other weaker nations suffering under the barbaric regime of the king of Assyria. Assyria had stolen, plundered, and committed acts of unconscionable atrocity. God acted in history to remove the oppressor and to restore the oppressed. Thus God's final message to Nineveh's king was brutal: "Three continents have reeled for decades from the irrational extremes of your passion. Shall those whose eyes you have gouged out shed tears at your death? Shall those whose ears and nose you have cut off lament now? Shall the tongues you have chopped off recite your praises?" No, the time had come in which "the offer of mercy must be superseded by divine judgment."[111]

In this context we find the true point of Nahum. God is the Lord of history who works in history to correct oppression and to lift up the oppressed. "Nineveh is no ordinary city for the prophet, nor is Assyria just another degenerating civilization. They stand for the ultimate supernatural evil that frustrates and suppresses the purposes and people of God. Their defeat is a sign of the victory of God and the basis for hope that his power and justice will ulti-

---

[109] Achtemeier, *Nahum–Malachi,* 28.

[110] Baker notes that "rejoicing is not in this context gleeful gloating at the misfortune of others (cf. Ps 22:17; Obad 12; Rev 11:10), an attitude which is unacceptable for the people of God. Rather, it is pleasure at the vindication of God and his promises" (*Nahum, Habakkuk, Zephaniah,* 23b, 40).

[111] Robertson, *Nahum, Habakkuk, and Zephaniah,* 130–31.

mately conquer all evil."[112]

Those who read the Book of Nahum should not miss the point that God cares for the weak and needy of the world and is working in history to correct oppression. Let us make sure that we recognize God's work and seek to correct oppression and participate in the work of God in his world. For us who read the Book of Nahum today, a strong message comes through. We can easily stand with Nahum and point the finger of guilt at our enemies. We quickly volunteer for God's army, hardly able to wait for his call to battle against the hated enemy. God calls us to another listening post as we read Nahum. He calls us to stand with the court of the king of Nineveh and listen to God's description of who we are in his sight. He calls us to take off our battle uniforms and watch God at work. "We must never forget that the whole Book of Nahum is a celebration of divine, not human, action. Nahum leaves vengeance in the hands of God."[113] So must we. When we listen to Nahum from this vantage point, something entirely unexpected happens. The hymn of hate is directed against us. We stand in the tension between the God who is full of wrath and yet good and slow to anger. We come to see that God is calling us to bear our cross, yes even to Calvary and death. We are not only "to resist evil, not only to correct it, but also sometimes simply to suffer it, confident in the assurance that God will finally cleanse his earth of all corruption."[114] Then for us Nahum becomes more than anything else a great call to repentance.

---

[112] Watts, "Joel, Obadiah, Jonah, Nahum, Habakkuk and Zephaniah," 120.
[113] Achtemeier, *Nahum–Malachi,* 29.
[114] Ibid.

Habakkuk

INTRODUCTION OUTLINE

INTRODUCTION

Habakkuk stands unique among the prophetic books of the Old Testament in form and content. Formally, Habakkuk's book records a dialog with God and a concluding hymn. Instead of speaking to the people for God, Habakkuk spoke to God for the people. In content, Habakkuk focused on the problem of injustice in God's world. He saw that evil never seemed to be punished and asked what God's response to such evil and suffering was going to be.

In his dialog with God, Habakkuk asked God directly how the wicked could go unpunished. God answered: You must wait to see the work I am about to do on the stage of world history. Next the prophet asked, How could God use an evil instrument like Babylon to punish his own poor people, who were surely more righteous than Babylon? Habakkuk's message is set within a backdrop of real people facing real questions about real human suffering. The prophet's questions prompted God's revelation. The revelation centered in words that have repeatedly transformed the world: the righteous shall live by their faithfulness to God.

1. The Historical Setting

Habakkuk was a contemporary of Jeremiah, Nahum, and Zephaniah. Each prophet served during a pivotal era in Judah's history: 625 B.C. to 575 B.C. In this fateful historical moment, Judah lost her national life and her religious center. Assyria faded from the historical scene, and Babylon took over. "Because she was a vassal of Egypt and a friend of Babylon, it seemed as if nothing could threaten the progress of Judah's prosperity."[1]

Habakkuk's ministry probably revolved around the two most significant events in the last quarter of the seventh century B.C. in the history of the ancient Near East—the fall of Nineveh to a coalition of Medes and Babylonians and the establishment of Babylon as the greatest power of the region. Israel, the Northern Kingdom, faced the Assyrian menace shortly after 740 B.C. and succumbed to it in 721 when the Assyrians destroyed the northern capital at Samaria and exiled the leading citizens across its vast empire (2 Kgs 17). Judah began facing Assyria seriously when King Ahaz of Judah refused to join Israel and Syria in a coalition against Assyria. Rather, Ahaz appealed to Tiglath-pileser of Assyria for help (2 Kgs 16:2–9; Isa 7:1–17; 8:4–8). This led to the defeat of Israel in 733 and the capture and exile of Damascus in 732. Ahaz had to pay tribute as a vassal of Assyria.

In 704 Sennacherib became king of Assyria, leading to widespread revolt. Hezekiah of Judah led in the revolts, was pinned like a bird in a cage in Jerusalem, but finally experienced miraculous divine deliverance (2 Kgs 18–20; Isa 39). The Bible crowns Manasseh as the most evil of Judah's kings (2 Kgs 21). Manasseh introduced Canaanite and Assyrian gods into the official Judean worship, even offering his own son as a burnt sacrifice to the Ammonite god Molech (2 Kgs 21:6). As an Assyrian vassal, he contributed forces to Ashurbanipal when the Assyrian king invaded and captured Egypt in 667 B.C. In 663 B.C. Ashurbanipal destroyed the Egyptian capital of Thebes (see Nah 3:8). Manasseh's fifty-five year reign ended with his death in 641 B.C.

[1] C. J. Barber, *Habakkuk and Zephaniah,* EvBC (Chicago: Moody, 1985), 14.

The two-year reign of his son Amon (641–639 B.C.) was no better religiously or politically.[2]

When Josiah (640–609 B.C.) came to the throne, the powerful Assyrian Empire had begun to crumble, allowing a new era of hope to dawn in Judah. Lack of leadership, particularly after the death of Ashurbanipal in 627, sent Assyria reeling. This placed all the Near East in ferment. "With a self-conscious and ambitious Egypt in the south, and with the movements of Scythian and other hordes in the north, everything was in the melting pot, and no one could have foreseen who would inherit the might of Assyria."[3]

Josiah came to the throne as an eight-year-old (2 Kgs 22:1). Not much is known of his early years. Apparently, wise and trusted advisors governed, steering Josiah and the nation to the dawning of a new era. Josiah's leadership toward political independence and religious reform coincides almost exactly with Assyria's decline as the leading world power. "Josiah rules during years in which Assyria fades but also those in which Babylon is not yet ready to rule as far west as Judah and in a time when Egypt does not yet attempt to rule the smaller nations north of the border. Judah thereby gets a rest from its constant role as political football."[4] In 627 B.C. Ashurbanipal died, and Josiah began to make major policy changes as he "began to seek the God of David his father" (2 Chr 34:3).

Josiah's reform had at least three components: (1) a consistent purge of foreign cults and practices, (2) destruction of the high places in the territory of the former Northern Kingdom as well as in the south, and (3) centralization of public worship in Jerusalem (2 Chr 34:3–7).[5] Apparently, Josiah renounced the gods of Assyria and rejected completely the syncretistic policies of his grandfather, Manasseh.[6] By removing the elements of the Assyrian state religion from

---

[2] For historical references see D. C. Browning, Jr., "Assyria, History and Religion of," *HBD,* 120–24; W. C. Kaiser, Jr., *A History of Israel* (Nashville: Broadman & Holman, 1998), 385–404. C. D. Evans, "Manasseh, King of Judah," *ABD* 4:496–99; A. K. Grayson, "Mesopotamia, History of (Assyria)," *ABD* 4:732–55; G. W. Ahlström, *The History of Ancient Palestine* (Minneapolis: Fortress, 1994), 607–38, 665–753; W. W. Hallo, W. K. Simpson, *The Ancient Near East* (New York: Harcourt Brace Jovanovich, 1971), 133–44; R. D. Haak, *Habakkuk* (Leiden: Brill, 1992), *VTS* 44:111–49.

[3] S. A. Cook, "The Fall and Rise of Judah," *CAJ*, 3d ed., 394.

[4] P. R. House, *1, 2 Kings,* NAC, vol. 8 (Nashville: Broadman & Holman, 1995), 382.

[5] J. Bright, *A History of Israel,* 3d ed. (Philadelphia: Westminster, 1981), 318–19; N. Lohfink lists ten issues involved in Josiah's reform ("The Cult Reform of Josiah of Judah: 1 Kings 22–23 as a Source for the History of Israelite Religion," *Ancient Israelite Religion,* ed. P. D. Miller, P. D. Hanson, and S. D. McBride [Philadelphia: Fortress, 1987], 465); also see House, *1, 2 Kings,* 388–89.

[6] G. E. Wright, *Biblical Archaeology,* rev. ed. (Philadelphia: Westminster, 1962), 176. For recent study of Josiah, see R. Althann, "Josiah," *ABD* 3:1015–18; Y. Suzuki, "A New Aspect on Occupation Policy by King Josiah. Assimilation and Codification in View of Yahwism," *AJBI* 18 (1992): 31–61; C. M. de Tillesse, "A reforma de Josias" *RBB* 6 (1989): 41–60; and "Joiaqim, repoussoir du "pieux" Josias: Parallélismes entre II Reg 22 et Jer 36," *ZAW* 105 (1993): 352–76; B. Gieselmann, "Die sogenannte josianische Reform in der gegenwärtigen Forschung," *ZAW* 106 (1994): 223–42.

the sanctuary, Josiah in effect revoked his vassal relationship. Religious reform became at the same time political reform.[7]

In 621 B.C. while repairing the temple, workers found the Book of the Law, most often identified as all or part of the Book of Deuteronomy.[8] This gave added impetus to the reform movement, providing clear evidence from ancient sources that such reform pleased God. Josiah called the people to the temple for a ceremony of covenant renewal, where they made a covenant before the Lord to walk after the Lord and to be obedient to his commands. Thus Josiah carried out the most thoroughgoing reform in Judah's history.[9] He transformed "the little state of Judah" into "the largest nation in western Palestine in the later part of the seventh century BCE."[10] One problem! "The leaders of the people ignored the spiritual reasons for their material prosperity and thought God's favor could be enjoyed without interruption."[11]

While Judah was asserting its independence and purifying its religion, Babylon and Assyria were changing positions of authority in world politics. After the death of Ashurbanipal, Assyria's fortunes immediately plummeted. Nabopolasser of Babylon sought and gained his independence. For the next ten years (626–615 B.C.), Babylon and Assyria attacked and counterattacked each other over Assyria's holdings in southern Mesopotamia. Eventually, Nabopolasser succeeded in taking Nippur and in freeing all of Sumer and Akkad.[12] In this same year a coalition of Medes and Babylonians systematically began to reduce the Assyrian Empire by destroying its major strongholds. By 614 B.C. Cyaxares, the Mede, had defeated Ashur, one of Assyria's capitals. Nineveh, the empire's main city, did not collapse until 612. Finally, in 610/609 B.C. the final bastion of Assyrian resistance crumbled as the Medes and Babylonians captured Haran.

Using the Tigris River as the boundary for the division of the Assyrian

---

[7] Note Ahlström's discussion (*History of Ancient Palestine,* 770–81).

[8] For a discussion of the contents of the Book of the Law, see House, *1, 2 Kings,* 382–84. Ahlström concludes, "The 'law book' of the Josianic period was neither part of the Book of Deuteronomy, nor of any other known biblical book" (*History of Ancient Palestine,* 777). Rather it was either written by Josiah's "own chancellery" or was a literary device of a postexilic narrator to authenticate Ezra's law code. E. H. Merrill says the Book of the Law "clearly consisted of at least Deuteronomy and likely the entire Pentateuch" (*Kingdom of Priests: A History of Old Testament Israel* [Grand Rapids: Baker, 1987], 444–45). Merrill then explains how the Torah could have been lost and then rediscovered.

[9] B. W. Anderson, *Understanding the Old Testament,* 2d ed. (Englewood Cliffs, N.J: Prentice-Hall, 1966), 308.

[10] Ahlström, *History of Ancient Palestine,* 763. See pp. 764–65 for a critical discussion of the extent of Josiah's territorial expansion. Ahlström sees Josiah as a "vassal or ally of Egypt" (p. 766).

[11] Barber, *Habakkuk and Zephaniah,* 14.

[12] G. Roux, *Ancient Iraq* (Baltimore: Penguin, 1964), 340; cp. Hallo and Simpson, *The Ancient Near East,* 144–49; A. K. Grayson, "Mesopotamia, History of (Babylonia)," *ABD* 4:755–77; Browning, "Babylon, History and Religion of," 141–44.

holdings, the Medes took everything to the north and east while the Babylonians received the territory to the west and south. The marriage of the daughter of Cyaxares to Nebuchadrezzar, the son of Nabopolasser, completed the political alliance in typical Near Eastern style.[13]

Egypt could not ignore the realignment of international power. In 609 B.C. Pharaoh Necho II went to Assyria's aid at Carchemish, where Ashur-uballit made one last effort to recapture Haran from the Babylonians. Egypt hoped to halt the Babylonian march westward and wrench control of Syria-Palestine for itself.[14] This placed Josiah in a difficult position. He apparently saw Egypt and Assyria as a strong threat to his religious reforms and desires for political independence.[15]

Josiah's attempts have been described as "suicidal"[16] and "foolish."[17] They resulted in death on the battlefield at Megiddo (2 Kgs 23:29). His army took his body back to Jerusalem in his chariot amid great lamentation (2 Chr 35:20–24). Rowton has tried to rescue Josiah's reputation, saying he succeeded in detaining Necho long enough that he could not aid the Assyrians: "Thus it seems very probably that the last of the great Jewish kings laid down his life in a truly heroic and entirely successful bid to avenge the dreadful wrongs his nation had suffered at the hands of Assyria."[18]

The people of the land[19] selected Josiah's son Jehoahaz as king rather than Eliakim, the firstborn. Evidently, they thought Jehoahaz would continue the struggle for independence while Eliakim would submit to Egypt.[20] Pharaoh Necho probably thought the same thing since after only a three-month reign Jehoahaz was summoned to Necho's headquarters at Riblah in central Syria. From there the Egyptians imprisoned Jehoahaz and took him to Egypt, where

---

[13] R. K. Harrison, *Old Testament Times* (Grand Rapid: Eerdmans, 1970), 244–45.

[14] There is no longer any doubt that Necho went up alongside to help the king of Assyria as RSV and later translations, including NIV and NKJV, translate instead of "against" the king of Assyria as the AV translates it (2 Kgs 23:29).

[15] Merrill talks of Josiah being loyal to Babylon (*Kingdom of Priests*). Bright emphasizes Josiah's fear of coming under Egyptian control (*A History of Israel,* 324–25). House suggests that Josiah wished to "stake absolute claim to what was once Israel and considers the Egyptian movement a threat to that desire" (*1, 2 Kings,* 391). See A. Malamat, "The Last Kings of Judah and the Fall of Jerusalem," *IEJ* 18 (1968): 137, n. 1.

[16] Bright, *A History of Israel,* 303.

[17] Roux, *Ancient Iraq,* 343. Merrill notes that the Chronicler intimates that Josiah opposed God's will (2 Chr 35:22; *Kingdom of Priests,* 446).

[18] M. B. Rowton, "Jeremiah and the Death of Josiah," *JNES* 10 (1951): 129.

[19] I.e., the leading circles of the population, especially those outside Jerusalem, who possessed full political rights and owned the land; see A. R. Hulst, "גּוֹי/עַם *ʿam/gōj* Volk," *THAT* 2:299–301; cp. L. Koehler and W. Baumgartner, *HALOT* 3:793. They often defended indigenous Judaic traditions over against foreign influences. See Lipinski, *TWAT* 6:190.

[20] H. W. Robinson, *The History of Israel* (London: Duckworth, 1938), 124. Malamat suggests a coup to place someone opposed to Egypt on the throne (*IEJ* 18 [1968]: 140).

he lived until his death (2 Kgs 23:33–34). Necho installed Eliakim on the throne of Judah, where he served as an Egyptian vassal. Necho changed his name to Jehoiakim (2 Kgs 23:34–35), another way of exercising control and establishing that Jehoiakim served the pharaoh.

Jehoiakim was certainly not a worthy successor to his father. Second Kings 24:4 describes him as a tyrant who shed innocent blood in Jerusalem. Jeremiah described him as an unjust and brutal despot whose chief interest was in the sumptuous enlargement of his palace (Jer 22:13–19). Available records show him as the only king of Judah who put a prophet of Yahweh to death. Not even wicked Manasseh could claim such notoriety.

For some years after the Battle of Megiddo, Necho maintained control over Syria and Palestine, primarily because the Babylonians were busy strengthening their positions in the Armenian mountains.[21] In 605 B.C. Nabopolasser entrusted his army to his son Nebuchadrezzar, who attacked and defeated the Egyptian army at Carchemish:[22] "The king of Egypt did march out from his own country again, because the king of Babylon had taken all his territory, from the Wadi of Egypt to the Euphrates River" (2 Kgs 24:7). Nebuchadnezzar chased the Egyptians across the Euphrates River to Hamath in Syria. The significance of this event must not be underestimated. With the victory, Babylon firmly established itself as the dominant world power. Also, it left all of Syria and Palestine open to Babylon's armies. Tiny Judah had a new overlord. Jehoiakim quickly changed his obedience from Necho to Nabopolasser.

An Aramaic letter found at Saqqara in Egypt in 1942 indicates that a neighboring king did not submit so readily. King Adon requested Pharaoh for urgent help for his beleaguered city. He described Nebuchadrezzar's advance as far as Aphek and warned Necho that the Babylonians were on the verge of setting a governor over the land.[23] Nebuchadrezzar might have pushed into Egypt had it not been for the death of his father. Instead, he quickly returned home in 605 to be proclaimed king. In 602 B.C. Jehoiakim rebelled, apparently supporting an Egyptian attempt that led to a defeat of the Babylonian army in 601.[24] Babylon reacted quickly (2 Kgs 24:1–2; 2 Chr 36:6). During the winter of 598/597 Babylonian troops, apparently strengthened by contingents from Israel's neighbors (2 Kgs 24:2), entered Judah and captured Jerusalem on March 16, 597 B.C. In

---

[21] Bright, *A History of Israel*, 325.

[22] Grayson notes that Egypt now stood alone, no reports of an Assyrian army ever being reported again (*ABD* 4:765).

[23] Bright, "A New Letter in Aramaic, Written to a Pharaoh of Egypt, *BA* 12 (1949): 47–48. W. H. Shea dates the letter to 603 B.C. ("Adon's Letter and the Babylonian Chronicle," *BASOR* 223 [1976]: 61–64). Merrill (*Kingdom of Priests*, 451, n. 56) relates the letter to a Babylonian invasion of Egypt in 601, following Malamat, *IEJ* 18 (1968): 142–43. Ahlström dates it sometime after 605 and probably before the battle with Egypt in 601 B.C. (*The History of Ancient Palestine*, 784). He notes that B. Porten and G. R. Hughes ("The Identity of King Adon," *BA* 44 [1981]) make it probable that Adon ruled Ekron.

[24] See Ahlström, *The History of Ancient Palestine*, 782.

the meantime, Jehoikim had died. Nebuchadnezzar took Jehoikim's son Jehoiachin, the new king, captive to Babylon and placed another son of Josiah on the throne, naming him Zedekiah.

These "catastrophic events of the last decades of the seventh century B.C. and the first decades of the sixth century B.C. left many people reeling and disillusioned. It was an agitated time, characterized by rapid political change, international turmoil, bloody military encounters, and a growing rebellion against the demands of the covenant by the great majority in Judah. Prophetic activity was feverish, not only with the ministries of people like Jeremiah, Nahum, Zephaniah, Huldah, and Ezekiel, but also with false prophets in abundance."[25]

2. Habakkuk, the Man

No records remain to tell us of Habakkuk except his book. His book reveals at least one thing: "a prophet with an unorthodox approach ... the role of the philosopher of religion."[26] The prophet's name means "to embrace" or "to caress."[27] The book gives no personal information about Habakkuk except to say he prayed courageously to God and was a *nabi'*, a prophet. Did this indicate an "official position in the religious community,"[28] that is what often

---

[25] J. N. B. Heflin, *Nahum, Habakkuk, Zephaniah, and Haggai,* BSC (Grand Rapids: Zondervan, 1985), 67.

[26] Ibid., 67.

[27] J. J. M. Roberts (*Nahum, Habakkuk, and Zephaniah: A Commentary,* OTL [Louisville: Westminster/John Knox, 1991], 86) refers the name to an Assyrian garden flower, a theory going back to M. Noth, *Die Israelitischen Personennamen,* BWANT 3/10 (Stuttgart: 1928), 231. Many modern scholars endorse this interpretation, including W. Rudolph (*Micha, Nahum, Habakuk, Zephanja,* KAT XIII 3 [Gutersloh: Gütersloher, 1975], 199), who notes one born in the era of Manasseh might well have an Akkadian name.

[28] W. S. LaSor, D. A. Hubbard, and F. W. Bush (*Old Testament Survey: The Message, Form, and Background of the Old Testament* [Grand Rapids: Eerdmans, 1982], 450). Jöcken (p. 5) quotes Küper (*Das Prophetentum des Alten Bundes* [Leipzig, 1870], 298–300) as pointing to previous writers who concluded that Habakkuk was a Levite active among the liturgical temple singers. For a description of the origin and calling of cultic prophets, see S. Mowinckel, *The Psalms in Israel's Worship* (Oxford: Blackwell, 1962), 2:53–73; he identifies both Nahum and Habakkuk as temple prophets or cult prophets (2:93, 147). Cp. J. Jeremias, *Kultprophetie uund Gerichtsverkündigung in der späten Königszeit Israels* (Neukirchen: Neukirchener, 1970), 90–104. From the evangelical side, W. A. Vangemeren (*Interpreting the Prophetic Word* [Grand Rapids: Academie, 1990], 41–46) rejects cult prophecy as an Israelite phenomenon. G. V. Smith (*The Prophets as Preachers* [Nashville: B & H, 1994], 181) identifies Habakkuk as "one of the Levites assigned to sing for temple services (see 2 Chr 25:1–8), referring to E. Achtemeier, *Nahum–Malachi,* INT (Atlanta: John Knox, 1986), 33–35. Barber (*Habakkuk and Zephaniah,* 15) also sees Habakkuk as a Levite temple singer. R. D. Patterson appears to lean toward identifying Habakkuk as a Levite working in the temple (*Nahum, Habakkuk, Zephaniah,* WEC, ed. K. Barker [Chicago: Moody, 1991], 130) but cannot find sufficient evidence to prove it (pp. 118–19); similarly R. L. Smith, *Micah–Malachi,* WBC 32 (Waco: Word, 1984), 93, 95. Heflin identifies Habakkuk as "a professional worship leader ... either as prophet, priest, or temple singer" (*Nahum, Habakkuk, Zephaniah, and Haggai,* 71–72). Rudolph gives the most vehement denial that any evidence points to Habakkuk as a cult prophet (*Micha, Nahum, Habakuk, Zephanja,* 193–94).

has been called a cult prophet? Szeles uses the simple word *nabiʾ* ("prophet") to conclude: "He was the LORD's spokesman then, called, trained, and commissioned to be his messenger. He had received his prophetic calling through the instrumentality of the liturgy in public worship, had grasped it as it applied to himself, as it was visually and audibly mediated to him. Thereupon he communicated it to the worshiping congregation (2:1–5)."[29] This leads to the conclusion that he was a "cultic prophet" at the Jerusalem temple.

Rudolph casts doubt upon this characterization, though the most recent commentaries all accept this conclusion."[30] Heflin goes so far as to say, "He may have composed liturgies and hymns for public worship as well as led the people in services at the temple."[31] Such a question cannot be answered so quickly and easily with the evidence at hand. Chapter 3 certainly represents a musical work complete with psalmic notations. If it appeared in the Psalms, few people would have difficulty seeing it as part of the temple worship. The natural place to carry on such a dialog with God as the Book of Habakkuk represents would be the temple, but this still does not mean that the prophet was on the temple staff. The prophet spoke readily and easily of the temple as the place to meet and worship God (2:20). To speak of temple or cult prophecy is to speak of a scholarly theory or conjecture. Nothing theologically forbids God to use a person on the temple staff as a prophet. Nor does it exclude worship services in the temple as places where God can reveal his word to the prophet and where the prophet can communicate the message to the worshipers. One would almost see the temple as the natural place for such revelation. Because prophets often criticized the cultic worship of Israel and Judah does not mean that they did not participate in it and even lead part of it. We must leave the possibility open that any one prophet had a staff position in the temple, but we can never dogmatically assert that this was the case. With Rudolph, "the least one can say is that he was a visionary."[32]

Another scholarly attempt is to place Habakkuk within certain "traditions" or "trajectories" in the Old Testament. Was he part of the wisdom tra-

[29] M. E. Szeles, *Wrath and Mercy: A Commentary on the Books of Habakkuk and Zephaniah*, ITC (Grand Rapids: Eerdmans, 1987).

[30] Ibid., 5.

[31] Heflin, *Nahum, Habakkuk, Zephaniah, and Haggai*, 72.

[32] Rudolph (*Micha, Nahum, Habakuk, Zephanja*, 3:199) based on 2:1 and 3:16. Achtemeier (*Nahum–Malachi*, 33–34) concludes that "prophets prayed for their people quite apart from the cult (cf. Amos, who is certainly not a cultic prophet), and cultic forms used in Habakkuk's book have sprung their usual structures. … Habakkuk is using cultic forms in a manner independent of cultic strictures, just as his contemporary Jeremiah also used them (cf. the lament of Jer 15:15–18 and its answer, vv. 19–21). We are not justified, therefore, in designating Habakkuk a 'cultic prophet'"; cp. Haak, *Habakkuk*, 110–11.

dition?[33] A few vocabulary words most frequently encountered in wisdom literature, appearance of the theodicy theme, and employment of the dialog format do not imprison the prophet in this wisdom tradition but only show that he belonged among the educated of Israel. Was Habakkuk part of the Isaianic tradition stretching from the ministry of Isaiah (740–701 or later) to the postexilic community?[34] Again, the evidence is suggestive but cannot prove more than that Habakkuk was well embedded in the prophetic tradition of Jerusalem. Should we label him a "disillusioned Deuteronomist"?[35] Certainly living in the shadow of Josiah's reform and Jehoiakim's destruction of the reform, Habakkuk understood deuteronomic theology, but comparisons of chap. 3 with Deuteronomy 33 and identity of the paralyzed Torah of 1:4 with the failure of God to fulfill the promises of Deuteronomy after Josiah obeyed the commandments cannot support the entire thesis that Habakkuk had expected Josiah's reform to bring fulfillment of God's promises only to be horribly disillusioned when it did not.

Another scholarly question centers on Habakkuk's relationship to the power structure of his day. G. Smith has pointed clearly to a solution here: "Habakkuk's prayer concerning oppression by the Judean political leaders (1:2–4) shows he was not a central prophet who maintained the perverted views of Jehoiakim's government.[36] R. Haak, however, wants to place Habakkuk square in the political infightings in Judah, saying 1:5–6 shows he was a member of the "pro-Babylonian party in Judah."[37]

Another approach to Habakkuk is to compare his representation of prophecy with those of other prophets. Working with the Twelve, House concludes: "Habakkuk represents a crucial point in the characterization of the prophet in the Twelve. Until this point all the prophets except Jonah accept the words and deeds of the Lord almost uncritically. Perhaps the prophets did not demur

[33] D. E. Gowan, "Habakkuk and Wisdom," *Perspective* IX (1968): 157–66; G. A. Tuttle, "Wisdom and Habakkuk," SBT 3 (1973): 3–14; M. E. W. Thompson, "Prayer, Oracle, and Theophany: The Book of Habakkuk," *TynBul* 44 (1993): 45–46.

[34] See particularly Thompson, "Prayer, Oracle, and Theophany," 46–50, and literature noted there.

[35] Johnson, *VT* 25 (1985): 264; see the discussion on 262–66.

[36] G. Smith, *Prophets as Preachers,* 182; see R. R. Wilson, *Prophecy and Society in Ancient Israel* (Philadelphia: Fortress, 1980), 278–79, for arguments that Habakkuk was a central prophet. Opposing a national enemy and even being part of the national cult would not necessarily mean a person supported national policy and maintained the government party line. The direct line of divine revelation superseded the party line.

[37] Haak, *Habakkuk*, 130. He sees Habakkuk supporting a deposed Jehoahaz while he was in Egyptian custody before he died (pp. 130–33). The prophecy would have been made between the battle of Carchemish in 605 and the recognition of Babylonian rule by Jehoiakim in 603, with Habakkuk being among those expecting an early arrival of Babylonian troops in Judah.

as long as some chance for repentance lingered, or as long as it was a foreign nation that was earmarked for destruction, but when the punishment comes to Judah, thus including the prophets themselves, questions arise. Habakkuk asks some very difficult questions. ... In the process he explodes any notion that the prophets are somehow wooden, lifeless characters, and may reveal how the prophets forged their orations."[38]

One thing appears clear about Habakkuk, even if it too rests on inference rather than clear statements of the text. Habakkuk was a person of great faith and great courage who dared take the theological teaching of his day and test it against the experiences of his own personal life and of the nation. "Habakkuk adopted the role of the philosopher of religion, seeking to understand the troubling times in light of his theological heritage. ... Whereas his colleagues served primarily as messengers from God to the people, Habakkuk took the concerns that troubled him and his fellow citizens to God."[39] Such action shows he was "an honest doubter, contemplative and speculative by nature ... [with] moral and ethical sensitivity ... [who] searched for truth ... maintained profound reverence for God ... with a deep personal faith."[40]

He refused to have simply a faith of the fathers that he received without reflection. He refused to have a God of the fathers whose actions could be predicted or else must be accepted as correct without further investigation. Habakkuk insisted upon confronting his God face to face and asking God the hard questions of life. He was not satisfied until answers came and dialog ensued. Only when he had wrestled in conversation with God and created a faith understanding of his own did he present a message to the public. What a message! It has continued to reform God's people in different ways up to the present time. An unknown man provided perhaps the Bible's most well-known message.

Probably because Scripture revealed so little about the prophet, tradition worked to create knowledge about him. Such traditions can hardly be taken at face value, but they do show Judaism's continued interest in Habakkuk and his unique form of prophecy. *Bel and the Dragon,* part of the additions to Daniel in the Apocrypha written about one hundred years before Christ, tells a story (vv. 33–39) of an angel telling Habakkuk to make a stew and carry it to Daniel in the lions' den. The angel carried the prophet by his hair from Judah to Babylon, blasting him along with his breath. Daniel thanked God for remembering him, and the angel returned Habakkuk to Judah. The Greek text even names Habakkuk's father as Jesus of the tribe of Levi. *The Lives of the Prophets,* a work written approximately during the lifetime of Jesus, also

---

[38] P. R. House, *The Unity of the Twelve*, JSOTSup 97, Bible and Literature Series 27 (Sheffield: Almond, 1990)196.

[39] Heflin, *Nahum, Habakkuk, Zephaniah, and Haggai,* 67.

[40] Ibid., 72–73.

places Habakkuk at the time of Daniel but says he belonged to the tribe of Simeon. About A.D. 1300 a Jewish writing, *Sefer ha-Zohar,* said Habakkuk was the son of the Shunammite woman whose life Elisha saved.[41]

3. Habakkuk, the Book

"Prophecy is a result of revelation given to a person who then proclaims the inspired message to the people. Often such revelation and inspiration are occasioned by conditions in the nation about which the prophet has been burdened."[42] Such is the traditional understanding of the origin of a biblical book. Critical study has offered a different picture. B. Childs summarizes it this way: "The frequent assumption of the historical critical method that the correct interpretation of a biblical text depends upon the critic's ability to establish a time-frame for its historical background breaks down in the case of Habakkuk."[43]

R. P. Carroll has characterized the book as a composite rather than a structured whole: "As a ragbag of traditional elements held together by vision and prayer, Habakkuk illustrates the way prophetic books have been put together in an apparently slapdash fashion."[44] Childs responds to such conclusions with the warning, "The danger is acute that a doctrinaire application of historical criticism not only fails to find an access into the heart of the book, but by raising a series of wrong questions it effectively blocks true insight."[45]

Achtemeier notes the adaptation of earlier materials, autobiographical and biographical materials, and subsequent use of materials in Israel's cult but still insists on the "book's internal unity."[46] Heflin claims: "The prophet has done a masterful job of fusing many diverse forms into a literary unit. The book contains elements of poetry, prophecy, wisdom, and liturgy. Habakkuk's framework is yet another literary form—autobiography. … The book could be yet another illustration of the literary ability of the Old Testament prophets. These unique and inspired men were able to take many literary forms and use them aptly to proclaim the message from God."[47]

Childs has shown that three distinct forms of literature appear nicely separated from one another:

1. Prophetic dialog with God (1:2–2:5) with two prophetic complaints

---

[41] See M. A. Sweeney, "Habakkuk, Book of," *ABD* 3:1–2.

[42] C. E. Armerding, "Habakkuk," EBC 7:494.

[43] B. Childs, *Introduction to the Old Testament as Scripture* (Philadelphia: Fortress, 1979), 454.

[44] R. P. Carroll, "Habakkuk," *A Dictionary of Biblical Interpretation,*" ed. R. J. Coggins and J. L. Houlden (London: SCM, 1990), 269.

[45] Childs, *Introduction to the Old Testament as Scripture,* 455.

[46] Achtemeier, *Nahum–Malachi,* 32.

[47] Heflin, *Nahum, Habakkuk, Zephaniah, and Haggai,* 74–75.

(1:2–4,12–17) balanced by two responses from heaven (1:5–11; 2:1–5).

2. Woe oracles (2:6–20) separated into individual oracles (2:6–8,9–11,12–14,15–18,19) with a concluding call to worship (v. 20).

3. The prophet's hymnic prayer (3:2–19a) introduced and concluded with psalms-like musical notations and interspersed with the Psalms' famous division marker, "Selah."[48] Childs also calls attention to the autobiographical framework of the book from 1:2 through 3:19, a framework that does not appear to lend itself to a cultic setting.[49]

Others reduce the structure to two major parts:

1. Dialog with God (1:1–2:20)
2. A Psalm or Prayer (3:1–19)[50]

M. Sweeney has developed this structural argument in its most detailed form.[51] He builds on the Hebrew notations in 1:1 (the "oracle" or pronouncement, *hāmmassaʾ*) and 3:1 (prayer, *tĕpillâ*) as inherent structural elements in the text. From this structural observation Sweeney concludes:

> "This form-critical reassessment of the structure, genre, and intent of the book of Habakkuk demonstrates that the book has a coherent structural unity and that its genre is based on the prophetic pronouncement *(maśśāʾ)* and a petitionary prayer *(tĕpillâ)*. The intent and setting center around an attempt to explain the rise of the oppressive Neo-Babylonian Empire in the late seventh century B.C.E. as an act of YHWH which does not contradict divine righteousness and fidelity to Judah. Hab. i-ii establishes that YHWH has raised the Chaldean Empire as part of a divine plan or 'deed' *(pōʿal)*, which is not immediately explained. These chapters also make clear that the Chaldeans will be punished for their acts of oppression. Hab. iii verifies that this punishment will take place, demonstrating YHWH's sovereignty over the world and ultimately, divine righteousness as well. The two parts of the book, the Prophetic Pronouncement in Hab. i-ii and the Prayer in Hab. iii, constitute a Prophetic Affirmation of Divine Sovereignty and Justice, the purpose of which is to convince its audience that YHWH is maintaining fidelity in a crisis situation.'[52]

The argument here appears to boil down to whether one wants to follow traditional form critical markers or whether one decides to look for literary markers in the present canonical form of the book. Interestingly, whichever of

---

[48] Childs, *Introduction to the Old Testament as Scripture*, 448. Such an approach appears in the works of Rudolph, *Micha, Nahum, Habakuk, Zephanja,* 195; Armerding, "Habakkuk," 7:495; K. Elliger, *Das Buch der zwölf kleinen Propheten II, ATD* 25 (Gøttingen: Vandenhoeck & Ruprecht, 1956), 23–55.

[49] Childs, *Introduction*, 452; R. L. Smith (*Micah–Malachi,* 96) appears to agree with Childs.

[50] See O. P. Robertson, NICOT (Grand Rapids: Eerdmans, 1990), 135–248; Heflin, *Nahum, Habakkuk, Zephaniah, and Haggai,* 80–109.

[51] "Structure, Genere, and Intent in the Book of Habakkuk," *VT* 41 (1991): 63–83; cp. *ABD* III, 3–5; see Szeles, *Wrath and Mercy.*

[52] Sweeney, "Structure …," 80–81.

these two choices one makes, the other subdivisions of the book remain virtually the same, resulting in the following structural outline:[53]

Title Verse: The Oracle of Habakkuk (1:1)

- I. Questions and Answers (1:2–2:5)
  1. Habakkuk's First Question: How Long Must I Call for Help? (1:2–4)
  2. God's First Answer: Look and Be Amazed (1:5–11)
  3. Habakkuk's Second Question: Why Do You Tolerate the Treacherous? (1:12–17)
  4. God's Second Answer: Write the Revelation of Righteousness (2:1–5)
- II. Anonymous, Scornful Words of Woe (2:6–20)
  1. Woe to the Extortioner (2:6–8)
  2. Woe to the Greedy and Arrogant (2:9–11)
  3. Woe to Those Who Build on Bloodshed (2:12–14)
  4. Woe to the Drunk and Violent (2:15–17)
  5. Woe to the Maker of an Idol (2:18–20)
- III. Habakkuk's Prayer (3:1–19)
  1. The Title Verse: A Prayer of the Prophet (3:1)
  2. Habakkuk's Confession and Petition: Renew Awesome Deeds (3:2)
  3. A Description of the Lord's Appearing in Angry Power (3:3–15)
  4. Habakkuk's Response to the Lord: I Wait Quivering and Patient (3:16)
  5. Habakkuk's Confidence in the Lord: God Is My Savior No Matter What (3:17–19)

The structure remains the same throughout most commentaries and interpreters, but the description of subsections varies to a minor degree. This will be discussed at the proper places in the following commentary, especially in relationship to the fifth word of woe.

4. The Date of the Book

R. L. Smith states the issue plainly: "We do not know when Habakkuk lived and preached."[54] The date of the book hinges on the interpretation of the wicked in Habakkuk 1. In the past various scholars have questioned the identity of the wicked in 1:2–4. The identification and resultant interpretation have

[53] R. L. Smith states, "The major units of the book are obvious" (*Micah–Malachi,* 94).

[54] R. L. Smith, *Micah–Malachi,* 94. The problem is complicated because the prophet speaks not only of the surprising rise of the Babylonians (612 to 605 B.C.) but also of the violent overrun of many small nations (2:5–17).

determined the approach to the remainder of the book.

One approach, taken by K. Budde, involved placing 1:5–11 after 2:1–4. This makes the woes of 2:6–20 refer to the Assyrians. Although popular in earlier times, this theory has lost favor because of the problem of moving the text and by historical difficulties.

Another popular approach, espoused by B. Duhm, solved the problem by making the nation spoken of in 1:5–11 (the Chaldeans) the Macedonians of Alexander the Great. The woes then referred directly to him. This approach hinges on the dubious possibility that Khasdim in 1:5 originally stood as Khittim. Duhm's hypothesis received a great deal of support until the discovery of the Dead Sea Scroll of Habakkuk confirmed the use of Khasdim (Chaldeans) in the text.[55]

More recently, Johnson has argued that the wicked in 1:4 must be foreigners, not people of Judah, and that 1:5–11 does not picture the Chaldeans as the solution to the problem of wickedness in 1:4. "Rather, the opening complaint of Habakkuk in 1:2–4 is a general statement of the injustice experienced for generations by Judah at the hands of foreign nations. But now, the prophet learns, the situation is becoming worse rather than better. The violence and havoc of the past will reach a climax with the coming of the Chaldeans, so that i 5–11 functions as a heightened form of the very complaint in i 2–4. … Yahweh, rather than bring an answer to the generations-old problem of theodicy, is making the problem more acute by a nonfulfillment of his promises which appears to be a paralysis of *tora*."[56]

Thompson argues the more traditional view that the wicked in 1:4 were Judeans who have brought internal corruption to Judean society so that the Jewish law has become ineffective.[57] Bruce interprets this more precisely as "the injustice of Jehoiakim's rule" and concludes that 1:12–17 was written "perhaps a few years later" than 1:2–4.[58]

---

[55] E. Sellin, *Introduction to the Old Testament* (London: Hodder & Stoughton, 1923), 182–84. For a list of scholarly identifications of the wicked in 1:4,13 see M. D. Johnson, "The Paralysis of Torah in Habakkuk 1:4," *VT* 35 (1985): 258.

[56] Johnson, 261. Sweeney ("Structure," 74) agrees with Johnson. Arguments against the unusual interpretation of Torah by Johnson and Sweeney will be given in the consideration of 1:4 in the commentary.

[57] Thompson, "Prayer, Oracle, and Theophany: The Book of Habakkuk," *TynBul* 44 (1993): 33–35; cp. J. G. Harris, "The Laments of Habakkuk's Prophecy," EvQ 45 (1973): 21–29; R. Smith, *Micah–Malachi,* 99; Armerding, "Habakkuk," 499; Achtemeier, *Nahum–Malachi,* 32; Rudolph (*Micha, Nahum, Habakuk, Zephanja*), who points to the Habakkuk Commentary from Qumran as the first to interpret the wicked in 1:4 as being from Judah; D. W. Baker, *Nahum, Habakkuk, Zephaniah,* ed. D. J. Wiseman (Downers Grove: InterVarsity, 1988), 46; J. J. M. Roberts, *Nahum, Habakkuk, and Zephaniah: A Commentary,* OTL (Louisville: Westminster/John Knox, 1991), 81–85, 90.

[58] F. F. Bruce, "Habakkuk," *The Minor Prophets*, ed. T. E. McComiskey, Vol. 2, 834.

A different argument for identifying the wicked and establishing a date has come from Patterson.[59] He maintains the view that the wicked reside in Judah[60] but returns to the view of Keil, following Jewish tradition that associated Habakkuk with the horrible king Manasseh, and argues that both Jeremiah and Zephaniah knew and used Habakkuk's prophecy. Viewing the reference to Babylon as inspired prophecy of the future rather than as prophecy based on signs of the times, Patterson pushes the date back to 652 B.C. shortly before King Ashurbanipal of Assyria mounted his western campaigns.[61]

Finally, Bullock represents a view that sees Habakkuk active in the early part of Josiah's ministry between 641 and 627, a time when people still could not believe what the prophet was saying about the Babylonians (1:6) but would still live to see it fulfilled (1:5). Such a view for Bullock relates to the known sins of Judah prior to Josiah's reform and does not weaken the predictive element of the prophecy.[62]

The almost consensus view sees the wicked in Judah itself (possibly Jehoiakim) and sees the Chaldeans as the instrument of the Lord to punish the wicked. The question appears to find its answer in one's view of prophecy. Namely, must prophecy have a strong predictive element pointing years ahead of itself as Bullock and Patterson argue, or does prophecy relate much more closely to the historical events of its time so that the contemporary audience has the opportunity and information to understand and identify with the message the prophet is delivering?[63]

For the present writer, the date of the book would appear to fall within the reign of Jehoiakim (609–598 B.C.), but a broader time span must be allowed as possible.[64] "Conditions during the life of the prophet would have progressed from excellent—with considerable material prosperity and even promise of spiritual revival—to the height of desperation as the net was drawn

[59] Patterson, *Nahum, Habakkuk, Zephaniah,* 115–17, 139–40.

[60] Ibid., 127–28.

[61] Jöcken (1–14) traces examples of dating Habakkuk to the time of Manasseh through the early Jewish tradition to C. Lapide in 1625; Keil in 1853; Reusch, 1859; Pusey, 1860; Küper in 1870; Kaulen, 1876; Baumgarnter, 1885; Knabenbauer, 1886; Cornely, 1887; Delitzsch, 1890; Sinker, 1890; Philippe, 1903; A. Jeremias, 1905; Schoepfer, 1906; Leimach, 1908; Zschokke, 1910; Lago y Gonzalez, 1911; and Göttsberger, 1928.

[62] C. H. Bullock, *An Introduction to the Old Testament Prophetic Books* (Chicago: Moody, 1986), 181–83. Jöcken (14) sets F. Delitzsch (1843) as the first to date Habakkuk to the time of Josiah, and more precisely to 629/628 B.C., the twelfth year of Josiah.

[63] See the discussion of Jöcken (13–14) with quotes from Delitzsch and Fohrer. Jöcken (13) refers to the old uncritical understanding of prophecy that is almost totally denied today.

[64] Armerding finds the best solution in "taking the sections of the dialogue as representative of Habakkuk's spiritual struggles over a long period of time, possibly beginning as early as 626 and continuing as late as 590 or after" ("Habakkuk," 493).

closer and closer around the helpless capital."[65] This would cover the time when the Chaldeans began to make their character and aims known but before they raised alarms in Judah. This broader time span might encompass the time from the death of Ashurbanipal of Assyria in 627 B.C. to the end of the reign of Jehoiakim in 598 B.C.[66]

The time must fit when the Lord's answer would "utterly amaze" the prophet (1:5). This would have been a time prior to the defeat of the Egyptians by Babylon at the Battle of Carchemish in 605 B.C. By that time discerning people had seen the handwriting on the wall concerning Babylon. Habakkuk 1:5–6 implies that that decisive moment had not arrived "so that the prophecy belongs probably to the years shortly preceding it, when the growing power of Nabopolassar's empire was beginning to manifest itself."[67] A probable date for the prophecy, then, would be just prior to the fall of Nineveh in 612 B.C. or shortly thereafter but definitely prior to 605 B.C. Keeping the date within the (evil) reign of Jehoiakim would call for a time between 609 and 605 B.C.

5. Literary Features of the Book

Habakkuk surprises the reader with two literary faces, the one given by its component parts and the other by its canonical context. We expect to discover neither one in the midst of the canon's collection of prophecy.

The component parts thrust the reader back into the realm of the Psalms. Questions such as "How long?" (1:2), "Why" (1:3,13), direct address to the Lord in prayer (1:12), descriptions of Yahweh's nature (1:12–14), the call to silent worship in the temple (2:20), the musical directions (3:1,19b), and even the prophetic oracle (2:2–5) appear to belong to temple worship and to the literature of the Psalter. Genre observation leads to the same conclusion, for community lament or complaint (1:2–4,12–17; cp. 2:1) dominates the book, and a theophanic hymn (chap. 3) closes it. Only the opening word *(hamaśśāʿ)*, first person divine speech (1:5–6), and the woes against a foreign nation (2:7–19) remotely remind us of other prophecy. Thompson can conclude, "Habakkuk is indeed the Old Testament's maverick prophecy!"[68]

Still the maverick prophecy has order and purpose. "Eclecticism is part and parcel of this book and the whole style and approach of its author."[69] The use

---

[65] Armerding, "Habakkuk," 493.

[66] S. R. Driver, *An Introduction to the Literature of the Old Testament* (Edinburgh: T & T Clark, 1892), 317–18.

[67] Ibid., 318.

[68] Thompson, "Prayer, Oracle, and Theophany," 53; cp. Heflin, who describes Habakkuk as a prophet with an "unorthodox approach" (*Nahum, Habakkuk, Zephaniah, and Haggai,* 67).

[69] Thompson, "Prayer, Oracle, and Theophany," 47.

of forms and language of the Psalms in the midst of prophecy has one explanation. "The only answers Habakkuk is able to give in response to his people's desperate sufferings are to be expressed in cultic terms, in the language of worship. … Habakkuk's resolution of his problem comes when he is able to believe that the Lord is present with him and his people, although they may at present find themselves beset with deep problems of life."[70] The language of divine presence is the language of worship, the language of God coming to be with his worshiping community.

Habakkuk's ties to the canon have come to the fore in recent study. The proposal of House deserves special attention. He has pointed to the neglect of the final form of the prophets in recent studies.[71] Employing new methods of literary criticism, House works out the genre, structure, plot, characterization, and narration of the Book of the Twelve. He finds that

> "Habakkuk deserves a special category all its own in many of the literary aspects of the Twelve. … Always a pivotal book, the work employs a unique narrative system. Though both Yahweh and Habakkuk speak in the book, autobiographical material also appears. … At least two symbolic purposes are served in Habakkuk's first-person sections. First Habakkuk represents the confusion the righteous remnant feels at the coming of the Day of Yahweh. Though no sin of theirs has precipitated judgment, they must learn to live by faith (2:4) and wait for salvation from the Lord (3:6). A second symbolic, or representative, feature of Habakkuk's struggles is that the reader observes how the prophet receives his oracle. The give-and-take between the Lord and the prophet chronicled in Habakkuk shows God's Word was not produced outside the arena of human pain. So Habakkuk represents the prophets' desire to gain a message from God, and the attempt of the righteous to grasp the ways of Yahweh."[72]

Thus House describes an "evident unity in the literary nature of the twelve books."[73] He defines this unity in terms of structure: "The Twelve are structured in a way that demonstrates the sin of Israel and the nations, the punishment of the sin, and the restoration of both from that sin. These three emphases represent the heart of the content of the prophetic genre. The Twelve's external structure therefore reflects its literary type."[74]

---

[70] Ibid., 51–52.

[71] House, *The Unity of the Twelve,* 10–11. Early in this century, "after breaking the text into pieces there is no attempt, however, to unite the fragments. Nor is there any notion of describing and interpreting the Twelve as a whole. … So much energy has now been expended on *dividing* the prophetic writings that the vision of a unified prophetic canon has almost completely disappeared" (p. 12).

[72] House, *The Unity of the Twelve*, 234.

[73] Ibid., 61–62.

[74] Ibid., 68. Note his reliance on R. Clements, "Patterns in the Prophetic Canon," *Canon and Authority*, ed. G. W. Coats and B. Long (Philadelphia: Fortress, 1977), 42–55.

House divides the Twelve into three groups, each highlighting one of the three emphases without totally neglecting the other two.[75]

Table 1: Structure of the Twelve according to House

Sin: Covenant and Cosmic	Punishment: Covenant and Cosmic	Restoration: Covenant and Cosmic
Hosea: Spiritual infidelity of covenant people	Nahum: Punishment of Nineveh as sign for all nations	Haggai: New temple as symbol of restored worship
Joel: Adds sins of all peoples	Habakkuk: Chastisement of Jerusalem	Zechariah: Restoration of Jerusalem and covenant people as holy to Yahweh
Amos: Names nations and details outward sins	Zephaniah: Summary: Israel and neighbors suffer Day of Yahweh but may call on Yahweh's name	Malachi: Covenant people must do something to bring about a new order brought by Messiah
Obadiah: Sin of nations and denouncing heartless neighbors		
Jonah: Inward-outward sin of nationalistic spiritual prejudice		
Micah: Summarizes sin and adds keys to repentance and faith		

In this interpretation of the structure of the Twelve, Hosea 1–3 foreshadows the claims of all the following prophets, Nahum, Habakkuk, and Zephaniah giving "more definite contours" to the punishment of Hos 3:4–5.[76] Habakkuk has the pivotal place in the center of the punishment section, being the "culmination of Hosea-Nahum" showing God will judge. The structure of complaint against Israel and against Babylon "perfectly illustrates the major components of the punishment motif. … If Nahum left any doubts about the punishment of the foreign nations, Habakkuk relieves them. Even mighty

[75] House, *The Unity of the Twelve*, 72. House admits: "It is impossible to declare with ultimate authority that the last compiler of the Twelve purposely shaped the corpus as discussed in this chapter. It is possible, though, to say that in their final canonical form these twelve diverse prophecies mesh together as a unit that unfolds the basic tenets of prophecy much more effectively than any single book of the group could alone" (p. 109).

[76] Ibid., 74.

Babylon, successor to Assyria as the major threat to Israel's security, has sinned and thereby come under God's wrath and judgment. The book also mentions the threat of punishment looming over the covenant people. They can, and will, suffer for their sins. Such ideas are startling to say the least, particularly in this section of the Twelve, since the focus so far has been on Assyria, a foreign country."[77] The prophet's questions "tie the book to predictions of judgment in Hosea-Micah, to the certainty of God's punishment of noncovenant states described in Nahum, and the inevitable chastisement of Jerusalem featured in Zephaniah."[78] Habakkuk shows God is able to give Israel up (see Hos 11:8) "in order to get them back later." Thus it is "the beginning of hope as well, since the Lord tends to redeem those He punishes."[79]

For House, Zephaniah summarizes Nahum-Zephaniah as Amos and Micah summarize the sin section. Zephaniah leaves open how God's future with Israel and the nations will unfold. Haggai, Zechariah, and Malachi "offer a consistent pattern for how restoration will take place."[80]

House contends that a recognizable plot unifies the Twelve. This plot centers on the conflict of Yahweh attempting to "forge Israel into a faithful nation," a goal achievable only when Israel keeps its covenant with God, a goal whose realization leads to a secondary goal of world redemption.[81] Habakkuk is at the apex of the crisis, signaling destruction for all the universe. Habakkuk represents the nadir of Israel's fortunes and those of the rest of the universe. It also heightens the tension brought about by Nahum. "The earlier parts of the Twelve explore the transgressions of the covenant people in much more detail than the inequities of the Gentiles. Since no mention of real repentance appears in Hosea–Nahum, it is reasonable to surmise that punishment must reach Israel and reach it soon. … Though the chosen people, Israel must now face the consequences of a repeated refusal to repent and return to the Lord. So the unthinkable will come to pass: even Israel will suffer punishment. Coupled with Nahum's statements about Assyria, this pronouncement brings the Twelve's plot almost as far down as it can go."[82] Still, some hope has been foreshadowed in 2:12–14 and 3:16–19, indicating that the plot is not yet finished.[83]

---

[77] House, *The Unity of the Twelve*, 93.
[78] Ibid., 92.
[79] Ibid., 91.
[80] Ibid., 96.
[81] Ibid., 117–18.
[82] Ibid., 145–46.
[83] Ibid., 147.

Table 2: Plot of the Twelve

Introduction	Complication	Crisis	Falling Action	Resolution
Hosea: broken covenant as spiritual prostitution	Amos: specific sins of Israel and of nations	Nahum: Assyria to be destroyed	Zephaniah: God will preserve remnant and convert nations through divine wrath	Haggai: rebuild temple
Joel: All nations must answer to God	Obadiah: Hating one's neighbor	Habakkuk: Babylon to conquer Judah		Zechariah: people show covenant love; purify Jerusalem
	Jonah: hating one's neighbor without pity	Crisis at apex in Habakkuk: if no further word comes, God will devastate the universe		Malachi: Israel will respond to new Elijah
	Micah: summary of Hosea–Jonah			Restoration complete: Israel and all creation reconciled to divine plan for them

House turns to the characterization in the Twelve and deals with four characters: Yahweh, the prophet, Israel as rebel and remnant, and the nations. He sees God as "an ever-growing, ever-more-important persona in the Twelve."[84] Habakkuk "brings together the various strands of the Twelve's characterization, much as it also brings the plot to its climax. … The divine characterization reaches a high point in Habakkuk from which it must either remain static or progress."[85] House concludes: "By any standard Habakkuk is a character of great depth and force who, because of these traits, pushes the Twelve's plot to its climatic point. The development of Habakkuk's character is achieved, as

[84] Ibid., 172.
[85] Ibid., 180.

is the development of the Twelve's plot, through his complaints. … During the process of testing the mind of God, the prophet develops from frustrated supporter (1:2) of the Lord to a satisfied, informed confidant of Yahweh (3:2,18–19)."[86] Similarly, Habakkuk became the "turning point" in the Twelve's characterization of Israel."[87] Israel must be destroyed for Israel to exist. Finally in characterization, "just as Habakkuk provides the crisis point of the Twelve's plot and the characterizations of Yahweh, the prophets, and Israel, so it also marks the highest point of Gentile power and arrogance before it punishes that pride and oppression. … Indeed, the Gentile persona has no redeeming traits. If anything, the character has grown in wickedness since Joel introduced it. … The once arrogant, lawless terrorizer of Yahweh's other vassals will be put in its place."[88]

House is not describing Habakkuk from the viewpoint of the prophet and his original audience. He describes the postexilic work of the "implied author."[89]

Nogalski, in particular, has forced us to ask questions concerning the ancient traditions that the final twelve books of the Old Testament prophetic canon form one book, not twelve.[90] Nogalski begins by noticing that several words and phrases from the end of one book reappear at the beginning of the next and concludes that this means one cannot assume that only the final form of each of the twelve books was then added to the larger collection that became the Book of the Twelve.[91] He sees two preexisting "multivolume corpora," namely Haggai and Zechariah 1–8 in one volume and Hosea, Amos, Micah, and Zephaniah in a "Deuteronomistic corpus." An editor created "significant touchstones" between Joel and Isaiah, creating a "Joel-related layer."

[86] Ibid., 196–97.

[87] Ibid., 206; see below in the theological discussion of the nature of the people of God.

[88] Ibid., 215.

[89] House, *The Unity of the Twelve*, 227. This person (p. 230) is proremnant and pro-Judah, who thinks the people have learned from previous mistakes so that he envisions a glorious future. Such a picture differs from Habakkuk himself, who gained certainty of God's eventual delivery of his people, but not with the glorious picture implied in House's "implied author."

[90] J. Nogalski's Zurich dissertation appeared in two separately titled volumes, *Literary Precursors to the Book of the Twelve*, BZAW 217, and *Redactional Processes in the Book of the Twelve*, BZAW 218 (Berlin/New York: de Gruyter, 1993. The former surveys previous work and decides that none of it represents a sufficient methodology to answer the question of how the Twelve became one book; cp. D. Schneider, *The Unity of the Book of the Twelve* (Ph.D. diss., Yale University, 1979), E. Bosshard, "Beobachtungen zum Zwölfprophetenbuch," *BN* 40 (1987): 30–62, and B. Jones, *The Formation of the Book of the Twelve: A Study in Text an d Canon*, SBLDS 149 (Atlanta: Scholars Press, 1995); A. Y. Lee, *The Canonical Unity of the Scroll of the Minor Prophets* (Ph. D. diss., Baylor University, 1985).

[91] Nogalski, *Literary Precursors*, 13–15. He opts for a variety of ways of catchwords entering the Twelve rather than for one consistent pattern accounting for them all: accident, collection principle, or a redaction principle.

This combined the Deuteronomistic corpus created after 587 B.C. and the Haggai–Zechariah corpus created about 500 B.C. and merged Joel, Obadiah, Nahum, Habakkuk, and Malachi into the resulting collection. Such a merger occurred between 400 and 350 B.C. After 332 B.C. Zechariah 9–14 and Jonah were added.

Table 3: Selected Redaction Theories

AUTHOR	PUBLICATION DATE	VERSES DATED LATE	COMMENTS
Gumpach	1852	1:15–17; 2:12–14	
Stade	1884	2:9–20; chap. 3	Late postexilic; others see chap. 3 as coming from temple hymnal
Giesebrecht	1890	1:5–11	Older oracle
Jeremias	1970	2:6a,8,10b,13–14,17,19b	Original oracles reinterpreted in postexile to anti-Babylonian, creating liturgy
Otto	1985	1:5–11,12b; 1:15–17,25bb,6a,8, 10b,13–14,17; 1:1; 2:18–20; 3:2,3–15 (using preexilic hymn), 16; 3:1,3,9,13,17–19	Five-step process based on formal; thematic contradiction of call of Babylon to punish and be punished
Rudolph	1975	2:6a,13a,14,17b,19; 3:6b–7	Argues strongly for basic unity
Roberts	1991	2:13a,14,18; 3:1,3,9,13,19	Unified composition by prophet or very good editor in light of post-597 experiences; reinterprets meaning, especially of 2:6–20
Achtemeier	1986	Later use in worship seen in 3:1,3,9,13,19	Later editors and prophet adapted earlier materials to universal work

Table 3: Selected Redaction Theories

AUTHOR	PUBLICATION DATE	VERSES DATED LATE	COMMENTS
Elliger	1955	Originated in time of and by prophet but not all parts from same time	Changing political situation means originally anti-Egyptian or even pro-Babylonian materials all seen as anti-Babylonian
R. L. Smith	1984	Unity	Some editing done later
Szeles	1987	Adopts Rudolph's position	Postexilic redactors
Heflin	1985	Unity	Messages and experiences over several years not necessarily written at one time; minor editorial revisions possible
Marti	1904	All redaction except 1:5–11, 14–15 (16)	four-source theory: 1:2–4,12a,13; 2:1–4 postexilic poetry; 1:5–10,14–15 from 605 B.C.; 2:5–19 about 540 B.C.; chap. 3 after 200 B.C.
Nogalski	1993	1:5–11,12, 15–17; 2:5b,6a,810b, 13–14, 16b–17, 18–19; 3:1–19	Brief original wisdom-related discussion of the wealth of the wicked expanded in "Joel-layer" bringing together Book of the Twelve

Habakkuk already existed with a recognizable structure as a "wisdom-oriented discussion concerning the prosperity of the wicked in Judah." The "Joel-related layer added a Babylonian commentary (1:5–11,12,15–17 and portions of the woe oracles in 2:5–19 and then added the concluding hymn in chap. 3. The Babylonian commentary imitates formulations from Nahum 3 with occasional allusions to Joel, while adapting Nahum's Assyria predictions to Babylon. The concluding hymn is modified in 3:16b–17, interpreting the theophany in light of Joel.[92]

Such a complex history of Habakkuk is not necessary. It represents a minimalist view in regard to the work of the original prophet and removes the "Babylonian commentary" into a period when Babylon had long vanished as the foe in focus for Israel.

The three brief chapters of the present Book of Habakkuk form a literary unity as we shall try to show below without excising major portions of the text. Especially, chap. 3 is essential for the book to be a meaningful piece of literature. Nogalski's original wisdom-oriented discussion is exactly that, a discussion, not a piece of literature with a structure of its own that would be preserved as a self-standing piece. As Heflin concludes: "The received text of Habakkuk, even with its difficulties, is open to meaningful interpretation. Efforts to change it to afford simpler explanations may in reality distort or negate the very message God intended!"[93]

A literary piece such as Habakkuk with eclectic literary genres and some type of ties to other parts of the Book of the Twelve automatically raises the issue of unity. Has a prophet's lifework been preserved by disciples or by a worship place that has incorporated some of its own new material into the prophetic work or has added material to tie the work to the rest of the Book of the Twelve? All too often scholars have been readily willing to describe parts of the book that did not belong to an original prophetic work. Marti even reduced the authentic sections of the book to eight verses.[94] Scholarly theories vary from the early consensus that chap. 3 was a late liturgical addition to more readily offered modern opinions that certain verses or parts of verses were added in the collection, redaction, or incorporation processes that finally produced the prophetic canon.

W. Rudolph, for example, holds to the unity of the book but still notes 2:6a; 2:13a,14; 2:17b; and the first two words of 2:19b as well as 3:6b with the first two words of 3:7 and 3:17 as later additions.[95] Roberts sees glosses in 2:13a,14,18; a transposition or gloss in 2:18; and the insertion of liturgical notations in 3:1,3,9,13,19. He also refers to an editor after 597 who "significantly reworked" some parts of the book to suit his purposes, turning, for instance, woe oracles against Judah in 2:6–20 into foreign nation oracles and

---

[92] Nogalski, *Redactional Processes, 274–80.*

[93] Heflin, *Nahum, Habakkuk, Zephaniah, and Haggai,* 78.

[94] See the discussion by E. Otto, "Die Theologie des Buches Habakuk," *VT* 35 (1985): 277–84. He notes the extreme position of K. Marti (*Das Dodekapropheton* [Tübingen: Mohr, 1904], 326ff.), who reduced the authentic words of Habakkuk to 1:5–10,14–15 (16). Cp. the extended discussion of Jöcken (116–240) on the literary critical epoch.

[95] Rudolph, *Micha, Nahum, Habakuk, Zephanja,* 3:195.

applying an archaic hymn in 3:3–15 to his purposes.[96] Achtemeier notes that the internal unity of the book has been preserved even as she points to the author's adaptation of earlier materials such as 2:5–20, a strong biographical and autobiographical emphasis (1:1–3,12; 2:1–2; 3:1,16,18–19) and subsequent use of portions of the book in worship (3:1,3,9,13,19), concluding that both Habakkuk himself and later editors "have given the work a universal and timeless validity which has made it a witness to every age."[97] Even the absence of chap. 3 from the famous Dead Sea Scrolls commentary has not placed a damper on the growing chorus of scholars defending the basic unity of the book, chap. 3 apparently not suiting the particular purposes of the Qumran community behind the Scrolls.[98]

The classical defense of the book's unity included the theory that the book represented a repentance liturgy from the time of Jehoiakim.[99] Eissfeldt gave the classical statement against combining liturgical usage and literary unity theories, arguing for a unified book that was not part of a liturgy.[100]

The essential unity of the book appears best as one looks at the literary devices the author has used to create a book. Such devices combined with the absence of normal oracular genres and the intricate meshing of very personal genres such as complaints, divine-human dialog, and first-person hymnic elements may point to writing as the first medium of communication used to make Habakkuk's message public.[101] Most prophetic books require dissecting into brief oracles in order to understand the message. Habakkuk almost demands that the reader read the entire book before the message becomes clear, the component parts serving more to support the entire message than to provide an individual message of their own. A summary of the literary work of the author should support this thesis.

Literary work can be analyzed in several ways. Close analysis of the Hebrew text of Habakkuk reveals numerous rhetorical devices the prophet

---

[96] Roberts, *Nahum, Habakkuk, and Zephaniah,* 84; cp. O. Eckart, "Die Stellung der Wehe-Worte in der Verkündigung des Propheten Habakkuk," *ZAW* 89 (1977): 73–107; J. Jeremias, *Kultprophetie und Gerichtsverkündigung in der späten Königszeit Israels,* WMANT 35 (Neukirchen: Neukirchener Verlag, 1970), 57–89.

[97] Achtemeier, *Nahum–Malachi,* 32.

[98] See the discussion of W. H. Brownlee, *The Text of Habakkuk in the Ancient Commentary from Qumran,* JBLMS XI (Philadelphia: SBL, 1959) and the references in Patterson (*Nahum, Habakkuk, Zephaniah,* 128–29); cp. Szeles, *Wrath and Mercy,* 9.

[99] P. Humbert, *Problèmes du livre d'Habacuc* (Neuchâtel, 1944), esp. 380ff.; cp. Otto, "Die Theologie des Buches Habakuk," 278.

[100] Eissfeldt, *The Old Testament: An Introduction* (New York: Harper & Row, 1965), 421.

[101] Schneider also argues for writing as the original medium of Habakkuk (*The Unity of the Book of the Twelve*).

employed to give artistic form and meaning to his message.[102] Such devices are more readily appreciated in chart form:

Table 4: Rhetorical Features

RHETORICAL FEATURE	VERSES	COMMENT
Proverb	1:9; 2:6	
Simile	1:8b,9b,14; 2:5; 3:4,14,19	
Metaphor	1:8a,9a,11a,15–17; 2:16; 3:8–10,11,14	
Allegory	2:15–16	
Metonymy	2:5; 3:2,9	Grave for death; Deeds for God; Waters for the Exodus event
Merismus	3:7	Tents and dwellings for all the enemies
Heniadys	1:15?; 2:2?[a]	Rejoices and is glad for gladly rejoices; Write and make plain for write plainly
Hyperbole	1:6–11[b]; 3:6b,11	Armies pictured larger than life; destruction pictured in apocalyptic terms
Paronomasia	2:19; 3:13–14a[c]	Parody of idols; Multiple meanings of *rō ʾš*, head, leader, top of house
Personification	1:7–11; 2:5,11; 3:2[d],5,7,10	Nation becomes individual people; wine becomes person; God's deeds, plague, tents, sun and moon
Rhetorical Question	1:12; 2:13,18; 3:8	Obvious answers: certainly
Repetition	1:15b–17	Two different words for net repeated

[102] See the review by Patterson (*Nahum, Habakkuk, Zephaniah,* 126) in addition to his review of the epic features of chap. 3 (pp. 122–25,267–72). The chart is based on Patterson's analysis.

Table 4: Rhetorical Features

RHETORICAL FEATURE	VERSES	COMMENT
Synecdoche	3:7	Tents and dwellings represent whole nation
Alliteration and Assonance	1:6,10; 2:6,7,15,18; 3:2	
Enjambment	1:13; 2:18; 3:4	
Gender-matched Parallelism	2:5; 3:3	
Staircase Parallelism	3:8	
Climatic Parallelism	3:2	
Pivot-pattern Parallelism	1:17	
Chiasmus	1:2,3,4; 2:1,6,9,14,16; 3:3	
Inclusio	2:4,20[e]	

a. Question marks follow Patterson. Certainly the English translations point to hendiadys, but the syntactical structure of Hebrew would also make the simple presentation without the conjunction possible.

b. The present writer would limit hyperbole itself to vv. 8–9,11, the other verses giving rather realistic descriptions.

c. See discussion below on 1:12,17.

d. Patterson lists 3:1 but apparently refers to the personification of God's deeds in 3:2.

e. See Patterson, *Nahum, Habakkuk, Zephaniah,* 205.

Such literary devices again reveal the literary ability of the prophet and his use of as many devices as possible to force the reader to unravel the complex nature of his message rather than simply looking for surface meaning. Such devices also make reading more pleasant to the ear and create an emotional atmosphere that is constantly changing throughout the book.

Table 5: Habakkuk as a Lament

Lament Components	Habakkuk Passages	Comments
Invocation (Ps 13:1)	1:2	
Plea to God for Help (Ps 13:1–2)	1:2; 1:17; 2:1	Watchtower represents symbolic plea for help

Table 5: Habakkuk as a Lament

Lament Components	Habakkuk Passages	Comments
Complaints (Ps 13:2)	1:3–4; 1:13–16; 2:6–19	Woes may be seen as complaints or as imprecation
Statement of trust in God (Ps 54:4)	1:12; 2:20	2:20 may be seen as statement of trust or confidence in response
Prophetic Oracle (Pss 14:3–4; 89:3–4,19–37; 91:14–16; 95:7d–11)	1:5–11; 2:2–5	
Confession of Sin (69:5) or Assertion of Innocence (Ps 17:3)		
Curse of enemies or imprecation (Ps 109:8–9)	2:6–19	
Confidence in divine response	3:2	
Hymn or Blessing	3:3–19	

The table above seeks to demonstrate that despite the many different elements from differing biblical genres apparent in the book, the final structure of the book represents a lament moving from complaints through prophetic oracle to curse to confidence to confessional praise. This writing prophet—in the literal sense of writing prophet—has produced a complex work that moves through most of the emotions of the human psyche and many of the genres of Hebrew literature. The superscriptions in 1:1 and 3:1 alert the reader to this complexity, showing that oracle and prayer have joined into a larger work. This work is a lament in form, inviting discouraged, suffering readers to join in with the prophet; but it is an oracle, indeed an oracle against foreign nations, in purpose. The prophet uses the lament form with its inherent ambiguity of complaint, curse, and praise to bring God's people to recognize God's power and God's promise in the midst of life's most horrific circumstances.

The book entitles itself an oracle, a *maśśāʾ*, preparing an alert reader for words against a foreign nation.[103] Opening verses do not represent what the reader expects from a *maśśāʾ*. Instead, one hears a lone voice lamenting in the

[103] See the study in the commentary on 1:1. The context of the Book of the Twelve strengthens this connotation of the word since the immediately preceding book, Nahum, is also entitled a *maśśāʾ* but in Nahum's usage, explicitly an *maśśāʾ* against Nineveh. Cp. J. D. W. Watts, "Superscriptions and Incipits in the Book of the Twelve," unpublished paper presented to the Consultation on the Book of the Twelve, SBL, 1994.

language of Psalms. The prophetic "therefore" *(ʿal-ken)* in v. 4 should warn the experienced reader of the prophets to look for a prediction of disaster.[104] Instead, it simply describes societal disaster facing the prophet's audience. Disaster need not be predicted; it has already occurred. Thus we have not an oracle pointing to the future but a lament horrified at past and present.

With 1:5 first person speech continues, but almost imperceptibly the speaker and tone change. Human lament gives way to divine instruction. The prophet is to learn God's future acts. These acts are described with the introductory *ki* used in prophetic judgment to provide a concluding characterization of the people facing God's punishment. This is made more urgent and radical with the Hebrew particle *hinnē*. True enough the description shows why these people should suffer God's judgment. The accent, however, created by repeated characterization, is on the nature of the instrument God uses to perform the unbelievable acts. No word of judgment is forthcoming.

Again, unexpectedly, God's conversation partner appears (v. 12), speaking this time in first person plural.[105] He uses a wordplay to address God, describing deity as *miqqedem,* a Hebrew word that can mean "in front of, before" (Ps 139:5), "from the east" (Gen 11:2), "from earlier days, days of old" (Jer 30:20), "from the primeval beginnings, ancient times" (Mic 5:2). Is this a reference to God's control of the east from where the frightening, evil enemy comes? to God's immediate presence before the prophet? to God's past history with his people? or to the God of the beginnings? Or is it intentionally vague to encompass all these meanings in the mind of the alert reader?

What a response to divine description of deadly enemies! The prophet makes a personal profession of faith, even claiming that he and his people will not die. Such is placed in contrast with actual events: God has sent Babylon to "execute judgment" or establish law and order (Hb. *mishpaṭ* as in 1:4) and to "punish" or settle quarrels. The prophet knows a different kind of God, one too pure to do such things. So he must, in good lament form, ask "why?" (v. 13). Again, he comes to a conclusion with the prophetic therefore *(ʿal-kēn)* in v. 15b, usually introducing the prediction of disaster in prophetic judgment oracles. What disaster! The enemy "rejoices and is glad." Again *ʿal-kēn* appears (v. 16). Again surprise. The enemy makes religious sacrifices to his fishing nets that enable him to "live in luxury." Again (v. 17) *ʿal-kēn* occurs but with a question mark attached and a wordplay following. "Emptying his net" involves the Hebrew *ḥerem*, which can mean a dragnet for fishing (Ezek 26:5) or also the spoils of holy war dedicated to the deity and forbidden for human use (Josh 22:20; 1 Sam 15:21). "Without mercy" can also mean "not

---

[104] See Butler, "Announcements of Judgment," *Cracking Old Testament Codes,* 157–76.

[105] Note the discussion of types of speeches in Nahum, Habakkuk, and Zephaniah by House, "Dramatic Coherence in Nahum, Habakkuk, and Zephaniah," unpublished paper presented to the Consultation on the Book of the Twelve, SBL, 1995.

sparing or keeping back." Thus the prophet ends his confession and lament with a haunting question: "Is it not therefore the case that the wicked enemy is emptying out his net, that is, pouring out his holy war sacrifice to God to kill the nations with no compassion and with no holding back?"

God's turn to answer is next if the pattern of 1:5 continues. But there is no voice. The prophet instead climbs on a watchtower to wait for God's answer. No prophetic form is present, but a dialog form introduces divine speech. God replies, but does he answer? He issues a command to the prophet. Write down the revelation that is coming, a revelation of a time in the future. Again (v. 4) the urgency of Hebrew *hinnê* introduces one of the Bible's most famous and most difficult to understand contrast statements containing the book's most important and difficult sentence. What follows maintains the element of formal surprise. If v. 4 is the revelation awaited; v. 5 returns to description of the enemy just as v. 4a apparently did.

Verse 6 then introduces another cast of characters into the plot, an indefinite "these, all of them" (lit.). Scornfully they speak for the next ten or eleven verses, pouring out woe oracles. What are such oracles doing in the mouths of common, anonymous people? They belong in the mouth of God or at least of his anointed, inspired prophet. Are these words of God or desperate hopes of a disconsolate, defeated, despairing people? Do they solve the prophet's laments and move him down from the watchtower? Do they represent curses or imprecations at home in the lament genre? Or are they another part of the puzzle of genres the prophet uses in mysterious ways, never fulfilling the proper task of the form, never coming to a formal conclusion, and never preparing formally for the genre that follows? What part do the cultic proclamations in 2:14,20 play in a collection of woe oracles uttered by an anonymous group? Do they do more than set the emotional stage for the climactic hymn in chap. 3?

Chapter 3 finally presents a complete form, a form that we expect to be called a "prayer of David" but find called a "prayer of Habakkuk." Here again the structure is dominated by the personal, biographical element, not the public proclamation element. The hymn itself is a first person hymn that incorporates elements of a theophanic or salvation history hymn alongside elements of lament (vv. 2b,8), personal confession (vv. 7,16–19), and second person description (vv. 9–15). The confessional part points directly to the problem of chaps. 1–2, the wicked enemy nation: "I will wait patiently for the day of calamity to come on the nation invading us" (v. 16). Finally, lament and complaint to God vanish, replaced by joyful praise (vv. 18–19).

Literary study leads to a surprising conclusion. The writer has joined together a multitude of basically incomplete forms and components, no one of which is complete in and of itself, to create a complex lament with cultic overtones that easily invites readers to join him in complaining to and then praising God. In so doing he has formed a masterful piece of literature with diverse characters and an enchanting plot pitting a prophet of lament and a God apparently acting contrary to his own character against a wicked enemy. This enemy is set up for destruction by the description of his evil acts but is promised destruction only by the woes of an anonymous choir. Prophetic intercession, prophetic proclamation, and prophetic silent waiting cannot supply the climax to the drama. Only a prayer describing God's coming in the past and thus preparing for his coming in the future can complete the prophetic message.

The prophet leaves his individualism to enter the domain of public worship and find the final answer to his lamentation. The answer comes not in action but in meditation. Still the prophet must wait, but he can wait with the praise that often concludes lamentation, the praise that grows out of worship, the praise that in the midst of the darkest situation can still confess that "I will be joyful in God my Savior."

6. The Text of the Book

The discovery of the Dead Sea Scrolls commentary on Habakkuk helps us understand the state of the text of the book much more clearly.[106] Smith concludes simply, "The Hebrew text of Habakkuk is in fair shape."[107] Heflin is not so restrained: "The Masoretic text has not been well preserved; it contains many obscure words and difficult passages."[108] Even the New Testament witnesses to textual distinctions in Habakkuk as seen in a comparison of 1:4 with 1 Cor 15:54; 1:5 with Acts 13:41; and 2:4 with Rom 1:17; Gal 3:11; and Heb 10:38. The New Testament in these places consistently quotes the Septuagint and its variations from the Masoretic Text.[109]

---

[106] Brownlee, *Text of Habakkuk,* 109–12 who documents nineteen major variants between the MT and the Dead Sea Scroll, according to Smith, *Micah–Malachi,* 96; see also Brownlee, "The Composition of Habakkuk," *Hommages a Andre Dupont-Sommer* (Paris: Librairie d'Amerique et d'Orrent Adrien-Maisonneuve, 1971), 255–75.

[107] Smith, *Micah–Malachi,* 96. Footnotes throughout the commentary will show some of the most important problems with the text, especially in the crucial passage 2:1–5 and in chap. 3. Smith points to four words that occur nowhere else in the Hebrew Bible and thus have given translators problems since the earliest Greek translation, namely, מעקל (1:4), מגמת (1:9), כפים (2:11) and חביון (3:4).

[108] Heflin, *Nahum, Habakkuk, Zephaniah, and Haggai,* 77, n. 6. Patterson (*Nahum, Habakkuk, Zephaniah,* 132) says the text "contains many difficulties," noting, "The difficulty of the text has defied the efforts of exegetes of all theological persuasions" (n. 39). Then on the next page (p. 133) he agrees with Smith's assessment noted above.

[109] See R. L. Smith, *Micah–Malachi,* 96.

7. Theological Insights

"With Habakkuk, prophecy moves into the interrogative mood. Whereas former prophets had declared the certainties of God to man, Habakkuk began asking questions of God on behalf of man."[110] Habakkuk provides theological insights in a more complex fashion than any other prophet.[111]

What are those theological insights? What questions does the prophet attempt to answer in this complex, unorthodox prophetic writing? Achtemeier lists traditional answers and says they do not explain the nature of the book. She shows that Habakkuk is not primarily about (1) the justice of God, a theme the prophet assumes rather than debates; (2) human doubt since the prophet maintains strong communion with God and expects the right answers from God; (3) human suffering and helplessness before the world's evil powers, that being the setting of the book not the theme.[112]

Achtemeier prefers to frame the primary purpose from a divine perspective: Habakkuk is "above all else a book about the purposes of God and about the realization of his will for his world."[113] She explicates this theme in terms of God's promises to Abraham; God's will for humans to have life abundantly; God's will for a human community of joy, security, and righteousness faithful to the divine will and lordship. In short, this is a book about the providence of God.[114]

Heflin approaches the same content from the human perspective. "Habakkuk is designed to show how a speculative mind can deal with the problem of theodicy and arrive at an answer for living."[115] The prophet stands between his people and his God. He is in many respects a mediator, but he is not an objective mediator. He favors both parties. He knows God's sovereignty and providence cannot be denied. He also knows God's people seem caught in an evil situation unlike anything God had promised his covenant people. He seeks to understand the purposes of God and the fortunes of his people at the same time. Like Job, Habakkuk's courageous acts of prayer and powerful conversations with God lead to theological reflection as much as do the contents of his language. Similarly, the forms of speech the prophet employs lead us to explore the meaning of revelation at a deeper level than is sometimes the case with the prophets. "His primary message was one of com-

[110] Ibid., 103.

[111] Otto seeks to fit his theological method to his complex history of tradition and redaction ("Die Theologie," 274–95). This is a necessary task if one must believe in such a complex process behind the production of such a brief biblical book, but the closer study of the literary structure of the book above makes such complex theological machinations unnecessary.

[112] Achtemeier, *Nahum–Malachi*, 31.

[113] Ibid.

[114] Ibid., 31–32.

[115] Heflin, *Nahum, Habakkuk, Zephaniah, and Haggai*, 73.

mitment to Yahweh even when a cruel, godless tyrant was poised on the border ready to overrun one's land."[116] This story of commitment under fire gives a universality to the prophet's message. "Habakkuk is a book for all faithful people, of whatever era, who find themselves living 'in the meantime'—in the time between the revelation of the promises of God and the fulfillment of those promises—in the time between their redemption, when God made his purposes clear, and the final time when that divine purpose will be realized in all the earth. As such, Habakkuk is a book from faith for faith."[117]

(1) Understanding through Honest Doubt and Prayer

"The old easy assurances that peace, health, long life, and prosperity were tokens of divine approval have collapsed in the face of experience, but Habakkuk, in hardship and privation, comes to know God more fully and to rejoice in him for his own sake and not for the benefits he bestows."[118] Habakkuk stood in a long line of godly people who dared to question God. Moses, Jeremiah, Job, and Habakkuk wanted to know about the work of God.

Habakkuk, like Job, screamed out at God's silence and shouted accusations at God, seeking to understand what appeared to be absolute injustice in a universe faith said stood under the rule of a sovereign, just God. "Your eyes are too pure to look on evil; you cannot tolerate wrong. Why then do you tolerate the treacherous? Why are you silent while the wicked swallow up those more righteous than themselves?" (1:13) The prophet's "doubts and questionings are not those of a fault-finding negative critic or a skeptic but the honest searchings of a holy prophet of God."[119] As Otto points out, the lament is made possible by the knowledge of the complete Otherness of Yahweh.[120]

In seeking to understand God with his probing questions, Habakkuk became what House calls a revelator with God and shows that "co-revelation does not come easily or in a historical vacuum. Habakkuk's report on God's actions comes after much search and sacrifice. His message will cause him pain along with the rest of Israel."[121]

God is the friend of the honest doubter who dares to talk to God rather than about him.[122] Prayer that includes an element of questioning God may be a

---

[116] Smith, *Micah–Malachi,* 97.

[117] Achtemeier, *Nahum–Malachi,* 32.

[118] Bruce, "Habakkuk," 835.

[119] Patterson, *Nahum, Habakkuk, Zephaniah,* 141.

[120] Otto, "Die Theologie," 285.

[121] House, *The Unity of the Twelve,* 197.

[122] Achtemeier comes at this from another perspective, seeing the prophet's questions as "not questions that rise out of doubt but out of lively faith in God, for the person who trusts in God and clings to his will knows what God's order for human society could mean. The faithful person has had a foretaste of that order" (*Nahum–Malachi,* 36).

means of increasing one's faith.[123] Expressing doubts and crying out about unfair situations in the universe show one's trust in God and one's confidence that God should and does have an answer to humanity's insoluble problems. Such an experience of doubting is not, however, "to be normative."[124] Such doubting, questioning faith is only a step to rejoicing, praising faith. It is not a way to avoid personal responsibility and action. "Habakkuk neither used his questions to shield himself from moral responsibilities nor shunned God's claims upon his life. He was genuinely perplexed by the unpredictable nature of God's dealings with him. He raised his protests actually because he thought so much of God and hungered and thirsted to see God's righteousness vindicated as well as his own. God's revelation of himself laid the ghost of the prophet's doubts and gave birth to a finer faith; the redeeming God had used his questions as a means of grace to draw Habakkuk closer to himself."[125]

(2) The Righteous Live by Faith

"The decisive point in Habakkuk is the power of his faith in God, that finally did triumph over all doubt. Yahweh is and remains the Lord of the world who directs the nations according to his will (1:5ff.), is the only Living One (2:18–19), who can call nations and rescind their call (3:5ff.), and he is and remains the Holy One and the Pure One (1:12–13), even when people at the moment do not understand him."[126] Habakkuk's willingness to question and therefore to know the God of the universe rather than settle for knowing the god of popular theology allowed him to see the reality of the world situation. God would judge Judah, but the judgment would not be final. God promised to spare a remnant based solely on their faithfulness to God, "their total dependence and dependability."[127] Habakkuk learned and sought to teach us that "faith and fact are not always compatible in the world of sense and sight, but that is not the whole world. There is a world of justice that only God fully comprehends. His people must accept by faith what they cannot confirm in fact."[128]

God's revelation to Habakkuk became the seminal idea for Paul's understanding of justification by faith. What Habakkuk learned to be God's principle of operation in the Babylonian invasion, Paul with inspired insight saw to

---

[123] Jeremiah, living in the same general time period, had serious questions. God used Jeremiah's questions in the midst of prayer to deepen Jeremiah's faith. Heflin says, "Doubts can express a maturing faith" (*Nahum, Habakkuk, Zephaniah, and Haggai,* 88).

[124] Patterson, *Nahum, Habakkuk, Zephaniah,* 131.

[125] LaSor, Hubbard, Bush, *Old Testament Survey,* 454.

[126] Rudolph, *Micha, Nahum, Habakuk, Zephanja,* 250.

[127] LaSor, Hubbard, Bush, *Old Testament Survey,* 453.

[128] Bullock, *An Introduction to the Old Testament Prophetic Books* (Chicago: Moody, 1986), 183.

be God's universal principle of salvation. Habakkuk's message prepared for the greater message to come (see Rom 1:17; Gal 3:11; Heb 10:38–39).[129]

(3) Worship as the Language of Revelation

Habakkuk's brief book amazes one who studies it closely. Normal prophetic forms of speech fade into the background. Habakkuk and the narrative-dominated Jonah are the only "minor prophets" not to use the revelatory "messenger formula," "Thus says Yahweh."[130] When prophetic forms occasionally reappear, they do so in functions strange to their original genre. Laments, theophany, and hymn forms take their place. Whether or not the prophet had a professional position in the temple, he had drunk deeply of Israel's worship patterns, rituals, forms, and contents. As so often with God's people, their songs formed the center of revelation rather than the words of God's preacher. In a moment of deepest need the prophet turned not to the words of Torah nor to history nor to previous prophecy for God's word for his generation's plight. Rather, he turned to familiar music of worship and familiar practices of praise. Then he determined God's word for himself and for his people.[131] As Thompson says, Habakkuk's resolution of his problem comes when he is able to believe that the Lord is present with him and his people although they may at present find themselves beset with deep problems of life.[132]

(4) God Is Just

Theological statements often come all too easy and have too little basis in the real struggles of life. Habakkuk knew the traditional theology of the fathers. He could easily take the place of one of Job's friends and describe how theology said the world was supposed to be and how God was supposed to react in holy justice to right the world's wrongs. One problem. God was silent, as he had been with Job. "Habakkuk is a significant theological treatise because of its interest in why God acts. The questions the prophet poses to the Lord are deep and telling. … Placed in the center of the punishment section [of the Twelve] this book completes God's most dreaded threats. Even Israel must suffer if the nation will not fulfill its covenant obligations."[133]

"The subject matter of the book of Habakkuk is theodicy: how can Yah-

---

[129] LaSor, Hubbard, Bush, *Old Testament Survey,* 453. See also S. L. Johnson, Jr., "The Gospel That Paul Preached," *BSac* 128 (1971): 327–40.

[130] House, *The Unity of the Twelve*, 186.

[131] "The only answers Habakkuk is able to give in response to his people's desperate sufferings are to be expressed in cultic terms, in the language of worship" (Thompson, "Prayer," 51).

[132] Ibid., 52.

[133] House, *The Unity of the Twelve*, 91

weh, he who is just, allow sufferings to continue to afflict his righteous people?"[134] How did one defend the justice and righteousness of God in a world where God no longer chose to speak or reveal himself or his ways? As Otto notes, "In view of the empirical situation of need, Habakkuk's understanding of God lost its self-evident quality. … The idea of God can become totally clear again only when the reality of the experienced world becomes totally clear."[135] Habakkuk dared to question all easy theological answers he had learned. He fought through real life situations with God. Only then did he affirm traditional theology, but it is a theology with firm roots in more than other people's traditions and textbooks.

Now he affirmed the justice of God on the basis of personal experience struggling with God and finding God in the midst of worship. "The prophet's probing of Yahweh's will dispels any thought that the Lord may not judge covenant and cosmic sin equally. The wicked of all nations will be punished."[136] On the other hand, "God is so great in His sovereignty He is even able to use human sin for His own purpose. … He did not force the Babylonians to assume the role of world conqueror. That was their own goal. … God allowed them to do what they themselves wanted to do, but He used it for His purposes."[137]

The prophet found that humans want to measure justice in the short term. God is just only if God acts according to our schedule and if God agrees with our evaluation of what is just and what is fair and who is evil and who is not fair. Habakkuk learned that God is just if one waits to see the long term work of God who in his sovereignty and eternity chooses to work according to his timetable and according to his understanding of the ways of his people and the needs of his people. His justice does not always work for every individual or even for every generation. To see God's justice one must take a stand on the watchtower and wait for God's timing and God's revelation. Still, one may find only divine presence and divine word. The divine action to bring justice and intercession may wait for another day or may bring judgment on the people who expected salvation. That is God's business. Habakkuk "showed that trials and perplexity were not incompatible with trust in God."[138]

(5) The Nature of God's Salvation

"Habakkuk is above all else a book about the purposes of God and about

---

[134] Thompson, "Prayer," 53. Achtemeier argues that it is not a theodicy and is not primarily about the justice of God (*Nahum–Malachi,* 31).

[135] Otto, "Die Theologie," 286.

[136] House, *The Unity of the Twelve*, 197.

[137] Heflin, *Nahum, Habakkuk, Zephaniah, and Haggai,* 84.

[138] Barber, *Habakkuk and Zephaniah,* 20.

the realization of his will for his world. … It is a book about a God whose will for humankind is that they have life and have it more abundantly. It is a book about God's desire that human beings live together in joy and security and righteousness, in a community ordered by his divine will and faithful to his divine lordship. … In short, Habakkuk is a book about the providence of God; that is, it is primarily concerned with how God is keeping his promises to his chosen people Israel and, through them, to humankind."[139]

To speak of God's purposes, God's saving will, God's providential provision and ordering, Habakkuk takes a tortuous path. Habakkuk's book is one long cry for help to a God who does not seem to be listening (1:2). It is a long description of enemies (1:6–11,13–16; 2:5,6b–19) whom God seems, at best, to ignore and, at worst, to use as his instruments of sovereignty in his world. The prophet and the faithful people who support him expect God to destroy such wickedness. The God they worship cannot tolerate such. Yet for a time God is silent.

Habakkuk finds a relationship with God as Savior even as God retains his silence on the field of human history. The prophet knows God as Savior even as he continues to wait for God's historical deliverance. Salvation depends on trust in God's word, in faithfully being righteous even when God does not appear to be (2:4). Salvation is not prosperity now. Salvation is trust in the midst of hardship while God plans his actions according to his ultimate knowledge and will. "Habakkuk's vision of God as the mighty conqueror of chaos endows him with hope for the future and instills within him the triumphant courage to endure a dismal present in the joyous confidence that this vision of God will prove reliable. … Nor have the intervening centuries robbed the book of its ability to give new courage to the modern believer in his or her struggle to live in the present. Its vision of the awesome divine warrior whose will is to save his people can and does still serve to refocus the modern believer's perceptions, enabling the believer to see through appearances and to fix his or her gaze on ultimate reality."[140]

(6) The Nature of Human History

Israel's confession of faith rested on the power of Yahweh to repeat the miracle of the Exodus and Conquest. Yahweh was the God who controlled history, the history of his people and the history of the universe. History in Habakkuk's day called this into question. "The prophet asked some of the most penetrating questions in all literature, and the answers are basic to a proper view of God and his relation to history."[141] "According to all that

[139] Achtemeier, *Nahum–Malachi,* 31–32.

[140] Roberts, *Nahum, Habakkuk, and Zephaniah,* 85

[141] Armerding, "Habakkuk," 495.

Habakkuk knew about God's holiness and covenant, Yahweh should have arisen to correct the situation, particularly in response to believing prayer for change by such as Habakkuk. Such correction had not been forthcoming, and the prayers of the righteous and the struggle for justice in the land seemed in vain, with the result that God's program of redemptive history was threatened." Thus Habakkuk and his people had "no clear vision of when and how Yahweh would continue his commitments to his line."[142]

All that Habakkuk does in his fight with God points us to the burning issue of our own day: where is God in a history drowning in human violence, human selfishness, and human sin? Is God's working in history only a thing of Bible times. Is our history self-determined by its human inhabitants. Achtemeier warns us of the horrible relevance of Habakkuk for us: "Such a word from God implies that the turmoil and violence and death in our societies may not be evidence of God's absence from our lives but instead the witness to his actual working in judgment as he pursues his purpose. No event in human history, therefore, is to be understood as completely divorced from his lordly action and will. God is always at work, always involved, always pressing forward toward his kingdom. But the means by which he chooses to pursue that goal may be as astounding as the destruction of a nation or as incomprehensible as the blood dripping from the figure of a man on a cross."[143] "One of the purposes of His ordering of the government of earth's history is that both classes of men—the righteous and the unrighteous—may be seen in clear distinction."[144]

Patterson points to a corollary of confessing God's participation in human history. God must be seen as involved in all of that history and not just the parts we commend or see as good. "God Himself must at times enter human history, using such social conventions as warfare to accomplish His purpose (3:13) in order that ultimately the earth may be "filled with the knowledge of the glory of the Lord' (2:14). Such knowledge justifies neither deliberate aggression nor warfare itself as a norm for relations between peoples."[145]

The struggle with God brought response, response that greatly modified Israel's view of their history and that of the nations. The nations too often saw history as cyclical, repetitious, and thus futilely going nowhere. The Bible describes history as linear "moving towards the goal of the Day of the Lord and the establishment of God's kingdom."[146] Within this linear history, certain appointed times carried special significance.

---

[142] Ibid., 494.

[143] Achtemeier, *Nahum–Malachi,* 38–39.

[144] Patterson, *Nahum, Habakkuk, Zephaniah,* 120.

[145] Ibid., 131.

[146] Baker, *Nahum, Habakkuk, Zephaniah,* 59.

(7) The Nature of Human Sin

"The central focus of Habakkuk's prophecy is on the relation of a sovereign and holy God to a sinful world, where society is permeated by godlessness and injustice. … Habakkuk can understand neither the gross sin of Judah nor God's seeming indifference to the rampant corruption he sees all around him."[147] The holy, pure God of Habakkuk reacted against the unholy, impure lives of both Judah and their enemies. The system of justice and righteousness he expected he did not find. Instead he found sin. This took many forms. Judah's sins could easily be categorized: violence, injustice, wrong, strife, conflict, a paralysis of law, perversion of justice, and mistreatment of the righteous. Likewise, the wicked Babylonians were guilty of proud ambition, covetousness, ruthlessness and cruelty, debauchery, and idolatry.

(8) Anger Is a Characteristic of Humans and of God

Lament is the language of anger (see Ps 137). Lament does not understand present situations and reacts in "righteous indignation." Righteous anger turns to God for help. Such help may come in the form of divine action. It may remain in the realm of divine silence. Human anger remembers the past anger of God (3:8,12) and calls for a repeat performance. Human anger wants death, destruction, and deliverance. Divine anger seeks justice, intercession, and discipline. Human anger responds to unhappy situations. Divine anger responds to human sin, oppression, and helplessness. Human anger seeks immediate action. Divine anger seeks human repentance. Human anger says, Act now. Divine anger says, I will act when people can recognize my action and respond as I desire. Habakkuk shows us human anger and divine anger. He also shows us how the language of prayer, whether it be that of lament or that of praise, can lead away from human anger to human patience, human righteousness, human faith, and human confession of God's salvation.

(9) The Nature of God's People

Two theological issues plagued Habakkuk: who are God's people, and what kind of God is Yahweh? Tradition told of a people of the covenant who treated friend and foe with love and kindness, not violence and injustice. Current history showed a people bent on disobeying every element of God's covenant law. God's revelation announced God would use wicked Babylon. Where were a people of God in all this? "In Habakkuk the first concrete signs of Israel's punishment emerge. Because the nation will be destroyed, thus forcing the righteous to suffer with the wicked, God must start over with a

---

[147] Patterson, *Nahum, Habakkuk, Zephaniah,* 119–20.

new group of people if Israel is to have any place in the world's future. Yahweh's comment that in difficult times 'the righteous will live by his faith' (2:4) indicates that a small segment of the people will survive the inevitable coming judgment."[148]

(10) God's Nature

"Habakkuk is above all else a book about the purposes of God and about the realization of his will for his world. … In short, Habakkuk is a book about the providence of God; that is, it is primarily concerned with how God is keeping his promises to his chosen people Israel and through them to humankind."[149] God's nature is Habakkuk's problem and yet his one certainty. Because he knows God so well, the prophet stands on his watchtower perplexed and amazed at God's actions, actions that defy his nature. His bewildered negative statements reveal his expectations and beliefs about God. God in normal times

- listens when his helpless people call (1:2)
- saves when his people suffer violence (1:2)
- removes injustice (1:3,5)
- tolerates no wrong or treachery (1:3,13)
- ensures that his Torah is protected and maintained (1:4)
- makes justice prevail among his people (1:4)
- delivers the righteous from the wicked (1:4)
- protects his people from ruthless enemies (1:5–11,17)
- protects his holy city from enemy armies (1:10)
- acts when the wicked seem to triumph (1:15)
- acts immediately without waiting (1:2; 2:6)
- reacts against worthless idols (2:18–19; cp. 1:11)

Positive statements, even statements that do not reflect present reality, share the prophet's personal confession about the nature of God. God is

- the Creator (1:14)
- eternal (1:12)
- a personal God, related in a personal relationship with the prophet (1:12)
- an awesomely holy God, pure and distinct from all creation (1:12)
- sovereign over history and all its nations (1:12; 2:13)
- a rock that can never be moved or changed (1:12)
- one who punishes disobedient people (1:12; 2:16)
- one whose purity makes him avoid all appearances of evil (1:13)
- one with no tolerance level for evil and wrongdoing (1:13)
- one who speaks with his prophets and reveals his plans (2:1)

[148] House, *The Unity of the Twelve*, 208.

[149] Achtemeier, *Nahum–Malachi*, 31–32.

- one who brings woe and destruction on all evil (2:6–19)
- planning salvation for the earth so that he can fill all his creation with his presence (1:14)
- at home in his temple on earth and in heaven (2:20)
- so awesome that people must be silent when he is present (2:20)

God speaks to his prophet and his people and reveals things about himself. God shows that he is

- planning to act in unbelievable ways (1:5)
- able and willing to use enemies for his purposes even when they are wicked (1:6)
- able and willing to reveal himself and his purposes to his people (2:2–3)
- Lord over his revelation and will bring it to pass in his own time (2:3)
- the one who always speaks the truth (2:3)
- the God of the righteous who serve him faithfully (2:4)

Meditation on God's past history also reveals much about the divine nature. He is

- famous so that people talk about what he has done for them (3:2)
- active with deeds that silence people awestruck (3:2)
- a God of wrath (3:2,12)
- one who comes to his needy people from his ancient dwelling place (3:3)
- the glorious one whose acts bring forth praise that fills the universe (3:3)
- so splendid in appearance that he dims the dawning sun (3:4)
- powerful (3:4)
- in control of all diseases (3:5)
- in control of all history, all nature, and all people (3:6–7)
- willing and able to show his anger against sinful peoples as exemplified in the exodus from Egypt (3:8–15)
- in control of all the chaotic waters and deeps (3:8–10)
- uses even the heavenly bodies for his purposes (3:11)
- our Savior from the enemy and the protector of our anointed leader (3:13,16)
- the source of all our strength (3:19).

SECTION OUTLINE

TITLE VERSE: THE ORACLE OF HABAKKUK (1:1)

I. QUESTIONS AND ANSWERS (1:2–2:5)

1. Habakkuk's First Question: How Long Must I Call for Help? (1:2–4)
2. God's First Answer: Look and Be Amazed (1:5–11)
   (1) The Revelation of God's Work (1:5–6)
   (2) The Description of the Babylonian Army (1:7–11)
3. Habakkuk's Second Question: Why Do You Tolerate the Treacherous? (1:12–17)
   (1) A Description of the Lord (1:12–13)
   (2) A Description of How the Babylonians Treat Other Nations (1:14–17)
4. God's Second Answer: Write the Revelation of Righteousness (2:1–5)
   (1) The Prophet on the Watchtower Awaiting an Answer (2:1)
   (2) The Lord Promising Revelation (2:2–3)
   (3) The Lord's Contrast of Wicked and Righteous (2:4–5)

Can any book be more up to date than one which questions the prosperity of the wicked and the demise of the righteous? Habakkuk asked the questions the suffering people of his day were asking. How can the wicked prosper? How can God not answer when the righteous suffer? More importantly, he was not content to hear human philosophies about these questions. He asked God to answer these questions.

The prophet's challenge to God makes the book unusual in the Old Testament, but not without precedent. In his confessions Jeremiah complained to God about the troubles he faced. Moses complained to God about God's apparent silence. Job complained about his suffering. The largest part of the Psalms addresses human laments to God about earthly injustice. The Book of Habakkuk deals not only with the prophet's questions but also with God's answers to the dilemma of individuals and of nations. The book closes with one of the most significant affirmations of faith in any religious book.

The initial section of Habakkuk (1:1–2:5) contains a series of challenges and questions by Habakkuk and answers from the Lord. Habakkuk questioned how God could remain silent in the presence of wickedness. How could God not punish the wicked in Judah? "How long Yahweh waits before moving against sin and why Yahweh waits must be answered if the earlier parts of the Twelve are to remain viable warnings."[1] God responded to Habakkuk's plea by showing what he would soon do in history, rousing the wicked Babylonians to punish Judah. God's surprising answer raised a second question: How could God use such a wicked instrument to punish Judah? God's reply has reverberated throughout the history of the church: the righteous will live by faithfulness.

THE ORACLE OF HABAKKUK (1:1)

[1]The oracle that Habakkuk the prophet received.

1:1 Prophetic books usually contain a superscription[2] or title verse with the essential information needed by the person hearing or reading the prophecy. In general the larger books contain more detailed information than the smaller books.[3]

The Book of Habakkuk contains only the most essential information. From the title verse the reader knows only that the message comes from a prophet[4] named Habakkuk,[5] who is otherwise unknown in the Old Testament. Neither the prophet's hometown (see Nah 1:1) nor his lineage (see Zeph 1:1) is known. Information about dating the prophet also is missing,[6] as is information about his audience (cp. Amos 1:1; Mic 1:1; Isa 1:1; and Nah 1:1).[7]

The reader knows only that the book contains the burden (oracle) that

---

[1] P. R. House, *The Unity of the Twelve,* JSOTSup 97, Bible and Literature Series 27 (Sheffield: Almond, 1990), 92.

[2] The exceptions are Ezekiel, Haggai, Zechariah, and Jonah. Each of these begins with information sounding like a superscription but actually being an integral part of the narrative itself, all but Jonah beginning with a dating formula; see G. M. Tucker, who notes similar superscriptions in nonprophetic books such as Nehemiah, Song of Songs, Proverbs, and Ecclesiastes ("Prophetic Superscriptions and the Growth of a Canon," *Canon and Authority,* ed. G. W. Coats and B. O. Long [Philadelphia: Fortress,1977], 58–59,); cp. J. D. W. Watts, "Superscriptions and Incipits in the Book of the Twelve," unpublished paper presented to the SBL Unity of the Twelve Group, 1994.

[3] Cp. the information given concerning Isaiah and that concerning Nahum. The Book of Jonah does not contain a title verse, probably because of the nature of the material. It contains information about the prophet rather than oracles by the prophet.

[4] Tucker notes that only Amos and Habakkuk supply information about the occupation of the prophet, and only Habakkuk is labeled as "the prophet" ("Prophetic Superscriptions and the Growth of a Canon," 61).

[5] See discussion in Introduction, "Habakkuk, the Man," p. 251.

[6] See Introduction, "Date of the Book," p. 257

[7] Watts notes that Habakkuk mentions the subject of prophecy only in 1:6: Chaldeans ("Superscriptions and Incipits in the Book of the Twelve," 5).

Habakkuk the prophet saw. "Oracle" or "burden" *(maśśāʾ)* [8] is a common way to describe prophetic material, especially material that deals with prophecy against foreign nations.[9] It is the least understood of the words describing the content of the prophetic books.[10] The word obviously describes prophetic utterances that primarily speak of foreign nations, but the word carries the idea of a load or burden, as if the prophet was burdened with the message he received from the Lord.[11] It has "negative, ominous tones" but in Habakkuk has "a broader meaning. ... It refers to all of the divine word received by the prophet, regardless of its nature ... (and) is synonymous with 'divine revelation.' "[12]

Weis has described a process producing such an oracle. A person, or persons, in the prophet's community asks a question about God's intervention or lack of it in some experience of the community. God gives the prophet the oracle as the response. An oracle is thus based on revelation concerning a forthcoming divine action. The oracle may give either insight into the future or directions for the audience's present actions.[13]

The title verse finds a structural parallel in 3:1. This raises the exegetical question: is 1:1 an introduction to the first two chapters of the book or to the

---

[8] See R. L. Smith, *Micah–Malachi,* WBC 32 (Waco: Word, 1984), 98. The natural setting of the term is agricultural and commercial, referring to the load or burden on the back of pack animals (Exod 23:5; 2 Kgs 5:17; 8:9; Isa 46:1–2; cp. Num 4:14–49); see W. C. Kaiser, *TWOT,* 601. Kaiser shows the term refers to prophetic threats or words heavy with doom even in Prov 30:1; 31:1 (p. 602). Still, the newest edition of KB, II, 604, and H.-P. Müller (*TWAT* 5:21–22) offer the translation *Ausspruch*, or "saying for the prophetic passages," arguing that Proverbs and Malachi along with other passages demand such a translation. Müller does emphasize that מַשָּׂא usually means oracle of judgment against foreign nations when it appears in prophecy (*TWAT,* 24). He points, however, to Jer 23:33; Ezek 12:10; and Hab 1:1 as counter examples against Judah and notes that this may indicate that the audience would also associate the term with the meaning "burden."

[9] Cp. Nah 1:1, which speaks of the downfall of Nineveh, and Isa 13:1, which begins a long section about foreign nations (Isa 13–23). "The oracle" (הַמַּשָּׂא) is characteristic of Isa 13–23, having been used ten times in these chapters of Isaiah but only once in the remainder of Isaiah (30:6).

[10] Tucker, "Prophetic Superscriptions and the Growth of a Canon," 64. Tucker draws the conclusion on the basis of indecisive etymology and usage. The other two terms so used are דָּבָר ("word," or in the plural, "words") and חָזוֹן ("vision"), the latter being the noun form related to the verb used in Hab 1:1.

[11] R. D. Weis defines the term as "prophetic exposition of divine revelation" ("Oracle," *ABD* 5:28); see his 1980 Claremont dissertation, *A Definition of the Genre Maśśaʾ in the Hebrew Bible*. He lists the eighteen passages the OT identifies with the term: 2 Kgs 9:26; Isa 13:2–14:23; 14:29–32; 15:1–16:12; 17:1–11; 19:1–25; 21:1–10,11–12,13–17; 22:1–14; 23:1–18; 30:6–7; Ezek 12:11–16; Nah 1:2–3:19; Hab 1:2–2:20; Zech 9:1–11:3; 12:1–14:21; Mal 1:2–3:24 (Eng. 1:2–4:6). Jer 23:33–38; Lam 2:14; and 2 Chr 24:27 use the term without reporting the speeches.

[12] J. N. B. Heflin, *Nahum, Habakkuk, Zephaniah, and Haggai,* BSC (Grand Rapids: Zondervan, 1985), 80–81.

[13] Weis, *ABD* 5:28–29 with bibliography; cp. M. Sweeney, *VT* 41 (1991): 65–66.

book as a whole?[14] The same phenomenon is found in Isa 1:1; 2:1; 13:1; 14:28; 15:1; 17:1; 21:1,11,13; 22:1; 23:1.[15] Chapter 3 contains its own introduction, calling the chapter a prayer of Habakkuk. It is most probable that both Habakkuk and Isaiah intend the original superscription to cover the entire canonical book, the following superscriptions being limited to the section or chapter they introduce.

Habakkuk's message burdened the prophet, and it burdened the righteous in Judah. How could righteous Josiah die at the hands of a pagan king? How could Jehoiakim ever reign in the place of Josiah on the throne of Judah? Habakkuk, burdened with the apparent success of the wicked, sought to unload his burden on the Lord. Through Habakkuk's questions, God spoke an eventual message of hope and deliverance to the people of Judah.

Although the name of a prophet often seemed to have significance in the Old Testament, Habakkuk's name appears to have been an exception. The name means "to embrace" or "to caress." An additional suggestion takes the name to have been a word for an Assyrian garden flower,[16] possibly used as a nickname.[17] In *Bel and the Dragon* the prophet is called "Habakkuk, son of Jesus of the tribe of Levi," a tradition linking Habakkuk to the priesthood.[18]

The title verse identifies Habakkuk as "the prophet," an unusual designation for the title verse of a prophetic book. Only Habakkuk, Haggai, and Zechariah are identified in this way in title verses. The Hebrew word for "prophet" *(nābîʾ)* has traditionally been interpreted as coming from a Hebrew root meaning "to bubble up," apparently indicating the overflowing message

---

[14] Watts ("Superscriptions and Incipits in the Book of the Twelve," 11) sees the Habakkuk superscription functioning to tie Habakkuk with Nahum, Zech 9:1; 12:1 and Malachi to the Book of the Twelve. In so doing he appears to rob Habakkuk of any type of superscription of its own, contrary to his earlier statement (p. 10) that "new superscriptions" at what he terms this "third (top) level" "are simply placed on top of others to relate books to one another." He explains this by concluding: "The process of building the Book of the Twelve accounts for the entire work on superscriptions in Joel, Micah, Nahum, Habakkuk, Zephaniah, and Malachi" (p. 12). Such conclusions leave too many books too different from the rest of the prophetic canon in their original form. In what way is מַשָּׂא "primary for Habakkuk"?

[15] For lists in Jeremiah see Watts, "Superscriptions and Incipits in the Book of the Twelve," 3, n. 1; note also his distinction of these from Ezekiel's "incipits." Tucker ("Prophetic Superscriptions and the Growth of a Canon," 58) points to Gen 5:1 and the Psalms as examples of a superscription serving as a chapter heading rather than as a book heading. He also notes that form critical criteria cannot solve the problem because "the form and content of the OT superscriptions vary considerably, although they ordinarily present information about the works they precede." Tucker (p. 62) points to three categories of titles, Habakkuk belonging with Nahum and Malachi, though the exact syntactical construction differs in each of these.

[16] J. J. M. Roberts, *Nahum, Habakkuk, and Zephaniah: A Commentary,* OTL (Louisville: Westminster/John Knox, 1991), 86. See Introduction, "Habakkuk, the Man," p. 251

[17] E. Achtemeier, *Nahum–Malachi,* IBC (Atlanta: John Knox, 1986), 34.

[18] E. A. Leslie, "Habakkuk," *IDB* (Nashville: Abingdon, 1962), 503; R. L. Smith, *Micah–Malachi,* WBC (Waco: Word, 1984), 93.

of the prophet. More recently Semitists have related *nābîʾ* to an Akkadian term meaning "to call," but the question remains whether this is active, one who calls (i.e., a speaker or preacher) or one who is called out by God. Most often contemporary scholars prefer the passive interpretation with the emphasis on the divine calling.[19] The prophet is God's "authorized spokesman" (Exod 6:28–7:2; Num 12:1–8; Deut 18:9–22) who according to Deuteronomy 13 and 18 must be an Israelite, must speak in God's name, must have supernatural knowledge about the future authenticated by God's fulfillment, must perform signs, and must have his words conform to those of Moses and other prophets.[20] These speakers for God had a job description: "The prophets were preachers who communicated God's words in order to transform their audience's thinking and social behavior. … They were persuading people to look at life in a radically different way (Jer 3:6–13)."[21]

In the Old Testament the term "prophet" could refer to the counterfeit as well as the genuine. In Jeremiah 28 both Jeremiah and the false prophet Hananiah are designated in the same way. The prophet proclaimed the message of the Lord and served as a spokesman for God, as Exod 4:14–16; 7:1 indicates. Prophets proclaimed a message that impacted the future and often made predictions, but the nature of the prophetic message primarily involved the contemporary society. Prophets were eyeball-to-eyeball preachers. They called contemporary people to repentance, and they expected the hearers to act on the word from the Lord. They preached to people of their own day, but the message continues to modern society.

How can a message over twenty-six hundred years old impact our contemporary world? (1) The prophetic message continues to speak to us because it is the message of God. Because it comes from God, it continues to communicate the ways of God to modern people. (2) The prophets forged their message in historical circumstances. The message of God came to real people in the everyday experiences of life as well as in times of crisis. (3) Though society has changed, human nature has not changed. People still need to know that God is at work in the historical situation. People continue to face the problem of sin and the necessity for repentance.

Habakkuk "received" (Hb. *ḥāzāh,* "saw") the oracle of the Lord. By translating "received," the NIV emphasizes the nature of the revelation. The prophet received the message from the Lord, possibly while in a prophetic trance or a related condition. The title verse of Nahum has a related word to

---

[19] J. Jeremias, *THAT,* II, 7; *HALOT.*

[20] See R. D. Culver, *TWOT,* 544–45, based on H. E. Freeman, *An Introduction to the Old Testament Prophets* (Chicago: Moody, 1968), 37–39.

[21] G. V. Smith, *The Prophets as Preachers* (Nashville: Broadman & Holman, 1994), 7; cp. the extended discussion by W. A. Vangemeren, *Interpreting the Prophetic Word* (Grand Rapids: Zondervan, 1990), 27–45.

describe "the book of the vision of Nahum." Use of the verb "to see" to describe the means of God's revelation is common in the prophets (Isa 1:1; Amos 1:1; Mic 1:1). At times a prophet is called a *ḥōzeh,* a "seer" (Amos 7:12; Mic 3:7; Isa 29:10; 2 Kgs 17:13; 1 Sam 9:9). The content of much of Habakkuk's message points to the emphasis here on reception rather than the visionary experience, for a prophecy dominated by lament and dialogue does not appear appropriately called a vision. Patterson thinks "Habakkuk's stress seems to be on his own participation in the revelatory process."[22]

The superscription then authorizes all that follows as powerful divine words even if their form and content would lead us to emphasize the human element of lament, complaint, questioning. God used the process of human questioning to enable the prophet to receive his word for his people.

I. QUESTIONS AND ANSWERS (1:2–2:5)

The Book of Habakkuk has a strange beginning for a prophetic book. Isaiah begins with God's complaint against his people. Jeremiah begins mysteriously with God's description of a prenatal call experience to which the prophet raises a lament. Ezekiel starts off with an eerie theophanic experience; Amos, with a more normal theophany followed by oracles against foreign nations including Israel and Judah. Hosea begins with God's invitation to marry a harlot. Joel begins by asking the people questions about the causes of current conditions. Obadiah opens with God's call to battle against Edom, introduced uniquely by plural voices. Micah announces a theophany. Nahum begins with a confession of faith in a jealous and avenging God of wrath. Zephaniah starts straightforwardly with an oracle of judgment. Haggai begins with God's condemning quotation of a complacent people's refusal to do his work. Zechariah introduces a call to repentance immediately. Malachi begins with God's confession of love for a people who do not believe him. God—his word, his actions, his coming, his call—opens prophetic books. But in Habakkuk the prophet's cry of complaint sounds forth hauntingly: "The prophet is weary—weary with the world as it is."[23] It warns the reader to expect something different here, to read closely between the lines. We must first determine why the prophet complains and ask what answer he expects.

The opening complaint finds a response rather than an answer, obviously

---

[22] R. D. Patterson, who argues that "the prophet at times apparently sees what God intends to do, agrees with God's revealed activities (sees them from God's point of view), and conveys in his own words the very words and message that God intends to be communicated to the prophet's audience" (*Nahum, Habakkuk, Zephaniah,* ed. K. Barker [Chicago: Moody, 1991], 137).

[23] Achtemeier, *Nahum–Malachi,* 36.

but not explicitly from God (1:5–11). "How long will God spare Israel? No longer than it takes to send the Babylonians against Jerusalem."[24] God's response expects amazement and disbelief from the prophet without explicitly involving Judah. The prophet responds as expected in amazement, having to check his own theological confession of faith before proceeding to question God (1:12–17). The prophet, not God, talks of punishment and judgment for Judah. Such punishment by such people the prophet cannot understand as the work of such a God as he worships. He must receive an answer, so he waits on God. The Lord explicitly replies (2:2–5), commissioning the prophet to write the revelation, a revelation centering on righteousness and faithfulness. Here the first major section of the book concludes with a description of the enemy's evil but not with a promise of victory. The section thus gives a sense of incompleteness, a sense of looking forward, while leaving an emotional aura of a disturbed world ruled by the wrong people. All the prophet and we find to hold on to is the mysterious call to righteousness and faithfulness.[25]

The section is tied together literarily. "The two perplexities of the prophet are begun with a question (1:2,12), and each of the answers starts with an imperative (1:5; 2:2)."[26]

Human nature tends to be filled with complaints, but human beings typically complain in the wrong directions. For example, we tend to talk about God rather than to talk to him; we tend to complain about God rather than complaining to him. Habakkuk took his complaints directly to God. He questioned how God could remain silent while the wicked prospered (Hab 1:2–4). When God answered Habakkuk's first complaint with the revelation that God would raise the Babylonians to punish wicked Judah (1:5–11), Habakkuk became even more perplexed. How could God use such a wicked instrument to punish the people of God (1:12–17)?

The very fact that Habakkuk took his complaints to God can help believers to be honest in prayer, taking all our burdens to the Lord. Habakkuk's experience shows that God is willing to hear our needs and to help us deal with our problems, even when he does not answer in the way that we expect or in the way that we ask.

1. Habakkuk's First Question: How Long Must I Call for Help? (1:2–4)

2How long, O LORD, must I call for help,
but you do not listen?
Or cry out to you, "Violence!"

---

[24] House, *The Unity of the Twelve*, 92.

[25] For fuller discussion of structure, see the Introduction.

[26] Patterson, *Nahum, Habakkuk, Zephaniah,* 122, who lists the various vocabulary elements tying the section together. These will be dealt with in commenting on the respective verses.

but you do not save?
[3]Why do you make me look at injustice?
Why do you tolerate wrong?
Destruction and violence are before me;
there is strife, and conflict abounds.

[4]Therefore the law is paralyzed,
and justice never prevails.
The wicked hem in the righteous,
so that justice is perverted.

1:2 A unique meter marks this opening prophetic cry, these verses representing the only instance of 3 + 2 meter in the book.[27] Habakkuk includes the invocation, "O LORD," and the complaint (vv. 2–3). There the formal elements end.[28] Rudolph notes that we cannot explain why except to say that Habakkuk refused to bind himself slavishly to a literary or liturgical scheme.[29] This is the traditional meter for the individual lament, the precise form of these verses. Verse 4 thus stands outside the lament pattern and also outside the metrical pattern, showing a 3 + 3 meter.[30] Verse 4b may incorporate a proverb from wisdom circles.[31] The content of v. 4, however, comes from the courtroom.

Verse 2 falls into two parallel parts, each asking the same kind of question in slightly different terms. This kind of synonymous parallelism characterized much of the poetry of the Old Testament.

The opening "tension of unanswered prayer"[32] sets the tone for the entire book. "Habakkuk here faces the dilemma that has confronted faithful people in every age—the dilemma of seemingly unanswered prayer for the healing of society. The prophet is one with all those persons who fervently pray for

---

[27] See Elliger, *Das Buch der zwölf kleinen Propheten II,* ATD 25 (Gøttingen: Vandenhoeck & Ruprecht, 1956), 27. E. S. Gerstenberger gives the most recent overview of the lament or complaint forms (*Psalms,* Part I with an Introduction to Cultic Poetry, FOTL 14 [Grand Rapids: Eerdmans, 1988], 11–14).

[28] Of the lament elements Gerstenberger lists, confession of sin or assertion of innocence, affirmation of confidence, plea or petition for help, imprecation against the enemies, acknowledgment of divine response, vow or pledge, hymnic elements, and an anticipated thanksgiving, do not appear in Habakkuk (*Psalms,* Part I 12). Patterson suggests that both here and in 1:12–2:1 the prophet has an "implied petition" (*Nahum, Habakkuk, Zephaniah,* 121). The traditional lament form includes an explicit petition.

[29] Rudolph, *Micha, Nahum, Habakuk, Zephanja,* 205.

[30] Already in v. 3 the last two words appear metrically superfluous so that Elliger marks them as a variant (*Das Buch der zwölf kleinen Propheten II,* 27).

[31] Ibid.

[32] C. E. Armerding, "Habakkuk," EBC 7:500. Note Patterson, *Nahum, Habakkuk, Zephaniah,* 140–41, who sees unanswered prayer as making the prophet wonder if he were out of fellowship with God: "He was an unhappy, perplexed, and greatly frustrated prophet."

peace in our world and who experience only war, who pray for God's good to come on earth and who find only human evil. But he is also one with every soul who has prayed for healing beside a sickbed only to be confronted with death; with every spouse who has prayed for love to come into a home and then found only hatred and anger; with every anxious person who has prayed for serenity but then been further disturbed and agitated."[33]

The central theme is justice, the word appearing twice in v. 4 and signifying "that world order ordained by God for the society of the covenant people. … Habakkuk's complaint is that the people of Judah … have abandoned the righteous order intended by God for their society, despite the fact that they renewed their covenant with the Lord and underwent a sweeping religious reform only twelve years earlier in the time of King Josiah."[34] The prophet's first complaint states such evils as violence, injustice, wrong, destruction, strife, and conflict. Such descriptions can be summarized simply: "The law is paralyzed, and justice never prevails" (v. 4). The picture is a courtroom scene where the guilty party brings so many false witnesses to court that the judge eventually gives a false verdict. This happens in the earthly courtroom all too often. The situation calls for intervention from the divine Judge, who is always just and guarantees justice for his people and his world. The problem is that such divine intervention does not come.[35] So the cry, How long?

Habakkuk's problem lay in what he knew about the Lord rather than in what he did not know. He knew that the Lord is holy and righteous. In the words of the great Old Testament text, Habakkuk knew the Lord to be a "compassionate and gracious God, slow to anger, abounding in love and faithfulness, maintaining love to thousands, and forgiving wickedness, rebellion, and sin. Yet he does not leave the guilty unpunished; he punishes the children and their children for the sin of the fathers to the third and fourth generation" (Exod 34:6–7). This passage gives the fullest description in the Old Testament of the holy God. How could this holy, pure (v. 13) God leave the guilty in Judah and Jerusalem unpunished? How could God continue to turn a deaf ear to the prophet's complaints? "The sorrow he felt on account of what he had seen had not been alleviated by any evidence of God's care or concern."[36]

Although Habakkuk asked a question to which he expected an answer, the question is primarily a complaint. The "how long" implies that the question

---

[33] Achtemeier, *Nahum–Malachi,* 35. Patterson follows Keil in translating "How long, O Lord, have I cried for help" to indicate "Habakkuk's past repeated cries to God" and to underscore "Habakkuk's frustration and exasperation with the whole state of affairs" (*Nahum, Habakkuk, Zephaniah,* 139, 141).

[34] Achtemeier, *Nahum–Malachi*, 34.

[35] See Elliger, *Das Buch der zwölf kleinen Propheten II,* 28–29.

[36] C. J. Barber, *Habakkuk and Zephaniah*, EvBC (Chicago: Moody, 1985), 26.

had been troubling the prophet for a long time. The prophet cried to God for help, but God had not heard his cry. In the Old Testament, "hearing," like most mental functions, implied more than simple hearing. It meant to hear and to respond. God had heard Habakkuk's cry, but he had not responded to the prophet's questioning complaint. The very sense of the question implies that Habakkuk expected that God would answer at some time in the future.

The second half of the verse continues the thought of the first half. Habakkuk used a different but similar Hebrew verb meaning "to cry." The second verb means "to cry out in distress or horror."[37] The prophet called out to God about the violence in the land. The wicked[38] oppressed the righteous, and God seemed not to care.

Violence (Hb. *ḥāmās*) is a key term punctuating the message of Habakkuk (1:2–3,9; 2:8,17a,17b). It "denotes flagrant violation of moral law by which man injures primarily his fellowman (e.g., Gen 6:11). Its underlying meaning is one of ethical wrong, of which physical brutality is only one possible expression (e.g., Judg 9:24)."[39]

When did such violence and oppression occur? Since God revealed the coming power of Babylon and its control of Judah, the latest possible date would have to be the Battle of Carchemish of approximately 605 B.C. After that battle every discerning person would know that the balance of power had shifted in the Near East. Babylon, not Egypt nor Assyria, would dictate the future of states such as Judah.

The earliest possible date for Habakkuk's outcry appears to have been the death of Josiah in 609 B.C. at the hands of Pharaoh Necho at the Battle of Megiddo (2 Kgs 23:29). Before his untimely death Josiah led the nation to a time of reform, removing the places of idolatrous worship and concentrating worship in Jerusalem, which apparently satisfied the teaching of the Book of Deuteronomy. In the appraisal of the writer of the Kings material, Josiah reigned as a good king because of his attempts at reformation (2 Kgs 22:2). Since going back prior to the ascension of Josiah (639 B.C.) appears too early for Habakkuk's complaints, the book must have originated between 609 and 605 B.C., most likely earlier rather than later in this period. Jeremiah knew Jehoiakim (who came to the throne in 609 B.C.) as a ruthless and merciless ruler. He cut up the scroll Jeremiah prepared and threatened the lives of Jere-

---

[37] D. J. Clark and H. A. Hatton, *A Handbook on the Books of Nahum, Habakkuk, and Zephaniah* (New York: UBS, 1989), 70.

[38] The history of research is dominated by attempts to identify the wicked here and in vv. 5–17. Rudolph eliminates the Babylonians as a candidate in 1:2–4 because God's answer cannot say he will send the Babylonians to get rid of the Babylonians (*Micha, Nahum, Habakuk, Zephanja,* 201). Thus Rudolph joins the roster of scholars reaching back to the Habakkuk commentary in Qumran to identify the wicked in 1:2–4 as a group within Judah.

[39] Armerding, "Habakkuk," 500.

miah and his scribe Baruch (Jer 36:20–26).[40]

The background of Jehoiakim's reign supports the anguish of Habakkuk. Of all Judah's evil kings, only of Jehoiakim is it said that he killed a prophet. Manasseh had shed much "innocent blood," but only Jehoiakim had a prophet killed who is specifically named in the Old Testament (Jer 26:20–23). No wonder Habakkuk cried "violence" and wondered when God would act on behalf on his people.

1:3 Habakkuk's additional question continued the thought of the passage. How could God allow the prophet to see such trouble?[41] The question implies that God's inactivity had allowed wicked people to dominate Judah. Such wickedness had come upon the whole land, including the prophet himself. The language picks up themes from Num 23:21 with similar verbs and objects.[42]

The second part of the question refers to God's inactivity. The prophet was incredulous: how could God look on trouble such as this and do nothing? The NIV has caught the force of the question: "Why do you tolerate wrong?" Though the interpretation seems free from difficulty, the remainder of v. 3 presents several problems for the translator.[43] The passage contains four nouns that indicate the problems in Judah during the reign of Jehoiakim. Jerusalem and Judah under the leadership of Jehoiakim could be described as a city of destruction and violence where contention and strife abound.

1:4 "The result of the abandonment of God's *mishpat* (justice) in Judean society is chaos":[44] the law is numbed, justice does not go out,[45] the wicked surround the righteous, and justice is perverted. No wonder the prophet complained about such a sorry state of affairs. With the breakdown of the social order, the nation lacked the elemental necessities for existence. When law is paralyzed and justice perverted, the righteous become the pawns of the wicked.

---

[40] For an appraisal of other options and a different conclusion see Patterson, *Nahum, Habakkuk, Zephaniah,* 139–40.

[41] The Hb. verb ראה is a *hiphil,* implying causation. The prophet blamed God for the continuation of the evil in Judah.

[42] See Armerding, "Habakkuk," 500, 502.

[43] The first part of the phrase contains two nouns (וְשֹׁד וְחָמָס, "destruction" and "violence") without a verb. In a passage that contains many examples of parallel thoughts, the translator naturally looks for a similar expression. The following phrase contains two nouns as well (רִיב וּמָדוֹן, "conflict" and "strife") but also two verbs. The critical notes to BHS suggest the possibility of a gloss or that several words may have dropped out of the text. The NIV interpretation is a reasonable one to treat וְשֹׁד וְחָמָס לְנֶגְדִּי as a verbless clause.

[44] Achtemeier, *Nahum–Malachi,* 35.

[45] R. L. Smith notes that לָנֶצַח usually means "forever" and thus as in this case with a negative modifier, "never" (*Micah–Malachi,* 98). In late Hebrew and Aramaic נֵצַח means "victory," a reading adopted by NEB here.

Who were the wicked?[46] Although some interpreters have looked to identify the wicked with Babylon,[47] most modern biblical scholars see the wicked as inhabitants in Judah, probably during the reign of Jehoiakim (609–598 B.C.). "There is nothing in this passage that points to a foreign nation. Those who hold such a view do so on other grounds."[48] As Armerding rightly points out, "Normally where 'justice' and social 'violence' are opposed, the 'wicked' are Israelites unless clearly identified in other terms (e.g., Exod 23:1–9; Isa 5:7–15)."[49] The terms "law" and "justice" would apply to Judah more naturally than to Babylon.

Armerding claims: "The law *(tôrāh)* may refer to any form of authoritative 'teaching' (e.g., Prov 3:1; 4:2); almost invariably it refers to God's 'law,' by which he reveals his will and directs the life of man. When used in the singular without clear definition, as here, 'law' signifies God's covenantal code established with Israel, given through Moses, and set forth particularly in the Book of Deuteronomy (e.g., Deut 1:5; 4:8; 17:18–19; 31:9; 33:4; Josh 8:31–32)."[50] This may be importing too precise a definition from the Pentateuch into prophecy. The "law" can refer to a number of different ideas such as the Ten Commandments, the law of Moses, or specific sets of law material. The most natural meaning is the "instruction" of God without reference to specific passages of Scripture.[51]

God's instructions had been violated. Habakkuk complained to God that the prophet dwelt in the midst of a people without moral restraints or abiding values. Does God have anything to say when society appears to be disintegrat-

---

[46] E. Nielsen sees two parties in Judah labeled righteous (supporters of Josiah and Jehoahaz, also called Shallum) and wicked (supporters of Jehoiakim and Egypt; "The Righteous and the Wicked in Habaqquq," *ST* 6 [1953]: 54–78). The basic problem is "lack of a rightful ruler" (p. 71). R. L. Smith rightly concludes: "There is not enough evidence to support Nielsen's conclusion. It is better to take a historical view and see the wicked in v. 4 as oppressors in Israel and the wicked in v. 13 as the Babylonians" (*Micah–Malachi,* 99).

[47] Johnson decides that "foreign military oppression of Judah has led to the conviction that the promises contained in the torah have been paralyzed and justice 'does not ever proceed' (i 4a) but rather has been 'bent' or twisted' (i 4c) … the injustice experienced for generations by Judah at the hands of foreign nations" (*VT* 35 [1985]: 260). He contends that Judah is identified as the wicked in v. 4 only through the mistaken idea that "transgressions of specific commandments are intended" (p. 262). For Johnson it is not a breaking of tora but a paralysis of tora, i.e., the failure of tora's promises, specifically in the days of Josiah and following the promises of Deuteronomy. Josiah met the requirements, but Habakkuk says God did not fulfill the promises as expected.

[48] R. L. Smith, *Micah–Malachi,* 99.

[49] Armerding, "Habakkuk," 499.

[50] Ibid., 500.

[51] Achtemeier is closer to reality in defining Torah as "the whole religious tradition of Israel, including her Deuteronomic law, her traditions of what God has done in her past life, and the ongoing guidance afforded her day by day through the preaching and teaching of priests and prophets" (*Nahum–Malachi,* 34–35).

ing? Is there a message from God for a wicked age? These became the questions of Habakkuk. Where is God and why is he not doing something?[52] The righteous in every age ask similar questions. One of the helpful lessons to be learned from Habakkuk is that God does know what is happening. He is not oblivious to wickedness in high places. In his time and in his way the Lord brings judgment on those who oppress the weak.

With the law paralyzed (lit., "numbed" or "ineffective"), justice cannot prevail.[53] In the Old Testament justice and righteousness are intertwined. Righteousness meant that a person met the demands of a relationship. Righteousness toward God meant meeting the demands of the relationship with God; righteousness toward a fellow human being meant meeting the demands of the relationship with another. Justice carried righteousness into the legal sphere. The prophets demanded righteousness in the gate, the place where justice was dispensed. In prophetic contexts such as the one under discussion, ethical and legal standards are the same.[54] Justice and righteousness "were the quintessence of the divine will. They embodied the central authority from which the coherence of the social order stemmed."[55] Law was "paralyzed" most extensively by "corruption of the religious and civil leadership of the nation" and not by foreign powers.[56]

The lack of justice meant that the wicked hemmed in the righteous. Without justice the righteous have little recourse. Not willing to resort to the devices of the wicked, the righteous suffer when justice does not prevail. The final verb (in v. 4) describes what happens when the law is paralyzed and justice is not carried out: the wicked hem in the righteous, and justice is "bent out of shape." Another meaning of the verb is that justice is made "crooked."[57] "The Israelites' rejection of God's authority mediated through the law merely exposed them to the harsher experience of his authority mediated through an alien people."[58]

2. God's First Answer: Look and Be Amazed (1:5–11)

Without warning to the reader, the speaker changed. Instead of the prophet questioning God, the Lord responded to the complaints of the prophet. "The

[52] R. L. Smith says, "The prophet was concerned about the unchecked power of evil, but that fact caused him to question the nature of his God who permitted such evil to go unpunished" (*Micah–Malachi*).

[53] Armerding ("Habakkuk," 500) is correct in noting the broad and varied connotations of מִשְׁפָּט, "implying the exercise not merely of legal processes but of all the functions of government."

[54] Achtemeier, "Righteousness in the OT," *IDB* 4:81.

[55] J. G. Harris, "The Laments of Habakkuk's Prophecy," *EvQ* 45 (1973): 24–25.

[56] Armerding, "Habakkuk," 500.

[57] BDB, 785.

[58] Armerding, "Habakkuk," 506.

answer God gives to those prayers is both comforting and confounding."[59] Though the Lord did not respond specifically to the prophet's questions (e.g., why the Lord tolerated evil), he addressed the basic thrust of the prophet's complaint. Habakkuk wanted to know what God would do about wickedness in Judah. The Lord responded in ways that amazed and frightened the prophet.[60]

God told the prophet that he was at work. Herein lies an amazing fact, especially for modern people. God is at work. In a world that only considers that humans are at work, God works. Alongside the "men at work" signs stands another, more important sign: "God at work."[61]

(1) The Revelation of God's Work (1:5–6)

5"Look at the nations and watch—
and be utterly amazed.
For I am going to do something in your days
that you would not believe,
even if you were told.
6I am raising up the Babylonians,
that ruthless and impetuous people,
who sweep across the whole earth
to seize dwelling places not their own.

1:5 Verses 5 and 6 have a 3 + 3 meter, though v. 5a could be read 3 + 2.[62] The expected form would be an oracle of salvation answering the preceding lament. Normally a priest or cult prophet would deliver such an oracle to the one offering the lament, but Habakkuk's response came directly from God.[63] Furthermore, that response involved not an oracle of salvation but an announcement of God's action in raising up a mighty, powerful, godless people to action.[64] This is presented in two parts: a call to look among the nations

---

[59] Achtemeier, *Nahum–Malachi,* 37.

[60] Patterson says God solved the prophet's perplexity by saying Judah's sin would be punished by the Babylonians but also added "an accompanying description of the ability of His agent of judgment to deliver the required punishment" (*Nahum, Habakkuk, Zephaniah,* 121–22). Sure he had no trouble convincing the prophet; this was a case of divine overkill.

[61] C. G. Chappell, *Meet These Men* (Nashville: Abingdon, 1956), 77.

[62] The LXX adds a further imperative in v. 5a: ἀφανίσθητε, "you will be made to disappear [i.e., "destroyed"]."

[63] Rudolph, with reference to Amos 3:7 and those special prophets to whom God reveals his plans and purposes (*Micha, Nahum, Habakuk, Zephanja*, 205). This is true even though God's answer addresses a plurality of people.

[64] See Elliger, *Das Buch der zwölf kleinen Propheten II,* 30. B. Childs says the salvation oracle has been turned on its head. "It does not offer the usual comfort but announces an attack by a cruel nation which will set Israel's wickedness right by a devastating judgment" (*Introduction to the Old Testament as Scripture* [Philadelphia: Fortress, 1979], 451). R. L. Smith notes that the oracle has neither the messenger formula nor the announcement of judgment (*Micah–Malachi,* 101).

(v. 5) and a description of the Chaldeans (vv. 6–11).[65] As Smith says, "one is left to assume that the coming of the Chaldeans is to punish Judah for the evil described in 1:2–4."[66] Verse 6 "sets forth the character of the Babylonians ('ruthless'), their conduct ('who sweep'), and their motivation ('to seize'), each element being elaborated in vv. 7–11."[67]

In the Hebrew text the first four verbs are plural imperatives ("be utterly amazed" translates two Hb. verbs which are different forms of the same root). The use of the imperatives emphasizes the urgency of the command as well as the incomprehensible nature of the revelation of the Lord. Such use also shows that God directed his answer to a group of people supporting the prophet, not just to the prophet himself. Prayer for help was and is the occupation of more than one person in God's community of faith.

The Lord instructed the prophet to look among the nations.[68] This must mean that God's work already could be seen by the person attuned to the "strange work" of the Lord (Isa 28:21). Does this imply that Babylon already had begun to move against the nations? Practically any date between 612 B.C. and 605 B.C. would fit such a context.[69]

God told Habakkuk to "be utterly amazed."[70] God would do a work "in your days," that is, soon or in the prophet's lifetime, which would astound him and all who witnessed the events from the perspective of the nation Judah. "I am going to do something" can be rendered more literally either "a deed is doing" or "doing a deed," supply (as the NIV) God as the subject.[71] The verb is a participle that can refer to present, continuous activity or the

---

[65] See R. L. Smith, *Micah–Malachi,* 101.

[66] Ibid. Johnson says 1:5–11 "functions as a heightened form of the very complaint in 1:2–4. … Yahweh, rather than bringing an answer to the generations-old problem of theodicy, is making the problem more acute by a nonfulfillment of his promises, which appears to be a paralysis of *tora*" (*VT* 35 [1985]: 261).

[67] Armerding, "Habakkuk," 502.

[68] The LXX gives an alternate reading for "among the nations" (בַּגּוֹיִם) taken up in Acts 13:41. By reading a *daleth* in place of the *waw,* the LXX translates οἱ καταφρονηταί, "despisers" (בֹּגְדִים). Such a reading comes from 1:13b and 2:5, according to Rudolph (*Micha, Nahum, Habakuk, Zephanja,* 203). This change makes the paragraph addressed to the wicked in Judah rather than to the prophet. Though the reading of the LXX makes sense and does fit the text, the reading of the MT better fits the situation and the remaining context. Another proposed rearrangement of the text affects the entire interpretation of the chapter. Some commentators make Hab 1:2–4 refer to the wickedness of the Assyrians rather than the wickedness of Jehoiakim or those in Judah. This was a popular approach in earlier times but seems to have been abandoned recently.

[69] See the historical section of the introduction for the background and activities of the new Babylonian kingdom.

[70] וְהִתַּמְּהוּ תְּמָהוּ consists of two imperatives, a *hitp.* followed by a *qal* of the same verb, תמה. It could be translated lit. "and look at each other in astonishment be astonished."

[71] The LXX adds the explicit first person pronoun as subject, but Patterson is correct in noting that Hebrew frequently omits it, here probably for metrical causes. He points to the similar construction without the pronoun in 2:10 (*Nahum, Habakkuk, Zephaniah,* 149).

immediate future. The point is that God is already at work. Habakkuk and his hearers would be surprised at the Lord's answer. Who could expect that the Lord would use such a wicked instrument to judge a nation more righteous than they?

Habakkuk argued in just this way in his next question (1:12–17). The Lord's answer indicates his sovereignty. He is not bound by the listener's whims or by their standards of "fairness." He responds according to his sovereign will. He is the Lord of history who works in history to accomplish his purpose.

Habakkuk's questions reflect the questions of many people. Especially when we deal with personal affronts, difficulties, and disappointments, we desire to know where God is and what he is doing. Habakkuk reminds us that God is at work. He is the Lord of the universe who works to accomplish his purpose in his world and in our lives.

1:6 Who could have believed that God's answer to the wickedness in Judah would be "Babylon"?[72] Who are these Chaldeans?[73] Chaldea lay in central and southeastern Mesopotamia between the lower stretches of the Tigris and Euphrates Rivers in modern Iraq, close to the border with Iran, touching the head of the Persian Gulf. Several Aramean tribes entered the area between 1000 and 900 B.C. They found a homeland with few natural resources, a flat alluvial plain, marsh lands, flooding, and hot summers. They rejected all urban society and its customs and manner of life but gradually developed military power under Merodach-Baladan and then a century later under Nabopolassar, who founded a Chaldean dynasty in Babylon, defeated the Assyrians, and captured Nineveh in 612 B.C. This was the Neo-Babylonian Empire.[74]

In case anyone needed a history lesson, the Lord described them as "ruthless" (or "bitter") and "impetuous" (or "hasty"),[75] that is, they were known for

---

[72] Note that the NIV does not translate the introductory particle, כִּי , meaning "because, for," or even "indeed." This ties v. 6 closely to v. 5, especially v. 5b, where the particle occurs twice with differing meanings, "because" and "even if" or "when."

[73] Scholarship has wrestled endlessly with the identification of the wicked enemy. P. Jöcken organizes his 524 pages of description of the history of Habakkuk research around theories of the wicked. Each theory must identify the people about whom Habakkuk complained in 1:2–4 and the wicked nation described in 1:5–11. Theories identify the two as Judah, Babylon; Assyria, Babylon; Judah, Scythians; Babylon, Babylon; Judah, powerful opponent of Babylon; Egypt, Babylon; Jewish prince in Nineveh, Medes; Judah, Egypt; Arabia, Arabia; Babylon, Persia; Seleuccids of Syria, eschatological battle; Greece, Greece. In most of these cases the interpretation can be directed against both countries or against the first country and in favor of the second, seen as the great deliverer from the conditions of 1:2–4 (*Das Buch Habakuk,* BBB 48 [Köln, Bonn: Hanstein, 1977]).

[74] See T. M. Martin, "Chaldea," *HBD,* 243. D. Browning, "Babylon, History and Religion of," *HBD,* 142–44; R. L. Smith, *Micah–Malachi,* 101.

[75] Patterson translates הַמַּר וְהַנִּמְהָר "fierce and fiery," following NJB in imitating the Hebrew play on sounds (*Nahum, Habakkuk, Zephaniah,* 150).

their cruelty and speed in conquering most of western Asia.[76] This was the nation whose armies marched through the expanse of the earth, enriching themselves at the expense of other nations.[77] Babylon proved to be a worthy successor to the Assyrian army with its thirst for power and plunder. "In effect the Lord's answer to 'violence' is 'violence,' as stipulated in the 'law,' whose paralysis with regard to injustice is only temporary (cf. Isa 55:11; 2 Tim 2:9)."[78]

"In this vivid description of a seemingly unstoppable power, one of Habakkuk's great theological themes begins to surface: Evil has within itself the seed of destruction. Babylon will not have the last word after all, for within the empire are self-destructive traits: greed (1:6), cruelty (1:7), arrogance and self-sufficiency (1:7), haughtiness (1:10), and blasphemy (1:11)."[79] Smith similarly explains, "God allows tyrants to spring up and flourish for a little while, but they become guilty by the abuse of their power and, like a plant before it is firmly rooted, God blows on them and they wither."[80] This is the God Hosea pictured as the husband, the family leader of Israel. The family leader has authority over much more than a family. He is sovereign over all the nations. He has the power and right to use a wicked foreign power to punish his wicked people.[81]

(2) The Description of the Babylonian Army (1:7–11)

7They are a feared and dreaded people;
they are a law to themselves
and promote their own honor.
8Their horses are swifter than leopards,
fiercer than wolves at dusk.

---

[76] A. B. Davidson, *Nahum, Habakkuk, and Zephaniah,* CBSC (Cambridge: University Press, 1899), 68. Properly speaking, the Chaldeans were not Babylonians, though they were Semitic. Elliger argues that the description of 1:5–11 does not really fit what we know of the Babylonian armies and thus originally referred to a general description of an enemy for whom the prophet had no specific identity (*Das Buch der zwölf kleinen Propheten II,* 31–32). Rather, the original reading was הַגִּבּוֹרִים, "the heroes," which the prophet later replaced with Chaldeans when the Babylonians came more clearly into the picture. In this explanation Habakkuk borrowed from Jeremiah's picture of the foe from the north in Jer 4–6 and may have seen Egypt as the one who caused trouble before it became clear that Babylon was the culprit. Rudolph shows that the following parallel statement in apposition, "that ruthless and impetuous people," demands a proper name. Rather, "heroes" is a later attempt to generalize the Chaldeans so that the verse could be applied to enemies long after the Chaldeans left the scene (*Micha, Nahum, Habakuk, Zephanja,* 203–4).

[77] The Hebrew uses third person singular in v. 6b, almost personifying the Babylonian army and the nation as a single individual; see Patterson, *Nahum, Habakkuk, Zephaniah,* 150.

[78] Armerding, "Habakkuk," 502. R. D. Haak uses 1:5–6 as the basis for placing Habakkuk squarely in the "pro-Babylonian party in Judah" (*Habakkuk,* VTSup 44 [Leiden: Brill, 1992], 130).

[79] Heflin, *Nahum, Habakkuk, Zephaniah, and Haggai,* 85.

[80] R. L. Smith, *Micah–Malachi,* 102.

[81] Cp. House, *The Unity of the Twelve*, 180.

Their cavalry gallops headlong;
their horsemen come from afar.
They fly like a vulture swooping to devour;
9they all come bent on violence.
Their hordes advance like a desert wind
and gather prisoners like sand.
10They deride kings
and scoff at rulers.
They laugh at all fortified cities;
they build earthen ramps and capture them.
11Then they sweep past like the wind and go on—
guilty men, whose own strength is their god."

1:7 These verses (1:7–11) vividly describe the arrogance (v. 7b) of the Babylonians along with their unrivaled military power. Peoples of the world rightfully dreaded the power of Babylon. Who tells Babylon what to do? Do they stand before a world court? No, they are a law unto themselves. They set their own rules about how they should treat other people. This means violence and terror. Their own strength is their god (1:11).[82] Babylon determined its own agenda and its timetable. "In short, they represent the epitome of heathen power, lawlessness and ruthlessness. Mighty Babylon does not concern itself with mercy, nor does it believe destruction will ever come its way."[83] It was this great nation that God called forth to punish the wicked in Judah and to show the power of God. "Judah has rejected God's *mispat* or order in its society (v. 4); therefore Babylonia's order (*mishpat,* v. 7, NIV "law") will be imposed upon it. Judah has opted for violence among its inhabitants (v. 2); therefore Babylonia's violence will be its punishment (v. 9). ... The punishment fits the sin."[84]

That God could use foreign nations for his purposes, even purposes of punishment for his people, did not surprise Habakkuk. Prophets long before him had taught that. The surprising, shocking news beyond understanding was that God would use a people who acted like this and would underline the terror and violence they would use.[85] "A nation that deified itself shall be an instrument of the true God!"[86]

God's actions to rouse up the Chaldeans to punish Judah emphasize other truths beyond those raised by the prophet. God is not confined to the nation Judah. Many people in the ancient Near East assumed that each nation had its

[82] Armerding describes it: "Their character was rooted in a self-sufficiency that acknowledged no superior authority and no dependency, which was tantamount to self-deification" ("Habakkuk," 503).

[83] House, *The Unity of the Twelve,* 215.

[84] Achtemeier, *Nahum–Malachi*, 38.

[85] See Rudolph, *Micha, Nahum, Habakuk, Zephanja,* 207.

[86] Ibid., 208.

gods. People who moved to Judah came under the sway of the God of Judah. Naaman asked for two mule loads of dirt to take with him to Syria, apparently so he could worship the Lord in Syria. He assumed that he had to be on the Lord's land in order to worship the Lord (2 Kgs 5:1–19).

God's raising the Chaldeans showed that he is sovereign over the whole earth. He is not confined to one nation or one people (cf. Amos 9:7). God can work through other peoples to accomplish his purpose. God used the Assyrians as the "rod of his anger" to punish recalcitrant Judah at an earlier time (Isa 10:5–15). He chose Cyrus the Mede to deliver the people of Judah from the exile imposed by the Babylonians (Isa 45:1). In Habakkuk's day God would use Babylon to punish Judah for its rebellion against the Lord.

1:8 The following verses describe the fierceness of the Babylonian army. Their horses and their soldiers seem larger than life. The sinister aspect accented here is the swiftness of the army, its ability to appear out of nowhere, accomplish its gruesome work, and suddenly vanish again.[87] A second emphasis is the army's resemblance to wild beasts of prey with their eagerness to attack, plunder, kill, and slip away to enjoy the spoils of the hunt.[88] Who could stand before armies of this magnitude?

The Lord first described the horses of the Babylonians.[89] Horses would frighten and fascinate the people of Judah and the surrounding region because of their relative scarcity in the area. Horses and chariots made sense in other areas, but not in the central hill country of Judah. The Philistines probably failed to dominate Israel because of the uselessness of the chariot in the hill country. On the Philistine plain horses and chariots ruled the day but proved worthless in mountainous terrain.

Babylon's horses struck fear in the hearts of the people of Judah.[90] Most of the biblical references to horses are connected to warfare. Using horses for agriculture or for pulling burdens was practically unknown.[91] The Lord described the horses as swifter than leopards and more fierce[92] than wolves at dusk. The literal Hebrew expression describes "wolves of the evening," that is, a hunting, feeding, hungry wolf. In Palestine wolves hunted during the evening hours, which meant that the wolves would be hungrier and more

---

[87] See Elliger, who describes the Babylonian army's work as child's play, magical (*Das Buch der zwölf kleinen Propheten II,* 31).

[88] See Rudolph, *Micha, Nahum, Habakuk, Zephanja,* 207.

[89] Rudolph claims that the Scythians supplied most of the cavalry for the Babylonian army.

[90] Armerding says, "If God's people refuse to fear him, they will ultimately be compelled to fear those less worthy of fear" ("Habakkuk," 503).

[91] J. A. Thompson, "Horse," *IDB,* 646–47.

[92] Patterson says וְחַדּוּ, "and they are fierce," is more accurately translated "sharp" or "keen" and refers to the "keen sensibilities of the wolf, alert to the prey and to every situation. As applied to horses it must refer to their skill and spiritedness in battle situations" (*Nahum, Habakkuk, Zephaniah,* 151).

fierce after not eating for a period of time.[93]

The second half of v. 8 presents several translation difficulties though the meaning is clear.[94] The Lord continued to describe the power of the army coming to attack Jerusalem and thus to punish the wickedness of Judah and Jerusalem. The second half of the verse describes the horses and their riders who would descend on Jerusalem.

The problem in translation revolves around the use of the word "horse," a different Hebrew word from the one used earlier in the verse. The word found in the second half of the verse can describe both the horse and its rider.[95] How should the verse be translated?

The context supports the idea that the horse (Hb. *pārāš*) in the first instance in the second half of the verse refers to the horse alone. The Hebrew text describes the horses "springing about" or "pawing the ground" (the Hb. verb can have either meaning). This seems to describe horses that would be nervous and ready to run.

The second use of the word *pārāš* appears to refer to the riders of the horses: "Their horsemen come from afar." The NIV seems to take a sensible view of the translation, making the first instance refer to the cavalry while the second word refers to the riders: "Their cavalry gallops headlong; their horsemen come from afar" (1:8).[96]

The last simile in the verse refers to the swift attack of the cavalry. They attacked like vultures swooping down to take their prey. Though "vulture" probably is the best translation, most English readers should think of the eagle, which is known for its power and strength. Like the suddenness of a bird of prey, the Chaldean army would attack Jerusalem and end the wickedness of Judah's leaders. God had indeed been at work in the world. The Lord revealed to the prophet that even in Habakkuk's day he was doing a work that would astound.

1:9 Babylon's purpose was clear. They were bent on violence, the same

[93] An alternate reading for "dusk" or "evening" is "desert," leading some translations to describe the fierceness of the horses as "wolves of the plain" (NEB). See the lengthy discussion by Rudolph, *Micha, Nahum, Habakuk, Zephanja,* 204, who, along with many scholars, adds a letter to Hb. עֶרֶב, "at dusk," to read עֲרָבָה, the steppe, the wilderness, so wolves of the wilderness.

[94] Rudolph follows Duhm and others in changing וּפָשׁוּ פָּרָשָׁיו, "their cavalry gallops," or "their war chariots gallop ahead," to פָּרָשֵׁי פָּרָשָׁיו combined then with the first word of the next line to create threefold alliteration and read "the horse with its rider gallops." R. L. Smith follows the Dead Sea Scroll and NEB as he reads וּפרשׁוּ, "they spring forward," for וּפרשׁיו, "horse with war chariot" (*Micah–Malachi,* 100). Rudolph says there is no reason to follow the Dead Sea Scrolls at this point (*Micha, Nahum, Habakuk, Zephanja,* 204). Elliger transposes lines in v. 8b after v. 9a on "stylistic and metrical grounds" (*Das Buch der zwölf kleinen Propheten II,* 29).

[95] פָּרָשׁ seems to refer to both the horse and the rider or the horse and the chariot and its driver, while סוּס indicates the horse alone.

[96] R. L. Smith translates "his horses paw the ground; they spring forward; they come from afar" (*Micah–Malachi*, 100).

Hebrew term the prophet used to describe the situation he complained to God about in v. 3 and about which he cried to God in v. 2. "They" in the Hebrew is "he," though the NIV and other translations are no doubt correct to refer to the army or cavalry of Babylon even though the last reference in the Hebrew was to the horses. The army of Babylon would sweep into Judah bent on plunder and destruction.

"Their hordes advance like a desert wind" is a conjecture in the NIV.[97] Since the first word in the line is found only once in the Old Testament, the translation has been almost impossible. The NIV carries the idea of the swiftness of the hordes that are bent on violence.[98]

The result would be clear. The Babylonians would sweep into the region with faces determined to take Jerusalem. The number of their captives would be like grains of sand. No wonder God told the prophet he would not believe what he was told.

1:10 Everyone should fear one in whom no fear exists. The Babylonian army mocked kings and made rulers objects of derision. They had "contempt for all other authority."[99] "They" (Hb. "he") is emphasized in the Hebrew text.[100] Though no one else would dare do so, *they* scoffed and made sport of the rulers of the people. If the army did not tremble before kings, what could the common people do?

---

[97] Armerding notes that "like a desert wind" rests more on the parallel passage in Jeremiah 4:11–13 than on the Hebrew text ("Habakkuk," 503). He prefers NASB "horde of faces," but note his seeming support for "desert wind" on p. 504.

[98] "Hordes" is a conjecture. The GNB and RSV change the Hb. word מְגַמַּת, an otherwise unknown word perhaps meaning "assembling" or "collecting" to a Hb. word meaning "terror"; thus terror goes before the approach of the army. Both translations also change the word for "desert wind" or "east wind" (קָדִימָה) to something meaning the approach of the enemy. While the RSV and GNB make sense in the context of the passage and do not appear to do violence to the text, the better approach appears to be that of the NIV and other translations, which acknowledge the difficulty of the text but attempt to draw meaning from the MT. R. L. Smith takes the word to mean "all," though the evidence he gives from BDB, 169, does not support this (*Micah–Malachi,* 100). Rudolph argues that to correct the first word which appears in the Dead Sea Scrolls also is methodologically incorrect (*Micha, Nahum, Habakuk, Zephanja,* 204). He connects the term to an Arabic one and translates: "their front presses forward." Patterson translates "very face is set forward," explaining that "final certainty is lacking" (*Nahum, Habakkuk, Zephaniah,* 144, 151–52). He bases his translation on context as much as anything else, tying to the preceding and succeeding lines and finding paronomasia between קָדִימָה and the following mention of sand. The commentary on the Dead Sea Scroll of Habakkuk supplies another alternative: "The set of their faces is like the east wind," meaning that the Babylonians' fierceness would be like that of the east wind that blew in from the desert. Habakkuk and others must have been struck by the fact that the debilitating east wind and the destructive Babylonian army came from the same general area (Clark and Hatton, *Nahum, Habakkuk, and Zephaniah,* 78).

[99] Armerding, "Habakkuk," 503.

[100] Patterson points the reference either to the personified Babylonian nation or to its king (*Nahum, Habakkuk, Zephaniah,* 153).

Nothing could stand before the Chaldean army. The Babylonians (again emphasized) laughed at the fortresses of the nations. Though Jerusalem presented a formidable stronghold, the Babylonians would scorn such defenses, overcoming them by throwing up siegeworks that would eventually overcome the city.

One method of defeating a walled city or fortress involved making a ramp of dirt[101] the attackers would climb and then overtake the city. The Romans took Masada with this strategy. The Babylonians followed the practices developed by the Assyrians in besieging a city. After building a ramp or a causeway, the attackers constructed war machines mounted on four or six wooden wheels. From these warriors could shoot directly at the defenders on the walls, or the machine could be used as a battering ram. At the same time, the walls of the besieged city would be undermined by digging a tunnel. At the appropriate time the full-scale assault would begin, led by heavily armed infantry scaling tall ladders. Archers then increased the attack with their arrows, which served to protect the infantry.[102] No wonder the Chaldean attackers scoffed at kings. No one seemed able to stand before them.

1:11 Though ordained of God to carry out his purpose (1:6,12), the Babylonians worshiped only might and the strength of their hands.[103] They bowed to no man and listened to no god. Thus the person coming under the sway of the army had little hope. This bitter and hasty army swept the earth like the wind and hurried on to plunder other nations.[104] "Such people acknowledge no accountability, seek no repentance, and offer no reparations, while violating the most fundamental order of created life.

The emphatic position of this statement about the godlessness of the Babylonians beckons the reader to expect more. This cannot be the entire

---

[101] The Hb. term for "earthen" is עָפָר "dust."

[102] J. W. Weavers, "War, Methods Of," *IDB,* 804–5.

[103] Dead Sea Scroll reads וישׂם for MT ואשׁם. NEB follows G. R. Driver, an influential member of the translation committee, in understanding this as from a dialectical form of שׁמם, "to be desolate, or appalled, horrified" ("Confused Hebrew Roots," in *Occident and Orient,* ed. B. Schindler [London: Taylor's, 1936], 75–77); see W. H. Brownlee, *The Text of Habakkuk in the Ancient Commentary from Qumran,* JBLMS (Philadelphia: Fortress, 1959), 22–24; others take it from שִׂים ("set"); Patterson, *Nahum, Habakkuk, Zephaniah,* 144, 153–54, translates "but he whose strength is his god will be held guilty"; see R. L. Smith, *Micah–Malachi,* 100.

[104] This interpretation appears to fit the context of the passage and to agree with the majority of interpreters, but the translational problems are more complex than the interpretation suggests. The following questions make the task of translation difficult: (1) "Wind" (רוּחַ) may also be translated as "mind" (KJV) or "spirit." Though most translators prefer "wind," they also add a letter to the MT to make the "wind" a simile ("like the wind") rather than the subject, which is possible. (2) Does "guilty men" (וְאָשֵׁם) go with the first half of the verse (as the *athnah* would suggest) or the latter half as the NIV and most translations suggest? For a fuller discussion consult Clark and Hatton, *Nahum, Habakkuk, and Zephaniah,* 80.

answer of God to the prophet's lament. Surely God will deal with the godless.[105]

3. Habakkuk's Second Question: Why Do You Tolerate the Treacherous? (1:12–17)

Habakkuk's second complaint reflects many features of the first:[106]

FIRST COMPLAINT	SECOND COMPLAINT	FEATURE
1:2	1:12	Invocation
1:2,3	1:12,13,17	Urgent Questions
1:2,3,4	1:12,13,15,17	Justice and Righteousness

This second complaint appears to come on the heels of the Lord's answer to Habakkuk's first complaint and seeks another answer to explain the first one. How could the Lord use the Babylonians, a wicked and unclean instrument, to carry out his purpose to punish the wickedness in Judah (1:12)?[107] Could the holy and just God do such a thing (1:13)?

The remainder of the complaint contains a description of how the Babylonians treated the nations it conquered (1:14–17).[108] The Babylonians caught men with a hook and gathered them with a seine. By the catch the Babylonians lived in luxury. Habakkuk ended the section by asking if the Babylonians could go on doing this with impunity.

(1) A Description of the Lord (1:12–13)

[12]O LORD, are you not from everlasting?
My God, my Holy One, we will not die.
O LORD, you have appointed them to execute judgment;
O Rock, you have ordained them to punish.

---

[105] See Elliger, *Das Buch der zwölf kleinen Propheten II,* 31. He claims that God's actions and the course of the world, that is, the actions of the world power, are not simply identical notions. There remains the question that must break out anew, the question of the meaning of the puzzle of world history whose irrationality has only increased.

[106] Armerding, "Habakkuk," 505. The note of confidence Armerding discusses in 1:12 and supposedly implicit in 1:2–4 stretches the evidence. The mood appears to be anything but one of confidence. It is one of questioning and horrified amazement at what the God he knows is doing rather than acting like the God of his confession of faith. Also the supposed *A-B-A* pattern of 1:12–2:1 makes both 1:12 and 2:1 confessions of faith. They certainly do not share similar structure, and the statement of God's election in v. 12 is not exactly a confession of faith.

[107] Armerding shows how linguistic, thematic, and structural parallels connect v. 13 with v. 6 and thus demand that the wicked enemy be the same in both verses ("Habakkuk," 506–7). "They are thus distinct from the 'wicked' in v. 4, just as the 'violence' and perverted justice in vv. 7,9 differ from that in vv. 2–4; and they represent a further dramatic embodiment of the lex talionis, the 'wicked' being judged through the 'wicked' (cf. Ezek 7:23–24).

[108] R. L. Smith argues that 1:12–17 "may have come later than the first" because "Babylon. . . is a ruthless world conqueror, not a new nation on the rise. A probable date for the origin of this section is 597 B.C." (*Micah–Malachi,* 95).

13Your eyes are too pure to look on evil;
you cannot tolerate wrong.
Why then do you tolerate the treacherous?
Why are you silent while the wicked
swallow up those more righteous than themselves?

1:12 The verses function as a resumption of the lament in vv. 2–3,[109] but they have neither the meter nor the formal characteristics of a lament.[110] Instead, the content is that of a confession of faith describing the characteristics of God. Even this form is altered by the use of interrogative mood and negative statements. Rudolph dates this a year or so after 605 when Nebuchadnezzar made regular military marches westward.[111] In explaining the text Rudolph relies on a major exegetical rule: a prophet or whoever speaks must be understood by his original audience.[112]

Habakkuk's complaint indicates the prophet's familiarity with both the Lord and the Babylonians. Israel's prophets showed an amazing understanding of how the world worked. They demonstrated knowledge of geography, history, and politics. They also served as conduits and tutors for who the Lord is and how he works in the world. Can the modern-day pastor be any less conversant in any of these areas? As Moses attested, "Would that all the Lord's people were prophets" (Num 11:29).

The prophets taught the people the ways of God, particularly concerning the current situations of the day. Because Habakkuk knew so much of the

[109] Patterson finds components of the lament genre here: invocation (v. 12), statement of the problem (vv. 13–17), closing declaration of the prophet's confidence in God (2:1; *Nahum, Habakkuk, Zephaniah,* 155). But this analysis omits too many basic elements of the genre; see note on 1:2. It also ties 2:1 to the previous section rather than the following section and baptizes it with an aura of confidence that may not fit well with the prophet's mood. Use of the Hb. root יכח as "bookends" in 1:12 ("punish") and in 2:1 ("complaint") is not sufficient evidence to isolate 1:12–2:1 as a unit.

[110] See Elliger, *Das Buch der zwölf kleinen Propheten II,* 34–35.

[111] Rudolph thinks the Babylonian campaigns gave the prophet opportunity to learn Babylon's military methods up close and thus gave content to vv. 14–17 (*Micha, Nahum, Habakuk, Zephanja,* 209). R. L. Smith notes that recent scholars who emphasize the cultic liturgy format of the book, which he does not, believe this second lament belonged to a cultic liturgy used in the New Year festival in Jerusalem about 602/601 "to protest Jehoiakim's usurpation of the role of Jehoahaz" (*Micah–Malachi,* 103). Smith correctly rejects this since the theory "leaves too much to imagination to be accepted as a viable option for the setting of this material."

[112] Rudolph, *Micha, Nahum, Habakuk, Zephanja,* 210. With this he rules out H. Schmidt, who understands the prayer in v. 12 to be that of an accused person and the "you shall not die" the answer of a judge setting the accused free (*ZAW* [1949/50]: 59). Such an interpretation interrupts the flow of the verse and does not give immediate sense to the audience. Similarly, Humbert and Jeremias seek to find royal language from Isaiah appearing in v. 12b and thus find a king in this passage. Again such interpretation goes far beyond what any average listener would detect in the passage.

Lord, he appeared incredulous concerning God's work among the nations. How could the holy and righteous God use an unholy instrument to punish Judah? Did this fit Habakkuk's understanding of God? The lament does not fundamentally deal with a situation in the outside world such as sickness or war for which the prophet can ask for a specific divine act. The heart of the problem is that the outside world of history contradicts the interior certainty of the nature of God himself. A holy, righteous God cannot endure the godless acts of a ruthless oppressor, can he?[113] Has the divine Rock lost the power to protect and serve as a refuge for his people? Habakkuk thus turned to lament to address God. Rudolph notes the contrast to Jeremiah, who in the same time period of the Babylonian victory at Carchemish in 605 recognized God's decision to use Nebuchadnezzar as a "servant of Yahweh" and to judge all nations and all prophets by whether they surrendered to Nebuchadnezzar or not (see Jer 27).[114]

Habakkuk's question dealt with the nature of God. "O LORD, are you not from everlasting?" Habakkuk used the covenant name of God in his address. The "I AM WHO I AM" (Exod 3:14) is the God who promised to be with his people. As God has been in the past, he will be in the future. The covenant name indicated eternal faithfulness and should "elicit confident dependence"[115] from those who call on the name of the Lord.

Habakkuk's question fits the use of the covenant name for God. The Lord is not a Johnny-come-lately God. He is from everlasting. The Lord always has been God. The Hebrew term for "everlasting" focuses particularly on God's past acts in Israel's salvation history.[116] God, being Israel's "eternal" God, knows the thoughts of human beings and works his righteousness in the world.

Knowing these things about God made Habakkuk perplexed. God is holy. Among the prophets Isaiah gave new emphasis to the holiness of God. While other nations thought of their gods as holy in the sense of "otherness," that is of being god and not flesh, Isaiah added the idea of perfect moral purity to the holiness of God. Other nations could speak of the otherness of their gods, but their gods might not be "good." Isaiah and Habakkuk knew that God is deity

---

[113] See Elliger, *Das Buch der zwölf kleinen Propheten II,* 34–35.

[114] Rudolph, *Micha, Nahum, Habakuk, Zephanja,* 208.

[115] J. H. Kennedy, "The Commission of Moses and the Christian Calling," 42. Kennedy renders "I AM THAT I AM" to mean "I shall continually be that which I always have been," a meaning that evokes confidence in God for the future as well as the past.

[116] R. L. Smith correctly points out that "the word קדם means 'former' or 'ancient' times (see Pss 44:1; 77:5,11; Isa 46:10; 37:27; Lam 2:17). The Hebrews did not think in abstract terms such as 'eternal'" (*Micah–Malachi,* 103). Cp. Armerding, "Habakkuk," 505–6; Patterson, on the other hand, uses Mic 5:2 to argue for "from everlasting" as the proper translation here for "conservative expositors" (*Nahum, Habakkuk, Zephaniah,* 163).

and not flesh and that he is perfect moral purity.[117] Such holiness is unchanging, separating all humans and all creatures and thus all sin from God. Nothing evil can stand before his holy purity. As Rudolph notes, he cannot distance himself even for the blink of an eye from his holiness.[118] If this is the case, the true description of God, how can he stand silent and inactive before the horribly evil and violent Babylonians?

Should the text read "we will not die" or "you will not die?"[119] "We will not die" indicates the prophet's certainty that God would leave a remnant though the Babylonians would take the land. As Patterson phrases it: "despite Israel's certain chastisement, God will remain faithful to His promise to the patriarchs (Gen 17:2–8; 26:3–5; 28:13–15), to Israel (Exod 3:3–15; 14:1–6; Deut 7:6; 14:1–2; 26:16–18), and to the house of David (2 Sam 7:12–29)."[120] "You will

---

[117] The first half of the verse presents some difficulty to the translator and to the interpreter. Should the question end with the terms of address "O Lord my God, my Holy One" (RSV) or as a separate sentence, "My God, my Holy One, we will not die" (NIV)? Either alternative makes sense. Rudolph (*Micha, Nahum, Habakuk, Zephanja,* 209) claims v. 12b must necessarily be an interrogative sentence whether marked or unmarked precisely as one in Hebrew, the interrogative *he* from v. 12a continuing to v. 12b or one having dropped out by haplography in v. 12b.

[118] Rudolph, *Micha, Nahum, Habakuk, Zephanja,* 210.

[119] The problem lies in the scribal emendations known as the *tikkune sopherim,* eighteen deliberate changes made by the scribes for fear of making unacceptable expressions about God. The rabbis listed Hab 1:12 as one such alteration. The scribes supposedly changed the text from "you will not die" to "we will not die" because of its disrespect toward God, placing God in the context of death. The change in Heb. would be only one letter. F. E. Deist portrayed the attitude of the scribes toward the text (*Witnesses to the Old Testament,* in *The Literature of the Old Testament* [Pretoria: NGBK, 1988], 5:27–28). Though the *tikkune sopherim* entailed deliberate changes in the text, the Masoretes apparently felt better about minor alterations than they did about irreverence. "The judgement of the Masoretes was well expressed in the following words by Rabbi Yohanan ben Zakkai: 'It is always better to take out a letter from the Torah rather than to be in danger of profaning the Name of God during public reading.'" In this passage Rudolph notes that the first person plural does not fit formally since it changes from second person reference to first person reference, but it also misses the point of the context. God is addressed as the one who does not die, who is, unlike humans, eternal and immortal. Another example of this kind of alteration is found in the text of Job, where Job's wife charged him to "bless God and die" (Job 2:9, MT). The scribes apparently saw the conflict in "cursing" God and changed the text to "bless." Most translations (including the NIV and RSV) translate "curse" with the *tikkune sopherim.* Armerding argues for the first person plural of the MT in v. 12, saying the "value of the alterations is, however, doubtful; and since the MT is supported here by the LXX and Symmachus and implicitly by 1 QpHab, there are no good grounds for abandoning its reading" ("Habakkuk," 510). Patterson discusses five theories of interpretation and then adds a sixth before reverting to translating the MT (*Nahum, Habakkuk, Zephaniah,* 157–58). For a fuller discussion see J. Weingreen, *Introduction to the Critical Study of the Hebrew Bible,* 25–29, and E. Wurthwein, *The Text of the Old Testament,* 18–19. For a discussion of Hab 1:12 see C. D. Ginsburg, *Introduction to the Massoretico–Critical Edition of the Hebrew Bible* (London: Trinitarian Bible Society, 1897); reprinted with prolegomenon by H. M. Orlinsky (New York: KTAV, 1966), 358, and E. R. Brotzman, *Old Testament Textual Criticism* (Grand Rapids: Baker, 1994), 117–18.

[120] Patterson, *Nahum, Habakkuk, Zephaniah,* 158.

not die" parallels the earlier statement that the Lord is from everlasting. This continues to describe the nature of God. He is from everlasting to everlasting.

The second half of v. 12 continues the description of the nature of God. Two vocatives begin the discussion of God's work with the Babylonians. The Lord is addressed as Yahweh, the covenant name discussed in the preceding paragraphs, and as the Rock, a common address for God in the Old Testament. Both "LORD" and "Rock" evoke feelings of permanence and stability.[121] The Rock was the protector of the covenant people. The New Testament applied the title to Christ (1 Cor 10:4; 1 Pet 2:6–8).

These two descriptions of God cut directly to the problem Habakkuk encountered. God had "appointed" and "ordained" Babylon to execute judgment[122] against Judah and to punish[123] the wicked in Jerusalem. How could the holy and everlasting God do such a thing? "Instead of reproof it appears that the Babylonians aim at extinction of their victims."[124]

The modern reader of the Bible might ask similar questions. How could God set up a godless nation to punish a nation filled with Christian churches? This was something of Habakkuk's dilemma. Habakkuk saw that the Babylonians had been established by God to do this. The Lord controlled history and worked his will among the nations. "Man may determine by his conduct how he will encounter God's sovereignty, but he cannot escape it!"[125] As Achtemeier reminds us, "International relations are understood to be always under the sovereignty of God. World history does not take place by chance, according to the Scriptures, nor are human beings ever the sole effectors of it. Human actions result in particular events, to be sure, but human actions are always also accompanied by God's effective actions as he works out his purpose."[126]

1:13 Verse 13 consists of two statements about God followed by two questions addressed to God. It begins and ends with a comparative statement: (lit.) "Purer are the eyes than seeing evil … when the wicked swallow those more righteous than them." The Hebrew term for wicked picks up the same term used for the guilty parties in Israel in v. 4b.[127] Similarly, the word for

---

[121] R. L. Smith says addressing Yahweh as a rock suggests that "he provides stability in an unstable age" (*Micah–Malachi,* 103).

[122] Armerding points out that "judgment" represents the same Hebrew word as "justice" in v. 4 and "law" in v. 7. It "implies the restoration of rule and authority through removal of the causes of disorder" ("Habakkuk," 506).

[123] Armerding points out that "punish" (Hb. יכח) has "the underlying judicial meaning of 'establishing what is just or right,' (and) generally implies a chastening that is redemptive rather than destructive" (ibid.).

[124] R. L. Smith, *Micah–Malachi,* 104.

[125] Armerding, "Habakkuk," 506.

[126] Achtemeier, *Nahum–Malachi,* 39.

[127] Rudolph asks, How can one who is wicked himself (רָשָׁע) carry out punishment on the wicked (רָשָׁע)? (*Micha, Nahum, Habakuk, Zephanja,* 210).

"tolerate wrong" repeats in from v. 3.

Habakkuk continued to describe God according to his holy nature. How could the holy God use the wickedness of a pagan people to punish Judah? How could God tolerate the wickedness of Babylon? God's "eyes" are too pure to look on evil. Here the eyes stand for the whole person. God is holy and cannot tolerate wrong. Yet God did tolerate the unrighteous and in fact used evil nations to accomplish his sovereign purpose. No wonder Habakkuk felt confused!

The prophets saw that God works in history to accomplish his purpose, even using godless nations to perform his designs. God used Assyria as the "rod of his anger" to chastise Judah in Isaiah's day (Isa 10:5–15) and worked through the designs of Cyrus the Persian to deliver those exiled to Babylon (Isa 44:28–45:7). Those who see only the short term always miss the significance of the work of God. Habakkuk, focusing on the short term, questioned how God could do such a thing.

God appeared to be doing the opposite of what Habakkuk believed of God. The God who is too pure to look on evil in fact tolerated the treacherous and stood silent[128] while the wicked swallowed up the righteous. "Sometimes the silences of God can be explained by the people's sins and their failure to repent. But that is not always true."[129] Judah, of course, could not be described as righteous (Hab 1:2–4), but in comparison to Babylon, Judah lived as a righteous nation. The Hebrew text uses a device for the comparative degree to show the contrast between "wicked" Babylon and "righteous" Judah.

Habakkuk used the metaphor of "swallowing up" to describe the wicked actions of Babylon, an apt description of the swiftness of the Babylonian army in overrunning other nations. God appeared to watch silently as these atrocities occurred.

(2) A Description of How the Babylonians Treat Other Nations (1:14–17)

14You have made men like fish in the sea,
like sea creatures that have no ruler.
15The wicked foe pulls all of them up with hooks,
he catches them in his net,
he gathers them up in his dragnet;
and so he rejoices and is glad.
16Therefore he sacrifices to his net
and burns incense to his dragnet,

---

[128] The Hebrew uses an asyndetic structure, that is one without the expected conjunction before the verb "you are silent." The NIV takes this as resumptive use of the opening interrogative, "Why?" Patterson (*Nahum, Habakkuk, Zephaniah,* 164) argues for the dramatic effect of asyndesis. One could almost translate, "Why then did you tolerate the treacherous in absolute silence?"

[129] R. L. Smith, *Micah–Malachi,* 104.

for by his net he lives in luxury
and enjoys the choicest food.
[17]Is he to keep on emptying his net,
destroying nations without mercy?

1:14 Habakkuk knew God, and he knew the events of the day. The remainder of the first chapter of Habakkuk describes how the Babylonians treated the nations they conquered. In figurative language the prophet stated the problem (1:14), described the setting (1:15–16), and raised the serious question about the future (1:17).[130] The grammatical structure shows the intricacy of the prophet's argument. He begins with direct address to God stating a proposition that is tied syntactically by a *waw* consecutive to the preceding questions of v. 13. Verse 15 then returns to third person singular describing the Babylonians, repeating the grammatical constructions of God's speech in 6b–11. The results of such actions are then given in a series of clauses introduced by "and so" (the adverbial particle *ʿal kēn*; 15b, 16a, 17a), the last of which is in the interrogative mode.[131] The argument thus runs: God, you made us like helpless fish without a leader; the enemy Babylonians took advantage of the situation; the natural result is his rejoicing, his self-worship because he is so prosperous so that we must ask if he is allowed to keep this up forever.

The continuing problem of evil in the world and God's involvement in it raised theological concerns for Habakkuk. Habakkuk knew that the Lord is the Sovereign of the universe. The Lord had made men like fish of the sea and like crawling things without one to guide them. Had the Creator now forgotten his creatures? Had the powerful Babylonians become so powerful they exercised control over what God had created? Are these godless people being rewarded more and more for their godless actions? Habakkuk's point seemed to be that people of the earth (Habakkuk uses the word *ʾādām* for human beings) are no less than the fish of sea, subject to the whims of the more powerful. Habakkuk's word translated "sea creatures" refers to swarming things in general whether in the sea or on land ("crawling things," such as ants, locusts, or other swarming insects, RSV).[132] These swarming things had no ruler and stood defenseless. "This is a forceful picture of the way other nations were helpless before the Babylonian armies."[133]

---

[130] The continuation of the question from v. 13 as in NJB, NEB, NASB, KJV, and NKJV is not necessary and misses the new direction of the prophet's argument as the change to narrative in REB as opposed to its NEB source shows.

[131] B. K. Waltke and M. O'Connor give a brief sentence about עַל־כֵּן clauses, saying, it "usually introduces a statement of later effects" (*An Introduction to Biblical Hebrew Syntax* [Winona Lake: Eisenbrauns, 1990], 666).

[132] "Sea creatures" translates Hb. רֶמֶשׂ that is usually translated "creatures that move along the ground" (Gen 1:24,26) but can refer to sea creatures also (Ps 104:25; cp. Gen 1:21).

[133] Clark and Hatton, *Nahum, Habakkuk, and Zephaniah,* 85.

1:15 Continuing the thought of the previous verse,[134] the prophet compared the people of Judah to the fish of the sea. Before the wicked foe the people of Judah would be as defenseless as fish caught on a hook or trapped in a net and dragged onto the shore. The Babylonians rejoiced[135] at their good fortune, catching men in nets. The "net" referred to a small net cast by one person while the "dragnet" would require a number of people to cast the net and pull it in a semicircle through the water.[136] How could God allow such behavior to go on? How could God cooperate with a people who had no consideration for other people but treated them as the lowliest of creatures (cp. Gen 6:20; 8:19; Ps 8:8–9) without anyone to protect them (Prov 6:7; 30:27) and whose capture brings no risk or danger.[137]

According to Achtemeier, Habakkuk's point is that such divine behavior does "not hasten the coming of God's order. It simply replaces a chaotic society with one that is totally godless—with the rule of a foreign people that makes it own might its god (1:11) and that worships that might as the source of its life (1:16). ... [God] has seemed to move even further distant from the goal of the establishment of his right order in the world, and Habakkuk cannot understand that any more than can we."[138]

1:16 The same Hebrew root *(ʾki)* connects this verse ("enjoys food") with v. 8 ("devour"). The same two words for "net" and "dragnet" are used in v. 16 as in v 15. Most peoples of the ancient Near East practiced sacrifice and the burning of incense.[139] The Hebrew word for sacrifice is used to describe a peace or communion offering (Lev 3). The worshiper brought the peace offering to the priest, who took part of the offering for himself and offered part to God. The remainder went to the worshiper who ate the offering with the priest

---

[134] Armerding ("Habakkuk," 506) notes that the "NIV's transition between vv. 12–13 and vv. 15–17 from a plural to a singular third-person subject is not present in the MT, where singular third-person forms predominate throughout. These verses are also linked by a continuity of theme, the image of devouring food pervading the passage." The NIV makes the transition by introducing "the wicked foe" into v. 15 when the Hebrew says literally, "all of it," consistent with its third singular.

[135] Armerding ("Habakkuk," 507) points to the religious contexts of "rejoice" and "be glad" to express praise and worship, especially when used together. "Be glad" appears in such a context in 3:18 also. The verbs affirms "what is valued and honored."

[136] Clark and Hatton, *Nahum, Habakkuk, and Zephaniah,* 86; Armerding, "Habakkuk," 507 is a bit more cautious in the identifications: "the precise identification of these nets is not certain, owing to their infrequent occurrence and their varied, overlapping functions. However, they appear to correspond to the two main types of net, the throw-net and the seine, used in NT times and up to the present in Palestine (cf. *ANEP,* pp. 33–34)." Patterson, *Nahum, Habakkuk, Zephaniah,* 165, uses Ezek 47:10 and Isa 19:8 to differentiate between nets used from the shore and those used on the water.

[137] See Rudolph, *Micha, Nahum, Habakuk, Zephanja,* 210.

[138] Achtemeier, *Nahum–Malachi*, 40.

[139] Armerding, "Habakkuk," 508, shows that the forms of the two verbs here when used together always refer to illegitimate worship (1 Kgs 22:43; 2 Kgs 12:3; 14:4; 15:4,35; 16:4).

while the offering went up in smoke to God as "an aroma pleasing to the LORD" (Lev 3:5). Burning incense symbolized prayer going up to God. Habakkuk described the Babylonians as sacrificing to the net and burning incense to the dragnet.[140]

The symbolism is quite clear. The Babylonians lived by the plunder of helpless peoples. In effect, the net and the dragnet became their gods, supplying the people of Babylon with the finest things that plundering the world could bring.[141] "The Babylonian rejoices and shouts for joy because of his success. Then he worships those things that make him rich and successful. How prone are people today to worship whatever makes them rich and successful?"[142]

1:17 In this context Habakkuk's complaint takes on profound meaning. How long can a holy, pure, immortal God remain silent? Can God use the Babylonians as instruments of his wrath? How long can Babylon continue[143] to empty its net?[144] "As will be evident, his views of God were right (cf. Ps

---

[140] Rudolph, *Micha, Nahum, Habakuk, Zephanja,* 211, notes that preserved sculptures shows their gods with nets in which they drag along their captured enemies.

[141] Armerding ("Habakkuk," 508) points out that both "luxury" and "choicest" represent Hb. terms meaning "fat." "Luxury" (שָׁמֵן) "is associated elsewhere with the prosperity of the wicked, whose well-being made them immune to any feeling of dependency or accountability."

[142] R. L. Smith, *Micah–Malachi,* 104.

[143] Most translators, including the NIV and Rudolph (*Micha, Nahum, Habakuk, Zephanja,* 209) follow the Dead Sea Scrolls and remove the *waw,* "and," before "keep on" (Hb. תָּמִיד) and connect it with the first line rather than the second line as the Masoretes appear to have done. Armerding argues that MT should be retained, coordinating the two clauses more closely as questions and as continuous action, while heightening the emphasis on the first question ("Habakkuk," 510). NASB represents the MT: "Will they therefore empty their net and continually slay nations without sparing?" but does not present the continuing action of the first half of the verse as does NIV. Patterson discusses the alternative interpretations at length and prefers the MT as the harsher reading, translating "and continually slay nations unsparingly" (*Nahum, Habakkuk, Zephaniah,* 155, 167). BHS suggests that some MSS and Dead Sea Scroll add the conjunction before the final negative ("without"), but this may represent another artistic use of asyndesis for dramatic effect. See note on v. 13.

[144] The Dead Sea Scroll of Habakkuk reads "sword" in place of "net." Rudolph accepts this since the fishing motif no longer appears in 17b and can be assumed to have been changed already in 17a (*Micha, Nahum, Habakuk, Zephanja,* 209). The verb of 17a (יָרִיק) usually appears with the sword imagery. R. L. Smith, however, probably is correct in saying, " 'Emptying his net' is a suitable metaphor here" (*Micah–Malachi,* 103). Armerding says "empty the net" and "draw the sword" are virtually identical in Hb. so that "possibly a double entendre is intended here," transitioning to 17b ("Habakkuk," 508). On text critical grounds Armerding retains MT as the more unusual, more difficult reading (p. 510). Both the LXX and Qumran agree that the verse is a statement instead of a question as in the Hb. text. Rudolph bluntly rejects this: "Removal of the question is not good" (*Micha, Nahum, Habakuk, Zephanja,* 209). Patterson agrees (*Nahum, Habakkuk, Zephaniah,* 167). The translator probably should retain the Masoretic reading because of the continuation of the fishing motif. Both readings convey the same image with the MT using figurative language instead of the nonfigurative language of Qumran and the LXX.

82; Isa 57:15), but his perspective was too limited. He had looked for the punishment of the wicked so that the prosperity of his people could be assured, but God, who knew the end from the beginning, looked for the punishment of Habakkuk's people so that they could be restored to fellowship."[145]

Habakkuk has two alternatives now. "He can allow his doubts to be either destructive or creative. He can use his doubts, struggles, and agonizing questions to turn from God and to renounce his faith. Or he can keep his hold on God, trusting him for an answer."[146]

4. God's Second Answer (2:1–5)

1I will stand at my watch
and station myself on the ramparts;
I will look to see what he will say to me,
and what answer I am to give to this complaint.
2Then the LORD replied:
"Write down the revelation
and make it plain on tablets
so that a herald may run with it.
3For the revelation awaits an appointed time;
it speaks of the end
and will not prove false.
Though it linger, wait for it;
it will certainly come and will not delay.

4"See, he is puffed up;
his desires are not upright—
but the righteous will live by his faith—
5indeed, wine betrays him;
he is arrogant and never at rest.
Because he is as greedy as the grave
and like death is never satisfied,
he gathers to himself all the nations
and takes captive all the peoples.

2:1 The second chapter opens with a prophetic announcement (v. 1) followed by a divine word (vv. 2–4)[147] to which is attached a separate description of the enemy, the nature of which scholars continue to debate. R. L. Smith notes that the passage implies some time passage since the first oracle, for there Babylon was just appearing on the scene as a conqueror, while here

---

145 Barber, *Habakkuk and Zephaniah*, 36.

146 Heflin, *Nahum, Habakkuk, Zephaniah, and Haggai*, 87.

147 R. L. Smith (*Micah–Malachi*, 105) classifies the form as "an oracle of response" without giving the formal elements or other examples of this genre.

it is seen as a ruthless oppressor.[148]

"There is no more important passage in Habakkuk than this one, and few in the OT more significant because of the later use of it by the apostle Paul and Martin Luther."[149] Habakkuk worried about God's silence, which he had to endure. That was part of the prophetic task. Not even a prophet could force God to answer what appeared to be a burning, immediate issue, even an issue defending God's (and the prophet's) honor (see Jer 28:11–12; 42:7; Job).[150] All the prophet could do was sit and wait for God's timing. That is Habakkuk's action here.

The final section of the communication with the Lord contains three parts. Part one appears to be preparatory (2:1). The prophet waited for the answer. The answer itself contained an introduction that provided instructions for the prophet (2:2–3) and the main part of the message from the Lord (2:4–5). Whether or not v. 5 should be grouped with the preceding or following verses is not clear. Though the verse seems anticlimactic to the profound message of v. 4, the text seems to fit better with the answer of the Lord in 2:1–4 than with the series of woes in 2:6–20. R. L. Smith correctly concludes: "Actually v. 5 should be seen as a transitional verse. It relates to both v. 4 and v. 6."[151] Later Smith claims that only v. 4 was written on the tablet, v. 5 being "an additional explanation by the prophet."[152] Elliger[153] emends the text to make v. 5 the first "woe" oracle. The Septuagint has v. 4 in first person, "my soul (desires)," and "my faith." Elliger accepts the first person reading of v. 4 as original, reading: "Behold, on the arrogant has my soul no pleasure." Patterson describes the prophet's "distinctive format: introductory formula (v. 2a), preliminary instructions (vv. 2b–3), general guiding principles (v. 4), and particular detailed application (vv. 5–20)."[154]

In preparation for the Lord's second answer, Habakkuk purposed to take his stand upon his watch[155] and to station himself upon the rampart. Both statements reflect a sense of purpose.[156] The resolve of the prophet may be taken literally.[157] He had a position, much like the military watchman who had a post

---

[148] R. L. Smith, *Micah–Malachi,* 106; cp. n. 74.

[149] Ibid., 105.

[150] See Rudolph, *Micha, Nahum, Habakuk, Zephanja,* 214.

[151] R. L. Smith, *Micah–Malachi,* 106.

[152] Ibid., 107.

[153] Elliger, Das Buch der zwölf kleinen Propheten II, 38–41.

[154] Patterson, *Nahum, Habakkuk, Zephaniah,* 122.

[155] Patterson says the noun מִשְׁמֶרֶת emphasizes the action, standing watch, more than the location, a watch post (*Nahum, Habakkuk, Zephaniah,* 168).

[156] The first verb in the Hb. text is a cohortative, reflecting a sense of intention. The second verb is reflexive *(hithpael),* meaning that the prophet would station himself.

[157] Armerding ("Habakkuk," 509) argues for a figurative rather than literal "watch" as does Achtemeier (*Nahum–Malachi*, 42), who denies this as a reference to the prophetic office as that of a watchman as seen in Jer 6:17; Ezek 3:17; 33:7–9, an office Achtemeier interprets as one of warning the people of God's war against their sin. Achtemeier appears, here, to limit the watchman office too specifically and not allow for a more comprehensive job description for the watchman.

above the city looking out for the approach of enemy armies (2 Kgs 9:17; cp. Nah 2:2; Jer 51:12).[158] Wherever his watch post was, the prophet went there to withdraw from normal society and concentrate specifically on God and what God would say when God decided to speak. The prophet knew he could not give an answer himself and would be permitted to speak again only when he received the divine decision. Thus he clearly possessed the gift to distinguish between the human and the divine voice in his innermost parts.[159] Here we see the nature of the prophetic office clearly. As Achtemeier phrases it, "Prophets have no independent wisdom of their own—they are dependent on the word of God (cf. Jer 42:5–7)—as we too are dependent for a true understanding of what God is doing and must ever search the word now given us in the Scriptures."[160]

The verse stresses the importance of the work of humans alongside the work of God. In the first half of the verse Habakkuk determined to station himself so as to receive the revelation of God. In the second half of the verse the prophet expected that God would indeed answer Habakkuk's complaint. Habakkuk needed "to know how to respond to God's ways, both in his assessment of injustice and in his conduct amid the consequences of injustice. He revealed a mature wisdom in his determination that this response be shaped by what God himself would say. It is a wise man who takes his questions about God to God for answers."[161]

Human responsibility and divine providence are complementary teachings in the Old Testament. These doctrines appear to run on parallel tracks, each necessary for the completion of the other. God certainly may work in his world without the cooperation of human instruments, but the biblical evidence indicates that God chooses to use the work of his chosen servants. For example, God used Moses' mother and sister to preserve Moses' life (Exod 2). Moses' mother devised a plan to save her child's life. At the same time the biblical text shows the providence of God in the life of the child. God apparently chose to work and also to use human instrumentality to deliver the child from the plan of Pharaoh.

The NIV follows the Hebrew text in the second half of the verse where the prophet would wait for the Lord's answer and for how the prophet would respond to his complaint. The ancient Syriac version, followed by a number of modern translations, makes the prophet wait for the Lord's answer and for

---

[158] This is one argument for seeing Habakkuk as a cult prophet, the assumption being that the prophet had a place in the temple where he waited for God to speak. Rudolph argues that such a position cannot be proved (*Micha, Nahum, Habakuk, Zephanja,* 214). By the same logic, neither can it be disproved. For prophets as watchmen see Isa 21:6–12; Ezek 3:17–21; 33:1–9; Hos 9:8; R. L. Smith, *Micah–Malachi,* 106.

[159] See Rudolph (*Micha, Nahum, Habakuk, Zephanja,* 21), who also notes that we do not know the criteria the people used to make such distinctions (cp. 2 Sam 7:3–4; Jer 15:10–21).

[160] Achtemeier, *Nahum–Malachi*, 42.

[161] Armerding, "Habakkuk," 509.

how God would respond to the prophet's complaint. Either reading is defensible in the text and from the standpoint of theology. Textually, the difference is only one Hebrew letter.[162]

In the reading of the Hebrew Text and the NIV, the prophet apparently determined to wait for God's answer and to seek to understand the question for himself. Though the other reading seems easier, the NIV is consistent with the personality of the prophet. Anyone who asks questions also tries to answer them. Habakkuk wanted an answer from God concerning God's work in the world. He also wanted to understand the character of God and his purpose in history.[163]

God answered the prophet's complaint by commanding that the prophet write the vision so that anyone running might read the message. God rewarded the prophet's willingness to wait and to watch to see the message of the Lord. God cares for the one who is willing to take his needs to the Lord. Habakkuk might be characterized as a doubter. Like Thomas among the disciples and Moses and Jeremiah of the Old Testament, Habakkuk questioned. The significant characteristic of each of these questioners is the willingness to talk to God rather than about God. Habakkuk's experience suggests that God will help with our questions and concerns.

How could the holy and just God tolerate the wickedness in Judah? More importantly, how could he tolerate the wickedness of Babylon against Judah? "Because of the way he gains his knowledge …, Habakkuk takes the reader into the council of God (cf. Jer 23:18) and demonstrates the process of how God 'reveals His plan to His servants the prophets' (Amos 3:7). Therefore,

---

[162] Commentators read the entire verse in different ways. Elliger omits "and I will look" as outside the meter and as a variant to מָצוֹר, "ramparts" (*Das Buch der zwölf kleinen Propheten II,* 38). Rudolph says "ramparts" or siege wall does not represent a good parallel to "watch" or "post." He changes the Hebrew pointing and translates, "watch." Elliger (ibid.) and R. L. Smith, *Micah–Malachi,* 104–5, follow the BHS suggestion to change the final verb to first person, while Rudolph says this is contextually correct but unnecessary, the first person of MT meaning the same thing, literally, "what I will bring back," thus "what I will receive" concerning my complaint. Patterson, *Nahum, Habakkuk, Zephaniah,* 161–62 lists the alternatives for translating תּוֹכַחַת either as "argument" (Ps 38:14) or "rebuke" (Ps 39:1), "reproof," Prov 1:23–25).

[163] Patterson translates "and how I can reply according to my reproof," explaining, "Habakkuk has expressed the fact that he understands God's intention to use the Chaldeans as his agent of reproof to Judah for their own good. Now he similarly expects divine correction to his own difficulties. Where genuine doubt and perplexities exist, God patiently brings the needed reproof (cf. Jon 4:10–11) and correction of man's thinking (cf. Ps 73:18–25). Such would also be Habakkuk's experience (cf. 3:17–19)" (*Nahum, Habakkuk, Zephaniah,* 155, 161). Barber notes the twofold possibility of Habakkuk's position. He may have been patiently, meekly waiting for God's answer to his complaint, or he may have been "fully aware that his words merited divine reproof. He fully expected God to censure him for his attitude" (Barber, *Habakkuk and Zephaniah,* 36). See also Armerding ("Habakkuk," 509), who argues for the latter on the basis of the root יכח used also in 1:12.

Habakkuk serves as revealer, interpreter, and guide, even as he fulfills the traditional function of a prophet (2:1)."[164] Armerding describes Habakkuk's role as "discharged in attentive, reverent prayer by the same conscientious watchfulness and persistence demanded of the literal watchman."[165] The vision he looked to see was something God would say, so that a close connection exists between prophetic seeing and prophetic saying. Visions could be transposed into sayings.

One of the wonders of Habakkuk's message is the engagement of God with his people. He answered Habakkuk. God dealt with the prophet's complaints and answered his concerns but in an expected way. He began with an imperative, not an indicative, a command to the prophet, not a word for the prophet. Like Job, Habakkuk seemed content that the God of the heavens is concerned with his people and answers from heaven. God's second response is more than an indication of concern; it is the answer for the ages. God is faithful and calls for faithfulness on the part of his people. Still, the answer does not yet address the prophetic questions, just as God's answers never addressed Job's issues.

2:2 The first two verbs of God's response are imperatives. God commanded the prophet to write the vision and to make the message plain on tablets. The writing material is not identified in the verse though the word for "tablets" is the same as that used in Exodus to describe the stone tablets of the Ten Commandments. Rudolph notes that we do not know if Israel used such tablets for public "bulletin board" announcements and that God had to insist on making the writing clear and plain because not every person could write and those who could did not always have enough practice materials to be able to write clearly and legibly without hard work.[166]

The remainder of the verse presents some difficulty. The Hebrew reads literally "in order that he will (or may) run the one reading it." The NIV takes this to mean that a herald may take the message and run with it from village to village. The note to the NIV text provides an additional possibility, "so that whoever reads it" may run with it. This reading indicates that the reader speedily obeys the message. Heflin contends that "the Hebrew here clearly puts the emphasis on the running of the reader, not the reading of the runner. … It means that the person who reads the message will adopt it as a guide for living … will run through life according to it."[167]

---

[164] House, *The Unity of the Twelve,* 197.

[165] Armerding, "Habakkuk," 509.

[166] Rudolph, *Micha, Nahum, Habakuk, Zephanja,* 215. On the other side, R. L. Smith says "writing on huge wooden tablets for public display was a form of publication" and refers to Isa 8:1; 30:8. He continues, "this may have been an early stage of writing notices on public walls. Such practice is still carried on in China and the Orient." (*Micah–Malachi,* 106). For באר ("to be plain") see Deut 1:5; 27:8, the only other uses of the verb. Heflin, *Nahum, Habakkuk, Zephaniah, and Haggai,* 89, says the issue was not legibility of handwriting but ease of understanding for the audience.

[167] Heflin, *Nahum, Habakkuk, Zephaniah, and Haggai,* 89–90.

The traditional interpretation seems best: make the message plain enough so the person running (Hb. participle) may read the message. The GNB supports this interpretation with the reading "so that it can be read at a glance." "In this respect it would be like a large modern advertisement beside a main road."[168]

2:3 Verses 2 and 3 prepared the prophet for the handling of the message. Verse 3 is the reason or motivation for v. 2. It guarantees certainty of the coming of the revelation and provides evidence of fulfillment for those who will experience that fulfillment. The content of the message is found in v. 4.

Impatience is the normal human response to God's promise to answer his people. God warned the prophet to wait on the prophecy. The answer of God would surely come, but the prophet should write down the message because from the prophet's point of view the prophecy might seem slow. The prophet was to "preserve it until its fulfillment could be demonstrated historically."[169] God had already decided upon a solution and would reveal it according to his timetable, but God was not indebted to any human to reveal the answer before he chose to. "Habakkuk, like all of us, was living 'between the times,' between the promise and the fulfillment."[170] Heflin notes that the end here "may refer to the termination of Babylonian power but, more likely, to the eschaton."[171]

The "revelation" (lit., "vision") of v. 2 is connected with the same word in v. 3 by use of the word "for." Though the appointed time of the revelation has not yet come, God reassured the prophet that the time would come. In fact, the revelation "hastens" or "pants" to the end. The NIV "speaks" fails to catch the certainty of the Hebrew verb, which literally reads, "And it will pant to the end and not lie."[172] "That which may seem delayed or halted by our reckoning has

---

[168] Clark and Hatton, *Nahum, Habakkuk, and Zephaniah,* 90; Elliger without textual comment translates, "so that one can easily read it" (*damit man geläufig sie lese*; *Das Buch der zwölf kleinen Propheten II).* Rudolph (*Micha, Nahum, Habakuk, Zephanja,* 211, 212) notes the verse neither means that the reader can read it while running by (this, according to Rudolph would require subject and verb to be transposed), nor does it mean that the reader should run away from it in order to announce its contents in a wider context (Brownlee, "The Composition of Habakkuk," *Hommages a Andre Dupont-Sommer* [Paris: Librairie d'Amerique et d'Orrent Adrien-Maisonneuve, 1971], 263) nor does it mean the reader runs, that is that the reader can find the religiously and culturally correct way of life [see J. M. Holt, "So He May Run Who Reads It," *JBL* 83 (1964): 301]. For Rudolph all these interpretations lay far from the context of the verse. He translates "so that one can read it easily" *(damit man es geläufig lesen kann).*

[169] Heflin, *Nahum, Habakkuk, Zephaniah, and Haggai,* 90. Achtemeier notes that "from the beginning of his work, God has seen its goal and completion" (*Nahum–Malachi*, 43).

[170] R. L. Smith, *Micah–Malachi,* 107.

[171] Heflin, *Nahum, Habakkuk, Zephaniah, and Haggai,* 90.

[172] Rudolph (*Micha, Nahum, Habakuk, Zephanja,*212) notes that the Dead Sea Scroll has confirmed the reading as from a verb meaning "pant after," but he contends that such a meaning does not fit the context. He suggests that Prov 12:17 is the closest parallel, giving a meaning of to make known, to state, thus leading to a translation much like NIV. Elliger (*Das Buch der zwölf kleinen Propheten II,* 38) questions his own conclusion as he translates *reist auf,* "set out after," claiming support from the LXX, but then says perhaps we can make do with the MT and translate *sie raunt vom Ende,* "it whispers of the end."

not been impeded at all. God's purpose cannot be thwarted."[173]

The prophet's humanity demanded that God provide a warning about impatience, one even more important to people living in the exhausting pace of modern society. Whether in prayer or prophecy, contemporary worshipers demand that God act according to the dizzying schedule of those pressed for time. God reminded the prophet of the certainty of the message[174] but without the promise of meeting Habakkuk's time schedule. "It does not mean that the future events predicted in the vision will come soon, without delay. Only God knows the time for such events. The comment rather means that the fulfillment will not miss God's scheduled time; it will not delay a moment beyond its appointed time."[175]

The answer may delay, but it is sure. "The world is not as God intended it, and God is setting it right. God's purpose cannot be thwarted (cf. Isa 55:10–11); it is speeding toward its completion. Indeed, those actions of God that seem to reverse his march toward his goal—as the Babylonian conquest of Judah seemed to Habakkuk to reverse that march (1:12–17)—may not be reversals at all but integral parts of God purpose to save his earth. Certainly Luke (21:24), Paul (Rom 9:22–24), and the author of 2 Peter (3:9) were sure that was true."[176]

2:4 Finally, God revealed the message itself. "It is short but comprehensive."[177] In the day of turmoil and destruction, the righteous person shall live by his faithfulness to God. The answer dealt with Habakkuk's frustrations and fears. Would God leave the guilty—in Judah and in Babylon—unpunished? Would the righteous be consumed with the wicked?

God answered the prophet by means of a strong contrast. The first half of the verse apparently refers to the wicked described in 1:7,11,13 (without using the term) while the second statement explicitly describes the righteous person.[178] By means of a strong contrast, the Lord answered the complaints

---

[173] Achtemeier, *Nahum–Malachi*, 43.

[174] The Hb. is an infinitive absolute followed by an imperfect. The two verbs could be translated "for it will indeed come" or with the NIV "it will certainly come."

[175] Heflin, *Nahum, Habakkuk, Zephaniah, and Haggai*, 90.

[176] Achtemeier, *Nahum–Malachi*, 43.

[177] Rudolph, *Micha, Nahum, Habakuk, Zephanja*, 216.

[178] The MT reads: "Behold, his *nepheš* (soul, desire) is puffed up (swollen), it is not upright in him." The NIV follows the Hb. somewhat while other translations diverge from the MT significantly. J. A. Emerton, "The Textual and Linguistic Problems of Habakkuk II. 4–5," *JTS* 28 (1977): 1–18, divides the consonants of the first verb and reads עף לה, reading עף as a participle meaning "to fly away," that is, "to die." R. L. Smith (*Micah–Malachi,* 105) says the subject has fallen out, so he reads העול, "the oppressor" with Wellhausen and others, but notes (p, 106) that this is the "easiest solution (which is not necessarily the best)." Elliger holds to the basic correctness of the MT, deleting the feminine ending on the second word as resulting from relating it to the following "soul." He translates, Sieh da an dem Vermessenen hast meine Seele keinen Gefallen, "behold, my soul has not pleasure in the arrogant" (*Das Buch der zwölf kleinen Propheten II)*. The soul refers to the whole person and not some abstract part of the person. For a discussion of "soul" see H. W. Wolff, *Anthropology of the Old Testament* (Philadelphia: Fortress, 1973), 10–25. Heflin, 92, notes the problem of a lack of subject in 4a and wants to generalize it to include "any who are not righteous, who do not live by faithfulness."

of the prophet. The one whose life is puffed up in pride and arrogance will die; the righteous, in contrast, by his faithfulness will live. Whether in Judah or Babylon, those in rebellion against God would die.[179] "Wherever human beings rely on something of this earth—whether it be intellectual achievement or wealth or military might or aesthetic ability and appreciation or pride of birth and status or even the ability to cope and solve problems and master the complexities of modern life—wherever confidence is placed in human prowess and not in God for the achievement of a satisfying and secure manner of living, there true life cannot be had."[180]

The righteous are those courageous enough to accept God's word of promise in a world dominated by the horrors of Babylonian power described in the preceding verses. To look for salvation in a world dominated by persecution requires faithfulness. World history may not indicate it, but God is leading his world to accomplish his purposes. The righteous are also those whose lives correspond to God's leadership.[181] The righteous are not perfect, but they do live according to their relationship with God. To be righteous means to meet the demands of a relationship. Righteousness toward God involves a strong ethical dimension—it is to meet the demands of God toward him and toward others. The righteous person will stand before God in the day of the judgment (cp. Ps 1) and will stand before God on his holy hill. Psalm 15 gives excellent examples of the behavior of the righteous. They use speech, money, and influence in positive ways. They recognize righteous acts and other righteous persons and treat them properly.[182]

The message to Habakkuk referred to the righteous person living by faithfulness—an important Old Testament term describing loyalty as well as truth and

---

[179] Achtemeier (*Nahum–Malachi,* 45) defines "puffed up" as the opposite of being faithful; it is "reliance on one's own self or personal resources to secure and sustain one's life."

[180] Ibid.

[181] B. Johnson ("צדק," *TWAT* 6:918–20) points to OT lists that give examples of what the life of the righteous look like (Exod 20; Pss 15; 24; Job 31; Ezek 18:5–9), concluding that righteousness characterizes the lifestyle *(Lebenswandel)* of a person (Isa 26:7; Ps 1:6; Job 17:9; Prov 2:20; 4:18; 20:7; Eccl 7:15). The righteous is one who upholds and conforms to the regulations and expectations of the covenant community. This is seen in the title of the entry by K. Koch, צדק, to be communally faithful, beneficial," *TLOT,* 2, 1046–62. Koch sees the righteous person as the "reputable citizen" (p. 1050). He is the innocent party in a dispute. But for Koch (p. 1059) Habakkuk is calling for faith in the prophetic word (cf. Ezek 14:14; 18:5–9,14–17,20).

[182] Achtemeier defines faithfulness as relationship more closely: "that does not mean moral steadfastness, rectitude, and earnestness. It does not signify the proper performance of ethical or cultic duties. Rather, faithfulness here means trust, dependence, clinging to God; it means living and moving and having one's being in him alone; it means relying on him for the breath one draws, for the direction one takes, for the decisions one makes, for the goals one sets, and for the outcome of one's living. ... Faithfulness means placing one's whole life in God's hands and trusting him to fulfill it, despite all outward and inward circumstances. ... Faithfulness is life by God's power rather than by one's own" (*Nahum–Malachi,* 46).

trust. Jepsen demonstrated that "faithfulness" *(ʾĕmûnâ)* is a way of acting that flows from inner stability. It indicated one's "own inner attitude and the conduct it produces." Thus it is a type of behavior characterized by genuineness, reliability, and conscientiousness. Jepsen used the terms "sincerity," "faithfulness," "reliability," and "stability" to describe the righteous person who lives by faithfulness.[183] The NIV, along with most other English translations, uses "faith" in the translation, probably to emphasize the importance of the text to the New Testament. "Habakkuk was not to wait with folded hands and bated breath for all this to happen. He was to live a life of faithfulness."[184]

"Faith in God was the key to consistent living, even though violence abounded and justice was perverted (1:2–4). That short statement helps believers to persevere even though God chastens them (1:5–11) and they cannot understand his ways (1:12–17). It provides a solution to the doubt they sometimes feel in His all-wise providence (2:1–3), and helps them to understand his righteous judgments (2:4–20). In the final analysis, faith provides the key to understanding the Lord's sovereign purpose, and it leads men to worship (3:1–19)."[185]

The New Testament writers quoted the verse three times (Rom 1:17; Gal 3:11; Heb 10:38).[186] Paul used this idea as the hallmark of his teaching concerning the primacy of faith in salvation. He took God's message to Habakkuk to its final emphasis: those who are judged righteous as a result of their faith shall live. Habakkuk's questions supplied Paul with his beginning and ending point that faith is the key. God recognizes the faithfulness (faith) of his people and gives life.

Habakkuk's revelation emphasized the life-giving nature of God. He cares for his people even when he appears distant and uninvolved. Though the revelation may take what appears to be an agonizingly long time to appear, wait for it. God knows and cares for his people.

2:5 The NIV and RSV take this verse as part of God's message to Habakkuk that immediately precedes.[187] Others (GNB) close the quotation at

---

[183] A. Jepsen, "אָמַן ʾāman, etc." *TDOT* 1:316–18; cp. H. Wildberger, "אמן ʾ*mn* firm, secure," *TLOT,* 147–51, who sees the basic meaning as "firmness," though "dependability, faithfulness" is the most frequent meaning in the texts." He sees the term at home in the salvation oracle given to war commanders and used in response to laments in worship with Hab 2:2–4 an example of the latter. People are called to trust the oracle promising deliverance. "Pious persons resist external threat and internal opposition with their faith" (p. 144).

[184] R. L. Smith, *Micah–Malachi,* 107.

[185] Barber, *Habakkuk and Zephaniah*, 39.

[186] For a discussion of the use of this text in the N., see D. S. Dockery, "The Use of Hab 2:4 in Rom 1:17: Some Hermeneutical and Theological Considerations," *Wesley Theological Review* 22 (1987): 24–36.

[187] Rudolph makes v. 5 the "concluding answer" (*abschliessende* Antwort), while Elliger vigorously denies all connection between vv. 4 and 5 (*Das Buch der zwölf kleinen Propheten II).* See also n. 101.

the end of 2:4, giving it either an independent section or one attached to the "woes" that follow.[188] Rudolph may well be correct in saying, "from the general principle that injustice will be punished, v. 5 makes the application to the Chaldeans and emphasizes that their role as a tool of punishment for Yahweh is only temporary, the last word about them having not yet been spoken. … That they cannot, despite all infringements on the rights of others (1:13b–17), reach, much less maintain, their goal of controlling the world is the comfort for the prophet which must for the present satisfy him."[189] Roberts sees v. 5 as linking back to 4a. He describes its meaning succinctly, "v. 5 seems to portray the outcome of a life not directed by God at all. … The reliability of the vision (v. 4) is set over against the deceitfulness of wealth and power."[190]

The Dead Sea Scroll of Habakkuk makes "wealth" *(hôn)* the subject of the opening line, a reading followed by a number of translations.[191] This change makes good sense, especially from the remainder of the verse, which describes the Babylonians as being as greedy as the grave. Both the NIV and RSV hold to the MT with its usage of "wine" *(hayyayin)*. Armerding admits "wine" is unexpected here but "is appropriate to the present verse, being associated with arrogance, unfulfilled greed, and social injustice elsewhere in the OT (e.g., 1 Sam 30:16; 1 Kgs 30:12,16; Prov 31:4–7; Isa 5:11–12,22–23; Amos 6:6). … indeed, the Babylonian regime was to be overthrown in just the circumstances of drunken pride portrayed here (cf. Dan 5:1–31)—such drunkenness being attested among ancient historians as characteristic of the Babylonians."[192]

The verse describes the arrogance of the Babylonians by looking back to the image of 1:13. Like death and the grave (Sheol), the Babylonians never have enough.[193] Sheol often is pictured as being greedy, always enlarging

---

[188] On textual issues and proposed emendations see Elliger, *Das Buch der zwölf kleinen Propheten II,* 41–45; Rudolph, *Micha, Nahum, Habakuk, Zephanja,* 213; J. A. Emerton, "The Textual and Linguistic Problems of Habakkuk II. 4–5," 1–18.

[189] Rudolph, *Micha, Nahum, Habakuk, Zephanja,* 216. Achtemeier sees 2:5–6a as transitional verses showing that the following woes are intended to illustrate the teaching of 2:4 (*Nahum–Malachi*, 48).

[190] Roberts, *Nahum, Habakkuk, and Zephaniah,* 116–17.

[191] Achtemeier (*Nahum–Malachi*) reads "wealth" as referring to 1:16, that of the "mighty man" in reference to 1:11. Such people cannot find the life of 2:4. Roberts (*Nahum, Habakkuk, and Zephaniah,* 113) says one can do nothing with the MT. He follows the Dead Sea Scrolls in reading ואף כי הון יבגוד, "How much more shall wealth deceive the arrogant man." This leads to translating the next line, "And he shall not succeed who has made his mouth as wide as Sheol." Such translation requires finding an Arabic cognate for ינוה.

[192] Armerding, "Habakkuk," 7:513.

[193] Armerding ("Habakkuk," 515) discusses the difficulty of determining the root meaning of ינוה (*yinweh*) "rest." This may come from Hb. נוה, "abode" or "habitation" or from an Arabic room meaning "to attain a goal." The LXX appears to support the Arabic derivation. Haak (*Habakkuk,* 59–61) seeks an ambiguous translation that will fit all the possibilities: "He surely does not stop."

itself to receive more of the dead. "Death never takes a holiday. The Babylonian, like death, continues to sweep the nations into his net (cf. 1:15)."[194]

The Babylonians sought more and more nations to devour, taking captives away to Babylon. Babylon, like Assyria before it, practiced exiling captives to far-away lands. The Babylonians added to this brutal practice by bringing captives from other lands to occupy the lands of those deported to other places. Roberts correctly notes, "This is no benign gathering in of the scattered and oppressed as imperialistic propaganda might wish to portray it; rather, it is a devouring of the nations that would destroy their identities as they are absorbed into the body of the Babylonian empire."[195]

Though probably not in Habakkuk's time frame or in Habakkuk's way, God proved himself faithful. Long after Habakkuk's lifetime and that of his audience, Babylon fell to Persia in 538 B.C. God is the Lord of history. He works in the world to defeat oppression and to deliver the oppressed. God showed himself ready to work on behalf of his people and to hear the needs of his people. Modern society seems even more complex and confusing than Habakkuk's. In this modern age God is faithful to his people. He remains the Lord of history, working to bring all people to him in faith and obedience. His working in history may appear as mysterious and inconsistent to us as it did to Habakkuk. The answer is not in rejecting God or in disconnecting him from our history. The answer is in waiting for his timing to bring about his purposes. Such waiting calls for faithfulness in having faith.

---

[194] R. L. Smith, *Micah–Malachi,* 108; Armerding ("Habakkuk," 514) sees the description as being the addiction to wine, an addiction that knows no limits and to which all other interests are sacrificed, but the Babylonians' addiction was to political and military ambition.

[195] Roberts, *Nahum, Habakkuk, and Zephaniah,* 117.

SECTION OUTLINE

II. WORDS OF WOE (2:6–20)
1. Woe to the Extortioner (2:6–8)
2. Woe to the Greedy and Arrogant (2:9–11)
3. Woe to Those Who Build on Bloodshed (2:12–14)
4. Woe to the Drunk and Violent (2:15–17)
5. Woe to the Maker of an Idol (2:18–20)

II. WORDS OF WOE (2:6–20)

What can a person do about the problem of evil in the world? When the wicked oppress the righteous, what can the righteous do? Habakkuk complained to God. He learned that God is vigilant, watching over his people. At first Habakkuk questioned the problem of evil in Judah (1:2–4). Later he questioned how God could allow wicked Babylon to overrun a nation more righteous than itself (1:12–17). Through an intense time of questioning, Habakkuk came to realize that God is the sovereign of the universe who watches over his world and watches over his word to perform it (Jer 1:11–12).

God punishes the wicked and delivers the oppressed, even when the wicked possess overwhelming power. Habakkuk 2:6–20 is a taunt or mocking song[1] placed artistically and unexpectedly in the mouths of the nations who had suffered from Babylon's excesses.[2] Patterson shows that each of the woe oracles have invective (vv. 6,9,12,15,19a), threat (vv. 7,11,13,16,20), and criticism (vv. 8,10,14,17–19b).[3] Except for the last section, each section begins with the word "woe" *(hoy),* a word with various shades of meaning.[4] The

---

[1] This includes a series of "woe oracles" described by R. M. Hals (*Ezekiel*, FOTL [Grand Rapids: Eerdmans], 358) as having two parts: (1) "the exclamation *hoy* ('woe') followed by a participle denoting the criticized action or a noun characterizing people in a negative way, and (2) a continuation with a variety of forms, including threats, accusations, or rhetorical questions."

[2] C. E. Armerding, "Habakkuk," EBC 7:495.

[3] R. D. Patterson, *Nahum, Habakkuk, Zephaniah,* WEC, ed. K. Barker (Chicago: Moody, 1991), 122.

[4] J. J. M. Roberts, *Nahum, Habakkuk, and Zephaniah: A Commentary,* OTL (Louisville: Westminster/John Knox, 1991), 114,118, says the basic meaning of the term is simply the attention getter, "Hey." This may be a basic lexical meaning, but it does not take note of the literary form or the emotional context. Within the woe oracles, הוֹי always signifies a sense of loss and condemnation. Thus *HALOT,* 242 defines הוֹי as a "grievous threatening cry of the prophets, " translating it "ah! alas!" D. A. Clines calls הוֹי "a general expression of dismay" (*The Dictionary of Classical Hebrew,* 2:503–4).

word carries the basic meaning of "judgment" or "lament." It "may be first identified as the introductory cry of a lament for the dead (1 Kgs 13:30; Jer 22:18)."[5] Thus it shows that the action under prophetic condemnation has the seeds of death within it.[6]

R. J. Clifford found fifty-three occurrences of *hoy* in the Old Testament. Of these he listed three possible uses: (1) to describe funeral laments (eight times), usually translated "alas"; (2) a cry to get attention (four times), usually translated "ho" or "ah"; (3) an announcement of doom (forty-one times and used only by the prophets), usually translated "woe to."[7] The wicked were under the judgment of God and therefore faced a time of ruin and mourning. The only thing left for an unrepentant people was to mourn the destruction of their lives.

The first four woes deal to some extent with the sin of greed and unjust gain. The fourth woe revolves primarily around drunkenness and violence but touches on the theme of misuse of people for the purpose of unjust gain. Habakkuk placed the taunts in five sections: against the extortioner (2:6–8); against the greedy and arrogant (2:9–11); against those who build on bloodshed (2:12–14); against the drunk and violent (2:15–17); and against the makers of idols (2:18–19).[8] It is climaxed "by a call for reverent submission to the Lord of history, who through all the vicissitudes of history remains seated in his holy temple (v. 20)."[9] Whether the woes refer to the wickedness in Babylon, Judah, or against any people who foster evil is not immediately clear.

One might shun a God who would pronounce such woes as too cruel or too holy or too full of dignity and honor. But as Robertson notes, "a part of his reality as the God of history includes his public vindication of the righteous and his public shaming of the wicked. His glory before all his creation is magnified by the establishment of honor for the humble and disgrace for the arrogant."[10]

The remainder of the Book of Habakkuk illustrates the truth of Hab 2:4: "See, he is puffed up; his desires are not upright—but the righteous will live by his faith." The series of woes confirms the truth of the Lord's message. The arrogant ultimately will fall under the weight of their sin; the righteous will live by faithfulness to God.

---

[5] E. Jenni, TLOT 1:357.

[6] Ibid., 358, quoting G. Wanke, "אוי und הוי," *ZAW* 78 (1966): 218.

[7] R. J. Clifford, "The Use of *Hoy* in the Prophets," *CBQ* 28 (1966): 458–64.

[8] C. J. Barber categorizes Babylon's sins as proud ambition (2:5–8), covetousness (2:9–11), ruthlessness and cruelty (2:12–14), debauchery (2:15–17), and idolatry (2:18–19) (*Habakkuk and Zephaniah,* EvBC [Chicago: Moody, 1985], 20).

[9] Armerding, "Habakkuk," 7:495.

[10] O. P. Robertson, *The Books of Nahum, Habakkuk, Zephaniah,* NICOT (Grand Rapids: Eerdmans, 1990), 185.

1. Woe to the Extortioner (2:6–8)

6"Will not all of them taunt him with ridicule and scorn, saying,
" 'Woe to him who piles up stolen goods
and makes himself wealthy by extortion!
How long must this go on?'
7Will not your debtors suddenly arise?
Will they not wake up and make you tremble?
Then you will become their victim.
8Because you have plundered many nations,
the peoples who are left will plunder you.
For you have shed man's blood;
you have destroyed lands and cities and everyone in them.

Woe is announced in v. 6 against him "who piles up stolen goods" and commits "exhortion." Then the *threat* is given in v. 7 that "debtors" will "arise," and they will "tremble." Verse 8 gives the *reason:* "you have plundered, … shed man's blood," and "destroyed."

2:6 The first part of the verse is an introduction to the entire section of woes. Since the verse contains pronouns without an immediate antecedent, the verse must refer back to 2:5, where the enemy's (Babylon's) arrogance is described. If this interpretation is correct, "them" refers to "all the nations" and "all the peoples" while "him" looks back to the enemy of 2:5.

The passage also could apply to any tyrant in any time period. In fact, the reader probably should understand the message in this way. The prophet probably had the Babylonians in mind, but the passage pronounces woe on any people who oppress others. "From God's reply it is evident that no wicked nation, covenant or cosmic, will escape divine wrath."[11]

Those who suffered under the heavy hand of Babylon would take up the taunt against the oppressor. The word "taunt" *(māšāl)* comes from a verb root meaning "to be like, to be similar" and often referred to a simple comparison. In the Old Testament the word has a number of interesting usages. It can mean something as harmless as a proverb (Prov 1:1; 10:1, the most common meaning of the Hb. word) or as unusual as Balaam's prophecy (Num 23:7,18). In the present context the taunt is identified further as being delivered in ridicule and scorn.[12] "Ridicule" translates a Hebrew term *(mĕlîṣâ)* that refers to "figurative language, allusive expression, proverb."[13] "Scorn" *(ḥîdôt)* represents a riddle or ambiguous saying and designates "something by enigmatic allu-

---

[11] P. R. House, *The Unity of the Twelve,* JSOTSup 97, Bible and Literature Series 27 (Sheffield: Almond, 1990), 93.

[12] V. P. Hamilton, "מָשַׁל *(māshal),*" *TWOT,* 1:533–34.

[13] *HALOT,* 590. The term occurs only here and in Prov 1:6 as well as in the apocryphal *Sir* 47:17. The root ליץ refers to boasting, scoffing, bragging speech (*HALOT,* 529).

sions."[14] All three terms belong to wisdom literature as seen in their combination in Prov 1:8. Babylon's enemies will use all types of enigmatic, mysterious, negative literary forms to condemn and ridicule the fallen world power. In typical biblical fashion those who suffered under oppression delivered the taunt against the oppressor. The judgment against the enemy fit the crime committed and reminded the oppressor of his oppression.

Though "woe" carries the idea of a lament, the lament is for a judgment that is certain to occur (rather than a wish that the evildoer be punished). The announcement of woe contains two assertions of evildoing interrupted by a question often asked in Scripture: "how long?" (cp. Isa 6:11). Some translations (e.g., NIV, GNB) place the question at the end of the verse while others (RSV, NASB) follow the Hebrew text with the incredulous question placed in the middle of the assertions concerning Babylon's evil. The position of the question in the middle of the woe may indicate the prophet's own frustrated reaction to all this, asking, if this is to come, why not today? More likely, it is a part of the woe oracle itself, showing the impatience of the nations as they wait for God to act against this dreaded, hated enemy.

The second assertion of guilt involved the taking of pledges. In ancient society a system of collateral developed that involved the giving of a pledge to insure the repayment of a loan. If the borrower could not or would not repay the loan, the lender kept the item pledged. The pledge often involved the simple belongings of peasants, such as a coat or cloak (Exod 22:25–28). Israel had strict rules regulating such practices (see Deut 24:10–13). How did Babylon gain wealth by the system of pledges? The language is certainly figurative here. Those whom the Babylonians plundered possibly saw the Babylonians as "borrowers" who were giving pledges. Later, when judgment came to Babylon, the pledges would be called in.[15] The phrase may be translated, "makes himself rich with loans" (NASB).[16]

A more likely interpretation involves the crime of extortion. The Babylonians seized the pledges of its victims and either kept the pledges or made the victims pay what they did not owe. Business and commerce always can be manipulated to gain unfair advantage. Habakkuk's message concerning modern commerce is clear: do not make your wealth or your living by unjust prac-

---

[14] *HALOT,* 309. See Judg 14:12–19; Num 12:8; 1 Kgs 10:1; Prov 1:6; Ezek 17:2; Dan 8:23. P. Humbert's proposal to read this as a verb form is adopted by *HALOT,* but this seeks to create too fine a form of Hebrew parallelism.

[15] J. J. M. Roberts argues for this position, saying, "the possessions it has obtained by conquest are thus seen, not as Babylon's own, but as simply on loan, as a burden of debt too heavy to pay back or to secure with pledges (*Nahum, Habakkuk, and Zephaniah: A Commentary,* OTL [Louisville: Westminster/John Knox, 1991], 119). He suggests that "the ambiguity may be an intentional device of the prophet to show the sudden fall of Babylon from creditor to debtor, from conqueror to conquered.

[16] R. L. Smith, *Micah–Malachi,* 111.

tices. Practice the business of just weights and just measures. Work to make an honest living without destroying the livelihoods of others.

Judgment would come to Babylon—or to any people who practice extortion and theft. Babylon, like Assyria before it (Nah 2:9; 3:1) and a multitude of tyrants since, piled up treasure at the expense of vanquished nations. Babylon's wealth flowed from the broken cities and broken lives of its neighbors. The first woe passage is a warning to those who are powerful. Power should be used to produce positive results. The criminal justice system of almost any nation permits all kinds of oppressive acts. Simply because a matter is legal does not make the matter right before God. When power becomes a tool to take advantage of others, "woe to you."

2:7 The person who lives by extorting others will surely experience the judgment of God. The punishment is an "in-kind" punishment, one in which the person taking advantage of others will be taken advantage of by those he oppressed. The wicked eventually receive a strong dose of their own medicine.

Both vv. 6 and 7 begin with the same Hebrew word, one indicating a negative rhetorical question.[17] Will not the debtors of Babylon arise and force Babylon to pay with interest?[18] The question serves as an emphatic assertion. Of course they will! Babylon should already be trembling in their boots rather than scornfully lording it over the nations they had captured.

The beginning of the woe referred to the Babylonians in the third person ("Woe to him"). In the succeeding verses the pronouns change to the second person ("Then you will become their victim"). This shift makes the judgment personal and powerful even though Habakkuk spoke primarily for the sake of the people of Judah rather than to the people of Babylon.

2:8 What Babylon had done to others, others would do to the Babylonians.[19] The Babylonians had set off a series of events that would not end until they had been plundered themselves. Violence does beget violence. National politics based simply on overwhelming power without care for people and with no determination to establish and uphold justice never endures. As Roberts insightfully writes, "the curse of war is far more pervasive than death, and in some ways the survivors feel its violence more profoundly than the dead."[20] The final verse of the first woe illustrates well the principle that

---

[17] B. K. Waltke and M. O'Connor discuss the use of הֲלוֹא, noting that most uses of the word fit the description of a double negative used to indicate a positive answer (*IBHS* § 40.3).

[18] Patterson follows the NIV footnote, saying נֹשְׁכֶיךָ is literally "those who bite you" and thus those you owe who keep nipping at your heels until he can take a full bite out of you and make you pay up in full (*Nahum, Habakkuk, Zephaniah,* 189–90).

[19] Roberts notes that the last line refers to the city in the singular, standing not for one particular city but for a class of lands and cities, those Babylon had treated with criminal violence (*Nahum, Habakkuk, and Zephaniah,* 114).

[20] Ibid., 120.

people and nations do sow what they reap (Gal 6:7). "Evil's inherent tendency is to self-destruct."[21]

2. Woe to the Greedy and Arrogant (2:9–11)

9"Woe to him who builds his realm by unjust gain
to set his nest on high,
to escape the clutches of ruin!
10You have plotted the ruin of many peoples,
shaming your own house and forfeiting your life.
11The stones of the wall will cry out,
and the beams of the woodwork will echo it.

Woe is announced in v. 9 against "him who builds" unjustly "to escape … ruin." Then the *threat* is given in v. 10 of shame and death, and also the *reason*: "plot[ting] the ruin of many peoples."

2:9 This second woe deals with building fortunes and power structures on unjust gain. As with the previous "woe," the second woe begins with the enemy described in the third person but with the last two verses of the woe moving to the second person.

The Hebrew reads literally, "Woe to the one cutting off an evil cut (material) for his house, to set on high his nest, to save himself from the hand of evil." The verb "cutting off" (a participle of *bṣ*ᶜ) may allude to a weaver cutting off a piece of material for sale.[22] An "evil cut" was shorter than promised and so involved cheating the customer. It is used more widely of making profits be cheating and violence.[23] The NIV applies this to the nation of Babylon by translating "realm" (lit., "house").[24] The Hebrew word can refer either to a house or to the occupant of a house, i.e., a family. The application could be more general to the house or family of the king along with his political advisors, military leaders, and economic powers. These built their "house" by taking unfair advantage of others. They and members of the family benefited from the unjust gain.[25] In this instance "house" apparently refers to both people and building since the people benefited from the unjust gain, but the "in-kind" judgment involved

---

[21] J. N. B. Heflin, *Nahum, Habakkuk, Zephaniah, and Haggai,* BSC (Grand Rapids: Zondervan, 1985), 93.

[22] *HALOT,* 147.

[23] Patterson, *Nahum, Habakkuk, Zephaniah,* 190.

[24] Note the literary artistry of using רע, "evil," both for what the condemned person was doing for his own house and that from which he was trying to escape.

[25] Hb. בצע referred to profits gained outside legal means. Exod 18:21 insists that Israelite leaders hate such gain. The prophet apparently applies such internal national standards to the international scene, expecting all national leaders to follow a self-evident system of values.

stones and woodwork crying out concerning the injustice.[26]

The "nest" symbolized the arrogance of the Babylonians. They built their nests "on high," a symbol of invincibility. Of all animals the eagle seemed most impervious to harm. The eagle built its nest "on high" and seemed to reign as lord over all that it surveyed. Habakkuk saw the people of Babylon in this way. They ruthlessly took from others and built houses and fortunes that appeared invincible. In their arrogance the Babylonians felt themselves to be untouchable by ruin or judgment.

Such an attitude permeates world history. Isaiah used the word "woe" as he described the proud of Judah who believed that they would not face judgment. Those people had made a "covenant with death," thinking somehow that judgment would not come to them (Isa 28:1,15). Pride, especially a feeling that we are above God himself, does not ennoble a people. Rather, arrogance takes away our dependence on God, leaving us to our own devices. "Doing our own thing" without regard for God is a sure prescription for ruin. How we have deceived ourselves! Security cannot be found in buildings, locks, or security systems. Security is found in dependence on God.

2:10 The Hebrew text reads literally, "You plan shame for your house, the ends of many peoples, and sinning against[27] your life/soul." With the repetition of "house," this verse is tied closely to the preceding one. Those building a house by unjust gain thought they brought fame, prominence, and power to themselves. Instead, their plans only shamed their house, that is their families, their ancestors, and their descendants. Destroying other peoples was a part of the security plan to isolate themselves from attack or danger. God saw the plan from a different perspective. Such a plan incurred guilt and thus promised sin's wages—death. Ending lives for others simply insured death for themselves. Rather than receiving adulation from the common people for wealth, the people brought shame on their house by the very actions that brought the wealth and provided the houses. Babylon's actions of scheming against the peoples of the world brought shame on the nation that would lead to the forfeiting of their own lives. Instead of building themselves up, they participated in the process of their own destruction.

Babylon—and modern peoples—must learn the cause-effect relationships in life. Our actions produce effects that may lead to death. The rich fool only thought that he was building larger barns to house more wealth. He did not

[26] O. R. Sellers, "House," *IDB* 2:657. Roberts says that since בצא carries with it the meaning of profits obtained illegally, רע, "evil," does not mean "unjust," this being redundant. Rather it is a noun "designating the disastrous impact of this action on the greedy man's house" and is to be translated, "to the ruin of your own house" (*Nahum, Habakkuk, and Zephaniah,* 114).

[27] חטא is sin or guilt. Patterson notes the tendency of some translators to "point to the metonymy here and translate with the following נַפְשֶׁךָ 'forfeiting your life' (cf. NIV, RSV) or prarphrase the line as 'You have worked your own ruin' (NJB)" (*Nahum, Habakkuk, Zephaniah,* 192).

consider that his very riches called out for his soul (Luke 12:13–21).

2:11 Throughout the Old Testament inanimate objects and the cosmos witnessed against those who rebelled against God (cf. Gen 4:10). On occasion God called on heaven and earth to witness the rebellion of human beings (Isa 1:2; Mic 6:1–2). The prophets especially appropriated this form to demonstrate the wickedness of human beings and the concern of God for the oppressed.

Babylon's wickedness was so great that even the wood[28] and the stone would cry out against their oppressive tactics. "The building is so much the result of wickedness that even its materials cannot forego protest."[29] Jeremiah preached a similar message of woe to the evil kings of Judah of his day, those who built houses without righteousness and upper rooms without justice. Specifically, Jeremiah condemned the same kind of extortion Habakkuk loathed in Babylon—that of using neighbor's services without pay and withholding wages (Jer 22:13–14). The messages of these contemporary prophets appears to indicate a rampant disregard for the needs of the powerless in society.

Habakkuk spoke about the wickedness of Babylon, but he spoke to the people of Judah. His message primarily involved the covenant community. Habakkuk spoke in terms that the people of Judah would understand. Houses in Palestine were constructed of such wood and stone. In Babylon brick replaced stone as the primary element of construction.

The prophet's tone invoked an incredulous element. When people built their wealth by unjust gain, even the building materials that housed their fortunes would cry out for justice. God is concerned with people. He cares for the needy of the land, reaching down even to the son of the handmaid, the lowest rung of society. Shame on those who oppress people, taking advantage of others in order to pile up unjust wealth.

3. Woe to Those Who Build on Bloodshed (2:12–14)

12"Woe to him who builds a city with bloodshed
and establishes a town by crime!
13Has not the LORD Almighty determined
that the people's labor is only fuel for the fire,
that the nations exhaust themselves for nothing?
14For the earth will be filled with the knowledge of the glory of the LORD,
as the waters cover the sea.

[28] Roberts (*Nahum, Habakkuk, and Zephaniah,* 115) shows the difficulty the early versions had in trying to translate כָּפִיס, "beam." Patterson follows NASB reading "rafters," saying the term "could conceivably imply any interior use of wood. … in ancient Mesopotamia the ceiling needed wood to augment the brick walls" (*Nahum, Habakkuk, Zephaniah,* 193) .

[29] J. D. W. Watts, *The Books of Joel, Obadiah, Jonah, Nahum, Habakkuk, and Zephaniah,* CBC (Cambridge: University Press, 1975), 139.

Woe is announced in v. 12 against "him who builds a city with bloodshed and ... crime." Then the *threat* is given in v. 13 that the Lord had "determined" their labor would be in vain. Verse 14 gives the *reason:* that "the earth will be filled" not with the crimes of men but "with the knowledge of the glory of the LORD."

House views these verses as crucial in the context of the Twelve.

> In many respects Hab 2:12–14 provides the climax of Hosea–Habakkuk. First, 2:12 proclaims the fate of all who attempt to abuse others (cf. Amos 1:1–2:3) to achieve their own wicked goals, which summarizes the concerns of Hosea, Amos, etc. Second, 2:13 demonstrates the sovereignty of God over the whole process of sin, punishment, and restoration described in the Twelve. ... Third, 2:14 explains the purpose and end result of all Yahweh's work in creation. What is sin but the rejection of the knowledge of God (cf. Hos 4:6). ... Renewal is as inevitable a result of punishment as punishment is of sin. Here the whole message of the Twelve hangs in the balance. Judgment is being poured out, the nations fall exhausted, the prophet bows in awe (Hab 2:20), and Yahweh reigns. What happens next hangs on the Lord's command.[30]

2:12 The third taunt builds on the first two and continues the idea of a people gaining wealth by unlawful and unethical means. Where the first two "woes" began in the third person and changed to the second, all of the third woe referred to the wicked in the third person. The woe ends with a description of the purpose of God in the world. The fifth woe ends in a similar fashion.

The NIV correctly interprets that the city has been built by shedding the blood of innocent victims and by committing grave crimes. For the Hebrew "to destroy a human life is the greatest evil, but the actual shedding of blood in murder imposes a special burden (see Gen 37:18ff.). ... The crime of shedding blood could be expiated only with blood, primarily that of the murderer (Gen 9:6; Num 35:31ff.). ... According to the general view, the power released when blood was shed brought about and demanded vengeance."[31] A land on which blood was shed could not be purified through sacrifice but only by shedding the blood of the murderer (Num 35:33). Thus a city or society built by bloodshed and oppression cannot endure.

"Crime" is literally "badness, malice, injustice"[32] or "perversity."[33] The law strictly prohibits it (Lev 19:15,35; Deut 25:16). The prophets repeatedly scream out against it (Isa 26:10; 59:3; Ezek 28:15; Hos 10:9,13; Mic 3:10). "It

[30] House, *The Unity of the Twelve*, 147. Opposed to this view stands Roberts, who argues that 2:14 along with 2:13a represents a gloss by a late editor who "did not interpret, much less understand, the whole text" (*Nahum, Habakkuk, and Zephaniah*, 122–24).

[31] B. Kedar-Kopfstein, "דָּם *dām*," *TDOT* 3:242.

[32] *HALOT* 798.

[33] R. Knierim, "עָוֶל *ʿāwel* perversity," *TLOT* 2: 849.

consistently involves crimes of a social, property, or commercial nature."[34] It is that which is incorrect or illegal. Thus again it belongs to the values all nations should recognize and follow. It is a characteristic that can never be associated with Israel's God (Ps 82:2; cp. Deut 32:4; Jer 2:5). To commit this crime is to ignore God's majesty (Isa 26:10).

Those who live on the weak and powerless ultimately collapse under the weight of oppression. This may be the meaning of the Fifth Commandment: "Honor your father and your mother, so that you may live long in the land the LORD your God is giving you" (Exod 20:12). The promise reflects living long in the land and appears to be a promise for a society that values life, especially life as reflected in families and the life of the old or weak. In contrast is the society built without the appreciation of life. That society will fail. Woe to the city, town, or society built on crime and bloodshed!

Micah chronicled the future of the city built on blood: "Therefore because of you, Zion will be plowed like a field, Jerusalem will become a heap of rubble, the temple hill a mound overgrown with thickets" (Mic 3:12).[35] The point is clear: the city (or society) built on blood will fail while the city built on the Lord will endure forever.

The people of Babylon acted toward the nations as criminals. "Bloodshed" may refer to warfare or mistreatment of captured peoples or to the practice of using slave labor for building projects, a vile practice that often caused extensive loss of life.

2:13 Habakkuk used a negative rhetorical question for the third time in the series of woes in Habakkuk 2. The first two occasions came in the first woe (the first word of Hab 2:6 and 2:7). The use of the negative with the interrogative particle forms a powerful positive statement.[36] The NIV leaves out a strong word of the Hebrew text, "behold" *(hinnê)*. Thisword calls attention to the text and directs the reader to give special attention. Waltke and O'Conner point out the use of the word as an exclamation of vivid immediacy.[37] Patterson follows Luther in seeing it as an "inferential particle" here: will it therefore not come to pass?"[38] The NASB seems to pick up on this by use of the word "indeed."

"Lord Almighty" (Yahweh *ṣĕbāʾôt*) is a special name for the God of Israel,

---

[34] Ibid., 2:850.

[35] Mic 3:9–12 reflects the prophet's condemnation of the leaders of the house of Judah who had built Jerusalem on bloodshed and wickedness (Micah used the same words for "bloodshed" and "crime" as Habakkuk, even using the participial form of "to build" that Habakkuk used). The chapter division in Micah is unfortunate since Mic 4:1–4 contrasts the city built on blood in Mic 3:9–12 with the city built on the Lord in 4:1–4.

[36] D. J. Clark and H. A. Hatton, *A Handbook on the Books of Nahum, Habakkuk, and Zephaniah* (New York: United Bible Societies, 1989), 104. See note at 2:6.

[37] Waltke and O'Conner, *IBHS* § 40.2.1.

[38] Patterson, *Nahum, Habakkuk, Zephaniah,* 197.

often translated Lord of Hosts. Only in 1:12 does Habakkuk use other titles for God. Thus here he calls special attention to this threat against Babylon. The basic term "hosts" along with the cognate verb refers to the mustering of troops for war but can also be used for service in cultic worship. It can extend to the heavenly realm of angels and stars (Gen 2:1; Ps 33:6; Isa 40:26). The point of reference for "hosts" when connected with the divine name Yahweh is debated. First Samuel 17:45 refers to the hosts as the armies of Israel, but the stars can also be part of God's army (Judg 5:20). God presides over the court of the host of heaven (1 Kgs 22:19; cp. Isa 6). T. Fretheim offers a mediating position, saying, "Hosts has reference to any group, human or divine, called upon by God to mediate a divine objective, which may or may not be military in nature."[39] A. S. van der Woude points to the divine title as "a characteristic designation for the God-King enthroned on the cherub throne (1 Sam 4:2; 2 Sam 6:2; cf. 2 Kgs 19:15; Pss 80:2; 99:1)." He concludes then that the term is a predicate of royal dominion, agreeing with J. P. Ross that as soon as Israel used the title for its God "it became the name of a god whose principle attribute was royal majesty."[40] The NIV follows this interpretation with its translation "LORD Almighty." Still, the association with war, with the Ark of the Covenant which led Israel to war, and the prophetic context threatening foreign armies all argue for a strong association between the divine title Lord of Hosts and military action. Babylon tried to protect themselves from ruin and to corner the market on economic power and wealth through military expeditions. Israel's Yahweh of Hosts controlled an army against which Babylon had no chance. Fighting Him was exhausting, profitless labor.

The force of the verse describes the futility of "getting and spending" without dependence on the Lord. Psalm 127:1 illustrates the principle Habakkuk declared: "Unless the LORD builds the house, / its builders labor in vain. / Unless the Lord watches over the city, / the watchman stand guard in vain."

Habakkuk used two parallel questions that expressed the same thought. The nations build and develop only to provide fuel for the fire. All that they labor for will come to naught. Jeremiah 51:58 contains similar language concerning Babylon, suggesting to some that both Habakkuk and Jeremiah referred to a popular proverb concerning Babylon. Davidson did not believe that Habakkuk quoted, nor did he believe necessarily that the words of the prophets came from a common source.[41] Whichever prophet first used the words, their appearance together in the canon of Scripture reinforces the consistency of God in pronouncing judgment on people who work for their own glory rather than for the majesty of the Lord of Hosts. All work not serving

[39] T. E. Fretheim, "Yahweh," *NIDOTTE* 4:1298.

[40] A. S. van der Woude, "צָבָא *ṣābāʾ* army," *TLOT* 2:1045.

[41] A. B. Davidson, *Nahum, Habakkuk, and Zephaniah,* CBSC (Cambridge: University Press, 1899), 80.

God's purposes is futile work good only for the flames of history forgotten.

2:14 Does God punish the wicked, or may evildoers commit iniquity with impunity (Hab 1:2–4)? For Habakkuk this constituted a major issue. God's answer to Habakkuk's complaint settled it. God works in the world to accomplish his purpose, but God's purpose goes beyond simply punishing the wicked. God desires that all the world know him. From the very beginning of Israel's history as a people, God declared his intention for all the world to know him (Exod 19:4–6).

Shame on those who build a city with bloodshed! Their labor will come to nothing, but God is at work doing a great thing: spreading the knowledge of himself. "The Lord declares that all punishment results as part of His plan to fill the earth with the knowledge of Himself. … Because God is righteous and sovereign, no sin can go unpunished lest God's glory be diminished and [His] name sink in esteem."[42]

The final verse of the third woe gives an uplifting and positive element to the woes. God will work to make himself known in all the earth. In Hebrew thought "knowledge" means more than information. "Knowledge is seen in fundamentally relational terms. … To know God is to be in a right relationship with him, with characteristics of love, trust, respect, and open communication."[43] Knowing involved intimacy and experience, being used in its most fundamental sense to describe the marriage relationship. For the earth to be filled with the knowledge of the glory of the Lord involved knowing God rather than simply knowing about God. Not to know God for Israel and for the nations invited His judgment (Ps 79:6; Jer 10:25). Thus the entire story of the Exodus centered on the fact that Pharaoh did not know God (Exod 5:2), but God wanted to introduce himself to Israel (Exod 6:6) and to Pharaoh and the Egyptians (Exod 7:5). Jeremiah also pictured a knowledge of the Lord that transcended geographical borders or conventional barriers (Jer 31:31–34). Ezekiel repeatedly uses the recognition formula, "and you shall know that I am Yahweh" to show that all God is doing has divine purpose behind it. That purpose is to introduce himself to Israel and to the nations.[44]

In the Old Testament "glory" is a "technical term for God's manifest presence"[45] (see Exod 16:7), often connected with the cloud (Exod 16:10) and

---

[42] House, *The Unity of the Twelve,* 93.

[43] Fretheim, "ידע," *NIDOTTE* 2:413.

[44] See R. M. Hals, *Ezekiel,* FOTL (Grand Rapids: Eerdmans, 1989), 362. The recognition formula often occurs as a part of a "prophetic proof saying"; see pp. 353–54; W. Zimmerli, "The Word of Divine Self-manifestation (Proof Saying), A Prophetic Genre," in *I Am Yahweh,* trans. D. W. Stott (Atlanta: John Knox, 1982), 99–110; Zimmerli, "Knowledge of God According to the Book of Ezekiel," *I Am Yahweh*, 29–98.

[45] C. J. Collins, "כבד," *NIDOTTE* 2:581. Note that כָּבוֹד means literally "heavy, having weight."

with the Ark of the Covenant. It can also be represented as a consuming fire (Exod 24:17). "Glory" also involves "honor" or position of power.[46] Habakkuk used the term in the sense of powerful presence.[47] All the earth would be filled with the knowledge of the manifest presence of God. For Ezekiel the "glory of the LORD" meant a manifestation of God. God's "glory" appeared to Ezekiel. He spoke of God's glory as that which he personally experienced: "Such was the appearance of the likeness of the glory of the LORD" (Ezek 1:28). The glory of the Lord "reveals his person and dignity, and the proper response to such a revelation is to give God honor or glory" (cp. Exod 33:18).[48]

Israel expected God's glory to fill their place of worship (Exod 40:34,35; 1 Kgs 8:11; 2 Chr 7:1–2; Ezek 10:4; 43:5; 44:4). Habakkuk joined a prophetic chorus calling for more. God's glory should be recognized as filling the entire universe (Num 14:21; Ps 72:19; Isa 6:3), letting all the people of the world experience and respond to God's manifest, weighty presence. The prophet wanted the knowledge of God to be as pervasive as the waters that fill the seas. For Christian believers the verse takes us in mind and heart to the work of Christ, who came into the world to make God known in the most unique way possible (cf. John 1:14; Eph 1:17). Through Christ the earth may be uniquely filled with the knowledge of the glory of the Lord.

4. Woe to the Drunk and Violent (2:15–17)

15"Woe to him who gives drink to his neighbors,
pouring it from the wineskin till they are drunk,
so that he can gaze on their naked bodies.
16You will be filled with shame instead of glory.
Now it is your turn! Drink and be exposed!
The cup from the LORD's right hand is coming around to you,
and disgrace will cover your glory.
17The violence you have done to Lebanon will overwhelm you,
and your destruction of animals will terrify you.
For you have shed man's blood;
you have destroyed lands and cities and everyone in them.

Woe is announced in v. 15 against "him who gives drink to his neighbors." Then the *threat* is given in v. 16 that he "will be filled with shame instead of glory." Verse 17 gives the *reason:* "the violence you have done to Lebanon."

---

[46] In such meaning the honor can be injured if not met with the proper response of respect and praise (Josh 7:29; 1 Sam 6:5; Isa 3:8; Mal 1:6; 2:2); see C. Westermann, "כבד *kbd* to be heavy," *TLOT* 2:596.

[47] E. Jacob, *Theology of the Old Testament* (London: Hodder & Stoughton, 1958), 79–82.

[48] Collins, "כָּבֵד," 2:582.

2:15 The fourth taunt, as with the first and second, begins in the third person and then changes to the second person. Babylon's sin involved the use of liquor, particularly for the purpose of manipulating other people, a device still widely practiced. As Robertson points out, "part of the depravity inherent in sin is its insistence on involving others in its debauchery."[49] The figure of a drinking party is clear, but its exact translation is debated. "Pouring it from the wineskin" is variously rendered: "mixing in your wrath" (Robertson[50]), "who mix in your venom" (NASB), "pressing him to your bottle" (NKJV; compare NLT), "pouring out your wrath" (NRSV).[51] It could be that the prophet intentionally played on the various possible meanings or associations of these words, all of which are appropriate in the drinking context.

The Old Testament pictures Babylon as a nation known for its drinking parties which often turned into wild orgies (Daniel 5). Babylon made the neighboring nations drink from the cup and then shamed those who became drunk. In this woe the liquor and orgy give a figurative picture of Babylon's practices. The Babylonians made the nations they conquered drink from the cup of their wrath, bringing shame and disgrace on the nation.

Parties of this kind did occur, of course, but for Habakkuk the practice symbolized a larger problem of relations between nations. Babylon took advantage of other nations, bringing shame on those conquered. More so than in other nations, in Israel nakedness symbolized shame. In their drinking parties, those who became drunk might expose themselves during their drunkenness thereby bringing shame on themselves, as Noah did (Gen 9:20–23). This is what Babylon had forced on the nations.

2:16 Verse sixteen builds on the preceding verse. "When the Lord deals with Babylon it is as its sovereign king. ... Because Babylon is 'puffed up' (2:4), 'arrogant' (2:5), 'restless' (2:5), and 'greedy' (2:5), God decides to reverse the nation's fortunes. ... Like Nineveh, Babylon will become a shadow of its former self, thus negating its intense pride."[52] What Babylon had done to others would be done to them. "Shame," nakedness, and drinking having played a prominent part in Babylon's sin, the prophet knew that these elements would play a significant part in Babylon's punishment.

---

[49] Robertson, *Nahum, Habakkuk, Zephaniah*, 201.

[50] Ibid.

[51] The problem comes from the Hb. phrase מְסַפֵּחַ חֲמָתְךָ. The verb ספח occurs only five times, and in the *piel* only here. In the *qal* it means "associate with" (1 Sam 2:36). See *HALOT,* 764, which suggests, following Elliger (p. 42), reading מִסַּף from סַף, "bowl." The MT of Job 14:19 reads סְפִיחֶיהָ, traditionally taken from a conjectured Hb. root based on an Arabic cognate meaning "outpouring." See BDB, 705. חֲמָתְךָ is often taken from חֵמָה, "heat, poison, wrath." If, however, חֲמָתְךָ is derived from חֵמֶת, then the meaning can be "skin" or" wine bottle" (Gen 21:14,19). Patterson summarizes the theories and argues for the NRSV translation (*Nahum, Habakkuk, Zephaniah,* 201–2).

[52] House, *The Unity of the Twelve*, 215.

The theme of drunkenness continues as in the preceding verse through the use of the verb "filled," a translation that misses the meaning of the Hebrew verb. In Hebrew the verb means to be satiated with food or drink (often in a good sense, e.g. Isa 66:11) or to be sated with drink (as here in the sense of drunkenness).[53] Babylon, the nation which had made others drink and become drunk, would become sated with disgrace, contempt, and shame. Babylon would be "ichabod," without glory (1 Sam 4:21). In this case, "glory" denotes honor. The nation which bought its honor by intrigue and power would substitute its honor for shame. The nation who thought they had spread their glory and honor across the known world would fall in shame before God's glory known throughout the universe (see v. 14).[54]

The following command appears unseemly to modern sensibilities, but the command conveys the reality of Babylon's punishment. Babylon had exposed others by encouraging drunkenness, now Babylon's genitals would be exposed.[55] Babylon did not practice circumcision. Exposing the sexual organs provided a double disgrace by opening the Babylonians to the shame of nakedness and divulging their lack of circumcision and thus lack of membership in God's covenant people.[56]

God himself would bring the punishment upon Babylon. Habakkuk dealt with the problem of the silence of God, but God did not remain silent. For Habakkuk, the judgment seemed slow (2:3), but God surely would bring judgment on the evil of Babylon.

In the Old Testament, the cup often symbolized judgment while the right hand indicated power. Jeremiah 15:15–29 describes God's causing the nations to drink from the cup of his wrath. The result of their drinking would be their falling to rise no more because of the sword which the Lord would send against them.[57] Christ picks up this same figure of speech in Matt 20:22;

---

[53] *CHALOT,* 348.

[54] Note how glory envelopes the verse beginning and end, tying back to the same term in v. 14.

[55] The word literally means "to leave the foreskin uncircumcised" in the *qal* stem of the verb. In the *niphal,* as found in Hab 2:16, it means "having a foreskin" (*CHALOT,* 283). The NIV uses the more socially acceptable term "exposed," a term which apparently conveys the idea of the Hb. verb. Other translations follow the Dead Sea Scrolls, the LXX, Aquila, the Vg., and the Syr. in using "and stagger." The letters are the same in both verbs but in a different order. Roberts notes that the Dead Sea Scrolls Habakkuk commentary plays on the concept of circumcision and thus knew the MT text tradition even if its Bible text does not reflect it. Robertson sees in the Scrolls and in some LXX manuscripts "ancient efforts to tone down what may have been regarded as a crude admonition" (*Nahum, Habakkuk, Zephaniah,* 202).

[56] Clark and Hatton, *Nahum, Habakkuk, and Zephaniah*, 107. Note Patterson, *Nahum, Habakkuk, Zephaniah,* 199: "not even in the marks of his body could the Chaldean claim covenant relationship with Yahweh."

[57] For other passages that describe drinking from the cup as a symbol of God's wrath see Jer 49:12; Obad 16; and Ps 75:8. For passages that use the right hand or the hand or the arm to symbolize power see Isa 9:12,17,21; 10:13.

26:42. "The wrath of the Father against the shameful sin of mankind finds a consummate manifestation in the outpouring of God's judgment on his own son. As repulsive as 'wrath' in God may appear to the sophistications of the modern mind, it is a scriptural reality that found awesome expression as the Son of God suffered in the sinner's place, drinking the cup of the fury of God."[58]

"Disgrace" at the end of the verse and "shame" at the beginning of the verse are related and may be a play on words.[59] While seeking glory, Babylon only would find disgrace. In modern society, seeking after sophistication and satisfaction often produces only shame and disgrace, but seeking after God and his righteousness produces the good things which only God can give (Matt 6:33). Our Lord knew the importance of putting things in their proper perspective, a lesson we continue to need to learn.

2:17 Babylon had done violence to Lebanon by destroying the forests and depriving the animals of habitat. As in previous woes, Babylon's punishment fit the crime. Now animals would terrify Babylon. "God takes note when his lowliest creatures are terrified by the brutalities of insensitive human beings. He hears the groanings of his entire creation, and will see that the whole created universe joins in the final redemption of mankind (Rom 8:19–21)."[60]

Lebanon became a proverbial expression for luxuriant growth and abundance. The term "Lebanon" referred to the Lebanon mountain range which produced thick forests known for their magnificent cedars and thriving animal life. Texts from as early as the third millennium show Lebanon as a major source of wood for temples and ships. "Even in prehistoric Egyptian tombs archaeologists have found coniferous wood that may have come from the Lebanon."[61]

Both the Assyrians and the Babylonians (Isa 14:8) used the forests of Lebanon as sources of abundant building materials. Sennacherib of Assyria and his servants vaunted themselves against God and boasted of taking the choice trees of Lebanon: "… I have gone up the heights of the mountains, to the far recesses of Lebanon; I felled its tallest cedars, its choicest cypresses..." (Isa 37:24, RSV). The reference to Lebanon would be only one such example of

---

[58] Robertson, *Nahum, Habakkuk, Zephaniah,*, 203.

[59] The Hb. words are קָלוֹן ("shame") and קִיקָלוֹן ("disgrace"). Robertson (*Nahum, Habakkuk, Zephaniah,* 204) sees the latter, which occurs only here in the MT, as a compound word the prophet constructed "to intensify the concept of disgrace to be experienced by the Chaldeans." Another way of reading the Hb. word for "disgrace" is to divide the word into two words and translate as "shameful spewing" (KJV) or "shameful vomiting" (HOTTP). This gives the idea of what drunkenness does when induced by the Babylonians and when induced by the Lord God. The Babylonian drunkenness produces vomiting while the Lord's punishment causes disgrace.

[60] Robertson, *Nahum, Habakkuk, Zephaniah,* 205.

[61] M. J. Mulder, "לְבָנוֹן *lĕbānôn*," *TDOT* 7:448–49.

how Babylon exploited and ravage the nations for its selfish interests. Babylon had manipulated its neighbors by giving them to drink from the wineskin and by using its power to take advantage of its neighbors. God had a clear message: "If the agent of God's judgment perpetrates the same wickedness he has been sent to punish, he too must receive the just judgment of God."[62] Theologians argue over what this concept of divine judgment means for our understanding of the nature of God. Robertson well states the issue: "This concept of the execution of reciprocal justice does not appeal to humanity. But it is God's way. By this way he proves himself to be impartial and righteous as judge. By this way he finally establishes himself as just and yet also the justifier of the ungodly who believe. For Jesus the Christ drank the cup of God's fury to the dregs, and so became the Savior of all who would renounce their own pride and violence, looking to him alone for salvation."[63]

The remainder of the verse emphasizes the sin of Babylon. The words are the same as the end of the first woe in Hab 2:8. "His will be a wanton disregard of the value of the natural world, the animal kingdom, and civilized humanity."[64]

Babylon's sin was against people and ultimately against God. They took advantage of the people of the land, thoughtlessly using up land and resources. God gave the land for the good of his people, but Babylon's destruction produced heartache and misery for generations and centuries to come. "The verse points to humanity's abuse of its authority over the rest of creation (Gen 1:28; Ps 8:6–9[5–8]). It is one thing to rule over creation, respecting it as God's creation entrusted to one for the moment (cf. Deut 22:6–7; 25:4; Prov 12:10; 27:23); it is quite another thing to exploit it unmercifully as though it belonged to one absolutely, as though one were not accountable for it to its creator."[65] Does God's judgment continue to those who thoughtlessly destroy the environment?

5. Woe to the Maker of an Idol (2:18–20)

18"Of what value is an idol, since a man has carved it?
Or an image that teaches lies?
For he who makes it trusts in his own creation;
he makes idols that cannot speak.
19Woe to him who says to wood, 'Come to life!'
Or to lifeless stone, 'Wake up!'
Can it give guidance?

[62] Patterson, *Nahum, Habakkuk, Zephaniah,* 201.
[63] Robertson, *Nahum, Habakkuk, Zephaniah,* 206.
[64] Patterson, *Nahum, Habakkuk, Zephaniah,* 200.
[65] Roberts, *Nahum, Habakkuk, and Zephaniah,* 125.

It is covered with gold and silver;
there is no breath in it.
[20]But the LORD is in his holy temple;
let all the earth be silent before him."

Woe is announced in v. 18 against the idol maker. Then the *threat* is given in v. 19 that the idol maker will be without revelation or guidance.[66] The *reason* is found in vv. 18–19: a god created by man is lifeless and must stand silent before the living God.

2:18 Unlike the former passages, the final woe begins the taunt before the word "woe" is used. While many translators and interpreters rearrange the text to place "Woe to him" at the beginning of the passage,[67] the text probably preserves the more effective arrangement. The prophet jumped right into idol worship without the pronouncement of judgment, giving the reader a sense of urgency and conveying the prophet's indignation at the abomination of worshiping "lies."

Babylon trusted in its many "gods," idols made of men's hands which were without power or strength. Habakkuk has prepared for this oracle against powerless gods in 1:11 and 2:16. In all three passages "the Babylonian has deified what is not divine, and in the long run, trust in any such false god will prove deceitful."[68] Not only Babylon needed to hear this. Judah did, too. They could easily assume Babylon's conquests had proved Babylon's gods superior to their God. Habakkuk's ironic picture assures them this is not the case.[69]

To trust "is a concept of central theological importance in the Old Testament. It expresses that which is, or at least should be, central in people's relationship with God."[70] Trust "almost always refers to a process at the foundation of existence. Whoever trusts, relies on something, and everything depends upon the reliability of the other; one seeks protection, and one stands or falls with that on which one relies."[71] God calls on his people to trust him at all times (Ps 62:8; cp. 115:9–11; Isa 26:3–4; 30:15). People are trusting folk, but choose the wrong things in which to place their trust—riches (Job

---

[66] Again here, Roberts sees an elliptical woe oracle without an explicit threat (*Nahum, Habakkuk, and Zephaniah,* 127).

[67] Cp. the verse order in JB and Moffatt. Roberts (*Nahum, Habakkuk, and Zephaniah,* 126) argues that v. 18 needs an introduction; "it can hardly stand alone to mark the transition to a new line of thought. As such it would be both awkward and unparalleled." This takes form criticism too far as a text critical tool and ignores the creative use of forms by biblical writers. The blatant change of subject matter along with the intentional break of form catches the reader's attention. See Robertson, *Nahum, Habakkuk, Zephaniah,* 207, for a defense of Habakkuk's literary creativity here.

[68] Roberts, *Nahum, Habakkuk, and Zephaniah,* 127.

[69] Ibid., 128.

[70] R. W. L. Moberly, "בטח," *NIDOTTE* 1:644.

[71] E. Gerstenberger, "בטח *bṭḥ* to trust," *TLOT* 1:228.

31:24; Prov 11:28); important people (Ps 146:3; cp. Jer 17:5–8); military fortifications (Deut 28:52; Jer 5:17); beauty (Ezek 16:15); in personal abilities (Prov 3:5; 28:26). One can even trust in evil (Isa 30:12). "The logic of biblical monotheism requires that all these things be used in the service of God and not set up as alternatives to him."[72]

Trust is not confined to God in the biblical revelation. Spouses (Prov 31:11), brothers (Jer 9:4) and friends can be trusted (Mic 7:5), but only in relationship to an ultimate trust in God. This trust in God is not an illusory, spiritual emotion. It relates to life crises, especially national ones (Pss 22:4–5; 25:1–2; 28:7; 31:14–15; Isa 36–37; Jer 39:18). But even trust in Yahweh can be misplaced if it is only ritualistic and not connected to genuine obedience (Jer 7:3–15).[73] Trust in God wipes away all fear (Pss 56:5,12; 25:2; 21:8). "Israelite tradition recognizes and demands an absolute, exclusive devotion to Yahweh; this trust in Yahweh includes *hope* of salvation (Job 11:18) and *faith* in the God of the fathers (Ps 22:4f.)."[74] Like Habakkuk, the prophets mocked the Babylonians for their worship of idols and the people of Judah for wanting to be like the Babylonians in their worship.[75]

What profit is an idol? This is the fundamental question and should be asked by everyone tempted to worship that which is false. Habakkuk saw a number of problems with idolatry. First, an idol is only something made by human beings. In the Hebrew text the word for "idol" and the verb "carved" are related. Worship an idol, and you receive from it what human beings can accomplish; but worship the Lord God, and you receive what the creator of the ends of the earth can accomplish.

Modern man may be most tempted to worship himself. The prophet Zechariah reminded Zerubbabel of the folly of self worship: "Not by might, nor by power, but by my Spirit, says the Lord of hosts" (Zech 4:6, RSV). Human beings can make things of wood and stone, but the Lord God can make human beings. Why not worship him? Modern man is even more tempted to worship

---

[72] Moberly, "בטח," 645. Note Gerstenberger's statement ("בטח *bṭḥ* to trust," 229) that the OT assumes "that one can successfully place confidence only in Yahweh, that no other entity can be an ultimate object of trust."

[73] See Gerstenberger, "בטח *bṭḥ* to trust," 229.

[74] Ibid., 230.

[75] Isaiah and Jeremiah scorned the Babylonians for idolatry. Of course, these prophets turned the lessons to be learned to the people of Israel and Judah who should have known better. Isaiah described the foolishness of idolatry in much the same way as Habakkuk, describing the making of an idol by cutting down a tree, carving the wood and finally overlaying the wood with metal (Isa 44:9–20). Isa 46:1–7 described two Babylonian gods being carried into exile before the invasion of Cyrus the Persian. Bel and Nebo sat helpless before the invader. Isaiah's message decried the foolishness of worshiping gods which have to be carried. Better to worship the God who can carry you! Jeremiah coined a word for the idols—they were *hăbālîm*, only breath. For Jeremiah, the idols lacked the power to do good or to do evil (Jer 10:5). They were nothing.

possessions, things made with human hands and coveted with human hearts. Such is idolatry (Eph 5:5). "Whenever a person's desire looks to the creature rather than the Creator, he is guilty of the same kind of foolishness. An insatiable desire for things not rightly possessed assumes that things can satisfy rather than God himself. Whenever a person sets his priorities on things made rather than on the Maker of things, he is guilty of idolatry."[76]

Second, idols teach nothing but lies. Habakkuk agreed with Jeremiah that idols are deaf and dumb objects. They neither hear men's petitions nor speak to human needs. They do nothing (Jer 10:5). Those who worship idols worship a lie. They are deluded by the ways of the world and deceived with false hope.

Third, making an idol means that the worshiper has made a god in his own image. But the worshiper of the Lord God has been created in the image of God. Worshiping an idol or image means that our god always will be too small because it will conform to our own image.

Fourth, the idol cannot speak or give guidance. Why should anyone cry out to that which is dumb? The idol cannot answer; it cannot save. The final word used for "idols" in the verse (*ʾĕlîlîm*) is a word meaning "nonentity" or "a nobody." The idols were "nothings." They could not speak, hear, guide, or save. Who, in his right mind, could worship an idol?

Preuss noted the way *ʾĕlîlîm* is used throughout the Old Testament to ridicule idols and surmised that the word was created expressly for the purpose of ridicule. Thus, the word is used to "contrast the power and greatness of Yahweh with the weakness and vanity of idols."[77]

2:19 The final woe indicates the total futility of idol worship. The entire woe is in the third person and indicates the sorrow of one crying out to a god which can neither stand nor hear. Like the prophets of Baal on Mount Carmel (1 Kgs 18:26–29), the worshipers of idols beg for a response but receive nothing. "But there was no response, no one answered, no one paid attention" (1 Kgs 18:29).

The word for "woe" may mean a word of judgment or a lament. In this instance both connotations fit the situation. Judgment surely must come on those who bow down before a block of wood (Isa 44:19), but how tragic for the person who cries in vain for the thing to arise and to save but without avail. Surely, the person who bows down before a block of wood should be pitied. Idols could be carved from wood and overlaid with silver or gold or hewn from a stone. They could be carried in festival parades and shown off in temple displays. They looked pretty and made their worshipers proud. Neither wood nor stone, however, could provide guidance for daily living or for the

---

[76] Robertson, *Nahum, Habakkuk, Zephaniah,* 209.

[77] H. D. Preuss, " אֱלִיל *ʾĕlîl,*" *TDOT* 1:285–87. Note that the final phrase of the verse, אֱלִילִים אִלְּמִים, "dumb idols," is a wordplay.

myriad difficult events in life.

The last line is more emphatic than the NIV rendering reflects. "There is no breath in it at all" would more adequately reflect the sense. In this context, "breath" (*rûaḥ*) meant life. An idol was a lifeless form. Snaith pointed out the peculiar significance of *rûaḥ*. He saw three particular points of emphasis. It stood for power, life, and came from God in contrast to coming from man.[78] Breath could refer to the idol's inability to give guidance or revelation. It lacked the ability to answer to the deepest needs of human beings. Lack of breath made the idol weaker than its "creator," for the true God had placed breath in man's nostrils (Gen 2:7).

2:20 What a contrast! The idol sits where it is put without the ability to hear or to respond, but the Lord resides by his almighty power in his holy temple ready to respond to the needs of his people.

For Habakkuk, the "temple" probably meant not only the temple in Jerusalem but also the heavenly sanctuary (Mic 1:2). From the heavenly temple, the Lord ruled over heaven and earth and received the honor due him alone. The proper response to such a God who is enthroned above the Cherubim is awed silence. The word for "keep silence" is "an onomatopoeic interjection with a force much like the English 'hush!' (cf. Zeph 1:7)."[79] The verse pictures the contrast between those who are no gods and the one who is in heaven ready to respond to human need and to human questions. Habakkuk himself knew from experience that he could take his questions to God's temple in heaven.

The last verse of the chapter serves as a fitting conclusion to the final woe as well as a conclusion to the entire series of woes.[80] Likewise, it points back to a prophet making demands of God, asking questions of God, and retreating to his watchtower to wait for God's answers, impatient at God's silence. Now the prophet hushes himself and all the world, willing to let God act in God's time and willing to wait for God to open his mouth when God chooses. This final verse of the chapter points the reader to the holy God enthroned in his holy temple and prepares the reader for the prayer of Habakkuk in chap. 3."Finally, God's holiness was vindicated, and the prophet was able to reconcile his theology with God's actions."[81] "Despite his apparent silence, he still remains with them; he has not lost control of their destiny. One should wait upon him in the awed silence that is often the most appropriate expression of true worship."[82]

---

[78] N. H. Snaith, *The Distinctive Ideas of the Old Testament* (Philadelphia: Westminster, 1946), 183–203.

[79] Patterson, *Nahum, Habakkuk, Zephaniah,* 209.

[80] Patterson sees v. 20 as "the chief lesson to be learned from the whole discussion. Verse 20 forms an inclusio with v. 4 that reveals the underlying thesis and its implication for the entire section: The Lord is a just and holy God who deals righteously with all people and is actively present in the flow of earth's history; therefore, He is to be acknowledged as God by all" (ibid., 205) .

[81] Barber, *Habakkuk and Zephaniah,* 20.

[82] Roberts, *Nahum, Habakkuk, and Zephaniah,* 128.

SECTION OUTLINE

III. HABAKKUK'S PRAYER (3:1–19)
1. The Title Verse (3:1)
2. Habakkuk's Petition (3:2)
3. A Description of the Lord's Appearing in Great Power (3:3–15)
4. Habakkuk's Response to the Lord (3:16)
5. Habakkuk's Confidence in the Lord (3:17–19)

III. HABAKKUK'S PRAYER (3:1–19)

The questions of life are many. Two of the most vexing are: Why do the righteous suffer and why does God often appear to remain silent. Having asked such questions, Habakkuk found answers in an unexpected fashion. He found he "must alter his perspective on the ways of God with mankind."[1] The ultimate answer to such difficult questions always takes the questioner back to God himself. Habakkuk questioned God, but ultimately the prophet came back to the profound answer for all the questions of life—he returned to the theme of the greatness and the majesty of God. "In chapter 3 his doubts have been satisfactorily answered. Here he breaks forth in prayer, praise, and joy. He makes a triumphant expression of undaunted faith."[2]

Dividing the chapter into paragraphs is a tentative process. Most translations differ on the divisions. The plan followed in this commentary appears reasonable from the standpoint of content and form though other proposals also make sense. Chapter 3 represents a cultic prayer composed of a superscription (v. 1), a petition for God to renew his work of salvation history (v. 2), a theophany (vv. 3–7), a battle description using traditional language to describe God against the forces of creation and history (vv. 8–15), and the prophet's statement of faith (vv. 16–19).[3]

---

[1] O. P. Robertson, *The Books of Nahum, Habakkuk, Zephaniah,* NICOT (Grand Rapids: Eerdmans, 1990), 212.

[2] J. N. B. Heflin, *Nahum, Habakkuk, Zephaniah, and Haggai,* BSC (Grand Rapids: Zondervan, 1985), 77.

[3] See R. L. Smith, *Micah–Malachi,* WBC (Waco: Word, 1984), 36, 95–96; on pp. 114–15 Smith says it is a combination of hymn, lament, thanksgiving, liturgy, and royal psalm and so best classified as a liturgy for the fall festival. J. J. M. Roberts finds a pattern here resembling the earlier patterns in chaps. 1–2: prophetic lament followed by divine response followed by renewed lament (*Nahum, Habakkuk, and Zephaniah: A Commentary,* OTL [Louisville: Westminster/John Knox, 1991], 148–49). This time, however, instead of the prophet bringing a lament, he offers an individual prayer of thanksgiving: invocation of Yahweh, statement of request or petition, vision report responding to the request, prophetic vow, and statement of confidence.

The language of this prayer stands apart from the preceding chapters and has caused great agitation among interpreters.[4] Albright demonstrated the antiquity of the psalm's language long ago.[5] In fact the language appears to point to two separate poems joined together (a theophanic hymn in vv. 3–7 and a victory song in vv. 8–15).[6] Armerding shows the relationship of Habakkuk's psalm to Exod 15; Deut 33; and Pss 18; 68; 77. He calls attention to the "remarkable power and enigmatic intensity … due in part to the depth of allusion that informs it: its few, compressed verses draw on the entire spectrum of salvation history, from Creation and Exodus to the final revelation of God's rule and judgment still awaiting fulfillment."[7] Robertson describes this as "a collage, a collecting of many images to convey an impression both of past experience and of future expectation … Moses' song, Deborah's song, David's song blend to provide a framework for anticipating the future."[8]

The prayer recorded in 3:1–19 celebrates the satisfactory answers the Lord offers to Habakkuk's complaints. "Habakkuk 1–2 appears to emphasize the human agents in the outworking of this pattern; chapter 3 reveals its inward dynamics in the sovereign agency of God, who implements the covenant through whatever earthly means he chooses. Together they form a compelling and tightly meshed testimony to the ways of God in judgment and in grace."[9] The Lord's righteousness and power are no longer challenged, and the prophet has learned the lesson of 2:4, as is evident in 3:19. At all points God has proved faithful. Regardless of how bleak the national situation becomes, Habakkuk promises to watch, wait, and hope for the Lord to act (3:16–18). As 1:5 promises, the prophet is amazed at God's answer (3:16), but this dismay is preferable "to a growing distrust in the sovereign God."[10] In this hymn of praise the prophet "extols the virtues of the Lord. God's power (3:2), glory (3:3), splendor (3:4), wrath (3:8), mercy (3:13), and grace (3:19) are celebrated."[11] Thus Robertson can see the entire psalm as a "poetic elaboration of 2:4. Despite all the cataclysmic calamities and judgments that shall come from the hand of God himself, 'the justified (by faith) shall live by his steadfast trust.' This permeating theme of the book now finds explicit elaboration in terms of the necessity of God's intervention for faith

[4] Roberts includes ninety-eight textual notes detailing scholarly questions about text critical issues (*Nahum, Habakkuk, and Zephaniah*, 130–48).

[5] W. F. Albright, "The Psalm of Habakkuk," *Studies in Old Testament Prophecy Dedicated to T. H. Robinson,* ed. H. H. Rowley (Edinburgh: T & T Clark, 1950), 1–8; cp. R.D. Patterson, *Nahum, Habakkuk, Zephaniah,* 122–23; idem, "The Psalm of Habakkuk," *GTJ* 8 (1987): 163–94.

[6] Patterson, *Nahum, Habakkuk, Zephaniah,* 124, 225–26, 268–70.

[7] C. E. Armerding, "Habakkuk," EBC 7:520.

[8] Robertson, *Nahum, Habakkuk, Zephaniah,* 219.

[9] Armerding, "Habakkuk," 7:522.

[10] P. R. House, *The Unity of the Twelve,* JSOTSup 97, Bible and Literature Series 27 (Sheffield: Almond, 1990), 93.

[11] Ibid., 147.

to be victorious. *Faith triumphant in life by the intervening power of God* may serve as a theme of this chapter."[12] But that theme stretches further than just the present crisis of Israel and Babylon. "The hymn really concerns God's final reckoning with the wicked and the establishment of his order in all the earth … of the time when God brings his purpose for the earth to completion."[13]

1. The Title Verse (3:1)

[1]A prayer of Habakkuk the prophet. On *shigionoth*.

3:1 The final chapter of Habakkuk differs from the preceding chapters in content and in form. The title verse and the final instructions to the director of music take the form of a psalm. The majestic descriptions of the Lord associate the chapter with one of the divisions of the Psalter. Psalms 17; 86; 90; 102; and 142 contain similar titles using the word "prayer." Like many of the titles of the psalms, the title verse contains the name of the person associated with the psalm with a preposition normally translated as "to" or "for." It is also frequently used, however, to express a genitive relation between an indefinite noun and a definite one, as here (cp. 1 Sam 16:18; 1 Kgs 5:15; Ps 3:1 and many other Psalms). It can thus indicate possession or source/authorship.

The first verse of the chapter parallels the opening verse of the prophecy of Habakkuk. Both identify the author as Habakkuk the prophet. The first section of the book contains the oracle or burden of the prophet while the last section contains the prayer of Habakkuk. Walker and Lund saw the entire Book of Habakkuk as a "closely knit chiastic structure throughout,"[14] a chiasmus with three parts I (1:1–2:5), II (2:6–20), and III (3:1–19).

Several Old Testament scholars have questioned whether Habakkuk 3 belonged to the original prophecy. The chapter is not part of the Habakkuk Commentary of the Dead Sea Scrolls (though it is found in the Greek Septuagint, which is roughly contemporary with the Dead Sea Scrolls). Whether the absence of chap. 3 in the Dead Sea Scrolls affects authorship remains unclear since the author of the Habakkuk commentary may have used only those parts of the Book of Habakkuk which suited his purposes and interests.[15]

Though the form and content of chap. 3 differs from the preceding chapters, the conclusion of the prophet answers the needs and questions raised earlier. The chapters, as found in the canon of the Old Testament, are unified thematically. Chapter three serves as the logical and fitting conclusion to the

---

[12] Robertson, *Nahum, Habakkuk, Zephaniah,* 214; cp. Roberts, *Nahum, Habakkuk, and Zephaniah,* 149, who sees 3:3–15 as "Yahweh's last response to Habakkuk, and that response is the vision promised in 2:2–3."

[13] E. Achtemeier, *Nahum–Malachi,* INT (Atlanta: John Knox, 1986), 54.

[14] H. H. Walker and N. W. Lund, "The Literary Structure of the Book of Habakkuk," *JBL* 53 (1934): 355–70.

book.[16] "The chapter is a unified piece that forms an integral part of the argument of the larger book of Habakkuk. Without it, the book remains a fragment with no resolution of the prophet's laments, and with no vision for the prophet to record as he has been commanded to do. There is no justification for treating Habakkuk 3 as an independent piece or for denying its traditional attribution to Habakkuk."[17]

The title verse also contains the curious expression "*shigionoth*," a transliteration from the Hebrew. Though the meaning of the word is unknown, scholars agree that it is most likely a musical notation.[18] The final sentence of the chapter supports this supposition. Many similar terms in titles to the psalms are now thought to be names identifying hymn tunes or instructions concerning the playing of the music which apparently accompanied the psalm.

J. H. Eaton speculated concerning the original and later use of the psalm. Based on the elements found in the first and last verses (concerning musical instruments and the word "psalm") and other elements such as *selah*,[19] he affirmed its liturgical use, assigning it to the time of the Autumnal Festival at the preexilic temple.[20] Eaton speculated specifically concerning the origin of the psalm. He viewed the king and people assembled to pray for salvation—

[15] J. De Waard, *A Comparative Study of the Old Testament Text in the Dead Sea Scrolls and in the New Testament* (Leiden: Brill, 1965), 17–21. See Roberts' textual discussion (*Nahum, Habakkuk, and Zephaniah,* 148); he notes that chap. 3 is found in the Murabba'at text and in the Greek scroll of Habakkuk found in Qumran. He concludes that "it is extremely doubtful that it [the absence of chap. 3 in the Dead Sea Scrolls Habakkuk Commentary] bears witness to a Hebrew manuscript tradition lacking the chapter."

[16] For fuller discussions of the issues see D. E. Gowan, *The Triumphant of Faith in Habakkuk*, (Atlanta: John Knox, 1976), 68–71. Gowan argued that the psalm may have been used in worship at a time contemporaneous with the prophet. See also Robertson (*Nahum, Habakkuk, Zephaniah,* 212–13), who argues that "the substance of the material in chap. 3 itself provides the strongest evidence for its connection with the first two chapters." Robertson does grant that the musical notations suggest that the chapter circulated independent of the first two chapters even though it belonged to the original form of the book (*Nahum, Habakkuk, Zephaniah,* 214).

[17] Roberts, *Nahum, Habakkuk, and Zephaniah,* 149, giving a conclusion that might not be expected in such a critical commentary. Roberts does see archaic language here and suggests that the prophet has adapted an ancient hymn that spoke of God's past acts for his purposes into a thanksgiving vision report that describes God's new, present coming to save. See also Patterson, *Nahum, Habakkuk, Zephaniah,* 230.

[18] Robertson (*Nahum, Habakkuk, Zephaniah,* 215) follows Keil and says it could refer to a kind of performance that would reflect the excitement that should accompany the celebration of a psalm with such a disturbing topic. *HALAT* 4:1314, list attempts to understand the term: (1) a lament as found in titles of prayers in Akk.; (2) an ecstatic poem or a song of an ecstatic, a meaning derived from שׁגה, "reel, stagger"; (3) to set something in great agitation or excitement, based on Arabic.

[19] J. H. Eaton, "The Origin and Meaning of Habakkuk 3," *ZAW* 76 (1964): 144–71. Eaton concluded that though the meaning of סֶלָה is "not yet agreed, its liturgical character can be safely assumed" (p. 159).

[20] Ibid., 168–70.

for rain and fertility of land as well as deliverance from social and political oppression. God spoke through the prophet. "He was empowered to see, hear, and declare the life-giving victory of God which would eventually be seen to shape the destiny of all." Eaton further questioned whether the prophet may have composed the psalm in advance or whether it came "as the spontaneous product of intense inspiration in this public setting."[21]

As to its continued use, Eaton suggested that the psalm was carefully preserved in oral and written form, passing into usage by the prophetic choirs. Habakkuk's motive for preservation involved his belief that the psalm meant "the culmination of his dialogue with God embodied in chaps. 1–2."[22]

Whatever value Eaton's theory may have, it is surely correct that in his prayer, the prophet is embodying his conviction that God is in his holy temple (2:20) and so prays to or even in that temple and that the prophet speaks in first person but represents the entire worshiping community as he prays.[23]

2. Habakkuk's Petition (3:2)

[2]LORD, I have heard of your fame;
I stand in awe of your deeds, O LORD.
Renew them in our day,
in our time make them known;
in wrath remember mercy.

3:2 Of the entire chapter, only this verse takes on the form of a petition for God to do something. The remainder of the prayer describes the greatness of God in the past and expresses the prophet's quiet confidence in the work of God. The prophet's petition is threefold: preserve life, provide understanding, and remember mercy.[24] Patterson has shown the many literary connections between v. 2 and v. 16, creating an envelope of first person language around the third person vision report of God's theophany in vv. 3–15.[25]

Israel based its religion on the work of God rather than any mystical experience. The prophet based both his confidence and his petition on the work of God in the past. God's leading the people of Israel out of Egypt provided hope and instilled confidence that God would continue to work in the future. Seeing the Egyptians dead on the seashore provided conclusive evidence of the protection of God. Israel could never have escaped from Egypt. Only God's intervention saved Israel. Habakkuk does not present a desire to return to the "good old days," however. He knows that "the best is yet to come."[26]

---

[21] Ibid., 168–69.
[22] Ibid., 169.
[23] See Robertson, *Nahum, Habakkuk, Zephaniah,* 214.
[24] Ibid., 218.
[25] Patterson, *Nahum, Habakkuk, Zephaniah,* 268.

Habakkuk "wants God's purpose to be fulfilled, God's work on earth to be done, God's actions to be seen clearly by faith in the passages of history. This prophet concentrates on God and not on human beings."[27] The prophet declared his awe at the work of God. "I stand in awe" translates the Hebrew verb *yarēʾtî*, "I fear." In the Old Testament, the fear of the Lord is the beginning of wisdom and a virtual synonym for "religion."[28] Deuteronomy shows that "hearing and fearing" may be regarded as the natural reaction to an experience with God.[29] "When one hears Yahweh's mighty work recited in the cult, the appropriate response is fear or awe and a desire to see those ancient marvels repeated in the present."[30]

Based on the work of God in the past, the prophet called on God to "renew" his deeds in the present day. "In our day" and "in our time" translate identical Hebrew expressions that begin their respective clauses, which call on God to renew his work and to make his deeds known "in the midst of years," a reference to the prophet's time period.[31] Habakkuk called on God to work in the present day in the way he had worked in the past.[32] In a sense, Habakkuk meant for God to work a new redemption from the tyranny of Babylon as he had delivered Israel from the old tyranny of Egypt. The prophet showed his profound knowledge of the ways of God. The Lord is a God who acts on behalf of his people. "He made known his ways to Moses, his deeds to the people of Israel" (Ps 103:7).

The last request involves the mercy of God. "Wrath" and "mercy" are picturesque words. "Wrath" comes from a root word which means "to tremble" or "to shake."[33] "Mercy" comes from a word associated with the womb, indicating the compassion and tenderness which Habakkuk requested from the Lord.[34] This clause can mean that the prophet wanted God (1) to show mercy even in the midst of his anger with Israel, or (2) to show mercy to Israel even when God was angry with Israel's enemies.[35] The former interpretation seems to fit the situation in Judah better than the latter. Roberts notes the "disturbing ambiguity in the concept of God's work" for God had called out the Babylo-

[26] W. P. Brown, *Obadiah through Malachi.* Westminster Bible Companion (Louisville: WJK, 1996), 95.

[27] Achtemeier, *Nahum–Malachi*, 54–55.

[28] D. D. Garland, "Habakkuk," BBC (Nashville: Broadman, 1972), 264.

[29] See Deut 13:12; 17:13; 19:20; 21:21; Robertson, *Nahum, Habakkuk, Zephaniah,* 216, who says, "fear is a significant indicator of the faith of the prophet."

[30] Roberts, *Nahum, Habakkuk, and Zephaniah,* 131.

[31] Robertson listed a number of other suggestions for the meaning of בְּקֶרֶב שָׁנִים ("in the midst of the years"), none of which seems satisfactory. He concludes that the phrase refers "to the time between the two acts of judgment revealed to Habakkuk in the process of his earlier dialogue" (*Nahum, Habakkuk, Zephaniah,* 217).

[32] "Renew" translates Hb. חַיֵּיהוּ, lit. "make him live" as Robertson renders it, seeing a connection back to 2:4 and saying this is an example of the prophet "pleading the promises" (ibid.).

nians to discipline Israel (1:5–6). "Thus while asking for the fulfillment of the promised vision, the prophet qualifies it with the request that it be accompanied by mercy. He wants a renewal of God's work, but his early work of deliverance as in the exodus and conquest, not that of his more recent work against Jerusalem" (cp. Isa 10:12; 28:21).[36]

3. A Description of the Lord's Appearing in Great Power (3:3–15)

[3]God came from Teman,
the Holy One from Mount Paran. Selah
His glory covered the heavens
and his praise filled the earth.
[4]His splendor was like the sunrise;
rays flashed from his hand,
where his power was hidden.
[5]Plague went before him;
pestilence followed his steps.
[6]He stood, and shook the earth;
he looked, and made the nations tremble.
The ancient mountains crumbled
and the age-old hills collapsed.
His ways are eternal.
[7]I saw the tents of Cushan in distress,
the dwellings of Midian in anguish.
[8]Were you angry with the rivers, O LORD?
Was your wrath against the streams?
Did you rage against the sea
when you rode with your horses
and your victorious chariots?
[9]You uncovered your bow,
you called for many arrows. Selah
You split the earth with rivers;
[10]the mountains saw you and writhed.
Torrents of water swept by;

---

33 Patterson, *Nahum, Habakkuk, Zephaniah,* 230. Robertson sees רגז indicating agitation, excitement, or disturbance, noting that it occurs four times in this poem (vv. 2,7,16). Here he sees it referring to a time when the foundations will be shaken and the people of God go into exile. Thus he translates "trembling" rather than wrath (*Nahum, Habakkuk, Zephaniah,* 218). Roberts sees the omission of the personal suffix as an indication of intentional double entendre: "When you renew your work, let your wrath, which has brought such turmoil upon us, be tempered by the memory of your mercy, so that your new work, the fulfillment of the vision, will mean our salvation" (*Nahum, Habakkuk, and Zephaniah,* 151).

34 L. J. Coppes, "רָחַם (*rāḥam*)," *TWOT* 2:841–43.

35 Clark and Hatton, *Nahum, Habakkuk, and Zephaniah* 116.

36 Roberts, *Nahum, Habakkuk, and Zephaniah,* 150–51.

the deep roared
and lifted its waves on high.

[11]Sun and moon stood still in the heavens
at the glint of your flying arrows,
at the lightning of your flashing spear.
[12]In wrath you strode through the earth
and in anger you threshed the nations.
[13]You came out to deliver your people,
to save your anointed one.
You crushed the leader of the land of wickedness,
you stripped him from head to foot. Selah
[14]With his own spear you pierced his head
when his warriors stormed out to scatter us,
gloating as though about to devour
the wretched who were in hiding.
[15]You trampled the sea with your horses,
churning the great waters.

3:3 God answered the prayer in verse two with a theophany in the following verses (Hab 3:3–15). "The passage forms the most extensive and elaborate theophany to be found in the Old Testament."[37] A theophany describes an appearance of God in great power and glory, often looking to the events of the exodus and the giving of the law on Mount Sinai.[38] Exodus 19 provides one of the best examples of a theophany:

> "Behold, I come to you in the thick cloud." (Exod 19:9)
> Then it came to pass on the third day, in the morning, that there were thunderings and lightnings, and a thick cloud on the mountain; and the sound of the trumpet was very loud, so that all the people who were in the camp trembled." (Exod 19:16)
> Now Mount Sinai was completely in smoke, because the Lord descended upon it in fire. Its smoke ascended like the smoke of a furnace, and the whole mountain quaked greatly. And when the blast of the trumpet sounded long and became louder and louder, Moses spoke, and God answered him by voice" (Exod 19:18–19, NKJV).

The parallels with Habakkuk's psalm are striking. Gowan thought of the theophany as a "composite of images drawn from the most awesome elements in the natural world, used freely and poetically in an effort to represent the emotional effect of experiencing the immediate presence of God himself."[39]

The verb tenses in the Hebrew challenge the interpreter to understand the

---

[37] Achtemeier, *Nahum–Malachi*, 56.
[38] Garland, "Habakkuk," 264.
[39] Gowan, *The Triumphant of Faith in Habakkuk*, 74.

significance of the passage. Is the passage future, present, or past? Verb tenses in Hebrew do not give past, present, or future time as much as aspectual distinctions.[40] Most of the verbs in the theophany are in the perfect tense, usually used in past time contexts. The NIV, following the KJV and RSV, translates the verbs in the past tense. Does this describe an event in the past or one coming at some point in the future?

One way of using the perfect tense is the "prophetic perfect" or "perfective of confidence," a way of describing something so certain that the prophet could speak of it as already accomplished.[41] A modern phrase which captures the essence of the "prophetic perfect" is to say that "it's money in the bank," that is, "you can count on it, it's sure to happen." This would mean that the events described would occur in the future while emphasizing the certainty of the occurrence.[42] Achtemeier argues exegetically and theologically for a present interpretation of the theophany, saying that the tradition saw the coming at the Exodus when Israel proclaimed God as their king (Exod 15:18), while "this time he comes as King over all the earth: His glorious manifestation so illumines the heavens that all the earth responds in praise (cf. Ps 48:10)."[43]

Whether or not the interpreter can determine past or present. God answered the prayer of Habakkuk and acted according to his sovereign purpose. Habakkuk felt the certainty of God's work. At the conclusion of the theophany, the prophet determined to wait for God's redemption (Hab 3:16). As Robertson notes, "Judgement had been central to Habakkuk's dialogue with the Almighty. But the whole point had been salvation for God's own in the context of judgment."[44]

Theophany may seem an unusual element to follow petition. Robertson makes the connection: "the prophet provides a framework of faith which will sustain him as well as all those suppliants that would join him through the ages."[45] The first two lines in the text obviously are parallel statements: "God came from Teman, the Holy One from Mount Paran." Teman designated a district of Edom, located to the southeast of Judah. Teman dominated the fertile, well-watered area and served as a crossroads for important trade routes.[46] In

---

[40] For a thorough discussion see Waltke and O'Connor, *IBHS* §29–31. For a more concise explanation see D. W. Bailey and J. O. Strange, *Biblical Hebrew Grammar* (New Orleans: Insight, 1985), 51–53.

[41] Waltke and O'Conner, *IBHS* § 30.5.1e.

[42] Roberts says that the prophet has changed the perspective of his ancient models such as Deut 33:2–5; Judg 5:4–5; Ps 68:8–9; Exod 15:14–16, which portray God's theophany as a past event. "Habakkuk portrays God's march as though it were happening in the present, before his very eyes" (*Nahum, Habakkuk, and Zephaniah,* 151).

[43] Achtemeier, *Nahum–Malachi*, 56.

[44] Robertson, *Nahum, Habakkuk, and Zephaniah,* 219.

[45] Ibid., 220.

[46] V. R. Gold, "Teman," *IDB* 4:533–34.

this context, Teman probably stands for the area of Edom as a whole.[47] Paran was a mountainous area southwest of Judah in the Sinai Peninsula and west of the Gulf of Aqaba.[48] Together, the two areas refer to God's coming in the past when he gave the law and led the people of Israel through the wilderness. Both areas are to the south of Judah. When the people of Israel left Egypt, God led them through these areas. Thus, the passage reminded the hearers and readers of the work of God in the past and his majestic power in making a nation of the Hebrews.[49] Interestingly, as Armerding mentions, Sinai does not appear here even though it is the fountainhead of theophanic language. This gives the theophanic allusion a certain imprecision: "it recalls, not the exact details of a past event, but the dynamics of that event as an analogy for another revelation of God's presence and power."[50]

The name for God, *ʾĕlôah*, used in this instance is a rare and archaic name which probably evoked memories of the work of God in ancient times when he led the patriarchs through the land and the people through the wilderness.[51] Patterson sees this usage as demonstrating the enemies' perspective. They saw God "not as Yahweh, Israel's covenant God, but as Eloah, the Creator (Deut 32:15) and the Lord of the earth (Pss 18:31; 114:7)."[52]

"The Holy One" is parallel to "God" and came into prominence as a title for God in the Book of Isaiah, who used the term (thirty times) as his favorite title for deity. He thought of the "Holy One" as perfect moral purity. According to E. Jacob, "The term holy one of Israel means above all else that Yahweh keeps close to Israel, that he could not abandon them without denying himself. ... The entire history of Israel is the work of holiness; it is not without reason that the prophet who forged the title holy one of Israel is also the one who best showed the realization of God's plan in history; illustrating the exclamation of the psalmist: 'Thy way, O God, is in holiness' (Pss 77:14; 68:25).[53] For Habakkuk this holiness implied another aspect of God, what Roberts calls the "radical and dangerous otherness of God, his separation and elevation over all possible rivals."[54]

Habakkuk had already complained that the holy God was not showing forth his holiness when he let an unholy nation like Babylon attack his people

---

[47] Jer 49:20; Ezek 25:13; Amos 1:12 show that Teman generally stood for the Edomite territory as a whole.

[48] J. L. Mihelic, "Paran," *IDB* 3:657.

[49] Robertson, *Nahum, Habakkuk, and Zephaniah,* 222.

[50] Armerding, "Habakkuk," 7:525.

[51] אֱלוֹהַ is found fifty-seven times in the Old Testament, forty-one times in the Book of Job, with most of the occurrences found in the dialogue. See H. Ringgren, "אֱלֹהִים *ʾĕlōhîm,*" *TDOT* 1:272.

[52] Patterson, *Nahum, Habakkuk, Zephaniah,* 232.

[53] E. Jacob, *Theology of the Old Testament* (New York: Harper & Brothers, 1958), 90.

[54] Roberts, *Nahum, Habakkuk, and Zephaniah,* 151.

(1:12). Now having seen the larger plan and purpose of God, the prophet could take up the ancient tradition of theophany and talk of the Holy One coming in salvation. He saw "the righteousness and holiness of God in action. With impartiality he shall strike down first the ungodly in Israel, and then the heathen Babylonian."[55] The poet continued his meaningful use of divine titles as he artfully switched to the personal divine name Yahweh in direct address in v. 8 and then to the climactic Yahweh Adonai, Yahweh Lord, or Sovereign Lord, in v. 19.[56]

"Selah" occurs in the middle of the verse and probably denotes the solemnity of the presence of God. How the word was used in ancient times remains a matter of speculation. The best suggestions involve some kind of musical notation, possibly a time for the orchestra to play while worshipers meditated on the profundity of the subject. This may be the case in Habakkuk's psalm as well as Psalm 85 where the only use of Selah follows a verse describing the forgiveness of God. Did the psalmist or those who used the psalm in the temple expect the people to consider the importance of God's forgiveness? Except for Habakkuk's prayer, the term does not occur outside the psalms.[57]

The last part of the verse consists of two parallel lines, which introduce the thunderstorm in the following verses.[58] Here "glory" does not represent the usual Hebrew term, *kābōd*, but *hôd*, a term that can be applied to humans (especially the Davidic king) and to natural elements as well as to God, showing evidence of power.[59] Often *hôd* is used to reveal God's majesty, sometimes to foreigners (Isa 30:30) or to the whole world as here in Habakkuk (cp. Pss 8:1; 148:13; 1 Chr 29:11). "To a greater or lesser degree, the expression implies the experience of astonishment and joy in all passages.[60] Such majesty calls inhabitants of earth to "bow in reverent submission."[61] In this instance, "glory" probably includes the bright shining light associated with the presence of God, a meaning which fits well with the reference to lightning in the following verse.

God's "praise" refers to his attributes which inspire the praise of men, a usage found in other places in the Old Testament (Isa 60:18; 62:7). Such praise comes out of "God's former or typical help Ps 22:3; cf. 106:2; Isa 63:7; Jer 20:13)."[62]

---

[55] Robertson, *Nahum, Habakkuk, Zephaniah*, 223.

[56] Ibid., 222.

[57] T. H. Robinson, *The Poetry of the Old Testament* (London: Duckworth, 1947), 44–45.

[58] W. G. E. Watson points out that the nouns in the first line are both masculine and those in the second one both feminine, which calls attention to the "polar word-pair," "heavens/earth," These elements together with the verbs express *merismus* and convey the idea of completeness (*Classical Hebrew Poetry*. JSOTSup [Sheffield: JSOT, 1986], 31).

[59] See C. J. Collins, "הוֹד," *NIDOTTE* 1:1016.

[60] D. Vetter, "הוֹדד *hôd* highness, majesty," *TLOT* 1:355.

[61] Collins, "הוֹד," 1:1016.

3:4 The opening words carry emotion without specifying the reality to which they refer. Literally, they read: "Bright light [*nōgāh*] as light [ʾ*ôr*] will be." Translators attempt to define the image of the Lord's brightness. Is it lightening that is in view (GNB), or sunlight (NASB, NRSV, CEV), or the dawn (REB, NIV)? The term *nōgāh* is ordinarily used "for the shining of the celestial luminaries (2 Sam 23:4; Isa 13:10; Joel 2:10; 3:15). Ezekiel uses it to describe the radiant brightness of the glory of God (Ezek 1:4,28; 10:4). The psalmist also employs the root to depict the divine theophany in a context parallel to that of Habakkuk 3:4 (Ps 18:12,28; cf. 2 Sam 22:13,29)."[63] The following line may indicate the brightness of lightning is referred to. But as Selman explains, "the precise form of the brightness of God's presence is less significant than the fact that wherever God is, he shines with unusual brilliance."[64] In either case the phrase appears to be a simile. The Lord's brightness can only be compared to something as bright or striking as lightning or the first rays of the sun on a clear day. "God himself is present in brilliant light and blazing fire at the center of the storm cloud (cf. Ezek 1:4–28), but the intensity of his presence, his face as it were, is veiled and obscured by an envelope of darkness and thick clouds. Yet his glory cannot be completely hidden. From the brightness of his presence lightning bolts blaze forth, and in their brilliant but flickering light, God's veil is momentarily pierced, and some hint of the awesomeness of that fiery presence is revealed."[65]

In the second line of the verse there is no verb corresponding to NIV "flashed," and the word "rays" is literally "horns." Nevertheless, the sense of the Hebrew is adequately rendered by the NIV. Under certain conditions light emanates from a source in rays that bear some resemblance to horns, as the light that came from Moses' face (Exod 34:29,30,35).[66] This image would be especially fitting if lightening was in view, which can be compared to horns. J. H. Eaton has shown from ancient Near Eastern iconography that the storm god was usually pictured with a lightning bolt in his hand. Habakkuk may be alluding to this common image of the majesty of God.[67]

Though the NIV deletes the words, the last line of the verse begins with "and there," referring to the hand where God hides his power. The line is literally "and there the hiding place of his power." The word for "hiding place" occurs only here, but it is usually derived from the verb for "hide oneself."[68]

---

[62] L. C. Allen, "הלל," *NIDOTTE* 1:1037. Israel was chosen to praise God (Jer 13:11) and bears an obligation to do so eternally (Pss 22:23; 78:4).

[63] Patterson, *Nahum, Habakkuk, Zephaniah,* 233.

[64] M. Selman, "נגה," *NIDOTTE* 3:18.

[65] Roberts, *Nahum, Habakkuk, and Zephaniah,* 153.

[66] Selman, "קרן," *NIDOTTE* 3:989–90; M. L. Brown, "קֶרֶן," *NIDOTTE* 3:990–92.

[67] J. H. Eaton, "The Origin and Meaning of Habakkuk 3," *ZAW* 76 (1964): 148. See also Roberts, *Nahum, Habakkuk, and Zephaniah,* 135.

A possible meaning of the phrase "hiding place of his power" is that even the splendor of the theophany was a gracious veiling of God's being (cf. Judg 13:22; Job 26:14)."[69] Even more helpful is Robertson's comment that "the concentration of power and light in the *hand* of God at the time of his coming emphasizes his readiness to move into action for his people."[70]

3:5 "Plague" and "pestilence"[71] often accompanied war.[72] The verse means that God commanded all the forces of nature and used them to demonstrate his mighty power. People of the ancient world would recognize the destructive power signified by these words. "Plague" (*deber*) is often mentioned in the Old Testament as a weapon the Lord uses against his enemies (cf. Exod 5:3; 9:15; Lev 26:25; Num 14:12; Deut 28:21; 2 Sam 24:15; Jer 14:12) as well as "pestilence" (*rešep*; Deut 32:24).[73]

3:6 Habakkuk's prayer continued with a picture of the triumphant God overthrowing his enemies. The main questions concern how Habakkuk used this picture of the Lord and whether Habakkuk saw a picture from the past or a vision for the future. The answer to the latter question is disputed. For example, Roberts saw the prayer as a vision which Habakkuk saw. Habakkuk 3:3–15 "no longer celebrates Yahweh's march as a past event, but describes this event as it is happening, as a visionary experience."[74] Patterson understood the prayer to be Habakkuk's celebration of the Lord's march from the south, an event which happened in the past.[75]

Habakkuk saw in a past event the work of God. God's power and majesty

---

[68] *HALOT,* 284–85.

[69] P. Jenson, "חֶבְיוֹן/חָבְיוֹן," *NIDOTTE* 2:6.

[70] Robertson, *Nahum, Habakkuk, Zephaniah,* 225. Roberts uses textual emendation and an understanding of חֶבְיוֹן as referring to "the veil or envelope of dark clouds and gloom within which God hides his glory" to translate the verse: "Brightness like lightning appears, / A double-pronged bolt projects from his hand, / He places the covering for his might." In this understanding, God is revealed in momentary brilliance and then vanishes in darkness.

[71] Roberts translates רֶשֶׁף as "fever" and notes the relationship to the West Semitic god Resheph associated with fever (*Nahum, Habakkuk, and Zephaniah,* 135). E. R. Clendenen explains that the Hb. word רֶשֶׁף basically means "flame" and that it "is sometimes associated with arrows (see Ps 76:4[3]), lightning (Ps 78:48), or pestilence (Deut 32:24; Hab 3:5)" ("Religious Background of the Old Testament," in *Foundations for Biblical Interpretation,* ed. D. S. Dockery et al. [Nashville: Broadman & Holman, 1994], 297). The god Resheph was often associated with the Mesopotamian god Nergal, "god of war, plagues, sudden death, and ruler of the realm of the dead (cf. Jer 39:3,13)" (p. 281).

[72] Roberts identifies "Plague and Fever" as members of Yahweh's military entourage who both precede and follow him in his march against his enemies and sees them as common features of literature of the ancient Near East (*Nahum, Habakkuk, and Zephaniah,* 154). They show God's intention to punish his enemies. Patterson, *Nahum, Habakkuk, Zephaniah,* 235, also sees these twin agents as personified members of God's retinue.

[73] Roberts, *Nahum, Habakkuk, and Zephaniah,* 154.

[74] Ibid., 149.

[75] Patterson, *Nahum, Habakkuk, Zephaniah,* 230–33.

were the answers to Habakkuk's needs. Having seen the awesome God who led his people from the south into the land of promise, Habakkuk saw that God could deal with the sin of Judah and with the arrogance of Babylon.

He saw the Lord standing and shaking the earth.[76] These descriptions are standard for theophanies (Exod 15:14–16; Nah 1:3–5; Joel 2:10). "In every image there is the essence of power barely held in check by the deity and a recognized danger to the mortal involved. The setting for these divine/human encounters also adds to the awe of the moment and the importance of the messages being conveyed."[77]

The descriptions, with those which follow, suggested to the prophet that the Lord is a powerful God who can withstand the onslaughts of the enemy and overcome evil with little more than a glance. "The 'mountains' and 'hills' are symbols of grandeur, permanence, and security in the 'earth' (e.g., Gen 49:26; Deut 33:15); yet they too are revealed as frail and impermanent ... Although they appear to be 'age-old', in truth God alone is eternal."[78]

3:7 For the first and only time in the theophany (vv. 3-15), the prophet spoke in the first person, emphasizing that whether in the past or in the present the passage is a vision of some kind which reassured Habakkuk of God's faithfulness. Cushan and Midian suffered great distress.[79] Roberts points out that these two lands are pictured neither as Yahweh's friends nor as his enemies per se. "They are simply portrayed as nomads encamped along the line of march of a terrifying army, fearful that it may turn its attention to them."[80]

Midian lay to the east of the Gulf of Aqaba, though the Midianites were a nomadic tribe often found to the west of the Gulf as well. "Cushan" occurs only here in this form. Moses' wife was referred to as a Cushite, but this may or may not have associations with Cushan. Some interpreters associate Cushan with the land of Cush (an area near the horn of Africa, normally associated with Ethiopia). Since the verse appears to contain parallel thoughts, the best interpretation equates Cushan with Midian.[81] Cushan could have been a tribe of Midian. Taken in this way, both names indicate the Lord's journey

---

[76] Anthropomorphisms are pervasive in the Old Testament. Though the interpreter may wonder about God standing, hearing, or speaking, "it is by no means a 'primitive' way of speaking of God." On the contrary, this figurative picture of God harmonizes easily with the most sublime texts of the Old Testament. See Jacob, *Theology of the Old Testament,* 39–40.

[77] V. H. Matthews, "Theophanies Cultic and Cosmic: 'Prepare to Meet Thy God!'" in *Israel's Apostasy and Restoration* (Grand Rapids: Baker, 1988), 307.

[78] Armerding, "Habakkuk," 7:527. The last line could be translated "His are the ways of eternity."

[79] אָוֶן, "distress," usually refers to sin or iniquity, but also means trouble or misfortune as shown in *DCH* 1:154. Patterson (*Nahum, Habakkuk, Zephaniah,* 237) takes תַּחַת אָוֶן as a geographical name, Tahath-Awen in southern Transjordan. With no further attestation of such a place, this is a long reach to solve an exegetical problem.

[80] Roberts, *Nahum, Habakkuk, and Zephaniah,* 155.

from the South and continue to show his power and majesty. The "dwellings" (lit., "tents"; Exod 26:1–13; 2 Sam 7:2; Isa 54:2; Jer 49:29; 1 Chr 17:1) of the nations trembled before him.

3:8 Patterson refers to 3:8–15 as a "victory ode that sings of the mighty strength of Israel's Redeemer."[82] But v. 8 interrupts the theophany proper for the prophet to question the Lord concerning the purpose of his coming. The answer may be hinted at in the last line (lit., "your chariots of victory/salvation"), but the answer is not given until v. 13 ("You came out to deliver your people …").

The syntax of the first three lines are variously understood. The most natural translation would be "Was/is it against rivers that Yahweh burned/burns? Or against rivers was/is your wrath? Or against the sea was/is your rage?"[83] The change from third to second person is not that unusual in Hebrew[84] and may help to convey "the transition from God's coming to God's actually being present."[85] Others consider "Yahweh" to be a vocative and the subject of the verb in the first line to be furnished by the nouns "wrath" and "rage" in the second and third lines.[86] Nevertheless, the point is that the Lord's coming cannot be understood as anger against the rivers and the sea, but as Habakkuk explains in v. 13 it is to save the Lord's people.[87] According to Achtemeier these rhetorical questions convey the thought that the Lord had not come "to turn the rivers to blood once again," nor "to divide the Reed Sea," nor "to heap up the Jordan … because those rivers and that sea have been subdued and the natural world now serves its Creator." Rather he had come to conquer the evil of all nations.[88] Some consider that the rivers and seas refer to cosmic forces;[89] others see a fig-

[81] Patterson affirmed that Cushan along with Midian existed in the southern part of Transjordan (*Nahum, Habakkuk, Zephaniah,* 237). A compound noun with כּוּשָׁן it is found in Judg 3:8–11 in the name "Cushan-Rishathaim," a name of an oppressor of Israel. See Robertson, *Nahum, Habakkuk, Zephaniah,* 228; D. W. Baker, "Cushan," *ABD* 1:1219–20.

[82] Patterson, *Nahum, Habakkuk, Zephaniah,* 238.

[83] For this use of אִם as "or" in an interrogative sentence cf. *IBHS* § 18.1c and the example from 1 Kgs 22:15. Cf. also Isa 10:15.

[84] Using a grammatical form whose gender, person, etc. is other than what is expected is called *enallage* (F. B. Huey, Jr. and B. Corley, *A Student's Dictionary for Biblical and Theological Studies* [Grand Rapids: Zondervan, 1983], 71). Patterson, *Nahum, Habakkuk, Zephaniah,* 240, cites M. H. Pope's example (*Song of Songs*. AB [Garden City, N.Y.: Doubleday, 1977], 303) from Song 1:4.

[85] Robertson, *Nahum, Habakkuk, and Zephaniah,* 230.

[86] R. D. Haak, *Habakkuk,* VTSup 44 (Leiden: Brill, 1992), 93. He also considers יְשׁוּעָה at the end of the verse to be a vocative, "O Savior!"; thus forming an inclusio.

[87] According to W. C. Kaiser, Jr., the answer is given even in v. 12. "His anger is directed towards the wickedness of the nations of the earth" (*Micah-Malachi,* CC [Dallas: Word, 1992], 185).

[88] Achtemeier, *Nahum-Malachi,* 57.

[89] See Roberts, *Nahum, Habakkuk, and Zephaniah,* 155, who sees the questions as identifying "Babylon with the primeval powers of chaos" and thus suggesting "that this new march of Yahweh is a fundamental reenactment of Yahweh's primeval victories from which there emerged an ordered world under God's kingship."

urative description of the Babylonians.[90] Most see the focus on divine interventions of the past as depicting God's action in the future. "As the Babylonian comes to heap judgment on God's people, he may expect an awesome retaliation from the same One who has smitten rivers and sea in the past."[91]

The horses and chariots upon which Habakkuk sees the Lord riding (the Hb. preposition *ʿal* usually means "upon" rather than "with") are figurative descriptions of God's mighty power, as he comes against his enemies like a powerful army.[92] GNB sees the horses and chariots as figurative descriptions of the Lord riding on the clouds. Scholars have often seen these images as rooted in Ugaritic texts reflecting the Canaanite mythology of Baal riding in the clouds, but "such allusions may be acknowledged as based on a possible but unestablished hypothesis."[93]

3:9 The theophany continues in vv. 9–12. Habakkuk continued to affirm the Lord's symbolic work in the midst of the storm. The verse begins with an emphatic description of the Lord revealing his bow (lit., "with nakedness you bare your bow").[94] As Robertson explains, "now his ire has been aroused, and he acts with the full force of his destructive powers."[95] In the Old Testament, the bow symbolized power and warfare. The same Hebrew word for "bow" is used of the rainbow in Gen 9:13–16. "The picture tempts one to see God taking up that battle bow that he laid aside, according to Genesis 9:13, and using the great deep this time to defeat the wicked."[96]

The second line of the verse presents several problems of translation.[97] The three Hebrew words each have several possible meanings, and their rela-

---

[90] R. L. Smith, *Micah-Malachi,* 116; Brown, *Obadiah through Malachi,* 95.

[91] Robertson, *Nahum, Habakkuk, and Zephaniah,* 231. See also Patterson, *Nahum, Habakkuk, Zephaniah,* 239. Baker cites Exod 13:17–14:31; Josh 3:13–17; 4:21–24; Isa 10:26; 43:16; 50:2; Job 26:12–13; Pss 29; 89:9–10 (*Nahum, Habakkuk, Zephaniah,* 72).

[92] The idea of God riding a chariot is also suggested by Ezekiel's vision of God's glory in the first chapter. The term "chariot" does not occur in Ezekiel's vision, but see L. E. Cooper, Sr., *Ezekiel,* NAC (Nashville: Broadman & Holman, 1994), 68–69, and 1 Chr 28:18. Also see 2 Kgs 6:14,17; Pss 18:9–10; 68:17; Isa 66:15; Jer 4:13; Zech 6:1–7.

[93] Robertson, *Nahum, Habakkuk, Zephaniah,* 232, who continues: "Nothing in the language of the chapter requires that a source be found outside the historical traditions of Israel, and it appears much more natural to identify the frame of reference in terms of the great saving acts of the Exodus." Roberts (*Nahum, Habakkuk, and Zephaniah,* 153–58) begins with v. 4 to show parallels with the language associated with the Canaanite storm god in Ug. materials and with other Near Eastern literature, particularly cosmic battles in creation epics. He argues that "the imagery of visions, after all, like the imagery of dreams, arises from the scenes and symbols familiar to one in his or her cultural context." Patterson, *Nahum, Habakkuk, Zephaniah,* 239, also notes the allusion to the Baal cycle but notes the distinction that Baal fights other gods, while Yahweh fights human opponents.

[94] See Patterson's discussion of the translation difficulties in this line (*Nahum, Habakkuk, Zephaniah,* 240–41).

[95] Robertson, *Nahum, Habakkuk, Zephaniah,* 233.

[96] Achtemeier, *Nahum-Malachi,* 57.

tionship to each other is not clear. Without emendation the first word *(šĕbuʿôt)* can mean either "sworn" or "oaths." It is sometimes emended to a word meaning "spears." The second word *(maṭṭôt)* can mean "staffs, sticks, rods," "arrows," or "tribes" (see comment on this word in v. 14). The last word *(ʾōmer)* can mean "word," "speech," or "decree."[98] The NIV translation, which is reasonable, may be derived from the more literal rendering, "sworn are the arrows with a word." Chisholm explains the sense that these figurative arrows of the Lord are divinely commissioned to do their work destroying his enemies, much as the Lord's sword is commissioned in Jer 47:6–7 (see also Deut 32:40–43). Similarly, "in Ugaritic mythology the weapons of Baal are formally commissioned to smite Yam, the god of the sea."[99]

Again the Selah occurs in the middle of the verse, possibly calling the hearer or reader to pause and meditate on the possibility of the Lord taking his bow in hand to deliver the people of Judah. God's great power demands the consideration of his people. That God works on behalf of sinful people (Hab 1:2–4) is an astounding truth. Paul stood amazed that Christ died not for the good but for sinners (Rom 5:8).

The last line of the verse changes the scene from preparation to engagement in battle as the Lord strikes "with awesome force."[100] The connection with the thunderstorm in vv. 4–6 continues as the prophet described the power of a torrential downpour to change the landscape by rushing waters that isolated one portion of the earth from another. In a dry, mountainous area, large amounts of water wreaked havoc on the countryside (Judg 5:21). The mention of rivers also reminded the readers of the way God had provided water in the wilderness. All of this section of the psalm alludes to God's leading the people from Egypt (cp. Ps 77:16–20).

3:10 Poetic language functions differently than prose, a fact which this verse demonstrates. The mountains writhed in pain at the power of God. Whether the writhing, a word often associated with the movements of a woman at childbirth (e.g., Deut 32:18; Isa 13:8; 26:17; Jer 4:31), occurs because of an earthquake or at the torrents of water is unclear. The latter makes more sense because of the remainder of the verse which refers to the raging waters.

The last two lines are literally, "He gave the deep its voice / high its hands

---

[97] According to T. Laetsch, *The Minor Prophets* (St. Louis: Concordia, 1956), 347, F. Delitzsch had found more than a hundred different interpretations of this line. See the discussion in B. Margulis, "The Psalm of Habakkuk: A Reconstruction and Interpretation," *ZAW* 82 (1970): 409–42. Margulis describes the second line as "patently impossible" (p. 420).

[98] See Robertson, *Nahum, Habakkuk, Zephaniah,* 234. He makes the significant point that a form of מַטֶּה occurs in v. 14 as an instrument of war. The NIV translates it there "spears."

[99] R. B. Chisholm, Jr., *Interpreting the Minor Prophets* (Grand Rapids: Zondervan, 1990), 195.

[100] Patterson, *Nahum, Habakkuk, Zephaniah,* 242.

he lifted." The "deep" is the same word used in Gen 1:2: "and darkness was upon the face of the deep." It also alludes to the flood that overwhelmed the earth in the days of Noah (Gen 7:11; 8:2). The word often refers to the forces of the sea which obey the Lord (Exod 15:5,8; Isa 51:10; Ezek 26:19; 31:15; Pss 33:7; 77:16; 135:6). The "hands" of the deep, that is, "its waves," the Lord lifted like weapons against the earth.

3:11 The Lord who does not change is sovereign over history, not only in the past but also in the present and future as he works for his own glory and the redemption of his people. The long day of Joshua, another time when the Lord's enemies were judged, is probably the background for the reference to the sun and the moon standing still in the heavens (Josh 10:12–13). The prophet Habakkuk saw the work of God in the past and knew that God would also work in the future. Our faithful God who does not change is a subject preached throughout the Old Testament.

Lines two and three are parallel to one another, saying essentially the same thing in slightly different words. The sun and the moon stood still as in awe before the Lord's power. The glint of the flying arrows and the lightning of the Lord's flashing spear produced a sight to stand entranced before. If the symbolism points to the thunderstorm, the sun and the moon would be hidden by the clouds, but the verse pictures the sun and the moon as hiding from the power of the Lord (literally) "in their lofty residence" (usually applied to God; 1 Kgs 8:13; 2 Chr 6:2; Isa 63:15; Ps 49:14).

3:12 From the description of the natural world, the prophet moved to the description of the inhabitants of the world.[101] In synonymous parallelism, the prophet described God as moving across the earth in anger. The verb translated "strode through" can mean to "march," as in Job 18:14 where the wicked is "marched off to the king of terrors." But when God is the subject, "he marches in indignation (Hab 3:12), to save his people (Isa 63:1) and to lead them through enemy territory toward the Land of Promise (Judg 5:4; Ps 68:7[8])." According to the latter two passages, "God's marching is to be celebrated."[102] "If the presence of God that spread across the sky sent the earth into cataclysmic upheaval, so much the more will God's power moving through the area bring down the ungodly nations."[103]

"Thresh[ing] the nations" reminded the people of a common, everyday occurrence. Oxen moved around a circular pit filled with wheat or barley to separate the ears of grain from the stalk by trampling on the grain. Sometimes the farmer attached a sledge behind the animal to speed up the threshing.

---

[101] Roberts (*Nahum, Habakkuk, and Zephaniah,* 156) says, "These human enemies are identified with the mythological representatives of chaos precisely to underline the cosmic significance of Yahweh's coming intervention."

[102] V. P. Hamilton, "צעד," *NIDOTTE* 3:824.

[103] Patterson, *Nahum, Habakkuk, Zephaniah,* 247.

Amos pronounced judgment against Damascus for threshing "Gilead with sledges having iron teeth" (Amos 1:3). The Bible often used threshing as a symbol of judgment (Isa 41:15; Mic 4:13). Micah spoke of God's judgment in terms of horns of iron and hooves of bronze. Habakkuk saw God the Master Farmer threshing the nations, throwing them away as useless chaff in order to preserve his chosen people.

3:13 Why did Habakkuk see the vision of the Lord's majesty? It foreshadowed the redemption of God's people. The purpose of the theophany is to provide assurance that God would crush the head of the wicked and deliver his people.

The first two lines are almost identical. The same Hebrew word is used for "to deliver" and "to save" (probably better rendered "for the deliverance of"). God worked on behalf of his people to save them from the hands of the oppressor. "Anointed" meant chosen of God for a particular purpose. The term "anointed one" was used of the high priest or the king as a member of the Davidic line but could also indicate another divinely selected individual, such as Cyrus in Isa 45:1.[104] In this context the term has multiple meanings. In reference to the exodus it would most likely point to Moses. But in Habakkuk's day it referred to God's anointed people in general and a hoped-for king/deliverer in particular.[105] In the context of sacred canon it looked forward to Messiah, fulfilled in the life, sufferings, death, resurrection, and salvation of Jesus of Nazareth.

A more literal translation of the last two lines of the verse may prove helpful: "You smashed [i.e., wound with a blow; Num 24:8,17; Judg 5:26; Pss 18:38; 68:21; 110:5–6] (the) head from [i.e., "of"] (the) house of (the) wicked; laying bare (the) foundation to (the) neck." Although the term "foundation" suggests that "house" might refer to a building, the phrase "head of a house" is used consistently in the Old Testament of the leader of a household or family.[106] In this context it must refer to the one opposing God's people

---

[104] The term מָשִׁיחַ is found five times in the Latter Prophets, Isa 45:1; Lam 4:20; Dan 9:25,26; Hab 3:13.

[105] According to G. Van Groningen, the OT "refers to the people of God as the anointed ones" here and in Ps 105:15; Lam 4:20. Here "the term *anointed ones* is equivalent to God's chosen covenant people, who were called to be a holy people, a royal priesthood (Exod 19:5–6), serving as God's mediating people among all the nations of the earth (Gen 12:3)" (*Messianic Revelation in the Old Testament* [Grand Rapids: Baker, 1990], 31). Patterson (*Nahum, Habakkuk, Zephaniah,* 247,252) sees the anointed one here as originally referring to Moses but then applicable by later generations to the ruling member of David's line. See Robertson's argument that the reference is to Isaiah's prophecy of Cyrus in Isa 45:1 and that the particle אֶת in אֶת־מְשִׁיחֶךָ is the preposition "with" (*Nahum, Habakkuk, Zephaniah,* 237–38). Also see the discussion by Armerding, "Habakkuk," 7:530–31.

[106] Robertson, *Nahum, Habakkuk, Zephaniah,* 239, who cites Exod 6:14; Num 7:2; 17; 18; Josh 22:14; 1 Chr 5:24; 7:7,9.

and from whom the Lord would deliver them. The verse does not refer to a "land of wickedness" (NIV) but to a wicked people opposing the Lord and his "anointed." Patterson argues that the historical context would suggest the Egyptian Pharaoh as the "head of the house of the wicked," but that the timeless nature of the passage encompasses "all the victories that the Lord gave to Israel" as well as application to the Babylonians and to eschatological forces who will oppose the Lord.[107] Robertson explains "laying bare foundation to neck" as "the undercutting of all supportive strength. The extension of this assault to the neck indicates the thoroughness of the destruction."[108]

The theophany continues to communicate the providence of God. Habakkuk looked to the past to see the deliverance of God in the present. Using the analogy of Habakkuk, people in modern times can see the coming deliverance of God. The same God who led the people of Israel from Egyptian bondage and worked on behalf of the people of Judah will lead believers from the bondage of sin. Though times appear to be the worst imaginable, God will lead his people.

3:14 The prophet continued the description of the defeat of God's enemies. God would defeat the enemy with his own "spear" (plural in Hb.), a way of making the punishment fit the crime as in the taunts (Hab 2:6–20).[109] The word for "spear" *(maṭṭeh)* is the same as "arrows" in 3:9. It is often used in the Old Testament of a shepherd's stick or staff (Num 20:11; 1 Sam 14:27,43) "or the staff of a leader of lower status than God or king, such as a priest, prince, or tribal leader."[110] Thus it could be a weapon of warfare (Isa 10:24; 30:32) or a symbol of authority (Jer 48:17; Ezek 19:11). Its association with a "bow" in Hab 3:9 or with "piercing" in 3:14 is unusual, leading to the contextual translations "arrows" and "spears" in the NIV (cp. "rods" and "spears" of NASB, "arrows" and "shafts" of NJB, and "arrows" in both verses of NRSV, REB, and NKJV). "Arrows" may be the best understanding here based on its use in v. 9.

The object of piercing in the Hebrew text (following the masoretic accents) is "the head of his warriors."[111] The word *pārāz* occurs only here, and its meaning is uncertain (also uncertain due to a textual problem is whether it is singular or plural). Besides "warriors" (NIV, NRSV, NJB), it is sometimes translated "leaders" (REB), "villages" (NKJV), or "throngs" (NASB).[112] The point is that whatever weapons or abilities are possessed by those who use

---

[107] Patterson, *Nahum, Habakkuk, Zephaniah,* 248.

[108] Robertson, *Nahum, Habakkuk, Zephaniah,* 240. Patterson understands it as "taking away the weapons and defenses" or better "severe wounding or loss of life," citing Ps 141:8 (NIV, "do not give me over to death"; but NASB, "do not leave me defenseless").

[109] The verb נקב, "pierce," occurs seven times in the *qal* referring to boring through or piercing something (2 Kgs 12:9[10]; 18:21=Isa 35:6; Hag 1:6; Job 40:24; 41:2[40:26]; and here). See G. A. Long, "נקב," *NIDOTTE* 3:149.

[110] D. M. Fouts, "מַטֶּה," *NIDOTTE* 2:924.

[111] Neither the NIV nor the BHS text scans this verse according to the masoretic accents.

them to oppose rather than to further God's work will find those weapons or abilities turned upon themselves. Robertson points to Haman who was hanged on the gallows he built to hang Mordecai (Esth 7:10), Daniel's enemies who were thrown into the lions' den they had intended to be his end (Dan 6:24), and David's enemies who would fall into the pit they had dug for him (Ps 7:12–16; see also Judg 9:19–20; 2 Chr 20:24; Isa 9:20). "Rather than being terrified at the strength of their enemies, God's people ought to rest confidently in the assurance that the strength of the enemies' power only displays their capacity to destroy themselves."[113] God will allow his enemy to "set his own trap."[114]

The remainder of v. 14 is extremely difficult textually. According to Roberts it is "quite obscure."[115] In the Hebrew text the next line is "they stormed to scatter me." According to Robertson "me" is most likely the prophet who in spite of his visionary state still sees himself as experiencing the onslaughts of the enemy.[116] Robertson's translation of the rest of the verse is perhaps the best attempt to understand the Hebrew as it stands: "Their rejoicing (is) / as one who devours the poor in secret."[117] The enemy's fiendishness, he says, is portrayed by the image of a wild animal who "lurks and then drags and devours its prey in secret."[118] The wicked sought to destroy the people of God and even gloated over the prospects. "Poor" or "wretched" could refer to those in physical need, but it often referred to godly people suffering at the hands of the arrogant.

3:15 An analysis of the prayer shows that vv. 9–12 speak of nature while vv. 13–14 describe the opponents of the people of God. Verse 15 returns to the theme of nature, particularly to the victory over the waters at the exodus. The entire verse describes the victory of God over his enemies.[119] "The LORD is a warrior, the LORD is his name. … Who among the gods is like you, O LORD?

---

[112] Robertson favors "throngs," arguing that "the use of related terms points to the multitudes who lived in tents on the open plains, in distinction from the more restricted number who lived in walled cities." So with this word Habakkuk represents "the horde-like character of the enemy" (*Nahum, Habakkuk, Zephaniah,* 230). See also R. L. Smith, *Micah-Malachi,* 113. Patterson favors "warriors" (*Nahum, Habakkuk, Zephaniah,* 253), as does Haak, *Habakkuk,* 99–100.

[113] Robertson, *Nahum, Habakkuk, Zephaniah,* 240.

[114] Kaiser, *Micah-Malachi,* 185.

[115] Roberts, *Nahum, Habakkuk, and Zephaniah,* 157, sees extensive corruption in this verse (detailed in pp. 143–45). Patterson agrees (*Nahum, Habakkuk, Zephaniah,* 254).

[116] Robertson, *Nahum, Habakkuk, Zephaniah,* 241. Patterson divides לַהֲפִיצֵנִי, "to scatter me," into two words, yielding לַהֲפִיץ צְנִיעַ, "to scatter the humble" (*Nahum, Habakkuk, Zephaniah,* 254).

[117] Robertson, *Nahum, Habakkuk, Zephaniah,* 230.

[118] Ibid., 241. See also Baker, *Nahum, Habakkuk, Zephaniah,* 75.

[119] Roberts (*Nahum, Habakkuk, and Zephaniah,* 157) sees here a description of Yahweh driving his chariot over the carcass of Sea and trampling it with his chariot horses, the enemy here being clearly identified with the personified Sea of the ancient myth.

Who is like you—majestic in holiness, awesome in glory, working wonders? ... In your unfailing love you will lead the people you have redeemed. In your strength you will guide them to your holy dwelling. ... The LORD will reign for ever and ever." (Exod 15:3,11,13,18). Israel's victorious Redeemer in the past "could be counted on to save once more a repentant and submissive people."[120] Habakkuk had received his answer. "God refuses to stand above the fray and idly watch human injustice run amok. God crosses time and space to enter into the sinful messiness of human existence to save those who are most victimized by the world's ways."[121]

4. Habakkuk's Response to the Lord (3:16)

16I heard and my heart pounded,
my lips quivered at the sound;
decay crept into my bones,
and my legs trembled.
Yet I will wait patiently for the day of calamity
to come on the nation invading us.

"Before any redemption or restoration takes place the prophet embodies his own observation that 'the righteous will live by his faith' (2:4), for at the end of the book Habakkuk waits patiently for a 'day of calamity to come on the nation invading us' (3:16) that has not yet arrived. Basically Habakkuk represents the reader here. Judgment has begun, and the followers of Yahweh must wait to see the results of God's wrath."[122]

3:16 Verse 16 echoes v. 2. In both verses the prophet speaks in the first person and uses the verb "I heard." Also repeated is the root *rgz,* occurring as a noun in v. 2 (*bĕrōgez,* "in wrath") and a verb in v. 16 (*wattirgaz,* "pounded"). Verse two precedes the theophany with a petition requesting that God repeat his mighty acts of the past. Verse 16 follows the theophany with the prophet's response to wait quietly for the evil to come on the Babylonians. Coming into the presence of the Lord produces awe and disturbance at the revelation of God (cp. Dan 7:28; 8:27). As the Lord said to Isaiah, "This is the one I esteem: he who is humble and contrite in spirit, and trembles at my word" (Isa 66:2b). "That response includes the typical reaction of terror in the presence of Yahweh's majesty, but it also indicates the prophet's willingness at last to await the fulfillment of the vision as he had been instructed in 2:3."[123]

The first half of the verse (i.e., as indicated by the Hb. accents; in the English text it is the first four lines) describes Habakkuk's reaction to God's

---

[120] Patterson, *Nahum, Habakkuk, Zephaniah,* 250.
[121] Brown, *Obadiah through Malachi,* 96.
[122] House, *The Unity of the Twelve,* 147.
[123] Roberts, *Nahum, Habakkuk, and Zephaniah,* 149.

revelation.[124] His heart (*beṭen,* lit., "belly" or "insides") "pounded" (lit., "trembled," the same verb, *rgz,* translated "[be] in anguish" in v. 7), his lips "quivered,"[125] his body went limp,[126] and his legs "trembled" (*rgz* again).[127]

Habakkuk's response fits the biblical model. When Isaiah received the vision of God in the temple, he felt his own worthlessness and recognized his sin (Isa 6:5–7; cp. Luke 5:8). Modern day experiences with God should produce the same feelings of reverence and unworthiness. Though culture and custom have changed since the days of Habakkuk, neither God nor human nature has changed. We should expect the same response to the genuine revelation of God as that experienced by the prophet.

The prophet also saw the real significance of the theophany—God stood as ready to aid Judah in Habakkuk's day as he did the people of Israel in ancient times.[128] "The implication is that God's people do not need to worry about the political situation, however bad it may seem, because God will never abandon them."[129] The final victory was in sight "when evil is no more and those faithful, who have relied on God, have inherited his Kingdom. In short, Habakkuk in this vision granted him foresees something of an equivalent of Armageddon (Rev 16–19)—evil fallen, God triumphant in his final battle with wrong."[130] When the realization came over the prophet, he could

---

[124] In the second line in the Hb. text "at the sound" (לְקוֹל) is prominently placed first in the clause. See Robertson's discussion of the significance of God's voice as it is elaborated in Ps 29 (*Nahum, Habakkuk, Zephaniah,* 243).

[125] The verb occurs only here and in 1 Sam 3:11; 2 Kgs 21:12; Jer 19:3. There the subject is the "ears" that shall "tingle" at the sound of bad news. Cf. R. H. O'Connell, "צלל," *NIDOTTE* 3:805–6.

[126] The same image of decay in the bones occurs in Prov 12:4; 14:30, the only other uses of רָקָב, "rottenness, decay." The verb is used of rotting wood in Isa 40:20.

[127] This fourth line of v. 16, וְתַחְתַּי אֶרְגָּז, is literally "and beneath me I trembled." BHS rejects the masoretic accents and places אשׁר in this clause rather than in the next, repointing it as אֲשֻׁרַי, "my steps." Thus it can serve as the subject of the repointed verb, יִרְגְּזוּ. Thus the NRSV translates, "and my steps tremble beneath me." Patterson repoints only אשׁר as אָשׁוּר, "[foot]step" yielding a literal "I experienced a trembling [foot]step [beneath me]," more smoothly, "And I moved with faltering footsteps" (*Nahum, Habakkuk, Zephaniah,* 258).

[128] Robertson has quite another view of the reason for Habakkuk's reaction to God's word. He translates אֲשֶׁר as "because" and explains Habakkuk's reaction as caused by "the terrible devastation that God's own people must undergo prior to their full possession of the premises" (*Nahum, Habakkuk, Zephaniah,* 243). The "calamity" (צָרָה, "adversity") he interprets as coming on God's people rather than on the Babylonians, translating, "because I must wait quietly / for the day of adversity, / for the coming up of the people / who will invade us" (p. 242). Armerding agrees that the cause of Habakkuk's "inward upheaval" was "the immanence of God's 'wrath' on Israel (v. 2) and … the uncertainty of any time-frame that accompanies the subsequent judgment on the enemy" ("Habakkuk," 7:532). "For Habakkuk to see such things that were veiled to his contemporaries was to experience distress. … To see beyond them, to the Holy One who appointed them, was to demonstrate the greatness of faith and to find strength to "wait quietly" (cf. 1:12; 2:2–4; 3:18–19)" (p. 533).

[129] Clark and Hatton, *Nahum, Habakkuk, and Zephaniah,* 134.

[130] Achtemeier, *Nahum–Malachi,* 58.

vow with assurance to "wait patiently" (lit., "rest"[131]), knowing that the situation was in the capable hands of an almighty God who would bring about his perfect will according to his eternal timetable. Habakkuk had prayed, and there was nothing further for him to do (Mic 7:7).

God answered Habakkuk's questions. How could God use a wicked people such as the Chaldeans to punish a nation more righteous than itself? God's answer was that though he might use Babylon to punish Judah's sins, he also would punish Babylon for its sin. "The day of calamity" would come on Babylon.[132] What an amazing transformation! Because the prophet had been honest with God and took his genuine questions to a caring God, Habakkuk began to look at the world from a different perspective. Habakkuk had moved from "how long?" (Hab 1:2) to "I will wait patiently."

5. Habakkuk's Confidence in the Lord (3:17–19)

17Though the fig tree does not bud
and there are no grapes on the vines,
though the olive crop fails
and the fields produce no food,
though there are no sheep in the pen
and no cattle in the stalls,
18yet I will rejoice in the LORD,
I will be joyful in God my Savior.
19The Sovereign LORD is my strength;
he makes my feet like the feet of a deer,
he enables me to go on the heights.

For the director of music. On my stringed instruments.

3:17 Of all the wonderful passages in the Old Testament, the climax to Habakkuk's psalm fits as one of the great affirmations of faith. His circumstances have not changed. The outer world with its evil conduct and rapacious

---

[131] In this sense the word is opposite in meaning to רָגַז, "tremble," as seen in Job 3:26. According to R. L. Harris, "נוּחַ (*nûaḥ*)," *TWOT* 2:562, נוח "signifies not only the absence of movement but being settled in a particular place (whether concrete or abstract) with overtones of finality, or (when speaking abstractly) of victory, salvation, etc." The word relates, he says, to "the presence of security."

[132] The NIV has interpreted the preposition in לְיוֹם as marking the object of the verb אָנוּחַ, indicating what the prophet was waiting for, i.e., a day of "calamity" to fall on the Babylonians. If following Patterson the preposition is considered one of specification ("with respect to") it could refer to the coming "calamity" to come on Judah when the Babylonians invaded. Patterson translates, "I will rest during the day of distress (and) / during the attack against the people invading us" (*Nahum, Habakkuk, Zephaniah,* 255). "In the midst of conflict and distress, the prophet rests securely in the knowledge of God's purposes" (p. 259).

warfare remains the same. God's people remain in time of lamentation.[133] The prophet, however, turns to praise. Why? He has heard God's voice and seen God's vision. He knows the ultimate outcome of history.[134] Thus vv. 17 and 18 serve as fitting climaxes to the psalm of Habakkuk and to the book as a whole. Here the prophet accepts God's program, thus resolving his contention with God expressed so strongly in chaps. 1–2. "Even with all the punishment imagery ..., the fact that the book concludes with the prophet rejoicing in the saving power and strength of God indicates that Habakkuk felt Yahweh's impulse to judge in no way dismisses the Lord's loving nature."[135]

The structure of the passage helps to determine the meaning. Verse 17 consists of six conditional clauses controlled by the word "though" (which in the Hb. text occurs only at the beginning of the verse). Did Habakkuk see these statements as possibilities or fact? Though the six clauses are introduced by "though," suggesting possibility, the events described appear too real to be seen as mere possibility. Could these events seem imminent? Did Habakkuk and the people of Judah face such catastrophes? Imminent possibilities help produce growing faith. Habakkuk demonstrated faith tested and refined by the genuine fires of life.

The six clauses of v. 17 seem to be in ascending order of severity, with the loss of figs ranking least and the loss of the herd in the stalls causing the greatest economic damage. Figs served as a delicacy in Israel, but their loss did not produce severe hardship. Grapes provided the daily drink, but again the loss of the fruit of the vine would produce inconvenience rather than privation. The olive crop on the other hand produced oil for cooking and lighting. Grain (barley and wheat) provided for the staple diet of Palestine. The failure of the fields to produce food might mean starvation for large segments of the population. Both sheep and cattle made up much of the wealth of Palestine. Sheep and goats provided wool and the occasional meat for the Israelite diet. Hebrews did not normally eat cattle, but they were used for preparing the soil for planting and other heavy work.

The loss of any of these individually might be survived. Together, the losses spelled economic disaster and devastating loss of hope—loss of their daily provisions, loss of their economic strength, loss of the Lord's blessing due to their sin (Lev 26; Deut 28; Amos 4:6–9; Hag 1:6–11). But Habakkuk knew that "man does not live on bread alone but on every word that comes from the mouth of the LORD" (Deut 8:3; see also Phil 3:7–8). "The entire

---

[133] The distressing circumstances described in v. 17 could be yet future, resulting from the invading Babylonians. "The passage describes a series of facts that shall transpire. These dreadful things shall happen" (Robertson, *Nahum, Habakkuk, Zephaniah,* 245).

[134] Cp. Achtemeier, *Nahum–Malachi*, 58.

[135] House, *The Unity of the Twelve*, 180.

present world order may pass away, but God's grace to his people shall endure."[136]

3:18 The sentence beginning with the six "concessive" ("though") clauses of v. 17 are continued in v. 18 with two clauses expressing contrast or "counterexpectation."[137] The contrastive sense of these clauses is indicated by the word order of the first clause (beginning *waʾănî*, "yet I"). In v. 18 the prophet gave his reaction to the imminent events. Let the nation face the worst economic disasters; still the prophet vowed to remain faithful to the God of his salvation.

By means of parallel statements, the prophet proclaimed his desire to serve the Lord and to honor him with his life. Emphasis is placed in the first clause on "in the LORD," which immediately follows the subject, "yet I." Though he might lose everything in this world which normally brings life and joy, Habakkuk vowed to rejoice in the Lord and to joy in God.[138]

More than "toughing it out" or "hanging in there" Habakkuk would be "joyful" in the God of his salvation (cf. Jas 1:2; Rom 8:35–37).[139] Habakkuk exhibited the kind of relationship with God which enjoyed the divine Person more than the things he could do for the prophet. He put God above the fray of life, rejoicing in him and worshiping him regardless of the circumstances. "The words for 'rejoicing' here represent strong emotions. Habakkuk had used them previously to express his anxiety over the unbridled avarice of the Chaldeans (1:14–15). His choice of them here underscores his repentant heart and triumphant faith. Together they express his resolve not merely to rest in the Lord's will through everything that would come to pass but to rejoice fully in his saving God. Israel's covenant Lord was yet on the throne; that meant eventual blessedness for prophet and people alike (cf. Deut 30:1–10)."[140]

In a world which sees almost everything in economic terms, believers need to consider the profundity of Habakkuk's faith. Though the worst things in life happen, believers need a faith which depends on the God of the universe and worships him as the true Lord of life.

3:19 Habakkuk's final words express his faith. The Lord would carry him through life. Habakkuk did not trust in the power of nature or in his own

---

[136] Robertson, *Nahum, Habakkuk, Zephaniah,* 245.

[137] Patterson understands the כִּי beginning v. 17 to be circumstantial (*Nahum, Habakkuk, Zephaniah,* 259), but this is made less likely by the semantic contrast between vv. 17 and 18.

[138] Note the same term עזל, "rejoice," is used with God as the object in Ps 28:7 ("my heart *leaps for joy*"); 68:4[5]; 96:12 ("let the fields *be jubilant*"); 149:5; Zeph 3:14.

[139] See M. Lloyd-Jones, *From Fear to Faith: Studies in the Book of Habakkuk* (London: Inter-Varsity, 1953), 68–69. Note William Cowper's poem based on these verses from Habakkuk, "In Him Confiding," set to music as "Sometimes a Light Surprises." The poem is quoted in Kaiser, *Micah-Malachi, 198–99.*

[140] Patterson, *Nahum, Habakkuk, Zephaniah,* 257.

ability to make money. He trusted in the Lord who is the Lord of nature. This is the only place outside the Psalms (16:2; 68:20; 109:21; 140:7; 141:8) that the phrase *yahweh ʾădōnāy* ("Sovereign LORD") occurs, expressing the divine personal name preceded by his title. The names emphasize the power and majesty of God. Habakkuk used the strongest names for God available. For this reason, the NIV translates the names as "The Sovereign LORD." "The Hebrew is 'Yahweh, my Lord' which links the traditions of covenant assurance with personal dedication and commitment."[141]

This God of nature who is all powerful provides the needs of life. In a land filled with places to stumble, Habakkuk emphasized the faithfulness of God. The hind (a female deer) was noted for its surefootedness in high places. Drawing on an image from Ps 18:34, Habakkuk acknowledged the protection of God in every experience of life. "Surefooted, untiring, bounding with energy, the Lord's people may expect to ascend the heights of victory despite their many severe setbacks. The heights of the earth, the places of conquest and domain, shall be the ultimate possession of God's people."[142]

In an unsure world, Habakkuk experienced the joy and peace of serving the sovereign Lord of creation. Habakkuk questioned God concerning his work and learned that God is indeed at work. The Lord God is at work accomplishing his purpose over the earth. Like Habakkuk, believers who live in unsettled times can find strength in the God who works in history to accomplish his purpose.

The book ends with a note common to psalms concerning the use of the psalm. Apparently, the psalms were set to music and used in the temple. The note to the "director of music" gave guidance concerning use of the psalm. The phrase is found fifty-five times in the titles of the psalms and is the second most often used phrase in the titles of the psalms. Except for the psalms and Habakkuk 3, the note to the "director of music" is not found in the Hebrew Bible. Robinson notes two other possible translations, "in regard to the musical rendering" and "for propitiation," but opts for the traditional "to the choirmaster" or to the "director of music."[143] "This psalm of submission was to be celebrated in the congregation throughout the generations. It was not merely a personal resolution of faith achieved by the prophet for himself alone."[144]

Patterson's conclusion is a fitting one: "God's prophet had walked a precarious path. But lest we condemn Habakkuk too readily, we need to remem-

[141] J. D. W. Watts, *The Books of Joel, Obadiah, Jonah, Nahum, Habakkuk, and Zephaniah,* CBC (Cambridge: University Press, 1975), 152.

[142] Robertson, *Nahum, Habakkuk, Zephaniah,* 247.

[143] Robinson, *The Poetry of the Old Testament,* 116–17.

[144] Robertson, *Nahum, Habakkuk, Zephaniah,* 247–48.

ber that the Lord did not do so; He merely corrected him. Ultimately Habakkuk's implanted faith bore spiritual fruit. … When times of doubt and discouragement come, as they inevitably do, the believer needs to come to God … and share his concerns with Him. Like Habakkuk, he needs to come to God's Word and get a fresh glimpse of who and what God is and so come to a place of renewed trust in the one who alone is truly God and therefore sufficient for all of life. May Habakkuk's test of faith and triumphant joy in his saving Lord be an inspiration and example to all who must travel life's road!"[145]

---

[145] Patterson, *Nahum, Habakkuk, Zephaniah,* 263.

Zephaniah

SECTION OUTLINE

1. The Historical Setting
2. Zephaniah, the Man
3. Zephaniah, the Book
4. The Date of the Book
5. The Message of Zephaniah
   (1) The Day of the Lord
   (2) The Nature of God
   (3) The Sovereignty of the Lord
   (4) Human Sin
   (5) The Mercy of the Lord
   (6) Israel as the People of God
   (7) The Nations as People of God
   (8) The Doctrine of the Remnant
7. The Text of Zephaniah

INTRODUCTION

The Book of Zephaniah[1] focuses on the needs of the people of God to live in righteousness before God. A people who do not respect the needs of the oppressed and care for genuine worship before God cannot long prosper. Zephaniah preached about the Day of the Lord and the impending judgment of the people of Judah. Zephaniah also believed in the sovereignty of God to preserve his remnant. Zephaniah delivered his message in the dark days before Josiah's reform became evident. His message ever reminds the reader that God desires humble submission unto him.

---

[1] For a recent overview of study of Zephaniah and the limited critical appreciation for it, see P. R. House, *Zephaniah, a Prophetic Drama,* Bible and Literature Series 16 (Sheffield: Almond Press, 1988), 9–14. He notes that Calvin and Luther set the agenda for Zephaniah study by focusing on author, situation, and date in Josiah's reign (p. 11).

1. The Historical Setting

For three-fourths of the seventh century B.C., the nation Judah was in a deep religious and political recession.[2] Both Ahaz and Hezekiah were submissive to the foreign policy of Assyria as directed by its two last strong kings—Esarhaddon, who invaded Egypt, and Ashurbanipal, who prided in his cultural achievements and dominated the smaller states of the Near East. Manasseh seemed willingly to accept subservience to Assyria and probably profited by adherence to his superiors. All kinds of vices returned to Judah during this wicked reign. According to the author of the Kings material, Manasseh led the people to do more evil than in Ahab's day or in the time when the Canaanites ruled the land (2 Kgs 21:9). Along with Assyrian divinities, the Baals and the Ammonite god Molech were served. Manasseh burned his own son as an offering to this god (2 Kgs 21:6). The two year reign of his son Amon was no better religiously or politically.[3]

Thus, when Josiah came to the throne and the powerful Assyrian Empire began to crumble,[4] a new era of hope began to dawn. This hope was short lived. Instead of providing independence and true religious reform, the last quarter of the seventh century B.C. proved to be "one of the most fateful periods of the ancient Near East, and particularly in the history of Judah."[5]

Even though the decline of Judah can be traced back to the reign of Manasseh and beyond, the beginning of Josiah's reign was a time of hope and optimism. Assyria was reeling because of its lack of effective leadership. All of the ancient Near East was in ferment. "With a self-conscious and ambitious Egypt in the south, and with the movements of Scythian and other hordes in the north, everything was in the melting pot, and no one could have foreseen who would inherit the might of Assyria."[6] Even before the death of Ashurbanipal, small nations were brash enough to revolt. In 641 B.C. Elam withheld its tribute. The assassination of Amon, king of Judah, in 640 may reflect a desire by many of the people of Judah to break away from their Assyrian overlords.[7] Malamat suspected that the plot was engineered by an anti-Assyrian party who undertook this means of striking for a change in national policy.[8] Other Judeans apparently felt that the time was not ripe for such a course of action. Thus, the people of the land executed the assailants of Amon and placed his

[2] For a current historical review see W. C. Kaiser, Jr., *A History of Israel* (Nashville: Broadman & Holman, 1998), 371–85.

[3] Cf. N. K. Gottwald, *A Light to the Nations* (New York: Harper & Row, 1959), 327–28.

[4] See Kaiser, *A History of Israel,* 385–95.

[5] A. Malamat, "A New Record of Nebuchadrezzar's Palestinian Campaigns," *IEJ* 6 (1956): 246.

[6] S. A. Cook, "The Fall and Rise of Judah," *CAH,* 3d. ed., 394.

[7] J. A. Thompson, *The Bible and Archaeology* (Grand Rapids: Eerdmans, 1962), 147.

[8] Malamat, "The Historical Background of the Assassination of Amon King of Judah," *IEJ* 3 (1953): 26–29.

eight year old son, Josiah, on the throne (2 Kgs 21:24).

Not much is known of the years when Josiah was still a child. Probably the kingdom was governed by wise and trusted advisors who steered Josiah and the nation to the dawning of a new era. The beginning of Judah's political independence and religious reform coincides almost exactly with Assyria's decline as the leading world power. In 627 B.C. Ashurbanipal died, and Josiah began to make major policy changes as he "began to seek the God of David his father" (2 Chr 34:3). Apparently, this indicates that he renounced the gods of Assyria and rejected completely the syncretistic policies of his grandfather, Manasseh.[9]

Josiah's second stage of reform took place when Ashur-etil-ilani, Ashurbanipal's son, died. "He began to purge Judah and Jerusalem of the high places, the Asherim, and the graven and the molten images. And they broke down the altars of the Baals in his presence: and he hewed down the incense altars which stood above them; and he broke in pieces the Asherim and the graven and the molten images, and he made dust of them and strewed it over the graves of those who had sacrificed to them. He also burned the bones of the priests and on their altars, and purged Judah and Jerusalem" (2 Chr 34:3–5).

The fact that this reform could be carried out as far to the north as Naphtali (2 Chr 34:6–7) indicates that Josiah also had military control over the Assyrian provinces of Samaria and Megiddo. Thus, while still a nominal vassal of Assyria, Josiah began a reunification of the Davidic rule over all of Palestine.[10] As long as he remained a nominal vassal of Assyria who controlled the provinces of Samaria and Megiddo as well as the tributary state of Judah, Josiah would be free to carry out his reforms. Therefore, there was no need at all for the reconquest of Northern Israel.[11]

Josiah's reform may have been as much political as religious. In reality, it would be very difficult to distinguish the two. By removing the elements of the Assyrian State religion from the sanctuary, Josiah, in effect, revoked his vassal relationship. Either Assyria still considered Josiah loyal, or else it was too weak to enforce its sovereignty over its vassals because no reprisal came from Assyria.[12]

There can be little doubt that Josiah's political and economic success increased enthusiasm for his religious reforms. When Jeremiah said, "Judah did not return to me with her whole heart, but in pretense, says the Lord" (Jer

[9] G. E. Wright, *Biblical Archaeology,* rev. ed. (Philadelphia: Westminster, 1962), 176.

[10] Y. Aharoni, *The Land of the Bible: A Historical Geography,* trans. A. F. Rainey (Philadelphia: Westminster, 1962), 47.

[11] W. F. Albright, "The Biblical Period," *The Jews: Their History,* ed. L. Finkelstein (New York: Schocken Books, 1949), 47.

[12] M. Noth, *The History of Israel,* trans. S. Godman (London: Adam & Charles Black, 1958), 171.

3:10), he may have been referring to the fact that the people were more anxious about Josiah's political accomplishments than they were in genuine experience of real religion.

Only a few scattered references can be found concerning the size of Josiah's kingdom. At some point during the reform, Bethel, which was formerly on the border of the Israelite kingdom and later on the boundary of the Samaritan province, was controlled by the Southern Kingdom. This conquest was one of the main points of Josiah's religious reformation (2 Kgs 23:4–15). In addition to asserting his authority over the old Davidic kingdom, Josiah also reached out into Philistine territory as Ekron and Japho formed part of his sphere of influence. These latter areas had not even belonged to the empire of David and Solomon.[13] When the Book of the Covenant was discovered in Josiah's eighteenth year and its far reaching reforms carried out, Josiah probably was the ruler of an independent state which included most of Palestine from the Negeb to Galilee.[14]

With the finding of the Book of the Law in 621 B.C., when the temple was being repaired, the main body of Josiah's religious reform began to take shape. These were probably not simple repairs, but repairs designed to remove from the Temple every trace of foreign influence. At any rate, a manuscript of the Law was found which contributed to the most thorough-going reform in Judah's history.[15] Apparently, this book was part or all of the Book of Deuteronomy.[16] After consulting with Huldah the prophetess as to the veracity of the book, Josiah summoned the people to the Temple for a ceremony of covenant renewal where they made a covenant before Yahweh to walk after Yahweh and to be obedient to his commandments. Anderson equated this experience with God with the story in Joshua 24 of the covenant renewal at Shechem and with the ancient covenant ceremony in Exod 24:3–8.[17] For the first time since the period of the Judges the people as a whole kept the Passover (2 Kgs 23:21–25). Evidently, the main purpose of the reform was "to revive the spirit and the legal tradition of the original Mosaic covenant as the ideology of the newly revived state."[18] Bright noted how Josiah carried out the reform: (1) there was a consistent purge of foreign cults and practices, (2) the high places were destroyed in both the north and the south, and (3) all public worship was centralized in Jerusalem.[19] For Josiah, himself, the reform

[13] Ibid., 273.

[14] Aharoni, *The Land of the Bible*, 250.

[15] B. W. Anderson, *Understanding the Old Testament,* 2d ed. (Englewood Cliffs: Prentice-Hall, 1966), 308.

[16] J. Bright, *A History of Israel,* 3d. ed. (Philadelphia: Westminster, 1959), 319.

[17] Anderson, *Understanding the Old Testament,* 308.

[18] Wright, *Biblical Archaeology,* 177.

[19] Bright, *A History of Israel,* 318–19.

probably indicated the final break with Assyria. His "declaration of independence from Assyria could hardly have been made in clearer terms!"[20] Even if this reform were mainly external, it must have made a profound impact on Judah and its people. It could conceivably have delayed its fall for a number of years.

While Judah was asserting its independence and purifying its religion, Babylon and Assyria were changing positions of authority in world politics. After the death of Ashurbanipal in 627 B.C., Assyria's fortunes immediately plummeted. Nabopolasser of Babylon sought and gained his independence in 626 B.C.

For the next ten years (626–615 B.C.) Babylon and Assyria attacked and counterattacked each other over Assyria's holdings in southern Mesopotamia. Eventually, Nabopolasser took Nippur and freed all of Sumer and Akkad.[21] In this same year a coalition of Medes and Babylonians systematically began to reduce the Assyrian Empire by destroying its major strongholds. By 614 B.C. Cyaxares, the Mede, had defeated Ashur, one of Assyria's capitals. However, the main city of the empire, Nineveh, did not collapse until 612. Finally, in 610/609 B.C. the final bastion of Assyrian resistance crumbled as the Medes and Babylonians captured Haran. "No one, as far as we know, sat on the ruins of Nineveh to write a lamentation."[22]

In 609 B.C. Egypt, under Pharaoh Necho II, went to the aid of Assyria at Carchemish to help Ashur-uballit in a last effort to retake Haran from the Babylonians. Egypt, consistent with its foreign policy, sought to gain firm control of Syria-Palestine. Josiah, naturally, opposed Egypt and Assyria because they posed a strong threat to his religious reforms and political independence.[23] Josiah resisted Necho and died in battle. Amid great lamentation, his body was taken back to Jerusalem in his chariot (2 Chr 35:20–24).

M. B. Rowton argued that Josiah's action detained Necho long enough to keep him from aiding the Assyrians. "Thus, it seems very probable that the last of the great Jewish kings laid down his life in a truly heroic and entirely successful bid to avenge the dreadful wrongs his nation had suffered at the hands of Assyria."[24]

2. Zephaniah, the Man

Like most of the minor prophets, we know little about the prophet

[20] Anderson, *Understanding the Old Testament,* 308–9.

[21] G. Roux, *Ancient Iraq* (Baltimore: Penguin, 1964), 340.

[22] Ibid., 342.

[23] H. H. Rowley, "The Prophet Jeremiah and the Book of Deuteronomy," *Studies in Old Testament Prophecy* (Edinburgh: T & T Clark, 1957), 162.

[24] M. B. Rowton, "Jeremiah and the Death of Josiah," *JNES* 10 (1951): 129.

Zephaniah. House says he is "almost invisible" in his own book.[25] The name itself means "the Lord hides," a possible reference to his birth during the evil reign of Manasseh, who shed much innocent blood among the people of Judah (2 Kgs 21:16; 24:4).[26] The reference in Kings to the shedding of blood may refer to Manasseh's having killed the prophets. Others see a reference to the practice of infant sacrifice during the time of Manasseh (see Jer 7:31). Zephaniah's parents may have been pious people who worshiped the Lord alone and longed for revival among the people of Judah. The name for their child may have been the prayer on their lips concerning the safety of their son.

Many commentators believe that Zephaniah came from the royal line of Judah. If this is not the case, why would the title verse follow the unusual practice in biblical prophecy of referring to the fourth generation of Zephaniah's ancestors?[27] If the Hezekiah referred to is the king of Judah (715–687 B.C.), then Josiah and Zephaniah would have been distant cousins who may have been close friends and allies. Zephaniah himself or his prophecies may have strongly affected Josiah or those advising him in the years prior to the reform movement.

Another reason suggested for taking the line of Zephaniah to the fourth generation concerns the reference to his being a "son of Cushi," which some might have interpreted as a "Cushite," that is, an Ethiopian. The biblical writer may have felt the need to establish the Israelite origin of the prophet. Fohrer accepted the latter position, arguing that if Hezekiah the king had been intended, then his royal status would have been mentioned. Hezekiah was a common name in Judah, and Fohrer believed that Zephaniah's ancestors were mentioned "to avoid the embarrassing misconception that Zephaniah's father,

---

[25] P. R. House, *The Unity of the Twelve,* Bible and Literature Series 27 (Sheffield: Almond Press, 1990), 117. House notes: "Part of the conflict in the Twelve exists in the lives of the prophets, for they must represent both God and the people, denounce sin and plead of mercy, ask questions and be men of faith, as well as reveal God's will and at the same time interpret it for the people. The prophets struggle to discover their identity much as the other non-divine characters attempt to find their place in God's order of existence."

[26] W. S. LaSor, D. A. Hubbard, and F. W. Bush, *Old Testament Survey: The Message, Form, and Background of the Old Testament* (Grand Rapids: Eerdmans, 1982), 431; J. D. W. Watts thinks the original meaning was a confession: Zaphon is Yahweh, identifying the old Canaanite god of the mythical mountain of the north, Zaphon, with Israel's God (*The Books of Joel, Obadiah, Jonah, Nahum, Habakkuk and Zephaniah,* CBC [Cambridge: University Press, 1975], 153). See also J. M. P. Smith, *A Critical and Exegetical Commentary on Zephaniah and Nahum,* ICC (Edinburgh: T & T Clark, 1911), 184. Patterson says the form of the name Zephaniah makes the connection to a foreign god unlikely and a connection between the name and the message of the book cannot be demonstrated (*Nahum, Habakkuk, Zephaniah,* 298). In the latter he argues against E. B. Pusey, *The Minor Prophets,* 2 vols. (Grand Rapids: Baker, 1953).

[27] See R. R. Wilson, *Prophecy and Society in Ancient Israel* (Philadelphia: Fortress, 1980), 279–80.

Cushi, was an Ethiopian and not a Judean."[28] A. Berlin considers the reasoning here to be "forced" and the conclusion improbable.[29] Against the theory is the fact that Cushi is used as a proper name in Jer 36:14 (see also "Cush the Benjamite" in Ps 7:1). Dillard and Longman respond that "the simple occurrence of this personal name is a slim basis to support" the connection of Cushi with Ethiopia. They conclude that "there can be little question" that Zephaniah's royal lineage "is the reason for the length of the genealogy."[30]

Prophets are known more for how they functioned than by explicit descriptions of who they were. "In Zephaniah the prophet is characterized in three ways: interpreter of God's wrath, proclaimer of worldwide destruction, and herald of coming restoration."[31] House sees the prophet taking center stage in the middle section of the book over against Yahweh, who occupies that place in the opening and closing sections. In the middle section "the prophet takes on the added dimension of an original proclaimer of judgment rather than remaining just an interpreter of God's anger." In the final section "Zephaniah gets to play the part all the prophets from Hosea to Habakkuk want to play …, he is allowed to ultimately reveal the lasting grace of God. Indeed, he leads the nation in celebrating the end of punishment. His character, long considered by scholars a gloomy individual, actually provides the means for leading the people to better times."[32] To put it another way, "at the start of the book he was a warning figure, while at the end he is an exhorter of the people. Thus, he is the complete prophet, combining judgment and salvation in his message."[33] House's summary points in the right direction: "Though very little can be said about the prophet's personality traits, his ability to fulfill several functions shows he is obedient, versatile, and totally prophetic."[34]

Is it thus totally impossible to know anything of Zephaniah, the man? Heflin thinks not, the book giving us a few clues about its human author. "Zephaniah was a man of intense passion and moral sensitivity … an opti-

---

[28] G. Fohrer, *Introduction to the Old Testament* (London SPCK, 1970), 416. See also E. Sellin, *Introduction to the Old Testament* (London: Hodder and Stoughton, 1923), 185; A. Bentzen, *Introduction to the Old Testament*. 2 vols. 2d ed. (Copenhagen: G. E. C. Gad, 1952), 2:153; J. Blenkinsopp, *A History of Prophecy in Israel* (Philadelphia: Westminster, 1983), 140.

[29] A. Berlin, *Zephaniah,* AB (N.Y.: Doubleday, 1994), 67. Nogalski, *Literary Precursors,* 182, discounts the idea of an African heritage for the prophet as ingenuous.

[30] R. B. Dillard and T. Longman III, *An Introduction to the Old Testament* (Grand Rapids: Zondervan, 1994), 415. R. K. Harrison also states: "There seems little doubt that he [king Hezekiah] was in fact intended to be understood by the reader. … There appears to be little ground for the supposition of Bentzen that Cushi his father was actually an Ethiopian, and that Zephaniah was a Negro slave in the service of the Temple" (*Introduction to the Old Testament* [Grand Rapids: Eerdmans, 1969], 939.

[31] House, *The Unity of the Twelve,* 198.

[32] Ibid.

[33] House, *Zephaniah*, 60.

[34] Ibid., 73.

mist, a joyful man who could call for song and praise (3:14) … man of profound spirituality … (1:2). . . .a man of great boldness and courage … (1:8: 3:3–4) … a youthful aristocrat."[35]

Heflin goes on to show that Zephaniah was a true member of the prophetic tradition, developing for his generation the themes of previous prophecy: "the 'day of Yahweh' concept (Amos 5:19–20; Zeph 1:14–2:3) … suffering of nature because of sin (Hos 4:1–3; Zeph 1:2–3) … the remnant community (Mic 5:7–8; Zeph 2:7; 3:11–13). But it was Isaiah who really contributed to Zephaniah's preaching."[36] Walker notes that the Book of Zephaniah has been viewed as a "compendium of the oracles of the prophets. … In repeating and summarizing much of the judgment and salvation material common to all the prophets, he did not hesitate to use distinctive expressions found in his predecessors" (e.g., cp. 1:7 with Hab 2:20; Joel 1:15; Isa 34:6; cf. 2:14 with Isa 13:21; 34:11; cp. 2:15 with Isa 47:8).[37]

Achtemeier takes another tact. She sees the language as close to that of the "Deuteronomic portions of Jeremiah." From this she concludes that: "it may be that Zephaniah was a member of that levitical-prophetic reform group that was responsible for the collection of Deuteronomy which gave rise to the Deuteronomic reform of 622/621 B.C.—a group that also included among its members Jeremiah."[38]

Such arguments about the personality traits and sociopolitical circles of the prophet remain highly subjective and open to question. What cannot be questioned is the prophet's obedience to God to carry forth the divine message no matter the content. He pronounced the darkest words of judgment and the sunniest words of hope as he faithfully followed his divine King.

3. Zephaniah, the Book

The Book of Zephaniah describes God's concern for righteous living by the nations and by the people of Judah. The book shows that God is active in history, judging sin and working in world events, leading history towards the day of the Lord in its multiple meanings of judgment on the wicked and hope for the righteous, humble remnant.

Zephaniah's internal structure has traditionally been considered to be tripartite. The first chapter, and frequently the first three verses of the second, is

---

[35] J. N. B. Heflin, *Nahum, Habakkuk, Zephaniah, and Haggai,* BSC (Grand Rapids: Zondervan, 1985), 119–20.

[36] Ibid., 125. Earlier he noted Isaiah's use of the remnant concept in Isa 7.

[37] L. Walker, "Zephaniah," EBC, 7:539–40.

[38] E. Achtemeier, *Nahum–Malachi,* INT (Atlanta: John Knox, 1986), 62; O. P. Robertson, *The Books of Nahum, Habakkuk, Zephaniah,* NICOT (Grand Rapids: Eerdmans, 1990), 27, also sees extensive dependence on Deuteronomy.

considered to announce and describe judgment against the nations and the nation of Judah on "the day of the LORD" (1:7). Then the second chapter or 2:4–15 declares judgment against the nations, specifically citing Philistia (vv. 4–7), Moab and Ammon (vv. 8–11), Cush (v. 12), and Assyria (vv. 13–15). Finally, the third chapter announces that out of judgment will come blessing and joy for a righteous remnant. The first eight verses of chap. 3 are sometimes considered part of the second division since they deal with judgment, specifically against Jerusalem, "the city of oppressors" (3:1).

Although critical scholars have generally regarded all or most of the first chapter as authentic, much of the second and especially the third chapter have usually been regarded as from a later hand. O. Kaiser, for example, representing a basic consensus of critical scholarship, saw a three-element eschatological pattern in Zephaniah consisting of an announcement of judgment against Judah and Jerusalem (1:2–2:3), oracles against foreign nations and Jerusalem (2:4–3:8), and oracles of salvation (3:9–20). But he could only assign to Zephaniah the judgment messages with any certainty. He questioned the authenticity of 3:1–13 and especially the universalism found in 2:11 and 3:9b–10.[39]

Conclusions concerning Zephaniah's redactional history have often been related to considerations of the history of the growth of the Book of the Twelve as a whole.[40] For example, J. Nogalski works with a model of the creation of the Book of the Twelve that has Zephaniah as crucial, for the book in his view participated both in a shaping of Hosea, Amos, Micah, and Zephaniah by Deuteronomistic editors during the middle of the exile, and it was involved in the editorial shaping that produced an expanded corpus including Joel, Obadiah, Nahum, Habakkuk, Haggai, Zechariah 1–8, and Malachi. Zephaniah is thus "the *turning point from pre-exilic to post-exilic situations*."[41] The Deuteronomistic corpus "centered heavily upon YHWH's judgment, and ultimately sought to advance a theological explanation for Jerusalem's destruction."[42] The Joel layer that expanded the Deuteronomistic corpus explained previous prophecies in light of the Babylonian crisis, showing that all the nations who divested Judah would be devastated, while those

[39] O. Kaiser, *Introduction to the Old Testament: A Presentation of its Results and Problems* (Minneapolis: Augsburg, 1975), 230–231. See the judgments of this approach made by E. J. Young, *An Introduction to the Old Testament* (Grand Rapids: Eerdmans, 1969), 274.

[40] For a brief history of research, see B. A. Jones, *The Formation of the Book of the Twelve: A Study in Text and Canon,* SBLDS (Atlanta: Scholars Press, 1995), 14–42.

[41] J. Nogalski, *Literary Precursors to the Book of the Twelve*, BZAW 217 (Berlin/New York: de Gruyter, 1993), 206. For a preliminary discussion of Nogalski and the contribution of P. R. House to this topic see the Introduction to Habakkuk: "Literary Features of the Book."

[42] Ibid., 280. In this collection Zephaniah 1:1–3:8 functioned as the "Southern parallel to Amos. It depicted YHWH's irreversible decision to bring judgment upon Judah and Jerusalem because the lesson from Hosea to Micah had not been heeded."

in Judah who repented would find their situation restored.[43]

P. House, on the other hand, has argued for the unity of the Book of the Twelve without recourse to redactional additions. In his view Zephaniah forms the concluding part of the middle section in the three-part structure of the Book of the Twelve. It joins Nahum and Habakkuk in emphasizing Punishment: Covenant and Cosmic.[44] It is a "pivotal book," confirming all the horrible expectations of judgment in Hosea–Micah and completing the carnage begun in Nahum and Habakkuk. "But from 3:8–20 Zephaniah introduces the reader to the possibilities of restoration outlined in Haggai–Malachi. ... The importance of Zephaniah as a plot-shaper in the Twelve can hardly be over-estimated."[45] For House, then, in the structure of the Book of the Twelve, "Zephaniah begins the process of falling action and resolution, but only after showing how complete God's judgment will be."[46]

Concerning the internal composition of Zephaniah, Nogalski finds two judgment layers in Zeph 1:2–2:3: the earlier and original focusing on Jerusalem and Judah, and the later looking to a universal judgment. This later layer is the tool for joining the Deuteronomistic corpus of the Book of the Twelve to the expanded corpus. Similar patterns of local judgment framed in universal judgment are found in Nahum 1 and Habakkuk 3, with all three passages reflecting language from Joel.[47] Habakkuk 3:16b "makes it clear that Judah will not escape punishment at the hands of the Babylonians. Precisely this thought creates the link between Habakkuk and Zephaniah. Zephaniah functions as the depiction of the Babylonian destruction of

---

[43] J. Nogalski describes the literary conclusions without giving a clear theological structure of the final compilation (*Redactional Processes in the Book of the Twelve*, BZAW 218 [New York: Walter de Gruyter, 1993], 275–78).

[44] House, *Unity*, 72.

[45] Ibid., 151. Cp. pp. 89, 95–96. House (pp. 93–94) contends that Zephaniah gathers the major elements of Nahum–Zephaniah in much the same way Amos and Micah summarize the emphases on sin in their section. Thus both Judah and the nations will suffer for their sins, the sins of the covenant nation and of the nations being listed.

[46] Ibid., 119. He notes (pp. 147–50): "At the conclusion of Habakkuk the reader, like the prophet, is waiting for Yahweh's redemption (3:16–19). Zephaniah's method of ending this suspense is to first dispel any possible doubts about the thoroughness of God's judgment. ... As a summary book, Zephaniah lists the many sinful groups, whether powerful or weak, in order to show that the nations will be as desolate as nature on the day of Yahweh. ... Zephaniah claims that individuals also face condemnation (1:4,8,12–13). None who sins can escape the Lord's wrath. ... *All creation* will be swept away. Though Zephaniah certainly pictures the Day of Yahweh as a time of extreme devastation, from the destruction unfolds a theme of forgiveness (3:8–9). ... The possibility of a redeemed remnant has become a completed picture of a new and powerful people. Once judgment is fully expended in 3:8 it becomes an avenue for Good to demonstrate mercy through the lives of the cleansed people. ... While the nations are not promised as much as the remnant, the fact that they can come to Yahweh at all is an incredible promise."

[47] See his summary in Nogalski, *Literary Precursors*, 198.

Jerusalem presumed in Hab 3:16b."[48]

For Nogalski, the original book began with 1:4, vv. 2–3 representing a different theology dependent upon the "P" account of creation and thus postexilic.[49] In chaps. 2–3 he sees the abrupt change that turns from judgment on the nations back to judgment on Jerusalem in 3:1–8. He sees a picture of a weakened Judah that is only a remnant (2:7,9) pointing to a time after the destruction of Jerusalem. He concludes that the oracles against the nations represent oracles from just before 700 B.C. that have been rewritten in some fashion by an editor seeking to provide hope for the remnant. Finally, he points to 3:9–20 as a unit with inner logic and cohesion but with a tenor quite distinct from all that precedes.[50]

Zephaniah 3 is crucial for Nogalski, for vv. 18–20 function in the combination of Zephaniah with Haggai, Zechariah 1–8, and Malachi as well as in adapting Mic 4:6–7 to the context of the larger collection and setting the stage for Haggai. The Zephaniah verses also contain allusions back to Joel. For Nogalski, then, the original Zephaniah corpus ended at 3:8a, to which was added 3:12–13, with 3:14–19 on the whole being part of the Deuteronomistic corpus. Later in the transmission of the Deuteronomistic corpus, 3:9–11 entered.[51]

Such concern over the redaction of the book brings strong response from scholars not convinced by such detailed and subjective analysis. Heflin says three reasons lead scholars to find inauthentic elements in the book: the understanding that one prophet could not announce judgment and then turn around and announce salvation, linguistic elements judged to have arisen only during the exilic and postexilic periods, and historical allusions such as 2:8 that belong to a different period of history. Heflin bluntly concludes: "Quite frankly, all of these arguments are arbitrary and subjective. They are often based on insufficient evidence. … No valid reason exists to deny any of the book to the prophet."[52] For Heflin, then, the book is not a gradual accretion of materials from different periods of history serving to unite different literary corpuses. Rather the book of Zephaniah "is a collection of sermons and sermon summaries from different periods in the prophet's life, joined together not so much by chronology as by purpose. The book is a literary unit that develops in logical sequence the major themes of judgment, purification, and restoration. The themes are incomplete without each other."[53]

[48] Ibid., 199.

[49] Ibid., 189.

[50] Ibid., 171–76.

[51] Ibid., 177–78.

[52] Heflin, *Nahum, Habakkuk, Zephaniah, and Haggai,* 121–24. See also Harrison, *Introduction to the Old Testament,* 942.

[53] Heflin, *Nahum, Habakkuk, Zephaniah, and Haggai,* 124.

Achtemeier reinforces Heflin's argument: "there is an organic wholeness about the book that argues against its overall arrangement by an editorial hand. The theme of sinful human pride runs through the whole work, and its separate parts are held together by similar and contrasting images. … Hebrew rhetorical structures prevent the separation of the supposed three parts of the book: 2:3 belongs inseparably with 2:4, and 3:8 joins with 3:9."[54]

Jones offers substantive critiques of the various attempts to bring structural, literary, and/or redactional unity to the Book of the Twelve. The methodologies of each of the scholars do not lend themselves to validation by other scholars; they rest on subjective bases; and they ignore other solutions to the problems such as access to common traditions, use of common cultic materials, literary dependency, or coincidence.[55] The theories dependent upon speculative redactional hypotheses become topheavy, building one hypothesis upon another and finding a farflung redactional unity by showing that the present literary contexts do not demonstrate such unity. The very complexity of the theories and of the processes outlined to develop texts also argues against the plausibility of the theories.[56]

Although J. J. M. Roberts considers the book in general to be original, "a clear statement of the message of Zephaniah," with few "late, secondary alterations to the composition,"[57] he nevertheless considers the work to be the

---

[54] Achtemeier, *Nahum–Malachi,* 62. She analyzes the book in six units: 1:2–6; 1:7–13; 1:14–18; 2:1–4; 2:5–15; 3:1–20. She does consider, however, 3:18–20 to "represent later Deuteronomic updatings of the work" (p. 62).

[55] Jones, *Formation of the Book of the Twelve*, 19–23.

[56] Ibid., 30. He is also critical of House's "formalist literary theory" as too simplistic, ignoring the complexity and fragmentary quality of the present texts. Rather, one must let remain "the individual and diverse elements of the Minor Prophets that do not fit into any unifying scheme; … the discordant features of the book cannot altogether be silenced" (p. 32, describing the work of H. Marks, "The Twelve Prophets," *The Literary Guide to the Bible,* ed. R. Alter and F. Kermode [Cambridge: Harvard University Press, 1987], 207–32). Cf. N. Gottwald, "Tragedy and Comedy in the Latter Prophets," *Semeia* 32 (1984), 83–96. Jones himself begins with the assumptions of S. Talmon that Qumran textual evidence allows one to conclude that "the stylistic techniques of ancient authors and the techniques used by copyists to introduce variations into the text were essentially identical" (p. 44, referring to S. Talmon, "The Textual Study of the Bible—A New Outlook, *Qumran and the History of the Biblical Text,* ed. S. Talmon and F. M. Cross, Jr. [Cambridge: Harvard University Press, 1975], 321–99). Cf. E. Ulrich, "The Canonical Process, Text Criticism, and Latter Stages in the Composition of the Bible," "*Sha'arei Talmon. Studies in the Bible, Qumran, and the Ancient Near East Presented to Shemaryahu Talmon,* ed. M. Fishbane and E. Tov (Winona Lake: Eisenbrauns, 1992), 267–91; and E. Tov, *Textual Criticism of the Hebrew Bible* (Minneapolis: Fortress, 1992). This gives Jones the goal that "text-critical materials therefore may provide an objective database for evaluating the kind of redactional changes that scholars have suggested for the Book of the Twelve" (p. 47).

[57] Roberts identifies "secondary additions" as "an explanatory gloss in 1:3 … a secondary transposition of verses at 2:4–5, and there are two late universalizing glosses at 2:11 and 3:10" (J. J. M. Roberts, *Nahum, Habakkuk, and Zephaniah: A Commentary,* OTL [Louisville: W/JK, 1991], 163).

result of "compositional editing" by which "the larger compositional structures within the book have been fashioned out of smaller, independent oracles, presumably given originally in an oral setting."[58]

A. Berlin objects that such a method which is "programmed *a priori* to discover small separate units" presumed to be original "trivializes the units and may totally miss the overarching literary interpretation of a pericope." She objects that Roberts' method "sees little purpose in searching for a line of thought sustained or developed over several contiguous oracles because he views the ordering of these oracles as more or less random; or even if there is a logic to the ordering (chronological or thematic), it is secondary and not to be used in understanding the meaning of the original unit." He thus "puts the emphasis on the individual units, denying any purpose to the collector of these units other than a naive recording of them" and "denies or minimizes the existence of the book *qua* book, a work in its own right with a coherent design." Berlin counters that "most if not all compilers, ancient and modern, have a purpose and seek to make their compilations coherent." [59]

All modern scholars begin their analysis of the book with the recognition that Zephaniah wrote totally in poetry.[60] House sees a prophetic drama with a comic plot.[61] The plot contains the following devices: Exposition (1:1–7), Complication (1:8–2:11), Climax of Crisis (2:12–3:5), Resolution of Crisis (3:6–13), and Falling Action and Conclusion (3:14–20). "Cosmic punishment is at the forefront" and "becomes more detailed as the book progresses."[62] This cosmic punishment is not the final message, however, for ultimately an international remnant will worship Yahweh (3:9) with Judah being restored (3:14–20). House summarizes the plot: God "wants Judah to be a nation that serves Him. That purpose is thwarted by the sin and idolatry of Judah and her

---

[58] Roberts, *Nahum, Habakkuk, and Zephaniah*, 161. The oracles against the nations in 2:4–15, e.g., "have been shaped into a loose compositional unity, but there are indications that that unity is not the rhetorical unity of their oral presentation. The oracles reflect no common form, and there are no recurring patterns to tie them together" (p. 195).

[59] A. Berlin, *Zephaniah: A New Translation with Introduction and Commentary,* AB (New York: Doubleday, 1994), 20–22. She notes that the oracles against the nations unit "exists now as a whole and there is no manuscript evidence that it ever existed otherwise; and that *viewing it as a whole yields an interpretation much more interesting and compelling than viewing it as a collection of separate parts"* (pp. 22–23).

[60] Cf. M. O'Connor, *Hebrew Verse Structure* (Winona Lake: Eisenbrauns, 1980), 240–62.

[61] House, *Zephaniah*, especially 91–116. House calls his method a "classicist method of discovering Zephaniah's genre" (p. 52). On pp. 105–116 House combines prophetic with comic to describe the sub-genre of the drama, showing particularly on p. 115 how the "characteristics of comic and prophetic literature fit together." Roberts, *Nahum, Habakkuk, and Zephaniah*, 161–62 vigorously denies House's results as "seriously flawed." Berlin notes the lack of evidence of drama in ancient Israel and prefers to understand the person shifts in Zephaniah as "a normal aspect of prophetic writing" (*Zephaniah,* 12).

[62] House, *Unity,* 94.

neighbors. Through the work of Yahweh, the severity of His day, and the salvation of the remnant, however, the Lord overcomes the obstacles to His purpose. Judah is restored, and even the heathen nations, those outside God's covenant, are invited to join the new society created by the day of the Lord. Justice and mercy prevail in this very inclusive plot instead of a sense of rigid law. In fact, the expectation of God's legalistic intractability is exposed by the plot's resolution. Joy prevails rather than a sense of fate."[63] House sees the change of speakers between Yahweh and the prophet as the "key to the book's structure."[64] "Each set of speeches has an artistic purpose, whether it is to present a problem, heighten suspense or tension, or conclude the work with a satisfactory resolution. Both speakers are important, for each actor's part is versatile enough to initiate plot elements or buttress the comments of the other. These structural achievements point to an author with a definite plan for presenting his story, and one who can carry out his plan with subtlety and ingenuity."[65]

W. Rudolph recognizes a dual focus in the book on nations and nation with promises of judgment and of salvation for each. He identifies an oracle threatening Judah (1:2–2:3) and an oracle against the nations (2:4–15) parallel to later threats against Jerusalem (3:1–7) and against the nations (3:8). The final part then reverses the subject and the order with a salvation oracle for the nations (3:9–10) and salvation for Israel in Judah and scattered among the nations (3:11–20).[66]

Patterson likewise recognizes Zephaniah's dual nature, finding it in both theme and structure. The message, he says, is to announce the day of the Lord as (1) a day of "judgment upon all nations and peoples, including God's own covenant people, due to their sins against God and mankind" and (2) "a day of purification for sin, when the redeemed of all nations shall join a regathered Israel in serving God and experiencing His blessings." This twofold message is reflected in the structure: 1:2–2:3 announces and describes the judgment and its severity, and 2:4–3:20 "depicts the extent and purposes of the judgment."[67]

J. A. Motyer follows the traditional three part scheme (1:2–2:3; 2:4–3:8; 3:9–20) but focuses on lexical and semantic repetition to discover "a complex chiastic format."[68] Especially prominent in his analysis is inclusio. He

---

[63] House, *Zephaniah*, 67–68.

[64] Ibid., 57. House thinks the speeches "reveal plot, movement, characterization, and genre." The speeches are determined simply by the use of first or third person for God.

[65] Ibid., 61.

[66] W. Rudolph, *Micha, Nahum, Habakuk, Zephanja,* KAT (Gütersloh: Gerd Mohn, 1975), 255.

[67] Patterson, *Nahum, Habakkuk, Zephaniah,* 281–82. See his chart and its explanation on pp. 282–85.

[68] J. A. Motyer, "Zephaniah," in *The Minor Prophets*, 3 vols., ed. T. E. McComiskey (Grand Rapids: Baker, 1993), 3:902. The following summary is taken from pp. 3:902–4.

observes that the first section (1:2–2:3) is framed by uses of the phrase "seek the LORD" in the first and last poems (2:6; 2:3). The second section is framed by repetition of "none will be left" (*mēʾên yôšēb*) in 2:5 and 3:6 and the Hebrew word *pāqad* (with opposite meanings) in 2:7 ("will care for them") and 3:7 ("my punishments come"). He also notes that the first two sections are framed by repetition of *kārat,* "cut" in 1:3–4 and 3:6–7. Sections two and three are framed by repetition of "restore their/your fortunes" in 2:7 and 3:20. The prominent word "day" (*yôm*; 1:7,8,9,10,14,15,16,18; 2:3) and the word "time" (*ʾēt*; 1:12) in the opening section both recur in the last section (3:8,11,16,19,20). Also framing the entire book are "matching expressions of universality," that is, "the face of the earth" in 1:2,3 and "all the earth" in 3:19,20, and the similar expressions "the word of the LORD" in 1:2 and "says the LORD" in 3:20.

> Significant contrasts include the false king (*malkām;* 1:5) and the true king (*melek yiśrāʾēl yhwh;* 3:15), the baffled warrior and the saving warrior (*gibbôr;* 1:14; 3:17), the name to be obliterated (1:4) and the admired name (3:19–20), Jerusalem under judgment (1:4,12) and Jerusalem restored to divine favor (3:14,16), the call to humility (*ʾănāwâ;* 2:3) and the humble people (*ʾānî;* 3:12), the prevalence of deceit (*mirmâ;* 1:9) and the city free of deceit (*tarmît;* 3:13).[69]

Thus Motyer argues that Zephaniah is "a coherent book presentation, a structured treatise on the theme of 'the day of the Lord.'"[70]

A study that likewise recognizes a threefold structure but places emphasis on the hortatory sections is that of R. B. Chisholm, Jr. Chisholm considers the three main sections to be 1:2–18; 2:4–3:7; and 3:10–20. These are linked, however, by two "hortatory hinges" that connect their respective larger sections together. The first two sections are hinged by the exhortation to seek the Lord in 2:1–3, which both concludes the section on the day of the Lord and introduces the woe oracles against the nations in 2:4–15 (note that 2:4 begins with *kî,* "for" in Hb.) and the woe oracle against Judah in 3:1–7. Then the exhortation to wait for the Lord in 3:8–9 both concludes the woe oracle against Judah (note the initial word "therefore") and also introduces the final

---

[69] Ibid., 3:904.

[70] Ibid., 3:901. For an intriguing variation of the threefold structure see I. J. Ball, Jr., "The Rhetorical Shape of Zephaniah," *Perspecitves on Language and Text,* ed. E. W. Conrad and E. G. Newing (Winona Lake: Eisenbrauns, 1987), 155–65. He identifies 2:1–7 as not only a summary of Zephaniah's message but also a structural miniature of the book: (1) warning of the coming day of the Lord (2:1–3; 1:2–18), (2) destruction of the enemy (2:4; 2:8–15), and (3) woe and salvation (2:5–7; 3:1–20). Ball has also elaborated this study in *Zephaniah: A Rhetorical Study* (Berkeley: Bibal, 1988).

restoration section.[71]

Current study of Zephaniah is thus pointing in two directions. One is the pivotal role it plays in the unified meaning of the Book of the Twelve. Such study has too often, however, been done on the basis of theories of extensive redactional work rather than on the basis of the logical structure, meaning, and purpose of the current prophetic canon. This means the second direction must be traveled before the first can be explored. This second direction is the literary structure and meaning of each book in the Book of the Twelve.

4. The Date of the Book

The opening verse tells us that Zephaniah proclaimed his message during the long and eventful reign of Josiah as king over Judah (639–609 B.C.). Much of the study of the prophetic book has centered on making the dating more exact or in finding a way to put aside the information in the opening verse and to find a time period that "better suited" the contents of the prophecy. Such a view sees the superscription as a later addition to the book by an editor without sufficient historical information

Calvin argued that the people did not follow Josiah's reforms completely so that Zephaniah represented the situation after 621, that is after the reforms.[72] Rudolph represents the view that places Zephaniah during and immediately after the reign of Manasseh (687–642 B.C.). He saw the prophet as an important instrument in starting Josiah's reforms. E. Achtemeier thinks Zephaniah spanned the years of Josiah's reign and was thus "the first prophetic voice to be heard in Judah since the time of Isaiah and Micah."[73] She places the first two chapters of the book shortly after 640 and the last chapter between 612 and 609.[74] Patterson looks at religious practices, worship failures, royalty enamored with foreign clothing, socioeconomic ills, political and religious corruption, and the youth of the king to point to a date parallel with Habakkuk about 635–630 B.C.[75] Heflin situates the prophet in the earli-

---

[71] R. B. Chisholm, Jr., *Interpreting the Minor Prophets* (Grand Rapids: Zondervan, 1990), 201–215. Similarly E. R. Clendenen recognizes a threefold structure "governed by the three exhortations to 'be silent' (1:7), 'gather' and 'seek the LORD' (2:1–3), and 'wait" (3:8)." Whereas the first exhortation is "sandwiched between two announcements of the Lord's wrath," the other two exhortations begin the second and third sections and are followed by explanations introduced by 'for'" ("Zephaniah," *Holman Concise Bible Commentary*, ed. D. S. Dockery [Nashville: Broadman & Holman, 1998], 377–78).

[72] For dating surveys, see House, *Zephaniah*, 11–12; Nogalski, *Literary Precursors*, 178–180.

[73] Achtemeier, *Nahum–Malachi*, 61.

[74] Ibid., 62.

[75] R. D. Patterson, *Nahum, Habakkuk, Zephaniah,* WEC (Chicago: Moody, 1991), 275–277.

est years of Josiah's reformation (thus 630–625).[76] Zephaniah's indictment of the king's son (but not the king) in 1:8 also fits well the time period early in Josiah's reign when politically astute religious leaders guided the young king.[77] G. A. Smith and J. M. P. Smith saw the Scythian invasion between 627 and 625 as the occasion for the book. Robertson places the prophet during the Josianic reformation after 622 because of extensive reliance on the language of Deuteronomy.[78]

Hyatt placed the date of the prophet two decades later during the reign of Jehoiakim, a view which requires the dismissal of the superscription to the book. He felt that placing the book during the reign of Josiah necessitated determining the oracles against the foreign nations to be secondary since he could not find a historical situation for the oracles during the reign of Josiah. "We are on even stronger ground in asserting that the international situation under Jehoiakim was more appropriate for Zephaniah's oracles than in the reign of Josiah, especially if we view the oracles against foreign nations as genuine."[79]

D. L. Williams agreed with Hyatt concerning the dating of the book during the reign of Jehoiakim, citing internal evidence but rejecting the evidence of the superscription. He saw Zephaniah ministering from 609 to 587 B.C. Williams emphasized the cultic materials of the book and saw Zephaniah as a priest, equating him with the priest Zephaniah mentioned in 2 Kgs 25:18; Jer 21:1; 29:25, 29; 37:3; 52:24; and Zech 6:10,14.[80] Nogalski thinks the late dating of Hyatt and Williams accounts for the "largest number of dating problems," while the superscription reference to Josiah is a part of the

[76] Heflin, *Nahum, Habakkuk, Zephaniah, and Haggai*, 115–18; J. D. W. Watts (*The Books of Joel, Obadiah, Jonah, Nahum, Habakkuk and Zephaniah*, CBC [Cambridge: University Press, 1975], 154) also sets Zephaniah early in Josiah's reign as one of the influencers of the reformation. He goes so far as to say (p. 155), "It is possible that Zephaniah planned the entire prophecy for presentation in temple services within the decade before Josiah's reform in 626 B.C." R. L. Smith, *Micah-Malachi*, 32, 123, favors a date of 627, but apparently without much enthusiasm. Roberts, *Nahum, Habakkuk, and Zephaniah*, 163–64, places the book early in Josiah's reign because of "Zephaniah's portrayal of the rampant syncretism and rapacious behavior among the royal and religious officials in Jerusalem (1:4–6,8–9; 3:3)." Motyer ("Zephaniah," 3:909) hints that Zephaniah could have been "the hidden influence within the palace from which the reform movement sprang."

[77] Kaiser, *Introduction to the Old Testament*, 229–30. Kaiser dated Zephaniah's prophecy as about 630 B.C., a view generally held. See also Fohrer (416) and Young (273).

[78] Robertson, *The Books of Nahum, Habakkuk, Zephaniah*, 30,32–34, 253–57.

[79] J. P. Hyatt, "The Date and Background of Zephaniah," *JNES* 7 (1948): 27; but see D. L. Christensen, "Zephaniah 2:4–15: A Theological Basis for Josiah's Program of Political Expansion," *CBQ* (1984): 669–82.

[80] D. L. Williams, "The Date of Zephaniah," *JBL* 82 (1963): 77–88.

Deuteronomistic editing.[81] On the extreme end of those arguing for a late date, L. P. Smith and E. L. Lacheman denied the book to Zephaniah, viewing the book as a pseudepigraphic work of 200 B.C.[82]

Whether Zephaniah preached throughout the reign of Josiah or during a brief period of time is not clear. But arguments against accepting the superscription's accuracy (regardless of its source) are not convincing. This is the earliest evidence of the date that we have. Since the book deals with the sin of the people of Judah, most commentators place the date before the religious reform of 621 B.C. After the beginning of the reform the actions pictured in 1:4–6 would have been less open and less prevalent. Zephaniah could have preached before 626 B.C. when the reform began to take greater prominence with the death of Ashurbanipal of Assyria.

5. The Message of Zephaniah

Zephaniah's message came to a people in need of a word from God. "No other prophet more forcefully describes judgment than this kinsman of royalty."[83] He proclaimed judgment against the abuses of the covenant people, but the prophet held out the possibility of repentance if the people turned to righteousness. Zephaniah called the people to humble themselves before the Lord that they might dwell before him. "Theologically, Zephaniah is not innovative, standing for mainstream Yahwism," but he has given us "a coherent, compelling eschatological vision."[84]

(1) The Day of the Lord

Like Amos (5:18–20) and Isaiah (2:12–22) before him, Zephaniah proclaimed the judgment of the day of the Lord (1:14–18), a judgment that would

[81] Nogalski, *Literary Precursors*, 180, where he lists seven reasons, for a date after Josiah and 183, n. 35, where he quotes K. Seybold (*Satirische Prophetie. Studien zum Buch Zefanja.* Stuttgarter Bibelstudien 120 [Stutttgart: Verlag Katholisches Bibelwerk, 1985], 79) as seeing 1:4–6 as the only passage that can be directly related to Josiah and then demonstrates that these verses did not come from Zephaniah but was imposed by Deuteronomistic editors deliberating over the material along with court annals. On p. 183 he notes: "The date of the formation of prophetic books must be taken separately from the question of the date of the prophet. In the case of Zeph. 1:1, the selection of Josiah could either be due to traditions about the prophet's ministry or to specific literary purposes." He then goes on to argue for literary purposes as the main factor, saying such a superscription looks back at the prophet from a chronological distance but contains genealogical traditions explainable only as coming from "someone who knew the prophet" (p. 184). He also sees the mention of Hezekiah as a literary addition linking Zephaniah to Mic 1:1.

[82] L. P. Smith and E. L. Lacheman, "The Authorship of the Book of Zephaniah," *JNES* 9 (1950): 137–42.

[83] Heflin, *Nahum, Habakkuk, Zephaniah, and Haggai*, 121.

[84] Motyer, "Zephaniah," 3:897.

affect all the earth including Judah. "Zephaniah is rooted in the flow of history, but his concern is only with the goal—the eschaton—the day when calamitous human efforts to run the world will coincide in an awesome climax with the Lord's purposes of judgment and hope."[85] Zephaniah pictured the day even more graphically than his predecessors as a day when the Lord would pour out the blood of sinners like dust and their flesh like dung (1:17). In that day, the possibility of escape would cease. Silver and gold would not deliver. Zephaniah carried the day of the Lord farther than either Isaiah or Amos. "No hint of restoration is found in this imagery."[86] At the time of the day of the Lord, Zephaniah proclaimed that God would make a full end of all the godless inhabitants of the earth (1:18). Heflin summarizees the day of the Lord as "imminent, terrible, and universal," devastating Judah, the nations, and nature.[87]

The imminency of this day of judgment, however, is somewhat in tension with its terrible and universal proportions. Chisholm resolves this tension by observing that the day of the Lord for Zephaniah had two horizons. Zephaniah's expectation of a terrible day in the immediate future is indicated by his references to its nearness (1:7,14) and by his specific references to such historical participants as Judah, Philistia, Moab, Ammon, Cush, and Assyria. "Thus in its initial phase Zephaniah's day of the Lord should be associated with the Babylonian conquest of the Near East in the late sixth and early fifth centuries B.C." On the other hand, other aspects of the day point to a time of fulfillment after Zephaniah's time, namely, the description of the judgment in such cosmic proportions and its "ultimate outcome," that is, the salvation of a people from Israel and all the nations to worship the Lord. Thus, although "the prophet presented a unified picture of the future," nevertheless, he was "blending together events both near and far away."[88]

In spite of the cosmic and universal extent of the judgment, God's purpose to purify a remnant is expressed in 3:9–13 as motivating God's people to "wait" (3:8). Believers were not to lose heart but to look for God's deliverance and to serve him "shoulder to shoulder" (3:9). Zephaniah thus rings forth a positive note to the day of the Lord. "It takes the ravages of the Day of Yahweh to melt away the wicked segment of the chosen people and bring forth the remnant."[89] By emphasizing both the positive and negative sides of the

---

[85] Ibid., 3:899.

[86] Robertson, *The Books of Nahum, Habakkuk, Zephaniah,* 22. He also states, "The message that can be disputed but cannot be missed is that God's judgment is retributive and not always restorative in nature. … In the end, his judgment has a character of rightness that has no further end beyond expressing the reality that a person or a nation shall receive from God's hand exactly what he deserves" (p. 21).

[87] Heflin, *Nahum, Habakkuk, Zephaniah, and Haggai,* 126.

[88] Chisholm, *Interpreting the Minor Prophets,* 216–17.

[89] House, *Unity,* 209.

day of the Lord as two sides of one coin, Zephaniah more fully develops this theme than does any other prophet.[90]

(2) The Nature of God

As D. W. Baker explains: "Even more encompassing than the day of the Lord in the structure of Zephaniah is 'the Lord' Yahweh himself. His name is not only in the book's opening phrase; it is also its final word, forming an envelope providing the parameters within which Zephaniah's whole message must be viewed. Zephaniah's prophecies in particular, and indeed all of Scripture, are theocentric."[91]

The Book of Zephaniah cleverly surprises the reader with its developing picture of God. The opening chapters reveal God as a righteous judge who is offended by moral and religious sins. "In Zephaniah the Twelve's image of Yahweh as punishing ruler and angry covenant spouse reaches its fruition. Here, Yahweh is, overwhelmingly, more a character of deeds than words."[92] But this is no impersonal deity mechanically applying a natural law. "Yahweh's personal anger leads to the actions he takes. ... When God is angry the whole creation trembles."[93]

Certainly no less than in Nahum and Habakkuk, in Zephaniah the central issue was the nature and character of God.[94] The people of Judah had not only blurred the essential distinction between Yahweh and the gods of the nations (1:4–5); they also regarded God as indifferent or possibly impotent. They assumed that he would do neither good nor evil, a common view held by modern society. But Zephaniah knew that God hates oppression, violence, and bloodshed (1:9; 3:1,3). "The Lord judges common people who no longer believe in His power, who say God will do nothing about Judah's sin (1:12). ... Yahweh will show how wrong it is to mistake His patience for a lack of power."[95]

(3) The Sovereignty of the Lord

Zephaniah's preaching against the foreign nations demonstrated the Lord's sovereignty over nations both near and far. In Zephaniah "Yahweh's main action is that of controlling history. He can sweep away the inhabitants of earth in the future because He created them at the beginning of time."[96] Such

[90] See Baker, *Nahum, Habakkuk, Zephaniah,* 84.
[91] D. W. Baker, "Zephaniah, Theology of," *EDBT,* 852.
[92] House, *Unity,* 181.
[93] House, *Zephaniah,* 78.
[94] See Robertson, *Nahum, Habakkuk, Zephaniah,* 20.
[95] House, *Zephaniah,* 77.
[96] Ibid., 76.

"sweeping" away of nations is not just one, general all–inclusive act. It is a series of particular acts against particular nations for particular reasons. Like Amos, Zephaniah believed that since God created all nations, they belong to him and are accountable to him. "God's justice is marvelously impartial. He will in no wise clear the guilty, whoever they may be."[97] Furthermore, he not only places limits on their evil but can direct that evil ultimately to serve him. And most importantly, God desires that all people worship him. For Zephaniah, "the Lord is from the outset a universal deity. He does not merely reign over Israel, but over all the earth. It is the whole earth He proposes 'to sweep away' (1:2), and He promises to punish foreign nations as well as Israel. Yahweh allows no rivals (1:4–6), punishing those who worship pagan gods (1:5). Supreme knowledge is also part of the Yahweh's character. He knows the thoughts of people (1:12–13) and the attitudes of nations (2:8–10)."[98]

This sovereign God is king (3:15) and savior (3:17). "Those very functions that once had been assigned to the scion of the line of David now revert to the person of God the Lord himself."[99] Thus as with his contemporary prophets Nahum and Habakkuk, Zephaniah makes no mention of Messiah. Messianic hope would have to come later. At the present all pictures of a human king seemed dark and dreary. For now, judgment was the word for the royal family (1:8).[100]

(4) Human Sin

"Zephaniah focuses on the spirit of wickedness in people,"[101] and divine sovereignty exercising itself over against human sin. Zephaniah sees a chain of human thought and action that calls forth divine action in the day of the Lord. Especially prevalent in the book is the sin of pride (2:10; 3:11),[102] which is found just as much in Judah as among the nations. It brings rebellion against divine authority (3:1–4) and becomes apparent in human insolence (2:15; 3:1–2,4), idolatry (1:4–6,8–9), and injustice (1:7–13; 3:3–5). Finally, it creates a lifestyle centered on self and not caring for others or for God

---

[97] Robertson, *Nahum, Habakkuk, Zephaniah,* 21.

[98] House, *Zephaniah*, 69.

[99] Robertson, *Nahum, Habakkuk, Zephaniah*, 19. He also states, "The most distinctive thing about the messianism of Nahum, Habakkuk, and Zephaniah is the absence of virtually a trace of messianism" (p. 17).

[100] Note the discussion of Robertson, *Nahum, Habakkuk, Zephaniah,* 18–19: "In the last hours before the Exile it is as though the Lord interrupts the movement toward Messiah to declare clearly that he alone can be king in Israel."

[101] Patterson, *Nahum, Habakkuk, Zephaniah*, 295.

[102] See the emphasis by Heflin, *Nahum, Habakkuk, Zephaniah, and Haggai*, 125, and Watts, "Joel, Obadiah, Jonah, Nahum, Habakkuk and Zephaniah," 154.

(1:6,12). "They do not in words deny God's existence, but rather deny his power in their actions."[103] Such a rebellious people are sinners, facing God's discipline.[104] "God cannot brook haughtiness and … people's only hope lay in recognizing their own frailty."[105]

"Dependence on the faith and piety of a preceding generation is not enough. A personal commitment to the covenant was needed by each successive king and each generation of Israel, as it still is for each generation in the church. Neither the twentieth-century church nor the Israel of the monarchy can be second-generation children of God. The commitment must be made individually and personally by everyone."[106]

(5) The Mercy of the Lord

In the final chapter we find what House calls a "radical switch from merciless judge to restoring creator."[107] The book of Zephaniah reminds us that in the midst of God's wrath there is always the possibility of redemption. The final six verses of that chapter show that "Israel's just but caring covenant God"[108] is with them, removing fear, delighting in the nation, quieting the people, rejoicing over them, rescuing and gathering the nation, giving them honor and praise, and restoring their fortunes. "Wrath is not forgotten, rather it is eliminated through the completion of judgment (3:8–9)."[109]

"Despite Yahweh's justifiable desire to punish both Israel and the nations, mercy is a major component of Zephaniah's characterization of the Lord. … Yahweh's willingness to spare anyone represents a great mercy in Zephaniah, since the heinous nature of worldwide corruption is so well documented. …There is even mercy for Israel's enemies, since all these can call on the Lord's name (3:9). … After, and because of, judgment, the merciful nature of God emerges."[110] This divine mercy and kindness, best displayed in the treatment of his enemies, "best defines His personality."[111] The merciful side of God appears in several images. The first is that of shepherd for hurting sheep creating a "resting place" for them (2:7). The second is the caring parent who cleanses the mouth or lips of the nations (3:9). Only when the child's lips are

---

[103] Baker, "Zephaniah, Theology of," 852. He also explains that "as many marriages are ruined by loss of interest, often leading to infidelity, so these two manifestations of trouble are present in the life of the nation that was betrothed to God."

[104] See Heflin, *Nahum, Habakkuk, Zephaniah, and Haggai*, 125.

[105] LaSor, et al. *Old Testament Survey*, 437.

[106] Baker, *Nahum, Habakkuk, Zephaniah*, 86.

[107] House, *Zephaniah,* 71.

[108] Baker, *Nahum, Habakkuk, Zephaniah*, 88.

[109] House, *Zephaniah,* 81.

[110] House, *Unity*, 181; cp. House, *Zephaniah*, 70.

[111] House, *Zephaniah,* 81.

cleansed, can the child properly speak to the divine Father. Finally, Zephaniah paints an image of a party, a celebration to which God and the prophet invite guests (3:15). Robertson can declare that 3:15–17 is the highlight of God's mercy and man's hope: "Not even in the glorious revelations of the new covenant can be found a fuller word of comfort."[112]

(6) Israel as the People of God

The tension in the Book of the Twelve, particularly in Zephaniah, is between the image Israel has of themselves and the reality which God shows through his prophet. "The Twelve's initial assessment of Israel is quite unflattering to say the least."[113] Their arrogance, for example, mirrored that of the nations (1:12; 3:11). They worshiped idols (1:4–6) and their leaders rejected the Lord's standards (3:2–7). Zephaniah maintains this negative picture of Israel in his opening sections, then turns to a contrasting one. The opening chapter pictures Judah's sin, particularly their idolatry, and its devastating effects. "Israel's reversal of covenant agreement causes a reversal of creation."[114] But then through judgment God's people are purified of sin and redeemed to worship and serve the Lord. "Due to the fires of judgment, the complacent, adulterous nature of Israel disappears, and a new, holy Israel emerges. … The rebel has been reborn as a righteous follower of Yahweh."[115]

(7) The Nations as People of God

Zephaniah does not limit the focus of his prophecy to Israel, the people of God. He spreads his net to include the nations of the world. As with Israel, so with the nations, Zephaniah paints two pictures, a before and after. First, Zeph 1:7 paints a haunting picture of the fate of the nations, a fate they share with disobedient Israel. All will be unwitting guests invited to Yahweh's sacrifice and finding once they arrive that they are the sacrificial animals. Their chief sin is pride and its result, taunting and mocking God's people. "They believe that the weakness of Jerusalem can be equated with the impotence of Yahweh."[116]

The second portrait of the nations is one of worship. God's purpose is expressed in 3:9–13 to purify from the nations a people united to worship him. Gentile inclusion in the Lord's salvation is especially prominent in Zephaniah.[117] God the king calls the nations, their speech cleansed of pride

---

[112] Robertson, *Nahum, Habakkuk, Zephaniah* 22.
[113] House, *Unity*, 204.
[114] House, *Zephaniah*, 63.
[115] House, *Unity*, 209.
[116] Ibid., 215.
[117] Robertson, *Nahum, Habakkuk, Zephaniah*, 24.

and idolatry, to a command performance in his temple. Outside the worship component the prophet paints few other strokes to identify how the nations decide to worship and to elaborate on their relationship to God and to his people. The one point is that "though ancient foes, Yahweh molds both covenant and cosmic peoples, mostly through judgment, into a single unit."[118]

(8) The Doctrine of the Remnant[119]

Zephaniah pictured a day when God's righteous remnant would dwell securely in the land as a humble people who took refuge in the name of the Lord (3:12–13). Interestingly, "the remnant is encouraged to seek meekness and righteousness in 2:3, but no mention is made of any overwhelming turn to the Lord. It is God's decision to cleanse them through the day of Yahweh that releases them."[120] As Robertson observes, Zephaniah's "Perhaps" in 2:3 "may appear to be a faint wisp of hope for those who seek the Lord in face of the burning wrath of God. But it is nonetheless there and provides encouragement to any sinner who truly has been moved (by God's Spirit) to seek the Lord."[121] God's cleansing action then brings the great change in the remnant. "An incredible change has occurred: God's judgment is the means of restoration. Only through punishment can restoration emerge. Thus 3:8–9 provides the knowledge that after Yahweh's day there will be blessings for the remnant."[122] And those blessings will bring God himself great pleasure. Robertson highlights the striking picture of "the Lord of love" presented in 3:17, "alternating between contented contemplation of the objects of his love and shouts of joy at the pleasure they bring."[123]

---

[118] House, *Unity*, 218. E. Jacob states, "The disentanglement of the remnant from its national trappings makes it into a splendid reality open to the heathen, or rather to the remnant among them (Zeph 3:9; Zech 14:16)" (*Theology of the Old Testament* [trans. A. W. Heathcote and P. J. Allcock; New York: Harper & Brothers, 1958], 324).

[119] See G. W. Anderson, "The Idea of the Remnant in the Book of Zephaniah," *Annual of the Swedish Theological Institute* 11 (1977–78): 11–14.

[120] House, *Zephaniah*, 70; cp. House, *Zephaniah*, 80: "Certain actions of the remnant mirror the goodness of Yahweh. The remnant *does* exhibit some humility and righteousness or God would not champion their cause. They are morally superior to the wicked of the earth because of their humility. ... From the point at which potential mercy is offered to the remnant, they become progressively more acceptable to God. ... Because of His mercy the remnant becomes what Israel should always have been. God's goodness bears fruit." Smith, *Micah-Malachi*, 123, notes: "There is no general call for repentance here. It seems the prophet has given up hope for the immediate deliverance of Judah as a whole. Only a remnant of the humble seekers after Yahweh might be hidden from the wrath of God on that day."

[121] Robertson, *Nahum, Habakkuk, Zephaniah*, 22. He continues that a "far more explicit ... sign of hope" is given in 3:15–17.

[122] House, *Unity*, 95–96. He notes that Haggai–Malachi shows how the blessings will materialize.

[123] Robertson, *Nahum, Habakkuk, Zephaniah*, 25.

(9) The Text of Zephaniah

Manuscript tradition is unanimous in including Zephaniah as one part of the larger unit, the Book of the Twelve. Its position within the twelve is also constant in the manuscript evidence, though some manuscripts, especially in the Greek tradition, have a unique order for the first six books, and one Qumran manuscript may reflect a collection where Malachi is not the final book.[124] Such a collection appears to have been known at least since the time of Jesus ben Sira about 200 B.C. (see *Sir* 48:10; 49:10). Luke appears to refer to such a collection in Acts 7:42–43; 13:40–41; 15:15.

The Hebrew text of Zephaniah is quite well preserved so that few, if any, changes to the text need be considered.[125]

OUTLINE OF ZEPHANIAH

Title Verse (1:1)

I. The Lord's Great Day of Judgment (1:2–2:3)
  1. Judgment against the Earth (1:2–3)
  2. Judgment against Judah (1:4–13)
  3. Judgment at the Great Day of the Lord (1:14–2:3)

II. The Judgment against the Nations (2:4–15)
  1. Judgment against Philistia (2:4–7)
  2. Judgment against Moab and Ammon (2:8–11)
  3. Judgment against Cush (2:12)
  4. Judgment against Assyria (2:13–15)

III. The Future of Jerusalem (3:1–20)
  1. The Destruction of the Rebellious (3:1–8)
  2. The Deliverance of the Righteous (3:9–13)
  3. The Joy of the City (3:14–20)

---

[124] Jones, *Formation,* 5–6.

[125] See Motyer, "Zephaniah," 3:900–901; Roberts, *Nahum, Habakkuk, and Zephaniah*, 163; Patterson, *Nahum, Habakkuk, Zephaniah*, 294; Rudolph, *Micha, Nahum, Habakuk, Zephanja,* 256.

SECTION OUTLINE

TITLE VERSE (1:1)

I. THE LORD'S GREAT DAY OF JUDGMENT (1:2–2:3)
   1. Judgment against the Earth (1:2–3)
   2. Judgment against Judah (1:4–13)
   3. Judgment at the Great Day of the Lord (1:14–2:3)
      (1) A Day of Wrath (1:14–18)
      (2) A Day for Repentance (2:1–3)

TITLE VERSE (1:1)

Zephaniah did not live in "the best of times; the worst of times."[1] Zephaniah simply lived in the worst of times. Manasseh ruled Judah for fifty-five years, long years of rebellion against the Lord and years of turning toward Assyrian gods. Manasseh introduced all kinds of evil into Judah. In this time Zephaniah was born. The brief reign of Ammon and the opening years of the boy-king Josiah brought little improvement. Zephaniah faithfully began pronouncing the word of the Lord in the worst of times.

Zephaniah's song had a dark melody of judgment. Again and again God announced judgment on a people who had turned away from him and turned toward all kinds of vile practices. What other choice did God have? God had given the people the blessings he promised to their father Abraham. He had given them prophets (whom they killed), priests, and the sages. He redeemed them in the exodus. He provided the law through Moses and gave the land under Joshua. God granted the tabernacle and the temple. God had done everything for the people of Jerusalem. If grace could not have its way, judgment would.

God promised judgment for an unrepentant people who set their faces toward rebellion. Zephaniah proclaimed God's message of judgment, which only eventually would issue in a period of hope.

[1]The word of the LORD that came to Zephaniah son of Cushi, the son of Gedaliah, the son of Amariah, the son of Hezekiah, during the reign of Josiah son of Amon king of Judah:

---

[1] C. Dickens, *A Tale of Two Cities,* reprint ed. (New York: Pocket Books, Inc., 1955), 3.

1:1 Most prophetic books in the Old Testament begin with a title verse that introduces the prophet, often briefly describing the time period of the prophet's ministry and how the message came to the prophet. The title verse to Zephaniah's prophecy describes the prophet's message as the word of the Lord that came to Zephaniah in the days of Josiah, king of Judah.[2]

Several prophetic books begin in a fashion similar to the Book of Zephaniah. "The word of the LORD" is the most common way to describe the message that came to a prophet (cp. Jer 1:2; Hos 1:1; Joel 1:1; Jonah 1:1; Mic 1:1; Hag 1:1; Zech 1:1; Mal 1:1). It emphasizes the uniqueness of the prophet's message—his message came from the Lord. The content of the prophetic literature illustrates how the prophets spoke for God in such a unique way as God's messengers that they prefaced their messages with "This is what the LORD says." Zephaniah's message followed the prophetic pattern. He received the word of the Lord and proclaimed that message when Josiah reigned as king of Judah.

The expression "word of the LORD" occurs 242 times in the Old Testament, 225 of these being a technical term for prophetic verbal revelation.[3] Often the expression also appears in the "call to attention" formula[4] that opens a public presentation and seeks to attract the audience's attention (Num 12:6; Pss 50:7; 81:9; Isa 1:10; Jer 10:1; Hos 4:1; Amos 3:1,13; 5:1; 7:16; 8:4; Mic 6:2; Jer 28:15). The word is the Lord's voluntary choice to make himself known, expressing his thought and his will. Through his word God shows the activity in which he is involved in his world. Once spoken, the word works out its message, never returning to God without having achieved its purpose (Isa 55:10–11).[5]

The word is good (Josh 21:45; 23:14–15; 1 Kgs 8:56; Isa 39:8; Jer 29:10;

---

[2] J. Nogalski argues that the superscription has no historical worth, being a stereotyped product of the Deuteronomistic school, and is to be compared to the superscriptions in Hosea, Joel, Jonah, and Micah (*Literary Precursors to the Book of the Twelve* [Berlin: Walter de Gruyter, 1993], 176–78, 181–87); cp. R. R. Wilson, *Prophecy and Society in Ancient Israel* (Philadelphia: Fortress, 1980), 145–66.

[3] G. Gerleman, "דָּבָר *dābār* word," *TLOT* 1:330. In the Pentateuch the term appears in Gen 15:1,4; Exod 9:20–21; Num 15:31; Deut 5:5. In the writing prophets it appears in the titles to books, quite rarely in prophetic address (Isa 1:10; 2:3=Mic 4:2; Hos 4:1; Amos 8:11–12) and in prophetic reports (Amos 7:16). At least 110 of the occurrences appear in the "Prophetic Word Formula —דְבַר יהוה + הָיָה + אֶל + the name of a prophet or a pronoun standing for the prophet—the word of Yahweh came or occurred to … (1 Sam 15:10; 1 Kgs 6:11; Jer 1:4 11; 2:1; 7:1; 11:1; 33:19,23; 35:12; 42:7; Ezek 6:1; 7:1; Hos 1:1; Joel 1:1; Mic 1:1).

[4] This consists of (1) a call to listen such as שִׁמְעוּ דְבַר־יְהוָה, "hear the word of Yahweh"; (2) a mention of those addressed such as בְּנֵי יִשְׂרָאֵל, "sons of Israel"; and (3) an indication of what is to be heard such as כִּי רִיב לַיהוָה עִם־יוֹשְׁבֵי הָאָרֶץ, "for Yahweh has a court case with the inhabitants of the land" (see Hos 4:1); cp. M. A. Sweeney, *Isaiah 1–39 with an Introduction to Prophetic Literature,* FOTL (Grand Rapids: Eerdmans, 1996), 544.

[5] Gerleman, "דָּבָר *dābār* word," 1:331–32.

33:14; Zech 1:13); upright (Ps 33:4; Neh 9:13); true (2 Sam 7:28; 1 Kgs 17:24); reliable (1 Kgs 8:26; 1 Chr 17:23; 2 Chr 1:9; 6:17); eternal (Ps 199:89); and even holy (Jer 23:9). His word brings creation into being (Pss 33:6,9; 104:7; 147:15–18). Once spoken the word of God stands forever (Isa 40:8). God watches to ensure that his word is realized in history (Jer 1:12; cp. Deut 18:22; Jer 28:9). This concept and understanding of the word of God "points out the absolute uniqueness of Israel's religion on the basis of personal contact with Yahweh—the transcendent, sovereign, creator God."[6]

The word is what characterizes a prophet just as wisdom does a wise man and torah does a priest (Jer 18:18). Thus people can go to a prophet seeking God (1 Sam 9:9; 2 Kgs 3:11) or seeking his word (1 Sam 16:23; 1 Kgs 14:5; 22:5; Jer 37:17; 38:14; 42:2; Amos 8:12). Such word comes when one stands in the council of God (Jer 23:18). The expectation is that the word received in God's council (cp. Isa 6) will be preached to the people (Jer 23:22,28) and will act like a hammer smashing a rock to pieces (Jer 23:29). The message may be preserved in writing also (Jer 36:2). The prophet digested God's word so that it became a vital part of his life (Jer 15:16).

Just because a prophet claims to have and to preach God's word does not mean he has done so. He may have stolen the word (Jer 23:30) or preached a word that did not come from God (Jer 23:16–17; Ezek 13:6). The prophet may be deluded or deceived (Ezek 14:9). A prophet may faithfully deliver God's word but not be believed or accepted (Jer 17:15; 29:19; 37:2; 44:16; Ezek 12:21–28; 33:30–31). The word can cause the prophet to suffer (Jer 20:8; 23:9).

The word is not guaranteed to Israel. The day will come when they will search and scurry to find it without results. They will suffer a famine of the word of God (Amos 8:11–12). Absence of God's word is in itself judgment (1 Sam 28:15–16; Mic 3:6; Ezek 7:26). It is a burning fire that consumes the people (Jer 5:14).[7]

The word "came" may convey more significance than would normally be assumed. In Hebrew the verb can mean that Zephaniah experienced the word or that the word happened to the prophet. "The word of the Lord became a living reality to Zephaniah."[8] Both ways of interpreting the word of the Lord that came to Zephaniah emphasize the unique nature of God's word. "We know nothing of the processes involved. This is a work of God. We do know, however, that it was the experience of specially prepared people (Jer 1:4) who were brought into divine fellowship (Isa 6:5–8; Ezek 1:28–2:2) and within that fellowship made privy to divine secrets (Jer 23:12,22; Amos 3:7). There was no crushing of human personality or overriding of human mental pro-

---

[6] H. D. Buckwalter, "Word," *EDBT,* 828.

[7] See W. H. Schmidt, "דָּבָר *dābhar,*" *TDOT* 3:103–25.

[8] J. A. Motyer, "Zephaniah," *The Minor Prophets,* ed. T. E. McComiskey (Grand Rapids: Baker, 1998), 3:908.

cesses; rather the prophetic state lifted the individual into the presence of God. This experience made the prophets more truly human than they were before, so that they were enabled to receive his revelation."[9] The word characterized Zephaniah's preaching and gave him authority to speak dangerous words in high places.[10] "Zephaniah was inspired to receive, understand, and then express the divine word without tarnishing its divine reality and truth."[11]

On the meaning of the name Zephaniah see the Introduction: "Zephaniah, the Man." Although Zephaniah twice mentioned the land of Cush (2:12; 3:10), and the Hebrew word *kûšî* usually refers to the land or people of Cush (except in Jer 36:14, where it is a proper name), there is no reason to place any ethnic associations on the name "Cushi" here (see "Zephaniah, the Man" in the Introduction).[12]

Neither the name "Gedaliah"[13] nor the name "Amariah" seem particularly noteworthy. Both names are compounds using the covenant name for God, and both appear frequently in the Old Testament. The name "Amariah" appears especially in the priest lists of the postexilic period.[14]

Only the Book of Zephaniah among the prophetic literature traces the genealogy of the prophet to the fourth generation, a method suggesting that the person named in the fourth generation was particularly noteworthy.[15] King Hezekiah, to whom this verse probably refers (see Introduction: "Zephaniah, the Man") reigned as king of Judah from 715–687 B.C. Zephaniah then would have been a member of Josiah's extended family and familiar with Jerusalem and the functions of the court (1:8–10; 3:3). He clearly appreciated the importance of Jerusalem to the people of God (3:14–20). Patterson suggested that the title "King of Judah" may have been omitted after Hezekiah's name out of respect for the reigning king Josiah.[16] A. Berlin

[9] Ibid. Motyer notes further: "If the prophet is to say something that appalls (1:2–3), shocks (1:10), horrifies (2:9), or seems too good to be true (3:8), he needs to be sure of his ground; he needs the authority of the divine word."

[10] Cp. R. D. Patterson, *Nahum, Habakkuk, Zephaniah,* WEC (Chicago: Moody, 1991), 298.

[11] Motyer, "Zephaniah," 908.

[12] Cf. A. Berlin, *Zephaniah,* AB (New York: Doubleday, 1994), 67. She notes the reference to "Cush, a Benjamite" in Ps 7:1.

[13] J. M. Ward, "Gedaliah," *IDB,* 360.

[14] F. T. Schumacher, "Amariah," *IDB*, 102–3.

[15] Nogalski (*Literary Precursors*, 182–83) argues that "since it would be inconceivable that the great-great grandfather of the prophet would have been alive, the name had to carry enough weight on its own merit to serve some function. Only if Hezekiah the king was intended could this name connote such special significance." Nogalski skates on thin scholarly ice as he tries to make the reference to Hezekiah a later addition to the superscription on the basis of ancient Near Eastern genealogies. His own evidence shows how weak is the argument that genealogies with only three previous generations have "considerably more attestation in ancient cultures" (p. 185; see n. 41 for evidence of a varied pattern without continuity or consistency).

[16] Patterson, *Nahum, Habakkuk, Zephaniah,* 279–81.

suggests that the genealogical connection to Hezekiah may have the point of connecting Zephaniah to his religious reforms, "which were not unlike those of Josiah." The superscription, then, "hints that Zephaniah's apparent support of religious reform in his own day has an origin in his family history. He was not a newcomer to the reform movement and was, perhaps, among those urging it even before Josiah instituted it."[17]

Josiah[18] reigned over Judah during some of the most significant days of the Southern Kingdom. He was a good king who entreated the Lord and removed the high places from the land (2 Kgs 18:4).[19] Manasseh, Hezekiah's son, had undone any good Hezekiah accomplished and had added to Judah's propensity to turn from the Lord to pagan worship. Manasseh (687–641 B.C.) influenced the people to follow pagan practices, even to the point of erecting altars for Baal and making an Asherah (2 Kgs 21:3).

Amon followed his father Manasseh and turned out to be as evil as his father. His servants killed him after only two years on the throne (2 Kgs 21:19–24). Josiah became king in the place of his father at eight years of age (2 Kgs 22:1–2). He probably received tutelage from godly priests who turned his thoughts to both political and religious reform.[20]

Zephaniah probably preached his word from the Lord in the early days of Josiah, before Josiah had the opportunity to institute his reforms and while the influences of Manasseh continued to consume the people. One wonders what effect Zephaniah's stern message of judgment had on Josiah, especially if Josiah and Zephaniah were related.

II. THE LORD'S GREAT DAY OF JUDGMENT (1:2–2:3)

Zephaniah's message appears strange and foreign to ears expecting to hear an easy message of hope. It is a realistic message that fit the world as it actually existed. The prophet saw the evil of his day and foresaw the final result of such evil. Evil like that of Judah called for a great day where the slate would be wiped clean and the evil would be swept away.

In a sense, Zephaniah bridged the years between the prophets of the past and the hope of the future age. Like the great eighth-century prophets,

[17] Berlin, *Zephaniah,* 65.

[18] Nogalski notes that Zephaniah is the last book in the Book of the Twelve whose superscription gives an explicitly preexilic date (*Literary Precursors*, 206).

[19] For a more detailed discussion of Josiah and his reforms, see the introduction. See also S. Herrmann, *A History of Israel in Old Testament Times* (Philadelphia: Fortress, 1975), 263–73. For an explanation of why Josiah was only three generations from Hezekiah whereas Zephaniah was four generations, see Berlin, Zephaniah, 68–69.

[20] Ibid., 261.

Zephaniah proclaimed a message of judgment against Israel and Judah. Zephaniah stood in a great line of prophets who proclaimed the evils of society and called for the people to repent (Jer 28:8–9). Failure to repent demanded a great day of judgment. Before Zephaniah, Amos preached a similar message against the social evils that unraveled the fabric of society. Amos had been the first to see the popularly viewed day of the Lord as a day of judgment rather than as a day of light (Amos 5:18–20).

Zephaniah followed in the footsteps of Amos but also extended the message. Zephaniah saw the logical end to the Lord's day of judgment—the Lord would purify his people, thus bringing hope in the midst of sorrow and pain (Zeph 3:14–20). Like the postexilic prophets, he recognized that God's work ends in victory rather than defeat. The prophets after the exile spoke victoriously of the salvation God would bring for his people, a theme revisited in the final chapter of the Book of Zephaniah.[21]

In opening his message of judgment, Zephaniah carefully moves from judgment against all the earth (1:1–3) to his real theme, judgment against Judah (1:3). He begins with a universal Prophetic Announcement of Judgment against the people, but in so doing he cuts the typical speech in half. He never gives reasons for the punishment of the whole earth. He simply announces punishment.[22] He then gives the fuller form of the Prophetic Announcement of Judgment against the people as he turns to Judah. Here the reasons for punishment become absolutely clear (vv. 4b–6). He then uses an ironic twist on a call to worship to introduce his major theme, that of the day of the Lord. This theme he also introduces in a curious fashion, describing it as a time of sacrifice when God himself is the officiating priest and those he has called to worship find themselves to be the sacrificial animals. The description then turns to lamentation and wailing (1:10–11) and the divine Priest's search to make sure he has not missed anyone (1:12–13). He concludes with a final Prophetic Announcement of Judgment against the people (1:14–18) with only a brief stroke of a reason for punishment (v. 17b).

The entire section concludes in a most unexpected way. The piled up Prophetic Announcements of Judgment against the people give way to a singular call to repentance (2:1–3). This creative use of prophetic forms is matched by a creative use of literary features: long, impressive, first-person speeches of God marked by alliteration and paronomasia (1:2), chiasmus and hyperbole (1:2–3), literary allusions (1:3), anthropopoeia (1:4,12–13), metaphor and simile (1:7,12; 2:1), lament (1:10–11), irony (1:11), merismus (1:12), personification (1:14), synecdoche (1:16), and repetition (1:2,3,14,15–16,18; 2:2,3).[23]

---

[21] J. D. W. Watts, *Joel, Obadiah, Jonah, Nahum Habakkuk and Zephaniah,* CBC (Cambridge: University Press, 1975), 155.

[22] See Sweeney, *Isaiah 1–39*, 530–31, and literature cited there.

[23] For the literary features see Patterson, *Nahum, Habakkuk, Zephaniah,* 297.

1. Judgment against the Earth (1:2–3)

2"I will sweep away everything
from the face of the earth,"
declares the LORD.
3"I will sweep away both men and animals;
I will sweep away the birds of the air
and the fish of the sea.
The wicked will have only heaps of rubble
when I cut off man from the face of the earth,"
declares the LORD.

1:2 The Lord's speech opens the book, establishing the tone for the first sections. Total destruction is the theme. The totality of the destruction appears again several times in the chapter, but especially in the last verse: "The whole world will be consumed, for he will make a sudden end of all who live in the earth." And yet there are indications later in the book that the total destruction theme may be hyperbolic. The possibility of the "humble of the land" surviving is suggested in 2:3. Then in chap. 3, although "no one will be left—no one at all" in the cities of the nations (3:6), the Lord also announces that he will "purify the lips of the peoples, that all of them may call on the name of the LORD and serve him shoulder to shoulder" (3:9). The Lord's people too will worship him after the earth is purged (3:10,20). As far as Judah is concerned, it is "those who rejoice in their pride" who will be removed, and "the meek and humble" will remain (3:11–12). Apparently the same will be true of the nations. Therefore the totality of destruction theme is hyperbolic, stressing by allusions to creation and the great flood that no corner of the earth will escape the Lord's judgment and that the renovation will be complete.[24]

Zephaniah "artfully reverses the order of creation, letting man the last made become man the first destroyed."[25] The two verses of the present section testify to the intention of God to undo creation.[26] Everything would be

---

[24] Cf. Patterson, *Nahum, Habakkuk, Zephaniah,* 300.

[25] Ibid., 299: "The coming destruction will begin with man, who has denied his Creator (1:6) and involved in his sin all that is under his domain. Man's sin is thus weighty, involving not only himself but his total environment."

[26] See M. De Roche, "Zephaniah I 2–3: The 'Sweeping' of Creation," *VT* 30 (1980): 104–9, who shows that previous scholars are correct in seeing that "from the face of the earth" points back to the flood account of Gen 6:7; 7:4; 8:8, that the opening words of Zeph 1:2 reflect Gen 8:21, that the play on words between man and earth (*ʾādām / ʾădāmâ*) points to Gen 2:7; 3:17,19, and that the order of destruction in Zeph 1:3 points back to a reversal of the order of creation in Gen 1:20–26. He also notes that "all" in Zeph 1:2 picks up an emphasis from Gen 2–3. Nogalski uses De Roche's evidence to date 1:2–3 postexilic since it depends on the "P" account of creation (*Literary Precursors*, 188).

swept away from the face of the earth.[27] "All living things are to be destroyed in this scouring of the world, so a picture of emptiness is projected."[28] By this picture "Zephaniah is proclaiming man's loss of dominion over all the earth, and more importantly, the *reversal of creation.* ... Yahweh's 'sweeping' will be just as bleak as his creating was abundant."[29] Nogalski notes that "the allusions to the creation and flood accounts are specifically selected for their emotional impact."[30]

The readers may have stood too secure in the promise of Gen 8:21 that God would not repeat the flood destruction. "God's people ought not to misunderstand (cf. v. 12) the old promise as indicating that God cannot again intervene to judge mankind."[31]

The prophet made sure that the reader and listener understood the one initiating the action. The Lord would be the One to sweep away everything. At the end of each verse, the prophet closed the section with "declares the LORD." The phrase describes an intimate communication from the Lord, with almost the force of whispering in the ear. This phrase, characteristic of prophetic speech, appears six times in the book (1:2,3,10; 2:9; 3:8,20). The first three emphasize God's judgment on the earth. The six occurrences together set apart the major themes of Zephaniah: judgment and mercy. "Only very pivotal speeches of Yahweh are chosen to receive this linguistic emphasis."[32]

By closing each verse with "declares the LORD," the prophet also communicated the certainty of the judgment. The one who created the world could reverse the process by wiping everything clean.

The Hebrew text emphasizes the intensity of the judgment. A good translation of the Hebrew text would be "I will indeed sweep away everything" or

---

[27] The first two words of v. 2, אָסֹף אָסֵף, use the same three consonants in Hb. but come from entirely different verbal roots—אסף, "gather or remove," and סוף, "come to an end" (or "cause to end" in *hiphil*). Repeated attempts by scholars to force the words to come from the same root offer a sad testimony in the history of scholarship to a desire to make the prophet prosaic and ordinary rather than skillful and unique. See Patterson, *Nahum, Habakkuk, Zephaniah,* 300, for a few of the scholarly emendations. Motyer warns against emendation, assuming we have here "a Hebrew idiom that we do not currently understand ... a colloquial usage involving anomalies similar to the familiar שָׁב שְׁבוּת (bring back captivity), arising perhaps from assonance (2:7; 3:20)" ("Zephaniah," 3:911).

[28] House, *Unity of the Twelve*, 148.

[29] De Roche, "Zephaniah I 2–3," 106–7.

[30] Nogalski, *Literary Precursors*, 200.

[31] Patterson, *Nahum, Habakkuk, Zephaniah,* 301.

[32] P. R. House, *Zephaniah: A Prophetic Drama*, JSOTSup 69 (Sheffield, Eng.: Almond Press, 1988), 86. Motyer says the phrase "often appears abruptly and even intrusively, as if it were a seal suddenly stamped down to validate the divine authenticity of what is being said" ("Zephaniah," 911).

"I will utterly sweep away everything."[33] Roberts follows T. H. Gaster in relating the verb to the festival of ingathering and thus seeing the word proclaimed during the festival: "The feast would not be what they expected; it was Yahweh who was going to do the gathering in."[34]

As the following verse attests, those things to be swept away were living creatures rather than inanimate objects. The judgment involved the whole world, not simply the land of Judah. Judgment against Judah follows in the next section (1:4–13).

The first hearers of the prophet's message must have been shocked at the severity of the judgment and that it would come from the Lord. The prophet used shock tactics to reinforce the message. At this point in the prophecy, Zephaniah had not made any accusations of wrongdoing. What had the people done to deserve this? The answer to the inevitable question comes quickly enough in the message but not without causing considerable consternation on the part of the hearers.

Motyer notes that "human nature remains impervious to the beneficial effects of good rulers and further reformations; it remains unchanged even by additional centuries of divine grace so that life in every aspect (1:3)—and indeed the planet itself (1:18; 3:8)—remains under divine judgment."[35]

1:3 God vowed to sweep away all the living creatures—man, beast, birds of the air, and fish of the sea. Presumably birds and fish would survive most natural disasters (fish survived the flood, Gen 6:7). To include birds and fish spotlights the severity of the judgment. God had created fish, birds, animals, and human beings in that order (Gen 1:20–28). The order of destruction is the exact opposite, indicating all that had been created would be "uncreated." As Nogalski notes, "The manner in which this unit [Zeph 1:2–3] utilizes these motifs [creation and flood] makes the imagery quite poignant. It draws upon the flood imagery as an actualization of YHWH's previous judgment, and its complete reversal of the creation motif heightens the intensity of the announced judgment."[36]

---

[33] אָסֹף אָסֵף, the infinitive absolute followed by the perfect tense, a device which serves in syntax to emphasize intensity. "The infinitive usually emphasizes not the meaning denoted by the verb's root but the force of the verb in context. When the verb makes an assertion, whatever its aspect, the notion of certainty is reinforced by the infinitive …" (Waltke and O'Connor, *IBHS* § 35.3.1b).

[34] Roberts, *Nahum, Habakkuk, and Zephaniah*, 169, following T. H. Gaster, *Myth, Legend, and Custom in the Old Testament* (New York: Harper & Row, 1969), 679, as well as A. S. Kapelrud, *The Message of the Prophet Zephaniah* (Oslo: Universitetsforlaget, 1975), 22.

[35] Motyer, "Zephaniah," 3:911.

[36] Nogalski, *Literary Precursors*, 188.

All that human ingenuity had formed would become a heap of ruins.[37] "Zephaniah traces judgment to its root cause (i.e., sin) and forecasts that the works of the wicked themselves will be swept away." "The wicked" is a general term to describe evildoers, the central theme of the last half of the verse. The wicked would have nothing left when God cut off human beings from the face of the earth.

The Hebrew word for "man" *(ʾādām)* means humankind in general.[38] Again the word comes from the creation account—Adam. This Adam will be cut off from the face of the earth—*ʾădāmâ*, picking up the wordplay from Genesis 1. This makes the verse parallel to v. 2.[39]

How can a message like that of Zephaniah square with the Christian gospel? Should not the church be less judgmental and more affirming? How can we understand the message of Zephaniah in such a modern age? E. Achtemeier gives an example of those who reject the relevance of Zephaniah's message. She recounts a sermon on Zeph 1:2 preached in 1939 by a British preacher who "softened the judgment announced by the prophet by pointing to our salvation in Christ."[40] The preacher compared the text with John 3:16 and then commented:

> Can we, "who profess and call ourselves Christians," doubt which of these sayings is from a spiritual standpoint the finer of the two?[41]

---

[37] The NASB translates the MT fairly literally: "And the ruins along with the wicked." The translation in the NIV is an attempt to render the sense of the Hb. text, though the footnote delineates the difficulty of the Hb. The RSV, NEB, and GNB make a slight change in the Hb. to get the reading, "I will overthrow the wicked" (RSV). House (*Zephaniah,* 127) follows BHS in emending וְהַמַּכְשֵׁלוֹת, "ruins" (occurring elsewhere only in Isa 3:6), to וְהִכְשַׁלְתִּי ("and I will make to stumble), but Berlin notes that "cause to stumble" "seems feeble compared with the other verbs of destruction in this verse" (*Zephaniah,* 73). Patterson shows various options while seeking to maintain the MT reading, which he translates as "the things that cause to stumble" (*Nahum, Habakkuk, Zephaniah,* 302). He analyzes this as a *hiphil* participle. He interprets this to mean: "Every false religious practice that has occasioned his falling will be destroyed." Motyer argues for the MT, seeing the present poem as balanced and Hebrew parallelism as not rigid enough to demand emendation here ("Zephaniah," 3:911–12). O. P. Robertson wants to take the MT reading literally, "stumbling blocks," rather than figuratively, "ruins." He concludes: "Beasts, birds, and fish, representative of the whole creation, have become for humanity an occasion of stumbling. … The prophet's reference may be to idols shaped after the form of created things" (*The Books of Nahum, Habakkuk, Zephaniah,* NICOT [Grand Rapids: Eerdmans, 1990], 259). Similarly Berlin, citing Deut 4:16–18, though she considers that it may be a gloss (*Zephaniah,* 73). Roberts follows many other commentators and the LXX in omitting the entire line as a late gloss that misunderstood the text (*Nahum, Habakkuk, and Zephaniah,* 167, 170).

[38] F. Maass, "אָדָם *ʾādhām,*" *TDOT* 1:75.

[39] See Patterson, *Nahum, Habakkuk, Zephaniah,* 300, who also points to the use of the Hb. letters *aleph* and *mem* twelve times each in a broad display of alliteration in these two verses.

[40] E. Achtemeier, *Nahum-Malachi*, IBC (Atlanta: John Knox, 1986), 33.

[41] Ibid.

> … there is surely nothing in His (Jesus') teaching to justify the supposition that He would have endorsed such a prophecy of general extermination. …[42]

As Achtemeier explains: "Zephaniah's radical pronouncements of God's judgment upon the whole earth were thereby rendered irrelevant and unimportant to the Christian reader or hearer of them."[43] But she continues to note that this sermon was preached when "there was taking root across the English channel in Nazi Germany a thorough-going perversion of the biblical faith" which "was finally done away only by being swept from the face of the earth."[44]

We acknowledge the ferocity and strange sound of these verses. At the same time, we must acknowledge the relevance of these verses for the believing community. God calls us to faith—and to obedience. Our lives must square with the Christian gospel at the point of obedience and faith as well as at the point of affirming sinners and pointing them to forgiveness in Christ Jesus.

2. Judgment against Judah (1:4–13)

4"I will stretch out my hand against Judah
and against all who live in Jerusalem.
I will cut off from this place every remnant of Baal,
the names of the pagan and the idolatrous priests—
5those who bow down on the roofs
to worship the starry host,
those who bow down and swear by the LORD
and who also swear by Molech,
6those who turn back from following the LORD
and neither seek the LORD nor inquire of him.
7Be silent before the Sovereign LORD,
for the day of the LORD is near.
The LORD has prepared a sacrifice;
he has consecrated those he has invited.
8On the day of the LORD's sacrifice
I will punish the princes
and the king's sons
and all those clad
in foreign clothes.
9On that day I will punish
all who avoid stepping on the threshold,
who fill the temple of their gods
with violence and deceit.

---

42 Ibid., 31.
43 Ibid.
44 Ibid., 63.

[10]"On that day," declares the LORD,
"a cry will go up from the Fish Gate,
wailing from the New Quarter,
and a loud crash from the hills.
[11]Wail, you who live in the market district;
all your merchants will be wiped out,
all who trade with silver will be ruined.
[12]At that time I will search Jerusalem with lamps
and punish those who are complacent,
who are like wine left on its dregs,
who think, 'The LORD will do nothing,
either good or bad.'
[13]Their wealth will be plundered,
their houses demolished.
They will build houses
but not live in them;
they will plant vineyards
but not drink the wine.

Separating this unit from 1:2–3 is done on the basis of content.[45] The grammatical structure of the Hebrew actually joins them together, using the same verb forms (perfect consecutive) found at the end of v. 3. Verses 4–6 form a subsection of the poem joined by the series of accusatives giving the charge against Judah.[46] This again shows the prophet's poetic skill as he gains attention with a statement on the judgment of the earth before zeroing in on his primary audience: Jerusalem. He repeats the prophetic form to gain attention and doubly emphasize the inevitability and the totality of the coming punishment. He then (v. 7) switches to imperative mood, issuing a solemn, silent call to worship before describing the worship situation that turns out to be a time of punishment and lamentation rather than praise and joy (vv. 7b–10). A second imperative (v. 11) issues a call to lamentation in view of God's action of seeking out any who may have missed his sacrifice (vv. 11–13).[47]

What a stunning surprise for Judah! "The scepter never was to depart from Judah (Gen 49:10). God had sworn that he never would remove a lamp from Jerusalem for the sake of his servant David (1 Kgs 11:13,36; cf. 15:4; 2 Kgs 8:19; 19:34; 20:6). It was unthinkable to a Judean that somehow the place of God's own enthronement on earth could ever fall."[48]

---

[45] According to Nogalski, "The imagery and intention of 1:4ff. change so dramatically that it is difficult to accept an original connection to 1:2f." (*Literary Precursors*, 189). He uses this argument to see the connecting "and" (Hb. *waw*) as part of the editorial process that he claims added 1:2–3 to the book at a later stage.

[46] The accusatives identify individual groups facing God's judgment for "abusing the YHWH cult in Jerusalem" (ibid.).

[47] See the structural comments of Patterson, *Nahum, Habakkuk, Zephaniah,* 307.

[48] Robertson, *Nahum, Habakkuk, and Zephaniah,* 261.

But Judah stood first in line for the judgment of God because of the Lord's proximity to the covenant people. They had benefited from the Lord's revelation of himself. Judah and Jerusalem received the blessings of God. They had the privilege of hearing the great prophets of God who preceded Zephaniah. They received tabernacle, temple, and law from the hand of the Lord. They heard the teaching of the priests. But their relationship with the Lord meant that they also must receive his judgment for their failure to heed his warning and instruction. The people's refusal to follow God and their choice to serve other gods is the reason for the judgment (1:4–6). "God is obviously quite angry at the present state of affairs, and His words come with great suddenness and vehemence."[49]

Most of the people may have believed that Judah's special relationship with God secured special treatment from God. Amos had reminded the people of his day that election meant election to service rather than election to privilege: "You only have I chosen of all the families of the earth; therefore I will punish you for all your sins" (Amos 5:18). "Whether religious officials (1:4), royalty (1:8), or common citizen who mistake God's mercy for indifference (1:12–13), none who sins can escape the Lord's wrath."[50]

1:4 The figure of God stretching out his hand against Judah pictured the judgment of God in a powerful way.[51] It reaches back to the exodus experience where God saved Israel by his outstretched hand or arm (Exod 3:19–20; 4:17; 6:1; 7:19; 13:3; 15:12; cp. 14:31; Deut 4:34; 5:15; 6:21; 7:8,19; 9:26; 11:2; 26:8; 34:12; Jer 32:21; Ps 136:12). This may be related to an Egyptian motif, the Amarna letters referring to the conquering arm of the Pharaoh.[52] Isaiah had used the same figure to describe the fury of Assyria which God would bring against Judah: "Yet for all this, his anger is not turned away, his hand is still upraised" (Isa 9:12, 17, 21; 10:4; cp. 5:25; Jer 21:5). The hand symbolized omnipotent power (Jer 32:17) and God's sovereign direction of history (Isa 14:26–27; Jer 27:5). He moved his hand in judgment against Israel and the nations (Exod 7:5; 1 Sam 5:6,11; Isa 19:16; 49; 22; Jer 6:12; Zech 2:9). The hand stretched against Judah symbolized the power of God brought to bear against the people of Judah and Jerusalem. "Not to see God's actions is a sign of deep spiritual darkness (Isa 5:12; Ps 28:5). ... People are capable of recognizing God's deeds in creation and in history and are obliged to draw conclu-

---

[49] House, *Zephaniah*, 58.

[50] Ibid., 149.

[51] A. S. van der Woude notes that the expression "the hand of God" occurs over two hundred times in the OT ("יָד *yād*, hand," *TLOT* 2:501).

[52] M. Dreytza, "יָד," *NIDOTTE* 2:403, referring to J. K. Hoffmeier, "The Arm of God Versus the Arm of Pharaoh in the Exodus Narratives," *Bib* 67 (1986): 378–87. For some reason van der Woude rejects the exodus as giving impetus to the expression in Israel ("יָד *yād* hand," 2:501).

sions out of these: to praise, fear, and trust him" (cp. Isa 26:11).[53]

For the first time Zephaniah began to delineate the kind of sins that aroused the wrath of God against his chosen people. He began "appropriately with an exclusive concentration on the sins committed directly against God in the worship practices of the people."[54] These included "religious error (vv. 4b–5), disloyalty (v. 5b), apostasy (v. 6a), and practical atheism (v. 6b). ... Six groups are singled out: Baalists, false priests, astral devotees (Zeph 1:4b–5a), syncretists (v. 5b), backsliders (v. 6a), and practical atheists (v. 6b). The first three are actively committed to other gods; the Lord has no place in their religion. The second three pretend a devotion that is actually unreal (v. 5b), have departed from a devotion they once professed (v. 6a), or have reached the ultimate irreligion where the Lord in not a living reality to them at all (v. 6b)."[55]

"Particularly offensive to Yahweh is syncretism, which in this instance results from mixing the worship of God with that of pagan gods (1:5) and from accepting foreign customs in Judah's court (1:8). Their worship has become as foreign as their clothing."[56] For centuries the people of Israel and Judah had worshiped the Lord while also giving allegiance to the Baal gods. Baalism held a powerful lock on the people of Israel and Judah. When the people entered Canaan from the wilderness of Sinai, the Canaanites remained in the land. The people of Israel learned to farm and to worship Baal from the Canaanites. The Canaanites believed that the Baals ensured the fertility of the land. The Canaanites probably believed that worshiping Baal did as much to produce a crop as breaking the ground, planting the seed, and harvesting the crop.

Still, as Josiah ascended the Judean throne, syncretism and idolatry reigned. "This idolatry infected the very center of Judah's religious life, the temple, where there were sacred cult objects kept for the worship of the Canaanite goddess Asherah (2 Kgs 23:4; 21:7) and statues dedicated to the sungod[sic] Shamash (2 Kgs 23:11), as well as altars for sacrifice to the Assyrian astral deities (2 Kgs 23:12; 21:4). At these idolatrous shrines, Judean priests led in worship."[57]

Baalism involved worship of a variety of gods on the high places. In the temples of Baal "sacred" priestesses served as prostitutes to provide for the fertility of the land.[58] According to Canaanite belief, Baal was the son of El. As god of fertility and storm, Baal provided the rain and the fertility of the

---

[53] Dreytza, "יָד," 2:403. God's hand can also express his protection and his creative power, but those meanings are not associated with the present context.

[54] Robertson, *Nahum, Habakkuk, and Zephaniah,* 262.

[55] Motyer, "Zephaniah," 3:913–14.

[56] House, *Zephaniah,* 149.

[57] Achtemeier, *Nahum–Malachi,* 64.

[58] M. J. Mulder, "בַּעַל *baʿal,*" *TDOT* 2:192–200.

land. Anat was Baal's consort. "It was believed that if Baal and Anat saw humans cohabiting on earth, they would be reminded of their own conjugal responsibilities. Their cosmic union would then produce on earth bountiful crops and increase the size of flocks and herds."[59] No wonder God vowed to stretch out his hand against Judah and Jerusalem and cut off the last trace of Baal worship! "The God who created in health and redeems in wholeness cannot be joined to a god who fertilizes the earth through sacred prostitution and who claims his portion by child sacrifice."[60]

Along with the last vestiges of Baalism, God promised to remove two groups mentioned in the last part of the verse—the pagan priests (who served Baal)[61] and the idolatrous priests (those who served the Lord and also gave allegiance to Baal). To cut off the "names" meant to cause these priests to be forgotten,[62] much in the same way that Isaiah spoke of giving those eunuchs who kept the Sabbath a "name," meaning that they would be remembered (Isa 56:4–5). "Instead of providing for the removal of sin, the priesthood instigated depravity of the worst sort."[63] The priests and the priesthood of Baal must go! Josiah put into practice Zephaniah's prophecy by removing the pagan priests (2 Kgs 23; 2 Chr 34).

The reader should not underestimate the abominable allure of Baalism. Baal could be read as a simple common name meaning "owner" (Exod 22:7; Job 31:39), "master" (Isa 1:3), "ruler" (Isa 16:8), or "husband" (Deut 24:4). Worship in the name of Baal could easily be understood as applying the name Baal to refer to Yahweh as owner, master, ruler, husband (cp. Isa 54:5; Jer 31:32; Hos 2:16). The worship of this god corrupted Israel for centuries. Elijah's contest on Mount Carmel involved the priests of Baal. The purpose for Elijah was to establish whether the Lord or Baal is God. Baalism obviously called into question the very nature of God (1 Kgs 18:21) by diluting the power of God and by giving worship and praise to another. While the word "baal" earlier had been a perfectly good Hebrew title meaning "lord," "master," or "husband," Hosea demanded complete abandonment of the name because of its evil associations (Hos 2:16–17).

---

[59] C. J. Barber, *Habakkuk and Zephaniah,* EBC (Chicago: Moody, 1985), 91.

[60] Robertson, *Nahum, Habakkuk, and Zephaniah,* 262–63.

[61] The Hb. term הַכְּמָרִים appears also in Hos 10:5 and 2 Kgs 22:5. Patterson says, "In all three cases the term refers to priests outside the established priesthood of Israel and has special connection with Baalism" (*Nahum, Habakkuk, Zephaniah,* 305). P. Jenson ("כֹּמֶר," *NIDOTTE* 2:662) notes an occurrence in the Jewish Elephantine papyri written after 500 B.C. in which the term refers to Egyptian priests in contrast with Jewish priests (כֹּהֲנִים). Motyer connects it to "one practicing a frenzied or ecstatic religion" ("Zephaniah," 3:912).

[62] Patterson points out that אֶת־שֵׁם הַכְּמָרִים עִם־הַכֹּהֲנִים "should probably be construed as apposition for emphatic amplification—even the names of the officiating priests connected with Baalism and the other false religions will be cut off" (*Nahum, Habakkuk, Zephaniah,* 305).

[63] Robertson, *Nahum, Habakkuk, and Zephaniah,* 263.

Later the people of Israel continued to worship Baal. They assumed that the bounty of nature resulted from him. Gomer, like Israel, had not acknowledged that the Lord "gave her the grain, the new wine and oil … [and] lavished on her the silver and gold—which they used for Baal" (Hos 2:8). "Such lack of concern about God's standards for proper worship leads to the belief that Yahweh is a powerless deity."[64]

As Motyer has pointed out, Baal worship has its modern reincarnations: "Baal was another name for the gross national product, and wherever people see bank balances, prosperity, a sound economy, productivity, and mounting exports as the essence of their security, Baal is still worshiped. … Wherever excitement in religion becomes an end in itself and wherever the cult of 'what helps' replaces joy in 'what's true,' Baal is worshiped."[65]

As late as the time of Jeremiah and Zephaniah, the people of Judah worshiped the nature gods. Only the exile in Babylon removed the worship of other gods from the land of Israel. God had swept everything clean, and the people of Israel returned to Jerusalem in the strong monotheistic faith which so characterizes the faith of New Testament times. If Zephaniah's message came early in the days of Josiah (640–609 B.C.) and provided impetus to the young king and his advisors, God's sweeping everything clean came only about fifty years after Zephaniah's preaching.[66]

1:5 God also stretched out his hand against those who bowed down on the housetops to the host of heaven. Many people in Judah apparently climbed to the flat roofs of their houses to worship the sun, the moon, and the stars, a practice as old as Babylon and as modern as the morning paper. Since so many of the heavenly bodies could be seen only at night, their worship was normally carried out at night (see Jer 19:13; 32:29).[67] The practice robbed God of the worship that uniquely belonged to him and deceived the worshipers into believing a lie. It also went against God's specific instructions (Deut 4:19; 17:3–7).[68] Such worship deprived the people of genuine guidance, the kind of wisdom that could make a difference in their lives and their very existence. This kind of worship would be cut off as well.

The holy God could not tolerate syncretism—the worship of the Lord and the worship of other gods at the same time. Worship in Zephaniah's day parallels much of the practice of modern society. Many people are not irreligious; they simply refuse to give allegiance to the Lord God alone. They too lose the guidance and strength of the living Lord, exchanging his blessings for the

[64] House, *Zephaniah,* 149.

[65] Motyer, "Zephaniah," 3:912.

[66] See the discussion of the historical background and date of Zephaniah in the introduction.

[67] See Roberts, *Nahum, Habakkuk, and Zephaniah,* 172–73.

[68] Jer 44:19 shows that this continued to be a temptation for Israel, especially the women, after they had fled from their homeland to Egypt.

impotence of pagan worship and daily horoscopes.

The Ammonites, Judah's neighbors to the east, worshiped Molech, a worship the Israelites shared especially during the reign of Manasseh when some of the people burned their sons and their daughters as an offering to Molech. Josiah's reform attempted to remove all such practices (2 Kgs 23:10), but these too seemed to persist until the fall of Jerusalem. But the Hebrew text reads *malkām,* "their king," emended to "Molech" by the NIV. It probably is better to translate "their king" here and understand it as referring to a pagan god.[69] "Zephaniah exposes an expressed loyalty to the Lord, while the actual basis of life is their king."[70] If this interpretation is correct, the "king" would be Baal. Israel swore loyalty "to" (lit. rendering of the Hb. preposition *lĕ*) Yahweh but too often swore allegiance "by" (Hb. preposition *bĕ*) the name of Baal.[71] Deuteronomy 6:13; 10:20 limited all oaths in Israel to those done in loyalty to Yahweh and sworn to by his name.

1:6 Verse 6 offers a new thought, "shifting the reader's attention from Judah's sinful devotion to other gods to Judah's neglect of Yahweh and the people's failure to seek direction from him."[72] Zephaniah also condemned those who apparently had not bowed down to the host of heaven or to the god Molech or to the gods of Baal. God determined to cut off those who turned back from following the Lord. Turning back from God involves "vacillating or faithless behavior toward people (Jer 38:22) or God (Ps 53:3). … It denotes a willful turning of oneself away or back from someone or something. When that someone is God (cf. Isa 59:12–13), it is a deadly condi-

[69] The vocalization of the MT, מַלְכָּם, favors the translation "their king." The KJV and RV took this as a proper noun, "Malcham" or "Malcam." Other translations use either "Milcom" (RSV, NEB) or "Molech" (NIV), referring to the god of the Ammonites. "Molech" may have derived from the writing of the Hb. consonants with the vowels of *bōšet,* meaning "shame." See the discussion of Patterson, who questions whether the popularity of Molech endured after the days of Solomon (1 Kgs 11:5,33), being overshadowed by Baalism (*Nahum, Habakkuk, Zephaniah,* 306). He follows the MT with good reason, understanding "their king" to point to Baal, worshiped in the place of the divine king Yahweh. Watts also reads "their king" but interprets it as a reference to a major Canaanite god known as Athtar in Ugarit, Chemosh in Moab, or Milcom in Ammon. Associated with the planet Venus, he could be one of the astral deities of v. 5 (*Joel, Obadiah, Jonah, Nahum Habakkuk and Zephaniah,* 158). See also E. R. Clendenen, "Religious Background of the Old Testament," in *Foundations for Biblical Interpretation,* ed. D. S. Dockery et al. (Nashville: Broadman & Holman, 1994), 298–99.

[70] Motyer, "Zephaniah," 3:913. Watts (*Joel, Obadiah, Jonah, Nahum Habakkuk and Zephaniah,* 157) sees a possible wordplay intended with the word שׁבע, "swear," being able to be read also as שׂבע, "be fed by." Thus Watts reads: "Those who bow down, who are fed by the Lord, but who swear by Milcom. This would picture priests whose support comes from their service in the temple of the Lord but whose genuine commitment is to a foreign deity."

[71] See the discussion of Robertson, *Nahum, Habakkuk, and Zephaniah,* 264–65.

[72] Roberts (*Nahum, Habakkuk, and Zephaniah,* 174), agreeing with Rudolph (*Micha, Nahum, Habakuk, Zephanja,* 266) that the verse should not be deleted as a later addition.

tion."[73] Although those condemned in this verse had not gone after other gods, they stood in judgment for doing nothing in the service of God. They no longer served the Lord God.

This is the story of many people's lives. Having started out well in service of God, they have become "weary in well doing" (Gal 6:9). They turned from the active service of the Lord to nothing.

"Seek" *(bqš)* and "inquire" *(drš)* frequently appear together (Deut 4:29; 2 Chr 20:3–4; Ps 105:3–4; Jer 29:13) and are difficult at times to differentiate. C. Chhetri understands that "when used together, *bqš* denotes seeking in a general sense while *drš* denotes inquiring of God with the view to repentance.[74] Robertson observes that "the combination of terms underscores the fact that worshiping the true God requires a conscious and directed effort. This intensity in devotion cannot be regarded as an option reserved for a pious minority."[75]

To "seek the Lord" normally means to worship him, but such worship is more than a one-time act. It "designates proper behavior before Yahweh, repentance and fear of God. 'It intends a state rather than an act.' "[76] At Sinai, God led Moses to provide a place where Israel could seek him (Exod 33:7). After Solomon dedicated the temple, God appeared to him and promised forgiveness for a people who sought him and turned from their wicked ways (2 Chr 7:14). To seek in this context involves prayer.[77] Such seeking is not limited to the temple but can occur even in exile by a people scattered for worshiping false gods (Deut 4:27–31; cp. Jer 29:13). In this case seeking clearly involves repentance, turning from false gods, and turning to the true God in worship at his holy place (Hos 3:5).

Going to the place of worship in and of itself is not truly seeking God (Hos 5:6). It must include ethical obedience (Zeph 2:3). People can seek God because God invites them to in his mercy and forgiveness (Deut 4:31) and has revealed himself to them (Isa 45:19). Ezra promised the protective presence of God to those seeking him (Ezra 8:22). The opposite of seeking in this context is to forsake him. Proverbs connects seeking God to understanding justice (Prov 28:5). "In sum, (1) seeking God requires turning from one's wicked ways and worshiping him in humility. (2) In prophetic thought, to seek God means to be in constant fellowship with God, to observe his commandments,

---

[73] Patterson, *Nahum, Habakkuk, Zephaniah,* 307. Roberts describes turning back as "to prove faithless, to treacherously desert one to whom one had a commitment (Isa 50:5; 59:13; Jer 38:22; Pss 44:18; 78:57)" (*Nahum, Habakkuk, and Zephaniah,* 173).

[74] C. Chhetri, "בקשׁ," *NIDOTTE* 1:725.

[75] Robertson, *Nahum, Habakkuk, and Zephaniah,* 265–66.

[76] G. Gerleman, "בקשׁ *bqš* pi. to seek," *TLOT* 1:253, quoting Westermann, *Keryma und Dogma*, 5.

[77] A prayer of intercession can also be involved in "seeking God" (2 Sam 12:16).

and to practice love and justice. (3) Sacrifices, no matter how lavish, cannot guarantee access to God for those who do not turn from evil ways and repent. (4) Even though the arrogant and sinful seek God, they never find him. (5) According to the Old Testament writers, ultimately it is God who chooses and seeks the lost to reveal himself to them, but the one who sincerely seeks him can hope to find him."[78]

To "inquire" of the Lord means to seek his guidance. The word referred early in Israel's life to seeking a prophetic word to relieve the distress of a crisis situation (1 Sam 9:9).[79] This often involved a king seeking a word about national survival from the prophet. The term can be used by an individual in a direct lament to God (Pss 22:27; 34:5; 69:33; 77:3; Job 5:8) or of a person seeking God's will in a very personal situation (Gen 25:22). Kings inquired of God before battle (2 Chr 18:4–7)[80] and about situations they did not understand (2 Chr 34:21,26).[81] It can also be used for inquiring of and relying on substitute gods, as Jer 8:2 well illustrates.[82] The word is a technical term for worship. It "became such a comprehensive designation for Yahweh worship that it often stands as the antithesis of idolatry (Isa 65:1,10; Jer 8:2; Zeph 1:6; Ezra 6:21; 2 Chr 12:14; 14:3; 17:4; 19:3; 22:9; 26:5; 30:19). But, at the same time, *drš yhwh* became synonymous with 'to fulfill God's will' or 'to keep the commandments' (1 Chr 22:19; 2 Chr 14:6a; 21:21; likewise Pss 14:2=53:5; 119:1,10)."[83] "Thus a loyal, positive, devoted commitment to Yahweh is

---

[78] Chhetri, "בקשׁ," 1:725–26. S. Wagner ("בִּקֵּשׁ," *TWAT* 1:763–64) points to the common phrase "to seek Yahweh's face" as belonging to a situation in which a worshiper entered the sanctuary to worship before the statue of the god or goddess. Such understanding was impossible in Israel because such images of the deity were forbidden. Rather, they had to depend on God to be present in the sanctuary as the worshipers came to seek him there. See 2 Sam 21:1; Hos 5:15; Pss 24:6; 27:8.

[79] See G. Gerleman and E. Ruprecht, "דרשׁ *drš* to inquire after," *TLOT* 1:347. Cp. 1 Kgs 14:1–18; 22; 2 Kgs 3; 8:7–15.

[80] Such inquiry did not automatically bring victory or divine help, especially when the king was not in the right relationship with God (Jer 21:2; 37:7–8; Ezek 17:7–8; 20:1,3).

[81] Inquiring of God becomes a major theme in Chronicles, being the type of relationship God expects with his people. דרשׁ appears twenty-seven times in 2 Chronicles referring to inquiring of God or being related to God. Kings are evaluated on whether they sought after God (2 Chr 12:14; 16:12; 19:3; 22:9; 26:5; 34:3). D. Denninger says, "The essential seeking that Chronicles requires points Israel to the temple in Jerusalem, while specifying a whole-hearted, humble relationship with Yahweh in each individual life" ("דרשׁ," *NIDOTTE* 1:997). Cf. also J. A. Thompson, *1, 2 Chronicles,* NAC (Nashville: Broadman & Holman, 1994), 266, who states that the phrase "defined one who was a member of the believing community" and "stood for one's whole duty toward God."

[82] One can seek the dead for help, but this certainly violates Yahweh's will (Deut 18:11; Isa 8:19; 19:3; 1 Chr 10:13). One could also inquire of false gods (2 Kgs 1). King Asa found condemnation when he consulted physicians rather than God (2 Chr 16:12). Isaiah (31:1) condemned Judah for depending on Egyptian military aid rather than inquiring of God. Seeking God in false ways while serving other gods brings God's destroying word (Ezek 14:7–10).

[83] Gerleman and Ruprech, "דרשׁ *drš,* to inquire after," 1:350.

expressed very generally by the expression 'seeking Yahweh.'"[84] It becomes closely tied to repentance (Deut 4:29; Ps 78:34; Isa 9:12; Amos 5:4–6; Hos 10:12; Jer 29:13). The Lord contended with people who neither served the Lord nor served other gods. They left behind the service of God. They ignored the Lord, falling prey to a practical atheism that rejected the power of God in their lives. Many people profess belief in God but live as atheists, neither seeking God in worship nor acknowledging him as the Lord of life. God vowed to cut off those who had turned to practical atheism.

The final group, those "who neither seek the Lord nor inquire of him," could be the most dangerous group of all. They have taken idolatry to its logical conclusion—a complete rejection of God and any acknowledgment in their lives. "Thus Judah had become a 'backslider' (v. 6), neglecting the only One who gave her life. God's reaction to her sin was to condemn her to that death she had chosen."[85]

1:7 The prophet recognized the intense anger God had displayed, so he "probes the character of God and finds there an opposition to sin that issues in death."[86] Zephaniah interjects a word of advice to the people, advice that immediately hushes any attempt at self-defense. In so doing the prophet, not Yahweh, becomes the speaker who introduces the book's central theme: the day of the Lord.[87] In preparation for the instruction of the Lord, the prophet counseled silence. In the Hebrew text the word for "silence" is an interjection usually translated as "hush!" or "keep silence."[88] The placing of the word at the beginning of the sentence and the use of "Sovereign Lord" emphasizes the importance of the demand. "'Be silent before the LORD God!' is the priestly cry before the sacrifice."[89] The sacrifice motif that follows joins this to the following section.[90] The prophet calls for "submission, fear, and consecration."[91] Since the day of the Lord was near, Zephaniah wanted all the people to think of the significance of the event and give God the awe due his holy name.

---

[84] Wagner, "דָּרַשׁ *dārash,* etc.," *TDOT* 3:300. Denninger argues that "seeking is a privilege and responsibility of belonging to the covenant community; it is not always cultic" ("דרשׁ," 1:995).

[85] Achtemeier, *Nahum–Malachi,* 65.

[86] Motyer, "Zephaniah," 3:917.

[87] House, *Zephaniah,* 58.

[88] BDB, 245.

[89] Achtemeier, *Nahum–Malachi,* 67; Roberts, *Nahum, Habakkuk, and Zephaniah,* 177, who points to Hab 2:20 and Zech 2:13. It is also used "in the presence of a person or event of great importance" (E. R. Clendenen, "Zephaniah," *Holman Concise Bible Commentary,* ed. D. S. Dockery [Nashville: Broadman & Holman, 1998], 382).

[90] Nogalski recognizes the common motif of sacrifice yet still argues that 1:7 belongs to a later redactional stratum even later than the Deuteronomistic corpus of the Book of the Twelve that he postulates (*Literary Precursors,* 189–90).

[91] Patterson, *Nahum, Habakkuk, Zephaniah,* 308.

The "Sovereign Lord" reflects the combination of the divine personal name "Yahweh" with the Hebrew title meaning "lord" or "master." It was common practice in the ancient Near East to use "Lord" in reference to a deity. Using both the name and the title indicates the personal nature and the power and majesty of God. Watts saw the use of the two names as a way of bringing the revealed truth of the God of the covenants—the covenant name—to the revelation of God as the sovereign lord of the universe.[92] By using the awesome divine title, Zephaniah shows the significance of his call for silence. He also shows that Yahweh is the true Lord, not Baal.[93] "Judah's true master was about to demonstrate the powerlessness of him who was no master at all. The last remnants of Baalism would be cut off. Therefore Judah and Jerusalem should be silent."[94]

The "day of the Lord"[95] reflected popular thought that went back for centuries among the people of Israel. VanHorn concluded that the day of the Lord was a product of covenant theology.[96] "The Day of the Lord is that time when for His glory and in accordance with His purposes God intervenes in human affairs in judgment against sin or for the deliverance of his own."[97] From a study of the concept of the day of the Lord, von Rad drew two conclusions: (1) that the day of the Lord embodied a pure event of war, the rising of the Lord against his enemies; and (2) that the concept is of old-Israelite origin, not from foreign sources.[98]

Judging by Amos's discussions concerning the day of the Lord, the people of his day must have seen the day as one of God's judgment against their enemies and a time of lightness and joy. Amos countered their optimism with a sober assessment of the day of the Lord. He said that it would be a day of "darkness, not light" (Amos 5:18). Amos compared the day with that of a man who fled from a lion only to run into a bear or retreated to the safety of his home only to be bitten by a snake (Amos 5:19). "Even though they expected

[92] J. W. Watts, *Old Testament Teaching* (Nashville: Broadman, 1967), 41.

[93] See discussion on v. 4.

[94] Patterson *Nahum, Habakkuk, Zephaniah,* 309.

[95] The specific expression "the day of Yahweh" occurs sixteen times: Isa 13:6,9; Ezek 13:5; Joel 1:15; 2:1,11; 3:4; 4:14; Amos 5:18,20; Obad 15; Zeph 1:7,14; Mal 3:23, but "the day" with several different modifications also describe this day. See E. Jenni, "יוֹם *yôm* day," *TLOT* 2:537–39, and the list of terms by Robertson, *Nahum, Habakkuk, and Zephaniah,* 272–73.

[96] W. W. VanHorn, "An Investigation of יום יהוה as It Relates to the Message of Amos" (Ph.D. diss, New Orleans Baptist Theological Seminary, 1987), 173.

[97] Patterson, *Nahum, Habakkuk, Zephaniah,* 310.

[98] G. von Rad, "The Origin of the Concept of the Day of Yahweh," *JSS* 4 (1959): 97–108; for a pungent description of holy war expectation and experience, see Achtemeier, *Nahum–Malachi,* 66. Robertson uses the imagery of Zephaniah 1 to connect the day of the Lord to the covenants of Noah, Abraham, and Moses (*NICOT,* 268). This may be placing too much weight on the language of images rather than on historical and theological references in the text.

their righteousness to be vindicated against their enemies, they were to discover that God's righteousness entailed his move against them."[99]

Isaiah understood the day of the Lord similarly as a day of God's judgment against the proud and the haughty among the people of Jacob (Isa 2:6–22). Isaiah's definition emphasized the central point—it is God's day: "The LORD Almighty has a day in store ..." (Isa 2:12). "The transferal of the concept from judgment prophecy to salvation prophecy and vice versa is facilitated by the essentially ambivalent nature of the day of Yahweh; it brings judgment upon the enemies of Yahweh and salvation for his people. The deciding factor depends upon the side to which Israel or the addressees belong. The concept of the day of Yahweh thus constitutes an essential point of contact between the prophetic proclamation of judgment and of salvation and demonstrates their inner unity."[100]

The day is not only a future day.[101] It can also refer to great events of the past. The fall of Jerusalem in 587 B.C. in fulfillment of prophecy was a "day of the Lord" (Lam 2:21). Isaiah saw the overthrow of Babylon as the day of the Lord (Isa 13:13,19). "Neither in prospect nor in retrospect was the day of the Lord fully realized. The prophets simply had in mind that these were events of such a dire nature that they exemplified a reality that would be fully demonstrated when the day finally came. But it is this ultimate day that preoccupies Zephaniah. His thinking is insistently universal (1:17a,18b; 2:11; 3:6,8b,9,20). He seems uninterested in identifying specific historical events. ... Zephaniah, whether under historical or theological prompting, has left us a tract on the day of the Lord—the climax alike of history, sin, and the purposes of God."[102]

Two centuries after Amos and Isaiah, Zephaniah saw the day of the Lord as a day when God would judge his people. "Zephaniah's own understanding of the Day of the Lord unfolds through a series of vivid images."[103] In these verses (7–13) he speaks of sacrifice, false worship, lamentation, personal search, and the looting of the wealthy. He thus gives new depth of meaning and unforgettable imagery to the depiction of God's day of judgment.

God's day could also be a day of salvation: return to paradise (Isa 35:1–10); new fertility (Joel 3:18); great harvest (Joel 2:24); God's removal of the enemy (Joel 2:20); restoration of Judah's fortunes (Zeph 2:7); the pouring of

---

[99] E. A. Martens, "Day of the Lord, God, Christ, the," *EDBT,* 148.

[100] Jenni, "יוֹם *yôm* day," 2:539.

[101] Patterson (*Nahum, Habakkuk, Zephaniah,* 310) prints an extensive list of passages for the day of the Lord as present (Joel 1:15), near future (Isa 2:12–22), future-eschatological (Isa 13:6,9), and primarily eschatological (Joel 3:14–15). Achtemeier (*Nahum–Malachi,* 66–67) lists eleven characteristics of the day of the Lord.

[102] Motyer, "Zephaniah," 3:918.

[103] House, *Zephaniah,* 148.

God's Spirit on the earth (Joel 2:29); the experience of God's loving presence (Zeph 3:17). Then all who call on the Lord's name will experience salvation and deliverance (Joel 2:32). These will include the Gentiles (Ps 96; Zeph 2:11; 3:9–10). Even creation itself will experience renewal (Joel 2:22,24).

The New Testament took up this language and referred to the "day of our Lord Jesus Christ" (1 Cor 1:8). His glory and salvation will be fully revealed. Pentecost was a "day of the Lord" (Acts 2:16–21; cp. Joel 2:28–32). Paul used this to refer to Christ's return to earth (2 Thess 2:1). "Whether the day is the parousia, or the climax of history and all things as in the 'day of God' when the dissolution of the heavens occurs (2 Pet 3:12), the 'day' will be characterized by the unquestioned and unmistakable presence of Almighty God."[104]

Martens neatly summarizes the meaning of the day of the Lord. It is a "day of God's vindication" when he is victorious over evil once and for all (Isa 2:17). It is a day when the questions of theodicy will be answered. The havoc evil has caused will be undone; "ambiguities will be resolved"; "evil will be trounced and evildoers will in the end receive their due." Finally, the prospect of the day coming "calls on believers especially to live in its light."[105]

The last half of v. 7 is filled with irony. The Lord had prepared a sacrifice[106] for his guests. His guests were the enemies of Israel; the sacrifice to be slaughtered was Israel itself. "To speak of the day of the Lord as a day of sacrifice (1:7–8) places it within the long biblical tradition that where there is sin there must also be death—and this because Yahweh is the Holy One."[107]

Zephaniah used the normal language associated with sacrifice. The word

---

[104] Martens, "Day of the Lord, God, Christ, the," 147.

[105] Ibid., 149, with reference to 2 Pet 3:11.

[106] Watts (*Joel, Obadiah, Jonah, Nahum Habakkuk and Zephaniah,* 159) says "sacrifice" is to be interpreted as "slaughter" for a feast rather than for a ritual sacrifice. This is part of his theory that the book was read at a great festival day. Thus for him the guests are the worshipers in the temple. The "king's sons" in v. 8 are sons of the god Melek, that is, cult officials of the god Melek. Foreign clothes are garments used in heathen worship. Stepping on the threshold becomes climbing up to the temple terrace or the holy of holies in astral worship. Roberts (*Nahum, Habakkuk, and Zephaniah,* 178) says placing v. 8 in the realm of pagan gods and their officials "seems farfetched and improbable." Achtemeier (*Nahum–Malachi,* 67–68) says the sacrifice is not that which follows a battle but is preparation for holy war, a consecration of the soldiers prior to battle, and a prelude to the call to repent in 2:1–3. Thus Judah is not the guest to be sacrificed. The guests are the mysterious members of God's army. Roberts (*Nahum, Habakkuk, and Zephaniah,* 177–78) is probably more on target when he writes: "The Judeans would not eat the sacrificial meal Yahweh was preparing, however, for the implication of Zephaniah's words is that Judah would be the sacrifice (cf. Isa 34:6–7; Jer 46:10)! Yawheh's guests, consecrated by him to eat the sacrifice (see 1 Sam 16:5 for this practice) would not be the Judeans, but either the foreign armies he would bring against Judah (Isa 13:3–5) or the birds and beasts of prey who would feed on the corpses of the dead (Ezek 19:17–20)."

[107] Motyer, "Zephaniah," 3:917.

for "sacrifice" *(zebaḥ)* is almost always used of a "sacrifice of slaughtered sheep, goat, or cattle to create communion between the god to whom the sacrifice is made and the partners of the sacrifice, and communion between the partners themselves."[108] Thus Zephaniah "takes the word of divine grace (the provision of a sacrifice for sin) and makes it the vehicle of the message of wrath: those who have long despised the sacrifice that God provides become the sacrifice their sin merits."[109]

Thus Patterson concludes: "The metaphor of the sacrificial banquet reinforces the announcement of the Day of the Lord and provides a ray of hope in the clouds of doom. As guests called to a sacrificial feast were to come with their uncleanness removed, so the Judahites are urged to respond to the invitation of Yahweh their host. Although judgment was coming, there was still time. By acknowledging God as their master and by responding in fear to the prospect of judgment in repentance from sin and repudiation of idolatry, God's people could join a believing remnant in coming to the feast as guests acceptable to Him. There was yet hope. … Guests who remained unrepentant, and hence unclean, would be disqualified and would, like those in Jehu's day (2 Kgs 10:18–28), discover that they were not only invited guests but also victims."[110]

1:8 Four of the next five verses either begin with or contain phrases that are similar. "On the day of the Lord's sacrifice" (v. 8),[111] "on that day" (vv. 9–10), and "at that time" (v. 12) refer to the day of the Lord's punishment of the wicked in Judah. References to God alternate between first and third person, giving critics like Rudolph occasion to look for editorial hands.[112] Robertson is correct in protesting that "this kind of variation occurs repeatedly throughout the book, and should be considered as a characteristic literary device for vivifying the Lord's own involvement."[113]

The verses contain a litany of lives filled with deceit and falsehood and the punishment for such rebellion. "First, the higher echelons of society are brought under judgment (1:8–9); then disaster strikes the city and the business community (1:10–11); finally, those under judgment are described, not by sta-

---

[108] *HALOT,* 262.

[109] Motyer, "Zephaniah," 3:917. The verb זבח is also used metaphysically "for slaying idolatrous priests on their own altars (1 Kgs 13:2 with 2 Kgs 23:20)" and "for slaughtering the rebellious nations in judgment as a feast for the scavenger birds (Ezek 39:17–19)" (R. E. Averbeck, "זבח," *NIDOTTE* 1:1069).

[110] Patterson, *Nahum, Habakkuk, Zephaniah,* 311–12.

[111] Roberts (*Nahum, Habakkuk, and Zephaniah,* 178) reviews reasons for seeing the opening line of v. 8 as an editorial addition and gives his own. Surely the change from third person to first person divine speech is not sufficient reason to declare this a later editorial addition. Rather, it furnishes the key terminology that ties the verse back to the preceding one and forward to vv. 8,10,12.

[112] Rudolph, *Micha, Nahum, Habakuk, Zephanja,* 264.

[113] Robertson, *Nahum, Habakkuk, and Zephaniah,* 275.

tus or function, but as the spiritual equivalents of the practical atheists in 1:6."[114] These verses "condemn Jerusalem's upper social class … and function well as a thematic counterpart to 1:4–6. Whereas 1:4–6 condemned cultic abuse, 1:8–12 focuses upon the upper class of Jerusalem. Both sections culminate in judgment upon those whose main failure was the lack of positive action (1:6,12)."[115]

Zephaniah used the same word for sacrifice as in the previous verse. The Lord would punish the princes and the king's sons. They would be fit for the sacrifice which the Lord planned. God's promise to punish literally states: "I will visit upon the princes and upon the sons of the king." In the Old Testament the verb *pāqad,* "to visit," often means to visit for good or to visit in judgment, as is the case in this instance.[116]

The "princes" refers to those members of the court who were the leaders of the government.[117] "The king's sons" probably did not mean literal sons but the royal family whether princes or others connected with the royal court.[118]

The time period for the delivery of Zephaniah's message impacts the interpretation of the royal family. Why is the king not mentioned? Was this delivered early in Josiah's reign when Josiah (640–609 B.C.) was only a child (cp. 2 Kgs 22:1)? If this was the case, the king may have been left out of the punishment because of his youth or because of his righteousness (2 Kgs 22:2). If Zephaniah descended from royal ancestry,[119] he would have known the conduct of the court and the reasons for God's visiting them in punishment.

Nothing particularly could be wrong with wearing the clothes of foreigners except for what that meant in Judah at the time.[120] Since the time of Manasseh (687–641 B.C.), Judah suffered under the vassalage of Assyria.

---

[114] Motyer, "Zephaniah," 3:917.

[115] Nogalski, *Literary Precursors*, 190; Robertson expresses it nicely: "The first in dignity, honor, office, and leadership shall be first to receive judgment" (*Nahum, Habakkuk, and Zephaniah,* 275).

[116] V. P. Hamilton, "פָּקַד (paqad)," etc. *TWOT* 2:731–32.

[117] Patterson (*Nahum, Habakkuk, Zephaniah,* 316) shows that שָׂרִים can include tribal chieftains (Num 21:18); court officials (1 Chr 22:17); district supervisors (1 Kgs 20:14–15); city officials (Judg 8:6); military leaders (1 Kgs 2:5; 2 Kgs 1:9–14); and religious leaders (Ezra 8:24).

[118] See Roberts, *Nahum, Habakkuk, and Zephaniah,* 178; Rudolph, *Micha, Nahum, Habakuk, Zephanja,* 267. Robertson (*Nahum, Habakkuk, and Zephaniah,* 275–76) contends that Zephaniah intentionally omitted reference to an obedient king Josiah and intentionally condemned his sons, three of whom would eventually be king of Judah; Patterson (*Nahum, Habakkuk, Zephaniah,* 317) dates the book early and refers the king's sons to sons of Josiah's predecessor Ammon.

[119] See Introduction: "Zephaniah, the Man."

[120] Roberts (*Nahum, Habakkuk, and Zephaniah,* 178–79) says one could interpret "the prophet's objection to foreign apparel as an attack on Judah's loss of self-identity as the people of Yahweh. Defenders of traditional culture often regard the importation of foreign styles in clothing as both a sign and a cause of corruption in the society's fundamental values." Roberts, however, prefers the religious interpretation.

Judah saw Israel overcome and taken into exile in 722 B.C. Later, Judah itself felt the power of Assyria. Manasseh, whether to appease Assyria or because of his own evil, erected Assyrian monuments and altars to other gods even in the temple of the Lord in Jerusalem (2 Kgs 21:3–8). Manasseh was deliberately attempting "to turn the religion of Yahwism into another polytheism."[121] Later, when Josiah began his reforms, he began to remove Assyrian influences from the temple.

Wearing the clothes of foreigners signified the desire to be like the Assyrians and others in every way, including the worship of pagan gods.[122] "The princely households [were] frivolously dazzled by supposed foreign sophistication. … The issue at stake was the distinctiveness of the people of God."[123] For this reason, God determined to visit those in judgment who clad themselves in foreign clothes.

1:9 The Lord continued to promise judgment for those who turn from him and turn toward other gods. Is this judgment against a different group of people than the preceding verse? Or are those who worship other gods and make themselves rich by fraud the same members of the royal family who sought to ingratiate themselves with foreigners? The latter probably fits the situation better. Of course, two or more groups could be included in this kind of evil, or the groups could overlap.

What exactly does it mean to "avoid stepping on the threshold"?[124] The NIV footnote equates this practice with the worship of Dagon among the Philistines as found in 1 Sam 5:4–5.[125] Many pagans believed that evil spirits resided at the threshold, waiting for someone to step on it and let them slip in.[126] This interpretation relates the practice in Judah with pagan worship,[127] perhaps for the same reasons as wearing foreign clothes in the preceding

---

[121] G. E. Wright, *Biblical Archaeology*, rev. ed (Philadelphia: Westminster, 1962), 175.

[122] Robertson insists that foreign clothing marked priests of each group of foreign gods so that the condemnation here is still of foreign worship (*Nahum, Habakkuk, and Zephaniah,* 276).

[123] Motyer, "Zephaniah," 3:919, who points to Israel's own national regulations of dress (Num 15:38; Deut 22:12) linked to religious loyalties (Num 15:39–40).

[124] Motyer determines that "הַמִּפְתָּן (the threshold) "remains imperfectly understood" (ibid.)

[125] Motyer says, "Zephaniah replaces the sober 'do not step on the threshold' (1 Sam 5:5) with a deliberately trivializing word in order to caricature the antics introduced into the Lord's worship" (ibid.). Roberts summarizes textual and exegetical attempts to define the term הַדּוֹלֵג, "the one who leaps" (*Nahum, Habakkuk, and Zephaniah,* 174–75). J. N. B. Heflin interprets the phrase in terms of the last half of the verse as referring to a call for social justice. "Henchmen" or associates of the political leaders are eager to carry out violence and deceit so they hurry over the thresholds of victims' houses in their hurry to plunder and rob and cheat (*Nahum, Habakkuk, Zephaniah, and Haggai,* BSC (Grand Rapids: Zondervan, 1985], 134). Similarly L. Walker, "Zephaniah," EBC 7:547.

[126] See Roberts, *Nahum, Habakkuk, and Zephaniah,* 179; Rudolph, *Micha, Nahum, Habakuk, Zephanja,* 268.

[127] Patterson also adopts this view with some hesitation (*Nahum, Habakkuk, Zephaniah,* 312–13).

verse.[128] "They observe the minutia of a senseless pagan law, but then run rampant over the basic ordinances of God in his own house."[129]

In this regard (that is, equating stepping over the threshold with wearing foreign clothes), some biblical scholars see vv. 8 and 9 as a chiasmus, where the first part of v. 8 goes with the last part of v. 9, and the two middle sections relate to one another. This is a feature often used in Hebrew literature and an effective means of communication. If the verses form a chiasmus, then those officials of v. 8 would be the same people who filled their master's houses with violence and deceit in v. 9.[130]

The second half of v. 9 speaks of those who fill (lit.) "the house of their masters" with (or by) violence and deceit. "The house of their masters" could mean the temple of a pagan god (NIV) or the house of the king, which would have been filled by killing and stealing. "Violence and deceit" is an adverbial phrase in Hebrew without a preposition. The phrase may be understood as a metonymy referring to *goods* obtained *by* "violence and deceit," which were deposited in "the house of their masters."[131]

The prophets of Israel and Judah demanded ethical behavior from members of the covenant community. Worshiping the Lord meant a great deal more than performing ritual. The prophets could not conceive of worship that did not affect relationships with other people and the practices of everyday life. Jeremiah, a contemporary of Zephaniah, was incredulous at the practices of some people who piously rejoiced in the temple yet performed all kinds of abominable practices during the week. "Will you steal and murder, commit adultery and perjury, burn incense to Baal and follow other gods you have not known, and then come and stand before me in this house, which bears my Name, and say, 'We are safe'—safe to do all these detestable things?" (Jer 7:9–11). Would God be any more pleased with the practices of Monday mornings or Saturday evenings in a land dotted with Christian churches?

1:10 Verses 10 and 11 fit together by noting the sorrow in the city and by calling on the people to wail in sorrow at the severity of the judgment. The verses are connected with those verses preceding and those following by use

---

[128] Roberts, *Nahum, Habakkuk, and Zephaniah,* 179; Motyer, "Zephaniah," 3:919: Just as the princes affected foreign dress, so the priests imported alien religious fetishes.

[129] Robertson, *Nahum, Habakkuk, and Zephaniah,* 278.

[130] J. D. W. Watts (*Joel, Obadiah, Jonah, Nahum Habakkuk and Zephaniah,* 159–60) takes the passage to mean those who climb on the holy of holies, possibly a common practice in astral worship.

[131] Motyer ("Zephaniah," 3:920) sees violence here as priests violently mishandling the law, while the deceit is priests deceiving those "who trustfully come for guidance" (Mal 2:7). Roberts (*Nahum, Habakkuk, and Zephaniah,* 179) shows that the ambiguity of house/lords is not significant since the temple would be part of the royal complex, and the king would ultimately control temple treasures. "Violence and deceit" could refer to the religious abuses of Manasseh; then the "house" would mean "temple."

of the phrase "on that day."

On the day of the Lord's judgment the sounds of attack and the cries of the people would be heard from around the city. The "cry," "wailing," and "a loud crash" are parallel terms. The "cry" and the "wailing" both describe the sounds of hurting people, while the "loud crash" from the hills may describe the sound of buildings falling at the onslaught of the enemy. "The *pleading* and *howling* arising from the areas of the *fish gate* and the *second quarter* of Jerusalem give expression to the utter despair of a people who have lost all hope in life. The judgment of God has now entered their own private district of town."[132]

The "Fish Gate" (Neh 3:3; 12:39) and the "New Quarter"[133] are not known precisely, but most interpreters assume their location in the northern section of the city. P. J. Nel agreed with the northwest location of the gate, citing the fishing trade from the Phoenician city of Tyre. "According to Neh 3:8 and 12:39 the Fishgate is located near the 'Old Gate' and the 'sheep Gate.' The latter is located toward the North-east."[134]

The geography of Jerusalem and of Palestine determined that most trouble would come from the north, the supposed area of the Fish Gate and the New Quarter. Palestine served as a land bridge with the Mediterranean Sea to the west and the desert to the east. All commerce was forced to follow the north-south trade routes in Palestine. Egypt lay to the south, and the other great powers (Assyria, Babylon, Syria, and non-Semitic peoples) had access to Palestine only from the north. Jeremiah spoke prominently of judgment that would come from the north. The "foe from the north" would bring destruction on Jerusalem (Jeremiah 4–6).[135] The Fish Gate "is chosen for its suitability to picture the final onslaught."[136]

---

[132] Robertson *Nahum, Habakkuk, and Zephaniah,* 278.

[133] G. A. Herion ("Second Quarter," *ABD* 5:1065) says: "It has long been suspected that this new addition to Jerusalem was constructed opposite the Tyropoeon Valley on the hill W of the old city of David and SW of the Temple Mount sometime during the reign of Hezekiah. … This expansion would have been designed to handle the increasing number of Israelite and Judean refugees fleeing the devastation of the Assyrian army." He notes of archaeological confirmation by Avigad's excavations including a defense wall, the extension nearly quadrupling Jerusalem's residential neighborhoods, bringing Jerusalem's population to twenty-five thousand. Cp. the older description of J. Gray, *I and II Kings*, OTL, 2d ed. (Philadelphia: Westminster, 1970), 726–27, quoted by Patterson, *Nahum, Habakkuk, Zephaniah,* 317. Heflin sees the four geographical points as representing the four quarters of the city or all of the city (*Nahum, Habakkuk, Zephaniah, and Haggai,* 135).

[134] P. J. Nel, "Structural and Conceptual Strategy in Zephaniah, Chapter 1," *JNSL* 15 (1989): 161. He concludes that the "hills" referred to the hilly area at the southern and eastern edges of the city. He also concluded that the "New Quarter" was located in the southwest. In these locations he saw the four wind directions, showing a total onslaught against Jerusalem.

[135] R. A. Bowman, "The North Country," *IDB* 3:560.

[136] Motyer, "Zephaniah," 3:920.

"Appropriate to the secular society that Jerusalem has become, God's destruction of his sinful people will start not at the temple but in the commercial quarter. … There in her commercial center—her ancient Wall Street—Jerusalem will experience God's first attack."[137] The loud crash from the hills is indefinite enough to call forth several explanations. It may be the echoes of war's devastation as the enemy ransacks the houses and business places and even the temple of Jerusalem.[138] Robertson views it as breaking down of the idols in the high places around Jerusalem.[139]

1:11 Zephaniah returns to the imperative mood (see v. 7), this time in an ironic tone. The judgment he announces should call the economic leaders of Judah to mourning and lamentation rites. Such rites should bring the community together to do what has already begun in the city streets (v. 10).[140] Instead, they will wail, but only for the money and possessions they have lost.[141]

In ancient cities, different trades and merchants often set up shop near one another (Jer 37:21, "the street of the bakers"). The "mortar" (market district, NIV), from a word meaning "to pound," may have referred to an area hollowed out where merchants gathered or to a vessel in which food could be pounded.[142] Since the following line refers to merchants, the NIV may give the best rendering by making this a place where commerce was carried out, probably in the Tyropoeon valley.[143]

In a number of different passages in the Old Testament, "Canaan" (*kĕnaʿan,* translated "merchants" here) and "Canaanites" referred to "mer-

---

[137] Achtemeier, *Nahum–Malachi,* 70.

[138] Patterson *Nahum, Habakkuk, Zephaniah,* 313, referring to T. Laetsch, *The Minor Prophets* (St. Louis: Concordia, 1956), 361.

[139] Robertson, *Nahum, Habakkuk, and Zephaniah,* 278–79.

[140] Patterson (*Nahum, Habakkuk, Zephaniah,* 307) emphasizes the future element of this section.

[141] Ibid., 314.

[142] From the earliest translations the term הַמַּכְתֵּשׁ has not been understood, being rendered as "pillars" (Vg), a proper noun (Syr, KJV), the Kidron River or brook (Tg), mortar (NASB, NRSV), hollow (NJB), market district (NIV, NLT, NCV), Lower Town (REB), Lower Hollow (CEV). See the discussion of Patterson, *Nahum, Habakkuk, Zephaniah,* 317–18. G. A. Herion ("Mortar, The," *ABD* 4:905) associates the time frame of the period of Josiah, its mention here with the Second Quarter, and the root meaning of "hollow," perhaps indicating a bowl-shaped depression. From this he concludes: "It is possible that this neighborhood was part of the W annex to the city of David and only came to be regarded as a "mortar" after neighborhoods were established on the eastern slopes of the W hill. In this case the "mortar" would likely be associated with (some portion of) the Tyropoeon Valley, which lay outside the city until the eighth century B.C." Cf. Berlin, *Zephaniah,* 87.

[143] Patterson supports this view (*Nahum, Habakkuk, Zephaniah,* 318) and quotes G. A. Smith, who placed the area in the upper part of the Tyropoeon Valley, an identification supported by a number of other sources. Robertson sees this as the all-inclusive term for Jerusalem: "Encircled by higher hills, Jerusalem itself may be compared to a mortar, a pounding place. God in his judgment shall grind the whole of the city as though it were encased in a mortar" (*Nahum, Habakkuk, and Zephaniah,* 279).

chants" or "traders."[144] The people of Canaan and the Phoenicians in particular were stereotyped as a merchant people. Motyer is probably correct in seeing a double meaning here: "They were people of the Lord, but in business they had become Canaanites!"[145]

In order to complete their financial transaction, traders weighed out silver using a system of weights and measures. Zephaniah called on the people to wail because the merchants would be "wiped out" (or "silenced") and the market place with its busyness from merchants trading would be "cut off" (NIV, "ruined"). "The cutting off of *all the dealers in silver* meant that the city as a center of culture, trade, luxury, beauty, and craftsmanship would come to an end."[146] The judgment of God against Judah would reach to all parts of society, especially to those who might be more tempted to trust in their own ability, creativity, or ingenuity. Motyer's warning here is appropriate: "Zephaniah is not showing an animus against trade or money-making. Rather he chooses a place normally alive with the buzz of conversation and humming with activity as a foil for the silence that will follow the devastation."[147]

1:12 Here is the central indictment of the book.[148] Zephaniah promised that the Lord would search out the "complacent," that is, all those who are self-secure and undisturbed. The NIV uses this interpretation[149] to explain the meaning of the Hebrew metaphor associated with wine making. The Hebrew reads literally, "I will visit upon the men who are thickening[150] on their dregs [i.e., like wine]."

In the wine-making process, fermented wine has to be poured from one vessel to another to separate the wine from the sediment (lees or "dregs"). If the wine is allowed to settle too long, it thickens and is ruined (cp. Jer 48:11–12, where the image is used of wine that is poured off too soon).[151] The meta-

---

[144] BDB, 488–89. כְּנַעַן is also used with the sense "merchants" and "traders" in Prov 31:24; Isa 23:8; Ezek 16:29; 17:4; Hos 12:7 [Hb. 12:8]; Zech 14:21. See Y. Aharoni, *The Land of the Bible: A Historical Geography*, trans. A. F. Rainey (Philadelphia: Westminster, 1967), 61.

[145] Motyer, "Zephaniah," 3:920.

[146] Robertson, *Nahum, Habakkuk, and Zephaniah,* 279.

[147] Motyer, "Zephaniah," 3:920. He adds: "In the Bible wealth is not a vice any more than poverty is a virtue, but the Bible asks three questions concerning wealth: How was it acquired? How is it being used? What is the attitude of the possessor to the possessions?"

[148] See Achtemeier, *Nahum–Malachi,* 69.

[149] Motyer ("Zephaniah," 921) notes that the NIV here follows BHS in emending הָאֲנָשִׁים, "men" to הַשַּׁאֲנַנִּים, "secure, complacent, undisturbed ones." Motyer's strong language may well be deserved here and in so many places where emendation is done for meter or parallelism: this "only proves that emendation can be insidious. The idea is suitable (though sufficiently present without being labored), but the change lacks manuscript evidence."

[150] קפא occurs elsewhere only in Exod 15:8 and Job 10:10. It refers to something that stiffens, thickens, or congeals (*HALOT,* 1117).

[151] D. J. Clark and H. A. Hatton, *A Handbook on the Books of Nahum, Habakkuk, and Zephaniah* (New York: UBS, 1989), 156. On the use in Jer 48:11–12 cf. Berlin, *Zephaniah,* 88.

phor in the Book of Zephaniah refers to those who have lived with uninterrupted prosperity and have become complacent. These are people who have deified themselves, thinking that their might and the power of their hands have gotten them wealth (Deut 8:10–18). "Many of Jerusalem's citizens had remained in their apostate lifestyle so long that they had become satisfied with it and then grown indifferent to genuine piety."[152] Moses warned the people of the danger of becoming proud and forgetting the Lord who brought them out of the land of Egypt (Deut 8:14).

"General apathy about God exists in the land, which the writer conveys with sight and sound imagery."[153] God promised to make a thorough search[154] of the city for those living in complacency. Invaders searched captured cities with small clay lamps, looking for any item of value. God would make the same kind of search for those who lived in practical atheism, believing that God did neither good nor evil.[155] In so doing Zephaniah may appear to deny God's basic characteristic as omniscient, all-knowing. In truth, he does just the opposite. He shows God can and will find everything about you. Nothing escapes God's attention (cp. Ps 139:1). "No absentee God, He will send an invading force that will search out and plunder Jerusalem. The implementation of the Lord's proclamation will come so quickly that all who have lived in pursuit of ill-gotten gain will not survive to enjoy their wealth. … In their preoccupation with self and riches they will lose them both (cf. Luke 12:16–21)."[156] As Achtemeier summarizes the teaching here: "In such societies, human beings have committed the ultimate idolatry—the final sin of trying to make themselves their own gods (cf. Gen 3:5)."[157]

While giving acknowledgment to the existence of God, many people ignore his lordship. In the modern mind "God" is a nebulous concept, lacking the ability to effect good or evil. People who think in this way might not question the existence of God but seriously question whether or not God works.

---

[152] Patterson, *Nahum, Habakkuk, Zephaniah,* 314–15. He explains that the sin is "one of indifference that goes beyond the smug self-satisfaction suggested by the word 'complacency' to an attitude that has hardened into deliberate disregard for the Lord and His standards" (p. 318). Roberts adds: "They had been secure so long in their wealth, despite their means of obtaining it, that they no longer took seriously any thought that Yahweh might affect the outcome of business or politics. They were self-sufficient, self-made men, and God was not a factor in their calculations (cf. Jas 4:13–17)" (*Nahum, Habakkuk, and Zephaniah,* 180–81). According to Berlin, "the people have become mired in their drinking and indulgent lifestyle" (*Zephaniah,* 87–88).

[153] House, *Zephaniah,* 58. Patterson says: "If not in theory, at least in practice, the people of Judah behaved like full-fledged pagans" (*Nahum, Habakkuk, Zephaniah,* 315).

[154] Motyer explains that the *piel* verb אֲחַפֵּשׂ here is "a true intensive," rendering "I will busy myself searching through" ("Zephaniah," 3:921).

[155] Motyer explains that the contrast between good and evil here is a Hebraic way of expressing totality by means of contrast, the conclusion being that God does nothing at all (ibid., 3:920).

[156] Patterson, *Nahum, Habakkuk, Zephaniah,* 315.

[157] Achtemeier, *Nahum–Malachi,* 69.

The faithful among the people of Israel knew the work of God. He worked to bring the world into existence, and he continues to work in his world. The prophets of the Old Testament, like the Christian authors of holy Scripture, affirmed the power of God to effect change as well as the will of God to work in his world. The Lord God works in history to accomplish his sovereign purpose.

1:13 This verse completes the preceding poem (vv. 8–12) but stands outside the poem's structure, not having the time reference in the opening line and not included in the poetic inclusio. The verse summarizes and characterizes the three groups condemned in vv. 8–12. Royal and temple personnel lose their palaces and wealth; the wealthy and the merchants lose their houses; and the ones resting on their lees in apathy cannot taste their wine.[158]

How ironic that the God who they said did "nothing, either good or bad" (Zeph 1:12) was at that moment preparing an aggressor who would search Jerusalem to punish those people and remove the wealth in which they trusted. In what would the people trust when their goods were plundered and their houses demolished?

Building houses and planting vineyards required hard work and patience. What a tragedy when the person expending the energy and waiting for the reward loses the reward! Zephaniah affirmed the truth that human effort apart from the blessing of God is futile. They had built houses for others to live in and planted vineyards so that others could drink the wine. The horror of such loss can be seen by the number of times this kind of judgment is described in the Old Testament (cp. Deut 28:30; Amos 5:11; Mic 6:15). "The day of the Lord will expose the transience of ownership, the insubstantiality of property, and the uncertainty that materialism will bring its promised fulfillments."[159]

Having warned against the destruction of every living creature on the face of the earth (Zeph 1:2–3), God also warned Judah of his wrath to come. God would finally remove the vestiges of Baalism and other forms of pagan worship from the city of Jerusalem and the land of Judah. The day of God's wrath would be so significant that the people should stand in silence before him. God promised to punish those in places of authority and those who trusted in material goods. The result would be destruction for all the people of Judah. "Yahweh's dispute with the nation is more specific now. He is dissatisfied with every possible kind of citizen. His complaint entails more than idolatry, with apathy, violence, and dishonesty prime reasons for

[158] See Nogalski, *Literary Precursors*, 190, who sees the verse as a Deuteronomistic addition dependent on Amos 5:11 that "deliberately parallels the fate of Jerusalem (as the symbol of Judah) with that of the Northern Kingdom" (p. 191).

[159] Motyer, "Zephaniah," 3:921.

judgment. *Who* God will judge is now spelled out, but *how* He will judge remains unclarified."[160]

1. Judgment at the Great Day of the Lord (1:14–2:3)

God's messenger, the prophet, brings news to God's people. His announcement is simple: the day of the Lord is at hand. References to that day appear ten times in five verses. This long section approaches apocalyptic language[161] as it details the day of the Lord as a day of intense judgment when nothing would stand before the Lord's wrath. Like Amos, Zephaniah saw the day of the Lord as a day of darkness and not light, a day when God's judgment would be poured out on a rebellious people. In that day wealth, youth, or power would prove useless (Amos 5:18–20). The prophet's message has a point. He gives more than pure description. He calls for immediate action (2:1–3).

(1) A Day of Wrath (1:14–18)

14"The great day of the LORD is near—
near and coming quickly.
Listen! The cry on the day of the LORD will be bitter,
the shouting of the warrior there.
15That day will be a day of wrath,
a day of distress and anguish,
a day of trouble and ruin,
a day of darkness and gloom,
a day of clouds and blackness,
16a day of trumpet and battle cry
against the fortified cities
and against the corner towers.
17I will bring distress on the people
and they will walk like blind men,
because they have sinned against the LORD.
Their blood will be poured out like dust
and their entrails like filth.
18Neither their silver nor their gold
will be able to save them
on the day of the LORD's wrath.
In the fire of his jealousy

---

[160] House, *Zephaniah,* 63.

[161] See the discussion and details by Patterson (*Nahum, Habakkuk, Zephaniah,* 320–21, with a chart showing the relationship of this section to Joel 2:1–11), who concludes: "Although Zephaniah is led by God to reiterate and recombine many thoughts concerning that day of judgment, he is also led to add fresh features. He does so with consummate literary artistry, and the effect is staggering."

the whole world will be consumed,
for he will make a sudden end
of all who live in the earth."

1:14 Zephaniah wanted to communicate the nearness of the great day of the Lord. The combination of "near" and "coming quickly" "indicates that the day of the Lord is not simply lurking at a distance but is moving quickly to its destined role. It is imminent (Joel 1:15). The first line repeats the exact words of v. 7 with the addition of the adjective "great." Von Rad noticed that in a highly repetitive phraseology, this phrase occurs even more repetitively and is firmly formulated. He believed that this phrase, too, came from the tradition of holy war, making up the "stereotyped call with which the troops were summoned to battle with Yahweh."[162]

The prophets proclaimed an urgent message that demanded immediate action. Like many people who depend on wealth or power, people in Judah in the seventh century B.C. expected their wealth to carry them through the evil time. Neither fortified cities (1:16) nor abundant wealth (1:18) could stand against the great day of the Lord. All the world would be consumed by the fire of God's jealousy.

With the day near and coming nearer, Judah could only repent and plead the mercy of God. Whether Zephaniah believed that Judah could be spared is unclear. He certainly believed that judgment could issue in a period of cleansing from which would come faith and dependence on God (3:9–10). In that day the haughty would be removed, and the meek and humble would worship God in peace (3:11–13).

Zephaniah's message must have had contemporary relevance. He probably intended his message to call sinners to repentance that God might stay his strange work (2:1–3) and to encourage the righteous concerning God's future work of grace.[163] The message had continuing meaning as Jesus came preaching the kingdom of God at hand (Mark 1:15). It continues speaking to God's people as we wait for the day of our Lord Jesus Christ and the final eschatological events.[164]

The second half of the verse begins an emphasis concerning the tragedy and sorrow of the day of the Lord which runs through v. 16. Translation of the two lines is difficult, but the rendering of A. Berlin is more faithful to the

---

[162] von Rad, "The Origin of the Concept of the Day of Yahweh," 107–8.

[163] For the phrase "the strange work of God" see Isa 28:21.

[164] D. A. Garrett states, "The day of the Lord is not *exclusively* any specific period of tribulation, deliverance, or final judgment. But each of these events can rightly be called the day of the Lord" (*Hosea, Joel,* NAC [Nashville: Broadman & Holman, 1997], 306).

Hebrew than is the NIV: "The sound of the day of the Lord: bitterly[165] shrieks then a warrior."[166] "Bitter" describes the experience of those who will suffer the Lord's judgment on that day (see also Isa 33:7; Amos 8:10).

The sound of the day of the Lord is a sound of agony, defeat, and hopelessness. The word for "warrior," *gibbôr*, is the word used of Samson and is part of the compound form of the "mighty God" in Isa 9:6. It is an intensive form, thus indicating a particularly strong person who can surpass others in carrying out great deeds.[167] The warrior's cries of fear and distress would show how great the anguish of that day, when not even the strongest could stand against the onslaught.[168]

1:15 The next two verses continue the description of the day of the Lord as a day of defeat and ruin by employing six brief phrases without the use of a main verb. Each phrase begins with the word *yôm,* "day." "This passage [vv. 15–16a] is probably the most classical description of Yahweh's day in Israelite literature."[169] Each *yôm* saying has a balanced (3 + 3) metrical structure. "Each saying has 7 syllables and the word *ywm* occurs 7 times. A complete stanza is thus formed."[170]

Zephaniah primarily described the day of the Lord as a day of devastating

---

[165] Although most modern translations read מַר, "bitter," as the predicate of the third clause (NRSV, "the sound of the day of the LORD *is bitter*"), the Masoretic accents connect it to the last clause of the verse. This is followed by the KJV and NASB ("Listen, the day of the LORD! In it the warrior cries out *bitterly*"). Note that the word קוֹל, "sound," beginning the third clause can function as an exclamation (*HALOT,* 1085, suggesting this verse as a possible case). צֹרֵחַ is a participle, "shouting," which can function either verbally (as NASB or NRSV, "the warrior *cries aloud* there") or nominally (NIV, "*the shouting* of the warrior there" or Patterson, "bitter is *the cry* of the warrior"; *Nahum, Habakkuk, Zephaniah,* 319). The placement of the adverb שָׁם, "there," between צֹרֵחַ, "shouting," and גִּבּוֹר, "warrior" makes the NIV rendering "shouting of the warrior" difficult. Patterson reads שָׁם as a relative particle, שׁ and the preposition מִן attached to the following word ("from/of the warrior"; *Nahum, Habakkuk, Zephaniah,* 326). He mentions as an alternative C. F. Whitley, "Has the Particle שׁם an Asseverative Force?" *Bib* 55 (1974): 394–98, who gives שָׁם emphatic force: "Yea, indeed." Berlin (*Zephaniah,* 85,89) follows the MT accentuation and reads שָׁם with a temporal sense "then" (citing *IBHS* § 39.3.1h). This is probably the best solution.

[166] Nogalski (*Literary Precursors*, 196) points to previous attempts to emend the text of "the shouting of the warrior" in v. 14. He opts for a redactional solution, taking 1:14,16–18a as an original poem into which 1:15–16a and 18b have been inserted to connect Zephaniah to the Deuteronomistic corpus of the Book of the Twelve. He thinks the "additions" add a universal note of judgment to a poem concerned entirely with Jerusalem and Judah.

[167] H. Kosmala, "גָּבַר *gābhar,*" etc., *TDOT* 2:373.

[168] Berlin, *Zephaniah,* 89. Motyer ("Zephaniah," 3:923) presents an alternative understanding: the warrior is God offended by sin and the person with whom sinners have to deal. Motyer sees human reactions beginning only in v. 17. Likewise Achtemeier (*Nahum–Malachi,* 71–72) sees the entire verse as announcing the war cry of the Divine Warrior encouraging his troops to start the battle (cf. Isa 42:13).

[169] Nel, "Structural and Conceptual Strategy in Zephaniah, Chapter 1," 164.

[170] Ibid.

defeat when the people of Judah would experience one tragedy after another. Verse 16 emphasizes the day as a day of battle against even the most secure positions. "The day of the Lord is not arbitrary; it is the logical outgrowth of what humankind is (1:17b); it will bring what humankind deserves (1:17a,c), and it will expose the uselessness of what humans trust (1:16b, 18a)."[171]

Zephaniah used wordplay extensively in this verse to add emphasis. The second and third lines employ it to call attention to the devastation to come.[172] In Hebrew the words "distress" *(ṣārâ)* and "anguish" *(mĕṣûqâ)* sound similar. Moffatt captured the poetic idea by translating as "stress and distress." In the same way, the words "trouble" *(šōʾâ)* and "ruin" *(mĕšôʾâ)* sound the same except that the word for "ruin" contains an extra syllable.

The fourth and fifth lines which begin with the word "day" do not contain the same play on words but emphasize the sorrow connected with the day of the Lord.[173] These are all "cosmic manifestations of the Lord's overwhelming presence. But the awful message of Zephaniah is that the covenant Lord has broken out on his Day, not in saving love toward his people—not to enter into fellowship with them as at Sinai—but in wrath and fury."[174]

"Wrath" *(ʿebrâ)* serves as the introductory and all-inclusive term describing the Lord's day. Such wrath comes because people have sinned (v. 17; cp. Ps 78:22).[175] The Hebrew *ʿebrâ* is a synonym of the more frequently occurring *ʾap* (about eighty times of God's anger, including Zeph 2:2,3; 3:8) and *ḥārôn* (about forty times of God's anger, including Zeph 2:2; 3:8). Twenty-one of its thirty-four occurrences appear in prophetic literature with God most often the subject.[176] A significant exception is Isa 14:6, where it is used of the king of Babylon "strik[ing] down peoples with unceasing blows" and with "relentless aggression." According to van Groningen, *ʿebrâ* "when used in relation to God … adds the nuance of the fierceness of God's wrath (Ps 78:49) expressed in an overwhelming and complete demonstration (Isa 13:9). God's wrath burns, overflows, sweeps away everything before it (Ezek

---

[171] Motyer, "Zephaniah," 3:923.

[172] Robertson, *Nahum, Habakkuk, and Zephaniah,* 283.

[173] Robertson sees the language here as reflecting that of the Sinai theophany, especially as Deuteronomy describes it: "Now those terrors from which Israel cringed shall be displayed again. But this time no mediator shall shield the nation from the consuming force of God's righteous judgments" (ibid., 284).

[174] Achtemeier, *Nahum–Malachi,* 72.

[175] K.-D. Schunck (*TWAT* 5:1038) notes that such anger is always Yahweh's reaction to human false behavior. Failure to obey God and his revelation of his will is the basic reason (Deut 3:26; Isa 9:18; Ezek 22:21; Ps 78:21,49). This can be specified as false worship (Ps 78:59; Jer 7:29) or social injustice (Hos 5:10; Ezek 22:31). Appearance of this wrath is most often described in terms of fire (Ps 78:21; Isa 9:18; Ezek 21:36; 22:21,31; 38:19; Hab 3:8).

[176] G. B. Struthers, *NIDOTTE* 3:316. See also B. E. Baloian, *Anger in the Old Testament*, 1992.

22:21,31)."[177] This verse so hauntingly describes the coming day of divine wrath that the opening line in the Latin Vulgate, *Dies irae, dies illa,* "day of wrath, that day," inspired a medieval hymn and then requiems by Mozart, Berlioz, and Verdi.[178]

"Darkness" is especially significant here: "The desolation touches the cosmos, making it what it was before the ordering hand of God transformed it—the light of sun and moon are gone. Humankind set out to rule without God, but this rule has brought back the primeval meaninglessness of Genesis 1:2."[179]

1:16 The trumpet[180] and the battle cry symbolized warfare. When these sounds reverberated through the city, the people knew to prepare for the battle (Judg 3:27). Jerusalem typified a fortified walled city reinforced by corner towers. If the enemy attacked such strong defenses, the people must have sensed that the remainder of the area had fallen, leaving the city without aid or reinforcements or hope. Zephaniah implied the imminent overthrow of the city. The enemy would not be slowed by walled cities and corner towers.

The certainty of the destruction came because of the character of the enemy. Whereas the immediate enemy turned out to be the mighty Babylonian army under the direction of Nebuchadrezzar, in reality it was the Lord himself fighting against the city. With God leading the charge, the city faced certain doom.

Herein lies the Hebrew concept of holy war. God led the fight against his enemies. In normal cases the concept of holy war gave tremendous comfort: "For the LORD your God is the one who goes with you to fight for you against your enemies to give you victory" (Deut 20:4). In this instance the whole idea is filled with bitter irony, for God would lead the charge against his own people.[181]

1:17 Why would God do such a thing? How could God lead the charge against his own people and destroy the city in which he caused his name to dwell (Deut 12:5)? Like Jeremiah and the writer of the Kings material, Zephaniah solved the theological conundrum by reminding the people of their sin (1:4–6). They had sinned against the Lord.

The poetic text contains five lines, with the first two lines and the last two lines paired. The middle line stands prominently alone in the middle, giving the reason for destruction (literally): "Because against the Lord they have sinned."

---

[177] G. van Groningen, "עָבַר (*ʿābar*)," *TWOT* 2:643.

[178] W. C. Kaiser, Jr., *Micah-Malachi* (Dallas: Word, 1992), 221.

[179] Motyer, "Zephaniah," 3:923.

[180] Motyer (ibid.) notes that "in Exod 19:16 the trumpet was a summons of grace to enter the divine presence. Typically Zephaniah reverses the symbolism. It is now the mustering of the Lord's host to battle (Jer 4:19; Amos 2:2)."

[181] L. E. Toombs, "Ideas of War," *IDB* 4:796–801.

Sin is first and foremost against God. David asserted the truth of this statement when he confessed his sin against God: "Against you, you only, have I sinned and done what is evil in your sight" (Ps 51:4). David had sinned against Bathsheba, Uriah, and the entire nation, but more than anyone else, he had sinned against God. "Humans may categorize their sins into the serious, the mediocre, and the insignificant. To Zephaniah (see Jas 2:10–11) the mere fact of sin excited and merited the whole weight of divine rage."[182] True sorrow for sin comes after repentance (Jer 31:19). Only after repentance can we see what our sin has done to God.

By shifting to the first person, Zephaniah showed the seriousness of sin and the determination of God to cleanse the people of Judah. Because of sin, God determined to bring his day of distress on the people. The result of the day of the Lord would be that the people (lit., "the man") would stumble and grope like blind men (Isa 59:10).[183] Being "poured out like dust" may reflect Lev 14:41, the only other biblical reference to pouring out dust. There it was a matter of the laws of impurity. "The lives of Zephaniah's audience, infected by sin, are unclean and will be treated as the unclean is treated."[184] The latter comparison of "entrails"[185] may mean that the dead bodies would be left where they fell, meaning that the total destruction left no one to bury them. Both sand and filth refer to that which is worthless.[186] The enemy would show "utter disdain" for their Judean victims.[187]

With this brief first-person speech, Yahweh has heightened the tension. The nation has no hope. "Judgment is so complete that it takes on grotesque proportions."[188]

1:18 In 1:18–2:7 the prophet issues his first long speech, referring to Yahweh in third person rather than in first. He introduces us to concepts vital to the plot of the book: "the possibility of escaping judgment and the condem-

---

[182] Motyer, "Zephaniah," 3:924.

[183] Patterson (*Nahum, Habakkuk, Zephaniah,* 324) notes the appropriate nature of the punishment: "Because they are blind ethically and spiritually (cf. Exod 23:8; Matt 15:14; Rom 2:19; 11:25; Eph 4:18; 1 John 2:11) and have sinned against God and His commandments, God's people will incur the just penalties of the covenant (Deut 28:28–30)."

[184] Motyer, "Zephaniah," 3:924, who admits: "This would explain a most unusual simile, but possibly the picture is that of helplessness before the onslaught (2 Kgs 13:7; Isa 41:2)." Berlin understands the imagery here as pointing to "carnage strewn over a broad area. ... The massacre will be so great that corpses will not be left intact; the remains will be in small fragments—specks and clumps—scattered over the landscape." She cites Ps 18:43 as a parallel (*Zephaniah,* 91).

[185] Patterson *Nahum, Habakkuk, Zephaniah,* 327; Motyer, "Zephaniah," 3:924; and *HALOT* 2:525 takes לְחֻמָם, "entrails," as "flesh" from an Arabic root.

[186] Patterson (*Nahum, Habakkuk, Zephaniah,* 324) explains: "Human life (flesh and blood) is thus reduced to a thing of no value, with even corpses being treated as despicable refuse (cf. Jer 9:20–22; 16:1–4; 25:32–33)."

[187] Roberts, *Nahum, Habakkuk, and Zephaniah,* 183.

[188] House, *Zephaniah,* 63.

nation of other kingdoms."[189] This represents one of the author's artistic uses of foreshadowing, pointing forward to the remnant concept he will develop in chap. 3 and the judgment of the nations that is to follow in chap. 2.

How could the people save themselves in such a terrible day? Cities often paid the attacker to leave the city intact. In some cases silver and gold might help dispel an enemy besieging the city. In this case silver and gold would be worthless. God himself would pour out his wrath, and the wealth would only get in the way.[190]

His wrath is a jealous or zealous wrath.[191] "The essence of "God himself is involved in this burning jealousy."[192] The Hebrew term *qinʾâ* has various usages that "share the notion of an intense, energetic state of mind, urging toward action. The cause of the *qnʾ* actions is the (possibly imagined) infringement of someone's rights or injury to the subject's honor."[193] It can refer to human envy (Gen 30:1; 37:11; cp. Ps 73:3). God can be compared to a jealous husband refusing to allow his people to commit idolatry, which is spiritual adultery. God is not jealous in the modern sense of being envious of that which rightfully belongs to someone else, but he is jealous in the Hebrew sense, earnestly desiring the honor that rightfully belongs to him. "The *qinʾâ* of God is the self-preservation of the sovereign, unapproachable, holy God. … [It] is not directed against the idols, but against the disloyal covenant partner. … [It] is not like that of the deceived husband against his rival, but rather like that of the lord/sovereign who does not tolerate anyone else next to him in the covenant with his subjects, and in that way he claims and maintains the exclusive relationship with his people. … It differs radically from the envy of gods known from the surrounding areas, which can be aimed at fellow gods or at worshipers. God's *qinʾâ* completely excludes other gods."[194] Therefore, bowing down or worshiping an idol calls for judgment since God is a jealous God (Exod 20:5; 34:14) who zealously desires the worship of his people. His holy jealousy means people cannot adequately worship and serve him but must rely on his loving faithfulness to them (Josh 24:19). His jealous wrath can be stopped from expressing itself in total annihilation (Num 25:11; cp. Ezek 16:42). In this sense the whole world will be consumed in the fire of God's jealousy since all have sinned and turned to their own evil ways.[195]

---

[189] Ibid., 59.

[190] Nel, "Structural and Conceptual Strategy in Zephaniah, Chapter 1," 166.

[191] H. G. L. Peels describes the range of meanings as "positive (advocate zealously for the benefit of someone else) and … negative … (bear a grudge against, resent) ("קנא," *NIDOTTE* 3:938)." Exod 20:5 illustrates each of these.

[192] Robertson, *Nahum, Habakkuk, and Zephaniah,* 286.

[193] Peels, "קנא," 3:938.

[194] Ibid., 3:939. G. Sauer informs us that "the ancient Near East spoke, at most, of the gods' envy of one another but never of a god's zeal in relation to his worshiper" (*TLOT* 3:1146).

[195] E. M. Good, "Jealousy," *IDB* 2:806–7.

Jealousy can also bring God's love to the fore in that he saves and delivers his people (Isa 42:13). "God's jealousy when offended issued in just retribution, but when stirred by his grace it resulted in eternal love."[196]

Zephaniah depicted the day of the Lord as a day of God's wrath against a wicked people addicted to rebellion against God. But exactly who will be consumed? The NIV's "the whole world" relieves the ambiguity of the Hebrew "all the land." Is this all the land of Judah[197] or the entire world?[198] The day appeared imminent and would come in the form of fire and battle even against the best fortified cities. Fire, "the symbol of active holiness (Exod 3:2–5), is God's holy outrage expressed in applied anger."[199] Nothing could prevent the judgment. Life as we know it will come to a sudden end.[200] Not even silver and gold would help in such a day of distress and ruin. In this opening chapter of the book, one side of God appears, the "angry deity who desires to smash the works of His own hands. ... Certainly no clearer picture of God on a rampage is possible."[201]

(2) A Day for Repentance (2:1–3)

1Gather together, gather together,
O shameful nation,
2before the appointed time arrives
and that day sweeps on like chaff,
before the fierce anger of the LORD comes upon you,
before the day of the LORD's wrath comes upon you.
3Seek the LORD, all you humble of the land,

---

[196] L. J. Coppes, "קָנָא (*qānāʾ*), etc.," *TWOT* 2:802.

[197] See REB; Watts, *Joel, Obadiah, Jonah, Nahum Habakkuk and Zephaniah,* 163. Robertson (*Nahum, Habakkuk, and Zephaniah,* 287) shows that the immediate context is concerned with Judah and not with the entire world, but he then argues for a universal meaning here. Roberts (*Nahum, Habakkuk, and Zephaniah,* 183–84) readily admits the ambiguity of the expression and uses a history of tradition approach. As an originally independent unit, it may have had a universal application or could have referred to Judah's enemies. In the present text, however, Roberts thinks the application is clearly to those previously addressed, namely, Judah and Jerusalem.

[198] Robertson points clear back to vv. 2–3 to claim a universal perspective for the larger context. He also interprets "all who live in the earth" as pointing to the universal picture, though this could also be translated "all who live in the land" (*Nahum, Habakkuk, and Zephaniah,* 287). Berlin explains similarly that "while the main focus of God's wrath is Judah, the Judeans are warned that they cannot escape because God's wrath will encompass the whole earth" (*Zephaniah,* 92).

[199] Motyer, "Zephaniah," 3:924.

[200] Motyer (ibid.) sees a double meaning here in נִבְהָלָה, both "yes, and suddenly accomplished" and "yes, and one to be dreaded." Roberts (*Nahum, Habakkuk, and Zephaniah,* 183) argues that the Hebrew term came to mean 'hasten" or "sudden" only as a late development under Aramaic influence, so he argues for the translation, "For he will made an end, a terrifying one," here, pointing to Gen 45:3; 2 Sam 4:1; Isa 13:8; 31:3; Ezek 26:18.

[201] House, *Zephaniah,* 70–71.

you who do what he commands.
Seek righteousness, seek humility;
perhaps you will be sheltered
on the day of the LORD's anger.

Grammar and syntax show a change of direction here as Zephaniah changes from declaring God's word to admonishing God's people. Three verses contain five admonitions.[202] The call to repent is replete with wordplays that can point in two directions.[203]

In the Old Testament prophecy reaches conclusions; it always contains a "therefore." Those who spoke the message of God demanded actions from the listeners.[204] After preaching a stern message of judgment, Zephaniah concluded with a "therefore" for the people. Having seen the coming judgment of God, the people of Judah should seek the Lord and seek righteousness. Zephaniah knew that only repentance and the mercy of God could avert the coming destruction. "Even this bit of mercy has a biting tone, however, since the author implies Judah has no closer relationship to Yahweh than other countries."[205]

2:1 Zephaniah "2:1–2 attempts to shock and insult Judahites into joining the remnant."[206] The first line consists of two words in Hebrew that are different forms of the same verb *qšš*, a rare word derived from the more common word *qaš*, "straw, stubble."[207] Berlin translates, "Gather together, gather like straw."[208] The people of Judah have been appointed as chaff to be cast out. They should gather themselves together in repentance in order to avert the judgment of God. The GNB puts the message in English idiom, "come to your senses."

---

[202] See Robertson, *Nahum, Habakkuk, and Zephaniah,* 289.

[203] Watts, *Joel, Obadiah, Jonah, Nahum Habakkuk and Zephaniah,* 164.

[204] Cf. Clendenen, "Interpreting the Minor Prophets for Preaching," *Faith and Mission* 13.1 (1995): 58–60.

[205] House, *Zephaniah,* 64.

[206] Ibid.

[207] *HALOT,* 1155.

[208] Berlin, *Zephaniah,* 95. As Patterson explains (*Nahum, Habakkuk, Zephaniah,* 330–31), these words "anticipate the reference to chaff blown away in line two of v. 2 (as well as the figure of threshing) and provide an image that can be adapted to the sociopolitical and religious needs of the community. The metaphor is of judgment likened to winnowing. As one gathers the straw left from the threshing sledge and separates the grain from the chaff in the winnowing process, so the people of God will be divided into believers (straw) and unbelievers (chaff) in the coming winds of divine judgment. It was a time of spiritual harvest, and Zephaniah's countrymen needed to assemble and 'gather straw.'" Robertson (*Nahum, Habakkuk, and Zephaniah,* 290) reads "gather yourselves together like stubble" and interprets it as a "derogatory address. Judah is worth no more than stubble. Its populace ought to bunch together in a manner that acknowledges this utter worthlessness."

A nation without shame (NRSV, "shameless)[209] should come to its senses. Patterson describes them: "They displayed a willful disregard for God and his standards and sought their own path."[210] Robertson adds: "Only a nation blinded to its own sin could feel no shame in the midst of such guiltiness. Tottering on the brink of utter destruction by the righteous judgments of God, the nation goes blithely on its way, oblivious to the calamities staring it in the face."[211] Zephaniah's questions must have been: "Can't you see what you're doing to yourself? Don't you see that the end of this is nothing but ruin?"

The magnitude of Judah's problem may be summed up by the use of one small Hebrew word. Zephaniah used the word *gôy* to describe Judah, a word normally used to describe the pagan nations rather than the people of God.[212] "Here Jerusalem is deliberately classed with the foreign nations, as it will be again in 3:1–7. It had become so foreign in its ways that it seemed to belong more to them than to God."[213] In every age believers must ask where their loyalties lie and how their lives are spent. Is it time for us to come to our senses?

2:2 Judah should come to its senses before the great day of judgment comes upon the people. The time of judgment, the appointed time of God's

---

[209] "Shameful" translates לֹא נִכְסָף. The verb כסף occurs only four other times and there seems to mean "long for" (Ps 17:12; Job 14:15 in the *qal;* Gen 31:30; Ps 84:3 in the *niphal* as here). The meaning "be ashamed" here is based on an Aramaic cognate meaning "become pale from embarrassment." Although Berlin translates "unwanted [by God]" with the verb's uses elsewhere (*Zephaniah,* 96; similarly Roberts, *Nahum, Habakkuk, and Zephaniah,* 187), Patterson (*Nahum, Habakkuk, Zephaniah,* 331) translates "wayward," basing it on an Akk. cognate that leads to the image of "threshed": "As grain must be broken off (threshed) into small pieces in preparation for winnowing, so a man must be broken spiritually (Pss 34:18; 51:18; 147:3) in submission to God if he is to be delivered. Motyer ("Zephaniah," 3:924) sees the term as "difficult to understand. … Normally meaning 'to long for' (Job 14:15), in certain contexts it requires the sense, 'to grow pale. … [This] may have emotional overtones depicting color draining away. … The verb has an absolute sense: insensitive, devoid of feeling: 'unresponsive to the Lord.'" Watts translates "who care for nothing" and relates it back to the description of God in 1:12 (*Joel, Obadiah, Jonah, Nahum Habakkuk and Zephaniah*, 164).

[210] Patterson, *Nahum, Habakkuk, Zephaniah,* 331.

[211] Robertson, *Nahum, Habakkuk, and Zephaniah,* 291.

[212] Some commentators link Zeph 2:1–3 with the following verses about Philistia rather than the preceding verses about Judah. Use of גּוֹי would therefore fit the reference to a foreign nation. G. J. Botterweck ("גּוֹי *gôy,*" *TDOT* 2:426–30) observed that עַם (people) and גּוֹי often are used as synonyms, but that גּוֹי normally designates a people according to political and territorial affiliation.

[213] Watts, *Joel, Obadiah, Jonah, Nahum Habakkuk and Zephaniah*, 164.

wrath, would sweep Judah away like the evening wind blows the chaff.[214] Judah must turn from its destructive behavior and return to the Lord.

The chaff or stubble referred to the worthless part of the wheat. After gathering the wheat into bundles, the harvesters carried the bundles to the threshing floor, where the wheat would be beaten in order to separate the kernel from the disposable parts of the stalk. Those threshing the grain threw all of this into the air where the brisk evening Palestinian wind would take the chaff away.

In a number of contexts the chaff described that which is worthless, only to be thrown away. Because of its wickedness, Judah stood in danger of becoming "like chaff that the wind blows away" (Ps 1:4).

2:3 Zephaniah's climactic message involved the necessity of repentance and the importance of looking to God in righteousness. Zephaniah used the verb "seek" three times in this verse, each time as an imperative. Judah must realize that "the only adequate refuge from the consuming wrath of Yahweh may be found in Yahweh himself."[215]

Seeking the Lord is almost a technical term that means to worship and obey the Lord.[216] The prophet further defined the term by calling on the people to seek righteousness and to seek humility. No person can seek the Lord without striving after right actions and displaying humility as corollaries. "Genuine seeking involves persistence until success is realized. It inevitably includes an unshaken trust in that which is being sought."[217]

Genuine worship of the Lord issues in right actions. In the Old Testament

---

[214] The first two lines are difficult. They could be rendered lit., "Before a decree is born, like chaff a day has passed away." The first line means "before the events decreed by the Lord take place," as the NIV seems to have taken it. Motyer says the NIV translation "that day sweeps on like chaff" is "inadmissible" because chaff "is never used in the Old Testament simply as a simile of speed but always of swift-acting divine judgment" ("Zephaniah," 3:926–27). He understands עבר to be used attributively, "the chaff that has passed away." יום is taken adverbially, "all at once." For a more complete discussion of the complexities of the verse and other possible solutions, Roberts (*Nahum, Habakkuk, and Zephaniah,* 187–88) gives a lengthy discussion of alternatives, then radically emends the MT and translates "before you are driven away like the passing chaff" (p. 185). Berlin responds: "The more the suggestions and emendations multiply, the less certain any one of them appears. Despite the fact that the MT does not yield good sense, I let it stand for lack of a convincing alternative" (*Zephaniah,* 97).

[215] Robertson, *Nahum, Habakkuk, and Zephaniah,* 293.

[216] See the discussion on 1:6. The imperative of בקש is also used with יהוה as its object in Ps 105:4 // 1 Chr 16:11. דרש is used similarly in Isa 55:6; Amos 5:4,6; Ps 105:4 // 1 Chr 16:11. Robertson notes that the plural form of the imperative here "may be regarded as a summons to worship. For only as the assembled community solemnly pledges the submission of its will to the will of Yahweh may a meaningful 'seeking' of the Lord be achieved. As his binding word of the covenant is rehearsed, as the sacrifices of praise and adoration are offered, the Lord may be found" (*Nahum, Habakkuk, and Zephaniah,* 293)

[217] Robertson, *Nahum, Habakkuk, and Zephaniah,* 293.

"righteousness" denotes actions that meet the demands of a relationship.[218] If the relationship is with God, then righteousness means meeting the demands of the relationship with God. Thus a genuine relationship with God implies the doing of right acts. The right acts are defined by God himself rather than by human beings. "Generally, the righteous man in Israel was the man who preserved the peace and wholeness of the community, because it was he who fulfilled the demands of communal living."[219] Stigers sees three aspects of personal relationships involved: (1) the ethical conduct of one person with another in fulfilling God's norms for such relationships (Job 29:12–15; Deut 24:13; Prov 14:34; Amos 5:15,24; Jer 22:1–4); (2) forensic conduct applying the law equally to every person regardless of social or economic class (Exod 23:7–8; 1 Chr 18:14; Prov 16:12; Isa 5:23); and (3) theocratic conduct of God and his people under the covenant whereby people obey God, and God deliv-

---

[218] Scholars vigorously debate the complex meaning of צדק. K. Koch ("צדק, *ṣdq* to be communally faithful, beneficial," *TLOT* 2:1046–62) describes a sphere of existence with actions that have built-in consequences (p. 1052). The universal king Yahweh permits his people to share in a power that surrounds him (Pss 9:5; 89:15–17; 99:4; 103:17–19). "Because cult members gifted with צדק conduct themselves in daily life in faithfulness to society and moral goodness, they produce welfare and victory for themselves and their environs by virtue of the sphere of influence in which the built-in consequences of action take place" (p. 1054). B. Johnson ("צָדַק, etc.," *TWAT* 6:903–23) sets forth a current distinction between juristic righteousness as conformity of conduct to a norm or standard and a relationship understanding in which righteousness becomes almost synonymous with deliverance and salvation. Righteousness involves God's active intervention to bring salvation (Ps 85:14; Isa 51:5) and yet is also something established, trustworthy, and reliable (Isa 1:21; Pss 89:15; 97:2). Righteousness is what God has commanded (Ps 119:138) and what man learns (Isa 26:9,10; Prov 1:3). It is also a legitimate claim a person can make (Deut 16:20; Ps 132:9; Job 19:14; Isa 64:4; Ps 15:2). Without righteousness one cannot claim membership in the community (Neh 2:20; Isa 5:23). The Decalogue in Exod 20 or the entrance liturgies in Pss 15; 24 show what it means to be righteous without establishing a standard, fixed list. Johnson argues that righteousness can stand in close relationship with the covenant, describing the form and results of positively ordered community relationships. God is righteous as he preserves the covenant community, while man is righteous as he lives according to the order of the God-given covenant community. D. J. Reimer ("צדק," *NIDOTTE* 3:744–69) gives an even more complex examination of passages concerning righteousness in the OT. His summary is that "the term appears to be used to refer to right comportment: status or behavior in accord with some implied norm" (p. 746). The interesting finding is that the norm remains implied and is seldom if ever explicit in the OT. Thus neither divine law nor divine covenant is in the center of attention in the language of righteousness. Righteousness is not necessarily tied to an action but can be part of a person's character, who the person is. It involves acting rightly on behalf of people in distress. God is the judge who determines who is right and eligible to remain in the community and who is wrong and thus forfeits right to community membership. Thus in the prophets (p. 764) "צדק revolves around the maintenance of relationship between God and people." Amos emphasizes the relationship in the human community; Hosea, in the community with God. "Ezek 18:5–9 gives the most comprehensive account of what this behavior looks like, joining matters of purity and equity and summarizing it with reference to divine statutes and ordinances" (p. 765).

[219] Achtemeier, "Righteousness in the OT," *IDB,* 81.

ers or disciplines his people (Deut 6:25; Ps 1:1–6; 31:1; Jer 11:20; Isa 45:21; 46:13).[220]

Being righteous toward other human beings means meeting the demands of the relationship with God and others. How we treat other people should never be divorced from the relationship with God. Rather, how we relate to others is defined by our relationship with God. For example, the two parts of the Ten Commandments are often illustrated as the first part defining the relationship with God and the second part defining the relationship with others—thus, the God-Man relationship and the Man-Man relationship. But the two parts must be understood to be closely connected. Only in the relationship with God do we live out correctly our relationship with others.[221]

Zephaniah wanted to see people seeking the Lord and as a result of their worship of God seeking right actions and profound dependence on God. Micah defined the proper relationship with God as acting justly, loving mercy, and walking humbly with God (Mic 6:8).

"Humility" refers to the "moral and spiritual condition of the godly" who have "absolute dependence on God."[222] The "humble" seek God, keep his commands, wait on God, and are guided by him. They are dependent on him in everything.[223] "They are conscious of divine approval and are confident that in the eschaton God will save them."[224] They are those "who can be pushed around and exploited by the influential, by vested interests (Ps 9:11–13). Spiritually they are ready to see themselves at the bottom of the heap in God's eyes, those who have no power to help themselves nor any influence to bring pressure on God (Pss 25:9; 149:4)."[225]

By the "humble of the land" Zephaniah referred to the minority of people in Judah who remained faithful to the Lord. These were people who did his "commands." In other words, these were much like the remnant in Elijah's day who had not sworn allegiance to Baal (1 Kgs 19:18). The humble had remained faithful to God, rejecting syncretistic worship (Zeph 1:4–6). As Patterson concludes: "Inward affliction of soul and outward circumstances of affliction play a vital part in developing true humility."[226]

The New Testament writers referred to the humble in much the same way. Jesus spoke in the Beatitudes of the "poor in spirit," the "meek" (gentle), and "those who hunger and thirst for righteousness" (Matt 5:3,5–6).

While Zephaniah did not hold out a promise for deliverance ("perhaps"),

---

[220] H. S. Stigers, "צָדֵק, etc.," *TWOT* 2:753–54.

[221] B. D. Napier, *The Book of Exodus,* LBC (Richmond: John Knox, 1963), 84–85.

[222] L. J. Coppes, "עָנָה (ʾānâ), etc.," *TWOT* 2:682–84.

[223] See Watts, *Joel, Obadiah, Jonah, Nahum Habakkuk and Zephaniah,* 165.

[224] Coppes, "עָנָה (ʾānâ), etc.," 2:683.

[225] Motyer, "Zephaniah," 3:927.

[226] Patterson, *Nahum, Habakkuk, Zephaniah,* 332.

he indicated the hope for deliverance for those who repented. "There is no promise. But it is a chance worth taking since no other option offers a possibility of survival."[227] Zephaniah presented the only hope for people in any age. On "the day of the Lord's anger" neither wealth nor station in life could deliver those who rebelled against God (Zeph 1:18). Those who responded to the prophetic message as God called them to do would be "sheltered."[228] Fortified cities would crumble before the Lord's attack, but his humble people would find shelter or literally be "hidden" in him. The verb *str* means "to hide oneself or others for the sake of protection from life-threatening situations."[229] This is not an escape from the day of the Lord. The day is not turned back. It cannot be. But shelter is available in that day.[230] "The way of salvation must provide satisfaction (Exod 12:12–13) and shelter (Exod 12:22–23)."[231]

Verse 3 "foreshadows the positive ending of the prophecy. At this point the reader cannot see the victory of 3:14–20, but there is some break in the gloomy picture. … Such as it is, this biting invitation is the book's first offer of redemption. Some resolution to the conflict is in sight."[232]

Living in greater affluence and stronger defenses leads us to a greater feeling of security. We trust in the wealth we have accumulated or in the power of security devices, but the answer to the needs of our day is the same as that of Zephaniah's age—we must turn to God in humble submission. No other device or plan can save. The message is the same in every age. We must "seek the LORD and live" (Amos 5:6).

---

[227] Watts, *Joel, Obadiah, Jonah, Nahum Habakkuk and Zephaniah*, 166.

[228] Patterson, *Nahum, Habakkuk, Zephaniah*, 332–33, takes תִּסָּתְרוּ as an "infixed t" form of the verb סוּר, "turn aside," a grammatical decision that is highly debatable. He translates "you will be delivered." NIV follows the traditional Hebrew grammarians and lexicons in reading this as a niphal form of סתר, "be hidden." See *HALOT* 2:771.

[229] A. E. Hill, "סתר," *NIDOTTE* 3:301.

[230] See Robertson, *Nahum, Habakkuk, and Zephaniah*, 288.

[231] Motyer, "Zephaniah," 3:928.

[232] House, *Zephaniah*, 64.

SECTION OUTLINE

II. THE JUDGMENT AGAINST THE NATIONS (2:4–15)
1. Judgment against Philistia (2:4–7)
2. Judgment against Moab and Ammon (2:8–11)
3. Judgment against Cush (2:12)
4. Judgment against Assyria (2:13–15)

II. THE JUDGMENT AGAINST THE NATIONS (2:4–15)

The Lord is the Lord of the whole earth. Every nation and every people belong to him. One of the truths to be learned from the following section is that all the earth is his (Exod 19:5), and all the earth comes under his jurisdiction.

The so-called major prophets (Isaiah, Jeremiah, and Ezekiel) also prophesied against the foreign nations. Among the minor prophets only Amos and Zephaniah proclaimed messages against several nations (the messages of Nahum and Obadiah involved the fortunes of a single foreign nation). Yet every prophetical book except Hosea contains judgment speeches against foreign nations. A large variety of genres can be used to announce the destruction of the enemy.[1] In Scripture such oracles often are collected together as here (Isa 13–23; Jer 46–51; Ezek 25–32; Amos 1–2). The formal use and origin of these oracles is debated. Sweeney locates them "initially in execration rituals to curse enemies (1 Kgs 22; Num 22–24) and later in liturgical announcements of YHWH's sovereignty (Pss 2; 46; 48; 76).[2]

Form critically, oracles (or prophecies) against a foreign nation are classi-

---

[1] M. A. Sweeney, *Isaiah 1–39 with an Introduction to Prophetic Literature,* FOTL (Grand Rapids: Eerdmans, 1996), 528–29) lists taunt (Isa 14:4–23; prophetic announcement (Isa 13–23; dirge (Ezek 27:1–36; 32:1–16); lamentation (Isa 15:1–9); summons to war (Isa 15:1–9).

[2] Sweeney, *Isaiah 1–39*, 529. More explicitly, he says: "The social setting of the prophecies concerning foreign nations appears to be in relation to war traditions in ancient Judah. … Such oracles were apparently delivered prior to a battle either to encourage the Israelite/Judean warriors and the king that YHWH had delivered their enemies into their hands (Deut 20:1–4; 1 Kgs 21) or as a means to curse enemies and to ensure their defeat." Sweeney goes on to note that a prophet like Isaiah did not foresee direct military confrontation between Judah and each nation mentioned. Rather Isaiah used this traditional literary form "as a means to present the Judean monarch with his views of the likely fate of the nations that stood to be invaded by the Assyrians. … Such oracles would clearly have been employed to discourage alliance with foreign nations and confrontation with Assyria."

fied according to their content much more than by their form. They announce Yahweh's present or immediately future act of punishment and formally address the foreign nation or its king. Most often they do not even give a reason for the destruction. The purpose is not to show that a nation deserves punishment or explain why a nation is receiving punishment. This may be a way of calling attention to the sin of Judah and the resulting judgment. Normally an oracle against a foreign nation has one major purpose: "to identify the destruction of the nation as an act of YHWH."[3] The collection of such oracles then serves "to announce the imposition of YHWH's rule in the world."[4] Hayes noted that the function of the speeches did not involve their being heard or acted on by the nations. Nor did their importance involve the nations' knowledge of the oracles. Hayes suggested that their importance should be sought in the "function they performed within the context of Israelite society."[5]

The significance of this section in Zephaniah may be indicated by the introductory word *kî*, "for," in Hebrew (not translated in the NIV). Although the word occasionally has an emphatic force and can then be rendered "indeed,"[6] its more common use is to indicate a connection between clauses or sentences.[7] Many translations (e.g., NASB, NRSV, NJB, NKJV) and commentaries consider "for" to be the best translation here and that this section serves as motivation for the call to repentance in 2:1–3. Robertson, for example, explains that "the Lord's devastation of other nations should make his people realize that they shall not escape his righteous retribution. On the other hand, the blessings accruing to Judah from God's judgment on their neighbors should inspire them to walk in righteousness before him. From still a third perspective, participation in the blessings of the Lord by the Gentiles should move Israel to a jealousy that will lead them back to the only true and living God."[8]

---

[3] Sweeney, *Isaiah 1–39*, 213.

[4] Ibid., 214.

[5] J. H. Hayes, "The Usage of the Oracles against the Nations in Ancient Israel," *JBL* 87 (1968): 81.

[6] R. L. Smith, *Micah–Malachi,* WBC. (Waco: Word, 1984), 133–34.

[7] See A. Harman, "Particles," *NIDOTTE* 4:1030.

[8] O. P. Robertson, *The Books of Nahum, Habakkuk, Zephaniah,* NICOT (Grand Rapids: Eerdmans, 1990), 296. See also A. Berlin, *Zephaniah,* AB (N.Y.: Doubleday, 1994), 99. W. Rudolph (*Micha, Nahum, Habakuk, Zephanja,* KAT [Gütersloh: Gerd Mohn, 1975], 279) and J. J. M. Roberts *(Nahum, Habakkuk, and Zephaniah: A Commentary,* OTL [Louisville: W/JK, 1991], 195) do not deny a causal sense for כִּי but judge it to be a later editorial attempt to provide a connection with the previous section. Motyer translates "for" but understands the section to be "an explanatory comment on the worldwide judgment threatened in the first section. … it describes how judgment will cover all the earth, justifies this divine action by making specific accusations, and qualifies judgment by an unexpected and unexplained note of hope (2:11; 3:8)" ("Zephaniah," in *The Minor Prophets*, 3 vols., ed. T. E. McComiskey (Grand Rapids: Baker, 1993), 3:931).

Zephaniah's words of judgment here are not against a chance grouping of nations. Like Amos before him (Amos 1–2), Zephaniah seemed to have had a definite purpose in his grouping of the nations. He chose nations close by (Philistia, Moab, Ammon) and far away (Cush, Assyria). He spoke of nations which surrounded Judah from all four points of the compass. He spoke of nations which concerned Judah because of their proximity, and he spoke of nations which concerned Judah because of their place in history. As Sweeney notes, "Zeph 2:4–15 includes those nations that were Josiah's major enemies or that Josiah intended to subjugate."[9]

Philistia lay to the west with Moab and Ammon to the East. Cush and Assyria were south and north of Judah. In the center of all this lay Judah. Zephaniah, in advising young King Josiah, showed that God would bring defeat to the king's enemies in every direction. Motyer categorizes these nations in interesting ways: "Here is a typical world: the militarily tough Philistines, the vaguely related (Gen 19:36–38) but unpredictable Moab and Ammon, the distant and hardly known Cush, and the superpower Assyria. Here is the world in its political diversity: the city-states of Philistia, the minor sovereignties of Moab and Ammon, and the monolithic imperialist Assyria. From all this Zephaniah stands back and sees that it is the Lord only who is sovereign, who decrees the destinies of all alike. His is a calm kingship, unswayed by worldly power, religious affiliation, proximity or remoteness on the face of the earth."[10]

Zephaniah employs artistic poetic figures to paint his pictures of the destructions of the nations. These include: metaphor and simile (2:4–7,9); irony (2:12); synecdoche (2:13); paronomasia (2:4,7); and literary allusions (2:4,9).[11]

1. Judgment against Philistia (2:4–7)[12]

4Gaza will be abandoned
and Ashkelon left in ruins.
At midday Ashdod will be emptied
and Ekron uprooted.
5Woe to you who live by the sea,
O Kerethite people;
the word of the LORD is against you,
O Canaan, land of the Philistines.

---

[9] Sweeney, *Isaiah 1–39*, 216.

[10] Motyer, "Zephaniah," 3:931.

[11] See R. D. Patterson, *Nahum, Habakkuk, Zephaniah,* WEC (Chicago: Moody, 1991), 335.

[12] For textual study and emendation suggestions in the text of 2:4–18, see Roberts, *Nahum, Habakkuk, and Zephaniah*, 191–94.

"I will destroy you,
and none will be left."

[6]The land by the sea, where the Kerethites dwell,
will be a place for shepherds and sheep pens.
[7]It will belong to the remnant of the house of Judah;
there they will find pasture.
In the evening they will lie down
in the houses of Ashkelon.
The LORD their God will care for them;
he will restore their fortunes.

The Philistines moved to the land of Canaan in large numbers about 1200 B.C. and lived in the same geographical region as the people of Israel. No natural borders separated the Philistines from the Israelites so the two groups interacted more than any of the other nations mentioned by Zephaniah.

Except for the early rivalry reflected in the period of Samuel, Saul, and David, the two groups lived in relative peace. The Philistines apparently migrated from the Mediterranean and continued their trading and fishing. The Israelites were not sailors (Jonah proves that fact) which means that the two groups did not struggle for the same resources and that they depended upon one another for their livelihood.

2:4 Zephaniah mentioned four of the five main Philistine cities. He excluded Gath, which may have perished by his time.[13] He probably used the four cities to represent the destruction to come on the entire area of Philistia.

Zephaniah basically moved from south to north in his description of the destruction. Gaza, the most remote Philistine city, lay fifty miles southwest of Jerusalem. Since the time of Sennacherib, Gaza had served as a vassal of Assyria and held Judean territory with the help of the Assyrians.[14] From Gaza, Zephaniah moved his prophecy progressively closer to Jerusalem, proclaiming the coming destruction of Ashkelon, Ashdod, and Ekron. Zephaniah's message came closer and closer to the covenant people who had rejected the true God for idols which do not profit.

The prophet used assonance, a poetic device based on similar sounds, to communicate his message. Gaza *(ʿazzâ)* would be abandoned *(ʿăzûbâ)* and

[13] Micah mentioned Gath prominently (Mic 1:10, 14). The city could have been destroyed by an Assyrian invasion. Amos indicated that the city may have suffered defeat by his day (Amos 6:2). W. F. Stinespring noted that Sargon II boasted of having destroyed Gath in connection with his campaign of 711 B.C. After that time Gath seems to have disappeared from history ("Gath," *IDB,* 355–56). Motyer ("Zephaniah," 3:931) attributes the decline of Gath to the military campaign of Uzziah (2 Chr 26:6). Roberts (*Nahum, Habakkuk, and Zephaniah,* 197) follows Rudolph (*Micha, Nahum, Habakuk, Zephanja,* 279) in seeing Gath as under Judean control at the time the oracle was originally delivered.

[14] Stinespring, "Gaza," *IDB,* 357–58.

Ekron *(ᶜeqrôn)* would be uprooted *(tēᶜāqēr)*.

Zephaniah proclaimed the judgment against Gaza as a city deserted, a statement meaning something like our saying that "grass would grow in the streets." The following statement, "Ashkelon left in ruins," is parallel to the pronouncement about Gaza. Both cities would suffer the same fate.

Nebuchadrezzar took both Gaza and Ashkelon. Ashkelon, laying twelve miles north of Gaza and ten miles south of Ashdod, recovered and became famous as a Hellenistic city.[15] Ashdod and Ekron fell at the same time but were also rebuilt at a later time.[16]

Two lines of thought on the significance of "midday" have been suggested. First, people often rested at noontime which was the hottest part of the day. The attack then would have come at noon surprising the city and making it an easy prey. The idea may have been the suddenness of the attack as perhaps in Jer 15:8.[17] Second, the attack concluded by noon, meaning that the city fell easily to the attacking forces. Taylor cited a reference from the Moabite stone, "And I fought against it from the break of dawn until noon, and I took it," as a reference to the ease of taking a city such as Ashdod.[18]

The second suggestion is more likely. Ashdod, like the other Philistine cities, would receive the judgment of the Lord God. The judgment emphasized here is loss of population, not the act of conquest and destruction. Roberts explains this: "the major problem with the Philistines was that they occupied territory claimed by Judah."[19]

2:5 "Woe" is a word meaning both judgment and lament. The word could introduce either a judgment speech or a word lamenting the fate of the city (cp. Nah 3:1; Hab 2:6–20). Of the fifty-three occurrences in the Old Testament, R. J. Clifford lists three possible uses for *hôy*: (1) to describe funeral laments (eight times), usually translated as "alas;" (2) a cry to get attention (four times), usually translated as "ho" or "ah"; and (3) an announcement of doom (forty-one times and used only by the prophets), usually translated as "woe to."[20] Zephaniah employed the latter usage. While no reason for the

---

[15] Id., "Ashkelon," *IDB*, 252–54.

[16] Patterson, *Nahum, Habakkuk, Zephaniah*, 339.

[17] Berlin, *Zephaniah*, 100.

[18] C. L. Taylor, Jr., "The Book of Zephaniah: Introduction and Exegesis," *IB* (New York: Abingdon, 1956), 1024; O. P. Robertson illustrates Esarhaddon's prideful boast of taking Memphis in only half a day, but then says neither surprise nor quickness of victory was in view. Rather he points to the emphasis on military superiority, so confident was he that no element of strategic surprise was necessary for victory. Frontal attack in broad daylight brings overwhelming victory to the superior forces (*The Books of Nahum, Habakkuk, Zephaniah*, NICOT [Grand Rapids: Eerdmans, 1990], 298).

[19] Roberts, *Nahum, Habakkuk, and Zephaniah*, 198.

[20] R. J. Clifford, "The Use of *hôy* in the Prophets," *CBQ* 28 (1966): 458–64. See the discussion on Nah 3:1.

judgment is mentioned, "the context shows the prophet has anything but affection for the Philistines."[21]

Zephaniah identified the Philistines as "Kerethites," a term that may identify a clan of the Philistines or may be associated with the island of Crete, from which most assume the Philistines migrated.[22] In Amos 9:7, Deut 2:13, and Jer 47:4, the Philistines are associated with Caphtor, which may have been Crete.[23] David recruited part of his bodyguard from the Kerethites (2 Sam 8:18). In the present context Zephaniah referred to the whole nation by the name of Kerethites.

Zephaniah also used the term "Canaan" with the Philistines, probably in the sense of their common fate with the Canaanites as a people to be driven out of the land. Canaan normally meant the region west of the Jordan River. Motyer points to Gen 9:25 to say that Zephaniah has brought Philistia under the curse of Canaan.[24] When Israel subdued the Philistines in the past, they were able to do so only because of the intervention of the Lord (1 Sam 7:13). Judah could know of the certain end of the Philistines because of the word of the Lord. The central couplet in this verse "traces all to the agency of the 'word of the Lord.' The divine agent in creation (Ps 33:6; see also Gen 1:3; Heb 12:3; 2 Pet 3:5) is the overmastering agent in history; in both arenas alike he 'spoke and it came to be' (Ps 33:9; Isa 13:3)."[25]

Like other parts of the Old Testament, Zephaniah presented the Lord as a dreaded warrior. The end of the Philistines was sure because the hand of the Lord was against them. For this same reason, the people of Judah could know that the day of the Lord would certainly come in judgment against those who rebel against the Lord. The same Lord also judges the people of the modern age who ignore God and his ways.

2:6 The totality of the destruction at the Lord's direction would be so great as to make the land of the Philistines a place for shepherds and sheep pens rather than one inhabited by a developed civilization.[26] "The picture of

---

[21] Ibid., 462.

[22] Roberts (*Nahum, Habakkuk, and Zephaniah,* 196) calls the Kerethites a "subgroup of the Philistines that apparently traced their origins to the island of Crete." They "were a dominant element in the Philistine population (1 Sam 30:14; 2 Sam 8:18; Ezek 25:16)." See C. S. Ehrlich, "Cherethites," *ABD* 1:898–99, and K. A. Kitchen, "Philistines," *Peoples of Old Testament Times,* ed. D. J. Wiseman (Oxford: University Press, 1973), 52:67.

[23] A. B. Davidson, *The Books of Nahum, Habakkuk and Zephaniah, with Introduction and Notes,* CBSC (Cambridge: University Press, 1899), 122–23. Cp. R. S. Hess, "Caphtor," *ABD* 1:869–70.

[24] Motyer, "Zephaniah," 3:932.

[25] Ibid.

[26] Robertson delineates the many attempts to emend or understand the difficult Hb. text of this verse, explaining that the NIV basically follows LXX rather than Hb. (*Nahum, Habakkuk, Zephaniah,* 300, n. 8). His own translation (p. 297) is: "The territory of the sea shall be pastures with caves for shepherds, with walled fences for flocks." Roberts offers a translation reflecting emendation to the text: "And the seacoast will become pastures, encampments for shepherds and folds for flocks" (*Nahum, Habakkuk, and Zephaniah,* 190, 192).

pastoral peace is probably an intentional contrast with the warlike reputation of the Philistine states."[27]

2:7 God would restore the fortunes of the people of Judah by giving to them the land of the Philistines. Far from abandoning his people, he intended to do good to them by caring for them. The metaphor "portrays the remnant of Judah lying down like sheep in the wasteland that was once Philistia. Before this pastoral image Yahweh only cares about Judah's destruction, but now is their shepherd who creates a haven for His 'sheep.'"[28]

God's magnificent promises of restoration involved the remnant of the house of Judah, probably a reference to the humble and submissive of the people of Judah (Zeph 2:3) rather than to a proud and arrogant group of returning exiles. "Remnant" can be a piece of wood left over from making idols (Isa 44:17) or a people who have survived a catastrophe (1 Chr 4:43; Isa 37:4; Jer 25:20). Theologically important is the remnant God uses after his discipline to participate with him in his universal plan of redemption (Gen 45:7; Isa 37:32; Mic 2:12; 4:7).[29] Baker rightly reminds us that the remnant doctrine is always two-sided: "exemplifying both the severity of God's punishment and also the graciousness of his mercy. Destruction will come, but no annihilation."[30] This remnant God will "care for." Here the literal Hebrew text is "Yahweh their God will visit them," picking up the same verb used to express God's visit to punish Judah in 1:8–9. God faithfully visits his people. The result and emotion of those visits depends on the people's faithfulness to their covenant love relationship with him.[31]

Roberts is certainly correct in emphasizing that this does not have to be a postexilic work giving hope to Judeans returning from Babylonian exile. Rather, in Zephaniah's day, Judah had lost its former glory and independence. Zephaniah has shown already that only a remnant of Judah could truly claim to be the people of God (2:1–3). Soon King Josiah would seek to claim Philistine cities as part of his expanded empire. Nothing serves as evidence against Zephaniah supporting the renewal of the Judean kingdom and looking forward to the grand day of Yahweh when full restoration would occur.[32]

The passage illustrates that while Zephaniah spoke against the Philistines,

---

[27] Motyer, "Zephaniah," 3:933.

[28] P. R. House, *Zephaniah: A Prophetic Drama.* JSOTSup 69 (Sheffield, Eng.: Almond Press, 1988), 149.

[29] See Motyer, "Zephaniah," 3:933. Cp. Isa 10:20–23; 11:11–16; Jer 23:1–8; 31:11–14,27–37; Ezek 11:13–20; 34:20–31; 37:15–28; Amos 5:15; Mic 2:12–13; 4:1–8; 5:7–8; 7:18–20; Zech 8:6–8; Zeph 3:9–20).

[30] D. W. Baker, *Nahum, Habakkuk, Zephaniah,* TOTC (Downers Grove: InterVarsity, 1988), 23b, 106.

[31] Cp. Robertson, *Nahum, Habakkuk, Zephaniah,* 301.

[32] See Roberts with reference to archaeological evidence that Josiah did indeed reach the Philistine coast in his expansion moves (*Nahum, Habakkuk, and Zephaniah,* 199).

he spoke for the sake of the people of Judah. "The word of the Lord is the central, determinative factor in the course of history (v. 5); the people of the Lord are the central concern that determines all his actions. The whole course of history is for their final welfare and their secure inheriting of his promises."[33]

2. Judgment against Moab and Ammon (2:8–11)

[8]"I have heard the insults of Moab
and the taunts of the Ammonites,
who insulted my people
and made threats against their land.
[9]Therefore, as surely as I live,"
declares the LORD Almighty, the God of Israel,
"surely Moab will become like Sodom,
the Ammonites like Gomorrah—
a place of weeds and salt pits,
a wasteland forever.
The remnant of my people will plunder them;
the survivors of my nation will inherit their land."

[10]This is what they will get in return for their pride,
for insulting and mocking the people of the LORD Almighty.
[11]The LORD will be awesome to them
when he destroys all the gods of the land.
The nations on every shore will worship him,
every one in its own land.

2:8 The voice of Yahweh returns with the unusual function of "filling out the *prophet's* message."[34] Such interchange between the functions of the prophetic speaker and the divine speaker show they work as "interchangeable revealers" so that "the word of the two is shown as one united word."[35] The people were to understand that these words were not the musings of an obscure prophet but the words of the Lord himself.

From an area southwest of Judah, Zephaniah moved east beyond the Jordan River. Both Moab and Ammon were Semitic people who descended from Abraham through his nephew Lot (Gen 19:36–38). The Ammonites[36] occupied the central area of the region beyond the Jordan, south of Gilead and north of Moab. [37]

---

[33] Motyer, "Zephaniah," 3:932.

[34] House, *Zephaniah*, 59.

[35] Ibid., 59.

[36] For Ammonites see R. W. Younker, "Ammonites," *Peoples of the Old Testament World,* ed. A. S. Hoerth, G. L. Mattingly, E. M. Yamauchi (Grand Rapids: Baker, 1994), 293–316.

[37] For Moabites see G. L. Mattingly, "Moabites," *Peoples of the Old Testament World,* 317–33.

They survived as an autonomous group until about 580 B.C.[38] The Moabites to the south lived on a large plateau overlooking the Dead Sea, at an elevation of ca. 3,000 feet and about 4,300 feet above the sea itself. From the plains of Moab, Moses glimpsed the land flowing with milk and honey which the Israelites took under the direction of Joshua. The region of Moab extended for about sixty miles from north to south and about thirty-five miles from east to west.[39]

The sin of Moab and Ammon involved some kind of territorial designs against the land of Judah which showed up in insults and threats against the people of Judah.[40] Sometime after Zephaniah's prophecy, Obadiah spoke the word of the Lord against Edom (Judah's neighbor to the south) for taking advantage of Judah's defeat at the hands of the Babylonians. They had cut off refugees fleeing the army of Nebuchadrezzar (Obad 14). God would not forget them nor his promises to his people. Despite the defeats that marked Israel's history, "Yahweh is still laying claim to his whole people and to all the territory he had once allotted to them."[41]

2:9 Sin always produces a "therefore." Moab and Ammon selfishly sought their own good and desired to steal from the people of Judah. God vowed to punish the people of Moab and Ammon for their evil. "Both nations have forgotten that to despise Judah is to despise God Himself."[42]

"Therefore, as I live"[43] introduces an oath on the part of the Lord to make Moab and Ammon as Sodom and Gomorrah, two cities destroyed by the Lord in the day of Abraham (Gen 19:23–28). Moab and Ammon came into existence when Lot escaped briefly before the destruction of Sodom and Gomorrah. After the loss of Lot's wife and his daughters' husbands, Lot's daughters found him in a drunken stupor and had sexual relations with their father. The children born became the ancestors of Moab and Ammon (Gen 19:29–38).

"The Lord's people have a well-founded security. The oath-taker is their God, 'the God of Israel'; they are his elect, 'my people'; and the oath rests on the surest foundation, the being ('as I live') and the omnipotence ('the Lord of Hosts') of God himself."[44] The severity of the oath and the determination of

---

[38] G. M. Landes, "Ammon, Ammonites," *IDB,* 108–14.

[39] E. D. Grohman, "Moab," *IDB,* 409–19. For a history of hostilities between Moab and Israel, see Motyer, "Zephaniah," 3:934.

[40] Robertson outlines the history of Moab and Ammon in bringing shame and reproach on Israel (*Nahum, Habakkuk, Zephaniah,* 303). See Gen 19:30–38; Num 22:3; 24:17; 1 Sam 11:1–2; 2 Sam 10:1–4; Neh 4:3; cp. 2:10,19; 4:7; Jer 40:14). He concludes: "Rather ironical is the fact that a people born of incest should be so determined to humiliate their neighboring relatives."

[41] Roberts, *Nahum, Habakkuk, and Zephaniah,* 200.

[42] House, *Zephaniah,* 65.

[43] Motyer calls this the second most common divine oath in the OT next to "I swear" ("Zephaniah," 3:934).

[44] Ibid.

the Lord to keep the oath are underscored by the use of two names for God. He is the "Lord of Hosts" (NIV, "Lord Almighty"), a term usually associated with military passages of Scripture which show the Lord as a God of the armies fighting on behalf of the people of Israel.[45] While the title carries military overtones, it also points to Yahweh's lordship over the entire universe. "He continually rules, but at times he directly intervenes to secure his own victory and insure the direction of history for the salvation of his people."[46]

The people of Judah knew well what the land of Sodom and Gomorrah had become. It was a land of weeds and salt pits, an infertile wasteland (cf. Deut 29:23).[47] Even today the area around the Dead Sea is an extremely desolate place. It is still a wasteland, though not even many weeds grow in the area. The only thing productive about the area was to dig pits around the sea allowing the water to fill the pits. After evaporation salt could be gathered from the pits.

The judgment against Moab and Ammon would be an in-kind judgment. The people of Moab and Ammon wanted to seize Israel's territory. Now the people of Judah would seize the territory of a greedy people. Motyer speaks of a "holy reality within the divine nature that the Lord's people cannot be mistreated with impunity. Every earthly hurt is registered in heaven, for whoever touches his people touches the apple of the Lord's eye (Zech 2:8)."[48]

Zephaniah's word of hope went out to the remnant of the people of Judah. These were the people who humbled themselves before God, turning to him in repentance. They were the heirs of humble Abraham who had let Lot choose this land in the first place when it rightfully belonged to Abraham's seed. "Now the land claimed by Lot's descendants shall revert to its rightful heir."[49]

Contrary to much of modern appraisals concerning the prophets, the prophets preached hope for God's people. Zephaniah, with all his fierceness, preached a strong message of hope, but his message contained hope for a repentant people who survived the fires of judgment. Zephaniah promised that

---

[45] The term "the LORD of hosts" is found prominently in the Books of Samuel, where the Lord promised to care for his people who suffered at the hands of the Philistines or some other oppressor. Notice especially David's vow in 1 Sam 17:45, where he went out against the Philistine giant in the name of the Lord of hosts, the God of the armies of Israel.

[46] J. E. Hartley, "צְבָאוֹת *(ṣĕbāʾôt)* etc., *TWOT* 2:751.

[47] The meaning of מִמְשַׁק, "place," is uncertain, occurring only here. *HALOT* (2:596) relates it to an Arabic word for red earth and translates it "ground." Motyer ("Zephaniah," 3:935) sees it related to the term in Gen 15:2 meaning "possession" and so translates "place of possession." Patterson (*Nahum, Habakkuk, Zephaniah,* 347) brings the Ug. enclitic *mem* into play here, resulting in what he locates as a *hiphil* participle of משׁק, meaning "overflowing," which he then reduces to "overrun." Hebrew חָרוּל, "weeds," is variously translated. Motyer lists "thistles, chickling, chickpea, and nettles" as possibilities but says that Job 30:7 makes "nettles" a "bit unlikely" ("Zephaniah," 3:935). *HALOT* 2:351 calls it a "tall wild artichoke."

[48] Motyer, "Zephaniah," 3:934.

[49] Robertson, *Nahum, Habakkuk, Zephaniah,* 305.

this group would inherit the land of God's enemies.

2:10 Zephaniah returned to the theme of insults and mockery found in v. 8. The verbs are the same in both verses. "Made threats" in v. 8 and "mocking" in v. 10 both translate Hebrew *gdl,* in its causative form, "make great." It refers to boasting or gloating, that is, making oneself out to be great (see Job 19:5; Pss 35:26; 38:17; 41:10; 55:13; Jer 48:26,42; Ezek 35:13; Obad 12). Thus v. 10 serves to recap and summarize all God had to say against Moab and Ammon.[50]

The verse begins literally, "This (will be) to them in place of their pride" (i.e., this is what they get). "This" refers to the total loss of everything of value described in v. 9. Pride will always be replaced eventually by the loss of everything that occasioned it. In a sense, mocking the people of the Lord Almighty really meant to mock the Lord himself. God so identified himself with his people as to take their hurt as his own.

2:11 Roberts typifies critical approaches to this verse, seeing it as an "isolated and apparently misplaced fragment" focusing on religious conversion rather than punishment and not being a natural continuation of God's oath."[51] Such an approach does not recognize that the hinge verse placed in the middle of the four oracles against the nations provides the prophetic focus to the entire section. God's judgment, even of foreign nations, has a purpose. Heschel pointed out that punishment has three aims: retribution, deterrence, and reformation.[52] For Moab and Ammon, the result would be (1) the destruction of the gods of the land and (2) the nations turning to the One who is God. The mention of the idolatry of the nations parallels Judah's idolatry in 1:4–6. "The sin of Israel and her neighbors is linked as one and the same" (cp. 2:13–3:5).[53]

The thrust of the verse must have caused quite a stir in Judah. Would the nations worship the Lord? Even more astounding, could they worship him outside of Jerusalem? Some rabbis questioned the validity of Ezekiel's call because it occurred outside the land of Israel. Many people who thought in the same way must have questioned Zephaniah's contention that other people could worship the Lord and do so in their own land.

This would occur after the time of judgment when the gods of the nations were shown for what they truly were and God became known for who he truly is. For "destroys" the Hebrew text uses a verb meaning "to make thin," apparently referring to a lack of food offered by the inhabitants of pagan lands.[54]

---

[50] See Roberts, *Nahum, Habakkuk, and Zephaniah,* 201.

[51] Ibid.

[52] A. J. Heschel, *The Prophets* (New York: Harper & Row, 1962), 2:187.

[53] House, *Zephaniah,* 59.

[54] See the discussion by Patterson, who eventually translates literally, "make lean" (for NIV's "destroy" (*Nahum, Habakkuk, Zephaniah,* 348). See also Robertson, *Nahum, Habakkuk, and Zephaniah,* 308.

Since judgment would take away the people of the land, the gods would waste away from lack of food. With the gods removed, the people would then begin to see the real rather than the counterfeit.

The real is "awesome." This conception of God has "very deep roots going back to the earliest periods of Zion's imperial theology (Pss 47:2; 76:7,12) and the royal cult in Jerusalem elaborated this conception with a clear claim for Yahweh's superiority over the gods of the other nations (Pss 89:7; 96:4)."[55] The Hebrew term is a passive form of the familiar verb meaning "to fear." The fear of God is central to Israelite worship and theology. The other side of this conception is that God is One whose nature is fearsome or awesome. Used in secular contexts the term can be translated, "terror," and refer to the desert (Deut 1:19; 8:15; Isa 21:1) or to enemy armies (Isa 18:2,7; Hab 1:7). God's acts are terrible or fearsome (Deut 10:21; Pss 65:6; 66:3,5; 139:14; 145:6; Zeph 2:11), especially the saving act of God at the Exodus (2 Sam 7:23; 1 Chr 17:21; Ps 106:22). The acts of the final day of the Lord are likewise terrible (Joel 2:11; Mal 4:5). Thus the Lord is One whose acts and person strike fear and terror into all who observe what he is doing and who he is (Exod 15:11; Deut 7:21; 10:17; 1 Chr 16:25; Neh 1:5; 4:18; 9:32; Pss 47:3; 68:36; 76:8,13; 89:8; 96:4; Isa 64:3; Dan 9:4).[56]

The end of each half of the verse contains a structural parallel. "All" the gods will be doomed, and "all" will worship him.[57] "Here in Zephaniah, the remnant of Israel moves out to the nations and forms in their lands the new people of God. The 'perhaps' of 2:3 has become a promise for the future in 2:5–15, and those who survive for the Kingdom of God will be those who have acknowledged his sovereignty by their humble, obedient, righteous seeking of their true Ruler (2:3)."[58] Zephaniah anticipated the theology of Paul who foresaw a time when all would bow before the Lord as Lord (Phil 2:9–11). The theme is visited again in 3:9.

The idea is also somewhat similar to the words of Isaiah who saw a time, also after Judah's restoration, when the Gentiles and even the eunuchs would offer sacrifices on the altar of the Lord in Jerusalem (Isa 56:1–7; also 53:8). Zephaniah, however, does not limit worship to pilgrimages to Jerusalem (Isa 2:3; 66:23). Each will worship Yahweh in his own land (cp. Isa 19:19–23; Mal 1:11).

This section begins to open a new side of God's character in Zephaniah. The angry God on a rampage against Judah[59] now condemns neighbors for mistreating Judah, shifting some of his wrath from Judah to the neighbors

---

[55] Roberts, *Nahum, Habakkuk, and Zephaniah,* 201–2.

[56] See M. V. van Pelt and W. C. Kaiser, Jr., "ירא," *NIDOTTE* 2:532.

[57] Baker, *Nahum, Habakkuk, Zephaniah,* 108.

[58] E. Achtemeier, *Nahum–Malachi,* INT (Atlanta: John Knox, 1986), 79.

[59] See 1:17 discussion.

and placing himself as Judah's protector. "God is still, supremely, a judge, but He is now a judge inclined to see some chance of releasing the defendant. ... Thus, the totally wrathful picture of God in 1:9–17 is tempered by the portrayal in 1:18–2:12 of Yahweh as still angry, but now offering a bit of hope."[60]

Robertson reminds us that in our day "the glorious day has come in which the sun never sets on the worshipers of the true God. Yet more shall come in fulfillment of these words. For we do not now see with absoluteness either the devastation of the wicked or the purification of worship."[61]

3. Judgment against Cush (2:12)

12"You too, O Cushites,
will be slain by my sword."

2:12 The "Cushites" referred to the people of the modern day Sudan and Ethiopia.[62] Zephaniah had now moved from west and east to south.[63] At least three explanations could be given for why the prophet singled out the people of Cush.[64] First, Zephaniah may have chosen the Cushites as a known people who lived on the edge of the world. Therefore, the power of God reached to the very ends of the world. This is one of the powerful messages of the book and of the section concerning the judgment of the foreign nations: the Lord is not confined to the land of Judah and the people of Israel. He is the Lord of the whole world.

Second, if Zephaniah had a special link with the Cushites (which is not likely; see comments on Zeph 1:1), the prophet may have used the name that meant something to him. Third, at an earlier time, an Ethiopian dynasty ruled Egypt (Isa 18:1–2; 20:3–4). Zephaniah may have spoken the message of God against Egypt, Judah's powerful neighbor to the south. This interpretation would balance the prophecy since Assyria, Judah's powerful neighbor to the

---

[60] House, *Zephaniah,* 71.

[61] Robertson, *Nahum, Habakkuk, Zephaniah,* 309.

[62] Originally referring to the region somewhere between the second and third cataracts of the Nile, Cush about 2000 B.C. became a general term referring to Nubia, south of Egypt. This general usage appears in Egyptian and Assyrian texts as well as the Hebrew Bible. Cushite kings controlled Egypt from 720 to about 663. See D. A. Hubbard, K. A. Kitchen, "Cush," *Baker Encyclopedia of Biblical Places*, ed. J. J. Bimson (Grand Rapids: Baker, 1995), 94–95.

[63] Patterson thinks Cush is an ironic touch to refer to all of Egypt which had been dominated by Cushite rulers for a century before the Assyrian conquests (*Nahum, Habakkuk, Zephaniah,* 349). This would avoid mentioning Egypt whose strength young King Josiah would eventually have to deal with and whose army would cause his death.

[64] Motyer ("Zephaniah," 3:936), somewhat uncharacteristically, sees this as an independent oracle "edited into its present position by Zephaniah in order to complete the north-south-east-west presentation of his worldview."

north, also received a message of condemnation.[65] "The citation of these two entities clearly draws the reader's attention away from the surrounding regions. This distraction functions meaningfully as an intentional device which sets up the oracle against Jerusalem (3:1–8a). It purposefully draws attention away from Judah in order to accentuate the fervor of the denunciation of Jerusalem which follows."[66]

Whatever the reason for choosing Cush and whatever the process by which the oracle achieved this position in the book, Zephaniah made a strong statement about the day of the Lord as he used the oracle. The day of the Lord has a "three-fold 'no-escape': no escape for any people, no escape from the wages of sin, no escape from divine confrontation."[67]

4. Judgment against Assyria (2:13–15)

13He will stretch out his hand against the north
and destroy Assyria,
leaving Nineveh utterly desolate
and dry as the desert.
14Flocks and herds will lie down there,
creatures of every kind.
The desert owl and the screech owl
will roost on her columns.
Their calls will echo through the windows,
rubble will be in the doorways,
the beams of cedar will be exposed.
15This is the carefree city
that lived in safety.
She said to herself,
"I am, and there is none besides me."
What a ruin she has become,
a lair for wild beasts!
All who pass by her scoff
and shake their fists.

2:13 Assyria,[68] with its dominant city Nineveh,[69] typified the enemies of the Lord and struck fear in the capitals of the smaller nations of the ancient

[65] D. J. Clark and H. A. Hatton, *A Handbook on the Books of Nahum, Habakkuk, and Zephaniah* (New York: United Bible Societies, 1989), 175–76.

[66] J. Nogalski, *Literary Precursors to the Book of the Twelve* (Berlin: Walter de Gruyter, 1993), 174–75. Note that Roberts quite honestly concludes: "We simply do not know what provoked this oracle" (*Nahum, Habakkuk, and Zephaniah,* 202).

[67] Motyer, "Zephaniah," 3:936.

[68] For Assyria see W. C. Gwaltney, Jr., "Assyrians," *Peoples of the Old Testament World,* 77–106.

[69] For Nineveh see commentary on Nah 1:1.

Near East. For more than a century, Assyria dominated the region and forced subservience from small nations such as Judah. Assyria took Damascus as early as 732 B.C. and destroyed Samaria in 722 B.C. Assyria forced many people from Samaria into exile in a number of scattered areas and brought other subject peoples to the area surrounding Samaria.

Therefore Zephaniah's message concerning Assyria and Nineveh served as a fitting climax to his prophecies concerning the foreign nations. By referring to Assyria, Zephaniah completed the compass. Having spoken of nations to the west, east, and south, he finished his messages by speaking of the most dreaded nation in the area of the north. Assyria actually lay northeast of Judah, but geography required the Assyrians to travel from the north to get to Judah.

Assyria's might had become legendary long before the time of Zephaniah. If the approach taken in this commentary is correct, Zephaniah preached of the fall of Assyria at about the same time as Nahum when no one else could have foreseen the downfall of the oppressor. Nahum concluded his message by addressing Nineveh and telling the warring nation that all who heard of Nineveh's downfall would clap their hands "for who has not felt your endless cruelty?" (Nah 3:19).

Nineveh actually fell in 612 B.C., not long after Zephaniah proclaimed these words, so he may have lived to see it. The destruction came at the hand of the Lord. Nineveh's fall and Assyria's ultimate destruction did not occur simply as coincidence. The Lord God, the sovereign Lord of history, stretched out his hand against the colossus of the north to leave the city and the nation desolate. Motyer sees an important principle here: "an 'interim fulfillment' like this guarantees all else that has been promised or threatened."[70]

The phrase "He will stretch out his hand"[71] is a figure of speech that symbolizes the power of the Lord and also indicates the active part the Lord would take in the downfall of the nation. Stretching out the hand was a favorite figure of speech of the prophets to symbolize God's power or strength. Isaiah used the figure prominently to indicate God's judgment (Isa 9:12,17,21; 10:4).[72]

"He" refers to the Lord even though the last direct reference to God came in v. 11. The prophets knew that the Lord is an actor in history. He created the world by his great power and brought the nation of Israel into existence. He brought the people of Israel from bondage in Egypt and gave them a land of their own. The prophets knew that God had not quit working in history when Israel settled in the land. He judged Israel and Judah, and he would judge Assyria as well.

---

[70] Motyer, "Zephaniah," 3:937.

[71] Berlin notes that the verbs in v. 13 are jussives and translates "let him stretch out his hand … let him make Nineveh a desolation" (*Zephaniah,* 114).

[72] R. L. Alden, "יָד *(yād)* etc.," *TWOT* 1:362–64. See commentary on 1:4.

Leaving Nineveh "utterly desolate and dry as a desert" meant the city would be utterly destroyed. The expression fit the city of Nineveh well since the city was located on the Tigris River with many canals adjacent to the city which supplied the city with water (Nah 2:8; 3:8). How ironic for the Lord to declare that Nineveh, the city with an endless water supply, would become like a wasteland as "dry as a desert."[73] Sin always affects the environment God has created. Ultimately, salvation will also bring renewal to the environment. Meanwhile, "the creation always sides with its Creator against the rebel. The holy life of God that makes 'nature' fertile (Ps 104:30) only grudgingly lends itself to the needs of sinful humans and ultimately will cease to do so. God's world will not forever support God's enemy."[74]

Nineveh was a great city (Jon 1:2, lit. "great unto God") yet the Lord would bring it to destruction. Though it had existed for centuries (Gen 10:11), the Lord would make it "dry as a desert." In 401 B.C., Xenophon visited the area from Greece and could find no trace of the city.[75]

2:14 Like Ashkelon (2:7) and Moab and Ammon (2:9), Zephaniah described Nineveh after its fall as a wilderness area without inhabitants. Instead of a bustling metropolis with commerce and travel, the area would be a pastoral scene with flocks and herds grazing where a large population had once resided. Creatures of every kind would roam over the area once known as Nineveh.[76] "Humankind holds its tenure on the earth only by holy obedience."[77]

Zephaniah pictured the grandeur of Nineveh as being in ruins with the desert owl and the screech owl roosting on the once magnificent columns of the palatial city.[78] The picture, of course, is of the columns overturned with

---

[73] F. E. Eakin, Jr., "Zephaniah," BBC (Nashville: Broadman, 1972), 285; Patterson, *Nahum, Habakkuk, Zephaniah,* 351.

[74] Motyer, "Zephaniah," 3:937.

[75] Clark and Hatton, *Nahum, Habakkuk, and Zephaniah,* 177.

[76] For "creatures of every kind" the MT reads "all the beasts of the nations." The KJV follows the MT, while the RSV apparently follows the reading of the Tg., using the phrase "beast of the field." The LXX (cited in *BHS*) also gives a reading similar to that found in the RSV. The NIV reading seems to understand the phrase to refer to the different species of animals or those that live in flocks or herds. Berlin notes that גּוֹי serves as a play on the word's use in v. 11 and exhibits irony in seeing Assyria "overrun by other nations' wildlife" (*Zephaniah,* 115).

[77] Motyer, "Zephaniah," 3:937.

[78] Both words are uncertain in meaning as can be seen by comparing versions. The "desert owl" (NIV) is referred to variously as a "cormorant" (a water bird, KJV), "vulture" (RSV), "pelican" (RV), "horned owl" (NEB), or "screech owl" (NASB). Clark and Hatton (*Nahum, Habakkuk, and Zephaniah,* 178), citing the use of the word as an unclean bird in Lev 11:18 and Deut 14:17 and as inhabiting deserted places in Ps 102:6 and Isa 34:11, think that some kind of owl best fits the usage found in the Old Testament. The second word ("screech owl") presents a similar conundrum. The translations present a variety of different animals: "bittern" (KJV), "hedgehog" (RSV), "porcupine" (RV), "bustard" (REB), and "desert owl" (NASB). For purposes of translation, the "screech owl" may be the best choice since the animal connotes the idea of a ruined and deserted area, exactly the idea that Zephaniah wanted to convey. For additional discussion of this issue see Clark and Hatton, *Nahum, Habakkuk, and Zephaniah,* 178–79.

animals lodging among them. In the mind of the hearer, Zephaniah portrayed a deserted city, inhabited only by wild animals whose calls[79] echo through the empty buildings[80] of the once proud city. "The environment was destroyed in verse 13, all human achievement follows in verse 14."[81]

Berlin explains that the Assyria oracle is more elaborate than the others in this section

> not only because we are reaching the climax of the prophecy, but because Assyrian cities and buildings were, indeed, more elaborate than anything that Philistia or Moab had to offer. Our verse reflects the reality of Assyrian palaces, with an ironic twist. They did contain beams and paneling of cedar and other types of wood; and, in addition to the huge statues of winged bulls and lions, and the ever-present reliefs of victorious campaigns, there were, especially in the time of Ashurbanipal when this art form reached its peak, reliefs of hunting scenes depicting many animals. … It is as if Zephaniah is playing on the artistic menagerie in Assyrian palaces and turning it into a vision of destruction and ruin.[82]

In such a vivid way, Zephaniah prophesied the end of Nineveh and the hope of Judah. With Nineveh on the wane and destined to destruction, Josiah and his godly advisors could proceed with their plans to reform the society of Judah, beginning with the temple in Jerusalem. Zephaniah's words, like those of Nahum, must have encouraged those who mourned over the ruin of Judah and the apostasy in Jerusalem. With Nineveh out of the way, Josiah could continue to call for the renewal of the nation.

2:15 Nineveh prided itself in its security and wealth. For generations the Assyrian army brought goods to Nineveh. The city enjoyed the spoils of war brought from conquered peoples. No one could remember a time of trouble, poverty, or insecurity. The city that would be destroyed and inhabited only by the beasts of the earth was this same city—a city of pride, one that dwelt securely. In pride the inhabitants of Nineveh said: "I am and there is none else." "These words claim a status of absolute power and complete independence that in no way properly characterizes finite humanity. … Such arrogant, self-centered blasphemy can only lead to ruin."[83] The people of Judah must

---

[79] Patterson describes the textual problems of v. 14 (*Nahum, Habakkuk, Zephaniah,* 355). He takes קוֹל, NIV "calls," as an interjection and translates (p. 351): Listen! (There is) singing in the window (but) rubble on the threshold." Contrast the conclusions of Roberts (*Nahum, Habakkuk, and Zephaniah,* 194), whose extended note concludes that קוֹל is a great owl that hoots.

[80] The last line of the verse has baffled translators and text critics. Roberts (*Nahum, Habakkuk, and Zephaniah,* 203) simply concludes that "both the text and the translation are uncertain." Exquisite cedar panels or carvings or other architectural masterpieces that had lined the majestic Assyrian temples and palaces would lie on the ground exposed to the wind and the rain and the scorching heat.

[81] Motyer, "Zephaniah," 937.

[82] Berlin, *Zephaniah,* 116.

[83] J. N. B. Heflin, *Nahum, Habakkuk, Zephaniah, and Haggai,* BSC (Grand Rapids: Zondervan, 1985), 145.

have thought of the words of the Lord when they heard these words. Repeatedly in the books of Deuteronomy and Isaiah we are told that, "the Lord is God; there is no other besides him" (Deut 4:35; see also Isa 45:5).

In the days of Isaiah, God had promised to punish the arrogance of Assyria. Though the Lord used the Assyrian as the rod of his anger, he also promised to punish Assyria because of such arrogance. "When the Lord has finished all his work against Mount Zion and Jerusalem, he will say, 'I will punish the king of Assyria for the willful pride of his heart and haughty look in his eyes" (Isa 10:12).

Assyria would become a city of desolation, suitable only for wild beasts. Zephaniah spoke about Assyria's future as if it had come to pass already (using the perfect "tense"). Nineveh's future held only pain and desolation. All who passed by the ancient city would shrink back in horror. Scoffing and shaking the fists (lit., "hand," echoing the word's use in v. 13 and thus framing these verses[84]) were gestures indicating revulsion, scorn, and horror.[85] Those who saw the ruin of Nineveh would feel shock that such destruction could occur as well as relief that the "city of blood" (Nah 3:1) had been removed from the scene.

The Lord is sovereign over the land of Israel and over the entire world. No one and no nation can stand before the Lord. Zephaniah promised that the Lord would punish the wicked in Judah, but he also would punish the nations as well. The city built on the blood of oppressed peoples would become a lair for the beasts of the field. "Because this nation exalted itself to the highest heaven, it must be brought to the lowest hell."[86]

Such is the fate of all those who live in defiance of the Lord God. But how is that defiance expressed? For Zephaniah, the basic expression is pride. As Achtemeier phrases it:

> Philistia's sin is not specifically mentioned but her proud arrogance and blasphemy against the God of Israel had already given birth to legend in Israel (cf. 1 Sam 17). And it is precisely the pride of the nations (cf. Gen 11:1–9) which primarily characterizes them in these oracles, and which is the object of the divine wrath on his Day (cf. Isa 2:6–20): pride of wealth, alluded to with he word 'Canaan' in verse 5, a synonym for greedy traders, and with the mention of fine 'cedar work' in verse 14; pride of power, embodied in the boasts and scoffings of Moab and Ammon (vv. 8,10; cf. Isa 16:6; Jer 48:7,14,17; 49:4) and in their grabs for territory (cf. Amos 1:13; Ezek 25:1–7); pride of independence

[84] Berlin, *Zephaniah,* 114.

[85] L. Walker ("Zephaniah," EBC 7:556) lists various ways of translating this gesture and admits "it is difficult to know exactly which emotion is reflected in this gesture." Motyer speaks of "gestures of derision" ("Zephaniah," 938). Patterson says the gesture is a wave of the hand not a shaking of the fist and indicates contempt (*Nahum, Habakkuk, Zephaniah,* 356).

[86] Robertson, *Nahum, Habakkuk, Zephaniah,* 314.

> and security and sovereignty, set forth in the taunt of verse 15 against Assyria (cf. Isa. 47:8,10). The nations exulted in their pride (v. 15; cf. Isa 22:2; 23:7; 32:13; Zeph 3:11), but God's exultation was to be the last word (3:17).[87]

We should remember that God punishes arrogance and oppression. He desires humble submission to him and right relationships toward others.

The oracles against foreign nations are implied calls for repentance to God's people. If foreign nations suffer for their pride and arrogance, will not God's people do so even more? If God is going to destroy foreign enemies, does that not open new opportunities for his people and encourage them in gratitude and hope to seek him and his righteousness and humility? If God's new picture of hope includes the Gentile nations along with the original people of God, should not his people jealously and zealously guard their relationship with him, making sure while new people are grafted in the old are not cut out?[88]

Who are the foreign nations against whom God's hand is stretched out today? We need again to hear the message of Zephaniah's preaching against foreign nations as succinctly summarized by Achtemeier: "The Word—the word here of Zephaniah, and the word in the rest of the Scriptures—the word made flesh in Jesus Christ—stands against us and our sinful pride. It will now and always so stand if we ignore it or reject it or think it a word intended only for someone else. And what a terrible pit that would be! For the word of the Lord throughout the Bible is a word intended to be for us and not against us—a word intended to restore our life and to lead us into quiet pastures and to allow us to lie down at evening time in peace and security. Therefore, 'seek the Lord … seek righteousness, seek humility.' "[89]

---

[87] Achtemeier, *Nahum–Malachi,* 77.
[88] See Robertson, *Nahum, Habakkuk, Zephaniah,* 296.
[89] Achtemeier, *Nahum–Malachi,* 79–80.

SECTION OUTLINE

III. THE FUTURE OF JERUSALEM (3:1–20)
  1. The Destruction of the Rebellious (3:1–8)
    (1) Jerusalem's Sin (3:1–4)
    (2) Jerusalem's Stubbornness (3:5–7)
    (3) Jerusalem's Hope (3:8)
  2. The Deliverance of the Righteous (3:9–13)
  3. The Joy of the City (3:14–20)

III. THE FUTURE OF JERUSALEM (3:1–20)

Sometimes life seems almost unbearable and completely hopeless. When we survey the current societal scene, we see crime out of control, families breaking up and pulling down the individual members of the family with them, and confusion and frustration on every side. Out of the darkness of our lives comes the dawn of God's love and care. Zephaniah promised that God had not finished with his people. When life seemed the toughest, God promised to provide.

Zephaniah prophesied in such a way as to be called the fiercest of the prophets. Yet, in his fierceness against the sin of the people, the prophet knew that God was at work creating a faithful remnant who would serve him with all their hearts. Out of the judgment would come a time when God would restore the fortunes of the humble and faithful of the people of Judah.

1. The Destruction of the Rebellious (3:1–8)

Zephaniah 3:1–8 "shocks the reader when it becomes undeniably clear (3:2) that it pronounces judgment upon Jerusalem and Judah," thus incorporating them into the oracles against foreign nations much as Amos incorporated Judah and then Israel in such a list in his opening chapters.[1]

These verses "presuppose the remaining oracles against the nations since YHWH indicates that the rationale behind the destruction of the other areas was to warn Jerusalem of impending judgment if she and her people did not change their tactics (3:6f.). The oracle presumes that this change did not

[1] J. Nogalski, *Literary Precursors to the Book of the Twelve* (Berlin: Walter de Gruyter, 1993), 280, n. 4.

occur, and that Jerusalem will be judged accordingly (3:8a)."[2]

Zephaniah—and the Lord—knew Jerusalem to be a rebellious and obstinate city. All of the leaders of the city took advantage of the poor and humble. Instead of heeding the words of the Lord, they looked for their own gain. Though they should have taken correction from the Lord, they went after their own stubborn ways. Their end would be God's wrath poured out on Jerusalem and on the whole world. Only then could the prophet begin to speak of hope for Jerusalem. Thus the prophet says, "the offenses of the city (3:2) and leaders (3:3–4) are inexcusable because of the indwelling God (3:5a–d)."[3]

(1) Jerusalem's Sin (3:1–4)

1Woe to the city of oppressors,
rebellious and defiled!
2She obeys no one,
she accepts no correction.
She does not trust in the LORD,
she does not draw near to her God.
3Her officials are roaring lions,
her rulers are evening wolves,
who leave nothing for the morning.
4Her prophets are arrogant;
they are treacherous men.
Her priests profane the sanctuary
and do violence to the law.

3:1 Roberts is surely correct in underlining the difficulty in separating chap. 3 into individual oracles.[4] Only two obvious introductory formulas occur—the woe oracle introduction of v. 1 and the call to praise or rejoice formula of v. 14. Other breaks are made according to shift in content rather than in form and structure.

Nahum identified Nineveh as the "city of blood" (Nah 3:1). Zephaniah's assessment of Jerusalem was not much different. Jerusalem was a "city of oppressors." The opening verse is all encompassing "addressing their relationship to God, to self, and to other people."[5]

In fact, the messages of the two prophets concerning the cities could be reversed without missing the point of the prophets. Nineveh was a city built on bloodshed, filled with lies and the spoils of warfare against oppressed peo-

---

[2] Ibid., 175.

[3] J. A. Motyer, "Zephaniah," 3 vols, *The Minor Prophets*, ed. T. E. McComiskey (Grand Rapids: Baker, 1998), 3:941.

[4] J. J. M. Roberts, *Nahum, Habakkuk, and Zephaniah: A Commentary*, OTL (Louisville: Westminster/John Knox, 1991), 204.

[5] Motyer, "Zephaniah," 941.

ples (Nah 3:1). On the other hand, Jerusalem, the city where God had chosen to have his name dwell, was a city filled with oppressors. In different ways, both cities took advantage of the weak. God's judgment would come against Jerusalem as surely as it would against Nineveh. This is made clear by the first word, "Woe," tying the announcement of punishment against Judah back to the opening oracle against the foreign nations. Judah is suddenly enveloped in the circle of nations foreign to God just as they had been in Amos 1–2. God's elect had been elected to disaster and destruction.

"Woe" can refer to a word of judgment, a funeral lament, or to a cry such as "ho" or "ah" which is used to gain attention. In the present context, the idea of judgment seems to fit the situation. Zephaniah used the same word in 2:5. There the word "woe" introduced a message of judgment against the foreign nations. In 3:1 the word introduced a message of judgment against the city of Jerusalem with invective (v. 1), criticism (vv. 2–4), and implied threat (vv. 5–7).[6] The theme of the third chapter as well as the theme for the book as a whole concerns the judgment of God against the city of Jerusalem.

For a brief time, the object of the prophet's judgment remained unclear. Zephaniah's words might have referred to a number of cities. By the time of v. 4, the prophet clearly referred to Jerusalem. "Prophets," "sanctuary," and "the law" (Zeph 3:4) are obvious references to the city of Jerusalem. The following verse left no doubt. The Lord was within the city, calling the people to righteous living. In v. 14, the prophet explicitly identified the city as Jerusalem.

The people of the city of Jerusalem in Zephaniah's day practiced oppression. They were rebellious,[7] and the city had defiled itself. The prophet used participles to indicate the present and continual practice of wrong actions toward others and toward God as well.[8] "Assyria's pride is balanced by Judah's disobedience, lack of faith, lack of devotion, injustice, and perversion of the law (3:2–4). In many ways God's people surpass Assyria in doing evil. … No matter how angry He may be with pagan nations Yahweh's chief complaint is with Judah."[9]

---

[6] For other instances of the use of "woe" see the commentary on Nah 3:1, Hab 2:6, and Zeph 2:5. Cp. R. D. Patterson, *Nahum, Habakkuk, Zephaniah,* WEC (Chicago: Moody, 1991), 357; T. C. Butler, "Announcements of Judgment," *Cracking Old Testament Codes*, ed. D. B. Sanday and R. L. Giese, Jr. (Nashville: Broadman & Holman, 1995), 163.

[7] The Hb. form here, מֹרְאָה, is unusual. מרא is traditionally considered a by-form of מרה, "rebel." *HALOT* 2:630 lists מרא as a separate verb that in later Hb. meant "soiled." Roberts shows the various proposals, notes the strong case for "soiled, excrement, sullied," but eventually opts for the traditional "rebellious" (*Nahum, Habakkuk, and Zephaniah*, 206).

[8] For some reason the NIV changes the word order from the Hb. text but without harm to the meaning of the verse. The Hb. reads, "Woe to the one (fem.) rebelling and being defiled; the oppressing city."

[9] P. R. House, *Zephaniah: A Prophetic Drama,* JSOTSup 69 (Sheffield, Eng.: Almond Press, 1988), 66.

Judah's sins are almost beyond belief for the people of God. For enemy nations God concentrated on matters of attitude—pride and arrogance. For his people, he concentrated on social injustice and breaking relationships. As rebels, they had disobeyed God, the Hebrew participle referring to rebellion against God in all but five of forty-five appearances in the Hebrew Bible. The occurrences are found primarily in texts referring to Israel's wilderness experience (Num 20:10,24; 27:14; Deut 1:26,43; 9:7,24; Pss 78:8,17,40,56; 106:7,33,43; Isa 63:10; Neh 9:26). Israel complained against God, wanting to return to Egypt rather than put up with what God provided in the wilderness. Rebellion includes refusal to obey God's commandment (1 Kgs 13:21; Lam 1:18; Ps 105:28; Num 20:24; 27:14). What the fathers began in the wilderness, Israel perpetuated. In God's eyes, "rebel" became their name.[10]

A rebellious people is a defiled or polluted people. Hebrew *gāʾal* most often refers to physical ritual defilement by murder (Num 31:19; Isa 59:3; 63:3) or use of unclean food (Dan 1:8; Mal 1:7,12) or by lack of proper priestly credentials (Ezra 2:62; Neh 7:64). It can refer to social injustice caused by political and religious leaders (Lam 4:13–14). Such defilement thus is "from any breech of moral or ceremonial law."[11] Zephaniah is certainly joining Lamentations in condemning public officials who have destroyed the poor for their own financial and political benefit.[12]

The social justice accusation takes center stage in the charge of oppression (Hb. *yônâ*). Here we are dealing with violent actions against the weakest members of society. The Mosaic law protects the aliens from oppression (Exod 22:21; Lev 19:33; Deut 23:16). Jeremiah (46:16; 50:16) used the term to describe the Jerusalem of his day, only shortly after the time of Zephaniah, if not Zephaniah's contemporary.[13] For Zephaniah, "it is clear from the following verses that the prophet is castigating violent officials, unjust judges, and deceitful prophets."[14] He is also showing the very nature of sin, for "the Hebrew order of these words serves to illustrate the way sin works. Sin is *rebellion* against God that *pollutes* or *defiles* the very being of the sinner, who then strikes out by *oppressing* others."[15]

Every generation faces this issue: how can we reform our social order? How can our nation become a better people. Zephaniah implies an answer:

---

[10] See V. P. Hamilton, "מָרָה *(mārâ)* etc.," *TWOT* 1:526.

[11] R. L. Harris, "גָּאַל *(gāʾal)* etc.," *TWOT* 1:145. Roberts sees גאל as "used especially of soiling one's hands or clothes with blood while committing an act of violence (Isa 59:3; 63:3; Lam 4:14)." Thus he sees Zephaniah referring to "unjust violence against the poor and powerless" (*Nahum, Habakkuk, and Zephaniah*, 212).

[12] See R. E. Averbeck, "גאל," *NIDOTTE* 1:795.

[13] See P. R. Gilchrist, "יָנָה *(yānâ)* etc.," *TWOT* 1:383.

[14] H. Ringgren, "יָנָה *yānâ*," *TDOT* 7:105.

[15] J. N. B. Heflin, *Nahum, Habakkuk, Zephaniah, and Haggai,* BSC (Grand Rapids: Zondervan, 1985), 146.

"true society arises from committed obedience (not rebellion) and from personal holiness (not defilement). … Social reformation arises from a return to God and to individual moral integrity. To seek to reform society in the hope that this will produce high standards and good people is to put the cart before the horse; it is converted and godly individuals that make good society."[16]

3:2 Zephaniah used a series of four negative phrases to describe how the people of Jerusalem acted wrongly toward God. Jerusalem was a city of oppressors, rebellious and defiled because she (referring to the city and to its inhabitants) refused to accept correction in general and specifically refused to listen to God.

The first two phrases contain general references to the obstinacy of Jerusalem. The city did not obey (literally, "listen to") anyone. Of course, Zephaniah meant that the people of Jerusalem did not listen to the Lord,[17] but he expressed it in general terms to emphasize their character. Zephaniah obviously saw the people of Jerusalem as stiff-necked, obstinate, going their own way without regard to God's leading in their lives. Can any nation with such arrogance survive? Zephaniah knew that the answer was "no."

In addition, the city also refused to accept correction. "Correction" (Hb. *mûsār*) has a wide sphere of meaning including discipline, instruction, and direction.[18] Here it includes "the several instances of affliction and rebuke that God sends into the lives of His own to accomplish their correction and spiritual growth (Prov 1:7–8; 3:11–12)."[19] Merrill describes the disciplined life as "the ideal, one that seeks after God and upholds standards of justice and fairness (Prov 1:3)."[20] Only fools refuse to take God's disciplining instructions (Prov 15:5,32).[21] The prophets constantly called the people to repentance and interpreted the nation's woes as warning and correction from God (Amos 4:6–11), but the people would not receive the discipline of God. Finally, "the punishment *[mûsār]* that brought us peace" was borne by God's Suffering Servant (Isa 53:5).

---

[16] Motyer, "Zephaniah," 3:942.

[17] Roberts sees this specifically as "the ruling classes' rejection of prophetic critiques of their behavior" (*Nahum, Habakkuk, and Zephaniah*, 212).

[18] Motyer, "Zephaniah," 3:942. Gilchrist calls it "correction which results in education" ("יָנָה *(yānâ)* etc.," 1:386). Cp. Lev 26:18,24,28; Prov 1:7–8; Deut 8:1–5; 11:1–15, where discipline is almost defined as God's great acts in Israel's history (cp. Hos 5:2; 7:12; Isa 8:11).

[19] Patterson, *Nahum, Habakkuk, Zephaniah,* 361. Cp. Jer 5:3; 7:28; E. H. Merrill concludes: "Fundamentally, it has to do with teaching/learning by exhortation and example, with warning as to the consequences of disobedience, and with the application of penalty following failure to adhere" ("יסר," *NIDOTTE* 2:480–81).

[20] Merrill, "יסר," 2:481.

[21] Note from Job 5:17–26 that even Eliphaz, one of Job's "friends," can speak the truth some of the time until he makes it into an ironclad rule that allows him to judge other people. Proverbs encourages us to seek, choose, and love such instruction from God (Prov 8:10; 12:1; 19:20; 23:23). This is true because as Merrill notes: "Discipline has a beneficent, restorative end. It issues from true love (Prov 13:24) even though the disobedient hate it (Prov 5:12)" ("יסר," 2:481).

Zephaniah's strongest indictment involved the specific act of not trusting God. "Trust" (Hb. *bāṭaḥ*) "expresses that sense of well-being and security which results from having something or someone in whom to place confidence."[22] A call to trust in God is central to biblical religion (Pss 62:8; 115:9–11; Isa 26:3–4; cp. 30:15). The Bible offers great promises to those who find such security in God and in him alone: deliverance from enemies (Ps 22:4–5; cp. 25:1–2; 28:7; 31:14–15; 86:2; Jer 39:18); answered prayer (1 Chr 5:20); straight paths for life (Prov 3:5–6); joy and gladness (Pss 16:9; 33:21); inner peace and absence of fear (Ps 4:8; Isa 26:3).[23] Such trust and hope in God separates relationship with Yahweh and pagan religions' relationships with their gods. "Unlike the pagan religions where unremitted anxiety was the rule, the Hebrew religion knew a God whose chief characteristic was faithfulness and trustworthiness (Deut 33:28; 1 Sam 12:11; Ps 27:3)."[24]

How could anyone not find trust and security in God who had experienced God's salvation the way Israel had? Roberts has the answer: "It was Jerusalem's attempt to find her security in wealth, in military power, in foreign alliances, or even in other gods—in short, in almost anything other than Yahweh himself—that led her to reject God's demands. Rather than draw near to her God in trust, she sought to establish her own security, and in so doing she refused God's offer of life (Isa 1:9) and turned from justice to trust in oppression."[25]

Like those in contemporary society, the people of Jerusalem put themselves in the place of God, preferring to trust in their own understanding rather than in God (Jer 17:5). To show the importance of trusting "in the Lord," the prophet placed "in the Lord" first in the Hebrew sentence Jerusalem stood condemned because "*in the Lord* she did not trust." No one can live without trust. We all rely on something—our friends, perhaps, or our job, our money, our skill, our intelligence, or our appearance. None of these things is worthy of our trust. According to vv. 3–4 the people of Judah clearly could not trust their leaders. "The ship of state that is piloted by a corrupt captain is a danger to itself and all those aboard it."[26] A look upward was their only hope.

---

[22] J. N. Oswalt, who notes that בָּטַח "does not connote that full-orbed intellectual and volitional response to revelation which is involved in 'faith,' rather stressing the feeling of being safe or secure" ("בָּטַח *(bāṭaḥ)* etc.," *TWOT* 1:101).

[23] Oswalt correctly warns that such rewards do not come automatically as a reward for trusting God ("בָּטַח *(bāṭaḥ)* etc.," 1:102). The reason we trust and the cause of our hope is not our merit but God's חֶסֶד, "his unswerving loyalty, his gracious kindness."

[24] Ibid. Oswalt adds: "This contrast between anxiety and confidence becomes all the more striking when one recalls that the pagan was never left without mechanisms whereby he felt he had some control over his destiny, while the devout Hebrew knew himself to be utterly without personal resources." Second Kings 18–19 illustrates the battle for trust between paganism and Yahwism.

[25] Roberts, *Nahum, Habakkuk, and Zephaniah*, 212.

[26] Patterson, *Nahum, Habakkuk, Zephaniah*, 359.

Zephaniah used the same grammatical device in the next line. "Unto her God" comes at the beginning of the sentence to underscore the importance of drawing near to God in obedience, faithfulness, and devotion.[27] Approaching God is not an automatic human response. God is holy, so drawing near may be dangerous (Gen 28:16–17; 32:30; Exod 3:5; 19:12; Lev 16:1–2; Num 1:51; Deut 4:11; 5:26–27; Josh 3:4; Judg 6:22–23). The wicked or godless cannot come near to God (Jer 12:2). Still, Israel had positive experiences: "Today we have seen that a man can live even if God speaks with him" (Deut 5:24). In time of decision Israel needed to draw near and inquire of Yahweh (1 Sam 14:36; cp. Isa 48:16) and hear his instructions (Lev 9:5). But what does Zephaniah mean they had failed to do? Is it Israel's normal use of the term in participation in the sacrificial offerings (see Lev 1:3; 7:20; 9:5)? Or has Zephaniah spiritualized the meaning, making it parallel to and synonymous with, "trust Yahweh, rest secure in him"? (Cp. Eccl 5:1). Motyer defines it as "the heart of biblical religion: peaceful enjoyment in the presence of the Holy God."[28] In the Old Testament the expression means to worship God, to focus attention on him in adoration and in prayer.[29]

On the surface, the accusation appears ludicrous. Jerusalem was the place where God made his name to dwell (2 Kgs 23:27). Jerusalem contained the temple with its altars and sacrificial system. At times of religious festival, Jerusalem swelled with people proclaiming their religious adherence. Yet, in Jerusalem, the people called by the name of the Lord did not draw near to him. Can we see ourselves in Zephaniah's words? While surrounded with all kinds of religious articles, we do not draw near to the Lord of the religion.

3:3 The problems in Jerusalem were not confined to the people at large. Those who should have led the people in righteous living became the worst offenders. They too lived in rebellion against the instruction of the Lord. The point of Zephaniah's singling out the officials and the rulers may have been the widespread perception that the people could trust in them. At a young age Jeremiah saw the widespread disobedience of the people. Having seen the rebellion of the weak in society, he determined to seek the great in society. He fully expected that they would be obedient to the Lord: "I thought, 'These are only the poor; they are foolish, for they do not know the way of the Lord, the requirements of their God. So I will go to the leaders and speak to them; surely they know the way of the Lord, the requirements of their God.' But with one accord they too had broken off the yoke and torn off the bonds" (Jer 5:4–5). The officials and rulers, even the prophets and priests (3:4) partici-

[27] J. D. W. Watts, *The Books of Joel, Obadiah, Jonah, Nahum, Habakkuk and Zephaniah*, CBC (Cambridge: University Press, 1975), 175.

[28] Motyer, "Zephaniah," 942.

[29] O. P. Robertson, *The Books of Nahum, Habakkuk, and Zephaniah,* NICOT (Grand Rapids: Eerdmans, 1990), 319.

pated in all that was wrong with the nation. Instead of giving leadership to the people in righteous living, the leaders led in the rebellion against God!

The "officials" and "rulers" designated the civil authorities in the community, whereas the following verse described the religious leaders of the covenant people. In Israel, no large break divided the secular from the religious. Civil leaders received authority from God and served as God's leaders. These leaders did not have special privileges. Their work was to do the Lord's work. The right of the king of Israel was to do right.[30] Anything less than dependence on God broke God's ideal for those leading the people of Israel.

By metaphorical language the prophet described the "officials" (lit., "princes") as roaring lions, apparently referring to the lion's taking of its prey. Those who should have exercised a fiduciary responsibility instead used their power to oppress people. Zephaniah likened the "rulers" (lit., "judges") to wolves who hunted in the evening. Wolves encountered during hunting time would be especially hungry.[31] Finding their prey, they would ravenously gnaw the meat off the bones, leaving nothing for the next day.[32] Like the evening wolves the judges were greedy for gain. They "picked the people clean" by their greed. "Nineveh was occupied by beasts (2:14a) to signify the absence of human occupants; in Jerusalem the beasts have already taken over! The leaders of the people were *mis*leaders.[33]

Surely Zephaniah's message continues to speak to a huge need in religious circles—the need for leaders who lead in righteousness and provide a positive example of the change for good that the Christ life can give to individuals and to society as a whole.

3:4 The problems in Jerusalem centered not only around the civil leaders but also around the religious leadership. Zephaniah condemned both groups for shirking their responsibilities. The prophets were "arrogant," a word referring to both pride and recklessness, as someone controlled by their passions who would do anything for personal gain (cf. Gen 49:4; Judg 9:4).[34] Jeremiah used the term of false prophets who would arrogantly and treacherously pass off their own ideas as God's word ((Jer 23:32)). By condemning the prophets for recklessness in speech, Zephaniah accused the prophets of neglecting the charge and call of God in their lives. The very thing they were supposed to do,

---

[30] For a discussion of this concept see W. Bailey, "The King and the Sinai Covenant," *Biblical Illustrator* (1984): 38–42.

[31] D. J. Clark and H. A. Hatton, *A Handbook on the Books of Nahum, Habakkuk, and Zephaniah* (New York: United Bible Societies, 1989), 186.

[32] Watts believes the Hb. means "since morning" and so can say: "These wolves have nocturnal hunting habits and begin their hunt in the evening when they are ravenous from an entire day without food" (*Joel, Obadiah, Jonah, Nahum, Habakkuk and Zephaniah,* 175). See Gen 49:27.

[33] Motyer, "Zephaniah," 3:943.

[34] Clark and Hatton, *Nahum, Habakkuk, and Zephaniah,* 186.

they failed to do. "They were speaking their own notions without waiting for the a word from Yahweh."[35]

The prophets were "treacherous" people who could not be trusted. "The word carries with it not only an indication of the lying deceit of Jerusalem's prophets (cf. Jer 28:1–17; 29:21–23) but the implication that such activity stems from a wanton disregard for God and His truth."[36] Without trust, the prophet did not have a message. Zephaniah charged that the prophets could not be trusted to lead the people in the word of the Lord.

The priests failed as well in their responsibility to carry out their calling from God. Instead of teaching the people the right way and bestowing reverence and awe before the things of God, they actually profaned the sanctuary and did violence to the instruction of the Lord (cp. Mal 1:7–10; 2:5–8).

Profaning the sanctuary may refer to a number of different practices which are actually known from the Old Testament. Nadab and Abihu, the sons of Aaron, offered unholy fire to the Lord (Lev 10:1–3) while the sons of Eli no doubt profaned the sanctuary by laying with the women who came to worship (1 Sam 2:22). In Zephaniah's day the priests apparently continued to allow and to encourage the use of pagan elements in the temple of the Lord (2 Kgs 23:4–20). All of these practices and many others would constitute profaning the sanctuary of the Lord.

The priests also failed to teach the law of the Lord, resulting in doing violence to the Law by neglecting its teaching. In the Old Testament, the *Torah* could mean any of several ideas depending on the context of the passage. The general use of the term refers to the "instruction" of the Lord, but the word may mean the teaching of the Pentateuch, the Ten Commandments, or to the entire Old Testament. The priests failed in teaching in all these areas.[37]

Roberts points out the most serious possibility, misuse of God's way of atonement. "The priests issued the rulings as to what sacrifices were acceptable in different situations, and their control of the means of propitiation and reintegration of an offender back into the cultic community gave them ample opportunity to abuse their authority for their own gain (cf. 1 Sam 2:12–17; Hos 4:4–8; Mic 3:11)."[38]

(2) Jerusalem's Stubbornness (3:5–7)

[5]The LORD within her is righteous;
he does no wrong.

---

[35] Roberts, *Nahum, Habakkuk, and Zephaniah*, 207.

[36] Patterson, *Nahum, Habakkuk, Zephaniah*, 362.

[37] W. Zimmerli, *Old Testament Theology in Outline*, trans. D. E. Green (Atlanta: John Knox, 1978), 93; Motyer says חמס here means "to do violence to the true meaning and intent of the law (contrast Mal 2:5–7) and thereby to wrong and hurt people" ("Zephaniah," 3:943).

[38] Roberts, *Nahum, Habakkuk, and Zephaniah*, 214.

Morning by morning he dispenses his justice,
and every new day he does not fail,
yet the unrighteous know no shame.

6"I have cut off nations;
their strongholds are demolished.
I have left their streets deserted,
with no one passing through.
Their cities are destroyed;
no one will be left—no one at all.
7I said to the city,
'Surely you will fear me
and accept correction!'
Then her dwelling would not be cut off,
nor all my punishments come upon her.
But they were still eager
to act corruptly in all they did.

3:5 In sharp contrast to the civil and religious leaders of the people, the Lord is righteous.[39] He does no wrong, and his righteous acts bring salvation to an oppressed, defiled people when they seek righteousness.[40] Had God given up on the people? Had he simply left them to their own devices without correction or guidance? Apparently not. The Lord was in the midst of Jerusalem. His presence signaled his desire for the people to repent. Judgment is the strange work of God, who desires to forgive and to restore.

God's goodness is constant. The constancy of God is a common theme throughout the Old Testament. "Because of the Lord's great love we are not consumed, for his compassions never fail. They are new every morning; great is your faithfulness" (Lam 3:23). "Morning by morning" literally reads "in the morning, in the morning," emphasizing the constancy of God righteous presence. "Despite the appearance that corruption prevails on every side, the Lord daily manifests his righteous judgments. Even the faithful remnant, suffering under the oppressive tyrannies of a depraved leadership, must acknowledge the daily realities of the Lord's justice. As faithfully as the Lord provided daily manna for his people during their trial period in the wilderness, so in the chaotic last days of Jerusalem the Lord's righteousness was coming to light."[41]

---

[39] See the discussion of righteousness in the commentary on 2:3. Motyer says: The Lord's righteousness is "his consistency of character (Ps 11:7), reliability in relation to his stated purposes (Neh 9:8), and correctness in all his actions (Ps 145:17)" ("Zephaniah," 3:944).

[40] B. Johnson reminds us that when God is designated as צַדִּיק, there appears consistently in the context an action through which he shows his righteousness (*TWAT* 6:917). See Isa 45:21. Part of the righteous intervention of God is his intervention to discipline an unrighteous people.

[41] Robertson, *Nahum, Habakkuk, and Zephaniah,* 322.

God gives his justice each new day. Righteousness is doing those acts which God himself requires because of the relationship with him. Justice takes the righteous acts to the legal sphere, insuring the care for the needy of society.[42] The affirmation of God's "justice" contains a play on words with the "rulers" of 3:3. Those who should have been dispensing justice (the rulers) are those who use their position to pick the people clean, leaving nothing to the morning (3:3). But the Lord dispenses justice every morning.[43] "Justice" is a word of such broad meaning and significance in the Old Testament that it is difficult to translate. It "can be used to designate almost any aspect of civil or religious government,"[44] for example: the act of deciding a case by a judge (Deut 25:1; Josh 20:6); place where a judge decides a case (1 Kgs 7:7); process of litigation (Job 22:4; Isa 3:14); a case or suit brought before the judge (1 Kgs 3:11; Job 13:18); the sentence or decision the judge announces (1 Kgs 20:40; Jer 26:11,16); the time the decision is made (Ps 1:5; Eccl 12:14); sovereign authority (Deut 1:17; Prov 16:33); the just claims of God (Isa 30:18; Ps 37:28); that which is right as that which agrees with God's character (Ps 106:37; Prov 12:5; Mic 6:8); an ordinance or law designed to establish justice in society (Exod 15:25; Isa 42:4; Deut 33:10); the just rights an individual possesses in the legal system (Deut 18:3; Jer 32:7).[45]

Because God is righteous, does no wrong, and daily dispenses justice, Israel should be secure. By implementing his word in their justice system, they could be sure every case was settled in righteousness and every person would receive his due.

Reality contrasted theory. A righteous, just God faced an unrighteous, self-centered people. Zephaniah's recitation of the goodness of God should have caused the unrighteous to meditate on their behavior. God had been so good, how could they continue in arrogance before God? They were shameless before the great God who manifested his goodness before them daily.

Verses 5–7 appear to revolve around the theme of Israel's knowledge of the goodness of the Lord and their need to turn from their sins. Seeing the righ-

---

[42] E. Achtemeier, "Righteousness in the Old Testament," *IDB*, 80–85.

[43] Patterson, *Nahum, Habakkuk, Zephaniah*, 362; Roberts sees the dispensing of justice in this case as the "continuing care over and ordering of nature … his commands that bring forth the morning, call the stars out by name, and dictate the rhythms of nature (Job 38:12,31–33; Isa 40:26; Ps 104:28–30)" (*Nahum, Habakkuk, and Zephaniah*, 214).

[44] R. D. Culver, "שָׁפַט *(shāpaṭ),*" *TWOT* 2:948.

[45] Ibid., 2:948–49. See the extended discussion also of R. Schultz, "Justice," *NIDOTTE* 4:837–46, with emphasis upon justice as that which is due one and with updated bibliography. He states succinctly: "Israel's injustice keeps divine justice from being manifested." He follows G. Liedke ("שׁפט *špṭ* to judge," *TLOT* 3:1392–99), who defines שָׁפַט as "an action that restores the disturbed order of a (legal) community." It involves a triangular act in which "two people or two groups of people whose interrelationship is not intact are restored to the state of שָׁלוֹם through a third party's שָׁפַט."

teousness of the Lord should have caused the people to feel the intense sorrow associated with sin (Jer 31:18–19). Yet they went on with their sin. Any rational person would have thought as the Lord did that the people would fear the Lord and accept his correction.

By accepting the correction of the Lord, the people could have averted the disaster. Instead of accepting God's chastisement, they persisted in their sin, thus insuring the judgment of God. In pride the wicked of vv. 3 and 4—the officials, rulers, prophets, and priests—carried on in their rebellion against God.

With 3:5 "the plot's conflict is fully presented. Both Judah and her neighbors stand against God, and will therefore be utterly destroyed on the day of Yahweh. A battle line is drawn between the prideful nations and the creator of those nations. One by one the offending nations are named and God's case against them stated. There is absolutely no hope for them, or creation, to stand. … The tension in the plot is extreme at this point, so some resolution is needed."[46]

3:6 What God had done in the past to others should have been a warning and an example to Jerusalem. God's punishment of the nations should have warned the people of Jerusalem of their failure to heed the covenant and of the sure destruction of the city. After all, God had "cut off" (the same word as used in 1:3) the nations. Now God would cut off the city of Jerusalem as well. The response of the people of Jerusalem should have been profound repentance. After seeing the judgment against the nations, how could Jerusalem not turn to the Lord?

The Book of Jeremiah shows that the people of Jerusalem suffered from a blind spot related to the Lord's warnings concerning the judgment of Judah and especially Jerusalem. From a theological perspective, they obviously thought that God could not destroy the temple and Jerusalem, where he had made his name to dwell. The biblical writers dealt with this problem in different ways. The writer of 1, 2 Kings showed that God punished Judah because of the people's rebellion against God (2 Kgs 24:20). Ezekiel accepted the destruction of Jerusalem by noting the departure of the Glory of the Lord. When the Glory of the Lord left the temple area, it signaled the coming destruction of the city (Ezek 11:22–23). Before the restoration of Jerusalem, the Glory of the Lord returned to Jerusalem (Ezek 43:1–5).

Zephaniah portrayed the destruction of the nations in vivid ways. Any person familiar with warfare in the Ancient Near East knew the significance of the prophet's descriptions. Zephaniah described a city whose defenses had been overrun and its citizens either dead or deported.

Though Zephaniah depicted the cities and nations of the gentile world, the

---

[46] House, *Zephaniah*, 66.

description fit what happened to Jerusalem only a few years later. Nebuchadrezzar took the city in such a resounding way that Jerusalem lay uninhabited. Nebuchadrezzar's army overran the strongholds of the city, tore down the walls, and destroyed the temple of the Lord. The word for "strongholds" is the same word used in 1:16 for "corner towers," a reference to the key point in the wall of the city. If the strongholds fell, the remainder of the city would fall as well.[47] Such a vivid description had to impress the people of Jerusalem. Could they not see what lay ahead?

3:7 The divine, "I said," as Motyer observes, "brings us right into the divine mind and heart."[48] God's speech, which began with the preceding verse, continues through v. 13. God spoke tenderly and compassionately to Jerusalem in the first person, seeking to avert the certain disaster.

Jerusalem's problem had been its lack of respect for God and its inability to accept correction (3:2). God demonstrated his power among the nations to bring Israel to fear him. Fear of God could border on sheer terror (Exod 3:6; 20:18), but this was not what God wanted (Exod 20:20). "While the normal meaning of fear as dread or terror is retained in the theological use of the terms, a special nuance of reverential awe or worshipful respect becomes the dominant notion."[49] Both the exodus (Exod 14:31) and the crossing of the Jordan (Josh 4:24) evoked fear from God's people. Fearing God was the first of God's list of requirements for his people (Deut 10:12–13). Hearing God's law in awesome rituals sought to bring the fear of Yahweh into the hearts of the people (Deut 31:12). Especially the king was to study God's Torah so he could learn to fear God (Deut 17:19). Wisdom taught that fearing God was the starting point for wisdom (Prov 1:7; 31:30). To fear God was parallel to and synonymous with obeying his precepts (Ps 119:63; cp. Deut 5:29; 6:2; 13:4). Those who fear God praise and glorify him (Ps 22:23). To fear God means to hold him in awe, to give to the Lord the honor due him. Bowling noted five usages of "fear" with the sense of awe and reverence being the predominant usage in the Old Testament. The person who fears God makes his fear work in terms of personal piety and righteousness. In many passages, fearing God and proper living are so closely connected that they seem to be synonyms. In the present verse this seems to be the case. Fearing God and accepting correction seem to follow one upon the other.[50]

---

[47] Patterson, *Nahum, Habakkuk, Zephaniah,* 362–363; Roberts sees Sennacherib's invasion of Judah in the reign of Hezekiah as the backdrop for Zephaniah's battle descriptions but only by emending the text to "their nation" instead of the MT "nations" (*Nahum, Habakkuk, and Zephaniah*, 214).

[48] Motyer, "Zephaniah," 3:947.

[49] E. H. Merrill, "Fear," *EDBT,* 248.

[50] A. Bowling, "יָרֵא *(yārēʾ)* etc.," *TWOT* 1:399–401. Merrill summarizes: "Usually, the fear of the Lord is an inducement to obedience and service: to fear God is to do his will. … The Lord as King demands and deserves the awesome respect of his people, a respect that issues in obedient service" ("Fear," 249).

Though Jerusalem had the example of the gentile nations, they continued to turn away from God and his leading for the city. The pronouns for Jerusalem begin with the second feminine singular in the first part of the verse but change to the third masculine plural in the last two lines. While this is awkward in English, the change occurs frequently and without fanfare in the Hebrew text.

The last line in the Hebrew text reads: "surely they rise early, they corrupt all their doings." The NIV rendering captures the eagerness[51] of the people of Jerusalem to run toward evil. The combination of "rise early" with the verb "corrupt" means that they were persistent in their evil. In becoming absorbed in corruption the people repeated the crime of the flood (Gen 6:12) and fulfilled the prophecy of Moses (Deut 31:29). [52]

The people of Jerusalem lived according to their own plans and planned to live apart from God. "Grace is offered, but frivolously spurned, a sobering epitaph for the city of David."[53] Making your own plans and ignoring God is a sure prescription for destruction whether living in the sixth century B.C. or the twenty-first century A.D.

(3) Jerusalem's Hope (3:8)

8Therefore wait for me," declares the LORD,
"for the day I will stand up to testify.
I have decided to assemble the nations,
to gather the kingdoms
and to pour out my wrath on them—
all my fierce anger.
The whole world will be consumed
by the fire of my jealous anger.

3:8 Judgment does not seem to be hopeful, but in the case of Jerusalem's rebellion, it was. The prophet changed from third masculine plural to second masculine plural, which he previously used in 2:1–3. Thus he appears to be addressing the same group here as there, the poor in the land who are humbled and seeking righteousness.[54] "Once judgment is fully expended in 3:8 it becomes an avenue for God to demonstrate mercy through the lives of the cleansed people."[55] The Lord had punished the nations to get them to repent, but

---

[51] See Patterson for a discussion of שׁכם, "eager." "Jeremiah employs the verb eleven times to picture God's eagerness to meet with His people. He rose, as it were, to be on hand at the beginning of each day, longing to meet with them—but to no avail. Zephaniah reports that the people were eager, 'rose early,' only to corrupt their ways further" (*Nahum, Habakkuk, Zephaniah,* 360).

[52] Cp. Robertson, *Nahum, Habakkuk, and Zephaniah,* 324.

[53] D. W. Baker, *Nahum, Habakkuk, Zephaniah,* TOTC (Downers Grove: InterVarsity, 1988), 114.

[54] See Roberts, *Nahum, Habakkuk, and Zephaniah,* 215.

[55] House, *The Unity of the Twelve,* 150.

the object lesson failed because the people continued to sin. "One final, cataclysmic day of wrath is therefore planned to dissolve all sin against the Lord. Such a judgment partially resolves the plot's conflict, but still leaves open the fate of the 'humble of the earth' mentioned in 2:3. Since all sinful people are removed in 3:8, the faithful remnant can now serve Yahweh with no hindrance."[56]

God apparently spoke to the righteous minority in Jerusalem. Though they faced the uncertainty of judgment which would come upon all the world, the only hope for the righteous lay in the judgment and mercy of God. So God counseled the righteous to wait on the Lord. God would indeed have his day when he would bring judgment on all the earth. What a picture! "The Lord, awaiting our fellowship and left disappointed!"[57]

Waiting for God's vindication is neither desirable nor easy. Yet, waiting on God is the only choice for those who love him and seek to live according to his commands. Patience is not natural, either for the wicked or the righteous, but God called on the people to wait on him for their deliverance—a deliverance which would come in the form of God's judgment against the nations. "We never go so far away, fall so deeply down, get so irretrievably lost that we are beyond his love, care, and remedial action."[58]

Sometimes the only hope comes in judgment.[59] "Zephaniah seems determined at this point to stress the enigmatic side of the Lord's ways. Somehow judgment and hope are both true."[60] This was the case in Zephaniah's day. When God poured out his fierce anger against the nations, then he would purify the lips of the peoples that all of them might call on the name of the Lord and serve him (3:9). The remnant—those meek and humble who trusted in the name of the Lord (3:12–13)—would endure the judgment. God would purify those who remained. These would be people whose lives matched their professions of faith. They would speak the truth; no deceit would be found in their mouths (3:13). When Jerusalem consisted of this kind of people—people who trusted God and obeyed him—the judgment would be worth the pain and trouble. Jerusalem's hope lay in God's work of judgment.

God himself would testify against the nations for their wickedness.[61] The

---

[56] House, *Zephaniah,* 66–67.

[57] Motyer, "Zephaniah," 3:948.

[58] Ibid.

[59] Roberts (*Nahum, Habakkuk, and Zephaniah*, 216) argues that the somewhat difficult grammar here with its unclear antecedents is saying that God will use the nations as his agents to punish the wicked rulers of Jerusalem already condemned in vv. 3 and 4 and mentioned again in the end of v. 7. This involves reading NIV's "the whole world" as "all the land," a reading made possible by the ambivalent meaning of הָאָרֶץ.

[60] Motyer, "Zephaniah," 3:948.

[61] In the second line the Hb. text reads "for the day of my rising for plunder" (cp. KJV). The LXX, followed by the NIV (also NASB, RSV, etc.), vocalized לְעֵד, "for a witness," rather than לְעַד, "for plunder." Berlin reads, לָעַד, "forever" (*Zephaniah,* 133).

concept of God's taking the witness stand is common in the Old Testament (Mic 1:2; Mal 3:5; Jer 29:23). God accused the nations of rebellion. They, therefore, stood guilty before God the righteous judge. God pledged to assemble the nations and to gather the kingdoms—but to gather them for the coming judgment. Not only Judah, but also the nations stood condemned before the Lord.

By the fire of God's jealous anger all the world would be consumed. For most of the English speaking world, "jealousy" is a vice, conjuring the idea of a jealous husband who maims or kills. In the Old Testament, God's jealousy denotes his desire to receive that which rightfully belongs to him, such as the praise and adoration of his people. Rather than being vices, God's jealousy and anger point often to "God's being moved to action on behalf of his own."[62]

In both general (1:8–18) and specific cases (2:4–3:8), the depravity of man can be met only by the wrath of God, since an integral part of his character is holiness and the inability to countenance sin."[63]

2. The Deliverance of the Righteous (3:9–13)

9"Then will I purify the lips of the peoples,
that all of them may call on the name of the LORD
and serve him shoulder to shoulder.
10From beyond the rivers of Cush
my worshipers, my scattered people,
will bring me offerings.
11On that day you will not be put to shame
for all the wrongs you have done to me,
because I will remove from this city
those who rejoice in their pride.
Never again will you be haughty
on my holy hill.
12But I will leave within you
the meek and humble,
who trust in the name of the LORD.
13The remnant of Israel will do no wrong;
they will speak no lies,
nor will deceit be found in their mouths.
They will eat and lie down
and no one will make them afraid."

The concluding units of Zephaniah change the tenor of the remainder of the book to one which treats Jerusalem more positively. They picture the

[62] Patterson, *Nahum, Habakkuk, Zephaniah,* 367–68.
[63] Baker, *Nahum, Habakkuk, Zephaniah,* 114–15.

removal of the threat, the delimitation of judgment, and the return of the inhabitants.[64] This strikes many as a logical contradiction. Robertson has to ask in light of the pictures of total wrath and destruction in 1:8 and 3:8: "If the Day would bring this cosmic destruction, what is the meaning of the reference to a fresh start for humanity?"[65] He can only answer by admitting: "Zephaniah simply does not resolve explicitly the tension that might be felt among various aspects of his message. He saw a destruction in judgment beyond any proportions that the world had experienced previously. He saw also a wondrous conversion among the nations of the world as well as among the scattered people of Israel. He does not explain how cosmic judgment and far-reaching salvation coordinate, but he faithfully proclaims both elements."[66] One can point to the historical demise and destruction of the foreign nations Zephaniah named as well as the destructions Jerusalem has suffered. Meanwhile, God continues to build up a remnant from Jerusalem and the nations prior to his final judgment. Theologically, we can echo Roberts: "Judgment is not the final word; it is simply a means to bring the people of Judah and Jerusalem back to an uncorrupted devotion to Yahweh."[67]

These concluding verses of the Book of Zephaniah contain additional teachings concerning the day of the Lord. These stand in stark contrast to the picture in 1:2–17 where an angry God rampaged against a sinful people. A series of divine "I will" statements there finds its parallel here in a series similar in grammatical structure but reversed in content and meaning.[68] "The same Lord is in action and the same day is being fulfilled, but, because the Lord so wills, the day is double-sided—and hope has the last word."[69]

The section falls into two portions (vv. 9–13 and vv. 14–20) connected by the use of "in that day" (vv. 11,16).[70] In the passage, vv. 9–10 speak of the nations while vv. 11–13 refer to Israel. In vv. 9–13 three first-person singular verbs of divine action carry the central message: "I will purify" (v. 9); "I will remove" (v. 11); and "I will leave within you" (v. 12).[71] The passage follows closely the picture of universal judgment in the preceding verse. Rather than

[64] Nogalski, *Literary Precursors*, 175. For scholarly debate on whether the last sections of Zephaniah can be attributed to the prophet or must be exilic/postexilic additions, see Introduction, "Zephaniah, the Book.

[65] Robertson, *Nahum, Habakkuk, and Zephaniah*, 327.

[66] Ibid. "See our discussion of this issue at 1:2.

[67] Roberts, *Nahum, Habakkuk, and Zephaniah*, 216. Achtemeier, *Nahum–Malachi*, 82, expresses the same thought: "God's word never ends with judgment, for God's goal for his world is finally not death but life. He is the God not of the dead but of the living. He is a God finally not of wrath but of love."

[68] See House, *Zephaniah*, 71.

[69] Motyer, "Zephaniah," 3:951.

[70] Patterson, *Nahum, Habakkuk, Zephaniah*, 374.

[71] See Motyer, "Zephaniah," 3:951.

being an end in itself, the judgment points to and helps to bring about the conversion of the nations. "When wrath is spent, the Lord will purify the foreign groups so they can serve their creator (3:9). ... There could be no greater kindness extended by a Hebrew prophet than these predictions."[72]

Baker points out that God's character as revealed in Zephaniah includes holiness, justice, righteousness, and an intolerance for sin; it also includes grace, love, and forgiveness. The remainder of the verses reveal the joy of that revelation.[73]

3:9 "In contrast to his roles as judge and bailiff, carrying out the decreed punishment (v. 8), Yahweh takes on a new role as saviour."[74] Zephaniah's masterful use of language continues. "The element of surprise in the message of hope is maintained. Logic would expect *kî* ("for," not translated in the NIV) to introduce further elaborations of judgment but instead it reaches back to the hint of blessing in 3:8a."[75] The effect of the judgment of the preceding verse would be the purification[76] of the peoples so that all could call on the name of the Lord. "In a miraculous turn of events the Gentiles are allowed access to God. Until this point, only 2:11 indicates that Yahweh cares for Judah's enemies, yet now they receive mercy."[77] "Lip" is singular in Hebrew and probably refers to the "speech" of the Gentile nations which have defiled their lips by the worship of false gods. In the future their speech would be pure as they called on the name of the Lord. "Ironically, judgment provides the needed renewal, since it cleanses the world of sin."[78]

Calling on the name of the Lord means reaching out in faith for his all sufficient grace. In some cases, the "name" referred to God's self-disclosure.[79]

---

[72] House, *The Unity of the Twelve,* 150.

[73] Baker, *Nahum, Habakkuk, Zephaniah,* 115.

[74] Ibid.

[75] Motyer, "Zephaniah," 3:951. Verse 9 begins with כִּי in Hb., which may be an emphatic use; but its following upon the exhortation in v. 8 argues for v. 9 to be taken as furnishing motivation for the exhortation.

[76] Motyer discovers another piece of Zephaniah's literary artistry in using the verb הפך, "turn, overthrow, change" (*HALOT* 1:253), "a characteristic verb of judgment ... almost a technical verb for what the Lord did at Sodom (Gen. 19:25,29; Deut 29:22; Jer 20:16; Amos 4:11). The usage here, however, is unique, for there is no other example where the verb is used to express 'to bring x back to y.' Zephaniah must therefore have chosen the verb deliberately because of its overtones of wrath: when more and more anger is to be expected, suddenly hope is shining, for light has dawned" (ibid.). Note the meaning "change," however in 1 Sam 10:9.

[77] House, *The Unity of the Twelve,* 149. Roberts argues that "of the peoples" is an early misreading of the text which originally read "to their people," that is, the people of the sinful leaders of Jerusalem. Basically, this decision is made from the context which Roberts reads as giving hope to Judah and Jerusalem (*Nahum, Habakkuk, and Zephaniah,* 216–17).

[78] House, *The Unity of the Twelve,* 151. House notes that the blessing of the nations "completes ideas like Mic 4:1–4 and abolishes the hatred of Obadiah and Jonah at the same time."

[79] W. C. Kaiser, "שֵׁם *(shēm), TWOT* 2:934–35.

Many commentators see a connection between the peoples being given pure speech and the corruption of speech at the Tower of Babel.[80]

Serving God "shoulder to shoulder" refers to the unity of the people who have received a common transformation of character. Genuine spiritual conversion results in peace (cp. James 3:13–18). The Hebrew says literally that they would serve with "one shoulder," thus with unity. Not only do the people serve in a unified whole, but it is universal—"all of them."

3:10 From the farthest regions ("beyond the rivers of Cush"), God's converted ones would bring offerings to the Lord. While the verse is easy to interpret generally, the specifics are difficult. "Cush" refers to the area of the upper Nile, including the area of the Sudan and part of Ethiopia (see comments on 2:12).[81] As God's judgment would go out to the ends of the earth (2:4–15), so also God's grace and forgiveness would go out to the most remote places.

Who are the worshipers? Are they the same group as "my scattered people" (lit., "daughter of my scattered ones")? The verse may be taken in three ways.[82] (1) Gentiles scattered throughout the world by their sin (Isa 18:7; 45:14; John 11:51–52) will bring offerings to God (understood as worshiping or paying homage to him) in their own lands as Zeph 2:11 suggests; (2) Judeans dispersed by the day of the Lord Zephaniah predicted return to Jerusalem giving themselves as an offering to God or renewing the Jewish sacrificial system. Achtemeier describes them: "as we have seen in Zeph 2:7,9, it is the remnant of Judah that moves out into foreign lands and inherits the earth. God's humble, dependent, righteous remnant will worship him throughout his creation, even in those regions beyond the limits of the imaginable world."[83] (3) Converted Gentiles, who as in Isa 66:20, bring dispersed Judeans back to their homeland as a thanksgiving offering for what God has done for them.[84] Patterson presents a similar resolution to the difficulty which seems to fit the text well: "converted Gentiles who 'call upon the name of the Lord' and 'serve Him shoulder to shoulder' will be 'My worshipers' who will 'bring My scattered ones' (the Jews) as 'My tribute.'"[85]

Roberts sees a historical problem here. He does not think Zephaniah's day would know many Jews dispersed as far away as Cush, so he sees this as a latter addition to the text from the time after the destruction of Jerusalem in 586.[86] More conservative approaches to the text accept this as inspired proph-

---

[80] Watts, *Joel, Obadiah, Jonah, Nahum, Habakkuk and Zephaniah,* 178; Baker, *Nahum, Habakkuk, Zephaniah,* 115; Robertson, *Nahum, Habakkuk, and Zephaniah,* 328–29.

[81] S. Cohen, "Cush," *IDB,* 751.

[82] Cf. Berlin, *Zephaniah,* 135, who favors the first interpretation.

[83] Achtemeier, *Nahum–Malachi,* 83.

[84] See Heflin, *Nahum, Habakkuk, Zephaniah, and Haggai,* 151–52.

[85] Patterson, *Nahum, Habakkuk, Zephaniah,* 371–72.

[86] Roberts, *Nahum, Habakkuk, and Zephaniah,* 218.

ecy pointing ahead beyond the prophet's days. Already Deut 4:27; 28:64 had looked forward to God's dispersing his disobedient people among the nations. Furthermore, living amid the power of Assyria and witnessing the cruel ways in which the Assyrians exiled captive nations, Zephaniah would have required little imagination to see what form the Lord's discipline of his people would take and what form the renewal of his people would take. An exiled, dispersed people had to be brought back home, but the new thing for Zephaniah was to see that they would not be alone in returning to God. God would purify the speech of foreigners who had rebuked and reviled the divine name so they could now join Judah in praising it.

3:11 Patterson sees the phrase "On that day" as introducing a subunit in this section and serving as a linking device for the section which follows (note v. 16). Phrases such as "in that day" often are used as formulae to introduce stanzas or strophes.[87]

In that future day after the judgment, Jerusalem ("you" is feminine singular) will no longer be put to shame because the unrepentant would be removed from her midst. The verse could have two meanings: (1) the repentant no longer would suffer shame and punishment because the wicked would be removed from the midst of Jerusalem; (2) because the wicked would be removed, the repentant would no longer need to feel shame for what had happened in the past.[88] On the whole, this seems to be the best interpretation.

No longer would Jerusalem be characterized by an arrogant and haughty class. God would remove "those who rejoice in their pride." The same Hebrew phrase is found in Isa 13:3 where the Medes were filled with pride for their victories in battle. Davidson saw the reference in Zephaniah as referring to the arrogant classes, whether prophets or politicians, who exult in their own might.[89] "In 2:3 Zephaniah had called for the poor and humble to seek the lord, suggesting that they might be hidden on the day of the Lord's wrath. Now in 3:11–12 he promises that in the new age there will be no haughty or proud people left in the kingdom of God, only the afflicted and poor."[90]

3:12 The Hebrew word for "I will leave" is the word from which we get the word "remnant," as in v. 13. God promised to remove the proud and haughty and to leave the meek and humble who "trust (lit., "take refuge"; cp. Ps 118:8) in the Lord. Those who trust in the Lord (3:12) are contrasted with the proud and arrogant who trust only in themselves and the might of their

---

[87] Patterson, *Nahum, Habakkuk, Zephaniah,* 374.

[88] F. E. Eakin, Jr., "Zephaniah," BBC (Nashville: Broadman, 1972), 288. Berlin explains, "God will remove Israel's guilt and shame by removing the cause of them—the prideful element of society" (*Zephaniah,* 135–36).

[89] A. B. Davidson, *The Books of Nahum, Habakkuk and Zephaniah, with Introduction and Notes,* CBSC (Cambridge: University Press, 1899), 133.

[90] R. Smith, *Micah–Malachi,* WBC 32 (Waco: Word, 1984), 142.

hand (3:11; cp. 2:3; 3:2).

The "meek" means one who is "poor," "weak," "afflicted," or "humble." It refers primarily to a person suffering from some kind of distress or disability.[91] On the other hand, the "humble" are those who are needy and who suffer from physical deprivation.[92] "To fully prepare the remnant to rule, though, Yahweh will remove the proud from the midst of the remnant (3:11), and then leave only the meek and humble (3:12). In conjunction with these actions, the Lord will 'rescue,' 'gather,' 'bring home,' and 'honor' Judah (3:19–20). This final act completes the restoration of God's people."[93] In almost every time period it is these who trust in the name of the Lord, probably because they recognize their abundant need and recognize the Lord's abundant resources.

3:13 With this verse "another integral part of the plot is now in place. Yahweh's remnant has moved into the realm of reality."[94] "Remnant" can refer in various contexts to that which is (1) neither morally good nor bad, (2) a remnant of the wicked, or (3) a righteous remnant. Most often the remnant refers to the faithful from the house of Israel, particularly those who will remain after the judgment.[95]

"Jerusalem's people, relying on God, will take on his character. He does no wrong (3:5) and neither will his new people (v. 13). Their faith in him will issue in the ethical transformation of their lives. … No one can meet the Lord and live without being changed into his new creation (cf. 2 Cor 5:17)."[96]

What a contrast with the former inhabitants of Jerusalem. They were "evening wolves," "arrogant," and "treacherous" (3:3–4). How could such changes occur? "A purging process must take place, whereby the old, proud people are removed in favor of a humble, holy remnant."[97] God had purified the lips of the remnant in Jerusalem; therefore, they would speak no lies nor would deceit be found in their mouths. God's decisive act of transformation would bring about decisive change in the humble and meek left in the land. "Although descendants of Jacob the supplanter, they finally have all guile removed."[98] As Heflin wisely points out: "This passage suggests, in embryonic fashion, the concept of regeneration as later developed in the New Testament."[99]

The last phrase came from shepherding. Sheep eat only when they feel safe

---

[91] L. J. Coppes, "עָנָה (ʾānâ) etc.," *TWOT* 2:682–84.
[92] Coppes, "דָּלַל (dālal) etc.," *TWOT* 1:190.
[93] House, *The Unity of the Twelve,* 150.
[94] House, *Zephaniah,* 60.
[95] G. G. Cohen, "שָׁאַר (shāʾar) etc.," *TWOT* 2:894–95.
[96] Achtemeier, *Nahum–Malachi,* 84.
[97] House, *Zephaniah,* 60.
[98] Robertson, *Nahum, Habakkuk, and Zephaniah,* 331.
[99] Heflin, *Nahum, Habakkuk, Zephaniah, and Haggai,* 153.

and unmolested. Thus, they can eat and lie down.[100] The last phrase, "and no one will make them afraid," is "a standing phrase to describe a condition of unmolested security."[101]

3. The Joy of the City (3:14–20)

14Sing, O Daughter of Zion;
shout aloud, O Israel!
Be glad and rejoice with all your heart,
O Daughter of Jerusalem!
15The LORD has taken away your punishment,
he has turned back your enemy.
The LORD, the King of Israel, is with you;
never again will you fear any harm.
16On that day they will say to Jerusalem,
"Do not fear, O Zion;
do not let your hands hang limp.
17The LORD your God is with you,
he is mighty to save.
He will take great delight in you,
he will quiet you with his love,
he will rejoice over you with singing."

18"The sorrows for the appointed feasts
I will remove from you;
they are a burden and a reproach to you.
19At that time I will deal
with all who oppressed you;
I will rescue the lame
and gather those who have been scattered.
I will give them praise and honor
in every land where they were put to shame.
20At that time I will gather you;
at that time I will bring you home.
I will give you honor and praise
among all the peoples of the earth
when I restore your fortunes
before your very eyes,"
says the LORD.

---

[100] Clark and Hatton, *Nahum, Habakkuk, and Zephaniah*, 196.

[101] S. R. Driver, *The Minor Prophets: Nahum, Habakkuk, Zephaniah, Haggai, Zechariah, Malachi,* CB (Edinburgh: T. C. & E. C. Jack, n. d.), 138. See Jer 30:10; 46:27: Ezek 34:28; 39:26; Mic 4:4; cp. Gen 15:11; Lev 26:5; Deut 28:26; 1 Kgs 4:25; Jer 7:33.

"The Book of Zephaniah ends in almost unimaginable joy."[102] The final section is unexpected by those who heard the words of the prophet (in spite of foreshadowings of blessing in 2:3,7,9; 3:9–13). This section falls under the maxim that with God all things are possible. This message of hope and encouragement comes only because God is the Lord. Here is what House calls the falling action of the book, a summary of the entire prophecy that explains "to a bewildered remnant what has happened and discloses Yahweh's pleasure with them. It also lets the reader know that all tension between the Lord and the nations is removed."[103]

These last verses are different from the remainder of the book, so different that many scholars have attributed them to an editor rather than to the prophet. But this new tone is possible because the faithful have passed through the fires of judgment. Now that the judgment has passed, the people may sing for joy at the blessings and goodness of God. "One of the most awesome descriptions of the wrath of God in judgment found anywhere in Scripture appears in the opening verses of Zephaniah. … One of the most moving descriptions of the love of God for his people found anywhere in Scripture appears in the closing verses of Zephaniah."[104]

The first part of the section speaks of the goodness of God in the third person. Then in vv. 18–20 God himself speaks to the remnant of Israel.

3:14 Zephaniah 3:14–17 functions "as a prophetic response to the divine pronouncements" in the preceding verses and "is a structurally self-contained unit based on its inner thematic chiasm and the prophetic speaker."[105] The command to rejoice apparently was used by town heralds calling the city to rejoice when messengers from the battlefield brought good news of victory and deliverance.[106] The term *rnn* ("sing") is closely connected to cultic praise of God for his past and expected acts of salvation and with the celebration of Yahweh's kingship.[107] It represents a cultic shout of praise.

The verse contains four imperative verbs that are similar in meaning ("sing," "shout aloud," "be glad," "rejoice") and three vocatives that refer to the people of Israel in general and Jerusalem in particular ("O Daughter of Zion," "O Israel," "O Daughter of Jerusalem"). R. L. Smith noted the similarities with enthronement psalms (Pss 47; 95; 97) but denied that this is an enthronement song. Rather, he saw the song as an oracle of salvation probably

---

[102] Achtemeier, *Nahum–Malachi,* 86.

[103] House, *Zephaniah,* 67.

[104] Robertson, *Nahum, Habakkuk, and Zephaniah,* 334.

[105] Nogalski, *Literary Precursors*, 203.

[106] See Roberts, *Nahum, Habakkuk, and Zephaniah,* 222, who points to Isa 52:7–10.

[107] See J. Hausmann, "רָנַן *rānan,*" *TWAT* 7:538–45.

delivered during the New Year festival.[108]

The redeemed people should be glad and rejoice with all their heart. In Hebrew, the term "heart" occurred in three basic ways: (1) the will of the individual; (2) the mind or the intellect; or (3) the emotions.[109] Zephaniah used the term with its latter meaning. With all their emotions the people should rejoice and be glad. Referring to the people as the daughter of Zion and the daughter of Jerusalem is a poetical personification. Driver noted its particular use where the people express vivid emotions (e.g. Isa 10:30; Jer 6:26; Zech 2:10, 9:9).[110]

3:15 Now the reasons for rejoicing are given. (1) the punishment and the enemy have been turned away, and (2) the Lord is king in the midst of the people, leaving nothing to fear (lit., "The king of Israel, Yahweh, is in your midst"[111]). No wonder the people can rejoice. The verbs are prophetic perfects or "perfectives of confidence," a device to speak of the certainty of the events.[112]

"Punishment" is literally "judgments," an apparent reference to the Lord's sentence of condemnation against the city. That has been "taken away." The "enemy" is not specified but may refer to those who collaborated with the Assyrians in the past; but it is most likely a collective singular referring to all Judah's enemies.[113]

The idea of the Lord as king is common in the Old Testament. Early in Old Testament history, Israel praised the Lord, who "will reign forever and ever" (Exod 15:18). The Lord manifested himself as "king over Jeshurun" (Deut 33:2–5). Gideon would not accept the people's desire to crown him king because "the LORD will rule over you" (Judg 8:23). What is striking in this context is that the Davidic king is missing, probably because of the failure of the earthly kingship and because of the presence of the divine king.[114]

"Through the unexpected salvation provided by the day of Yahweh her sin is forgiven, her enemies are defeated, and her future is secured."[115] God's salvation from sin here is total. As Motyer astutely observes: "It is one thing to deal with sin within the sinner so that conscience no longer accuses (Zeph

[108] R. L. Smith, *Micah–Malachi,* 143–44. Baker speaks of a "self-contained little psalm [that] could have been written by Zephaniah for this prophecy, or it could have been adopted from its previous use in the liturgy of God's people as a fitting response to Yahweh's grace bestowed once again upon his people" (*Nahum, Habakkuk, Zephaniah,* 117). He compares it to songs of salvation in Ps 98; Isa 12:1–6; 52:7–10.

[109] H. W. Wolff, *Anthropology of the Old Testament* (Philadelphia: Fortress, 1973), 40–58.

[110] Driver, *The Minor Prophets,* 138.

[111] Berlin notes that forms of בְּקֶרֶב occur in 3:3,5,11,12,17. The sinners who were once in Jerusalem's midst have been replaced by the Lord (*Zephaniah,* 143).

[112] Waltke and O'Conner, *IBHS* § 30.5.1e; Driver, *The Minor Prophets,* 138.

[113] Waltke and O'Conner, *IBHS* § 7.2.2; Berlin, *Zephaniah,* 143.

[114] Robertson, *Nahum, Habakkuk, and Zephaniah,* 337. Cf. also Isa 44:6.

[115] House, *Zephaniah,* 67.

3:11): this is the guiltiness of sin. It is a different thing to deal with sin as it outrages the holy character of God: this is the offense of sin, and it constitutes a deeper and more necessary work, for there can be no salvation until God is satisfied." He adds that the Lord's presence (lit.) "in your midst" is "the objective verification of his inward satisfaction over his people. There is nothing now to alienate the Holy One; at-one-ment has been achieved."[116]

3:16 "On that day" refers to the day when the judgment was complete and God's blessings completely manifest (note v. 11). Then Zion, a synonym for Jerusalem which specifically referred to the temple mount, will have no reason to fear. "Do not fear" is the essential element in the "reassurance formula" and often a component of the "prophetic announcement of salvation" or "promise of salvation." Here the formula may be combined with the assurance of divine presence, "I am with you" as occurs here and in Isa 43:5. This is usually followed by a "future transformation" and a "basis for reassurance."[117] The future transformation appears in vv. 18–20 as God describes what he will do for his people. This is preceded by the basis for reassurance in v. 17 describing the character, love, and joy of God.

The expression "do not let your hands hang limp" is unfamiliar to our culture. In Hebrew thought the hand symbolized strength or power. Letting the hands hang limp referred to a feeling of weakness or powerlessness, a sense of discouragement. In other contexts, hands hanging limp or being "gone" (Deut 32:36) indicated loss of power.[118] Thus "the Lord's salvation is comprehensive: fear is banished as to its objective causes (3:15: 'evil'), its subjective reality (3:16: 'not fear'), and its immobilizing effect (listlessness)."[119]

3:17 Verses 17 and 18 make the transition from speaking about God in the third person to God's speaking in the first person. The first word of 3:17 is the divine personal name for the Lord. The reason why the people can rejoice is that the Lord is in their midst. Here "all tension built over the threatened judgment is relieved as the foreshadowing changes to fulfilled promise. By using this method of interrelating promise and completion the book's structure is tightly bound by allusion and concrete image."[120]

The word translated "mighty" is *gibbôr*, an adjective usually used as a noun,

---

[116] Motyer, "Zephaniah," 3:956–57.

[117] See the discussions by W. A. VanGemeren, "Oracles of Salvation," *Cracking Old Testament Codes,* ed. D. B. Sandy and R. L. Giese, Jr. (Nashville: Broadman & Holman, 1995), 139–55; C. Westermann, *Prophetic Oracles of Salvation in the Old Testament*, trans. K. Crim (Louisville: Westminster/John Knox, 1991); Sweeney, *Isaiah 1–39,* 531.

[118] R. H. Alden, "יָד *(yād)* etc.," *TWOT* 1:362–64. Cf. 2 Sam 4:1; Isa 13:7; Jer 6:24; 50:43; Ezek 7:17; 21:12; Ezra 4:4; Neh 6:9; 2 Chr 15:7. Berlin gives the meaning "to be afraid, discouraged, in despair, unable to act" (*Zephaniah,* 144).

[119] Motyer, "Zephaniah," 3:957.

[120] House, *Zephaniah*, 60–61. "Commentators who deny a message of hope to preexilic prophets simply fail to grasp the theology of the name of Yahweh on which the prophetic ministry rested: his name forbids him to be only judge or redeemer; he must be both" (Motyer, "Zephaniah," 3:957).

often translated "hero" or "warrior" as in 1:14. It is used most frequently with military activities to describe one "who has already distinguished himself by performing heroic deeds."[121] In this case the word speaks of God who is "a warrior who brings salvation."[122] In other contexts as well, God is spoken of as a "mighty God" (*ʾēl gibbôr*; cf. Isa 9:6[Hb. 5]; 10:21). So here the Divine Warrior has declared peace. He will issue no more battle cries. He will wreak no more havoc. His people have no reason for fear except a healthy "fear of the Lord" (see 3:7,15–16). He has accomplished his purpose. He has vanquished the proud. The holy, humble remnant now seek him in righteousness. The cultic cry has become reality: "The Lord reigns, let the earth be glad; let the distant shores rejoice" (Ps 97:1). "The Lord reigns, let the nations tremble; he sits enthroned between the cherubim, let the earth shake. Great is the Lord in Zion; he is exalted over all the nations. Let them praise your great and awesome name—he is holy" (Ps 99:1–3).

The remainder of the verse speaks tenderly of God's love for his people. "Three parallel lines each containing three phrases express the deepest inner joy and satisfaction of God himself in his love for his people ... that the Holy One should experience ecstasy over the sinner is incomprehensible."[123] Robertson called the verse the John 3:16 of the Old Testament.[124] Here we have the "reasons for their deliverance," namely God's satisfaction with the remnant and Yahweh's own power to save."[125]

The last three lines should be taken together.[126] The general sense of the verse is plain: God's delight in those whom he has redeemed. The middle phrase has presented particular difficulty. How is it that God will "quiet you with his love?"[127] Without changing the MT as do some, the best alternative seems to be to follow the flow of the verse: God delights, he quiets, bursts into song over

---

[121] H. Kosmala, "גָּבַר *gābhar* etc.," *TDOT* 2:374.

[122] This is Berlin's translation. She cites Jer 14:9 as a notable parallel (*Zephaniah,* 145).

[123] Robertson, *Nahum, Habakkuk, and Zephaniah,* 339–40.

[124] Ibid., 339.

[125] House, *Zephaniah*, 67.

[126] Roberts transposes the last two lines of v. 17 to restore parallelism but in so doing misses the progression of thought here. His transposition then forces him to emend the text at several other places unnecessarily (*Nahum, Habakkuk, and Zephaniah*, 220).

[127] Patterson (*Nahum, Habakkuk, Zephaniah,* 383) lists six options for interpretation: (1) God will keep silent about or cover up people's sins; (2) God's silence due to the overwhelming depths of his love; (3) God's preoccupation with planning good for Israel; (4) God's resting in his love; (5) God's giving peace and silence to the believer; and (6) God's singing out of the joy of his concern. The difficulty of the phrase has led to several suggestions concerning alternate readings. BHS suggests יְחַדֵּשׁ "he will renew," which requires only minor adjustments to the Hb.. Patterson, while hesitant to abandon the MT, accepts this reading (*Nahum, Habakkuk, Zephaniah,* 383–384). T. H. Gaster rejected this reading as spoiling the point of the contrast between keeping silent and bursting into song and suggests following the MT, rendering: "Though now He be keeping silent about His love, He will then joy over thee in a burst of song" ("Two Textual Emendations," *ExpTim* 78 [1966–67]: 267).

you.[128] Robertson explains the meaning in the following way: "*he will be quiet (over you) in his love*. The only essential difficulty with this rendering is found in the vividness of the phraseology. To consider Almighty God sinking in contemplations of love over a once-wretched human being can hardly be absorbed by the human mind." But that is exactly the point of the verse—God delights in you. The verb is most often intransitive, depicting the inward condition of the subject rather than depicting quietness conveyed to another.[129] "Yahweh joins the people's singing and soothes them by expressing love."[130] This amazing love of God for human beings is inexplicable. Human minds would never dream up such a God. Human actions or human character could never deserve such love. God's love comes in his quiet absorption because this is who God is. In the core of his being, God is love (1 John 4:8). Zephaniah thus sings the prelude to the cross kind of love Jesus reveals, a love that "surpasses knowledge" (Eph 3:19). How can this not cause God's people to praise! "Surely the greatest reason for them to offer praise is found here. They are to rejoice in Him because He, their gracious King and Savior, rejoices in them."[131]

3:18 The sense of the passage seems clear even though the verse is difficult to translate. Students of the Hebrew text question the division of the verses between v. 17 and v. 18. Most modern translations follow the Septuagint and take the first phrase of v. 18 with v. 17 as the end of the message begun in v. 16. The NIV does not follow this approach but places it in a footnote.[132] J. M. P. Smith called the phrase "unintelligible"[133] while Keil called every clause "difficult."[134]

Only Yahweh speaks in 3:18–20. At this point He summarizes His acts of grace by saying He will deal with Israel's oppressors, save her cripples, and bring her scattered people home. The prophecy's plot is now also complete. "It seems a strange ending, for the book's beginning suggested an unhappy

---

[128] Motyer sees a progression here: "From the feeling of joy to the silence of adoration to vocal exultation" ("Zephaniah," 3:958).

[129] Robertson, *Nahum, Habakkuk, and Zephaniah,* 340.

[130] House, *The Unity of the Twelve,* 150.

[131] Heflin, *Nahum, Habakkuk, Zephaniah, and Haggai,* 155.

[132] For a thorough discussion of this problem see Clark and Hatton, *Nahum, Habakkuk, and Zephaniah,* 201–2; M. Tsevat, "Some Biblical Notes," *HUCA* 24 (1952–53): 111–12; Patterson, *Nahum, Habakkuk, Zephaniah,* 384–86. Nogalski, *Literary Precursors*, 204 argues that vv. 14–17 represent a self-contained chiastic unit, whereas 18–20 is a unit closely tied by catchwords to Haggai 1. Motyer ("Zephaniah," 3:960) follows BDB (387) in seeing the *niphal* participle of יגה’, "to be grieved," as does NIV. *HALOT* 2:385 recognizes that this is the form in the MT but advises to emend the text after the LXX to כְּיוֹם מוֹעֵד, "as on a day of festival" (cf. NRSV in 3:17).

[133] J. M. P. Smith, *A Critical and Exegetical Commentary on Nahum,* 258.

[134] C. F. Keil, *The Twelve Minor Prophets: Biblical Commentary on the Old Testament,* trans. J. Martin (Grand Rapids: Eerdmans, 1954), 2:162. According to Berlin, "This verse is unintelligible" but "it seems to mean that God has removed those in Jerusalem who were a reproach to her" (*Zephaniah,* 145).

conclusion. The writer shows his artistic skill by changing the expected into something surprising and different."[135]

The prophet pictures a day when all of the sorrows associated with the people's sin and judgment would be removed. What are these "sorrows"? Do they refer to sorrow over the loss of Jerusalem as well as the feasts associated with it? Critical scholars simply refer the verse to the postexilic community of diaspora Jews outside Jerusalem who cannot attend the festivals.[136] The verb translated "remove" normally means "gather." The object is the participle "grieving," which can refer to "those grieving" (KJV, "them that are sorrowful") rather than the NIV "sorrows" (see NIV margin). Nogalski sees the picture of Jerusalem inhabitants "wandering rather aimlessly with no one to gather them together for cultic celebrations. … YHWH promises Zion he will gather those who are suffering under these deplorable conditions, a promise which is realized very shortly with the description of the construction of the temple at the instigation of Haggai."[137] Whatever grief the prophet sees among the people of God, he promises relief. Enemy destruction will vanish. Worship opportunities will be purified and renewed. Social injustice will disappear from Israel's agenda. God's elect people will participate in joy and thanksgiving in God's appointed times of worship. People will rejoice, and God will be glorified.

3:19 The NIV changed the word order to convey a smooth English rendering. The Hebrew begins with *hinĕnî,* "Behold me!" followed by a participle. This construction usually has the sense, "I am about to … / I am going to …" God announced that he was about to do something about Jerusalem's oppressors.

Who are those who oppress Zion? Are they Jews or foreigners? Although Jews cannot be ruled out (cf. 3:1), the context here implies outside oppressors of Zion.[138] Thus Nogalski wants to see the entire book of Zephaniah with its description of "unparalleled destruction" as "the literary foreshadowing of the Babylonian destruction."[139] In 3:19, however, the use of "all" for the oppressors widens the picture and points to a literary dependence on Isa 60:14 to include everyone who had ever afflicted Zion, including Assyrians as emphasized in Nah 1:12 and Babylonians, as well as neighbors who took

---

[135] House, *Zephaniah,* 61.

[136] See Nogalski, *Literary Precursors*, 204, who refers to W. Rudolph, *Micha, Nahum, Habakuk, Zephanja,* KAT (Gutersloh: Gütersloher, 1975), 3:293–98.

[137] Nogalski, *Literary Precursors*, 205.

[138] Nogalski, *Literary Precursors*, 206, who says within the confines of the Book of Zephaniah, "the identity of the group oppressing Zion is very difficult to determine," so that commentators such as Rudolph, *Micha, Nahum, Habakuk, Zephanja,* 299, simply leave the group unidentified.

[139] Ibid., 206.

advantage of Jerusalem when the Babylonians attacked.[140] The people would no longer suffer oppression because the Lord would gather them and bring them home (3:20).

The reference to the lame and the banished is a chiastic structure which could be translated as follows: "I will save the lame and the banished I will gather." This probably refers to the following verse which asserts that the exiles would return to their home. If the weak could make the trip "home," then all other segments of the population would receive assurance as well. Motyer is probably on track as he sees here the motif of the final pilgrimage to Zion (Isa 35). "No personal inability will be allowed to prevent the Lord's pilgrims from coming safely home. Rather, the Lord will provide everything necessary for them (Isa 42:16; Jer 31:7–9)."[141]

A change in status (returning home) would also result in a change in reputation. Israel had been profaned by the experience of the exile. God promised a time when they would not experience shame again. Instead praise and honor would be the order of the day.[142]

3:20 The first part of the verse closely approximates the preceding verse. God would return the people to their land and the people would experience praise and renown rather than shame and reproach. The day of the Lord is complete, "marked by the liberation of the people of God from everything that ever bound them or injured their well-being."[143]

In language reminiscent of other promises of restoration from exile (Amos 9:14–15; Ezek 36:34–37), God promised to restore the fortunes of the people of Israel. He would again make them prosperous in the land. The restoration would occur "before your very eyes," that is, in your own day. How could the people know that this would indeed come to pass? The Lord had spoken. The message was God's and not man's.

The promise of Zephaniah found its immediate fulfillment in the return from the seventy years of exile of which Zephaniah's contemporary, Jeremiah, spoke. At that time the people were rescued and the reputation of the people restored.

The book ends where it began with a scene of the reversal of the whole world order. It began with cataclysmic overthrow. It ended with the blessings of God's people being returned to the land.[144] "God's restoration of the nation in chapter three is as complete as His destruction of the world in chap-

[140] Ibid., 207. He concludes finally that Zeph 3:19 is a quotation of Mic 4:6–7 and reverses the punishment announced in Mic 7:11–13 so that it brings the punishment motif to a resolution. As such Nogalski seeks Zeph 3:19 as part of the Deuteronomistic edition (p. 208).

[141] Motyer, "Zephaniah," 3:961.

[142] Clark and Hatton, *Nahum, Habakkuk, and Zephaniah,* 203.

[143] Motyer, "Zephaniah," 3:962.

[144] Patterson, *Nahum, Habakkuk, Zephaniah,* 347.

ter one. He is now a judge who pardons."[145]

In some sense, the fulfillment describes the glorious promise of the Messianic age when the Lord promised through his Son to "take great delight in you, … quiet you with his love, [and] … rejoice over you with singing" (Zeph 3:17).

[145] House, *Zephaniah,* 71.

Selected Bibliography

Books and Commentaries

Achtemeier, E. *Nahum–Malachi,* INT. Atlanta: John Knox, 1986.

Alfaro, J. I. *Justice and Loyalty: A Commentary on the Book of Micah.* ITC. Grand Rapids: Eerdmans, 1989.

Allen, L. C. *The Books of Joel ... Micah.* NICOT. Grand Rapids: Eerdmans, 1976.

Archer, G. L., Jr. "Micah." In *The New Bible Commentary Revised.* Edited by D. Guthrie et al. Grand Rapids: Eerdmans, 1970.

Armerding, C. E. "Habakkuk." Vol. 7. In EBC.

Baker, D. W. *Nahum, Habakkuk, Zephaniah.* TOTC. Downers Grove: InterVarsity, 1988.

Barber, C. J. *Habakkuk and Zephaniah.* EvBC. Chicago: Moody, 1985.

Barker, K. L. Gen. ed. *The NIV Study Bible.* Grand Rapids: Zondervan, 1995.

Boadt, L. *Reading the Old Testament.* New York: Paulist, 1984.

Boice, J. M. *The Minor Prophets.* 2 vols. Grand Rapids: Kregel, 1996.

Brown, W. P. *Obadiah through Malachi.* Westminster Bible Companion. Louisville: Westminster John Knox, 1996.

Brownlee, W. H. *The Text of Habakkuk in the Ancient Commentary from Qumran.* JBLMS. Philadelphia: Fortress, 1959.

Bullock, C. H. *An Introduction to the Old Testament Prophetic Books.* Chicago: Moody, 1986.

Calkins, R. *The Modern Message of the Minor Prophets.* New York: Harper & Brothers, 1947.

Carlson, E. L. "Micah." In *The Wycliffe Bible Commentary.* Edited by C. F. Pfeiffer and E. F. Harrison. Chicago: Moody, 1962.

Cathcart, K. J. *Nahum in the Light of Northwest Semitic.* Rome: Biblical Institute Press, 1973.

Cathcart, K. J. and R. P. Gordon. *The Targum of the Minor Prophets.* Wilmington: Michael Glazier, 1989.

Chisholm, R. B., Jr. *Interpreting the Minor Prophets.* Grand Rapids: Zondervan, 1990.

Clark, D. J. and H. A. Hatton. *A Handbook on the Books of Nahum, Habakkuk, and Zephaniah.* New York: United Bible Societies, 1989.

Clark, D. J., and N. Mundhenk. *A Handbook on the Books of Obadiah and Micah.* New York: United Bible Societies, 1982.

Clark, D. J. "Micah." In *The International Bible Commentary.* Edited by F. F. Bruce et al. Grand Rapids: Zondervan, 1986.

Coggins, R. J. and S. P. Re'emi. *Israel among the Nations.* ITC. Grand Rapids: Eerdmans, 1985.

Craigie, P. C. *Twelve Prophets.* 2 vols. Philadelphia: Westminster, 1985.

Deane, W. J. et al. "Micah." In *The Pulpit Commentary.* 23 vols. Edited by H. D. M. Spence and J. S. Exell. Vol. 14: "Amos to Malachi." Grand Rapids: Eerdmans,

1983 reprint.

Eakin, F. E., Jr. "Zephaniah." BBC. Nashville: Broadman, 1972.

Elliger, K. *Das Buch der zwölf kleinen Propheten II.* ATD 25. Gøttingen: Vandenhoeck & Ruprecht, 1956.

Fausset, A. R. "Jeremiah-Malachi." In *A Commentary Critical, Experimental and Practical on the Old and New Testaments.* 6 vols. By P. Jamieson, A. R. Fausset, and D. Brown. Grand Rapids: Eerdmans, 1967.

Feinberg, C. L. *The Minor Prophets.* Chicago: Moody, 1976.

Gloag, P. J. *The Messianic Prophecies.* Edinburgh: T & T Clark, 1879.

Graffy, A. *A Prophet Confronts His People: The Disputation Speech in the Prophets.* AnBib 104. Rome: Biblical Institute Press, 1984.

Haak, R. D. *Habakkuk.* Leiden: Brill, 1992. *VTS* 44.

Hagstrom, D. G. *The Coherence of the Book of Micah: A Literary Analysis.* SBLDS 89. Atlanta: Scholars Press, 1988.

Heflin, J. N. B. *Nahum, Habakkuk, Zephaniah, and Haggai.* BSC. Grand Rapids: Zondervan, 1985.

Hillers, D. R. *Micah.* Her. Philadelphia: Fortress, 1984.

House, P. R. *The Unity of the Twelve.* JSOTSup 97. Bible and Literature Series 27. Sheffield: Almond, 1990.

———. *Zephaniah: A Prophetic Drama.* JSOTSup 69. Sheffield, Eng.: Almond Press, 1988.

Jeremias, J. *Kultprophetie und Gerichtsverkündigung in der späten Königszeit Israels,* WMANT 35. Neukirchen: Neukirchener Verlag, 1970.

Jones, B. A. *The Formation of the Book of the Twelve: A Study in Text an d Canon,* SBLDS 149. Atlanta: Scholars Press, 1995.

Kaiser, W. C., Jr. *Micah-Malachi.* Dallas: Word, 1992.

Keil, C. F. "The Twelve Minor Prophets." 2 vols. In *Biblical Commentary on the Old Testament.* By C. F. Keil and F. Delitzsch. Translated by J. Martin. Grand Rapids: Eerdmans, 1949.

Kelley, P. H. *Micah ... Malachi.* Vol. 14. LBBC. Nashville: Broadman, 1984.

King, P. J. *Amos, Hosea, Micah—An Archaeological Commentary.* Philadelphia: Westminster, 1988.

Lee, A. Y. "The Canonical Unity of the Scroll of the Minor Prophets." Ph.D. diss., Baylor University, 1985.

Lewis, J. P. *The Minor Prophets.* Grand Rapids: Baker, 1966.

Limburg, J. *Hosea-Micah.* INT. Atlanta: John Knox, 1988.

Longman, T. III. "Micah." In *Evangelical Commentary on the Bible.* Edited by W. A. Elwell. Grand Rapids: Baker, 1989.

———. "Nahum." in *The Minor Prophets: An Exegetical and Expository Commentary.* Edited by T. E. McComiskey. Grand Rapids: Baker, 1993.

Maier, W. A. *The Book of Nahum: A Commentary.* St. Louis: Concordia, 1959.

Martin, J. A. "Micah." In *The Bible Knowledge Commentary: Old Testament.* Edited by J. F. Walvoord and R. B. Zuck. Wheaton: Victor, 1985.

Mays, J. L. *Micah.* OTL. Philadelphia: Westminster, 1976.

McComiskey, T. E. *The Covenants of Promise.* Grand Rapids: Baker, 1985.

———. "Micah." In EBC. 12 vols. Edited by F. E. Gaebelein et al. Grand Rapids:

Zondervan, 1985.

Motyer, J. A. "Zephaniah." Vol. 3. *The Minor Prophets.* Edited by T. E. McComiskey. Grand Rapids: Baker, 1998.

Nogalski, J. *Literary Precursors to the Book of the Twelve.* Berlin: Walter de Gruyter, 1993.

———. *Redactional Processes in the Book of the Twelve,* BZAW 218. Berlin/New York: Walter de Gruyter, 1993.

Orelli, C. von. *The Twelve Minor Prophets.* Translated by J. S. Banks. Minneapolis: Klock & Klock, 1977 repr. of 1897 ed.

Patterson, R. D. *Nahum, Habakkuk, Zephaniah,* WEC. Edited by K. Barker. Chicago: Moody, 1991.

Pusey, E. B. *The Minor Prophets.* 2 vols. Grand Rapids: Baker, 1950 reprint

von Rad, G. *The Message of the Prophets.* London: SCM, 1968.

Riggs, J. R. *Micah.* BSC. Grand Rapids: Zondervan, 1987.

Roberts, J. J. M. *Nahum, Habakkuk, and Zephaniah: A Commentary.* OTL. Louisville: Westminster/John Knox, 1991.

Robertson, O. P. *The Books of Nahum, Habakkuk, Zephaniah.* NICOT. Grand Rapids: Eerdmans, 1990.

Robinson, G. L. *The Twelve Minor Prophets.* Grand Rapids: Baker, 1967 repr. of 1926 ed.

Rudolph, W. *Micha, Nahum, Habakuk, Zephanja,* KAT XIII 3. Gutersloh: Gütersloher, 1975.

Schneider, D. *The Unity of the Book of the Twelve* (Ph.D. diss., Yale University, 1979).

Smith, G. A. *The Book of the Twelve Prophets.* London: Hodder & Stoughton, 1898.

Smith, G. V. *The Prophets as Preachers.* Nashville: Broadman & Holman, 1994.

Smith, J. E. *The Minor Prophets.* Joplin: College Press, 1994.

Smith, J. M. P. *A Critical and Exegetical Commentary on the Books of Micah ...* ICC. Edinburgh: T & T Clark, 1911.

Smith, R. L. *Micah–Malachi,* WBC 32. Waco: Word, 1984.

Szeles, M. E. *Wrath and Mercy: A Commentary on the Books of Habakkuk and Zephaniah.* ITC. Grand Rapids: Eerdmans, 1987.

VanGemeren, W. A. *Interpreting the Prophetic Word.* Grand Rapids: Zondervan, 1990.

Van Groningen, G. *Messianic Revelation in the Old Testament.* Grand Rapids: Baker, 1990.

Vawter, B. *Amos, Hosea, Micah.* Wilmington: M. Glazier, 1981.

Waltke, B. K. *Micah: An Introduction and Commentary.* In *Obadiah, Jonah, and Micah.* By D. W. Baker, T. D. Alexander, and B. K. Waltke. TOTC. Downers Grove: InterVarsity, 1988.

———. "Micah." In *The Minor Prophets.* 3 vols. Edited by T. E. McComiskey. Grand Rapids: Baker, 1993.

Watts, J. D. W. *The Books of Joel, Obadiah, Jonah, Nahum, Habakkuk and Zephaniah.* CBC. Cambridge: University Press, 1975.

Watts, J. W. and P. R. House, eds. *Forming Prophetic Literature: Essays on Isaiah and the Twelve in Honor of John D. W. Watts.* JSOTSup 235. Sheffield, Eng.: Academic Press, 1996.

Westermann, C. *Basic Forms of Prophetic Speech.* Translated by H. C. White. London:

Lutterworth, 1967.
Willis, J. T. "The Structure, Setting, and Interrelationships of the Pericopes in the Book of Micah." Ph.D. dissertation. Vanderbilt University, 1966.
Wilson, R. R. *Prophecy and Society in Ancient Israel.* Philadelphia: Fortress, 1980.
Wolff, H. W. *Micah: A Commentary.* Translated by G. Stansell. Minneapolis: Augsburg, 1990.

Articles and Journals

Barker, K. L. "False Dichotomies between the Testaments." *JETS* 25 (March 1982): 3–16.
———. "Praise." In *Cracking Old Testament Codes.* Edited by D. B. Sandy and R. L. Giese, Jr. Nashville: Broadman & Holman, 1995.
———. "The Scope and Center of Old and New Testament Theology and Hope." In *Dispensationalism, Israel and the Church.* Edited by C. A. Blaising and D. L. Bock. Grand Rapids: Zondervan, 1992.
Brownlee, W. H. "The Composition of Habakkuk," *Hommages a Andre Dupont-Sommer.* Paris: Librairie d'Amerique et d'Orrent Adrien-Maisonneuve, 1971.
Butler, T. C. "Announcements of Judgment." In *Cracking Old Testament Codes.* Edited by D. B. Sandy and R. L. Giese, Jr. Nashville: Broadman & Holman, 1995, 157–76.
Carroll, R. P. "Habakkuk." In *A Dictionary of Biblical Interpretation.*" Edited by R. J. Coggins and J. L. Houlden. London: SCM, 1990.
Clements, R. "Patterns in the Prophetic Canon." In *Canon and Authority.* Edited by G. W. Coats and B. Long. Philadelphia: Fortress, 1977.
De Roche, M. "Yahweh's *Rib* against Israel: A Reassessment of the So-Called 'Prophetic Lawsuit' in the Preexilic Prophets." *JBL* 102 (1983): 563–74.
Eaton, J. H. "The Origin and Meaning of Habakkuk 3." *ZAW* 76 (1964).
Gerstenberger, E. "The Woe Oracles of the Prophets." *JBL* 81 (1962).
Gowan, D. E. "Habakkuk and Wisdom." *Perspective* IX (1968).
Harris, J. G. "The Laments of Habakkuk's Prophecy." *EvQ* 45 (1973).
Helmbold, A. K. "Micah the Prophet." In *ZPEB*. Edited by M. C. Tenney et al. 5 vols. Grand Rapids: Zondervan, 1975, 4:213–16.
Huffmon, H. B. "The Treaty Background of Hebrew *Yada*ᶜ." *BASOR* 181 (1966): 31–37.
Johnson, M. D. "The Paralysis of Torah in Habakkuk 1:4," *VT* 35 (1985).
Leslie, E. A. "Habakkuk." *IDB*. Nashville: Abingdon, 1962.
Longman, T. III. "Lament." In *Cracking Old Testament Codes.* Edited by D. B. Sandy and R. L. Giese, Jr. Nashville: Broadman & Holman, 1995, 197–215.
Nielsen, E. "The Righteous and the Wicked in Habaqquq." *ST* 6 (1953).
Otto, E. "Die Theologie des Buches Habakuk." *VT* 35 (1985): 277–84.
Patterson, R. D. "Old Testament Prophecy." In *A Complete Literary Guide to the Bible.* Edited by L. Ryken and T. Longman III. Grand Rapids: Zondervan, 1993, 296–309.
Ramsey, G. W. "Speech-Forms in Hebrew Law and Prophetic Oracles." *JBL* 96 (1977): 45–58.
Renaud, B. "La composition du livre de Nahum: Une proposition." *ZAW* 99 (1987).

Shaw, C. S. "Micah 1:10–16 Reconsidered." *JBL* 106 (1987): 223–29.

Stern, E. "Israel at the Close of the Period of the Monarchy: An Archaeological Survey." *BA* 38 (1975): 26–54.

Sweeney, M. A. "Concerning the Structure and Generic Character of the Book of Nahum." *ZAW* 104 (1992).

________. "Habakkuk, Book of," *ABD* 3:1–2

Thompson, M. E. W. "Prayer, Oracle, and Theophany: The Book of Habakkuk." *TynBul* 44 (1993).

Tucker, G. M. "Prophetic Superscriptions and the Growth of a Canon." In *Canon and Authority.* Edited by G. W. Coats and B. O. Long. Philadelphia: Fortress, 1977.

Tuttle, G. A. "Wisdom and Habakkuk." *SBT* 3 (1973).

VanGemeren, W. A. "Oracles of Salvation." In *Cracking Old Testament Codes.* Edited by D. B. Sandy and R. L. Giese, Jr. Nashville: Broadman & Holman, 1995, 139–55.

Waltke, B. K. "Theology of Micah." In *Evangelical Dictionary of Biblical Theology.* Edited by W. A. Elwell. Grand Rapids: Baker, 1996, 525–27.

Willis, J. T. "The Structure of Mic. 3–5 and the Function of Mic. 5: 9–14 in the Book." *ZAW* 81 (1969): 191–214.

———. "Structure, Genre, and Intent in the Book of Habakkuk." *VT* 41 (1991): 63–83.

Selected Subject Index

Person Index

Selected Scripture Index

Proverbs